Series: Of Islands and Women
Number 5

Sardinia

Also by Susanna Hoe

Lady in the Chamber (Collins 1971)

God Save the Tsar (Michael Joseph/St Martin's Press 1978)

The Man Who Gave His Company Away: A Biography of Ernest Bader, Founder of the Scott Bader Commonwealth (Heinemann 1978)

The Private Life of Old Hong Kong: Western Women in the British Colony 1841–1941 (Oxford University Press 1991)

Chinese Footprints: Exploring Women's History in China, Hong Kong and Macau (Roundhouse Publications Asia 1996)

Stories for Eva: A Reader for Chinese Women Learning English (Hong Kong Language Fund 1997)

The Taking of Hong Kong: Charles and Clara Elliot in China Waters (with Derek Roebuck) (Curzon Press 1999; Hong Kong University Press 2009)

Women at the Siege, Peking 1900 (HOLO Books 2000)

At Home in Paradise: A House and Garden in Papua New Guinea (HOLO Books 2003)

Madeira: Women, History, Books and Places (HOLO Books 2004)

Crete: Women, History, Books and Places (HOLO Books 2005)

Watching the Flag Come Down: An Englishwoman in Hong Kong 1987–97 (HOLO Books 2007)

Tasmania: Women, History, Books and Places (HOLO Books 2010)

Travels in Tandem: The Writing of Women and Men Who Travelled Together (HOLO Books 2012)

Malta: Women, History, Books and Places (HOLO Books 2015)

Women in Disputes: A History of European Women in Mediation and Arbitration (with Derek Roebuck) (HOLO Books 2018)

Sardinia

Women, History, Books and Places

Susanna Hoe

HOLO BOOKS
THE WOMEN'S HISTORY PRESS
OXFORD

First published 2022 by
HOLO Books: The Women's History Press
Clarendon House
52 Cornmarket
Oxford OX1 3HJ

email:holobooks@yahoo.co.uk
www.holobooks.co.uk
and www.centralbooks.com

Copyright © Susanna Hoe 2022

The right of Susanna Hoe to be identified as the author
of this work has been asserted by her in accordance with the
Copyright, Designs and Patents Act 1988

British Cataloguing in Publication Data
A catalogue record for this book is available from the British Library

ISBN 978-1-9196318-0-6   (pbk)
ISBN 978-1-9196318-2-0   (e-book)
ISBN 978-1-9196318-1-3   (Kindle)

This book is printed on paper suitable for recycling and made from fully managed
and sustained forest sources. Logging, pulping and manufacturing processes are
expected to conform to the environmental regulations of the country of origin.

Produced and typeset for HOLO Books by
Stanford DTP Services, Northampton, England
Printed in the UK

In Memory of my Husband Derek Roebuck. Together we travelled the World and Worlds. Sardinia was the last foreign place on which he left his footprints.

Contents

Illustrations   x
Preface   xii
Acknowledgements   xiv
Author's Note   xvii
Map 1   xix
Map 2   xx

Introduction   1

1 The Earliest Women c.170000 BC–850 BC   4
The Stone Age c.170000 BC–c.5300 BC; Neolithic Women
4700 BC–4000 BC; The Copper Age 3200 BC–2700 BC; Nuragic
Women and the Bronze Age 1600 BC–850 BC

2 From Late Nuragic Women to the Romans 850 BC–AD 257   25
Early Iron Age Nuragic Developments; The Arrival of the Phoenicians;
Carthaginian Sardinia; Women of Roman Sardinia (Scaurus and Aris's
Wife, Fundania Galla of Tharros, Atilia Pomptilla, Claudia Acte,
Berenice and Sea Silk, Favonia Vera of Nora and Maxima Flavia Publicia)

3 From Early Christians to Muslims AD 314–1077   48
Early Christian Martyrs (Santa Rosa, Santa Giusta, Giustina and
Enedina, Santa Restituta); Evidence from Christian Tomb Inscriptions,
Fourth and Fifth Centuries (Flavia Cyriace and Septimia Musa of Porto
Torres); Pope Gregory the Great and the Resolution of Women's Disputes
591–604 (Pomponiana, Theodosia, Juliana, Catella, Desideria, Gavina
and Sirica); Islamic Sardinia (Mujāhid's mother, Jūt, and Maryam)

4 Abbesses, *Giudicesse* and Benefactors 1065–1420   60
Introduction: *Giudicati*; Donna Tocoele and Santa Maria di
Bonarcado; Sardinian Women through the *Condaghi*; Abbesses of
San Pietro di Silki; The *Giudici* of Logudoro-Torres and *Giudicessa*
Adelasia; the Fate of San Pietro di Silki; Cagliari and the *Giudicessa*
Benedetta; *Giudicessa* Eleonora and the *Giudicato* d'Arborea

5 Spanish Sardinia, Feudalism, Violence and Scandal 1478–1720   86
Introduction: Spain in Sardinia; The Jews of Alghero 1322–1492;
Violante Carroz, Contessa di Quirra – *La Sanguinaria* 1456–1511;
Rosa Gambella, Woman of Legends 1440–1482; Pirate Raid on
Bonorcili 1527; Accusations of Witchcraft 1534–1606; A Century of
Disasters; The Miller's Daughter 1657–1662; Costanza Pamphili and
her Letter from Sardinia 1662–1664; Francesca Zatrillas: *Cherchez
la Femme* 1651–1673; Rosaria Guiso's Lament; the End of Spanish
Sardinia

6 Sardinia under the House of Savoy 1720–1861 108
Introduction: Dukes of Savoy, Kings of Sardinia; Corruption, the
Tonduts and Rebellion in Sassari 1733–1780; Women and Feudal
Rights Under Savoy 1723–1836; The Sardinian Vespers – *Sa Die de
Sa Sardigna* – Rebellion 1793–1796; War and Royal Exile in Sardinia;
The Cholera Epidemic of 1855 in Sassari

7 Vendetta, Vengeance, *Banditesse* and Resistance 1733–1917 138
Introduction; Feuds, Vengeance and Reconciliation as Seen by
Foreigners; The Sardo and Sardinian View; *Banditesse*: Sardinian
Women Bandits; Dr Adelasia Cocco in Barbagia; *Accabadora*: Woman
of Violence?; Paskedda Selis Zau and Uprising Against Enclosure:
de Su Connottu 1868

8 From Tabarca to Carloforte, San Pietro 1738–1918 162
Introduction; Tabarca 1540–1737; San Pietro 1738; September 1798;
The Story of Francesca Rosso (Jenet Lela Beia) 1798–1806; Return to
Freedom 1803; The Story of Anna Porcile 1798–1826; The Nightmare
Returns 1815: Sant'Antioco; Bey Mother Jenet Lea Beia Reunited with
Family 1837–1848; 29 April 1918

9 The Other Islands: La Maddalena and Tavolara 177
Introduction; William Craig, Women Lichen Collectors and the La
Maddalena Family; Emma Collins and Garibaldi; Garibaldi on Caprera:
Wives, Mistresses and Daughters 1855–1959; Maria Webber Tamponi;
From La Maddalena to Tavolara: The Royal Bertoleoni Dynasty

10 Women and Sardinia's Economic Development 1735–1919 202
Introduction; Donna Francesca Sanna Sulis, the Lady of the Mulberry
Trees; The Pernis Family 1832–1941; Sardinia's Mining Sisterhood
1851–1918 (Introduction; Elena Poinsel and the Rosas Mine; Zely
Sanna-Castoldi, Montevecchio and its Women Workers; Helen Dunstan
Wright, Idina Brassey and the Ingurtosu Mine)

11 More Foreign Women in Sardinia 1848–1966 228
Introduction; Mary Davey 1848–1850; The Piercy Family 1872–1966;
Isabelle Eberhardt 1900–1904; The Strange Case of Ellen Giles
1906–1914; Anna Rose Giles and Georgiana Goddard King
1906–1939; Amelie Posse-Brázdová, Alghero 1915–1916; Ethiopians
Exiled to Asinara 1937–1940

12 The Twentieth Century: Literature, Politics, War, Science
and Art 1875–1950 261
Introduction; Late Nineteenth and Early Twentieth Century
Developments; The First World War and the National Women's Union
(*l'Unione Femminile Nazionale*) 1915–1924; Science and Art between
the Wars

13 Anti-Fascism 1920–1943   286
Introduction: Fascism and its Appearance in Italy and Sardinia; The
Sardinian Connection (Joyce Lussu, Ines Berlinguer, Lina Merlin, Sister
Giuseppina Demuro and Fulvia Riccardino); *La Triade Femminista
Sardista Antifascista* (Mariangela Maccioni, Graziella Sechi Giacobbe,
Marianna Bussalai)

14 Post-War Women and Politics 1945–1946   313
Introduction; Bastianina Martini Mussu; Nadia Gallico Spano; Maria
Giulia Cocco; Ninetta Bartoli; Margherita Sanna

Bibliography   325
Index   339

Illustrations

1. Venus of Macomer — 5
2. *Dea Madre* Macomer — 8
3. *Donna* or *Madre con Ucciso* — 17
4a. Portatrice di Brocca — 22
4b. Portatrici d'Acqua, Golfo Aranci, 1916 — 22
5. Wooden statuette — 24
6. Goddess Tanit — 28
7. Ceramic bottle, Tharros — 32
8. Lugherras oil lamp — 34
9. Claudia Calliste funeral urn — 41
10. Favonia Vera stele, Nora — 46
11. Empress Constantina Augusta coin — 52
12. Statue of Giudicessa Eleonora d'Arborea — 85
13. Page of letter from Costanza Pamphili — 100
14. Ippolita Ludovisi — 101
15. Donna Francesca Zatrillas — 105
16. Duchess Benavente — 113
17. Giovanna Roberti Nin Carcassona, 1866 — 115
18. Campanile di S Eulalia, 1938 — 120
19. Queen Clotilde — 123
20a. Princess Maria Cristina, 1790 — 131
20b. Queen Maria Carolina of Naples, 1791 — 131
21. *Ritratto Famiglia de Raimondo de Quesada di San Saturnino, c.1828* — 134
22. Cavalcade of horsemen and horsewomen — 141
23. Lucia Delitala — 148
24. Mariantonia Serra — 150
25. *Sagezza Antica*, Orgosolo — 155
26. Orgosolo women with embroidered aprons — 157
27. Simulacrum of Madonna of the Slave — 168
28. Last page of Anna Porcile letter, 1805 — 169
29. Millelire House, by William Craig, post-1848 — 179
30. Baroness Espérance von Schwartz (Elpis Melena) — 187
31. Francesca Armosino, Clelia and Malio — 191
32. Edwardian woman on terrace of Villa Tamponi, Golfo Aranci — 197
33. King Carlo I and Bertoleoni family — 200
34. Mirra Pernis — 207
35a. '*Via Roma a Cagliari*' — 208
35b. Anna Marongiu — 208
36. Donna Maddalena Vacca Salazar, Milis — 210
37. Women collecting oranges — 211
38. Zely Sanna Castoldi — 214
39. Women workers inside Map of Sardinia — 216

40.	Maria and Attilio Mariani, c.1911	218
41.	Helen and Charles Wright	220
42.	Idina and Thomas Brassey	221
43.	Villa Idina, Ingurtosu, 2017	226
44.	Vera Mameli Piercy and Giorgina as a child	233
45.	Sarah Piercy (née Davies)	234
46.	A page from Florence Piercy's diary	236
47.	Piercy family in Sard costume	238
48.	Young Vera sitting on a wall	241
49.	Isabelle Eberhardt	245
50.	Ellen Giles	247
51.	Georgiana King	250
52.	Amelie Posse-Brázdová and Oki on balcony	254
53.	Grazia Deledda	266
54a.	Lina Pernis and little Enrico	269
54b.	Lina Pernis and her husband Enrico	269
55.	Eva Mameli	274
56.	Nicolina Deledda	274
57.	Coroneo sisters	276
58.	Altara sisters: Iride, Lavinia, Edina, 1937	278
59.	Women with corbulas on their heads	282
60.	Maria Lai	284
61.	Joyce and Emilio Lussu	291
62.	Ines Berlinguer	295
63.	Sister Giuseppina	299
64.	Mariangela Maccioni	303
65.	Graziella Sechi Giacobbe	305
66.	Marianna Bussalai	310
67.	Nadia Gallico Spano	314
68.	Ninetta Bartoli	319
69.	Margherita Sanna	320
70.	'The Community Laundry Tub'	322

Preface

'On the benches of my elementary school', wrote Marianna Bussalai, noted Sardinian anti-Fascist and advocate of self-determination, 'I felt humiliated, wondering why, in the history of Italy, Sardinia was never mentioned. I deduced that Sardinia was not Italy, and had to have a separate history.'

Chapter 13 will show that Marianna Bussalai intended for Sardinia more than its own history. But to be ignored is often the fate of an island detached from a larger country of which it is, nevertheless, deemed to be a part. Tasmania, for example, the last but one of my books in this series 'Of Islands and Women', has sometimes been left off maps of Australia, and even looked down on by mainlanders. I am writing this preface while we are all in isolation because of the Covid-19 pandemic. Anxious that our 'children' and grandchildren are far away from us in Hobart, mostly medics, Derek and I have been given some solace at the news that Tasmania has lifted the drawbridge over the 'moat' between the island and the mainland: Australians arriving by sea to the north are required to go into 14 days' quarantine. Tasmania's history, as well as that of Sardinia, is, indeed, separate.

Then, of course, there is the fact that so many histories of a place are seen through male eyes; they are histories of what men did. This series, 'Of Islands and Women', is a determined effort to show an island's history, instead, through that of women, about women.

I never intended to write *Sardinia: Women, History, Books and Places*. Derek, so patient and, indeed, invaluable, in trailing around islands for my research, suggested it as an attractive place simply to go on holiday. All I knew of it was that rich people went there to the Costa Smeralda – and that is the last time I shall mention that area. And wasn't there something about poverty and malaria? What is more, I had never heard of any historical women there and quite fancied a real holiday which, because of the previous four books and return research visits to the islands concerned, we had not had for some years.

Before the days of the internet, I had for many years picked up books about islands in second-hand bookshops. I was not, therefore, surprised to find on my bookshelves Mary Delane's *Sardinia: The Undefeated Island*. She mentioned arriving in Golfo Aranci, on a peninsula in the north-east of the island, and staying at the Villa Margherita. She made it sound so attractive that, although her account was published in 1968, I put that name and place into a browser and found that, in a later manifestation, it still existed, and looked and sounded ideal. I booked and we went, and we were disappointed neither with the hotel nor with the place.

But then, of course, I started to discover Sardinia's very long and fascinating history and its extraordinary women, and there was no going back: I had to start my research and then, after a few years, to write. My only problem really, has been the language. So much is written in English about Madeira, Crete and Malta (and obviously Tasmania) that, with the help, too, of Derek's ancient Greek and Latin, I had access, even, to Portuguese and modern Greek. But my Italian was six months dunking in the language at Perugia's University for Foreigners when I was 17 – a lifetime away. Somehow I have coped – dredging my memory, practice, the help of kind informants who have become friends, and, I'm afraid to say, sometimes, 'Google translate', which often needs knocking into better shape.

For the other books in this series, Derek and I have returned several times to the island concerned and, while much of each book has been its history, a substantial second part has been detailed itineraries. That has not been possible for Sardinia. Our first visit was limited to Golfo Aranci, La Maddalena Archipelago and Olbia where, having written in advance to a publisher for some information, we made our first Sardinian informant turned friend. He and many others are thanked in the acknowledgements.

The second visit was a year later, in the autumn of 2017, to Cagliari, and I got around the capital, and within striking distance of it, a fair bit, but it is rather a large island. What is more, by then Derek's health had begun to limit journeys. Kind friends took us to Nora, and drove me north-westwards to where women were involved in the mining ventures. But we had to back out of a couple of days in Alghero. I managed to book a 10-day tour round the island in 2018, but had to cancel it, and it has since proved impossible to return. As far as practicable, therefore, I have added place to the text of the history section. I explain in the Author's Note what the future might hold.

Clearly, though, I had no option but to write about Sardinia and the women who have made its history and its places.

Since drafting this Preface in March 2020, and after Derek's approval of it, I put it aside to continue writing chapters. Derek read, corrected and commented on all up to, and including, chapter 12. He much looked forward to reading 13 and 14 and, indeed, told me to hurry up and finish writing so that he could. But on 27 April, my beloved of 41 years died. Travelling and writing, let alone living, will, and can never be, the same. I have, not surprisingly, dedicated this book to the memory of my late husband, Derek Roebuck.

Oxford
August 2021

Acknowledgements

As usual, it is impossible to thank sufficiently those who have helped me during the rather long drawn-out completion of this book, but I shall at least try. My first thanks have to go to Owain Wright, scholar of Italian history, whom I first contacted about a couple of articles he had written on Sardinia. Some time later, when I got in touch with him again, I had the nerve to ask him if he would be good enough to read the whole completed text; generously he agreed. None of the remaining errors of any kind can be laid at his door, but there would have been many more without his eagle eye.

Informants are always the life-blood of my endeavours. The most patient and determined has been Pietrina Rubanu of Orgosolo, expert on its famous murals, who, with her unremitting research nose, made sure that the life and death of Paska Devaddis was as accurate as possible. She not only saw me through several versions of the story as she dug deeper, but she was also always ready to answer questions and translate from a Barbagia dialect concerning other aspects of the region. Bill Rolston put me in touch with Pietrina following my reading of an article by him about the murals, and has given me permission to use his fine photograph of one of them. Maurizio Piga, one of the earliest upon whom I could call, was not just invaluable for deciphering and translating the long Anna Porcile letter, but also available to translate even odd words about which I sent him any number of *cris de coeur* over the years; we could discuss in person particular aspects of Sardinian history as well. The Porcile letter was sent to me by Marco Sioli who also helped me with the rest of the Tabarca chapter. Eugenia Tognotti, known for her studies on Sardinia's infectious diseases, helped my writing up of the Sassari cholera epidemic of 1855.

Oxford college librarian and scholar, Sardinian Catherine Costa, provided me with the translation of one of the dialect poems I have used, added to my knowledge of an issue, as well as lending me an essential book – greater generosity has no one! Particular thanks are due to Maria Antonella Casula of the *Memoriale* Giusepe Garibaldi, Caprera. I discovered that she had translated into Italian Mary Davey's *Icnusa* which contains an account of an event concerning the Santa Caterina Convent, in the Castello, Cagliari. When hunting down the convent, I accosted two staff members who kindly showed me round its later incarnation as the Santa Caterina School. They also introduced me to the headteacher, Anna Pusceddu, and I told them about the convent incident. I asked Maria Antonella if she would send her translation to Anna, which she unhesitatingly did. She also read my chapter on La Maddalena and Caprera. Historian of that island archipelago, Alberto Sega, was endlessly patient with my questions, as was Brian Walsh who had researched, and written about, the details of James Philip Webber's life there, and thus those of Maria Tamponi.

Sandro Saba drove me to find the places connected with mining and women's involvement in Sardinia's economy, such as the long-neglected

Villa Idina (Brassey). He also bought me the invaluable book about the women workers at the nearby Montevecchio mine. He and Rachael Cockrell accompanied Derek and me to the archaeological site of Nora and she took the photograph of the Favonia Vera stele there. Rachael also helped sort out the current situation regarding the San Francisco church. Anna Maria Spinas Pernis and Edoardo Spinas Pernis, today's members of the Pernis family, invited us to their adjoining apartments, and made sure, with family tree and photographs, that I was able to give the women of that family something of their due. The late Angelo Merridda also helped me with the Pernis family, and made sure that I included the town of Milis, sending me an image of one of its distinguished women. Cristina Muntoni, whom I first contacted when I found one of her pieces on the late-lamented and invaluable *DonnaSarda* website, continued to give me useful sisterly insights. Finally of those to be specially thanked in detail is Dario Maiore of Taphros Publishers who was my very first Sardinian contact when I was still unbelievably ill-informed. With his interest and kindness, he put my feet on the first step of my research, giving me not only an invaluable book, but also, accompanied by Mario Spanu Babay, he took me to my first archaeological site.

I am no less grateful to the following who, in one way or another, have helped me: whether it has been giving permission to quote, sending me articles they have written, acting as an intermediary, answering questions, often at some length, or getting me out of a technological hole. Often their names also appear in the bibliography. Abhilasha (Amazon Advantage), Antonella Anedda Angioy, Laura Baccaro, Silvia Benussi, Alison Blaszak, Travis Bruce, Stephanie Budin, Bruna and Mario Bussa, Caroline Castiglione, Valentina Chirtoca, Vincenzo Cincotta, Maria Bastiana Cocco, Annalena Cogoni, Tiziana Cossu (Kew Gardens, London), Francesca Desogus (Historical Archives, Cagliari), Staff at the Dickens House Museum, London, Rubens D'Oriano, Stephen Dyson, John Foot, Francesca (The Italian Bookshop, London), Maria Fusaro, Laura Galoppini, Michele Hobart, Jamie McKendrick, Paola Mancini, Amira Meir (Beit Berl College, Jerusalem), Marco Milanese, Monica Morbidelli (Ministry for Cultural Heritage and Archives, Rome), Caroline Moorehead, Ivo and Xanthe Mosley, Anna Maria Oppo (Historical Archives, Cagliari), Gian Giacomo Ortu, Nellie Phoca-Cosmetatou, Enrico Pusceddu, Renata (The Italian Bookshop, London), Paola Ruggeri, Santa Chiara Convent (Oristano), Lara Saritzu (National Archaeological Museum of Cagliari), Staff of the British Library, London, particularly Alison, Giovanni Strinna, Francesca Vardeu, Vera (Hotel Flora, Cagliari), Colin Walker (Bodleian Library, Oxford), Corrado Zedda.

When the text of this book was already with the editor, with Covid-19 restrictions lifted, I tried to follow up information that there was a hoard of Tharros finds at the British Museum, London. I was thwarted in this attempt. But my long-standing friend, Jane Taylor, with her Museum connection, did a much better job for me than I could have done; she was helped by Museum Curator James Fraser. I thank them both.

Those whose names follow provided me with images (of portraits, photographs or documents), often without charging, further details of which are credited in the list of illustrations: Daniela Ciccu (Library, University of Cagliari) (Marongiu portrait and Via Roma, Cagliari), Antonio Fois (ILISSO Edizioni), Giorgina Giustiniani, Ilaria Cioli (Vatican Apostolic Library, Rome), Rohan Jayasekera (Bexhill Museum), Lara Joffe (Kent History and Library Centre), Davide Mariani (Museo Stazione dell'Arte, Ulassai), Paulo Marongiu and heirs of Anna Marongiu Pernis, Marina Morra (Museo e Real Bosco di Capodimonti, Naples), Eric Pumroy (Bryn Mawr College Library, Pennsylvania), Gianni Usai (Italian translator of Amelie Posse-Brázdová). I particularly thank Bob Mcintyre who, with great generosity, scanned several images and sorted others out in ways beyond me.

As always, it is difficult to express enough thanks to Susan Faircloth and Dave Stanford for their tireless efforts to make this book publishable. Neither I, nor HOLO Books, could manage without their long-standing patience, kindness, experience and expertise.

Derek, as usual, provided translations of Latin quotations and obscure legal terms. Each of us has always ended the Acknowledgements of our books by saying how much the other's contribution to our research and writing has meant. For this first of HOLO Books' titles by either of us to be published since Derek's death on 27 April 2020, neither words nor sentiments exist. He has been my everything, in writing and in life, since March 1979. I hope to continue publishing and, indeed, to complete and publish a manuscript which Derek was unable to finish. HOLO Books, with its two imprints, The Women's History Press and the Arbitration Press, and their publications, are some sort of a monument to our time together.

Author's Note

This series 'Of Islands and Women', with its sub-title 'Women, History, Books and Places', has developed its own style over the years. Some explanations are, therefore, probably helpful. Many women appear – sometimes it might seem too many in a particular chapter – but I do not apologise for that. It might be the only time that their place in history in recorded in context. Historical women's names of those connected with Sardinia or Italy are in bold on their first appearance, including in quotations. This is intended to make it clear when the details of another woman start, especially those whose stories are told in some detail. I tend to use first names after women are first introduced. I am more formal with my contemporaries, and they are not in bold. Women mentioned only once in the text, even in bold, may not be in the Index.

There are, as usual, intentionally no footnotes or endnotes, which may be irritating for a scholarly reader. Instead, I put sources within the text; this is intended to make the book accessible to the general reader, but I also hope that scholars or Sardinians will find those sources, together with the bibliography, sufficient. I hope they will also find what I have written as accurate as the facts and my understanding allow. Many alleged facts, it has to be said, are contradicted by other alleged facts. I have had to use my nous.

If a scholar conversant with a particular aspect of Sardinian history feels that something I have written is out-of-date, I can only apologise. So much material, new and old, becomes constantly, and more than ever, available, that I have had to leave a chapter to speak for itself at the time of writing. Exceptions are where a kind expert reading my draft has pointed out what should usefully be included or changed, or where something I came across later obviously demanded it.

Previous titles in the series have consisted of a historical section and a shorter section of itineraries, marrying relevant information in the two sections. As explained in the Preface, I have not been able to visit Sardinia often enough to present the places with first-hand accuracy. There are, therefore, no itineraries; instead, where practical, I have put details of a particular place where it fits within the historical section. Once it becomes possible to travel safely again, I hope to return to Sardinia and, as far as possible, rectify the omission. If so, I shall put the itineraries on the publisher's website – www.holobooks.co.uk.

The Bibliography is rather extensive and may seem, at first sight, unduly complicated. It is split into several sections. If the author or title you seek is not immediately obvious, persevere. By this system, I hope to guide the reader into the sort of book or article that best suits their purpose, as I have drawn on books of appeal to the general reader and books and articles by scholars indiscriminately in the text. The internet, though it has to be used with discretion, is an invaluable hunting ground for information about women, who still tend to be neglected in the re-creating of history; the internet may be the only source. As proliferation of internet material increases over the years, that section of the bibliography is long. Many scholarly articles in the section devoted to them, called 'Specialist Works …' can also be found on the internet. Even some otherwise difficult to access historical travel accounts can be found there.

Where historical sums of money are mentioned, no attempt is made to suggest their value in any currency today; indeed, it would be impossible to do so.

This is not a guidebook and, therefore, the two maps, one of Sardinia, and the other of its place in the wider world, are simply guidance to the main places mentioned.

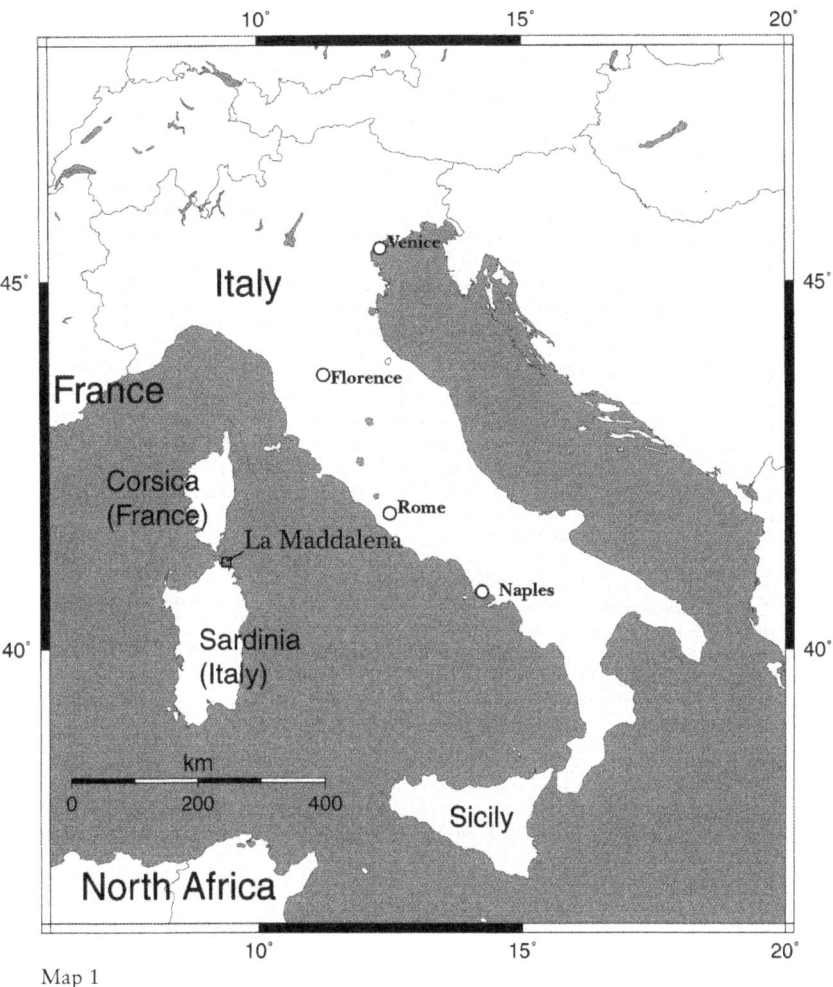

Map 1

xx *Sardinia*

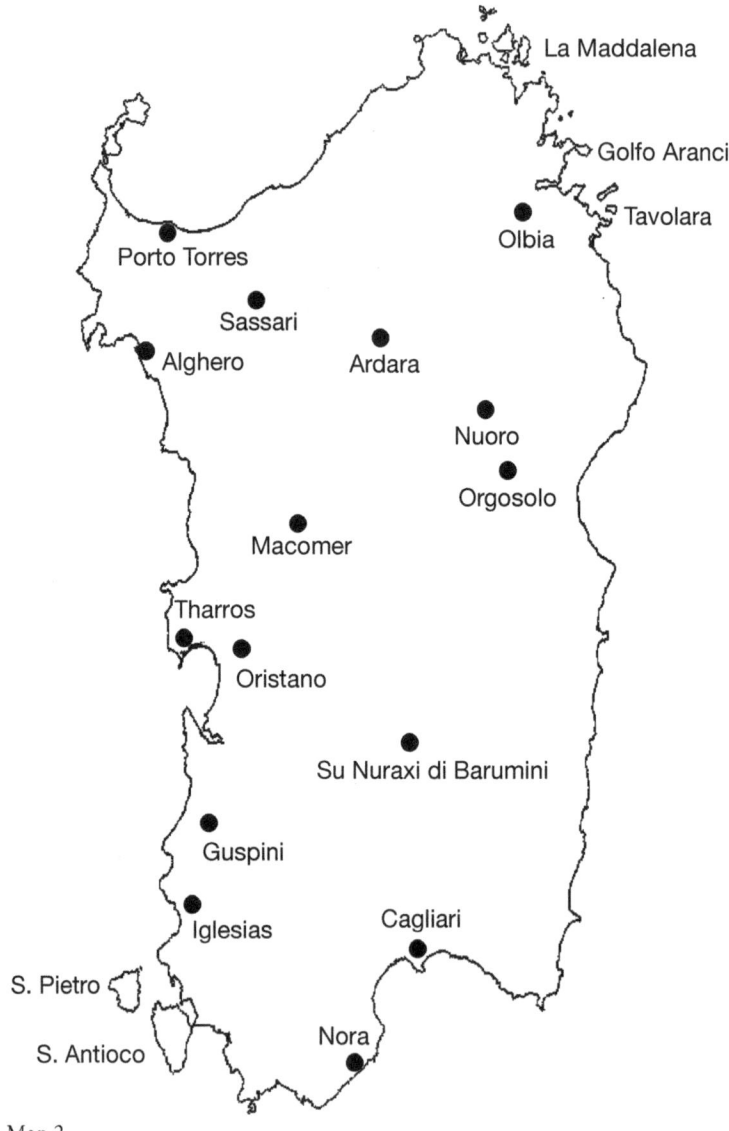

Map 2

Introduction

Islands differ in many respects from the mainland country of which they are often a part, it hardly needs saying. Because of their geographical separateness from anywhere else, and the sea that surrounds them, they have developed in their own way; and their histories are particular to themselves. Sometimes, as Sardinian Marianna Bussalai's quotation that opens my preface suggests, they insist upon, and celebrate, that difference. Some Sardinian writers even call mainland Italy the 'Continent', as if it were a completely separate entity, and the people from there 'Continentals'.

That Sardinian trait of separateness has even been obvious to perceptive foreigners. Swedish Amelie Posse-Brázdová, exiled to Sardinia from the Italian mainland as an enemy alien in 1915, wrote in *Sardinian Sideshow* (1933):

> For many centuries the Sardinians had been so fooled and exploited by the Italians, especially the Genoese merchants, that in the end they began to look upon them as their worst enemies. Neither were they any too pleased with the officials whom the mainland sent over with all their tiresome, new-fangled laws and orders. The Sardinians are untamed and proud, and they find it very difficult to bow to the authority of others. They have a poise and dignity which strike one at the first glance, a certain noble austerity that contrasts sharply with the flexible, gesticulating liveliness of the southern Italian.

How 'Continentals' viewed and treated Sardinia and Sardinians emerges from the chapters that follow.

Amelie's delightful account is one of the few over the centuries to give us a contemporary foreign woman's view of the island. Many more men have visited it, and left their version, and some have pontificated without even going there. Perhaps few are more damning than the opening words of the French writer MH Monier's *Lettres Sur La Sardaigne* (1849) when he told a friend of his planned visit:

> But, good heavens, what is this Sardinia? An abandoned island, a sad country, unhealthy and not fit to be lived in. Why don't you go to Athens instead, to Constantinople, to Jerusalem! These are at least places that offer some interest.

I have to be frank: though I ploughed my way through to the end of Monier's account, it does not make Sardinia live and breathe, the way English Mary Davey's does, written at much the same time.

What I have really appreciated when starting to research and then write about an island is coming across an early named woman foreigner who, arriving inadvertently upon its seashore, left a historical footprint, one which I could use in the introduction to continue a perhaps self-indulgent stamp on the series 'Of Islands and Women'. It worked for Madeira, Crete and Tasmania. As for Malta, it was a woman denizen, an early artist, whose name has been given to a crater on the planet Mercury who gave the introduction that quirk. For Sardinia, the arrival of the woman concerned goes against the historical chronology, and you might think it a legend – as some stories about Sardinia are – were there not physical evidence to suggest something approaching confirmation.

By AD 1000, when the Princess of Navarra is usually said to have arrived, Sardinia already had a rich history stretching back many thousands of years, including the emergence of the Nuragic people – so uniquely Sardinian in about 1600 BC. As early as Roman times, named Roman women about whom a fair amount is known, lived there. But the princess's arrival coincided with three centuries of invasion by Berbers from North Africa and some limited settlement by Muslims. In 1015 Mujāhid of Denia was to mount yet another invasion. Although Christianity had been well established on the island for some centuries, particularly well-documented concerning women in the sixth century, it was in abeyance until later in the eleventh century.

The Princess of Navarra had been exiled, or incarcerated, by her father, a nameless king, apparently for wanting to marry an unsuitable man – a servant. The name 'King of Navarra' – a Basque kingdom on the Spanish Pyrenean border with France – appears for the first time in 987, though a kingdom under another name already existed there. In 1000 the king was killed in battle, and a minor ascended the throne, which doesn't help identification. Exile of women to Sardinia was not new – more than one Roman had been – but the princess's way of arrival was.

One night, while the guards were asleep, the princess escaped from the tower in which, one version has it, she had been locked, and, with her forbidden love, who was waiting for her nearby with a boat, set sail, destination unknown. A terrible storm blew up, as it always does in such stories. The princess prayed to the Virgin Mary to save them, and promised that if she did so, a church would be built on their exact landing place.

I'm a little concerned about the logistics of this version. The only sea the Basque country has access to is the Bay of Biscay, certainly a piece of water prone to storms. But to get to Sardinia from there would mean a voyage round Spain and Portugal and through the Straits of Gibraltar to the Mediterranean, and then round the south of Sardinia and halfway up the east coast of the island to where the battered boat came ashore. Nevertheless, in the eleventh century, the church of Santa Maria Navarrese was built there, between today's Baunei and Tortoli, with a village growing up around it. And the legend of the Princess of Navarra is firmly attached to it. A question remains unanswered: what happened to the princess thereafter?

The history of Sardinia is full of legends and myths, many of which have survived years of oral tradition, and some of which probably have some basis in fact. It is untangling the historical web which is sometimes frustrating, but mostly rewarding, fun even. Some questions that arise are never answered, and have to remain dangling, and hoping an answer will eventually arrive.

This introduction is written by a foreigner, and leans mainly on other foreigners' opinions and visits to Sardinia. The reconstructed history that follows is also sieved through the mind of a foreign writer. That needs to be taken into account though, happily, there is now considerable research done, and material written, by Sardinians and other Italians about the position of women in Sardinia, particularly individuals. This is what I have for the most part been able to draw on.

Foreignness more generally is part of the mix in what follows because of foreign invasions, incursions, colonising, exploiting, settling, enforced union and arriving over the centuries. That mix, and reaction to it, is part of what helped forge Sardinian women with a distinctive Sardinian history. This was reinforced from time to time by an independence, including the ownership of land, and status within the family, not enjoyed by contemporary women elsewhere in Europe, particularly mainland Italy.

1 – The Earliest Women *c.*170000 BC–850 BC

The Stone Age *c.*170000 BC–*c.*53000 BC

Basic flint tools have been found in Sardinia dating back to the early Stone Age, 170000–160000 BC; they belonged to members of hunter-gatherer bands who then roamed the island. These hominids, or proto-humans, arrived when sea levels had been lowered by the glacification of Europe, with Corsica as a probable stop on the way. It is possible to imagine the females of these bands foraging for roots, berries, nuts, leaves and herbs, while the males hunted fauna, typically of the insular dwarf kind – elephant, pig, hippo – as well as a type of hare (since named *prolagus Sardus*) and large field mouse. Fish and shellfish would also have been part of their diet.

In Stephen Dyson and Robert J Rowland jr, *Shepherds, Sailors and Conquerors: Archaeology and History in Sardinia from the Stone Age to the Middle Ages* (2007), Stephen Dyson explains that this early population appears to have been extinct when the first *homo sapiens* arrived on the island, evidence for which dates to around 13000 BC. By this time, the large game too were probably extinct, but there was still plenty of protein available.

Some time during the Stone Age, probably 15000–10000 BC, an early Sardinian carved the statuette known as the Venus of Macomer. The archaeological and technical details of this extraordinary early object were explored through her fieldwork by the Italian prehistorian Margherita Mussi and described in 'The Venus of Macomer: A Little Known Prehistoric Figurine from Sardinia' (2003).

On the outskirts of Macomer (Nuoro Province) a local farmer illegally dug in a small cave in an orchard in a gorge of the river S'Adde and found the asymmetrical statuette, approximately 14 cm (5.5 in) tall, carved from local basalt. It has large buttocks, distinct thighs, straight kneeless legs and one breast. Strangest of all is its animal head, deduced to represent *prolagus Sardus*. As for its significance, Margherita Mussi suggests that it is 'of a model and a set of beliefs developed far away, elsewhere in continental Europe'. At least the statuette has a name, but is it possible to determine anything about the life of the women of Macomer from its existence?

The Venus can be seen in the National Archaeological Museum of Cagliari. Its catalogue shows that the dating of the Venus is not universally agreed; the fourth millennium BC is also suggested.

Another lowering of the Mediterranean facilitated the arrival of a new population during this prehistoric period. Ecological changes improved resources. Sardinian obsidian (volcanic glass used for fine tools), found particularly at sites such as Monte Arci on the Gulf of Oristano, dates from the eighth century BC; Dyson notes that identifiably Sardinian obsidian is found elsewhere in Europe and may well have been traded, though its extraction and the process of distribution are not easy to reconstruct. Internally its

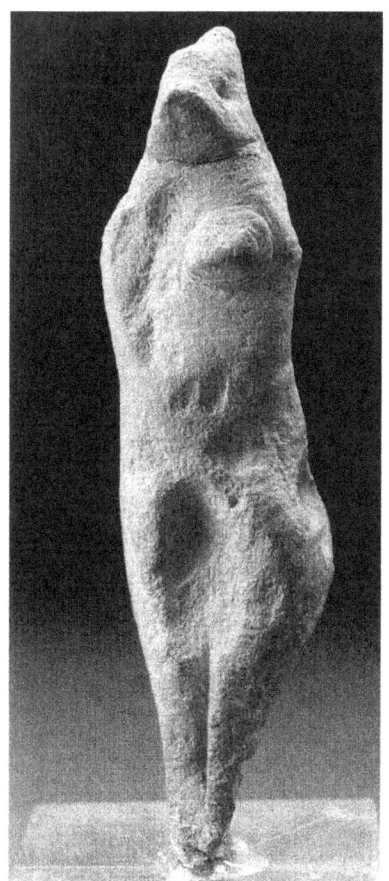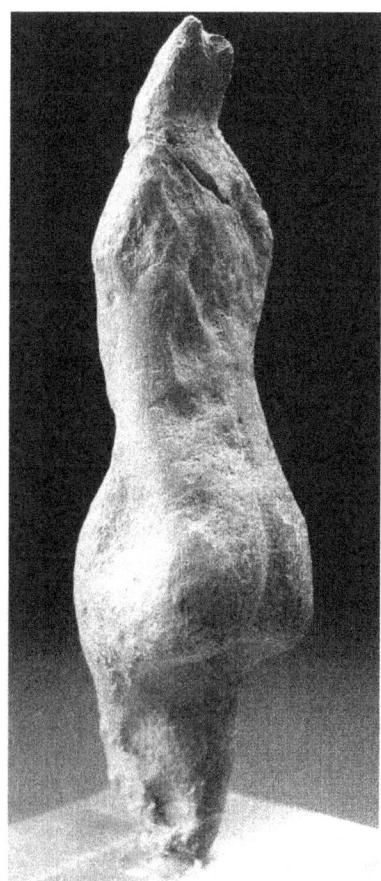

1. Venus of Macomer, from Bernardini, *Il Museo Archeologico Nazionale di Cagliari*

distribution probably took place through a network of mobile bands meeting at the borders of their territories. Ideas would have been exchanged as well as trade goods. The life of women then can only be surmised.

Neolithic Women 4700 BC–4000 BC

The Neolithic period in Sardinia dates from about 4700 BC. Its main feature is semi-permanent settlement facilitated by small-scale agriculture, livestock raising and ceramics, arising from the exchange of goods and ideas. And at last there is more tangible evidence of women. Dyson writes, 'Women were likely to have been the potters in those Neolithic societies, and processes of raiding and exchange could easily have brought women with ceramic skills to Sardinia in small but adequate numbers.' The word 'raiding' is not easy to gloss over.

Leading up to 1984, an archaeologist found evidence in Filiestru cave, 30 miles south of today's Sassari, of continuity of Neolithic exchange and habitation for millennia, through to the Nuragic period. A thousand fragments of obsidian and cardinal pottery ware were found, 7 per cent of which were decorated. This was done with the use of 'cockle shell to incise patterns on the highly burnished surface of vessels. Most of the pottery fragments, though, were from undecorated round bottomed vessels with red ochre slips or washes and small vertical or horizontal handles.' The method used may have been the result of exchange more widely in the Mediterranean or, as Dyson writes, emphasising who made the vessels, 'the arrival of a few female potters could have brought the relatively simple technology to the island'. But he also warns that much of the detail for this period is based on hypothesis.

As domestic animals were gradually introduced, women would have been responsible, it is fair to assume, not only for tending them, but also for making use of their skins and wool. The bones in Filiestru cave were 'heavily weighted towards sheep, a new animal for Sardinia, with some pigs and goats. Wild deer were also present.' Women would have been involved, too, in the increasing cultivation of produce; indeed, there is evidence from a more generalised study and one about Malta, that their involvement in agriculture was key to its introduction and progress. Margaret Ehrenberg, archaeologist and anthropologist in women's studies programmes, writes in *Women in Prehistory* (1995):

> The discovery of farming techniques is usually assumed to have been made by men, but it is in fact very much more likely to have been made by women. On the basis of anthropological evidence for societies still living foraging life-styles and those living by simple, non-mechanised farming, taken in conjunction with direct archaeological evidence, it seems probable that it was women who made the first observations of plant behaviour, and worked out, presumably by long trial and error, how to grow and tend crops.

Giulia Battiti Sorlini, an Italian specialising in archaeomythology, in 'The Megalithic Temples of Malta' (1986), felt that prehistoric women gatherers

> Might have noticed certain peculiarities and recurrences about certain grasses that could not only be gathered, but also stored and pounded to provide staple food on a yearly basis. This discovery might have brought about the so-called agricultural revolution and one of the most radical changes in the way of life of our forebears.

Later ceramic fragments of the Bonu Ighinu (4700–4000 BC) period have punched and incised decorative elements, the pottery and ritual caves suggesting cultural and societal continuity. The Bonu Ighinu period seems to have reached its apex around 4500 BC. As it expanded into the Ozieri period, villages appeared consisting of a number of timber and reed huts. The village of Cuccuru S'Arriu near Tharros, close to both the Gulf of Oristano and the

Cabras lagoon, also had a necropolis of single-room chamber tombs cut into sandstone. These contained skeletons, pottery and lithics (stone objects), some of them stone bracelets and armlets, and were covered with red ochre, as well as obese female statuettes. The goods may suggest a belief in afterlife and developing social differences. Again Dyson, often drawing on the work of archaeologists, warns about the need for care in interpreting. Regarding the female statuettes, he writes:

> The stone statuettes found at Bonu Ighinu sites are of special interest. They are relatively small, measuring some 11.5–18 cm [4.5–7 in] in height. Some have their arms folded across the belly, while others have them positioned at the side. The style is abstractly geometric with only minimal indications of anatomy. They have evoked the same range of interpretations from wife substitute to mother goddess that characterize all early female images in the Mediterranean. ...
>
> ...The appearance of the stone figures ... has also been used to argue for Sardinian contacts with other parts of the Mediterranean. ... It is also likely that the expansion of trade fostered the development of low-level hierarchies within the Bonu Ighinu communities. The burials with their status goods may well reflect that.

Examples of the statuettes, commonly captioned 'Mother Goddess' (*Dea Madre*), are in the Cagliari Archaeological Museum. Finds at this site also date from the culture that followed.

The Sardinian Neolithic period culminated in the Ozieri culture, named for a cave at Ozieri in the north-central part of the island, but Ozieri sites have also been documented more widely. Although most were to the south-west, their proliferation elsewhere suggests population growth leading to settlement expansion. The lack of defences round these unwalled, open-air villages argues for limited tension and warfare which would have affected women positively: they could continue bringing up children, making pottery, cultivation and involvement with domesticated animals without fear.

'The signature Ozieri artefact is a ceramic vessel with a bicoloured surface slip and a complex incised surface decoration.' A variety of closed and open forms were produced, including tripod vessels. The motifs on this pottery, considered fine for its time, included zigzags, triangles, festoons (chains or garlands), spirals, and circles, as well as representations of human figures. Some regional differences are noted, women potters perhaps harking back to their forebears who had arrived from different places.

Typical of the Ozieri period is the best known site of San Gemiliano-Sestu, close to a lagoon and the Gulf of Cagliari, on an undulating ridge facing a well-watered plain. It consisted of at least 60 huts, most of them less than 3m in diameter, spread over an area of about 220m by 200m. Close as the village was to Monte Arci, obsidian tools predominated. As Dyson remarks, 'there seem to have been differences in the types of objects found in specific

8 Sardinia

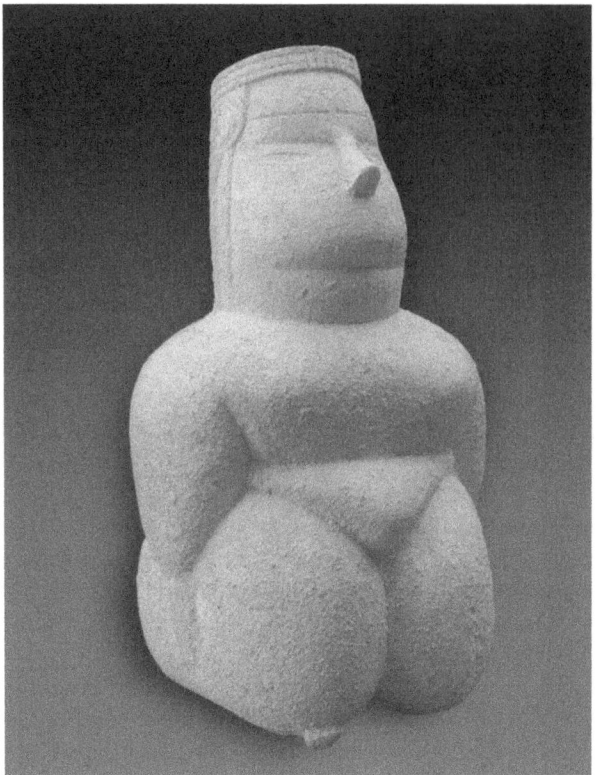

2. *Dea Madre* Macomer, from Bernardini, *Il Museo Archeologico Nazionale di Cagliari*

huts, suggesting specialized activity areas within the community'; these include more signs of women's life, particularly their work: 'Loom weights and spindle whorls attest to the importance of weaving.'

Diet seems to have expanded: animal remains found include those of wild deer, boar and moufflon (a species of horned sheep still found in Sardinia), as well as cattle, swine and sheep. There appear too remains of grain, including a variety of barley – though this may not have been an innovation – and legumes. Sea shells were numerous, presumably attesting to shellfish; at another village site the remains of sea products predominate over those of animal bones, 'suggesting a strongly maritime-based sustenance economy'.

Late Ozieri culture led into that of metal technology and was in transition through the eneolithic (Copper Age) to the better-known Nuragic period. An innovation of late and post-Ozieri culture is the menhir, literally 'men-stone', '*hir-long*', in the French Breton language; they are not found only in Sardinia. Menhir are, as the name implies, tall monoliths, often decorated with carved human faces, both female and male, linked with fertility rites, and are a feature of the Sardinian landscape.

A useful place to see menhirs is the open-air archaeological museum in the grounds of the Aymerich Palace in the Laconi commune 70 km (45 miles) east of Oristano – a palace with connections – see chapter 5. Among the menhirs are those from the Genna Arrele archaeological site, one of which has distinct female breasts. Most fascinating is the 5m tall menhir Luxia Arrabiosa (Angry Lucy) found at the hamlet of Terrazzu, 500m from the village of Villaperuccio in the Carbonia Iglesias province of south-western Sardinia.

There are different versions of the legend of **Luxia Arrabiosa**, the simplest being that she was a giant who planned to build a bridge across from the mainland to the nearby island of today's Sant'Antioco. Setting out, she carried the necessary stone on her head, while one arm was spinning flax and the other held a baby to her breast. But finding that there was already a bridge there, she returned to Terrazzu and, in a fit of pique, threw the boulder to the ground. Is it fair to assume that the depiction of her represents the multi-tasking of women then and, even, that her actions give a hint of their attitudes?

Also near the village of Villaperuccio is the Ozieri necropolis, the biggest in Sardinia, of Montessu which contains 35 *Domus de Janas* (house of fairies or witches), containing 12 sanctuary tombs, resembling a round house in their layout, built in the 4th millennium (4250–3350 BC). Corpses were buried with common life objects such as jewels and tools. The *Tomba di Corna* (tomb of horns), in which red and ochre painting can still be seen on side walls, has, as well as carved horns, symbols of the Mother Goddess. The bulls' horn decorations may, according to Dyson, represent an emerging local aristocracy with power based on the control of oxen and cattle.

The Copper Age 3200 BC–2700 BC

From the earliest times, Sardinia was rich in copper and silver. Ozieri-decorated ceramics show that high temperature kiln firing was used, and this was, therefore, suitable for metal smelting. Dyson suggests that 'Sardinian craftsmen pioneered certain forms of metal production, especially silver' and that the Mediterranean obsidian trade fostered further exchanges of materials and technological innovations. In several Ozieri sites silver and copper objects, dating from the fourth millennium, have been found, probably used for rituals. The presence of metal jewellery in some of the immediate post-Ozieri burials shows that the smiths were producing new types of status goods. Whether or not jewellery was worn exclusively by women is a moot point. The presence of metal weapons as grave goods is limited.

Just as some of the Ozieri sites show signs of earlier Neolithic habitation, the huts continued to be occupied during the succeeding Monte Claro period (2700–2200 BC), the cultures are sometimes difficult to differentiate. It is pottery ware that suggests a cultural shift: Monte Claro vessels generally have rows of grooved channels or fluting incised on their surface. Once again, though, there are regional differences. If that reflected women's work and lives, an increase in copper weapons, such as daggers, as grave goods would more naturally reflect that of men.

Biriai, near Oliena, well into the centre of the island and more to the east than other villages, is the most interesting of those of Monte Claro culture. The settlement consisted of large rectangular apsidal (vaulted) huts facing east-south-east. Finds have included numerous millstones and loom weights attesting to grain preparation and wool working, traditionally women's work. In *The Periphery in the Center: Sardinia in the Ancient and Medieval Worlds* (2001), Robert Rowland suggests that there may be evidence for use of a rudimentary pottery wheel on two objects found at Biriai. The huts were close to a 'high place' about which Dyson writes that it may have been 'associated with its cult, serving either as dwellings for sacerdotal specialists or temporary dwellings for pilgrims or worshippers'. Perhaps to enable easy access, it is noticeable that there were no walls.

Sometimes burial practices continued from Ozieri to Monte Claro. This is illustrated by a tomb unearthed at Serra Is Araus-Cabras, east of Oristano. The entrance to the tomb was sealed with a slightly curved sandstone stele, the four protuberances on which may represent the breasts of the fertility-funerary goddess. The stele is now held in Oristano's archaeological museum.

Linking Monte Claro culture and the following Bonnanaro culture is that known as Bell Beaker, which appeared in Sardinia around 2100 BC. Its name derives from its distinctive pottery, shaped like an upturned bell or a beaker and incised with triangles, dashes, wolf's teeth, and zigzag motifs. This campaniform ceramic, which first arose in Portugal, spread throughout Europe; from Sardinia it went to Sicily. It may well be that its emergence did not signify the arrival of new people, sometimes called Beaker Folk, but was another form of prestige goods imported for the Sardinian elite via increasingly well-established trade networks. The artefacts were connected with mortuary rituals and have usually been found in burial places such as *Domus de Janas*. Whatever their significance and origin, a Sardinian woman scholar in Oxford, to whom I turned for information, remembered a general study arguing that 'the beautifully incised ceramic campaniform had to be made by women'.

Bonnanaro culture (1800–1600 BC), named after the commune of Bonnanaro in the province of Sassari where its first site was discovered in 1889, is often described as the first stage of the Nuragic civilisation and early Bronze Age (2200–1800 BC). Its sites are mostly burial, many of them in Sardinia's south-western mining area. Its ceramics, with handles, were smooth and linear without decoration; as so often, it is the ceramics that tend to define the culture, which otherwise has traces of those which preceded it, as well as that which followed. These, though, do not seem to have been imported; is it fair to assume that it was Sardinian women who were still the potters? The consensus among archaeologists is positive, but it can only be an assumption. A friend tells me of her Moldovan grandmother who still made her own cooking pots at the age of 84.

One large burial contained copper grave goods such as awls, punches, pins and daggers; this may have been that of a large, rich extended family, or several connected warrior families. In other burials fewer weapons have been found. The houses were of stone with roofs of wood and branches. About 2000 human skeletons have been unearthed allowing physical attributes and diseases to be deduced. The women averaged 1.59 metres (5 ft 2 in) in height, the men 1.62 metres (5 ft 3 in). The population suffered from osteoporosis, anaemia, caries and tumours.

That is a generalised sketch of some aspects of Bonnanaro life and death. But in 1961 the Nuoro Cave Group (Gruppo Grotte Nuorese) made a chance finding that was totally specific. It was of a skeleton entombed in a natural cave in the steep limestone side of Lanaittu Valley near Dorgali in the east and, happily, the skeleton was of a woman. She was entombed alone which suggests that she must have been someone special and such a burial is, it appears, unique. In describing her in some detail I am drawing on Flavia Lo Schiavo and Matteo Milletti's chapter 'The Nuragic Women: Facts and Hypotheses' (2016).

Flavia Lo Schiavo, doyenne of Sardinian, particularly Bronze Age, archaeology, paints a slightly eerie picture:

The name of the site is Sisaia or S'Isaia, which means 'the she-ancestor' or 'the foremother', 'the Witch', as if the place were known and the name given when the body was not buried but simply laid down on the ground at the beginning of the second millennium BC, and from that time, never more visited or disturbed.

More prosaic is the account of **Sisaia's** grave goods which consisted of 'an impasto (hand-made coarse clay) pan and bowl, a granite grindstone and the remains of burned branches of an earth place where wood fires were frequently lit, and the ashes allowed to collect over time; remains of animal bones were also present.' What those objects suggest to me is that, however special Sisaia's status, she was used in life to undertake the domestic tasks that need confirmation that they were women's work.

Forensic examination of the skeleton revealed much about Sisaia's health, or lack of it. She had spinal arthrosis (osteoarthritis), a large tumour on the sacrum, and the left shoulder-blade, ulna and humerus were broken and badly healed from 'a traumatic episode (possibly a violent blow and a consequent fending-fracture). Moreover, a series of Harris lines on the tibiae and femurs show that the growth during her infancy and childhood was not continuous and healthy.' She was 150 cm (5 ft) tall, which is considered short for the Bonnanaro period. She had never given birth and, poor thing, was 'quite ugly because of a strong dental prognathism (the teeth were in very bad condition)'. There is evidence from the more general picture of people, noted from their skeletons of that time, of trepanning of the skull; and Sisaia, too, had undergone the same procedure, 'the small round piece of bone cut from her skull then replaced in a successful case of Bronze age autografting'. It may have been for medical purposes, or to release evil spirits; usually the holes can still be seen in the skulls, unlike in Sisaia's case.

Sisaia's cave is sometimes called 'Tomb of the Witch', which leads one to speculate that she might have practised as a healer. If so, was it relatively common for particular women to do so? It could account for her being regarded as other, a little feared, even in death. The reference to a witch may suggest that they were part of the cultures dating back at least to the *Domus da Janas*, translated as fairies and witches.

Flavia Lo Schiavo ends the detailed description of what Sisaia had gone through by suggesting that,

> after having embodied an almost supernatural resistance to the worst possible occurrence – the people of her tribe found a far-away place to lay down the body, exceptionally with grave goods and food (in order to deter her spirit from going haunting [sic] for food and offerings?) and never more did anyone dare to disturb her.

The importance of the finding of Sisaia, with so much that can be deduced from her skeleton, is that we have a real woman, however exceptional, whom we can visualise in flesh and blood and let the imagination wander about the life she had led.

Nuragic Women and the Bronze Age 1600 BC–850 BC

Sardinia is often known promotionally as *l'Isola dei Nuraghi* (Island of the *Nuraghi*) which confirms what the Nuragic period is to Sardinians, and how important a part it plays in tourism. This is not surprising, as there are 7000–8000 or so sites scattered about the landscape (5000 others may have been destroyed). Dyson suggests what it also means for Sardinian archaeologists: '[The Nuragic period] is a defining moment in Sardinian history, when a culture very distinctive to the island emerged and provided an archaeological unity and purpose.'

Given the various interpretations of the most visible feature of the period – the megalithic tower (*nuraghe*) – the most simple and generalised description by two 1890 scholars, quoted by Rowland (2001), is a useful introduction, however much individual sites, and parts of them, may now be seen to differ in composition and purpose:

> Nuraghs therefore were the Sardinian *pyrgos* (tower or castle keep) of the family or tribe, according to their greater or smaller size. They formed the village centre, around and within which clustered the population; where light tenements and farm houses, with huge yards for cattle and sheep, were spread over a vast area, and encompassed by rude outer walls. Here too, were to be found workshops for manufacturing arms, implements, and utensils in bronze and in all probability a small stock in trade.

A more up-to-date, similarly useful description comes from 'Ancient Copper and Bronze in Sardinia: Excavation and Analysis' (1976) by the late Miriam S Balmuth, the first archaeologist from the United States in Sardinia, spearheading ground-breaking excavations there in 1975; she also inspired many of those, often her students, who followed her there. She wrote of

> *nuraghi*, large towers in the shape of truncated cones, constructed of massive stones, and often surrounded by subsidiary towers and sometimes by villages. The period of their construction and use is now generally dated from 1500 to 500 BC.

Gary Webster, quoting the work of a colleague, adds a refinement in *A Prehistory of Sardinia 2300–500 BC* (c.1996):

> In spite of the enormous amount of nuraghi and the architectural idea and concept they have in common, each nuraghe is unique, determined by function, and environmental circumstances, location, geography, choice of material etc.

When the Nuragic settlements began to emerge in the mid to late second millennium BC, they tended to do so in the uplands where there was decent soil and enough water, particularly from springs, for agriculture, pastoralism and hunting – wild animals still being plentiful. The acorns from large stands of oak would have supplied food for pigs and mash for other livestock and for dough.

Over the centuries the settlements spread more widely and by the height of the later Bronze Age the population has been estimated at 450000–600000. During the course of the later second millennium, the elites of some *nuraghi* were able to amass considerable wealth and power leading, as Dyson says, 'to the building of more complex Nuragic compounds and the accumulation of a richer and more varied material culture'.

Webster adds, almost in passing, an element concerning the accumulation of wealth and power that shows a dark side; he describes how they tended to be based on livestock, and elaborates:

> The localization of large numbers of related males, in these communities operating as fraternal and corporate interest groups, no doubt had other advantages [than influence and prestige] such as greater defensive security, enhanced military competitiveness (raiding for livestock, wives and other wealth) and perhaps an increased ability to launch well-protected trade ventures.

Once again, as for earlier times, the suggestion occurs of raiding parties seizing women and trading them as a commodity. We are left with only our imagination to comprehend the enormity of that experience for them, though details that follow of the finds excavated from Nuragic sites will suggest what they might have been torn from. And raiding does tie in with the warrior society – for which evidence presented in some studies will be included below.

It is necessary, though, at this stage to introduce a caveat concerning interpretations of a warrior society, and this is best seen with the help of the Lo Schiavo/Milletti chapter. They remark in their introduction that one should be aware of the traditional emphasis on 'patriarchal prerogatives and on warriors, thus on the men of the Nuragic peoples'. At the same time, they point out the danger, too, in swinging too far the other way, on attributing to Neolithic cultures a 'matriarchal structure' and the 'cult of the mother goddess'.

The difficulty of dating the Nuragic sites hinders determining when a *nuraghe* reached certain stages of its structure and cultural development. Su Nuraxi-Barumini at the foot of the Giara plateau is the best known, and is now a UNESCO World Heritage Site. Its tower, originally about 6 metres (20 ft) high, dates from the middle Bronze Age, but the whole complex has cultural layers lasting from 1500 to the sixth century BC. The village that developed around the tower eventually consisted of some 200 circular huts with dry stone walls and conical roofs made of wood and branches. In some huts even ovens, wells and fireplaces have been found intact, as well as millstones, pestles, loom weights, clay spindle whorls and, my favourite, a stamp for decorating bread. These would presumably have been part of women's domestic life. There were also ornaments in bone, ivory, amber and bronze, and fragments of a clay female head, now in the Cagliari archaeological museum.

More generally, excavations of almost every Nuragic village has produced evidence of objects to do with wool processing and cheese making, as well as grinding implements and storage vessels and some remains of grain, barley, grapes and almonds. With all these activities, which it is natural from our point of view to ascribe to women, Flavia Lo Schiavo's mild warning against such assumptions should be borne in mind:

> From the archaeological point of view, as well as from the anthropological one, there is no trace of any kind of discrimination against women, not only in material culture but also in symbology. It is so extreme that … it is not easy to ascribe to women even the most traditional of feminine tasks, namely spinning and weaving.

Having accepted that, what has been deduced about women's clothes from the bronze figurines that are about to be introduced does suggest that women were concerned about, and involved in, the sort of material culture typical throughout the ages. And later in her chapter, Flavia Lo Schiavo tends both to undermine and to reinforce her warning. One of her examples, from her own 1976 work, is intriguing: she writes of 'One single fingerprint on the interior of an impasto pan made when the coarse clay was moist …

is the only document of possible domestic and female pottery production.' She goes on to write, illustrating her long experience and careful thought:

> Bread-making and baking, traditionally attributed to women, now form part of a more solid hypothesis after the discovery in the 2014 excavations of Nuraghe Arrubiu-Orroli of two clay baking plates and an earthplace. In the same Tower C many grind-stones and pestles were found, together with many spindle whorls, stressing the designation of the room for feminine activities.

Because of the thousands of Nuragic sites, continuing excavation, and changes of interpretation, those sites with a female connection are given precedence here, particularly those in which female bronze figurines have been excavated. In *La Donna Nuragica: Studio della bronzistica figurata (The Nuragic Woman: A Study of the Bronze Figurine* [2005]), Elisabetta Alba illustrates 37 of these finds, identifies where they were found, if known, and indicates where they can be seen.

Bronze making became increasingly prevalent; large numbers of stone moulds for the casting of metal objects have been found all over the island. As regards the bronze figurines, Dyson suggests that the lack of archaeological context makes the dating of most of them difficult, particularly as Nuragic sites have been looted and the bronzes have appeared without provenance on the international antiquities market, or are sometimes poorly provenanced in museum collections. Of Elisabetta Alba's list of 37, 10 are without provenance. And, because of their popularity, there are forgeries.

A similar, if particular, problem has affected excavation of the so-called 'Giants' Tombs'. Drawing on a preview of the work of archaeological historian Ornella Fanzo, Flavia Lo Schiavo (2013) notes of the hundreds of this most common form of Nuragic funeral practice that most of them have been 'destroyed by clandestine digging in the past, those properly excavated are few and even less were properly studied'. The same has applied to human bones. What is noticeable, though, is that women from the later Bonnanaro period 'and throughout the Nuragic period, had access to the same burial with the same ritual as men, with no distinction of gender and age'.

The fallback for interpretation, therefore, is often figurines. In 'Clay Human Figurines from "Nuragi" Sardinia' (2009) Andrea Babbi introduces figurines of coarse clay, crudely rendering the human shape, some female. He makes an interesting contrast with the figurines in bronze when he writes:

> Often the criterion for gathering the antiquities was based on their aesthetical value. The crude modelling and humble substance of the clay specimens could have cut them off from the antiquarian market. As a consequence, today these artefacts could be underestimated.

Although I concentrate on the bronze figurines said to be female, and they make up only a fifth of the figurines found, there were also warriors and archers, implying the bellicose nature of Bronze Age Sardinian society. But more peacefully, there were also musicians and dancers, fantastical beings, animals of all kinds and boats. The purpose of the bronze figurines is still debated, as indeed is that of the clay, but their frequent appearance in what are thought to have been sacred sites, especially wells, suggests that they were offerings, perhaps made in fulfilment of vows.

The question that nags concerning the clay figurines is, who made them? The bronze figurines required technology, including very high heat, not so the clay. Andrea Babbi makes no suggestion, apart from comparing similar artefacts in other parts of Europe, and reflecting on 'regional networks'. But could it have been the women making the offerings, quickly and roughly fashioning something appropriate from the clay they used for modelling household ceramics, not long before setting out for the sacred well? Perhaps there was an immediate and personal necessity.

Sacred wells (*pozzi*) were, it is deduced, dedicated to water-worship and played a significant part in Nuragic culture; at least 50 have been documented. One of the smallest and best preserved is what Elisabetta Alba calls Su Tempiesu sa Costa 'e Sa Binza, more simply known as Su Tempiesu-Orune. It was unearthed near today's Orune, north of Nuoro in eastern Sardinia, on a steep and solitary ridge. Dating to the second millennium BC, its preservation is due to a landslide which buried it for centuries.

The water from the spring gushing from the rockface was channelled into the main chamber, then out into a smaller pool. From this sacred site emerged numerous bronze votive offerings, among them one that Elisabetta Alba calls 'A Couple Making an Offering' (*Coppia di Offerenti*) – two bronze figures (a woman and a man) on the same base. It is kept in the Museo Speleo-Archaeologico di Nuoro. There is a co-operative office at the site and reproductions of some of the objects that have been found are kept in a small museum there.

One of the most intriguing female figurines also comes from eastern Sardinia, from the site Sa Domu'e S'Orcu, near Ursueli, a small town in the mountains of Ogliastra. Elisabetta Alba calls the figurine of a woman cradling a male figure on her lap, *Donna con Giovane Adulto* (Woman with Youth). It is more commonly known, for example captioned by the Cagliari archaeological museum, as *Madre dell'Ucciso* (Mother of the Slain). The museum elaborates on its website, drawing on archaeologist Giovanni Lilliu's *Sculture della Sardegna Nuragica* (2008):

> The little Nuragic statue, of intense emotion and charm, represents a woman, dressed in a tunic with frills, sitting on a stool, holding a naked boy wearing a cap who holds on his chest a dagger in a sheath.
>
> In 1931 archaeologist Antonio Taramelli stated that if the male figure is dead, then we could be in front of a Pietà. This hypothesis is strengthened by the fact that this statue was found in a holy cave, thus suggesting the idea of a religious rite involving a [devoted] mother offering in sacrifice her son covered in a mantle resembling a shroud.

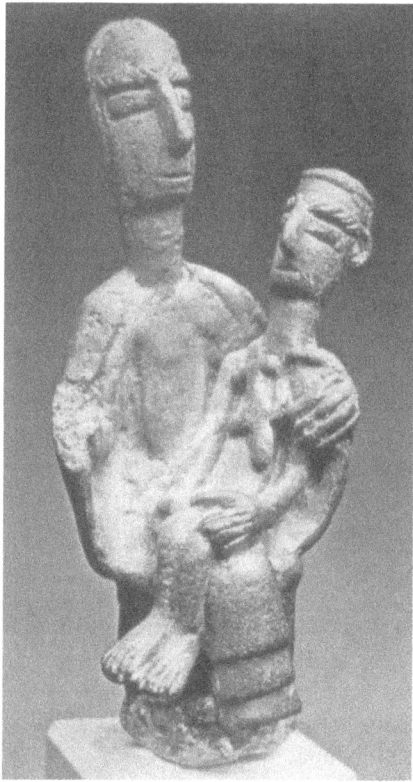

3. *Donna* or *Madre con Ucciso*, from Dyson, *Shepherds, Sailors and Conquerors*

On the other hand, Giovanni Lilliu simply talks of a mother holding her dead son, maybe killed in a fight in the oak woods in consequence of particular blood rituals.

Christopher Hayden uses a different (1982) interpretation of this figurine by the late doyen of Sardinian archaeology, Lilliu, to make a point in 'Public and Domestic: The Social Background to the Development of Gender in Prehistoric Sardinia' (1998); he begins his piece with Lilliu's quotation:

... an arcane and anguished story of death. The son, in the lap of his mother, wrapped in her cloak that seems a shroud, is a young warrior, dead, abandoned in her arms, face rigid, body naked ...

And he comments:

The romanticism of Lilliu's interpretation of *la madre dell'ucciso* ... reflects the ease with which it seems we can read its meaning. In part that ease stems from the apparent familiarity of the gender roles it seems to illustrate: the man, his status signified by the dagger he wears on his chest, is presented as a warrior, the woman is presented, if we follow Lilliu, as the caring mother. The two figures are thus referred to very different spheres of life: the role of the young warrior lies in the public sphere of conflict with outsiders, the mother's within the domestic sphere – the care of the family.

While it is easy, he suggests, to follow Lilliu, it is, nevertheless, highly problematic. Another archaeologist, for example, has it that the young warrior is, rather, recovering from his wounds. And the difficulties of interpretation go deeper:

> Although the contexts in which this and many of the other *bronzetti* have been found – sacred caves and wells, temples, as well as occasionally in tombs, nuraghi and other contexts – allow us to exclude many of the possible interpretations of figurines … and suggests that many of them had some kind of ritual role, many details of their significance remain obscure.

He wonders if they represent particular individuals from actual mythological events, or if they are idealised generic figures, and ends this point with 'The notion, implicit in attempts to make straightforward inferences about Nuragic society from these figures of art representing everyday life, is probably anachronistic.'

Whatever the reservations about interpretation, excavation and study of finds demand the attempt, so that archaeologists build on each other's work often through time and space. However scientific that process may be, there is a place for imagination between the cracks. In *Viaggio in Sardegna: Undici Percorsi nell'Isola che non si Vede* (2014; 'Voyage in Sardinia: Eleven Unseen Byways') Michela Murgia quotes from Sergio Atzeni's posthumously published novel *Passavamo Sulla Terra Leggeri* (2009; 'We Passed Lightly on the Earth') in which a narrator tells an acquaintance the story of Sardinia from mythical times to the fifteenth century.

She was taken by how he imagined women warriors, queens of the *nuraghi*, in Sardinian prehistory. He recounts how Lea of Se covered the *nuraghe* with wood, cork and branches, making a dark space where she gave birth to Usir. There the two rested for 30 days and 30 nights. The thirty-first night was moonless so Lea and Usir left. The story continues,

> Usir grew and saw with the eyes of the eagle, he talked with horses, he was challenged thirty times by invincible warriors and thirty times he won and killed. Never had the island had a fighter like him. Many women of Se decided to give birth to warriors, many women of many villages decided to give birth to fighters, every mother, at least for a son, imitated Lea of Se: they gave birth in the nuraghe enclosed for thirty days and thirty nights with their newborn.

Michela Murgia sums up what she has quoted:

> The importance of the feminine element in the Nuragic culture emerges constantly, also in the traces related to the cult, finding significant expression in bronze and in stone. But it is in the latter that most important testimonies of that ancient polytheistic faith have remained impressed, capable of attributing to how the masculine and feminine complement each other, and play an essential role in the world.

Not far from Su Nuraxi-Barumini, at the edge of the Giara Plateau, and dating to the second millennium BC is the Nuragic settlement of Santa Vittoria with its commanding view of the surrounding countryside. The *Guide to Archaeological Sites in Sardinia* (2010) gives it the prominence of two pages of description and illustrations and suggests that it was probably a political and trading centre. Giovanni Lilliu called it 'One of the most important, fascinating and evocative monuments of Nuragic civilisation'.

It includes perhaps the most imposing of the Nuragic shrines, part of a bigger complex of houses, a feasting enclosure, one for meeting that consists of five large circular huts, an enclosure where disputes were resolved (*Recinto di Giustizio*), a chief's hut, a foundry and a temple close to the sacred well. This is approached by a keyhole shaped paved vestibule with benches along each side; 13 steps lead down to it. Dyson writes that 'the complex of features suggests a variety of cultic functions associated not only with water but also with animal fertility and social and political cohesion'.

The cult of water plays a significant role in the many interpretations of Nuragic culture. Michela Murgia introduces us to the legend, or myth, of **Maria Giusta**. Her story was originally told by 90-year Maddalena Deriu of Macomer to Francesco Enna. He published it as '*Parstoria di Maria Giusta*' in *Sos Contos de Foghile* (1984; 'Folkloric Stories'). It was then spread more widely, through a 2000 symposium, by Enedina Sanna whose mission as historian and storyteller is to unearth, publicise and preserve the oral cultural history of her island. These are the bare bones of Maria Giusta's story, originally told in dialect verse:

> While out looking for firewood, she saw a holm oak fall and burst into flames next to a nearby well. From an axe without a handle abandoned in the middle of the forest appeared a 'fairy' who said to the woman 'throw the double-edged axe into the well and water will flow'.
>
> The woman, after drinking from the well, forgot everything. When summer came, everyone was thirsty, including her son who, overcome by the drought, went limp like a lily. The woman, desperate, returned to the well and heard a voice say '*S'abba non sachet/si sambene no paschet*' ('water is not born/if blood does not feed'). The woman understood, jumped into the well and the water flowed freely.

The bronze offerings at Santa Vittoria include three female figurines. Elisabetta Alba calls two of them, without the need for translation, *'Donna con Adolescente'* and *'Donna con Bambino'*. She calls the third, and 25 other female figurines from various sites, *'Donna in Preghiera'* ('Woman in Prayer'); but the National Archaeological Museum in Cagliari talks of priestesses, and in *Viaggio in Sardegna* Michela Murgia uses the term *Sacerdotessa* (priestess). The archaeological guide calls her 'preaching woman' under the details for the Sacred Well of Coni (Nuragus, Cagliari). This difference is one of many interpretations of findings in the archaeology of Sardinia's prehistory.

Of interest is the head-covering of most of these figurines, in particular those of the *'Donne in Preghiera'*, priestesses or preachers. One figurine found with most of its body missing but head and long neck whole at S'Arrideli (Terralba, Oristano), and housed now in the Cagliari archaeological museum, has a hat uncannily resembling a sombrero. Another, provenance unknown, now in the National Museum of Copenhagen collection, wears a hat strikingly similar to the black, broad-brimmed one worn by some priests today. Did ordinary Nuragic women praying wear such a statement-making head-covering? If they did, what times they must have been!

In *Il Popolo di Bronzo* (2005), Angela Demontis calls both those hats sombreros and illustrates each of the 18 figurines. Opposite each illustration she includes a descriptive text. Her drawings show what the original would have looked like from several viewpoints, back and front, with and without hat; with and without long cloak and its ornamentation and, peeping out beneath, the pleated frill of an undergarment, or dress, and sandals; with and without hood; the figurine's arms and hands in various poses. Neither does she hesitate to add her two possible interpretations of the so-called 'Mother of the Slain': she wonders if the woman, instead of being a mother, is a priestly healer (*una sacerdotessa-guaritrice*); or is it part of a ritual, the passing of boy to warrior manhood?

Another female figurine, whose provenance is given as 'German Art Market 2000', priced at $18000, wears a different hat; her ensemble is described, this time in words:

> Her clothing seems rather complex: over a tunic striped with vertical lines that falls just to her ankles, she wears an over-garment that covers her to her knees; to complete, a large cloak, whose fabric is decorated with horizontal lines and small dashes, is placed on her shoulders, thus hiding her torso. Her head is covered with a large headpiece that is shaped like a bell.

The description continues with what she is doing, and her function:

> Her left hand, raised towards the viewer is interpreted as a gesture of worship or salutation to a divinity. In her other hand, she holds a seemingly flat object, perhaps a cake or a cup, offered as an ex-voto. ... Because

of her peaceful pose, her hand gestures and in particular her intricate clothing, including the pointed headpiece, this figure can probably be identified as a priestess.

Some figurines wear a stole and Flavia Lo Schiavo adds another possibility to whether or not such a woman was formally a priestess. It has to do with two figurines wearing a stole: they may have belonged to a priestly class or, 'as seems more likely, simply individuals – whether men or women – perhaps of elevated rank who have taken over this function'.

There is another aspect to the sacred wells: the astronomical care with which at least those that came later in the Nuragic period were built (the late Bronze Age – eleventh to tenth century BC). Arnold Lebeuf introduces this feature in his article 'The Nuragic Well of Santa Cristina …' (2008) (where no bronze female figurines have apparently been found, but of three made of clay, one is female). He writes of 'Priestesses for a Moon cult and sacrificial victims'. Is it possible to link that sacrifice to the Maria Giusta story?

Santa Cristina, a Nuragic site set in a park with hundred-year-old olive trees, is in the commune of Paulilatina, province of Oristano. Michela Murgia writes in *Viaggio in Sardegna* that it is more complex than other wells and suggests that 'it is in all probability one of the mature expressions of the civilization that built it, so advanced as to reveal architectural and astronomical knowledge that is still astonishing today'. She goes on to explain that nothing in its structure was left to chance, and that this is confirmed by the most recent astronomical studies on the orientation of the well. She continues with the fact that it is

> now verified that every eighteen and a half years, the moon when it is full projects on the bottom of the well the whole of its shape through the hole that overhangs the dome covering the well, the *tholos* (conical tower). The last time this striking event occurred on 3 January 2007, in the presence of scholars of the phenomenon and a large crowd of the curious and followers of cults of neo-pagan derivation; to see it again it will be necessary to wait until 2025.

The *Guide to Archaeological Sites in Sardinia* (2010) talks more of 'water worship' and adds that 'during the winter nights the moon rays filter through the well, reflecting on the water pool'.

My favourite of all the female figurines – one more obviously a woman than some listed and illustrated by Elisabetta Alba – is the one she calls 'Donna Offerente' ('Woman Making an Offering'), found at the rather inaccessible hill site of Cabu Abbas (Olbia). She is a tall thin woman with arms raised to hold a two-handled clay jar or amphora on her head. In the Cagliari archaeological museum she is labelled *Portatrice d'Acqua* ('Woman Water Carrier') and, with her bronze stick-like body, you do suspect that she inspired the sculptor Modigliani (whose father had Sardinian connections).

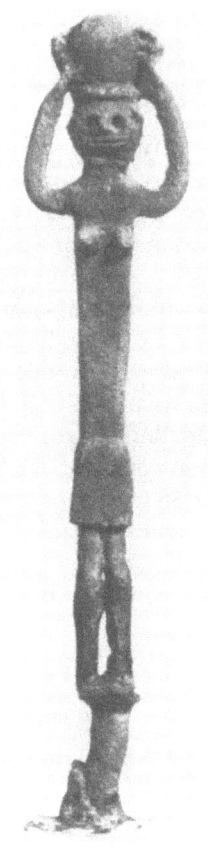 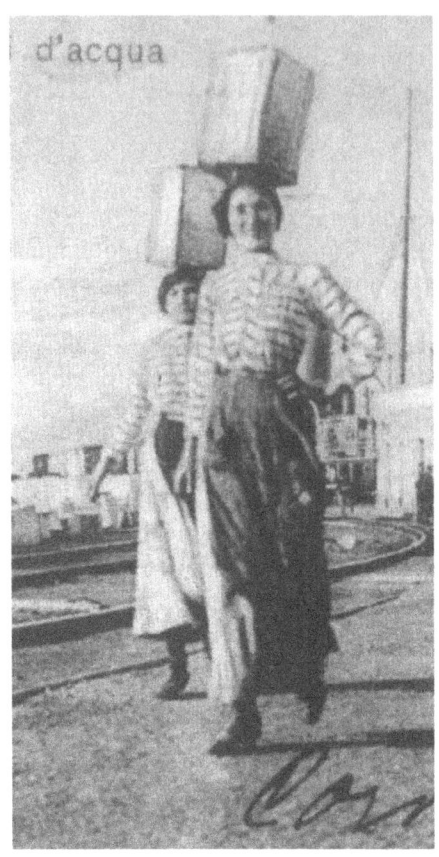

4a. Portatrice di Brocca, from Alba, *La Donna Nuragica*

4b. Portatrici d'Acqua, Golfo Aranci, 1916, from Babay, *Figari*

The reason I particularly like her is that in Mario Spanu Babay's *Figari: Storie del Golfo e di Golfo Aranci* (2004) there is a 1916 photograph, probably a postcard, captioned *Golfo Aranci – Portatrice d'Acqua*. It shows two women with square tin vessels balanced on their heads, and they are smiling; they are happy to be photographed thus. The two images shown here of women water carriers from much the same location make a marvellous link between the long-distant past and the near present. Photographs of women carrying objects on their heads even today are common.

Elisabetta Alba also captions a bronze figurine, one of five females found in the Nuragic sanctuary of Abini (Teti, Nuoro), *Donna Offerente* and that is more obvious: the woman is holding out a large, lovingly depicted focaccia as an offering. What I had not realised until I saw Angela Demontis's drawings of this figurine is that she is wearing a dress similar to that worn by the Snake Goddess and other Minoan women at much the same time. As an illustration in my *Crete: Women, History, Books and Places* (2003) shows, the upper part of the dress is a tight bodice that leaves the breasts bare.

Minoan women too affected extravagant head covering; in that illustration it is a bit like a windsock. Scholars speculate on a connection between Sardinia and Crete when they explore influences and trade.

From the Albini site a female clay figurine also emerged. These rough and ready figurines tend to be kept in museum storage.

Angela Demontis features another bronze figurine from that site whose hat is even more particular than the sombrero; this tall, pointed confection, with its wide brim, she calls, 'Witches Hat'. She also draws the woman hatless but, unusually, with the four long braids, two of each pulled from behind the ears to hang down in front. She discusses at some length evidence of a similar hairstyle found in tombs in various parts of the east, such as mummies preserved by dryness dating back 4000 years found in the Taklamakan desert in Xinjiang, western China. What is more, they wore not only long cloaks, but also tall (70cm/2ft) conical, blue-grey felt hats.

The last figurine to be mentioned here defies interpretation, and almost description. It was excavated in 1938 in an unrecorded archaeological layer of the Nuragic sacred well Sa Testa just outside Olbia (Gallura). It is not of bronze or clay, and how I came upon its image was an occasion early on in my first visit to Sardinia, when my research was very much in its infancy.

I was sitting with my husband, Derek Roebuck, in the Olbia office of Taphros, the publisher of *Gallura Orientale: Preistoria e Protostoria* (Eastern Gallura: Prehistory and Early History; 2010) by the archaeologist Paola Mancini. Dario Maiore had just generously given me the book to help in my research for this one. With us, too, was local author Mario Spanu Babay. When I turned the pages and came upon the statuette it immediately seemed female to me; but it did not say that it was. The caption merely read 'Wooden Statuette' and Paola Mancini's text only noted that it had been found with materials between Late Bronze Age and the Final Bronze Age and into the Roman age. She ended that the wooden statuette was controversial both chronologically and culturally.

I passed the book round, without saying what my impression was. But each of my three companions pronounced it female. Of course, they knew that I wanted it to be!

I wrote to Paola Mancini who put me on to an article about *Kouroi* in Sardinia by Rubens D'Oriano to whom I wrote; he replied:

> For me [it] is not datable and not attributable to a precise cultural ambit (Etruscan? Greek? Phoenician? Punic? Roman?), nor can it be sexually ascribed because it is too simply realised. ... really it is little more than a puppet, very badly made, hardly delineated.

But at least one source mentioned in his article suggests that the juniper wood statuette could be Punic and, more importantly, 'a female figurine'.

Following that session our two new friends drove me to the nearby Pozzo La Testa discovered in the 1930s when shepherds were searching for freshwater springs. This was my first view of a Nuragic sacred well. I have

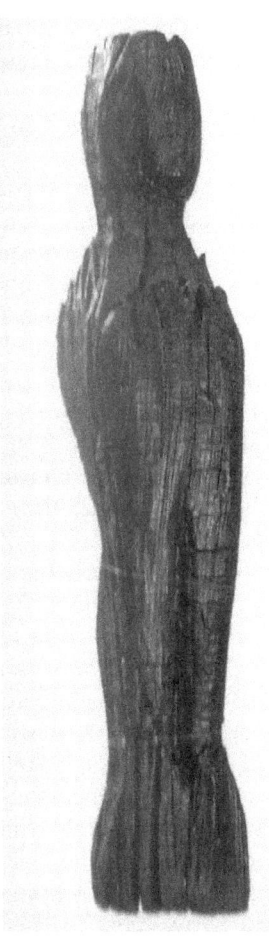

visited it again via YouTube, as many sites can pleasingly and effortlessly be visited.

Happily, the lack of clear context for the statuette, and the various periods from which it could be, allows an introduction to what befell Sardinia next – the arrival and settling of Phoenicians, Carthaginians, Romans and even early Christians, for the Santa Cristina site is named for the Christian church close to the Nuragic sanctuary and, next to the Santa Vittoria, is a Punic-Roman temple and a Byzantine church rebuilt in the eleventh to the twelfth century AD. Sa Testa continued in use until the Roman period. It should also be said that the Nuragic people did not disappear with the arrival of others; they will appear again in the next chapter.

5. Wooden statuette, from Mancini, *Gallura Orientale*

2 – From Late Nuragic Women to the Romans 850 BC–AD 257

Early Iron Age Nuragic Developments

The Nuragic people did not suddenly disappear with the arrival of the Phoenicians from the Levant between 850 and 510 BC, nor indeed when those originating from Tyre and Sidon were succeeded by the Carthaginians from North Africa in about 509 BC. The last vestiges even survived into Roman times.

In an effort to distinguish different Nuragic phases, archaeologists have given them Roman numerals; the phases relevant to this chapter are Nuragic IV, sometimes called proto-historical or Late Nuragic, and the last, Nuragic V, or Final Nuragic.

Not surprisingly some Nuragic sites continued to develop throughout the five phases, as did the lifestyle, politics, economy and culture of the people. As usual, though, dating is difficult and finds and interpretations of them mentioned in the last chapter are clearly relevant to this later period. They are included earlier to make a coherent Nuragic and place narrative. The simplified developments described here are most obviously of the later stages. Andrea Babbi's article about clay figurines links at least one of them to the Final Bronze, Early Iron Age.

Su Nuraxi-Barumini, the settlement mentioned in chapter 1 as perhaps the most impressive and a UNESCO world heritage site, developed into an Iron Age one, and Gary Webster suggests how it reveals the 'emergence of true socio-economic classes'. He writes, too, of a 'pre-eminent "aristocratic" family' with hierarchical zones in structures round the central *nuraghe*, including 'poorer peasant families'.

Webster introduces the idea of polygynous households – the presence of more than one married woman – adding, 'There is good written evidence that some Sards retained concubines (*concuvas*) as late as the thirteenth century AD much to the distress of proselytizing Christian missionaries.' Such concepts, like other interpretations, tend to rest on comparisons with other cultures, not only in Europe, so may not be helpful to include in this more straightforward account. And Webster further adds, 'To conclude from this that such arrangements reduced the status of women in these societies generally, or inhibited their political aspirations would be a mistake ... That Iron Age Nuragic women attained ... elevated civico-ritual positions seems likely from the evidence of the votive bronzes.'

In her conclusion, Flavia Lo Schiavo re-emphasises her interpretation of women and Nuragic culture when she writes 'Equal treatment and isonomy seem to be the secret of Nuragic welfare'. Isonomy means literally equality under the law; Nuragic people may not have had law as we know it, but they will have had customary law and a means of dispute resolution as the *Recinta di Giudizio* at Su Nuraxi-Barumini suggests.

In this naturally developing society, domestic livestock continued to play an important part in wealth, prestige and competition, always bearing in mind that competition, and the fighting that it suggests, were unlikely to improve the well-being of women and children, not only of the 'client' families, but even of the most 'aristocratic'.

Apart from their wealth value, livestock were, of course, also important for wool, hair, milk and perhaps blood. Mention has already been made of finds of loom weights and spindle whorls; these were in both clay and stone and of varying sizes and shapes (biconical, spheroid, tubular). A rather nice quotation with an almost irretrievable provenance gives a flavour. It comes originally from the Roman historian Claudius Aelianus of the second century AD, and is finally quoted by Webster:

> Nymphadores says that Sardinia is an excellent mother of flocks. The goats which she nourishes are animals deserving admiration, for the natives clothe themselves in their skins and these offer them protection, and in winter the skins keep them warm, and in the summer by some mysterious natural property keep them cool. The hair on the hides actually grows to the length of a cubit.

Nymphadores, who does not vouchsafe who she or he is, in spite of determined search, suggests that the Sards were able to keep cool wearing skins, but hot summers and the need for suitable clothing has been bothering me. I wondered about flax which was commonly grown elsewhere for the weaving of linen, and managed to hunt down enough evidence of it in Sardinia at the time to be worth mentioning, not forgetting, of course, the earlier legend of Luxia Arrabiosa with 'one arm spinning flax'.

The Nuragic site of Sa Osa was not identified until 2008 when a road was being constructed between Oristano and Cabras, a short distance from the coastline of the Gulf of Oristano, and close to the river. In the Late Nuragic well there that archaeologists call N, they have excavated finds preserved in the groundwater. According to an online account by Alessandro Usai (2012), these included 'fragments of fish, fragments of wood and cork, raw and processed, grape seed, fig, cereals, legumes, probably also olive and plum'. No flax. But, undeterred, I found another description: 'From the well N come the seeds of different plant species (carbonized cereals, cultivated vines, blackthorn, fig, **flax**, melon etc.)' (emphasis added). So perhaps the women were preparing not only wool to make garments, but also flax.

All those other finds suggest what women would be cultivating, harvesting and cooking, not forgetting the excavation at Su Nuraxi of ovens, millstones, pestles and stamps for decorating bread, the baking of which in quantity seems to have been important. Additions to the diet of cattle, caprines (a type of goat) and swine were hedgehog, fox, rabbit, hare, wild deer and fish, as well as wild and domestic fowl and wild weeds, mallow, catchfly and knotweed.

More generally, household specialists included not only bakers but also cobblers, leatherworkers, oil producers, carpenters and lithic workers – in any one of which specialisms women could also have played a part. The households were both self-sufficient and ready to exchange any surplus. As Webster explains, competition among chiefly households expanded from 'control of familial labour and livestock holdings ... to include control of native products such as metals [and] trade exotica'.

The Arrival of the Phoenicians

The previous paragraphs provide a sketch of the Nuragic people inhabiting Sardinia when the Phoenician traders started to arrive. They did so in different ways; for example, initially Sardinia merely provided ports of call on their way to trade in the Iberian peninsula. Increasingly, though, they started to settle, establishing new colonies on promontories or islands – at Nora, Caralis (Cagliari), Sulcis (the island of Sant'Antioco) and Tharros. Mostly the new settlers were peaceful; Webster gives an intimation of what changed for the Sards as a result of this incursion from the eastern Mediterranean:

> First, apart from new people, settlements and goods, Phoenician traders and settlers introduced an entirely novel set of standards by which native populations evaluated prestige and the quality of existing lifestyles: it is mostly simply termed 'Orientalized culture'.

There is at least one anomaly which is introduced by the finding, in a vineyard in 1771, of what is called the Nora Stone – to be seen in Cagliari's archaeological museum. Nora, on the Capo di Pula to the south-west of Cagliari, was perhaps the earliest Phoenician settlement to be established, some time between the ninth and eighth centuries BC. Scholars argue about the translation of the stone's inscription, but it does suggest military action and perhaps conquest, at least of those Sards living in that area. There is evidence of worship of the goddess Tanit at several Phoenician sites; at Nora there are the remains of the foundations of a temple to her. Part of ancient Nora has been reclaimed by the sea; the remains of a stele dedicated to a Roman woman, to be described later in this chapter, almost teeter on the edge.

How the Phoenicians related more peaceably with the Sards than at Nora is also suggested by Webster:

> Some no doubt married into Phoenician families and became the first Phoenicio-Sard elites, as the not infrequent finds of native artefacts within otherwise wholly Phoenician contexts ... may attest.

Scholarship continues to advance: in 'Ancient Phoenician DNA Tells a Story of Settlement and Female Mobility' (2018), Tessa Gregory takes the doubt away when she writes of skeletal finds at the Phoenician settlement of Monte Sirai (Carbonia), established opposite that on Sant'Antioco in about 750 BC.

> The genetic comparison showed evidence that some lineages of indigenous Sardinians continued after Phoenician settlement [there] which suggests that integration between Sardinians and Phoenicians occurred there. [The archaeologists] also discovered evidence of new, unique mitochondrial lineages in Sardinia and Lebanon, which may indicate the movement of women from sites in the Middle East or North Africa to Sardinia and the movement of European women to Lebanon. Given their findings, the authors suggest that there was a degree of female mobility and genetic diversity in Phoenician communities, indicating that migration and cultural assimilation were common occurrences.

Tessa Gregory in her short internet piece makes more accessible to the uninitiated the findings described in scholarly detail in the research article by many archaeologists (three of whom, Lisa Matisoo-Smith, Olga Kardailsky and Rosanna Oquin, were women), 'Ancient Mitogenomes of Phoenicians from Sardinia and Lebanon: A Story of Settlement, Integration, and Female Mobility' (2018). She ends with the words of one of the article's co-authors: 'This DNA evidence reflects the inclusive and multicultural nature of Phoenician society. They were never conquerors, they were explorers and traders.'

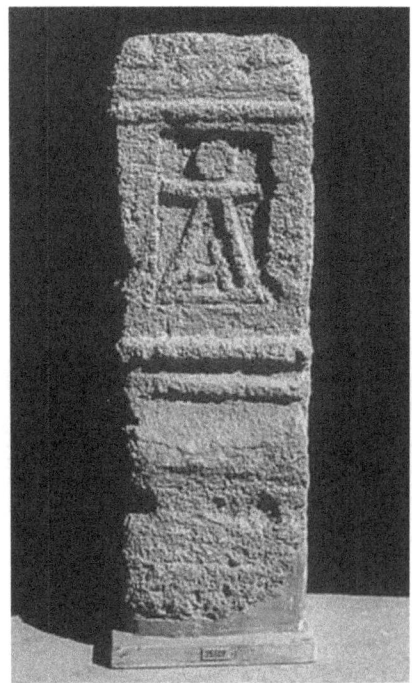

6. Goddess Tanit, from Bernardini, *Il Museo Archeologico Nazionale di Cagliari*

They did, however, apparently dismantle part of the complex *nuraghe* on Monte Sirai and, as Stephen Dyson (2007) says, a portion of it may have been turned into a shrine to the goddess Astarte; and the necropolis in which Phoenician skeletons were found was established in the Nuragic village. In 1962, a local boy came across a female figure carved on a stele of the tophet (the open-air sanctuary where terracotta cinery urns containing the ashes of premature babies or foetuses were kept; the rate of child mortality was high). A statue of the goddess was excavated in 1964; it is now in the Cagliari archaeological museum.

In other Phoenician settlements, indigenous material appears in graves, again suggesting peaceful interaction. At Sant'Imbenia, Alghero – a major centre for bronze production – a village grew up adjacent to a *nuraghe* containing eighth–seventh century BC Phoenician *amphoras* and Levantine cooking pots; there, too, there seems to have been 'a peaceful interaction between the Phoenicians and local Nuragic inhabitants'. All such evidence benefitted both Nuragic and Phoenician women and their families and might, indeed, have led to inter-relationships.

The Phoenician settlement of Tharros provides different evidence of interaction. Dyson writes that its citizens engaged in trade 'with the natives of the interior' and that it is 'documented by the development of the jewellery industry' during the seventh–sixth centuries BC. Graves were 'crudely plundered' in the nineteenth century AD, producing 'massive evidence for local Egyptianizing such as scarabs'. Dyson presumes that these pieces of jewellery were used as valuable items in trade between the Phoenicians and Nuragic natives. But, once they were traded, who was wearing them? As so often, one cannot make assumptions; it was not necessarily women, or only women, either Phoenician or Nuragic. Finally, Dyson suggests that Phoenicians could only survive by developing a high degree of accommodation with the 'natives'.

Carthaginian Sardinia

Phoenician hegemony of the eastern Mediterranean had been disrupted by the sixth century BC; power had shifted to Punic Carthage in North Africa. In the middle of that century, an expeditionary force arrived in Sardinia in reaction to Greek colonial aggression in the north-west Mediterranean. Sardinia was seen as both an important Punic power base and a source of minerals, grain and mercenaries. That force was defeated by either the Phoenicians or the Sards, or combined forces.

The *Nora Tourist Guide* (2016), available at the archaeological site, intimates that Nora was where the expedition landed:

> The Carthaginians did not find [its] conquest easy because the Nuragic people offered a strong resistance. When the Punics reached their goal, they destroyed almost all of the cultural heritage of the pre-existent population. This is the reason why in the promontory of Pula there is not much left of the ancient Nuragic inhabitants.

As for the temple dedicated to the goddess Tanit, the foundations of which remain, that could be either Phoenician or Punic, the two peoples being ethnically and religiously closely related. The vessel depicting a seated woman which that guidebook illustrates and dates rather unhelpfully '7th–3rd century BC', suggests Greek influence. There is also a stele excavated from the *tophet* depicting a woman holding a tambourine; another, also with tambourine, stands in profile. Like the Nora Stone, they are now in the Cagliari archaeological museum.

It does not take much imagination to realise that, every time there was fighting, women and their families suffered. The father of their children might be killed or badly wounded; obtaining everyday necessities would be made more difficult. What part women might play in defence of their place has apparently left no evidence, nor even speculation in the sparse written sources upon which the historical reconstruction of this time is based. Archaeology provides no help either.

In spite of Phoenician resistance, over the following century the Carthaginians prevailed, controlling not only the coastal Phoenician settlements, but parts of the interior too. An initially uneasy occupation was to last over 300 years. The old Phoenician wall at Nora was rebuilt, and the fortifications of the citadel at Caralis (Cagliari) have been dated to the fourth–third centuries BC. The walls at Monte Sirai were strengthened c.360 BC; the Phoenician settlement had been completely destroyed at some time around 520 BC. The new Punic settlement was not built over in later periods because it was abandoned about 110 BC following Roman military rule, making it particularly accessible to archaeologists.

Monte Sirai is especially interesting in reconstructing an account of women. A dozen new Punic families had initially settled there and relations with their neighbours appear to have been peaceful. An anonymous Master's thesis, I suspect by a woman, presented in an Ancient History and Classical Archaeology department, possibly in Britain, led me to a research paper, introducing us to a specific woman. 'A case of semi-combusted pregnant female in the Phoenician-Punic necropolis of Monte Sirai' (2015) had several co-authors, one of whom was Assumpció Malgosa i Morea, professor of physical anthropology at the Autonomous University of Barcelona.

The paper concerning the pregnant female describes the complete skeletal remains, excavated in T316 grave, of a woman aged between 20 and 25. She may have been given a name informally among those discovering her, but that would not be serious for their paper. I shall call her **Dido**, named after the Queen of Carthage. This Dido was subjected to an 'incomplete heat treatment according to a funerary practice, perhaps limited to the period of early 5th century BCE'. The anthropological examination came first: it deduced that Dido was about five foot (1.5m) tall; the foetus was in good condition, the pregnancy being of 38–40 gestational weeks, and 'skeletons from both individuals did not present signs of long-term disease or trauma, and no signs of pathologies related to the pregnancy or the labour could be diagnosed'.

The anonymous Master's scholar suggests that Dido

> may have been of a higher status in society, as she seems ... not to have endured a life of physical labour, and may also have, by inference, had access to a better diet. Indeed, it seems from the evidence available that she died from complications during childbirth.'

The scholar is grateful to the co-authors of the research paper, as their work relates to her or his own: 'This is also of particular importance to this paper, as it is one of the few times that we have evidence for the lives of

Sardinian women during the Punic period.' What Dido also does is to enable us to see women of this period as individuals in the way that Sisaia of the Bonnanaro period did. It should be noted, though, that the scholar cannot be certain if Dido and the others buried on Monte Sirai were of Carthaginian origin, or 'whether they were indigenous Sardinians adopting elements of Punic culture with regard to burial rites'.

Another tomb at Monte Sirai bears the symbol of the goddess Tanit, but upside down. The Carthaginians also brought the cult of the goddess Demeter to Sardinia, using pre-existing Nuragic sites for her worship.

In Paolo Bernardini and others, *Museo Archaeologico Nazionale di Cagliari* (2016) are illustrations of several grave goods relevant to women and the places in this chapter. Influences from the wider Mediterranean are noteworthy. The Greek influence mentioned at Nora is shown in a wide-mouthed, two-handled cup excavated from a Punic tomb on Mount Sirai; it is captioned 'greco-oriental'. Of the two stele excavated from the *tophet* there, one is captioned 'Stele with an Egyptian-style frame and a woman holding a tambourine'; of the other the authors are less ready, for some reason, to call the figure a woman; it is captioned 'stele with an architrave decorated with dentils and a central figure expressed in cursive and impressionistic style'.

From the *tophet* sanctuary on Sulcis, off the coast opposite Monte Sirai, come two stele: one woman, holding a lotus, stands in bas relief between Cypriot-style columns with a winged sun disc on the lintel. The lotus, at least in ancient Egypt, could symbolise the deceased entering the underworld and the process of rebirth, regeneration and reincarnation. The other stele is of marble, set inside a tuff (volcanic detritus) niche in the Greek style. The woman, in a tunic with peplum, holds the Egyptian *ankh*, or symbol of life, in her right hand. Are the images on the stele in the *tophet* sanctuary dedicated to dead babies or those of a particular mother who has lost her child or are they, perhaps, symbolic of bereaved mothers more generally? A third artefact, this time from a tomb in the necropolis, is a *protome* – a Greek word seemingly adopted by other European languages referring to the sculpture of a head, similar to a gargoyle.

A cornucopia of artefacts has been excavated from the wonderfully positioned Tharros, built on the edge of the Sinis peninsula and approached from today's Oristano and then Cabras. The Carthaginians prized this old Phoenician settlement for its agricultural potential and that of trading inland up the river Tirso. Disagreement continues over whether or not the Carthaginians introduced the large grain-producing farms more commonly known in the Roman period as *latifondi* (large estates), and worked by slave labour, or if they merely encouraged further proliferation of the existing small ones. There is some evidence that the malaria that was to plague Sardinia up to the middle of the twentieth century was introduced by the workers the Carthaginians brought from North Africa. It may, though, have already existed in earlier Nuragic times.

The most intriguing Punic artefact found at Tharros is a ceramic bottle made in Attica (the province of Athens) 490–480 BC, with only the rim and a bit of the neck broken off. The neck swells into a woman's head, and then narrows to her own neck, ending with the base of the bottle. The painted inky arched eyebrows, almond-shaped eyes, nose and mouth are as new, below a ceramic fuzz of hair topped by a sort of painted diadem. The vessel may have held liquid to sustain the deceased in the afterlife, and the broken top could have been part of a funerary ritual.

Further finds at Tharros include three female figurines. The description of one is quite simple: it is in the Greco-Egyptian style. The head of the second, in the Egyptian style, is adorned with a ceramic kerchief decorated with shells, and has a suspension hole at the top. The third is in the Greek style, influenced by Rodia in Crete. A veil is held in place by a diadem, and there are sideways suspension holes. There are two images of free-standing terracotta women, one with a tambourine, the other clutches a lotus flower to her breast. Many gold objects were also excavated from Tharros; it is unclear who owned or wore them, but one is a pendant depicting two of three Egyptian sister goddesses, Iside and Hathor, pressing their hands to their breasts.

That cornucopia of finds in the National Archaeological Museum, Cagliari, should be larger, but uncontrolled excavations and looting took place in the middle of the nineteenth century. Those taking part included an English Lord, a Frenchman, Italian mainlanders and local denizens of Cabras. As a result, finds from Tharros are today in the British Museum, the Borely Museum in Marseille and in the *Museo Reali*, Turin. You can see some of the British Museum's Tharros holdings, including dazzling gold jewellery in a not-readily-accessible publication by RD Barnett, *Tharros: A Catalogue of Material in the British Museum* (1987). It is a large, heavy, copiously illustrated volume containing not only gold jewellery but also female terracotta figurines. This is the ultimate scholarly work, but not exactly user-friendly.

I recently became the proud possessor of a copy of this fine book, thanks to Jane Taylor, not only a long-standing friend but also a professional photographer and historian of Middle Eastern archaeological sites. Through her

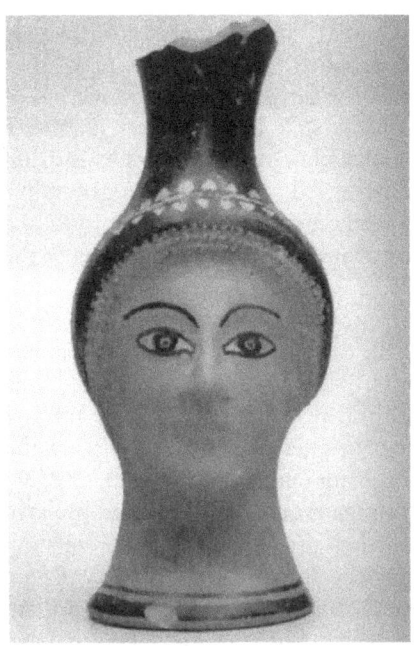

7. Ceramic bottle, Tharros, from Bernardini, *Il Museo Archeologico Nazionale di Cagliari*

British Museum connections, she was able to see so much more than I would have done. I had earlier gone to the museum hoping to see at least what Barnett described, but was thwarted by a heatwave that closed the relevant gallery. Jane, more successful, sent me images of what she saw, in particular in room 57 – several Phoenician finds from Tharros, including women terracotta figurines similar to those I've already described, one of whom is a terracotta votive offering, pregnant and seated, with gold and beaded jewellery, a plaque dedicated to the goddess Astarte and a faience hedgehog perfume flask, surely the most enviable object. One showcase in room 71 contains a preponderance of male Nuragic finds; and in room 73 there are some Sicilian-made female figurines, at least one of which was exported to Tharros. The hedgehog, too, was imported, this time from Rhodes.

Another area ready for exploitation was on the north-east coast where the Punic settlement of Olbia was established and developed as an urban centre during the middle years of the fourth century BC. From there, trade routes led to Etruria, Latium, Marseille, southern Italy, Attica and Carthage. Olbia was to prove of interest in Roman times, particularly through the life there of a Roman woman in semi-exile.

Women of Roman Sardinia (Scaurus and Aris's Wife, Fundania Galla of Tharros, Atilia Pomptilla, Claudia Acte, Berenice and Sea Silk, Favonia Vera of Nora and Maxima Flavia Publicia)

Although Roman domination of Sardinia was to last 694 years, it did not happen overnight. There were years of the sort of invasion and fighting, between Romans and Carthaginians, and Sardinians in the eastern mountains (Barbagia), that make women's lives so difficult. In 238 BC, the Carthaginians, with whom the Romans had been vying in the Mediterranean, particularly over trade routes, were defeated in the first Punic War; this led to the surrender of Sardinia, which became a Roman province. The Romans conquered the Nuragic-Phoenician-Punic settlement of Tharros that year. The first Roman *praetor* (provincial governor) arrived in 227 BC, but it is not obvious if such officials brought their wives and families to Sardinia.

In 215 BC, Sardinian rebels sought help from Carthage. In that period, two coins were minted: one had the head of a young woman on one side; on the other side was the head of a bull. Who the woman was I have not seen established. But Sardinia was subdued, and minerals, wool, cloth, cheese, horses, timber and grain were sent to Rome. The cult of Ceres (Greek Demeter's Roman *alter ego*) united ethnic groups in the countryside where sanctuaries devoted to her were established; among other duties she was goddess of agriculture. There is a bust of Ceres in the Cagliari archaeological museum, but it does not say where it was found.

The working villa of S'Imalconadu, one of several around Olbia, was developed between 150 and 140 BC to produce wine, grain and oil and to raise livestock. A granite block has been discovered there with the symbol of Tanit embossed on it. The estate is described and illustrated in Paola Mancini's

Gallura Orientale. The Tanit block is in the National Archaeological Museum of Sassari.

There is some disagreement among scholars concerning the system of slave-based *latifondi* – large-scale farms primarily producing grain to be sent to Rome, though Sardinia was drawn into the Roman tax and market economy, leading to increased imports and exports. And slavery seems to have been a feature, particularly following the brutal Roman campaign of 177 BC when many Sardinians were killed, and many sent as slaves to Rome. These would have included women and, as will become apparent, there were female slaves in Sardinia.

At Lugherras (Paulilatino) where the Carthaginians had built a temple to Demeter on top of the hill, it was transformed into a temple to include her daughter Kore. There, too, figurines of Ceres were excavated in 1906. The Romans introduced oil lamps and incense burners to Sardinia, often in the shape of a woman's head. One theory has it that because the artefacts were excavated at Lugherras, that Sardinian name was given to them. Another source has it that the site was named after the lamps in the Logudorese dialect. There are two atmospheric short films of the site available on YouTube.

The Punic city of Caralis became an important administrative centre under the Romans, so much so that, in the second century BC, they built a theatre-temple complex apparently dedicated to the goddess Venus and her lover Adonis who died after being bitten by a bear. During the building of the post office between Piazza del Carmine and Vico Malta, the ruins came to light. In them were found dozens of terracotta statuettes, fragments of a ritual bed, and a large quantity of raw coral, an extraordinary picture of which you can see in Carla Cossu's 2017 internet article about the excavation, completed by Simonetta Angiolillo. Ground coral could be used medicinally and as an amulet. Dyson suggests that the temple-theatre and its connotations testify 'to close contacts between the elite of Caralis and that of the mainland'. Unfortunately, there is no longer anything to see in Vico Malta.

Those remains and finds are intrinsically interesting and revealing, but it is the emergence

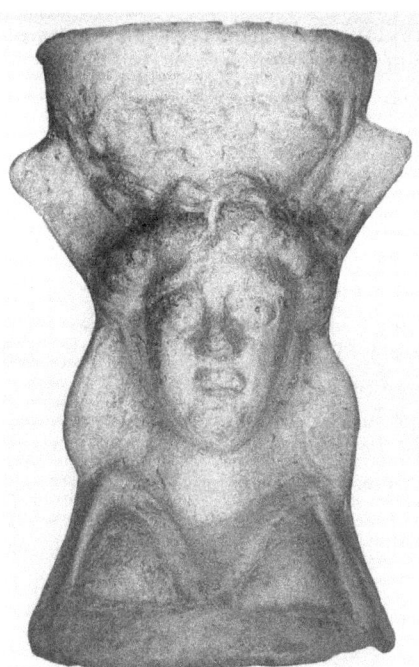

8. Lugherras oil lamp, from Dyson, *Shepherds, Sailors and Conquerors*

in the sources of individual women, most of them named, and enough details of their life to fascinate, that is particularly important. They have something to say not only about Roman Sardinia, but also about Rome itself.

The most useful introduction to individual women in Roman Sardinia is to be found in a piece written by Paola Ruggeri and Maria Bastiana Cocco to celebrate International Women's Day, 8 March 2012. '*Nel Segno di Sardo: Donne di Potere, Donne di popolo*' ('In a Sign of Sardo: Powerful women, women of the people') enables us to delve further into the lives of women of all kinds. The first, chronologically, lived in Nora when Marcus Emilius Scauros was first *praetor* (56 BC) and then *propraetor* (55 BC) of Sardinia. In 55 BC, he was accused by the Sardinians of extortion (illegal taxation), corruption, maladministration, sexual transgression and violence in his province. At his trial, at which his treatment of a particular Sardinian woman was included in the prosecution, he was defended by Cicero.

In *The Case for the Prosecution in the Ciceronian Era* (2002), Michael C Alexander unravels Cicero's oration 'pro Scauro' in more detail than other sources, showing the separate but related involvement of two women – **Bostar's mother** and **Aris's wife**, a noblewoman of Nora of Punic origin. By leaving them unnamed, Cicero further demeaned them. Although the man Bostar, a rich citizen of Nora, was planning to leave Sardinia before Scaurus arrived, nevertheless he dined with the *praetor* and died by poison that same evening. The prosecution claimed that the motive was financial, 'and thus strictly relevant to the extortion case, possibly by Scaurus distributing the late Bostar's estate'. Cicero, for the defence, reviled Bostar's mother. He also related how Aris (Arine) had fled Sardinia, leaving his wife behind; she then committed suicide. Alexander simplifies the intricacies of the story:

> The connection between the two incidents is the fact that the mother of Bostar is present in court … apparently as a witness. Cicero charges that she and Aris planned to marry at Rome, once the wife of Aris was out of the way. Whereas the prosecution alleged that the wife of Aris had committed suicide to protect her chastity against the designs of Scaurus.

Cicero ridiculed this suggestion: how could any man desire such 'an ugly old woman'? He argued that she committed suicide when she discovered her husband's perfidy, 'or a freedman of Aris was commissioned to murder her in such a way that her death would appear to be suicide'. The freedman concerned had hastened to Rome to tell Aris of his wife's death. Hearing of it, Aris immediately married Bostar's mother.

The women were not the only ones insulted by Cicero: the Sardinians as a whole were reminded of their African, Punic, heritage and – referring to the Carthaginians against whom Rome had waged two wars – were, thus, untrustworthy; many of them had been transported to Sardinia as punishment for their crimes. He labelled them powerless in resources, treacherous by descent (*fides punica*). Because of Cicero's fame as an orator, the insult stuck among Romans. The prosecution case was not helped by the lack of any Roman among the Sardinians who came to testify. Cicero was successful in getting Scaurus acquitted. It would be little consolation to the Sardinians that in 53 BC Scaurus was accused of shameless bribery and sent into exile.

Antonella Anedda included the poem 'Against Scauro', written in the Sardo language, in her anthology *Archipelago* (2014); the footnote to the English translation, which faces the version in Sardo, suggests that Scaurus raped Aris's wife. These lines show that Cicero's slur still hurts in the twenty-first century:

> How can I write of Rome in one or seven days
> – a glut of beauty, taste and linen tunics.
> Maybe those Sards, 20 centuries ago, felt this
> when they came to plead for justice against Scaurus.
>
> 'A truthless people … land where even honey is gall'
>
> Cicero said in his oration. But his name, now
> tiny and rapid, flits among the stones, and just as
> then, witnesses die, the bee labours on.
> Honey endures – a tongue of salt, arbutus, thistle.

The connection between Sardinia and Africa and the critical judgments made on the island's people were to long outlast Scaurus and Roman times. In his article 'Between Italy and Africa: British Perspectives on Nineteenth-Century Sardinia' (2013) Owain Wright gives a taste of what British visitors were to write about the 'primitiveness' of Sardinians, and often with reference to women.

Marcus Terentius Varro (116–27 BC) was 80 years old when he wrote the first volume – *De Re Rustica* (36 BC) – of his three-volume seminal work *Rerum Rusticarum Libri Tres* (Three Books on Agriculture). He was not only an agronomist, but also a historian, philologist and poet. It may not be extraordinary that he should have dedicated his work to his much younger wife, **Fundania Galla**, daughter of scholar Gaius Fundanius, but there was much more to the dedication. He wrote in the preface (translated and presented with the Latin in the 1934 Loeb edition):

> Since you have bought an estate and wish to make it profitable by good cultivation, and ask that I concern myself with the matter, I will make the attempt; and in such wise as to advise you with regard to the proper practice not only while I live but even after my death … Therefore I shall write for you three handbooks to which you may turn whenever you wish to know, in a given case, how you ought to proceed in farming.

What makes Fundania Galla of special interest is that her property was in Sardinia, at Tharros. In his preface, Varro then invokes the help of various deities – Tellus (mother of earth), Sol and Luna (who looked after planting and harvesting), Ceres, Flora (goddess of flowers), Minerva (protector of olive groves) and Venus (protector of gardens). He continues:

> Having duly invoked these divinities, I shall relate the conversation which we had recently about agriculture, from which you may learn what you ought to do; and if matters in which you are interested are not treated, I shall indicate the writers, both Greek and Roman, from whom you may learn them.

Varro then details those other books from which she can learn, confirming, if we needed it, that his wife was a highly erudite and educated woman – perhaps one of the reasons he had married her.

Near the end of his long preface, in which he converses with other scholars, including his father-in-law, he advises his wife:

> You should have some knowledge of [the elements of the universe] before you cast your seed, which is the first step in all production. Equipped with this knowledge, the farmer should aim at two goals, profit and pleasure; the object of the first is material return, and of the second enjoyment. The profitable plays a more important role than the pleasurable; and yet for the most part the methods of cultivation which improve the aspect of the land, such as the planting of fruit and olive trees in rows, make it not only more profitable but also more saleable, and add to the value of the estate.

What adds to the accessibility of Fundania Galla's story, as told through her husband's obvious faith in her abilities, is the hint of her property on the great coastal road that ran from Tharros to Othaca (later Santa Giusta). This comes in the form of an inscription found in the nineteenth century, and seen transcribed in, for example, Maria Bastiana Cocco's thesis presented to the University of Sassari '*Servi e Liberti nella Sardegna Romana alla Luce della Documentazione Epigrafica*' (2009-10):

> ----/ [---]us Fundan(iae) / Gallae disp(ensator) templum / et maceriem item / pomar(ium) impens(a) sua fecit idemq(ue) dedicavit.

From this, together with Varro's preface, it has been possible to glean a fuller version by, for example Maria Bastianna Cocco's supervisor, Paola Ruggeri, in '*Un Nuovo Bollo Laterizio dalla Necropoli Romana di Monte Carru Alghero* (SS)' (2019), and Anna Ardu in '*Tharros in Età Romana*' (nd). It appears, therefore, that Fundania Galla's bailiff (*dispensator*) constructed for her, out of privately made bricks, a large rustic walled villa and temple with apple orchard dedicated to Pomona (goddess of abundance of orchard fruit). Taking all the details together, it is hard to imagine Fundania Galla not spending time there herself, supervising, her husband's volumes beside her, perhaps increasingly so after his death when he was 89. Is that being fanciful? Many Romans owning *latifondi* in Sardinia never went near them. Fundania Galla's bailiff might well have been a slave or freedman.

Not far from Tharros, about 35 km (about 22 miles) east of Oristano, is the farming and shepherding village of Aidomaggiore. From there comes an inscription dating from the first century BC and mentioned in the 8 March 2012 sketch of women's history in Roman times by Paola Ruggeri and Maria Bastiana Cocco. It not only tells of the Sardinian-born slave **Qdabinel**, but allows her name and thus a hint of her story to survive, for the authors deduce that she died on the same estate where she had worked, and she probably spoke either the Punic or the Nuragic language. How she came to be a slave is not so easy to discern.

If Fundania Galla did go to Sardinia, it would have been of her own volition; it was not always so: the island so near Rome across the sea, was also a place of exile. In the first century AD a wife, a noblewoman, **Atilia Pomptilla**, and husband, Lucio Cassio Filippo, went into exile in Caralis, probably because of politics that affected his Roman Cassius family. Gaius Cassius Longinus was involved in the murder of Caesar, and the Emperor Nero exiled a jurist of the same name to Sardinia in AD 65; he was not, apparently, the father of Lucio Cassio Filippo but they were probably closely related.

We would know nothing of the couple's exile but for the funerary hypogeum in today's Viale Sant'Avendrace, known as 'the Vipers Cave' (*Grotto delle Vipere*) or 'the Atilia Pomptilla Sepulchre'. It is worth visiting, not only for the romance attached to it, but also for its survival. That one can visit it at all and, indeed, learn the story that it tells, depended on chance, as so much in the recreation of history from archaeological remains or documents does. The Piedmonese soldier and naturalist Alberto della Marmora who was on active service in Sardinia in the 1820s, wrote in *Viaggio in Sardegna* (1860):

> This tomb is no longer in its original state of integrity, because for a long time it had been dug around to extract the rock and cut stone which is of good quality here. I can say, without boasting too much, that in 1822 I stopped the destructive hand of the work supervisors. They had already done their worst to a nearby grave, and they would have done the same with the other, if I had not caused the viceroy, with his authority, to intervene and prevent the complete destruction.

The street where the sepulchre is located is a very ordinary, modern one on the outskirts of Cagliari. On the day I went, the sepulchre was covered in scaffolding, and it was closed for restoration; I could only gain an impression from the gate, not seeing the inscriptions on each side in Greek and Latin, nor even the entwined snakes which give it its name.

The inscriptions tell how, when her husband was gravely ill, probably with malaria, Atilia Pomptilla offered her own life to the gods in order to save his. And so it came to pass that he got better and she died, aged 62, after 42 years of marriage. The inscriptions not only relate that sacrifice of a devoted wife, but also, at length, and in flowery language, reveal the devotion of the husband for his dead wife and his longing to join her. Typical are these lines: 'From your ashes, Pomptilla, violets and lilies flourish and may you bloom again in the petals of the rose, of the fragrant crocus, of the eternal amaranth.' Scholars have supposed all sorts of Greek or Egyptian mythological connections for the entwined vipers, but Maria Bastiana Cocco is satisfied that they simply symbolise the couple's love for each other.

The same author, in her chapter on slavery in Sardinia, '*La Schiavitù nella Sardegna* (2016), notes from a further, emotional, inscription in the sepulchre that a special bond appeared to exist between Atilia and two of her freedmen who tended it. From the way they are addressed, she is led to suggest that Atilia and her husband may have been childless and compensated for that.

Perhaps the best known, and most written about, Roman woman in Sardinia is **Claudia Augusti Liberata Acte**, often just known as Acte or Atte; she was in semi-exile there, not for what she had committed, but because of who she was: the lover of Emperor Nero. He became Roman emperor in AD 54; a year later, against his mother Agrippina's wishes, jealous of her own influence with him, he was introduced to Atte by his tutor, in order to prevent the 17-year-old from engaging in risky sexual exploits, and to maintain his own influence.

Atte's life has been pieced together by several scholars; among the most accessible is Paola Ruggeri's 2015 Facebook post, '*La Liberta Amata da Nerone, Claudia Atte*', a simplified version of a 1995 article she wrote with the eminent historian of Sardinia, Attilio Mastino. Atte was born in Asia Minor, date unknown, in the Roman province of Bithynia (then Greek; today in Turkey), and bought as a slave there. She was possibly adopted and freed by Nero's great-uncle, Emperor Claudius; she may then have become an actress, and she and Nero could have met in theatrical surroundings. Their relationship was kept secret so as not to damage Nero's politically expedient marriage to Octavia. Their passion for each other lasted three years; indeed, Nero even hoped to marry Atte, and bribed ex-consuls to prepare to swear that she was of royal birth.

Nero gave Atte estates in Italy, probably in Egypt, and in Sardinia, in Olbia and Mores (ancient Hafa; between today's Sassari and Ozieri), so that she was able to accumulate considerable wealth, though she is supposed not to have tried to influence affairs of state; nor did she have power-hungry relatives. When, however, Nero decided to repudiate Octavia and marry Poppea, Atte either decided herself to go into voluntary exile, or was encouraged to do so; she settled in Sardinia in AD 63.

Atte seems to have first visited her Sardinian properties, which belonged to Nero's dynastic family, in AD 55, and it was there, particularly in Olbia, that she really came into her own: she showed herself to be a successful entrepreneur, for example, setting up brick- and tile-making factories; bricks stamped with her trade-mark *Actes Aug(usti)/l(iberta)* have been found all over the island. She also had *latifondi* around Olbia producing wheat. She became part not only of the local economy, but of its politics too. While Atte is said to have steered clear of meddling in politics in Rome, as a *latifondista* she seems not to have been so reticent in Sardinia. In another facebook post *'Esiliati in Sardegna: Claudia Atte, la Liberta Amata da Nerone ad Olbia'* (2017), Paola Ruggeri wrote of AD 56:

> It is probable that Liberta Atte also played a role in the condemnation of the Prosecutor of Sardinia Vipsanio Lenate, accused by some wealthy island landowners of having administered the province with rapacity and called to respond to the crime of extortion under Calpurna law.

Not far from Olbia, just off the charming tourist resort of Golfo Aranci, is the island of Figarolo. In *Figari*, Mario Spano Babay implies that Atte had a villa there, where she retired during the hot season in Olbia. In 1882, the archaeologist Pietro Tamponi, excavating there, made a discovery the importance of which, he wrote, was little in itself, except to show that the island had been inhabited in Roman times. He found an oval pool, or bath, lined with crushed rustic bricks; and other remains of buildings came to light when an island ring road was constructed. Mario Spano Babay wrote, 'Could this have been Atte's villa?'

Not surprisingly, reading this and being able to quiz the author about it, I did so in some excitement. But he was not prepared to indulge me wholeheartedly: it was only a possibility, he insisted. Nevertheless, as we were staying in Golfo Aranci, I made plans to go on a boat trip round the island just before we were leaving. Unfortunately, it came to nothing: the weather was too inclement; the trip was cancelled. It is not scholarly of me to persist in imagining Atte there.

Other, more tangible, evidence of Atte survives. She had slaves in her household, and probably in her brick factories too. One woman at least, **Claudia Pythias Acteniana**, a slave of Nero's, had gone with Atte to Sardinia, and it seems that many others also accompanied her. In the National Archaeological Museum, Cagliari, found in 1881 in the countryside near Olbia, is a marble funeral urn inscribed with a dedication by her mother, Acteniana, to **Claudia Calliste** who died in Sardinia aged 21 years, 10 months and 14 days. The name Acteniana links her to Atte (Acte). Acteniana became a *Libertà*, freedwoman, although it is not clear if it was by Atte or Nero's hand. Other slaves in her entourage were also freed. There is mention of Christianity, at least among her slaves, and at least in *Myself My Sepulchre* (1969), a fictionalised autobiography of Nero by Mary Teresa Ronalds; modern scholarship finds it improbable that Atte herself was a Christian.

There was a failed coup against Nero at the games to celebrate the goddess Ceres on 19 April AD 65. In thanksgiving Atte is said to have built a small temple in Olbia dedicated to Ceres. All that remains is a lintel in Sardinian granite inscribed with Atte's dedication, now kept at the Camposanto monument, Pisa. Also found at Olbia is a bust of the young Nero, the commissioning of which is attributed to Atte, to celebrate their years of happiness together.

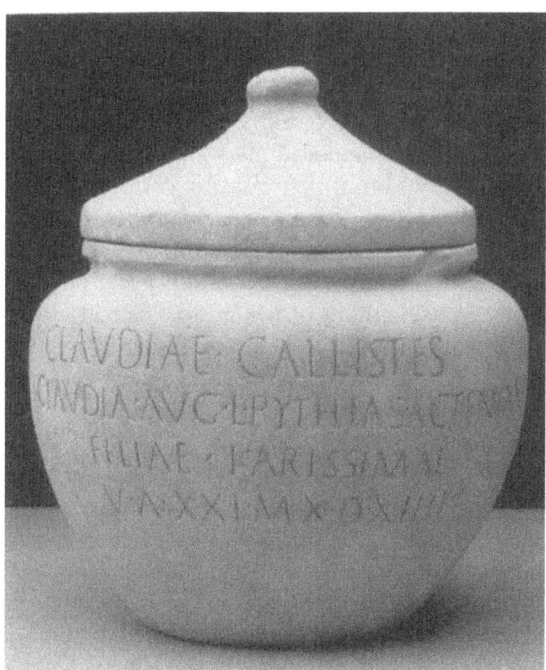

9. Claudia Calliste funeral urn, from Bernardini, *Il Museo Archeologico Nazionale di Cagliari*

Another coup was attempted in AD 68; although it was not successful in its immediate aim, Nero fled Rome. He was tried in his absence and condemned to death. Instead, he committed suicide. It is said that Atte returned from Sardinia and organised, with his old nurse, the burial of the emperor's ashes on the Pincian Hills at the Campo Marzo. She is even said to have paid for the funerary rites.

Maria Bastiana Cocco details, in her thesis '*Servi e Liberti Nella Sardegna Romana*', how under Nero's successor, Emperor Vespasian, Nero's family lands in Sardinia, which he had given to Atte, became the property of the Flavian dynasty founded by Vespasian. Property included not only lands and factories but also slaves, and Claudia Augusti Libertà Pythias Acteniana seems to have been among them. The Flavian stamp began to appear on local tiles. Flavian freedmen and women constituted an important family in Caralis, as indicated, for example, by a funerary altar dedicated by Titus Flavius Martialis, to his son, his daughter **Flavia Primitiva**, and his wife **Flavia Auxesis Martialis**. Although their functions are not mentioned, they are assumed to have had precise duties.

How Atte dealt with these losses does not seem to be recorded. But Attilio Mastino explains in *Storia della Sardegna Antica* (2009) that she was not killed as, presumably, she might have been, nor did she suffer *damnatio memoriae* after her death, whenever that was. This would have meant that she would be excluded from all official accounts, and her name removed from inscriptions and documents. It was a form of dishonour that could be passed by the Roman senate on traitors or others who brought discredit to the Roman state.

Her life until AD 68, but not after, is explored, as much as the Roman sources and archaeological evidence allow, not only by scholars but also in literature. Alexander Dumas' first novel is entitled *Acte* (1838), and she appears in the novel by Nobel Prize winner Henryk Sienkiewicz, *Quo Vadis* (1895), about two fictional Christians who suffer Nero's persecution.

While evidence of what became of Atte in reality seems to be lacking, Attilio Mastino does suggest something of her legacy. Her brick- and tile-making factories seem to have continued functioning under Flavian proprietors and, as a result, 'the entrepreneurial experience of Atte would have borne fruit and the island would have opened up to trade and export of high quality craft products'.

Several facts have contrived to create what is most likely a myth on the island of Sant'Antioco (earlier Sulcis). In AD 19, in the reign of the Roman emperor Tiberius (AD 14–37), 4000 Roman-freed Jews were transported to southern Sardinia, as confirmed by catacombs containing Hebrew tombs on Sant'Antioco. Engraved on the front of one of them is the name Beronice. This is a common enough Roman name, but the story has grown up that she was in fact **Berenice** (AD 28–post 81), Queen of Chalcis (Cilicia – in today's Syria), Princess of Judea, whose family ruled the Roman province of Judea between 38 BC and AD 92. She has become linked to the production of sea-silk (*byssus*), a very fine cloth woven from the filaments of the long beard of the large bivalve *Pinna nobilis*, and dating back to antiquity. Indeed, perhaps the last weaver of sea-silk, a Jewish exponent born in 1955 on Sant'Antioco, is wedded to this theory. In an article of September 2015 in *BBC History Magazine*, 'Chiara Vigo: The Last Woman Who Makes Sea Silk', Max Paradiso writes,

> According to Vigo, the skill was brought to Sant'Antioco by Princess Berenice, great-granddaughter of the Biblical Herod, Herod the Great, during the second half of the first century.

Berenice's life is certainly one of partly concocted stories. In AD 64 Nero had appointed as procurator of the province of Judea a man who systematically discriminated against the Jews in favour of the Greek population, as well as being corrupt, particularly in the way he imposed taxes. Having been first married at 13, and since twice widowed, the second time, aged 20, after marriage to an older brother of her father, Berenice then lived with her brother, King Herod Agrippa II. There is evidence, in fact, that she ruled jointly with him; for example, they sat together in judgment against the apostle Paul, and exonerated him.

When the Jewish Revolt broke out in AD 66, Berenice, hair shorn and barefoot, and putting herself in danger of being killed, travelled to Jerusalem and attempted to mediate. The royal couple's palace was burnt down and they gave themselves up to the Romans. Emperor Nero sent Vespasian to put down the revolt; he took his son Titus with him and, in AD 68, Berenice and Titus, 11 years her junior, began a relationship, leading to her historical reputation as a traitor to her people. When Vespasian went back to Rome and, in AD 68, soon after Nero's death, became emperor, Titus was left in charge.

In AD 70, the rebellion over, the Second Temple destroyed, approximately a million dead, and 97000 taken into slavery, a triumphant Titus returned to Rome. In AD 75 Agrippa went to Rome, taking Berenice with him. She resumed her relationship with Titus, moving into his palace, and acting in every respect as his wife. To give an idea of her status, Quintilius, like Cicero a leading exponent of legal rhetoric, writes 'some have been judges in cases where their own interests were involved ... when I appeared on behalf of Queen Beronice, actually pleaded before her'.

Not surprisingly, the relationship between Titus and Berenice did not meet with Roman approval: the eastern queen was seen as an intrusive outsider. Titus gave in to pressure and sent her away. When he succeeded his father as emperor in AD 79, she returned to Rome, but had to leave again. Titus may have intended to send for her again, but he died in AD 81, after reigning barely two years.

What became of Berenice is unknown for certain, though much is written about her. Were her two periods of enforced exile, or the second, spent in Sardinia? Maybe; maybe not. Can it be dismissed out of hand? A 2007 article in *La Nuova Sardegna – 'Il Mistero dei "beronicenses": antichi cortigani della regina?'* (Mystery of the 'beronicenses': were they the queen's courtiers of antiquity?') – supports the thesis that Queen Berenice was in Sant'Antioco (Sulcis). Carlo Floris writes:

> The Beronicenses who would have constituted a distinctive community in the Roman city of Sulcis, recorded by the Greek geographer Claudio Tolomeo in the second century AD, would have been the courtiers of the Jewish queen Beronice, or Veronica, the companion repudiated at the time of Emperor Titus's coronation and exiled to ancient Sulcis with all her followers.

Floris calls Berenice the Jewish Queen; although Princess of Judea she was, like Herod, not Jewish. Claudio Tolomeo (AD 100–*c*.170), usually known simply as Ptolomy, Greco-Roman mathematician, astronomer, geographer and poet, published *Geographia* (*c*.AD 15), giving details, among other matters, of the extent of the Roman Empire. This Berenice suggestion is not universally accepted, but a Sant'Antioco website goes further: it speculates: 'Now could it be that the tragic destiny of Beronice, lady of legend and history, found a happy end on Sant'Antioco? If such were the case, did she have a part in the saga of Sea-Silk?'

The works featuring Berenice are too long to list, but the 1791 opera by Mozart, *La Clemenza di Tito*, has her being sent back to Jerusalem by Titus.

Would a man who loved her have done that, given that the Jews regarded her as a traitor? And, as has been demonstrated, Sardinia was a place of Roman exile.

The wider story of sea-silk, Chiara Vigo's part in it and, indeed, that of her grandmother **Maddalena Rosina Mereu**, is told in several articles to be found on the internet. A good example is the anonymous '*Quel Tessuto Che Viene de Mare*' (2004; 'That Fabric that Comes from the Sea') in the archive of the *Nuova Sardegna*. There is also a book – *La Seta del Mare – Il Bisso* (2004) by professor of Italian history, Evangelina Campi.

It has already been made clear that women in Roman Sardinia, at least Roman women, owned land there: Fundania Galla in the last century BC, Claudia Acte in the first century AD. This practice continued in the second century AD. Among such women, as Maria Bastiana Cocco writes in '*La Schiavatù nella Sardegna*' (2017), was **Iunia Rufina** from an important senatorial family (*Iunii Rufini*). She owned farms in the commune of Neoneli, 35 km (22 miles) north-east of Oristano. There is no evidence that she visited her properties, but her bailiff, again a slave or freedman, marked products such as roof tiles, bricks and ceramics with her seal. Her farms employed a number of slaves who also marked their names on what they made.

The International Women's Day piece by Paola Ruggeri and Maria Bastiana Cocco names two other women who owned Sardinian properties: **Antonia Rouphina** from Bonorva, south-east of Sassari, and **Claudia Galla** from Fonni in Barbagia. It also names two women slaves, their names discovered by their marks on tiles or bricks. Of **Honorata** we know only that she was linked to the possession of a farm by an unnamed female member of the Sardinian ruling class in Garulus Vetus (today's Padria, south of Sassari); and **Germana** about whom even less seems to be known except that her name appears in Tegula (Teulada) south-west of Cagliari.

Although slaves were primarily of economic benefit, it was possible for close relationships, if only of loyalty, to be formed between mistress and slave. That bond has already been alluded to in the story of Atilia Pomptilla in the first century AD. An epitaph from Nora at the end of the second century AD is another example. Freedwoman **Aurelia Victoria**, who may have been freed by her mistress, the 60-year-old widow of independent means **Aelia Cara Marcellina**, took care of her burial, praising her as an 'incomparable patron'. The admiring epitaph hints at a woman without guardianship (*tutela*) and, therefore, with a certain autonomy.

For most of the first century AD, the inhabitants of Nora had not been granted Roman citizenship because the Punic settlement was not yet subdued, but in AD 79 it was granted. By the time it was the home of Aurelia Victoria and Aelia Cara Marcellina and, in the third century, Favonia Vera, it had become a well-built Roman town beside the sea with all the facilities, including a temple, an open-air theatre seating 700–1000 spectators, and numerous public baths. The excavated remains of these are well illustrated in the Nora guidebook, including wonderful mosaics. The day I went, a heavy rainstorm made it rather difficult to appreciate from under a hood.

The text of the Nora guidebook does, though, illustrate the sort of controversies that can arise from interpretation when it notes of 'a Roman building, that was probably a reconstruction of a Punic temple':

> You can see the remains of three rooms attached to the temple where probably the Roman ladies went in secret to take on the rite of religious prostitution, that the Carthaginians used to adopt in honour of Ashtart.

It is possible to find descriptions of so-called 'sacred prostitution', but it is also possible to come across Stephanie Budin's *The Myth of Sacred Prostitution in Antiquity* (2008) and, indeed, to communicate with the author concerning Sardinia. She is clear, even about the Punic goddess: 'The idea that a cult of Astart would encompass ritual prostitution is based on several flawed and circular arguments.' Astart is not even a love goddess, she explains. Drawing on evidence of her cult in Mediterranean islands and countries she shows that she is more a 'warrior goddess'. She ends the chapter:

> Because authors believe that sacred prostitution existed, evidence is tweaked and manipulated to place references to that institution into texts, inscriptions, and even ... architectural structures. This then creates new 'evidence' that will then be used to support further hypotheses concerning the relevance of sacred prostitution to various texts, inscriptions, and architectural structures, until it seems that there is a whole world of evidence supporting the existence of sacred prostitution in the ancient world. And so the myth survives and grows.

Stephanie Budin based that chapter mainly on two Italian archaeological sites, Pyrgi and Rapino. She does not mention Sardinia there or in the book. So I emailed her with the Nora quotation; she replied: ' What you have in Sardinia is the same situation you have in Pyrgi – a temple associated with a Semitic people who worship Astart that has rooms around it.' As regards the rooms, that same chapter, talking of Pyrgi notes:

> In contrast to these faulty arguments for sacred prostitution in Pyrgi, and thus the presence of a sacred brothel of sorts, a far simpler explanation has been offered for the series of rooms by Temple B. Quite simply, they may have served as *Katagogion*, a hostel or 'motel' for those visiting the sanctuary.

The guidebook does not mention Favonia Vera, nor the stone with its inscription about her now on the edge of the sea near the remains of the theatre, in what would have been the forum. And it is important not to confuse the priestess (*flaminica*) Favonia Vera with sacred prostitution.

46 *Sardinia*

Attilio Mastino describes all that is known about her in *Storia della Sardegna Antica*.

Favonia Vera was the daughter of priest Marcus Favonia Callisto, 'probably' a freedman of Marci Favonii di Terracina, a Roman notable of Nora. The stone I saw seems to be what remains of a statue, placed by her father, in honour of Favonia Vera. She was celebrated as a priestess of the cult of the deified Empress Livia and the goddess Juno. It was in Juno's honour that she donated a house in Caralis (Cagliari) for the use of the citizens of Nora, both as accommodation and support when they had to travel there on public or private business.

Vestal virgins were in a special category of their own as priestesses in charge of maintaining the sacred fire within the Temple of Vesta, goddess of the hearth, of home and family, worshipped in every Roman household. Her priestesses were selected from distinguished patrician families some time between the ages of three and ten, and they served for 30 years. They were then free to marry, and to marry one was highly prestigious. They were held in high regard and, while their behaviour had to be above reproach, particularly sexually, they were granted various benefits commensurate with

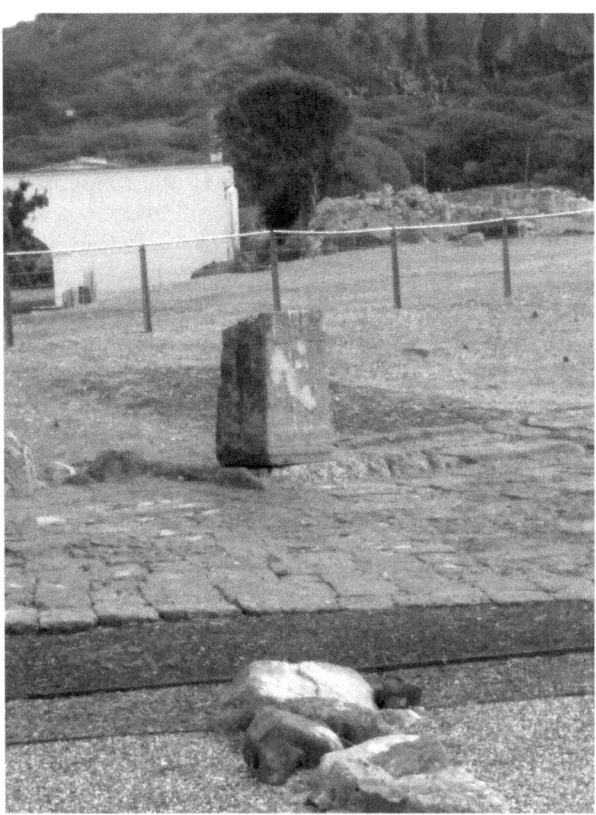

10. Favonia Vera stele, Nora, photograph by Rachael Cockrell

their status. They had, for example, front row seats at the games, whereas other women were normally relegated to the back, and they were allowed to move around Rome in a carriage. They lived in the House of the Vestal Virgins on the Roman Forum and close to the temple itself.

The order of vestal virgins was led by a senior member, the *Virgo Vestalis Maxima*. Such a one was **Maxima Flavia Publicia** who held the position *c*.247–257. There is considerable evidence of the learned and charitable Flavia Publicia, carefully explored and detailed in Paola Ruggeri's *La Vestale Massima Flavia Publicia: una protagonista della millenaria Saecularis Aetas* (2015). Most, but not all, inscriptions providing clues are found in Rome, including on the base of a statue in the remains of the atrium of the House of Vesta.

Flavia Publicia's connection with Sardinia comes from a find made between 2006 and 2007 during work on the basin of the commercial port of Porto Torres (ancient Turris Libinsonis) in the north of the island. It consists of a small bronze plate, with a portrait in profile of a veiled Flavia Publicia in the centre, which would have been attached to her vessel the *Porphyris* under the captaincy of her slave Eudromus. The plate exempted her vessel from port duties, one of the perks granted to the *Maxima* by the Emperor. It is suggested that her vessel would have been carrying grain back from Sardinia to Rome in time for the Games, the support of which was one of the *Maxima*'s obligations. Late second-century AD grain warehouses have been found in Porto Torres, indicating its commercial importance to the Romans who founded the port. A similar Flavia Publicia plate, dated *c*.247, is in New York's Metropolitan Museum of Art, this time exempting her from the tax on a horse or bull for pulling a cart or a plough.

The comparatively recent finding of the connection between *Maxima* Flavia Publicia and Sardinia has, not surprisingly, raised interest and been a cause for celebration, for example on International Women's Day in 2017. On that occasion, archaeologist and superintendent of Sardinia's archaeological heritage, Gabriella Gasperetti, described the finding of the plate in the harbour, drawing on her article with Attilio Mastino, *Viaggi, Navi e Porti Della Sardinia e Della Corsica Attraverso La Documentazione Epigrafica* (2014). She was followed by Paola Ruggeri, who talked of Flavia Publicia herself. The Porto Torres plate is in its archaeological museum.

The situation in Sardinia and, indeed, throughout Italy and the Roman Empire was to change with the recognition of Christianity as its religion. The Order of the Vestals, for example, was disbanded in AD 394, when non-Christian cults were banned.

3 – From Early Christians to Muslims AD 314–1077

Early Christian Martyrs (Santa Rosa, Santa Giusta, Giustina and Enedina, Santa Restituta)

During the reign of Roman Emperor Constantine the Great (AD 306–37) Christianity gradually became the dominant religion in the empire. Possibly influenced by his Christian mother, Helena, he was an instigator of the Edict of Milan of 313 which decriminalised Christian worship. The following year it became the recognised religion in Sardinia. As chapter 2 related, there may well have been earlier signs of it there: the seeds of Christianity may have arrived with the 4000 Jews exiled in the early years of the first century AD to the island of Sulcis (later Sant'Antioco) off the main island's south-western coast, and there were intimations of it among Acte's slaves. Christians were certainly persecuted in earlier years.

Details of women martyrs are mostly sketchy or legendary. The earliest of them, dying as a martyr according to popular belief in the second century AD, was **Santa Rosa**. Much better known is her son Antiochus, the martyr known as Sant'Antioco, who died *c.*AD 127. The family was originally from North Africa. There, Rosa converted to Christianity and brought Antiochus up in that faith. His father disapproved and, failing to make his son recant, pressured him into becoming a doctor, which he did, to some renown. But, because he refused to make sacrifices to pagan gods, he was exiled to Sulcis. Rosa must have accompanied him.

In Sardinia, Antiochus was forced to work in the lead mines on the mainland opposite Sulcis island. Eventually, once again for refusing to recant, he was imprisoned and martyred on Sulcis, which is how the island came to be called Sant'Antioco. He was buried in the catacombs, formerly Punic burial chambers, under what became Basilica di Sant'Antioco Martir. Christians of all strata of society were buried there too between the second and seventh centuries. Further along from Antioco's burial chamber is the smaller one of Santa Rosa, though the bodies of the two were apparently stolen. Their lives are celebrated as far away as Palmas Arborea, a few miles south-east of Oristano, Santa Rosa on 12 April. The catacombs are open to the public.

The best known of the women saints connected with Sardinia is **Santa Giusta** who not only has a town named after her in Oristano province, but has 11 churches dedicated to her scattered around the island. She may have lived between AD 117 and 138, but some accounts have her martyred under the Emperor Nero in the first century AD, others under Diocletian in the fourth century. I am mostly drawing on the 2017 internet account by Claudia Sanna, *'Il Culto di Santa Giusta, Santa Giustina e Santa Enedina in*

Sardegna', which refers to the earliest account of Santa Giusta's vicissitudes written in Spanish in 1616 by Antonio Martis.

Giusta came from a rich aristocratic family of the town that was later to bear her name, and she lived with her widowed mother **Cleodonia**. Giusta became a Christian aged 12, perhaps converted by a bishop, perhaps drawn to the faith through family slaves. Unable to make her change her mind, Cleodonia, who was firmly pagan, locked her in the cellar of their house and otherwise ill-treated her. While she was there, several miracles occurred which convinced her mother to free her. Shortly after, Cleodonia died. Meanwhile, two other noblewomen, **Giustina** and **Enedina**, hearing of Giusta's faith, also converted. Another source says that they were her maids, presumably slaves.

More trials were to come: a pagan suitor employed spells to try and get Giusta to marry him. Instead, she prayed to God for help. This came in the form of an earthquake, followed by floods in which the suitor and other idolaters were drowned. Finally, Giusta herself also died – one internet source says in AD 130 – and, following her, Giustina did so too on 20 July and Enedina on 26 September. Santa Giusta's life and faith are celebrated annually on 14 May, the day of her death.

Basilica Santa Giusta was built between 1135 and 1145, it is said on the site of where she had been incarcerated, and where she was buried. In the fourth and third centuries BC there had been a temple dedicated to Demeter and Persephone on that same site. Though the name of the Phoenician-Punic town of Othoca was changed to Santa Giusta, other sources suggest she might have been from Caralis (Cagliari) or Turris Libisonis (Porto Torres), or that her remains were reburied in Cagliari. A North African connection is also suggested for all three martyred women.

Santa Restituta was born in Carthage, or Teniza, another town in what is now Tunisia, and martyred under Diocletian some time between 284 and 305. How her cult spread to Italy may be associated with the expulsion of Christians from North Africa under a Vandal king. The power of Rome had declined, and that of the Germanic Vandals had risen by the early fifth century, and Sardinia began to be a place of refuge. The Vandals of North Africa occupied Caralis and other coastal towns between 456 and 476, so that grain could not be exported to Rome. Rome regained dominance briefly, but then once again the Vandals took over. During that time the prosperous city of Olbia was destroyed, but it is not clear how much violence more generally was involved; the evidence of their stay is open to interpretation. Although the Vandals set up a Caralis-based administrative system in Sardinia, headed by a governor, I have found no evidence of Vandal women who may have settled. Some Sardinian-Roman landowners kept their landholdings in return for lump-sum payments but, as usual, unsettled times would have led to unsettled lives for women of all strata of society trying to safeguard their families. The Christian dioceses that had come into existence in the Roman period still functioned under the Vandals.

One of the several places that Restituta relics are said to have been brought in the fifth century is Caralis. Certainly, the Crypt of Santa Restituta can be found at 14 Via Sant'Efisio, in the Stampace district, almost at the end of Largo Carlo Felice. Stampace was the political centre of the town through the late Roman period, and is also the location of the Punic Venus temple-theatre described in chapter 2. There is even an internet source that claims that Restituta's martyrdom, imprisonment and torture took place there. This is given some support by Rossana Martorelli in her chapter (in Hobart, ed., 2017): 'Cagliari: Historiography and History of the Archaeology of Cagliari'. She writes:

> According to a popular tradition, it is believed that Saint Restituta was the mother of Bishop Eusebio, and she lived in a cave named after her in the district of Stampace. Unfortunately, in 1607, Monserrat Rosselló [Spanish jurist and bibliophile] with the help of Salvatore Mostellino [Doctor of Laws] excavated the site and depleted it, using nonscientific methods.

In 1614 some embellishment work was done. The altar was raised and three recesses were built. In the centre was placed a statue of Santa Restituta, while originally on either side were statues of Sardinian-born Bishop Eusebio of Vercelli and his sister **Abbess Eusebia**. While Rossana Martorelli noted the suggestion that the bishop was Restituta's son, other sources talk only of a mother who took him to Rome after his father was martyred. Abbess Eusebia does appear to have been his sister, but the convent he founded for her is unlikely to have been in Sardinia; details about her are elusive. Eusebio may also have been martyred.

There was also, according to a Cagliari tourism website, an area in the crypt called *Schola Sanctae Restitutae* where, again according to tradition, 'the saint would have given lessons to the children of the neighbourhood'. On a minor altar were originally simulacrums of the saints Giusta, Giustina and Enedina.

The relics of Santa Restituta were taken for safekeeping to the church of Sant'Anna during the Second World War, when her crypt was used as a bomb shelter, and only rediscovered in 1997 in a seventeenth-century wooden urn covered with fabric and bearing a scroll that identified them. Whatever the confusion of facts, which so often leads to the creation of legends, the crypt is traditionally a place revered for its healing powers. Santa Restituta's feast day is 17 May.

Evidence from Christian Tomb Inscriptions, Fourth and Fifth Centuries (Flavia Cyriace and Septimia Musa of Porto Torres)

Finds in the Porto Torres area of Christian sepulchres and their inscriptions provide some insight into the unexceptional but faith-based lives of women there in the fourth and fifth centuries. Two inscriptions, and the women they describe, are usefully detailed by Maria Bastiana Cocco in *Servi e Liberti*

Nella Sardegna Romana. Both inscriptions are to be seen in the Porto Torres archaeological museum.

Flavia Cyriace, daughter of **Flavia Arnobia** (Arnovia) and a father simply given as M, lived in the first half of the fourth century. Her husband Demeter had inscribed on the slab of marble that fronted her sarcophagus words dedicated to his life's companion in whose arms he had wished to grow old. He said that she died in peace in the third hour of the night, aged 26 years and 14 days. As the pure and careful custodian of the most beautifully adorned gifts, she was leaving her worldly goods to the poor, rather than to her family. She was always generous towards the Christian community. The names of the family suggest that they may have been of Greek origin; they may also have been freed slaves.

The adjacent tombs of wife and husband **Septimia Musa** and Dionisius were discovered in 1963, during the construction of a small villa on the road towards Balai beach. They lived and died towards the end of the fourth century, or the beginning of the fifth, and Septimia Musa died first. It was possible to deduce that Dionisius was her husband, that their children were Esychius and Valeria, and that it was he who had ordered the inscription to her. She was said to be 'a good woman', who died aged 47 years, 5 months and 15 days. And there was a prayer that she be refreshed in the name of Christ. Maria Bastiana Cocco gives a vivid description of the mosaics fronting Septimia Musa's tomb, the colours, including doves of intense blue glass tessera in various tones. What research into other inscriptions of the time and place have also allowed is to suggest the social origins of the group, and of imperial nobles and those with Greek names, as well as the Christian community in which they lived.

Just as Maxima Flavia Publicia was celebrated on an International Women's Day, so on St Valentine's day in 2012, Maria Bastiana Cocco told the love stories of Flavia Cyriace and Demeter, and Septimia Musa and Dionisius.

The Vandal period ended in 534 when the Emperor Justinian's troops defeated them near Carthage, and the Byzantine era in Sardinia and elsewhere began.

Pope Gregory the Great and the Resolution of Women's Disputes 591–604 (Pomponiana, Theodosia, Juliana, Catella, Desideria, Gavina and Sirica)

The information for this part of chapter 3 came in a rather roundabout way. In the middle of my research for this book, I was inveigled away to write a book with my husband, published in 2018 as *Women in Disputes: A History of European Women in Mediation and Arbitration*. That was already at the printers when, back in my Sardinia research, I came across the letters of Pope Gregory about Sardinian women, their disputes, and how they might be resolved. It was too late for my findings to go into our book on mediation and arbitration, so I wrote an article – 'Pope Gregory the Great and the Disputes of Sardinian Women 591-604' – for the journal *Arbitration International*, which has just been published as I write. It is upon that article that I draw.

In 534, the Emperor Justinian incorporated Sardinia into the Byzantine Empire, the Eastern Roman Empire, the capital of which was Constantinople (today's Istanbul). Pope Gregory, though based in Rome, had connections in the new capital: he knew the Emperor Maurice from a stay there, as well as his two sisters, and he was godfather to one of the emperor's sons by his wife **Constantina Augusta**. Because she had special oversight of Sardinia's government, in particular its taxation and the appointment of judges, Gregory was able to write to her about the island. He did so at some length in September 594 about the continuing problems of paganism and sacrilegious practices, in spite of the bishops he had sent over to take matters in hand. 'You must mention these things to your most pious lord at an appropriate time,' he wrote, 'so that a great weight of sin such as this may be lifted from his soul, from the empire, and from his children.'

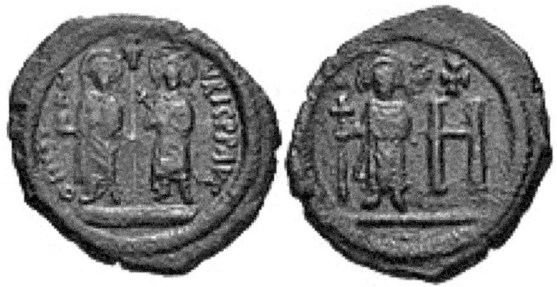

11. Empress Constantina Augusta coin, from the internet

But usually Gregory's letters about Sardinia were written directly to someone in authority there, and of the 41 letters concerning the island, 11 were about women, most of them religious, several of them abbesses. He seems to have had a special connection with, and concern for, women, and the letters to Sardinia encapsulate the lives of a certain stratum of society and, particularly, their problems. His attitude towards women may have stemmed from his upbringing among strong women, his mother, her sister and his father's three sisters – his father being much occupied with affairs of property and state.

The most interesting Sardinian woman, and the one about whom he wrote most letters, five of them over the years, was Abbess **Pomponiana**, a widow with a widowed daughter called **Matriona**. The first letter was written in June 591 to Theodorus, Byzantine Duke (*Dux*) of Sardinia, commander of the army, calling on him to arbitrate a dispute between the abbess and the mother of her deceased son-in-law, Epiphanius, who wished to annul his will concerning the disposition of his property. It does not appear that Pomponiana, who was obviously a woman of some spirit and determination, was satisfied with his efforts, if any. That is not surprising as the *Dux* has been accused of showing injustice and violence towards the clergy and people of Sardinia, so much so that the Pope complained strongly to the emperor and to the governor of Africa whose province included Sardinia.

It was only a month later that Gregory wrote to Januarius, Bishop of Caralis, on Pomponiana's behalf. This time, her complaint was more general: 'Know you that Pomponiana, a religious woman, has represented to us through one of her people, that she endures many grievances continually and unreasonably from certain men.' Once again, the Pope called for the matter to be arbitrated.

It seems that Januarius, too, failed to satisfy Pomponiana. At much the same time, the aristocratic nun **Theodosia** had a complaint, so the pope invited the two women to Rome; it is noteworthy the connections the two were able to call upon to petition the pope directly and, indeed, to bring about what must have been a fascinating meeting. Unfortunately, there appears to be no record.

For seven years there seems to have been nothing to bother the pope concerning Pomponiana, but then it becomes clear that there is still a problem regarding her late son-in-law's will, and the plans for his property next door to her convent; there was certainly a tangle that needed to be unravelled. In October 600, Gregory wrote to Januarius about his having forbidden the building of a monastery in contravention of the will of Epiphanius, a one-time reader in his church. It is clear that Januarius had been fearful about a monastery being built next door to a convent, and the possible implications of misbehaviour between nuns and monks. The pope had approved at the time, but now Pomponiana wanted to remove the nuns from the convent and return them to their original convents, and to establish a community of monks in their place. Januarius was instructed to comply with this, to resolve the dispute through the good offices of a mediator, Vitalis.

By 603, poor Januarius was old and sick, so Gregory wrote to Vitalis: 'In the case concerning the convent of St Hermes, constructed in the home of the religious lady Pomponiana, it must be treated with tactfulness rather than with strictness.' This was something in which Vitalis was a past master, the pope flattered him. Gregory was concerned about the well-being of the nuns, but there was another point: 'Furthermore, that religious lady Pomponiana has complained to us that [you], together with our most reverend brother and fellow-bishop Januarius, have unjustly taken away the inheritance of her late son-in-law.'

In his will, Epiphanius had appointed his wife Matriona to be the beneficiary of income from the convent to be founded in their home; then there were items to which Matriona also had a right: 'So far no income from this has benefitted either [Pomponiana's] daughter or the convent.' If there was any problem putting this right, Vitalis was to pass the matter to arbitrators – 'to chosen ones' – to do so. It is rather unsatisfactory that we do not know how Pomponiana's problems ended; nevertheless, those five letters show not only how hard the pope tried to resolve them for her through arbitration and mediation, but also hint at the power of an abbess, well connected or not, in the early days of the establishment of the Christian Church in Sardinia.

In that first letter of June 591, Gregory asked *Dux* Theodorus to arrange for arbitrators to settle the case of **Juliana**, abbess of the Convent of St Vitus. Like Pomponiana, she had her own means of approaching the pope to put her case and, like her, her problem concerned rights to her convent. This time the matter directly concerned the *Dux*, for Gregory had learned that 'the legal document proving possession of the … convent is being held by Donatus, a relative of yours'. Because Donatus felt he was under the protection of the *Dux*, 'he does not deign to submit to being examined in court'. The *Dux* or, as Gregory would have it, 'Your glorious self must order this same official to appear before a court of arbitration with the … abbess.'

This letter confirms the adverse reputation of *Dux* Theodorus, as well as adding to evidence of corruption prevalent in Sardinia, including in the Church. Unfortunately, as is so often the way with records of arbitration, there is no indication of the outcome of Juliana's case.

Catella was a 'religious woman' with a son serving in the Church in Rome – another woman with a direct line to the pope. In July 591, Gregory had occasion to write to Januarius about her complaint, with a similar suggestion as to its resolution, without the 'annoyance of legal proceedings'. Catella was 'being troubled by the exactions and molestations of certain persons'. Gregory looked to Januarius to give Catella his protection and that her problem should be 'terminated by your judgment'.

The nun **Theodosia**, who had been invited to visit the pope in Rome with Pomponiana in May 593, had almost as complicated a problem as hers. Presumably as a follow-up to the visit, Gregory wrote to Januarius in September that year. Theodosia's problem also concerned the wishes of the deceased, this time her late husband Stephen who wished a convent to be built on a farm called Piscinas, 'recently under the control of the hostelry of the late Bishop Thomas'. The tenant was willing for this to happen, but the owner seemed reluctant. Gregory explained, 'We have agreed therefore that she should construct a convent in a house belonging to her, which she claims to own in Cagliari.' That presented a problem of its own because 'some guests and casual visitors are overrunning her home'. Januarius was asked to sort things out.

A further letter, undated, shows the matter to be somewhat difficult to resolve, or Theodosia somewhat contrary, as it presented different facts; this time it is a monastery for monks that is at issue: that is what Stephen had set out in his will. 'But,' Gregory wrote, 'it is said that his desire is so far unaccomplished owing to the delay of the honourable lady Theodosia, his heiress.' The Bishop's Fraternity was to 'admonish the … lady: within a year she must establish a monastery as has been directed'. If Theodosia came forward with excuses, the Bishop's Fraternity should take over.

Theodosia's case rumbled on, and changed course again. In September 594, Gregory wrote about it once more, this time to Bishop Felix and Abbot

Cyriacus, his trusted agents. It is hardly surprising that the letter was not to Januarius:

> The tenor of the report submitted to you explains adequately the complaint of Theodosia, a religious woman, in which we have read a good many charges against our brother and fellow-bishop Januarius, and ones not befitting the clemency of a priest, stating that after she had founded a monastery for the monks, everything pertaining to avarice, disturbance and prejudice is said to have appeared at the time of the actual dedication of the oratory.

After suggesting a resolution, Gregory ends, 'In this way, after you have settled that venerable place in a decent and regular manner ... we may neither be shaken by the frequent complaint of the ... religious woman over the non-fulfilment of her desires...'.

Misbehaviour between nuns and monks Gregory calls 'snares of the old enemy'; he even talks of it as adultery, presumably a reference to a nun being the bride of Christ. Nuns, it transpires, were 'forced to go on their own to public officials for their land taxes and other dues, and are forced to run through villages and farms on men's business to supplement their incomes'. He continues in his letter of September 593:

> If any of these nuns, through their earlier freedom, or through an evil custom of impunity, has either been seduced in the past or will be dragged down into the abyss of adultery in the future, we want her to suffer the severity of appropriate punishment, and then be consigned to another stricter convent of virgins, to do penance.

The seducer was not to get away scot-free:

> But the man who is found in some wicked act with women of this sort must be deprived of communion, if he is a layman. If he is a cleric, he must also be removed from his office and be confined to a monastery, to bewail his failures in self-control for evermore.

Another Stephen appears in a letter to Bishop Mariniano in October 599: he, 'a famous gentleman', had complained that a man called Peter, 'an extremely wicked person, had finally persuaded one of Stephen's relatives, with diabolical intent, to leave her convent'.

The pope's notary had organised for the errant nun to return to her convent and to resume wearing her habit; but it did not last: 'that extremely wicked man again used unfair techniques to lure her out of the convent once more, and until now he has been keeping her shamelessly in his house'. Gregory then spelt out to the bishop what action he had to take, getting several men able to persuade wicked Peter to let the nameless nun return to her convent – in other words, that they should mediate. As for wicked Peter:

'In this way we could then write to the royal city [Constantinople] asking that the offence which managed to escape being punished as it should be, receive its just retribution.'

Most of Gregory's letters concerned the problems of religious women, but the letter he wrote to Januarius in 599 shows that there were exceptions; indeed, it seems that as long as a woman could find a way to approach the pope, he would respond, and the Bishop's Fraternity could themselves be in the firing line:

> The most distinguished lady **Nerida** has complained to us that your Fraternity does not blush to exact from her a hundred soldi for the burial of her daughter, and would bring upon her the additional vexation of expense over and above her groans of sorrow.

This behaviour was all the more reprehensible: 'especially as she tells us that Hortulanus, to whom she asserts she bore this daughter, had formerly been munificent to your Church in no small degree'.

Pomponiana and Theodosia were by no means the only women to visit Gregory in Rome about their disputes, as his letter to Januarius of September 602 confirms. This time an abbot was the other party, and the Fraternity were to be involved in the resolution. The pope explained: 'The **abbess Desideria**, who bears this letter, came here complaining that the fortune of her parents, and equally that of her brother, rightly belonged to her but were being unjustly retained by the abbot John.' There followed exactly what had to be done for the matter to be decided, 'that she is spared any odium over favour or negligence, and after your decision no lawsuit remains between them'.

There seemed to be no end to church corruption, as an undated letter shows:

> We have learnt ... that a certain widow left her substance to the monastery of St Julian, and that this substance has been plundered by one of your clerks who used to direct the actions of the deceased woman while she lived, and that he now evades making restitution.

This was followed by an exhortation that matters be put right.

A long and complicated letter to Januarius of March 599 concerns a report by **Gavina**, abbess of the convent of Saints Gavin and Luxorius and her predecessor **Abbess Sirica**. It is mostly about whether or not nuns could make wills, and various ramifications if, against the rules, they did, and how any fallout might be resolved. It also mentions the bishop's archpriest, another Epiphanius 'who came to visit us'. One of the morsels of gossip with which this visitor regaled the pope concerned the fact that Abbess Sirica 'up to the day of her death had been unwilling to wear the monastic habit, but had continued to wear the sort of dresses used by elderly widows in that place'.

That reference to the visit of the archpriest suggests the extents of Gregory's network of informants on the island, not all men. Raimondo Turtas, in his chapter 'The Sardinian Church' (in Hobart, ed., 2017), writes that 'Communication across the Tyrrhenian sea seems to have still been easy, with the pope's trusted informers, many of them women, travelling to Rome to meet him in person.' Thus, when women such as Abbess Pomponiana and the rich aristocratic nun Theodosia visited him in Rome, he was not only listening to the details of their problem, interesting to him in themselves, but also taking in other levels of what was going on in Sardinia.

Without Pope Gregory's letters we would probably know little, if anything, about Sardinian women in the late sixth or early seventh century. It was to be several centuries more before there are any details of the lives of the women there, though much was to happen to the island. While Pomponiana and the other abbesses seem to have held the status rather informally, in spite of their influence and connections, when we catch up with later abbesses and, indeed, other women of high status, it was more formalised.

Islamic Sardinia (Mujāhid's mother, Jūt, and Maryam)

The Mediterranean was always likely to be a cauldron of competing interests, trade and otherwise, the competitors changing over the centuries. In AD 698, Christian Carthage fell to Arab invaders, moving potential hostility nearer to Sardinia. The first recorded Arab raid was on Sant'Antioco in 705, and such raids continued through the eighth century and into the early ninth. Those of 807 and 813 resulted in the destruction of property, the enslavement of Sards and their transportation to Muslim North Africa. This led to the Sardinian population moving away from the coast. Once again, it is necessary to use one's imagination concerning women, enslaved and transported, or the upheaval of their established lives and families on the island.

Both Dyson, in *Shepherds, Sailors and Conquerors*, and Corrado Zedda in his chapter 'A Revision of Sardinian History Between the Eleventh and Twelfth Centuries' (in Hobart, ed., 2017) describe archaeological evidence of Islamic attack and presence, particularly in areas such as Tharros, but there was no attempt to conquer and settle the island, and any sign of Muslim women is lacking. Zedda suggests the Arabs' rationale:

> incursions were a feature of careful Islamic strategy, designed to put strong, simultaneous pressure on various fronts of the Byzantine Empire. ... Islamic leaders must have anticipated the gradual dissolution of the island's Roman and Justinian infrastructures, which had remained predominantly stable until the mid-eighth century.

In this they were successful: refugees from Byzantine Mediterranean provinces arrived to find shelter, administrators, soldiers, ecclesiastics and civilians, but there is no specific mention of women. Internally there was a tussle between Rome and Constantinople, between Roman Catholicism and Greek Orthodoxy, between Latin and Greek. Of how Abbess Pomponiana's successors may have been involved there seems to be no record.

Even in the eleventh century, I can find only two examples that give some flavour of the presence of women, this time Muslim. The most useful description of them and, indeed, of their historical context, comes from Travis Bruce's articles: 'The politics of violence and trade: Denia and Pisa in the eleventh century' (2006) and 'The Taifa of Denia and the Medieval Mediterranean' (2010). As ports and cities expanded, and new powers emerged, competition between them over sea routes and territory increased. Typical was that between the newly independent town of Denia, an Islamic town on the east coat of Spain, south of Valencia, and opposite the Balearic Islands, and re-awakening Christian Pisa. With Genoa, Pisa had interests in Sardinia. The two powers began to clash in 1005, and again in 1011. By this time there was a new ruler of what had become the *taifa* (Moorish Kingdom) of Denia, freed slave Mujāhid al-Amiri.

Pisan and Islamic sources, not surprisingly, tell the story differently, but it seems that Mujāhid, having increased his power base by taking the Balearic Islands, sought to further legitimise his position in Islamic terms not only by further conquest but also by securing the important trade route on which Sardinia was pivotal. It was similarly important to Pisa and Genoa. What is more, an Islamic presence on Sardinia would be just across the water from them.

Mujāhid's 405/1015 raid on Sardinia was, therefore, repelled, though there is some evidence that he left a foothold there. The following year, he returned with 120 vessels and 1000 Balearic horses – this was no mere raid. He targeted the south-eastern coast, killing a personage, disputably the local ruler, and took the Cagliari area as his territory. He intended his occupation to be permanent. Some evidence for this seems to be that he sent for his mother, Jūt, her sister, his aunt, and his son, Ali. There is no mention of his wife.

Mujāhid's occupation of Sardinia was short lived, lasting perhaps only a year. The Pisans and Genoese fought back. As Bruce (2006) writes:

> Mujāhid's ultimate defeat and expulsion, however, was as much an act of nature as the result of the combined fleets of Pisa and Genoa. Outnumbered, Mujāhid sought to flee when his fleet was smashed by a storm against the rocks of an ill-chosen cove. The Pisans and Genoese were easily able to pick apart the remains, and capturedMujāhid's mother and his future heir.

Mujāhid's mother and her sister seem to have been Sardinian; Bruce writes, 'His mother would choose to remain among "her people", indicating the taifa ruler's possible ethnic origins, while his son would remain a hostage for a number of years.' Following my email to Travis Bruce when his articles had no name for the Mujāhid's mother, he gave me that and added, 'A later poem insults Ali by referring to his father as the son of Sardinian Fishermen. The extent to which we should take that literally is limited, but it's probably indicative.'

That there was an established eleventh-century presence of Muslim women on Sardinia is confirmed by a just-legible funerary stele in two pieces dated 470/1077. It was found in Assemini, a commune now in the Metropolitan City of Cagliari, about 7 km (4.2 miles) to the north-west, on the plain of Cixerri. The church of San Giovanni there, Bruce suggests, was, in the Islamic period, a mosque: 'The church's basic structure resembles primitive North African mosques, while the semi-circular apse, which is found in only two other churches on the island, is consistent with Mihrāb in a mosque's directional orientation.' The stele was carved for **Maryam**, the daughter of Atiyya al-Sarrāj, a saddler. Her father, then, was not simply a raider or slave, but a craftsman. In a village with approximately thirty to fifty inhabitants, the Muslim community must have comprised a large proportion of the local population, one prosperous enough to afford a competent sculptor. One other stele has been found in Assemini, and others elsewhere on the island, all marking male deaths.

Sard people had moved from the coastal areas to escape raids when many were enslaved and transported. But in spite of the evidence of Islamic settlement, it does not appear that they, or Christian believers in particular, suffered further during the later Islamic period. The following chapter shows that Christianity and women of status flourished in the Middle Ages. It is fair to assume, too, that Muslim women, or girls, such as Maryam, were able to live relatively freely.

4 – Abbesses, *Giudicesse* and Benefactors 1065–1420

Introduction: *Giudicati*

From the second half of the eleventh century until early in the fifteenth is the time of the *giudici*, four rulers of four distinct Sardinian territories, the *giudicati* (judicatures). These were Cagliari in the south stretching to the east; Arborea, in the west, stretching across the centre and based in Oristano; Logudoro-Torres in the north-west, eventually centred on Sassari; and Gallura in the north-east, centred on Olbia (over time called both Civita and Terranova).

There is some debate among historians concerning the date of fully functioning *giudicati*, for there were earlier intimations of their formation. An 864 letter from Pope Nicholas mentions Sardinian *giudici*, but not independent *giudicati*. This issue may be connected to the question, too, of when Byzantine sovereignty ended. A papal letter of 1073 from John VIII recognises the division of the island into the four units, providing a useful date for the existence of formal *giudicati*, and it coincided with the subdivision into ecclesiastical provinces overseen from Rome. The population of Sardinia then is estimated at 330000.

The term *giudice* derives from the Byzantine *judex* or *provincialis iudex* (governor) and is sometimes translated as 'judge', but it was more akin to a petty sovereign. The *giudice* and court, as the system developed, travelled around their *giudicato* cementing their power by responding to the needs of their people, dispensing justice, supervising the layers of bureaucracy, and controlling the nobles who, nevertheless, had some influence through an assembly, a proto-parliament, the *Corona de Logu*.

Each *giudicato* had its own political identity, often according to outside influence, such as that caused by the rivalry between Pisa and Genoa, previously so united against Islamic power on their doorstep. Not easy to disentangle are the relationships between the *giudicati*, sometimes determined through marriage, and sometimes through merger following conflict. In the chapter 'Establishing Power and Law in Medieval and Modern Sardinia' (in Hobart, ed., 2017), Gian Giacomo Ortu suggests that 'from the late twelfth century on, there was not a single *giudice* who did not concoct a plan to rule the island under one sceptre'. The position of *giudice* was also attractive to ambitious men from the mainland who might obtain it through marriage to a *giudicato* heiress. Family names can become quite bewildering, particularly as offspring could take that of their mother, father or grandparents. Ortu gives the example of the four brothers of **Barbara de Gunale**, each with a different surname. I will try and keep it simple, as well as steer a comprehensible course through the minefield of often conflicting sources. It will mean omitting most of the political inter-*giudicati* shenanigans and power-and-land-grabbing from the mainland and Spain that would be included in a more comprehensive and academic study.

Of particular note is that women could informally inherit or obtain the highest position – *Giudicessa (Judikessa)*. Eleonora d'Arborea is still considered one of the most important personages in Sardinian history, her place among notable woman European rulers of her time rather neglected. Benedetta of Cagliari was her father's heir (1214); Adelasia of Torres succeeded her brother by an election between her and a sister (1236). It cannot have been clear cut: Ortu writes, 'Women were excluded from the throne, but in the absence of direct male heirs, they could transfer power to a son and assume guardianship if he had not yet reached maturity.' That may have applied to Eleonora, but she did have that power to make the transfer and assume guardianship, and, indeed, to rule. It was not the case with Benedetta and Adelasia who seem to have come more naturally to the position. As was so often the case where women historically were concerned, the law was not necessarily the reality.

The period also saw an influx of nuns and monks, and relations between convents (usually called female monasteries), monasteries (for monks) and connections between monasteries and *giudici*. These could be in the form of benefaction, often by the consort of the *giudice*, who could be a person of substance in her own right.

Donna Tocoele and Santa Maria di Bonarcado

The earliest known example of this was **Donna**, or 'Queen' **Tocoele** (Tocode, Focode), wife of Gonario Comita I de Salanis, the first *giudice* of Arborea and Torres before the formal recognition of the *giudicati* as distinct units, and the separation of Arborea and Torres. In 1065, before the building of what would become the Abbey of Santa Maria di Bonarcado, Tocoele gave land for the rebuilding of the seventh- or eighth-century sanctuary of San Pietru, transforming it into a church dedicated to the Madonna di Bonacattu. The Byzantine sanctuary had been built using the remains of an earlier Roman villa.

The land was that of the villa Miili picinnu, in the area bounded by the villages of Bonarcado, Senaghe, Narbolia and Milis, in the lee of Montiferru and within striking distance of today's Gulf of Oristano. And it belonged to Tocoele herself. There seems to be no information about her background and how she became an obviously rich landowner, though, as will become clear, women landowners were not at all uncommon. With Tocoele's donation went the surrounding vineyards and workers, slaves and free, to ensure their continued cultivation. Tocoele intended to be buried in the church which was to contain her funerary monument. Beside it were the remains of a *nuraghe*. The little church stands 3 km (1.8 miles) from Milis on the road to Narbolia.

The memory of Tocoele is still integral to the area through the archaeological and cultural project named after her. The surround of the logo TOCOELE seen horizontally represents the landscape of Montiferru seen from the sea but, turned upright, it shows a woman's profile, the sail on the sea becoming her eyelashes. The face is that of Tocoele.

With the arrival of the Camaldolese monks from Pisa and the foundation in 1110 of the much grander Abbey of Santa Maria di Bonarcado, Costantino de Lacon-Serra, *giudice* of Arborea from 1131 to 1147, and his consort **Anna de Zori** (Thori, b. *c.*1080) confirmed the donation of the *domus* of San Pietru de Miili made by Donna Tocoele. Pietro II, *giudice* of Arborea 1211–1224, and his consort **Diana Visconti** from Pisa (m.1222), added to the Santa Maria di Bonarcado lands. These details were to be contained in the *Condaghe di Santa Maria di Bonarcado*, the first document in the local dialect.

In its internet entry the Municipality of Bonarcado describes what can be seen today:

> Jewels of this small village of Montiferru are the Byzantine sanctuary and the Romanesque church both dedicated to Santa Maria di Bonarcado: a religious complex that overlooks a delightful square in the historic centre and home to the island's oldest Marian cult.

Sardinian Women through the *Condaghi*

The main sources for the period are several *condaghi*, administrative documents, or registers, of various monasteries. They record acquisitions of property by donation, sale or exchange, and various acts relating to serfs and litigations, thus providing invaluable social and economic detail. In *The Periphery in the Center: Sardinia in the Ancient and Medieval Worlds* (2001), Robert Rowland sums up their usefulness in the recreation of women's lives:

> One aspect of landowning and land-disposing that seems to have been overlooked by students of women in the medieval world is the role played by women in Sardinia ... women had more control over property than had been recognised. ... It would seem that Sardinian women were more independent than their contemporaries anywhere on the continent.

A drawback of the *condaghi* is that they are virtually dateless. Scholars have worked out some dates, according to context, such as which *giudice* was in power in that place at that time; but even then, the entries may not be chronological. Because they were written in the language of the time, they are impenetrable to the uninitiated; even where there is an Italian translation, some words have been deemed better left in the original; I will explain them where necessary. A more general drawback is that they cover only Arborea and Logudoro-Torres, and that patchily.

Abbesses of San Pietro di Silki

While the monastery of Santa Maria di Bonarcado in Arborea was for monks, that of San Pietro di Silki, built between 1065 and 1082 on the outskirts of Sassari, in the *giudicato* of Logudoro-Torres, was for nuns. The first of them came from the Benedictine motherhouse near Livorno in Pisan Tuscany, Santa Maria di Asca, travelling from the port of Piombino. In due course the Silki nuns and, indeed, its abbesses, were Sardinian, but there continued to be a close relationship between the two convents, the wealth of each being pertinent to the other. The best source for the link between them is Giovanni Strinna's chapter '*Monache viaggiatrici tra Sardegna e Toscana*' (2018; Travelling Nuns ...); the *Condaghe di San Pietro di Silki* fills in details used by other scholars concerning the activities of the Sardinian convent, particularly those of its abbesses responsible for keeping the record.

The *Condaghe* certainly records land transactions and litigations, and its best known abbess, perhaps the most litigious, was **Massimilla**. She held the position for an exceptionally long time; Strinna calculates that it was from 1127 to 1191. In 1180, the only date vouchsafed about her by the *Condaghe*, she was over 80 and still active. The entries during her tenure exceed those for any other abbess and, indeed, she took great care to make sure that there was a proper convent record, including collating those previously scattered.

Not only is Massimilla reminiscent of abbesses such as litigious Pomponiana five centuries earlier but, as then, mediation was also a method used for resolving disputes. This leads to a simple explanation in English of two terms used in the *Condaghe*: *campania/campaniare* means reconciliation/to mediate. *Salto* means literally a leap or jump in Italian, but coming from the Latin into Logudorese it was a form of leasehold land to be used as pasture, or kept as a small forest, normally on a hill. Some other terms I have had to guess at with the help of a Latin-literate husband.

One source implies, by juxtaposition, that when Massimilla took a legal conflict with the archbishop of Torres over possession of the church and assets of San Giovane di Usune to the *Corona de Logu*, the case was mediated by the *giudice* Gonario II of Torres (di Lacon-Serra; giudice in name 1127; in fact 1140) and several bishops. The outcome is unclear, as Francesco Artizzu explains in '*Un Approccio al Condaghe di San Pietro di Silki*' (2013), because the text of the *condaghe* at that point was spoiled and, therefore, illegible.

Some of abbess Massimilla's disputes seem to have been litigated (*kertu/kertos*). One dated 1130–1147, between her and the sons of Mariano de Castavar, concerned the inheritance of **Maria Flaca**. It was complicated by the fact that a long time previously Maria stole from the church of Santa Maria di Codrongianos. Then a compensation of 40 *sollos* was handed to Massimilla. The de Castavar case appears to have been won by Massimilla. It is not clear if this was something personal to her, or if it affected the convent, most probably the latter. In some ways, the stealing by Maria Flaca from the church is the most interesting fact to emerge from the case. Was she in desperate poverty, was that common, or was she simply a kleptomaniac? That she had left something to be inherited seems to belie poverty, but not necessarily.

Giudice Gonario was also the judge in a much more detailed case involving Massimilla. It is told in the *condaghe*, but made more accessible by the journalist and historical novelist Vindice Lecis in *Buiakesos: Le Guardie del Giudice* (Guards of the Judge) (2014). The novel is about this whole period, including much else that went on in the *giudicato* of Logudoro-Torres. And when his version is seen side by side with the original and the translation into Italian (which exists on the internet in three columns – 'Processo per il Possesso di Servi' (2013)), it is possible to see not only his exact source, but also his elaboration. To make the case and, indeed, Massimilla, live, it is worth this stray from the factual *condaghe* record into fiction, for it describes an attempt at rebellion against their lot by workers on the estates of the San Pietro di Silki convent, and thus against the status quo of the time. Servitude was linked not to the soil, but to labour.

On the day in question, some time between 1130 and 1147, in front of the Basilica San Gavino in Porto Torres, *Giudice* Gonario, sitting as judge, surrounded by his guard, had before him ten torn parchments, 'greasy and threadbare'. In front of him stood a crowd of some 200 workers in 'worn tunics', heads of families, wives and children. The novel gives only a few names so as not to bog down the narrative; the *condaghe* gives many, at least 26 of them women, several of them sisters; the record needed to note the names of the rebels.

The crowd awaited judgment in the case they had brought against their employer, represented by Massimilla, abbess of San Pietro di Silki with its vast estates on which they worked. They had decided to challenge the authority of the most powerful abbey in Sardinia. One morning at the end of August, therefore, they had refused to start working on the convent lands. Now, before the *giudice*, they demanded to farm the land for themselves, as free tenants, rather than as servants (serfs) of the convent. Indeed they had cards which appeared to confirm their condition as free. What they really wanted was to improve the harsh conditions in which they lived.

Massimilla, not surprisingly, was having none of it: it threatened not only the wealth of the Benedictines but the social order of the island itself. First she tried to dissuade them. When that failed – they had no intention of working for the convent as their parents had before them – she moved to create a hostile climate against the claimants and she was present on the day, supported by witnesses of equal rank whose names resonated throughout the *giudicato*. The rebellion must not be allowed to spread. Gonario himself had a lot to lose; he decided, therefore, that he needed more time and adjourned the case for six months. Massimilla used that time to sow division among the workers.

On the appointed day six months later, Massimilla arrived at the venue in a covered cart with her supporters. When the hearing began, the workers were called but none came forward. Everyone waited. For political reasons,

Gonario was anxious not to find in favour of the landed aristocracy. He asked what he should do. As night fell the convent prosecutor asked what the *giudice* intended. After a further wait, Massimilla played her trump card: she presented one of the convent serfs who swore that the claimants were servants of the convent's family and not, as they asserted, free tenants. Gonario had no choice but, with some irritation, to find in favour of the convent, and made it clear that the case was closed; if the rebels tried to present their cards in future, they would not be recognised.

A few days later, Massimilla wrote up the case in the convent's *condaghe*, listing the names of the rebels, among whom was **Susanna Carta**. She is worth mentioning specially because there were other entries concerning her, this time in the *condaghe* of the Vallombrosa abbey of S Michele di Salvennor, as detailed by Alessandro Soddu in '*I pàperos ("poveri") nella Sardegna giudicale (XI–XII secolo)*' (2009). The entries are dated 1130–1140, giving no indication of whether or not it was before or after Susanna had been involved in the San Pietro di Silki rebellion, and assuming that there was only one Susanna Carta at the time; Susanna was a common name. It is worth noting the dates, though, because Gonorio II, who judged the other case, only became active as *giudice* in 1140. As the abbey was not given to the Vallombrosa monks until 1139, it may at least be possible to date the entries to 1139–40. In the first entry, the abbot records the successful marriage of Susanna Carta, servant of the church of San Salvatore, a dependence of S Michele, with Gosantine de Eti Guerra. But then, learning that the latter was a servant '*de pauperos*', the abbot of San Michele sent his '*mandator*' to dissolve the marriage, denying Gostantine the rights to the couple's offspring.

Massimilla had dealings, too, with Gonario's son, Barisone II (*giudice* (1153/4–1186), as an entry in the *Condaghe di San Pietro di Silki* makes clear:

> I, Massimilla, abbess of San Pietro di Silki renew this *condaghe* of San Quirico di Sauren, which was very worn down, and I have asked permission of my lord, the *giudice* Barisone de Lacon, to renew it, and he, as a good man, he agreed to do it again, and I have done according to the will of God and the *giudice*.

This renewal may or may not be the same as that of the *Condaghe di San Pietro di Silki* itself which appears to have taken place in 1180, also with the authorisation of *Giudice* Barisone. It is worth noting that the authorisation included Barisone's second wife, **Preziosa de Orrubu** (*c.*1120, m.1153, d.1183), and their son Costantino. The wife, or consort, of a *giudice* was known as a *giudicessa* and often, though not in this case, the male was ruling because of his wife's inheritance of the *giudicato*. Strinna does suggest that the inclusion of Preziosa and Costantino was more a diplomatic nicety towards the *giudice*, rather than an example of her status as someone who should be consulted. Evidence follows, however, that gives some credence to her status as a valued partner.

Massimilla was helped with the renewal of the *condaghe* by **Sister Bullia Fava**, member of a great Pisan family. She may well have been responsible for writing up the record more generally, an example of official acceptance of female literacy. The renewal gave the abbess the opportunity to note how, under her administration, the convent's assets had increased, and to suggest future plans. In 'La Comunità Rurali nella Sardegna Medievale (Secoli XI–XV)' (2004), Carla Ferrante and Antonello Mattone describe how, for example, Massimilla had acquired from Gunnari de Thori half the *salto* d'Arave, paying two pounds of silver, and from Comita de Thori Gardis, the *salto* of the River Turthebi, which was under concession, for half a pound of silver, with the balance a domesticated ox. On other occasions, textiles and articles of clothing were exchanged, both produced by the nuns or brought over from the Tuscan motherhouse. It is worth looking for surviving examples of this work in the Antica Palazzo di Città (Palace Museum), Cagliari.

Massimilla was not the only abbess of San Pietro di Silki; indeed, the *condaghe* lists its abbesses, apparently chronologically: **Teodora** (1), **Massimilla**, **Jena**, **Speciosa**, **Maria**, **Benvenuta**, **Teodora** (II), **Preziosa**, **Agnese**, and **Susanna**. It is easy for there to be confusion between the two Teodoras, one of whom seems to have been abbess for 20 years. I am assuming it is the second because the first mention of her in Francesco Artizzu's writing on the *Condaghe di San Pietro di Silki* is 1210 when she wrote a memorandum. It concerned, in a matter left partly in the original Logudorese, the return to the convent by *Giudice* Comita of the *domus* of Ogotzi which had been taken from it for a repayment in a judgment of his brother and predecessor, Costantino II. Comita returned ownership to the convent, with all its pertinences, for the salvation of his own soul and that of his dead brother.

Like Massimilla before her, Teodora involved herself in the families of those workers tied to the convent. Ithikor Varitho had had children with the handmaid of the prior Stephen of Guzule. Teodora agreed with the prior an appropriate division of the children. The situation had arisen because the convent and priory were close neighbours. Teodora is involved in the similar case of the children of **Susanna Vacca**, servant of San Pietro, and Jacopu Batkillu of San Nicola. As useful as the insight into the cold power of an abbess is the inkling one gets of the forlorn lives of women rather lower in the pecking order.

Strinna suggests that Teodora was not as diplomatic as Massimilla had been: in one instance, writing on behalf of Santa Maria de Asca she omitted the name of the Sardinian convent.

A straightforward memorandum records the donation to the convent by wife and husband, **Susanna de Thori**, and Comita de Thori de Tauerra, with the approval of their children, of a sixth part of the *salto* of Terri, and the same of the *salto* of Urcone. As is clear, land was sometimes acquired by donation, but just as often by barter, one of the functions of the abbess being to increase, as well as maintain, the wealth of the convent; indeed, the religious establishments became a major economic force, the Church and the monasteries, it has been estimated, eventually owning 40 per cent of Sardinia's land. In a case which Carla Ferrante dates to 1126, so it must refer to the first Teodora, the abbess bartered the *salto* of Tigesi from the men of Tigesi for 40 pigs and 80 sheep. The *salto* came with servants both tied and free.

And what land the convent owned, the abbess was determined to keep. The successor of Teodora II, abbess Preziosa, records a case against Saltaro de Nuchetu who claimed before the court of the Unchinos a parcel of land which appeared to belong to the convent whose ownership was recognised.

Abbesses were not the only women with a vested interest in land. It has been clear that women owned land in Sardinia from at least Roman times, and that that continued into the Middle Ages, as the earlier quotation from Rowland (2001) shows. And women of all strata of society could own land. He illustrates his point with an undated family saga from the *Condaghe di San Pietro di Silki*.

When Comita d'Iscanu was on his deathbed, he donated a vineyard to the Church and his health improved. This happened twice more; each time meriting a different entry in the *condaghe*. When it happened again he became more generous, donating everything he possessed in Silki – lands, vineyards and serfs' labour – to San Pietro and San Gavino, half each. Comita remained on his deathbed until another entry when he gave his garden with a spring and grove of nut trees, and his part of a grove of mulberries. Eventually, having exhausted his possessions, he became a monk. In the very next entry, his mother, **Donna Vittoria de Iscanu**, brought him to the convent saying 'If God and San Pietro heal my son, San Pietro will have as reward my uncultivated land of Presnaki and all the fruit trees that are there, both mine and those belonging to my brothers.' God obviously listened because Vittoria was as good as her word. Rowland comments:

> The story of Comita d'Iscanu is instructive on various matters, not least the role played by Donna Vittoria, who finally took the situation in hand, convinced her brothers to donate their share of what was presumably common patrimony (or ... matrimony, ie, property inherited from the mother) to secure [the] healing of their nephew. Nor is Donna Vittoria unique or rare, since women of all classes and conditions, not only the rich and powerful, give, sell, buy and share property; they are frequently noted as proprietors of contiguous properties, and they initiate litigation.

It may have been mainly women accorded in the records the title *donna* who donated property of note to the church, but, just as the well-off and noble sold and donated properties, so did the poor and non-noble, including serfs. **Maria Canba**, for example, donated an abandoned vineyard to celebrate Masses for her daughter 'who had been taken away to Pisa'. Rowland provides much more detail about the intricacies of women and property, from relations between spouses and siblings, to parts of a serf's labour that went with property, together with brief illustrations. One of the latter is revealing; this must be a different Susanna de Zori/Thori, or a different marriage:

> Dericcor de Gitil, along with his wife **Susanna de Zori**, was noteworthily generous in donating to S Pietro di Silki half of everything he had in Silki – people (*omines*), lands and vineyards – the people, as we learn from the next entry, consisted of two serfs entire, four halves of serfs, eleven quarters, and four days' worth of some others, with a total value of some 120 *sollos*.

Dyson, in his joint book with Rowland, completed and published after the latter's death, suggests that 'Calculations from the *condaghi* indicate that some 20-25% of the property in rural Sardinia was controlled by women'. But all was not rosy for women, and it is necessary to remember that slavery still existed in Sardinia, in this case in the *giudicato* of Logudoro-Torres; as Dyson records:

> It appears that the slave trade preyed predominantly on women, valuable as servants and concubines for the affluent of Pisa and Genoa. One of the earliest references to Pisans in the *condaghi* is to Pteru de Sune of Sassari, who had seized a young woman and sold her to the Pisans.

That may be what had happened to Maria Canba for whom a Mass was said.

The *Giudici* of Logudoro-Torres and *Giudicessa* Adelasia

The *giudicessa* in her own right, **Adelasia** (1207–1259), does not come first chronologically of the three powerful *giudicesse* to be highlighted in this chapter. But it seems appropriate to include her and her antecedents of the *Giudicato* of Logudoro-Torres here as it follows the part *Giudice* Gonario II and his son Barisone II played in the life of the convent of San Pietro di Silki and its abbesses.

Not only was Gonario the judge in cases concerning Abbess Massimilla, but his mother and wife deserve mention, partly because his birth is connected to 'the most famous and spectacular medieval church on the island' or 'the most important Romanesque site on the island'. He was born between 1110 and 1114; Santa Trinità di Saccargi was founded in 1112, built over the ruins of a pre-existing monastery, and consecrated in 1116.

Some nine months before Gonario's birth, his father, *Giudice* Costantino I of Torres, and his second wife, **Marcusa de Gunale** (b.1065), were on a pilgrimage to San Gavino in Porto Torres. They despaired of ever having a living child, after several had died within their first year. During the night, they saw a sacred apparition which told them that they could have the desired child if they built a monastery on the site where they had rested.

Not only was the basilica, with its black and white striped stone facings, the result, so was future *Giudice* Gonario II.

Costantino died in 1127/8 while his son was still a minor, so Gonario was brought up in the Palace of Ardara, seat of the *giudicato*, among the court of his mother's ladies; she ruled as regent, together with Itticore Gambella. Politics, however, put the lad's life in danger, so he was given Pisan protection and then taken to Pisa where he was educated by *Cavalieri* Ugo da Ebraica. When he was 17 he married that nobleman's daughter, **Maria Ebraica**. In due course, he left for Sardinia and, with Pisan military support, marched on Ardara and re-claimed his inheritance. Construction began of a new, more secure palace at Goceano. Both Ardara and Goceano palaces feature later in this chapter in the Logudoro story. Gonario and Maria had four children, including the future *giudice* Barisone II, and Peter, who was to become *giudice* of Cagliari. In 1136, Maria donated the church of San Michele di Therricellu to the Benedictine monks from Montecassino with whom the *giudici* of Logudoro had close connections. The location of this church is lost in the mists of time. In later life, Marcusa travelled to Messina in Sicily and founded the Hospital of St John Overseas. There she died and was buried.

It has already been suggested that Barisone's wife, Preziosa de Orrubu, was more than a mother of *giudicato* heirs. The only extant secular *condaghe* is that of her husband (*Condaghe di Barisone II*). It records how, in 1190, Barisone, Preziosa and their eldest son Costantino (already ruling in tandem with his father) were responsible for the foundation of the Hospital of San Leonardo di Bosove in the northern outskirts of Sassari as a leper hospice connected to San Leonardo di Stagno Hospital near Livorno on the Italian mainland.

Protomes (outer effigies) of Preziosa and Barisone's family seem uniquely to have been carved on the façade of the Romanesque church of Sant'Antioco di Bisarcio situated on a volcanic hill between Ozieri and Ardara. It was rebuilt and re-consecrated, after being damaged by fire, in 1174, and that must have been when the family's *protomes* were erected. Barbara Mastino, in her article in *Nuova Sardegna*, '*Sulla basilica di Bisarcio I ritratti dell'età giudicale*' (2013) writes of how Barisone, Costantino, **Susanna**, Comita and Itticore were identified by the scholar Gian Gabriele Cau in 2012/13. But that of Preziosa was missing, withdrawn in 1958 because it was so worn, and given up for lost. It re-appeared in 1997, presented by the caretaker and his family, and is now part of the Diocesan Museum of Sacred Art in San Michele Church, Sassari.

There have already been several examples of the memory of its historical characters being kept alive in Sardinia. In August 2006, a medieval parade took place in Porto Torres. The long procession wended its way to San Gavino past *Turritani* lining the street. The 'Kings and queens, monks and abbesses, knights and admirals' played by local denizens included Gonario II, Barisone II accompanied by his wife Preziosa and daughter Susanna and 'Silki's Abbess', perhaps Massimilla, perhaps Teodora II. The church service was followed by a medieval feast which included roast suckling pig and 'good wine'.

It might be useful in the lead-up to *Giudicessa* Adelasia to reinforce what I have already intimated with a quotation from Marco Tangheroni's 'Sardinia and Corsica from the Mid-Twelfth to the Early Fourteenth Century' (1995):

> The political situation in Sardinia remained extremely complicated as a result of constant dynastic problems, the conflict between the various states, the repercussions of the struggles among the leading Pisan families and the permanent enmity between Pisa and Genoa.

Unfortunately, these complications are sometimes exacerbated by conflicting sources about, for example, who was who, and who married whom, particularly when the *giudicati* become entwined. Even with these complications, the women deserve to find their place here.

To detail the rather unhappy reign (1186/1191–1198) of *Giudice* Costantino II, son of Preziosa and Barisone II, would be inappropriate here. Suffice it to say that it consisted of political and military conflict between *giudicati*. But it would be unfair to omit the fate of Costantino's second wife, the Catalan **Prunisinda** (d.1195). One of the conflicts was with Guglielmo I of Massa, *giudice* of Cagliari, who had acquired the *giudicato* by marriage to **Adelaide de Malaspina**. In 1194, he had occasion to invade Logudoro-Torres, attack and take Goceano, and imprison Prunisinda. The archbishop of Pisa tried to mediate between the two *giudici*, a mediation which was to include the release of Prunisinda, but Costantino broke the peace and was excommunicated. Meanwhile Prunisinda, having been taken to Santa Igia, the seat of the Cagliari *giudicato*, was imprisoned there and, a year later, died of starvation.

Where Prunisinda suffered can no longer be visited. Santa Igia was destroyed by the Pisans in 1258. Although archaeological excavations took place in the 1980s, the site was then covered up to allow the construction of an elevated road. But, when the Cathedral of Santa Maria of Cagliari was built by the Pisans in what became their stronghold, apparently the altar of Santa Cecilia from the Santa Igia (Cecilia, Illia) cathedral was transferred there.

Costantino, who died without an heir in a battle against Guglielmo of Cagliari, was succeeded by his brother Comita III who came to terms with Guglielmo by marrying off his heir, later Marianus II of Logudoro-Torres, to Guglielmo's daughter, **Agnes of Massa**. Should she be seen as a mere pawn in a struggle between men, or might she have had some say? Might she, indeed, have felt that she was benefitting both sides in creating peace? In any case, she makes a link between the *giudicati* which becomes even clearer in the Cagliari section of this chapter. Agnes's son became Barisone III of Logudoro-Torres, and her daughter Adelasia *Giudicessa* in her own right between 1236 and 1259.

What is unusual about Adelasia's elevation is how she came to be elected. It happened because of conflict in the period 1233–1238 between pro-Pisan and pro-Genoese factions in Logudoro-Torres. In the middle of this conflict, in 1236, Adelasia's brother, *Giudice* Barisone III, was assassinated during a riot. Under the terms of their father's will, in any such eventuality an election should be held and the outcome left to the Logudorese magnates. They had to choose between Adelasia and her sister, and unanimously chose Adelasia. Was it because of her intrinsic qualities – she had been educated to take her place in the *giudicato* – or was it because of who she was married to, and who her sister was married to?

In 1219, Adelasia, barely 13 years old, had been married off to Ubaldo Visconti. Before his marriage, he was already heir to the *giudicato* of Gallura, his mother being **Elena of Lacon** (d.1218), *Giudicessa* of Gallura in her own right (1202/3–1218); indeed, she is sometimes described as 'the first queen regnant of Sardinia' though her husband, Pisan Lamberto Visconti, sought to eclipse her. One example of that was that Adelasia's marriage was a result of a pact between her father and her husband. Ubaldo came into his Gallura inheritance in 1225. According to Tangheroni, when marriage to Adelasia was first mooted, Ubaldo was already married to Benedetta of Cagliari (whose period as *giudicessa* will follow), but the pope 'obligingly' annulled the marriage. Ubaldo was made joint *giudice* with Adelasia in 1236.

In 1237, the pope sent his chaplain to Torres to receive recognition from its *giudicessa* of papal suzerainty over her *giudicato*, as well as the lands in Pisa, Massa and Corsica that she had inherited from her grandfather, Guglielmo I of Cagliari. It was a grand occasion in the palace of Ardara before a large crowd from the *giudicato*'s religious establishments. Ubaldo died of a high fever, possibly poisoned, the following year.

Although *giudicessa* in her own right, and although she 'ruled' for over 20 years, in many ways Adelasia was a pawn, almost more noted for her several marriages than for any achievements. Following Ubaldo's death, she quickly married Guelfo dei Porcari who was well in with the Holy See. When he, too, died, Emperor Frederick II, influenced by Genoese advice, convinced her to marry his natural son Enzo of Swabia and create a Kingdom of Sardinia; indeed, the couple were titled Queen and King. But Enzo, who was 20 years younger than Adelasia, soon left Sardinia to fight against Bologna; during a battle he was taken prisoner and remained there until his death. In 1245/6, their marriage was annulled.

A summary of Adelasia's life suggests that, saddened and tired of active government, she retired to her castle of Goceano. But that phrase, 'active government' does suggest that there must have been more to her than unsuccessful marriages. There is a suggestion in the entry for her life on the *DonnaSarda* website, and confirmed elsewhere, that she was baulked in any attempt to govern by Enzo's ecclesiastical adviser, the Sardinian Michele Zanche, who remained behind at her court when her husband left Sardinia. He is said to have taken it upon himself to grasp the reins of power as firmly as he could. Much of Zanche's otherwise mysterious part in Adelasia's rule has been overtaken by how he is depicted, by name, in Dante's *Inferno*: he is a swindler who ends up in the eighth circle of Hell. He may well have been involved in the assassination of Adelasia's brother.

Adelasia died in her Ardara palace in 1259. Her tomb is at the foot of the main altar, where the *giudici* traditionally took their oath of office, in the church of Santa Maria del Regno, Ardara. There, in 1238, she had married Enzo. The church itself contains even more of the *giudicato*'s history.

The church had been erected in the eleventh century by **Georgia, princess of Torres**, sister of Comita II, who ruled from 1038 to 1060, and was said to be the founder of the Logudoro-Torres *giudici*, even before the formal recognition of the four separate *giudicati* in 1073. (Comita's sister is not to be confused with his daughter of the same name.) Georgia is said to have been a woman of strong character and some standing who emerges from the folk tradition of the *giudicato*, and is noted in the *Condaghe di San Gavino*, as being involved in financial matters, in agriculture, and in encouraging building. Goffreddo Casalis' *Dizionario Geografico – Storica* ... (1833) when describing Ardara has this to say about 'the famous heroine': in addition to her having been responsible for both church and palace, she showed 'prudence and valour in leading the army against the *giudice* of Gallura'.

It is ironic that Georgia's achievements should emerge from the mist, and perhaps myth, of time, when little is noted of those of Adelasia. Not only did Adelasia leave no heir, but she was the last *giudice* of Logudoro-Torres. Some of her territory was taken by the *giudicato* of Arborea; most of it was divided amongst the Doria, Malaspina and Spinola families, who all held it from Genoa.

These incoming families from the mainland were steadily building up their power. The Tuscan Malaspina family were already in Sardinia by 1123, when they built the grand Castello Malaspina in Bosa, a little town on the banks of the Temo. Only a skeleton remains of the original structure – imposing walls and a series of brick towers; inside is a fourth-century chapel. Adelaide Malaspina has already been mentioned in passing as the wife of *Giudice* Guglielmo I of Cagliari, and will re-appear in the next section. A member of the Doria family married Susanna, daughter of Preziosa de Orrubu and *Giudice* Barisone II of Torres; another will appear as the husband of *Giudicessa* Eleonora d'Arborea. Sassari, which had become the Torres *giudicato*'s seat of government, expelled its Pisan governor with the support of the Doria, refortified its defences, and adopted a republican model of government in alliance with Genoa.

The Fate of San Pietro di Silki

That concise description of what followed Adelasia's death obscures the turmoil that ensued. Giovanni Strinna details how it affected the nuns of San Pietro di Silki outside the walls of Sassari. For a start, the expansion of the town led to the annexation of the abbey complex. The Genoese takeover followed Pisan defeat at the Battle of Meloria in 1284; the break in the relationship between Sassari and Pisa directly affected the convent with its own links to its Pisan motherhouse. Citizens of Sassari took convent land and harassed the nuns. There was nothing for it but to retreat across the sea to Santa Maria de Asca and join other Sardinian nuns who had already taken refuge there as soon as there was political instability in Logudoro-Torres. They entrusted their funds to their male prosecutor, though there still appears to have been a prioress at the convent in 1340, and she held the assets of the convent of San Leonardo di Bosove which belonged to the Order of St Clare.

Meanwhile, in the motherhouse in Tuscany, a Sardinian, **Paola**, rose to become abbess not only of the nuns from Silki, but of the Tuscans as well. All went well for five years, but then a papal legate gave in to the demands of **Costanza Peruzzi da Calci** from the Pisan convent of Santa Agnese to become abbess of Asca; he reported that he had done so because the position was vacant.

A battle royal ensued: though now exiled from the convent, Paola was not giving way without a fight. Although elderly, she travelled from Tuscany to Avignon in France, then the papal seat, accompanied only by another exile, the nun **Caterina de Valle**. In 1335, the pope, moved by this gesture, commissioned the prelate from Cagliari to reinstate Paola at the head of both convents. There is a record of 1342 confirming that this took place.

Intimations of the final days of the convent of San Pietro di Silki are given in Roberto Sana's *'Il Condaghe Svela il Medioevo Silki, I Benedettini Raccontano'* (2014; 'The Condaghe unveils the Medieval Silki, the Benedictines Tell'). At the beginning of the fifteenth century, when some nuns had obviously returned to Silki, or reoccupied it locally, the last of them, **Antonia**, left on a pilgrimage to the Holy Land to genuflect in front of the Holy Sepulchre. She did not return.

That seems to have been the end of the convent, with its history of strong and purposeful women in charge of a great abbey and its possessions: in 1467 it became a monastery inhabited by Franciscan friars. They are still there today in what has been substantially rebuilt over the centuries. Little, if anything, remains of the convent in what is now the Church of the Madonna delle Grazie, and the village of Silki no longer exists.

Cagliari and the *Giudicessa* Benedetta

San Pietro di Silki was not the only convent to become a monastery. With the influx of nuns and monks, there was a certain jockeying for position and more tangible assets. Thus it was that at the beginning of the twelfth century, as Raimondo Turtas tells it without enough detail in 'The Sardinian Church' (in Hobart, ed., 2017), there was the 'indecorous expulsion of certain nuns from a *monasterium castrum*'. Their convent, on the heights of Cagliari, was turned over to the French Victorine monks who arrived from Marseille. Giovanni Strinna, in *'La Carta di Nicita e la Clausula Defensionis'* (2009), implicates *Giudice* Mariano II Torchitorio II (reigned 1103–1130) who 'chased the nuns from the *monasterium castorium Amani judicis* to offer their premises to the Victorines'.

Corrado Zedda in '"*Amani judicis*" o "*la manu judicis*"' (2012) not only clarifies the meaning of *Amani judicis* – simply, by the hand of the *giudice* – but also provides enough detail to engage more fully with what happened to the nuns:

> In his letter, Archbishop Guglielmo tells Pope Gelasio, in bitter tones and with an abundance of detail, of the deplorable state in which the church of Cagliari, once honourable and powerful, has suffered, due to the loathing suffered by the lay and the support of the giudice Marianus Torchitorio, at that time ruling in Cagliari, and the arrogance of the Marseilles monks, who held assets of the archdiocese; among other things, the newly arrived monks who had recently entered a female monastery (*monasterium castarum*), from which the abbess and the nuns had been hunted. In previous years, Pope Pasquale II himself intervened in the dispute, but the results had been modest and the judge Mariano and his wife **Preziosa [Lacon-Gunale]** had in reality continued their behaviour.

This affinity with the Victorines of Marseille was not new; it had a family history: Marianus's grandfather, *Giudice* Orzocco Torchitorio I and his wife **Vera**, made donations to the Order in France. But what no one seems to clarify is, who were the nuns who were chased out of their convent? And their abbess? And where did they go? Strinna suggests that what is for ease called a convent could at that time have been a few houses round a church. Were the nuns then homeless? It is worth noting, however, the status of the two *giudicesse*, Preziosa and Vera – the evidence that they had a definite role to play alongside their husbands in the *giudicato*.

Marianus's son, Costantino II of Cagliari, was to support Western monasticism in his *giudicato* for the economic, technological, ecclesiastical, agricultural and educational advances they brought, as well as their ties to Western Europe.

Benedetta (*c*.1194–1232/3), *Giudicessa* of Cagliari in her own right from 1214 until her death, did not descend or inherit straightforwardly from Costantino. Her right to the *giudicato* is a prime example of the complicated intermarriage, how royal women conferred rights on their husband between the *giudicati,* and how complicated a web was woven – one which I have tried to simplify.

By Costantino's marriage to **Sardinia of Arborea**, he had three daughters. The eldest, who remains nameless, married Pietro of Torres, already briefly mentioned as one of the sons of *Giudice* Gonario II of Logudoro-Torres, and brother of *Giudice* Bariosone II. He was, by her right, to become *Giudice* Pietro Torchitorio III of Cagliari (reigned 1163–1188), but at least one source suggests that it was a joint husband and wife rule.

That was almost immaterial because, not long after the beginning of their rule, Pietro Torchitorio was embroiled in inter-*giudicati* conflict with Arborea whose *giudici* laid claim to Cagliari, well stirred up by the Pisans and Genoese vying for control. Finally, in 1188, Pietro was deposed and imprisoned by Guglielmo of Massa and never heard of again. What happened to his unnamed wife, from whom he held the right to rule, seems to have concerned no one, either then or now.

Her sister, **Georgia**, the second of the royal Cagliari daughters, married Oberta di Massa from the mainland. It was their son Guglielmo who, having deposed Pietro, then followed his brother-in-law as *Giudice* Guglielmo I of Cagliari. We are already familiar with Guglielmo from his attack on Logudoro-Torres, and capture and imprisonment of Prunisinda in 1194. We know, too, that his daughter by Adelaide de Malaspina, Agnese of Massa, married Marianus, later *giudice* of Logudoro-Torres, to secure peace between the two *giudicati*. Benedetta was Guglielmo's third daughter. Aged 20, she inherited the *giudicato* of Cagliari on her father's death in 1214, and was consecrated in the presence of the high clergy and grandees of the *giudicato*. She swore an oath not to diminish the territory of the *giudicato*, nor to alienate its castles, nor to make foreign alliances without their consent.

We may think that *Giudicessa* Adelasia of Logudoro-Torres, with her three over-ambitious husbands, was over-married; Benedetta was similarly beset, but with four of them. She married the first, Barisone of Arborea, in June 1214, the marriage being seen, as so often, as securing peace between *giudicati*. In the same year, he inherited the *giudicato* of Arborea, becoming *Giudice* Barisone III of Arborea and *Giudice* Torchitorio IV of Cagliari by right of his marriage to Benedetta. They ruled their two *giudicati* jointly, each being cited in the acts of the other in their own *giudicato*. Benedetta made homage to the Holy See, recognising its rights over Sardinia and her *giudicato*, and the couple made donations, including lands, to various churches.

It took only a year for trouble to befall Benedetta: she favoured Sardinians over Pisans for positions in her government and preferred to cultivate the economy of Sardinia over that of the Republic of Pisa. This reversed the trend earlier set by *Giudice* Marianus II Torchitorio II who had released the Pisan merchants from customs duties and made later charters also in favour of Pisan commerce in gratitude for their support when he was briefly usurped. In 1215 Pisa retaliated against Benedetta's policy. In that same year, Pisan Lamberto Visconti, who has already appeared as husband and joint ruler of *Giudicessa* Elena of Gallura, assembled a fleet and landed an army at Cagliari, taking and fortifying the hilltop of Santa Gilla. Benedetta was forced to flee to Santa Igia, seat of the *giudicato*.

In June 1216, in a gesture of appeasement, she made a donation to the Cathedral of Pisa but the following year Lamberto's brother, Ubaldo Visconti, forced her to accept terms surrendering Cagliari, at that time mostly occupied by Pisan merchants. The victors built the Castel di Castro (the Castello) on the heights there, having acquired the concession of the land from Benedetta. She received Cagliari back as fief from Pisa. Later she asked the pope to intervene to annul the act conceding the land for the Castello, appreciating the constant threat that it posed, but without success.

When conflict continued between Sardinians and Pisans in Cagliari, Benedetta and Barisone made an alliance with Comita III of Torres and the Republic of Genoa then already installed there, as the Logudoro-Torres section above described, in the hopes of expelling the Pisans. When Marianus, Benedetta's brother-in-law, succeeded as *giudice* in 1218, he continued his *giudicato's* support.

In the spring of 1217, Barisone died, leaving Benedetta widowed with a son only a few months old. The following year, Ubaldo Visconti arranged for her to marry his also widowed brother, Lamberto of Gallura; the wedding took place in April 1220. But the pope, who had earlier been helpful towards Benedetta in the face of Pisan power-ambition, annulled the marriage. She promised not to contract new marriages without his consent and renewed her oath of fidelity to the Holy See.

Francesco Artizzu, in his Benedetta entry in *The Biographical Dictionary of Italians* (1966), suggests that for a couple of years, 1225–1226, she was able to govern relatively unimpeded. But then Ubaldo Visconti turned his attention again to Cagliari. In spite of her promise to the pope regarding remarriage, in order to protect herself, Benedetta remarried in 1227, this time to Enrico di Ceola of the Capraia Pisan family who was able to obtain papal favour. But he died in 1229 and the following year Benedetta married another Pisan noble, Rinaldo de Glandis; that marriage, too, was declared valid. These two husbands do not appear to have become *giudici* by their wife's right, but they may have interfered in the government behind the scenes, or perhaps Benedetta appreciated their counsel. What she felt about the turnover of husbands by death or annulment has to be left to conjecture.

In spite of the marriages that Benedetta may have expected to provide her with some sort of protection, violence in Cagliari forced her to flee first to Santa Igia, then to Massa, her ancestral home on the mainland. There she died in late 1232 or early 1233, not yet 40 years old. By February 1233, the pope had given away Massa, and Cagliari was divided by the Visconti, the Capraia family of her third husband, and the della Gherardesca, all Pisans.

Benedetta's son, still a minor, became *Giudice* Guglielmo II, with his Aunt Agnes and her husband Marianus II, *giudice* of Logudoro-Torres, as regent. In 1235, Guglielmo obtained his majority and voluntarily submitted to Pisa. This ensured that his reign (1232–1254) was relatively peaceful, though he did make war on the Visconti of Gallura until 1244 with the support of Agnes's second husband, Ranieri della Gherardesca.

In 1258, when *giudice* Guglielmo III of Cagliari turned pro-Genoese, Santa Igia was besieged and then destroyed, by Pisan and Sardinian troops from the other three *giudicati*, and salt was poured over the rubble. The *giudicato* was divided between them, the Pisans retaining the *Castel di Castro* in Cagliari. The campaign to save the archaeological site of Santa Igia is mentioned above, following the earlier description of Prunisinda's imprisonment by Guglielmo I and her death there. As for the inhabitants of what had grown to be a sizeable town since the people of Caralis (Cagliari) had earlier moved there to escape the predations of raiders from the sea, they were scattered to the winds. They found refuge in the new town of Villa di Chiesa (later Iglesias) near the river Cixerri, and in the district of Stampace, built west of Castel di Castro. Others settled in what is today the Sant'Avendrace district.

Benedetta's son, Guglielmo II, could be said to have reigned, not ruled. Benedetta, *giudicessa* for 18 years, tried to do both, but was not given much chance to be a successful ruler. Looking at her tenure, it has to be said that being a female ruler, of the *giudicato* of Cagliari at that time anyway, had its obstacles, but we know nothing of how she felt. Her entry on the late much-lamented *DonnaSarda* website (Cristina Muntoni, '*Benedetta, la Giudicessa di Cagliari che cedette Castello ai Pisani*' (2015)) may be the only source to spell out this lack:

> What psychological turmoil this woman experienced, and whether or not she was a pawn amidst the intriguing politicians and power-hungry men, or a woman capable of deciding and fully responsible for her choices, perhaps we will never know. No personal letter can reveal the nuances of her emotions, because the documents that have been received and from which we can reconstruct her history are only official ones kept in the State archives of Florence and Massa.

Giudicessa Eleonora and the *Giudicato* d'Arborea

Eleonora d'Arborea (Eleonora of Arborea) (*c*.1340–1404) either had rather more luck as ruler of her *giudicato* than Benedetta, or had a stronger character and more intelligence to meet her vicissitudes. And, having done that, she left behind a legacy that was to sustain the whole of Sardinia until 1827. Her rule certainly started less auspiciously than those of Adelasia of Logudoro-Torres, or Benedetta. But, apart from her own qualities, Eleonora came into the world supported by strong women who could be called role models.

The first of these women was her aunt, **Costanza di Saluzzo** (?–1348). Eleonora was only eight years old when Costanza died, and it is not clear that she influenced her niece in person, but accounts of Costanza's achievements and character with which Eleonora grew up would, not unnaturally, have had some bearing on her development.

Costanza's mother was **Sibilla Peralta** (1258 or ?1262–1321), a noble Catalan; her father, Marchese Filippo di Saluzzo, was from subalpine nobility, related to the kings of Aragon. Underlying all that follows is that in 1297, without consultation in Sardinia, or the right to do so, Pope Boniface VIII had granted 'The Kingdom of Sardinia and Corsica' to the King of Aragon in return for Sicily; indeed, there is evidence that Costanza's father held the title of Governor of Sardinia. Certainly much of Sardinia, taken by force of arms over time, fell under the suzerainty of Aragon.

In 1328, Costanza, whose birth date seems to be unknown, married Pietro Serra de Bas of Arborea who was to succeed his father as *Giudice* Pietro III in 1336; his birth date is also elusive. Of their reign together, Luca Demontis noted that 'His government was [one] of peace, in which [the couple] devoted their efforts to the improvement of the kingdom.' There are few details of the reign except what is in Demontis's article, *'Costanza di Saluzzo regina-giudicessa d'Arborea et fondatrice del Monastero di Santa Chiara ...(1343)'* (2018).

There is a suggestion that the Clarisse – the nuns of the Order of the Poor Clares – had been in Sardinia since some time between 1260 and 1264, but no substantiation. Costanza and Pietro's founding and building of the convent and church of Santa Chiara in Oristano in 1343 is, however, well documented, and is their joint monument. For it, they obtained particular papal privileges. It was to perform several functions. It was seen as a place of retreat for the royal family, including Pietro's mother **Benedetta** (details apparently unknown), sister **Maria**, and two other 'virtuous women'. Its nuns were to pray for them, not only personally but there was civic and political value to their prayers, for the safety of the *giudicato*, and 'as an indispensable resource for the proper functioning of the state'.

Thirteen nuns had arrived from Pisa by 1345, though the recorded names that follow are dated between 1368 and 1373: **Abbess Ceccha de li Stroci, Nicolita Exeo,** and **Sisters Nicolina d'Arezzo, Caterina Doria, Clara Passegi, Margherita Conton, Benedetta de Serra**. This last may have been a member of the royal family and was abbess in 1371.

Giudice Pietro's reign lasted barely 11 years: he died in 1347 and, on his death, Costanza retired to the convent they had founded. She did not long outlast him, dying in her retreat early the following year. And she is buried there, as a plaque in Latin records: 'Here lies a remarkable lady, Costanza di Saluzzo, once *giudicessa* of Arborea, who died on 18 February 1348'. To come across the Santa Chiara in the back streets of Oristano (*Via Santa Chiara*) enables the visitor to gain some feeling for this woman's life, indeed, it seems, according to their website, that it is possible today to stay in the convent.

Early in their marriage, possibly in 1339, Pietro had given Costanza the convent of Santa Chiara in Molins de Rei, on the banks of the lower Llobregat, in Catalonia. This Costanza bequeathed to the Oristano nuns. But they found that distance made it difficult to administer and, therefore, in 1367 they sold it to Queen Eleanor of Aragon.

Just as Costanza was to set an example to a later generation, the strong royal women of Arborea who had gone before her no doubt similarly did so to her. Donna Tocoele, *giudicessa* of Arborea, has already been mentioned at the beginning of this chapter. In 1065, she provided the land and enabled the establishment of the Monastery of Santa Maria di Bonarcado. Five years later, because of attacks from the sea, the seat of the *giudicato* moved from Tharros to Oristano, just as the *giudicato* of Cagliari had moved from Caralis to Santa Igia.

Abbess Sardinia de Lacon of the convent of San Pietro di Zuri (Ghilarza district of Oristano) presents a bit of a mystery. One 2012 source suggests that she was a member of a collateral branch of the ruling family of Arborea because she has left no trace in the medieval genealogies of Sardinia. But Luca Demontis, publishing in 2018, proposes differently – that she could be the second wife of *Giudice* Pietro II (reigned 1211–1241), left a widow in 1241 and, therefore, mother of *Giudice* Mariano II (1241–1297). He goes on to explain,

> When the person who commissioned a building, king or queen, was elderly or remained in a state of widowhood, it was not uncommon that they found within the walls of the monastery the sort of retreat that the life of the court prevented them from finding, sometimes wearing the dress of the Order in which they were a guest.

Whoever Donna Sardinia was, there is a plaque on the front of the church reading, translated from the Latin:

In the year of our Lord 1291, this church was built and consecrated in honour of the Blessed Peter the Apostle of Rome, at the time of Judge Mariano of Arborea ... at the same time, the abbess, Donna Sardinia de Lacon was a worker. The builder was master Anselmo di Como.

Anna Pistuddi, a scholar of the Sardinian medieval period, asked by a member of the audience she was addressing, what was meant by 'worker (*operare*)', replied, that it referred to the person 'who collected the necessary funds to complete the architectural work and managed the expenses connected to it'.

There is more to this church, distinguished by the red ochre of the volcanic rock with which it was built, than meets the eye. Originally, it was on the floor of a valley but in 1923 a dam, or artificial lake, Omodeo, was constructed on the river Tirso which would have inundated it, so it was dismantled and re-assembled on the hill where it now stands. The old village of Zuri is at the bottom of the lake, but a new one was also constructed. Ghilarza was the home place of philosopher Antonio Gramsci, whose mother, **Giuseppina Marcias** (1861–1932) was from a landowning family from Sorgono in the province of Nuoro.

When Costanza di Saluzzo's husband, *Giudice* Pietro III, died in 1347, he was succeeded by his brother as *Giudice* Mariano IV (reigned 1347–1376). Eleven or so years earlier, in 1336, 19-year-old Mariano de Bas-Serra was in Barcelona, at the court of the new king of Aragon, Pedro IV, in order to obtain a prince's education. There he met 18-year-old **Timbora** (Timborata) **di Roccaberti** (1318–1361 or 1364) who belonged to one of the most influential families of Catalonia: she was the daughter of **Beatrice di Serralonga**, Baroness of Cabrenys, and Dalmatius IV of Roccaberti. With the consent of her parents, Timbora and Mariano were married, the bridegroom being given the rank of Count of Goceana and Marmilla by the king, who considered the *giudici* of Arborea as Aragon's vassals, though Sardinians considered themselves allies. Goceana, earlier the seat of the *giudicato* of Logudoro-Torres, had been, as already noted, taken by Arborea on the death of *Giudicessa* Adelasia in 1259, and the disintegration of her *giudicato*.

The newly married couple spent some years in Catalonia at Timbora's feudal property in the village of Molins de Rei (with its Santa Chiara convent). In the Castle of Molins, Timbora gave birth to four children, including Eleonora. In 1342, the family moved to Oristano, to the court of Mariano's brother *Giudice* Pietro and Costanza di Saluzzo, though they also used the castle at Goceano in the county from which they took their rank at that time. It was then that Eleonora would have come to know her aunt.

In 1347, on Pietro's death, Mariano and Timbora reached Oristano for him to become *giudice* and for her to be crowned *giudicessa*. She set about giving her daughters a similar education to that of her son Ugone. She herself was not only well educated, literate in Latin and Catalan, but also highly intelligent and strong-willed. Mariano never hesitated to send her as ambassador to wherever a crisis occurred; indeed, she had a prominent role in politics more generally, particularly in Arborea's attempts to shake off the Catalan yoke, so as to affirm the autonomy of Arborea; this in spite of being a Catalan herself. It is not clear that she was always diplomatic: Ortu (in Hobart, ed., 2017) describes how, when she was handed down a mandate by the governor of Sardinia, the Aragonese nobleman Bernat de Cabrera, she 'left him threatening a storm'. Though the alliance with Aragon had been in effect for more than fifty years, the couple realised that the political aim of its king was nothing less than the annexation of Sardinia, a yoke to be resisted.

Even before Mariano became *giudice*, the pope allowed Timbora to visit any convent once a year with ten honest women. On becoming *giudice*, Mariano completed Santa Chiara's construction, and in 1356 the pope allowed Timbora the 'privilege' of visiting the convent seven times a year with her daughters, Eleonora and **Beatrice**, and four honest women. Hanging corbels (carved stone brackets) in the church probably depict Costanza and Timbora and their husbands. Timbora died either in 1361, the last recorded mention of her, or 1364, only in her forties. In 1368, Mariano endowed the convent in perpetuity. I have not seen it suggested but it seems likely that it was in Timbora's memory. His reign ended with his death from bubonic plague in 1376.

In extolling the virtues and strengths of the women who may have influenced Eleonora, it would be unfair to downplay those of her father. He is often called Mariano the Great, and his 28-year reign was largely successful, particularly for his initiation of the *Carta de Logu* which his daughter was to update, develop, refine and enact, and for which she is renowned.

Following Mariano's death, his heir was not Eleonora but her brother; he became Ugone III and in many ways continued the moderate policies of his father. The wife he married in 1363, from the da Vico ruling family of Viterbo on the mainland, died in 1369, perhaps in childbirth, leaving a daughter, **Benedetta** (c.1369–1383) who became her father's heir to the *giudicato*.

In spite of following in his father's footsteps, Ugone also continued to oppose Pedro IV of Aragon by warring against Catalonia's parts of Sardinia. To this end he raised taxes and enforced rigid military conscription. This aroused the enmity of Sardinian nobles who, seven years into his reign, incited the poor to revolt. In 1383, this led not only to the assassination of Ugone, but also to that of 14-year-old Benedetta. How this took place is unclear, perhaps in a riot, perhaps in an ambush. A republic was declared which set out to expand the laws initiated by Mariano. Eleonora, who had been in Genoa, immediately left for Oristano.

Ugone was succeeded by his nephew, Eleonora's six-year-old son Federico, elected by the nobles in the *Corona*, with Eleonora as regent. In 1376, the year of her father's death, and her brother Ugone's succession, Eleonora had married Brancaleone Doria. Although he was probably born in Sardinia, where the Doria family had become well established, owning large swathes of the island, they were from Genoa. That is an alliance which both her father and brother sought, though Brancaleone was also a vassal of the king of Aragon who had, for example, given him the title Count Monteleone. Assuming that Eleonora was born in 1340, as is usually deduced, though the date is sometimes given as 1347, she was already 36 by then, late for a first marriage. Given what we know of her, it is likely that she would have been involved in the decision concerning a politically advantageous marriage. Federico was born a year later at Castelgenovese (today Castelsardo) on the north coast and seat of the Doria fiefdom where both Eleonora and Brancaleone had castles. A second son, Mariano, was born there in 1378.

From the beginning in 1383, as regent for Federico, Eleonora acted as *giudicessa*, and signed documents as such. In 'Eleanora of Arborea' (2015), Marina Ebrahim describes how, when the king of Aragon addressed her as Countess of Monteleone, so that she would know her place, she replied, '*Giudicessa* of Arborea'. Not surprisingly, given her importance in the creation of a distinctive Sardinian identity, much has been written about Eleonora, without much to go on. Some is particularly adulatory; some seeks to demystify.

The American art historian Georgiana King whose *Sardinian Painting* (1923) entailed travelling around the island's medieval churches, wrote of Eleonora: 'She was a great-hearted lady; her ready wit, her sound sense, her personal courage, her sure judgement are remembered and glorified still.' Georgiana was a suffragette, so was pleased to find a powerful woman in Sardinia. But I have seen a rather vicious denunciation of Eleonora online. More nuanced is journalist Stefania de Michele's well-researched historical novel *L'Arcano Minore Eleonora d'Arborea: Tra Mito e Realità* (2010). One has to steer a sensible course through often contradictory sources. This I also had to do when including Eleonora in *Women in Disputes: A History* of *European Women in Mediation and Arbitration* (2018), written with my husband.

But, to get to the heart of Eleonora, one's best bet may be the gloriously produced version of the *Carta de Logu* in the original language, with, alongside, an Italian translation and historical context by Francesco Cesare Casula (2008). I bought my copy in a to-be-recommended bookshop in Cagliari – *Libreria Miele Amaro*, Via Giuseppe Manno.

At the start of her rule, Eleonora set about scotching the uprising that had brought down her brother and securing her son's *giudicato*. Describing this, Virginia Lalli writes, in an accessible chapter, 'Eleonora of Arborea' in *Women in Law* (2014):

> Eleonora travelled across the whole island to visit the territory's castles and burgs, granting tax exemptions in return for acceptance and firmly intervening to reorganize and expand the Judicate. She summoned the magistrates, the elders and the entire population of free men and serfs, asking them for an oath of loyalty to her son Federico. The initiative was successful: thousands of soldiers arrived to defend her in the name of justice and of the Sardinian people. The financial resources of the Doria family allowed her to pay officials to train the army.

However peaceful that was, Eleonora, and her husband Brancaleone, who was also involved in governing, continued the warring with Aragon pursued by her father and brother. Sources differ over what happened then: Brancaleone was either taken hostage and held in Barcelona, or he was captured and imprisoned in the Torre del Elefante in the Castello of Cagliari which, with much of Sardinia, was under Aragonese jurisdiction. Brancaleone begged Eleonora to capitulate; she refused but did try to arrange, through bribery, for his escape, unsuccessfully. He was not released for seven years. At some stage, too, young Federico was also imprisoned, and died there in 1387; other sources say that she had been unwilling to give Federico up as a hostage to gain the freedom of Brancaleone. On Federico's death, however it happened, his brother, nine-year-old Mariano, became *giudice*, once again with Eleonora as regent and *de facto giudicessa*.

Pedro IV of Aragon had died the same year as young *Giudice* Federico and, the following year, after fruitless conflict, Eleonora signed a pact with Aragon in the Chiesa San Francesco which borders the Piazza Eleonora d'Arborea in Oristano. It brought peace and safeguarded Mariano's rule. But war broke out again in March 1392; Eleanor and Brancaleone, who had been released in 1390, were accused of perjury and rebellion and sentenced to death. The Arborean army, led by Brancaleone, had taken Sardinian territory held by Aragon. Negotiations took place back and forth between Oristano and Aragon. It was in that year, in order to re-establish order in the *giudicato* that Eleonora enacted the revision of the *Carta de Logu* that she had been working on; it had last been revised by her father 16 years previously.

The 1392 *Carta* was surprisingly modern for its time. One of the 198 clauses encoded 'provisions on disputes and suits'; another, that prison should be followed quickly by a fair trial; and another that the death penalty was limited to a few cases. Some clauses were more down to earth, taking into account the agricultural nature of the *giudicato* and its inhabitants. The area around Oristano was a particularly fertile part of the island. Several were framed in order to prevent disputes in the countryside, between rural workers of all kinds: they included 'provisions for protecting cereal crops, the fencing of vineyards and agricultural fields, against trespassing animals', because disputes between farmers and cattlemen were rife.

Other clauses were to prevent inheritance disputes. Virginia Lalli is useful for her translation into English and paraphrasing of several clauses, for example, 'no descendants, whether adult or child, could be excluded from the inheritance process without a legitimate reason; daughters enjoyed the same inheritance rights as sons'. And there was a clause relating to rape: marriage could redress the wrong only if the woman approved of the man; if rejected, the man still had to provide a dowry suited to the woman's station. Most revolutionary was the introduction of equality before the law.

Some clauses give an insight into the difference in the lives of Sardinian women and those on the mainland, or coming from the mainland to settle in Sardinia, known as 'Pisan'. It is worth pursuing, because that difference more generally concerning the status of women is said to pervade Sardinia even today.

In Laura Galoppini's chapter 'Overview of Sardinian History (500–1500)' (in Hobart, ed., 2017) she clarifies this difference concerning types of marriage: 'For example, a marriage contract could be distinguished as being *a sa sardisca*, based on the communion of goods or profits, in contrast to a dowry contract, that is *a sa pisanisca*.' In *Marriage and the Family in Italy* (1991), Marzio Barbagli elaborates:

> Historians of civil law have claimed that in Sardinia women 'were accorded a dignity and judicial status that found few comparisons in other parts of Italy'. A form of marriage contract *a sa sardisca* ('in the Sardinian custom') survived in Sardinia which established the communal ownership of property between marriage partners. Sardinian lawyers contrasted this with what was called the marriage contract *a sa pisanisca* ('in the Pisan custom'), which was based on the dowry system standard in most parts of Italy.

The Sardinian form of marriage allowed a wife to enter into contracts, incur debts and dispose of her own property, with or without the consent of her husband, provided she could prove to three relatives that she was not being rash. In contrast, the dowry system prevented the wife, whose father had paid the dowry, from disposing of any property involved, or entering into any obligation either with or without her husband's consent.

Clause XCIX of the revised *Carta de Logu* is headed, 'On Women, married the "Sardinian" [*Sardesco*] way, or with a dowry, who die leaving any living young child':

> We order, moreover, that if any woman marries according to the 'sardesco' custom or with a dowry, dying leaving any living child, if that child would die before the age of eighteen, then let his father succeed him in the inheritance; and similarly, let the mother succeed the deceased young child in the inheritance of those goods and items left by a deceased father, only exception being made if the father or the mother deceased had left a will, in which case the will of the testament be lawfully executed according to the will of the testator.

Of great importance was the fact that the *Carta de Logu* was in the Sardinian language. Each local administrator had to create two copies at his own expense, one of them, as Marina Ebrahim explains, 'was available to the population, who could use it to check the behaviour of the judges and the application of the law'.

It is not clear exactly which clauses, particularly those affecting women, owe their content to Eleonora herself. But whatever her own intrinsic qualities and insights, it is not hard to suggest the influences on her of women such as her mother Timbora. There is evidence, for example, that both had a good regard for themselves when slighted in their diplomatic dealings with men. Hints of Eleonora's rounded character can be glimpsed in her interest in ornithology, so much so that she legislated for the protection of a species of falcon which came to be named *Falco eleonorae* by a nineteenth-century ornothologist. The falcons can most easily be seen in the summer on the island of San Pietro where they nest among the rocks.

On the death of Juan I of Aragon in 1396, Eleonora concluded a peace agreement with his successor Martìn I. Arborea, thanks to her, was the last of the four *giudicati* to survive. She died of plague in 1404; no other details of her death seem to be available. But with her death Sardinian independence became merely a dream, and Arborea did not long outlast her. Her son Mariano died three years later, and Brancaleone in 1409. Mariano was succeeded as *giudice* by the grandson of Eleonora's sister, Beatrice, who, only recently arrived on the island, was defeated in battle by the Aragonese under Martìn. By 1420, Sardinia was 'Spanish' (Spain was not yet an entity that would include Aragon).

It is not surprising that Eleonora became seen as a Sardinian hero in the fight for independence, sometimes compared with Joan of Arc, exalted in poetry, and with a nineteenth-century statue of her, right arm raised, dominating the small but atmospheric Piazza Eleonora d'Arborea in the centre of Oristano.

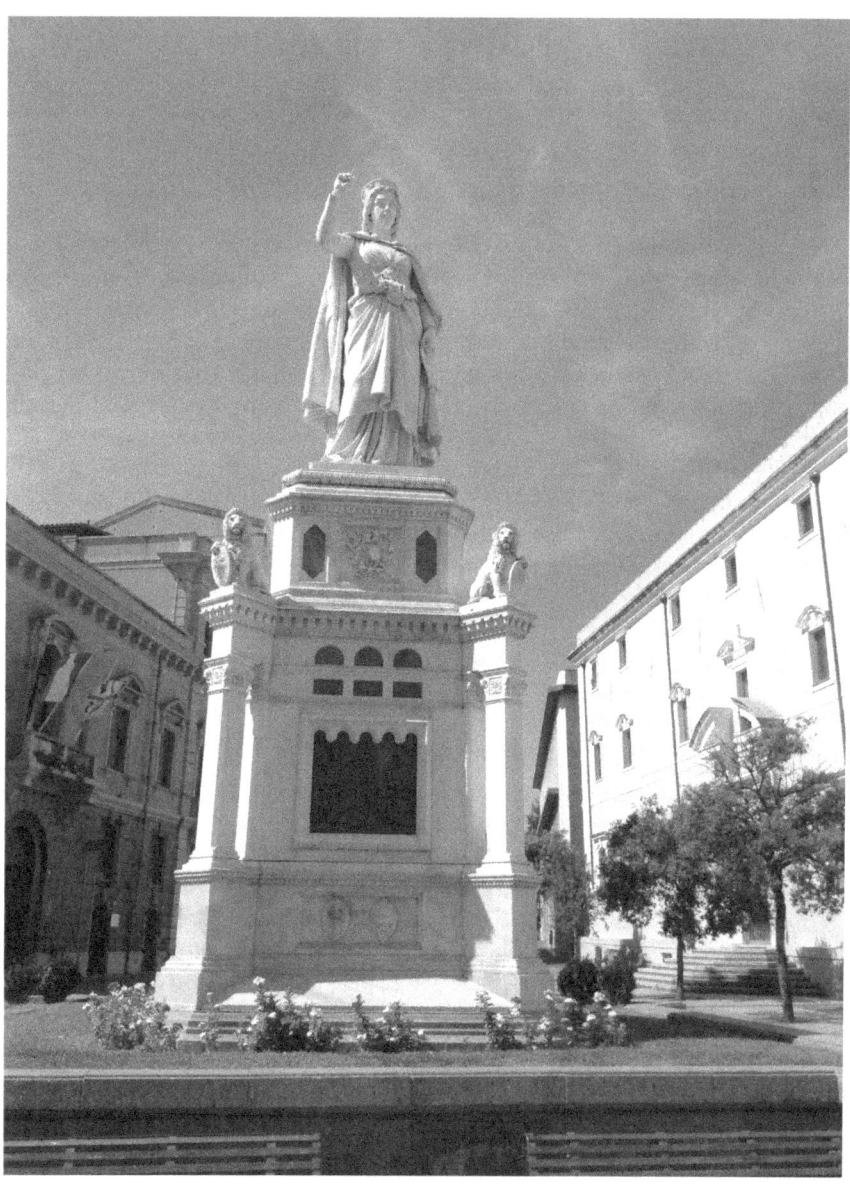

12. Statue of Giudicessa Eleonora d'Arborea, photograph by the author

5 – Spanish Sardinia, Feudalism, Violence and Scandal 1478–1720

Introduction: Spain in Sardinia

Spain was not an entity until 1479, following the marriage in 1469 of **Isabella, Queen of Castile** (1451–1504) and Ferdinand of Aragon. This is a usually accepted fact which is, nevertheless, finely tuned by scholars. And, in chapter 4, which covered the years 1065–1409, Spain in Sardinia was more accurately the Aragonese from Catalonia. They had had a hold over Sardinia since 1297, when Pope Boniface VII granted the 'Kingdom of Sardinia and Corsica' to the king of Aragon in exchange for Sicily. But there was more to it than that. Laura Galoppini quotes a source recalling that the 'pope was the one who, in order to marry off one of his nieces, enfeoffed Sardinia and gave his niece's hand in marriage to the king of the Aragonese'.

This niece was, I deduce, **Blanche of Anjou** (1290–1310), daughter of Charles II of Naples and Maria of Hungary. She married Jaime II of Aragon in 1295, aged 15, and thereafter gave birth to eight children, including the *infante* Alfonso. In 1310, she served as regent, or 'Queen-Lieutenant' of Aragon during her husband's absence. She was pregnant at the time and died giving birth to their ninth child.

In 1322, Jaime II formed an alliance with the *Giudicato* of Arborea, at the same time preparing to conquer the island because of its strategic value. The following year, he sent his son, the *infante* Alfonso, at the head of an army occupying 60 galleys to do so. Of particular interest to us is that Alfonso was accompanied by his wife, **Dona Teresa de Entenza, Countess of Urgell** (1300–1327), whom he had married when she was 14. Presumably she left their three young children behind, and may even have been pregnant with a fourth, a daughter born in 1323. We cannot know what motivated her to follow her husband on such a possibly dangerous venture.

Alfonso's forces succeeded in conquering the Pisan territories of Cagliari and Gallura, but the town of Villa di Chiesa (today's Iglesias) was only taken after a siege of eight months. When the troops entered the city, everything edible had been consumed. The suffering of women and children will have been unimaginable. Teresa must have known about this, but once again, we can know nothing of her feelings.

The victors, though, were also paying a heavy price: half the troops died from malaria, endemic in Sardinia for centuries both before and after; indeed, Alfonso himself came down with it and was nursed by Teresa before she too was taken ill. When Cagliari itself fell, Aragon's control was absolute for the time being and the royal couple returned home, only for Teresa to die in 1327 while giving birth to her seventh child. Her father-in-law died a few days later and the widowed Alfonso became Alfonso IV.

Thereafter, the power of the kings of Aragon in Sardinia, and the land over which they had control, waxed and waned. While initially Arborea was in collusion with Aragon, in order to safeguard its autonomy, eventually the *giudicato* of Arborea, as briefly alluded to in chapter 4, had to fight to regain as much of the island as was in their sphere.

In 1353, the Aragonese nobleman Bernat II of Cabrera, with whom Timbora de Roccaberti had a diplomatic disagreement (see chapter 4), took the town of Alghero, formerly in Logudoro-Torres, but by then part of Arborea. After later trouble, indigenous inhabitants were sent elsewhere. Meanwhile Catalan colonists were encouraged to settle there, and it remained Catalan thereafter. Even today Alghero tends to be more Catalan than Sardinian in its architecture, language and culture.

In 1409, five years after the death of *Giudicessa* Eleonora, *Infante* Martìn of Aragon landed in Sardinia at the head of an army of 8000 foot soldiers and 3000 cavalrymen. The Sardinian army, led by Eleonora's great-nephew Guillaume of Narbonne, *giudice* of Arborea, was composed mostly of mercenaries, including the renowned Genoese crossbowmen and other units from France and northern Italy. Martìn's troops, though fewer, were better trained and led. At the Battle of Sanluri, 5000 of the Sardinian army were killed, 4000 taken prisoner. The 500 soldiers of the Sanluri garrison who had escaped with *Giudice* Guillaume to San Gavino di Monreale were slaughtered there. It is worth pausing to think of their wives, mothers, sisters, sweethearts and children, many of whom would have been left destitute as well as grief-stricken.

The Battle of Sanluri is detailed not only because it marked the end of any independence then left to Sardinia, but also because of the legend of Giovanna of Sanluri. The victorious Martìn, though married, decided to celebrate his victory with a beautiful local damsel. It may or may not have been with her consent; there is some evidence that his troops raped and pillaged after the battle. Such was the extent of Martìn's celebration that he was in a weakened state when he caught malaria, as Aragon's invaders had before him. He was taken to Cagliari but, in spite of the ministrations of four physicians, he died on 25 July. Giovanna is said to have survived but, having wreaked Sardinian revenge on the invader, intentionally or inadvertently, she disappears from history.

The Battle of Macomer of 1478 concluded the Aragonese conquest of Sardinia. It was consolidated under Spanish rule which was to last until 1720. But, as Giovanni Murgia explains in 'Spanish Sardinia: Conflicts and Alliances' (in Hobart, ed., 2017), 'With the expansionist agenda of the Spanish Crown, Sardinia lost the importance it had once enjoyed under the Kingdom of Aragon'. With the suppression of opposition within the island, feudalism gradually unfolded during the sixteenth century. There was opposition to Spanish rule, including to the influx of Spanish landowners, often Castilian, often absent, and class conflict. This chapter, though, does not detail the story of Spanish Sardinia; rather, it picks out women who made their mark, some of them Spanish incomers, and incidents relevant to

Sardinian women as a whole. Thus, hints of life more generally are revealed. Violence and scandal were often a feature.

The Jews of Alghero 1322–1492

There is more than one kind of violence, and what befell the Jews of Sardinia and, indeed, those of elsewhere in 1492, illustrates that.

The first Jews, 4000 of them, arrived in Sardinia in AD 19, in the reign of the Roman emperor Tiberius and settled on the island of Sulcis. During the time of Gregory the Great and his letters to Sardinia, 591–604, he had occasion to write to Bishop Januarius of Cagliari concerning an incident in which some 'disorderly' Christians had taken possession of the Cagliari Synagogue and placed images of Christ and the Virgin Mary there. Januarius was instructed to right the wrong and make sure it was not repeated. Not much is known about the Jewish community thereafter until the Catalan period.

The Aragonese king had granted them privileges, and many had arrived from Barcelona, Majorca and elsewhere. Among the new settlers were families – 30 to 40 of which arrived in 1322. Between 1370 and the early fifteenth century, other Jewish merchant families arrived from France and assumed an important role in, for example, the coral trade. As *The Jewish Encyclopedia* explains,

> Especially favoured were the Jews of Alghero, for whom King Alfonso and his successors showed marked friendliness by exempting them from payment of customs duties and by urging the Governor to protect their business interests.

Two scholars provide more specific details, Marco Milanese, in his chapter 'Catalan Alghero' (in Hobart, ed., 2017) and the foremost scholar of the Jews in Sardinia, Cecilia Tasca, in *'La comunita ebraica di Alghero tra "300" e "400"'* (1990). There is not much mention of women, but one couple, who acted together in land matters, emerges: they were **Bet** (or Beth or Set) **Bassach** and her husband Jacob (Giacomo). As in large Catalan colonies, Jews were divided into three classes, rich merchants and doctors, commercial and professional, and small artisanal.

Jacob was a rich merchant, owner with Bet of land and buildings which the couple purchased between 1376 and 1381. This presumably lent status to Bet, as did the several servants they acquired. But, as Cecilia Tasca suggests, their acquisitions also attracted enmity from Christians. Although the Bassachs' residence was bounded on each side by Christian homes, this must account for the contretemps in 1376 between Jacob and a Christian barber, Pietro Seguert, in which Jacob drew his sword and wounded his opponent. As if to dispute general enmity, Marco Milanese writes that the Bassachs' Christian neighbours are significant 'for interpreting relations between the Christian and Jewish community, as well as the demographic of the Jewish quarter'.

By 1381, Jacob was secretary of the community (*aljama*); it was in that year that documentation notes that he and Bet sold a plot of land in the street leading to the castle for the building of a synagogue and school. By 1448, the synagogue needed expanding because by then more than 700 families lived in the Jewish quarter. In 1455 the Jewish cemetery was enlarged.

Alghero was not the only town with a Jewish community; Jews also settled in Cagliari, Oristano and Sassari, and the smaller towns of Bosa, Borutta, Macomer and Iglesias. But after 1430 they were not treated as well as those in Alghero. In spite of that, when in 1471 the king of Aragon learned that there were not enough houses in the *juderia* of Cagliari, he accepted the plea of Anstruch Farsis, who seems to have lived there between at least 1456 and 1474, to allow him to take up residence in a house with a shop among Christians near the gate of the *Juderia* and the Torre del Elefante. There he could live with his family and carry on his trade. Who his family consisted of, Cecilia Tasca does not mention, but digging comes up with a sister, **Ester**, and her son Jacob Camon. There is one other record of Anstruch Farsis, that in 1470 he and Giovanni Filippi asked that their dispute be arbitrated by Dalmazzo Marquet and Antonio Esglesies. It is frustrating not to know the subject of the dispute; presumably Filippi was a Christian.

However well Jews had managed to rub along with Christians until then, the day was approaching when their lives would be turned upside down. Isabella and Ferdinand of Spain issued a decree on 31 March 1492 for the expulsion of Jews from their territories, which included Sardinia. The decree said in part:

> It is agreed and resolved that all Jews and Jewesses be ordered to leave our kingdoms and that they not be allowed to return. We further order in this edict that all Jews and Jewesses of whatsoever age that reside in our domain and territories leave with their sons and daughters, servants and relatives, large or small, of all ages, by the end of July of this year.

The penalty for not complying was death; nor could anyone defend or hide 'any Jew or Jewess'. Many Jews did, indeed, go into exile, and it is not necessary to imagine what that was like, for women, men and children: accounts of involuntary exile abound. There was, however, an alternative to exile: that was conversion to Christianity and, as recently discovered documents reveal, a fair number of those in Sardinia took this option. Conversions are divided into two kinds, those who did so before 1492 (15 in Alghero and 26 in Cagliari's Castello), when restrictions were imposed on Jews in 1485 and those who did so after.

Perhaps the best known family to convert following the expulsion order was the Carcassona. They are first mentioned in Alghero in 1422 with the name of Samuele who arrived from Provence and immediately became the *aljama*'s secretary and holder of the right to collect the king's taxes. He had four sons and an unnamed wife. And those sons, too, had wives, for their descendants converted to Christianity and remained in Sardinia from then. They integrated and even maintained some of their former privileges.

The name of one pre-conversion Carcassona wife emerges from a 1456 marriage contract (*ketubah*). The fragmentary document was found in a book binding in the library of the University of Sassari by Professor Amira Meir of Beit Berl College, Jerusalem. She published it in *Materia Giudaica* in 2009, publicised it at conferences thereafter, and it is available online. **Bella bat Merwanha ha-Sheniri** was to become the daughter-in-law of Samuele's third son, Zarquillo, when she married Shelomo ben Zarch de Carcassona on 9 January 'in the city of Alghero on the seashore'. The groom promised the bride that he 'will provide for you and bury you and will give you to eat according to the custom of Jewish men'. Bella remained owner of her entire dowry, as was the custom among the Jews of Aragon. It is possible that she and Shelomo were still alive in 1492, and had to make the momentous decision to convert to Christianity. After the extended family's conversion, the names of wives come thick and fast in the records.

Before 1492, Shelomo's uncle, the youngest of the four brothers, Salomone, known as Nin, built the family palace on the Via Sant'Erasmo, the main street of the Jewish Quarter. It was so luxurious that Ferdinand II, he who was responsible for the expulsion order, wrote to the viceroy of Sardinia that the house of 'Nin de Carcassona' be held to accommodate him. The palace still stands; indeed, between 2014 and 2018, it was the Michelin-starred Restaurant O, under master chef Eoghain O'Neill, who had been encouraged to choose Sardinia by his Italian wife.

In 1641, the Alghero Jewish synagogue was converted into the Santa Chiara church, with a convent attached for the Order of the Isabellines, the reformed Poor Clares. Initially the convent housed only three nuns who arrived from the Sassari Santa Chiara – **Abbess Angela Sussarello y Boyl**, **Marquesa Manca de Prada** and **Hipolita Tavera**. When the Order was dissolved in 1855, the convent was turned into a hospital which, in 1902, included the church of the Holy Cross. In 1909 that was pulled down and the entire hospital rebuilt as *Ospedale Marino* 'Regina Margherita'.

At the beginning of the twenty-first century, the remains of the Jewish Quarter, 1350–1492, were archaeologically unearthed, with the involvement of Marco Milanese, and the complex re-opened as Piazza della Juharia in 2013.

Violante Carroz, Contessa di Quirra – *La Sanguinaria* 1456–1511

In the year that Bella married into the Jewish Carcassona family of Alghero, 1456, **Violante Carroz** (1456–1511) was born in Valencia to Violante de Centelles, who died when her daughter was three, and Count Giacomo di Quirra. Violante was 13 in 1469 when her father died and she inherited the title Contessa di Quirra; by the time she died, aged 55, she was known as *La Sanguinaria* – 'the Bloody One' – subject of several contradictory stories, particularly concerning her end. With the Quirra title, she inherited several castles, vast tracts of Sardinia and the wealth that went with them. She was a larger than life example of the incoming Spanish landowner who was not always there but reaped the benefits.

The first Carroz to come into wealth did so in 1240 when he was awarded large properties in the kingdom of Valencia, and it was he who set out with his four sons in the train of Jaime II of Aragon in 1323 to conquer Sardinia. He was suitably rewarded. In 1323, one of his sons was granted the Castle of Ogliastra in central Sardinia; in 1349, another was rewarded with the castle of Quirra in the south-east and made Conte di Quirra in 1363; the castle of San Michele, on a hill overlooking Cagliari, also came into the possession of the extended Carroz family, as did Castle Barumeli in Ales, a small town south of Oristano. Another family member, Nicolo Carroz d'Arborea, from the cadet branch of the family, was appointed Viceroy of Sardinia (1460–1479), representing the Crown of Aragon.

The Viceroy, as executor of her father's will, became guardian to Violante, Contessa di Quirra, when she inherited the Carroz feudal possessions in Sardinia. She spent time in her castles and is also said, depending on the source, to have died in each of them, as well as in a Cagliari convent. She has, therefore, left behind mysteries, ghosts and myths, explored in numerous publications, including Maria-Merce Costa's *Violante Carros: Contessa di Quirra*, republished in 2004 in three languages – Catalan, Italian and Sardo. She is not to be confused, as so often happens, with an earlier **Violante Carroz** (1372–1408) in Sardinia.

In spite of her wealth and position, Violante's life was not easy. In the year of her father's death, her guardian married her off to his son Dalmazzo Carroz who died in 1478. That same year, she married a cousin of her dead husband, Filippo de Castre-se. This marriage may have provided some happiness, and resulted in two sons, but Filippo died three years later – the euphemism 'disappeared' may have another significance. Whatever happened, it led to conflict with her mother-in-law. Violante travelled to Barcelona and did not return to Sardinia for 15 (or five) years.

Back on the island, Violante moved between her castles, San Michele in Cagliari, Barumeli in Ales and Quirra near the village of Villaputzu (Sarrabus province), with its view of the coast and valleys from 296m (970 ft) up Monte Cudias. There she felt most at ease. In Cagliari where she was not popular on account of her foreignness, wealth, position, and the fact that she was a woman with power, there was nothing but trouble: family litigation over assets, financial woes and another court case concerning the extended family's tombs, including her own, in the Cagliari church of San Francesco.

In 1503 both sons died. Violante drew up a will leaving her estates to a maternal nephew and a niece. She returned to Barcelona to put her travails before the king. But it would appear that the deaths of her sons and the court cases may have sent her over the edge. In 1509 an event took place in one of her castles, that was to lead to her title *La Sanguinaria*. The truth of what happened may never be known because there are so many versions; she may, for a start, have been at any one of her castles.

The cause of what happened is impossible to disentangle, but the outcome was that her curate, or the local priest, Giovanni Castangia, was seen hanging from the castle walls, and left there. Was it because he rejected an amorous advance from Violante? Or was his to her offensive? Did he take her to task, and threaten to report her to some higher authority concerning an amorous adventure – betrayal of a third husband, perhaps? A diplomat is mentioned. Did she have him hanged, or did he commit suicide? All these suggestions have been put forward. Not surprisingly, it was assumed that the hanging was the doing of that wicked woman.

As for Violante's punishment, she was, for a start, excommunicated by the bishop of Ales. That town does seem to be pivotal because it is known that Violante, perhaps as a form of penance, funded the building of the Cathedral of Saints Peter and Paul there. What happened next? Was she put under house arrest, but where? Did she commit herself to the Convent of San Francesco, and die there? She is said to have made a bequest to it. Did she throw herself from the battlements of her castle St Michele, or those of the castle Quirra, now in ruins? She was, anyway, buried outside the walls of San Francesco church, in a sepulchre engraved with her coat of arms, no longer extant.

Much of the convent of San Francesco was destroyed when lightning struck the bell tower in 1871. This led to the collapse of the roof truss in January 1885, marking the beginning of the almost complete destruction of the complex after it had been used as a *carabinieri* barracks. As I write what remains is now the *Niu* (Nest) restaurant at 56 Corso Vittorio Emanuele II; the internal courtyard is also accessible from the Via Mameli. I haven't had the chance to visit it, but it is clear from photographs that there is enough of the church and the vaulted cloister left to let one's imagination roam. Violante's ghost haunts all those places where she had her being. The castle San Michele, with its fine view over Cagliari, is left not only standing but still impressive, available to visit as an arts and cultural centre. After Violante, the Quirra title descended through the female line until 1857.

What I never see mentioned are the labourers that worked on her properties, and their families, the servants who waited on her, perhaps mostly women. Were they tied to a particular castle, or did some of them join her 'royal progress' from castle to castle, perhaps even accompany her to Barcelona? And how much was she involved in the administration of her vast estates?

The *DonnaSarda* website's biographical entries always tried to find good in their women, so for Violante Carroz, Contessa di Quirra, Annachiara Atzei says:

> We like to imagine her a strong and courageous woman who was able to redeem herself from her sad fate, fighting in life to affirm herself. A woman who has entered history and myth because of her wealth, her power and her impenetrable way of being.

Rosa Gambella, Woman of Legends 1440–1482

If Violante Carroz was bloodstained, that is nothing compared with the blood that flowed where **Rosa Gambella** (d.1482) and her family were concerned. Her life started well: her grandfather, Gonario Gambella, a Sassari knight, member of its oligarchy and ambassador to the Aragonese court, was enfeoffed in 1440 by the king as Lord of Romangia, a territory on the north coast of Sardinia. Her father, married to Catalan **Juana Pertegas** in 1433, was his heir and Rosa, the eldest of three daughters, would inherit from him. Rosa married well: Don Angelo de Marongiu was Lord of Oppia and Costavalle which he had won as a result of the 1478 Battle of Macomer in which he had played a leading role. It was not necessarily a happy marriage, though; the main attraction seems to have been Rosa's inheritance, and he tended to neglect her. A son, Doncicello Salvatore, was born the same year.

In 1479, the year Sardinia became formally Spanish, following Macomer, widower Ximene Perez Escrivá de Romani arrived as viceroy. He seems to have taken one look at the beautiful Rosa and, indeed, her possessions as Lord of Romangia, and decided he must have her. Perhaps she felt the same – who knows? Her story is legendary and somewhat embroidered by Enrico Costa in his historical novel *Rosa Gambella* (1897). That same year, Don Angelo was murdered, stabbed while praying next to his wife in the Sassari cathedral of St Nicholas. It is assumed that Perez was behind it, that even Rosa was involved. But it could just as easily have been assassins in retaliation for his being on the wrong side at Macomer. That same year Rosa's son, and heir to both parents, died.

In 1480, Rosa married Perez, not only that but he somehow persuaded her, by public deed, to make over her possessions to him. That was by no means the end: in 1482, Rosa, too, was murdered. If Perez thought he would get away with holding on to Rosa's patrimony, he had not reckoned with her sisters, **Maddalena** (d.1490) and **Marchesa**, who took legal action in Madrid against him. Maddalena had also married well, twice, and Marchesa was married to the brother of Rosa's first husband. Perez retaliated by pronouncing the death sentence on his accusers who were 'guilty of rebellion'. He was called home to answer the charges; later he was sent to Cagliari to answer the same charges. Eventually he was recalled because of theft from the public exchequer. One account says that he sold his rights to Rosa's estate to Maddalena's second husband, a merchant with whom he had some involvement. All seems to have ended well for him because, although his term as viceroy ended in 1483, he had a second term, 1484–1487.

Because so much of the story is legendary, it is best not to pursue the family tangle further, though, once again, it is worth asking what happened to the labourers, servants and slaves attached to Rosa's various possessions. One of her properties, known as the Palazzo Vecchio (Palatta Ezzu, Old Palace) is in the historical centre of Sennori, four miles north-east of Sassari – the village of San Basilio, on the corner of Via Veneto and Via San Basilio. It is also known as Rosa Gambella's palace, though the family never lived there, preferring Sassari, where Rosa died, and Sorso, a little town nearby on the coast, also in the historical territory of Romangia.

Pirate Raid on Bonorcili 1527

Note has already been made of how whole populations of a place moved further inland to escape the predations of raiders. And throughout the centuries raids from one part or another of the Muslim world continued. The raid described here is another of the stories of Sardinia that have seeped into its legends.

On an April night in 1527, Saracen pirates came ashore in the area of Terralba, on the Campidano plain which extends across most of the distance between Cagliari and Oristano. We have details of what happened in particular to the village of Bonorcili on the Mogoro river, earlier a Roman fort and, with its ancient church of Sant'Anastasia, a place of some importance during the *giudicato* of Arborea.

The inhabitants were asleep when the raiders struck. They broke down doors, raped, killed, looted and then razed the village; they even crucified the priest. Few were saved from the massacre. One other known victim was Sofia, daughter of a wealthy landowner. It is not necessary to suggest what happened to her before she was stabbed to death, suffice it to say that her name lives on as **Sofia Bonorcili** among the few remains of the village, including those of Sant'Anastasia. She is said to have been buried in a white robe, her arms folded across her chest where the dagger that killed her still lodged.

One woman at least was among the few who managed to escape to nearby Mogoro. She was **Giuanna Zonca** who fled carrying with her a silver cross and a sacred garment from the church; indeed, in a vain attempt to resume her life, she was to donate land for the building of a house for the Mogoro priest, and she gave the artefacts she had rescued to the church of San Bernardino. She is remembered not so much for those donations, but for her love for her lost village. She wrote a poem in her local language, the essence of which is 'Take me back to Bonorcili, where I left my heart.'

An illustration of the confusion over details that makes the history of Sardinia difficult to reconstruct with total accuracy emerged by chance when I searched for more about Sant'Anastasia church in Bonorcili. I learnt that all this area formed, from 1504, one of the possessions of the notorious Donna Violante Carroz. Not only that, but the Sant'Anastasia account suggests that Giovanni Castangia, the chaplain she was alleged to have had hanged, was that of Bonorcili's church, and it may have been suicide. This account explains that, having been excommunicated, on 2 March 1510, Violante obtained pardons from the family of the chaplain and the King of Aragon, noted with a public act in the village parish church. Bonorcili is not marked on even large scale maps today, presumably because it is but a ruin, but Mogoro is; Ales, one of the other locations where the hanging was said to have taken place, is a few miles to the north-east.

In 1798 a much larger pirate raid than that on Bonorcili was to take place on the island of Sant'Antioco, with even more repercussions; it is described in chapter 8.

Accusations of Witchcraft 1534–1606

'Aiming high, the Inquisition first tried to concoct a case of witchcraft involving the wife of the actual viceroy Cardona …' writes Giovanni Murgia (in 'Spanish Sardinia: Conflicts and Alliances'). A clue dropped very much in passing which cannot be ignored, not just out of interest in the case of Donna Cardona, but because of the themes of both witchcraft and the Inquisition.

Witchcraft was a thread running through Sardinia's history, as with many other places. Chapter 1 mentions the *Domus de Janas*, translated as house of fairies or witches, dating from at least 4250–3350 BC. Then there is the skeleton of a woman from the Bonaro culture, 1800–1600 BC, named by archaeologists Sisaia – she ancestor or witch – found entombed in an isolated cave sometimes called 'Tomb of the witch'.

The introduction of the Holy Office, the Inquisition, based in the Palace of Sassari, is attributed to 1492, not long after the island formally became Spanish territory. Witchcraft was an aspect of its function of rooting out heresy by any means.

Antonio Folch de Cardona y Enriquez, cadet son of the 1st Duke of Cardona, was viceroy of Sardinia between 1534 and 1549. His wife was **Anna Maria de Requesens de Soler y Enriquez de Velasco** (c.1500–1577), sometimes simply called **Maria Cardona**, from an equally distinguished Spanish family – her father was Galceran de Requesens, Conde de Palamos, and her ancestors highly renowned in Catalonia; her mother was **Beatriz Enriquez de Velasco**.

Not only was Maria grand, she was also good; she lived an unostentatious and virtuous life, establishing philanthropic foundations and endowing a convent, as Edward Campion detailed in his funeral oration for her in 1577. The convent was the Santa Lucia in the Castello (Martini Street), Cagliari. It was built in 1539 to house 12 Poor Clare nuns from Barcelona led **by Sister Angela Madrigal**. With the passage of time their number increased to 40, concentrating on the education of young women of the nobility of Cagliari.

How much time Maria Cardona spent in Sardinia is not clear; indeed, a lack of dates concerning her birth and marriage, and firm dates for the births of her children, does not help. The couple had seven children before Don Antonio died in 1555. Their first son was born c.1530, their eldest daughter, Margarita, c.1535. At any time in Sardinia between 1534 and 1549, Maria must have been pregnant, or giving birth, there or returning to Spain especially, to four more daughters and another son.

How then did she come to be accused of witchcraft? Not surprisingly, it was political, and against her husband and, indeed, the vicegeral centralised bureaucracy, and the Holy Office, the whole riddled with Spanish nepotism. Although Cardona did not apparently spend the whole time in Sardinia, leading up to his 1545 parliament *(stamenti)*, there had also been a series of bad years in Sardinia, creating a general state of poverty. One example of the harshness of the regime was the corporal punishment in the form of mutilation meted out by the military for such crimes as the theft of cattle.

The spark to the accusation appears to have had something to do with a particular case of corruption. The anti-Cardona faction decided to implicate Maria Cardona. Forty women witnesses appeared before the inquisition, resulting in confessions, probably extracted under torture. But in December 1545, the case against Maria and, indeed, the original allegedly corrupt official fizzled out; on 8 December the *viceregina* affair was ended with a public ceremony in which its political motivation was made explicit from the pulpit of the cathedral. The women who had borne false witness were punished.

It is worth noting that whatever accusations were levelled at Maria Cardona in Sardinia, the mud cannot have stuck, given her life afterwards, involving as it did the highest reaches of the Holy Roman Empire. Maria of Austria, Holy Roman Empress, was Spanish born, and the son who was to become Rudolf II spent time at the Spanish Court of his maternal uncle, Philip II, from the age of 11 in 1563 until he was 19. According to the funeral oration for Maria Cardona, she looked after Rudolf 'from his youth' and he, as a pupil, 'had drunk the raindrops of her goodness'.

The imperial link was even stronger than that. Under the name Maria de Requesens, and as chief lady-in-waiting until her death in 1577, possibly at the age of 77, she organised Maria of Austria's Spanish court. Her daughter, **Margaret Folch de Cardona y Requesens** (*c*.1535–1609), wife of a German diplomat, chamberlain to the emperor, was another lady-in-waiting. Her second daughter, **Anna de Cardona, Baroness de Sant Boi** (*c*.1540–after 1583), possibly Sardinian born, married twice into the Sardinian-Spanish aristocracy. What is disappointing, is never to hear the voice of Maria Cardona; what was it like, with her privileged background and exalted status, to be accused of witchcraft in a place like Sardinia?

Those accused of witchcraft in Sardinia were usually from a different level of society, as the story of **Julia Casu Masia Porcu**, better known as **Julia Carta** (b.*c*.1561) shows. She was born in Mores (Sassari), the daughter of Calvador Casu, a bricklayer, and **Giorgia de Ruda Porcu Sini**. Poor and illiterate, at 25 she married widower and farmer Costantino Nuvole, inheriting a stepson and moving to nearby Siligo. She had seven children but only one son survived.

Julia's mother had taught her a Sardinian woman's domestic duties – sewing, weaving and spinning – but she obviously exuded some special 'other', for her grandmother had handed on to her more particular arts, those of divining and healing, including the making of protective amulets – a healer being known as a *bruxia*. These arts were reinforced by day to day practice within her community. Because there were some *bruxie* who were alleged to be able to make people sick and to die, such arts were dangerous. It only needed your 'patient' to die, for accusations to be levelled, and so it happened to Julia, accused of casting a spell on a woman. The local priest did his best to find evidence against her. It was said that, instead of confessing her sins to him, she did so in a place in tune with nature, and when she was healing, she recited a prayer of her own, while invoking the aid of the Virgin Mary.

At the age of 35, in 1596, Julia appeared before the Inquisition, accused of 'magical and heretical practices'. Five named women appeared as witnesses, together with the priest and others – witnesses whom, the day before, Julia may have healed. This was typical of the Inquisition's methods. In the cells abuse was commonplace; confessions took place under torture, the accused was said to be in league with the devil. The process was convoluted and endless. Finally, Julia was sentenced to three years, with the imposition of spiritual penances and the wearing of a penitential habit that marked social death for her and her family.

Julia was, between 1604 and 1606, accused of witchcraft for a second time and tried. She was lucky to escape the inquisitorial bonfire. She is still mentioned in documents in 1614, but for the last time – she then disappears from history, her story having illustrated an aspect of life under the Holy Office for a certain type of woman and, indeed, even of women who may not have practised as a healer, but were accused for some other motive. The museum – 'The Witch House' at 9 Via Monte (the old town hall) in Bidoni – includes Julia's story among those detailing legends of sorcery and the devil between the fourteenth and sixteenth centuries.

A Century of Disasters

Disasters, particularly epidemics, were not unusual in Sardinia, and that was on top of endemic malaria that both killed and sapped the energy of its people. Plague, known in Europe as the Black Death, led to thousands of deaths between 1347 and 1353. Alghero was beset by plague in 1582/83; it lasted eight months but, by good management, its spread was halted. There is a suggestion, though, that the local authorities augmented the death rate to obtain a tax reduction. That is as may be, but several names of those who died are known. A sailor from Barcelona may have been the harbinger; after his death, two women, a widow called **Cifra** (Crippa) and her mother **Grazia**, who was assisting her in the Sant'Antonio Hospital, died one after the other. The Sant'Antonio also served as a *lazaretto* to isolate plague patients. Then the widow Cifra's son died, followed by a disabled woman, an old woman and a young daughter of the widow Cifra.

But seventeenth-century Sardinia seems to have been even worse hit, and that was compounded by the Thirty Years War (1618–1648) which caused upheaval throughout Europe. Sardinia was not a particular target though the French attempted an invasion of Oristano in 1637 which was repulsed. But the Spanish nobility, settled or with properties on the island, recruited from the rural population. Giovanni Murgia suggests that, from 1628 to 1650, between 10000 and 12000 soldiers were killed. This led not only to families being torn apart, but also to the loss of labourers, which in turn affected both the rural economy and that of the island more generally.

Other victims of the French invasion of 1637 were the nuns of Oristano's Santa Chiara, the convent founded by Costanza di Saluzzo described in chapter 4. The nuns were forced to flee, some taking refuge in the nearby commune of Villaurbana, others taken in by the Laconi family, which may well mean the parents of the Marquis of Laconi who features in the later, Zatrillas, section of this chapter. On the nuns' return, like other families in the city they found the church and convent desecrated, furniture and vestments removed, all the rooms ruined and furnishings missing or destroyed. But it was not necessarily the work of the French invaders – who suffered at least 800 deaths as they sought to re-embark, leaving behind many prisoners and a part of the booty they had pillaged. It may well have been the work of the Sardinian 'liberators' of Oristano: oral tradition of the convent mentions an unfaithful sacristan to whom the nuns had entrusted the keys and the custody of a number of golden shields concealed before their flight, but which were no longer to be found.

Excessive rain or drought led to a plague of locusts in 1638, destroying all vegetation in its wake. Between 1652 and 1657, plague spread uncontrollably across Sardinia, leading to a drop in population, particularly in Cagliari, estimated at 50 per cent. Women caught it, but they would also have been in the forefront of nursing family members. Famine because of drought descended in 1680/81, and 32 per cent of the population died of starvation; the crop of 1680 was the worst ever. Unfavourable harvests followed, slowing recovery. Once again, women would have been in the front line trying to feed their families, haunting the local market, foraging, striving to grow produce. Starvation was, of course, a factor in those years, but malnutrition would also have been rampant leading to weakness and, through that, to vulnerability to diseases, and then the spread of them, which could also be killers.

These disasters form a backdrop to the lives of women, both those for whom Sardinia was home, and those who spent time there.

The Miller's Daughter 1657–1662

As well as natural disasters, the Spanish viceroy (1657–1661), Francisco Moura, 3rd Marquis of Castel Rodrigo, Duke of Nocera, had to deal with criminals, more generally known as bandits, with which Sardinia was plagued, and with the killings for which they were responsible.

I can find no evidence that he was accompanied by his second wife and two daughters, the elder of whom was seven, when he arrived in Sardinia to take up his post. As he was there for four years, either he visited them in Spain or they spent time with him in Cagliari without the ripples caused by some vicereines.

To combat the violence of bandits, Castel Rodrigo issued an edict which forbade the carrying of weapons, and threatened with the death penalty those who armed themselves. One of these bandits came from Gallura, and was known as Giovanni Galluresu. He became a hero when he was in charge of a watchtower in the town of Santa Teresa Gallura on the northern tip of the island. On Easter eve 1658, he defended his post alone against the attack of three Saracen vessels. The viceroy rewarded him with the title *Alcade* (municipal magistrate) of the town.

But Giovanni was an orphan and in search of his roots he got into bad company, turning to banditry. Legal execution was not the only means of ending such criminality: there was also trickery. Giovanni was sweet on the nameless daughter of a nameless miller of the commune of Osilo in the province of Sassari. It is not clear if she was complicit but, using her, the authorities laid a trap for Giovanni.

One morning, at dawn, some time in 1662, as he came out of the mill, having visited his Osilese, the trap closed on him. He defended himself vigorously, but was felled by several musket balls. His corpse was then subjected to treatment in line with the viceroy's edict. Not surprisingly, the romantic story burnished his heroic reputation and has led to at least one romantic novel.

Costanza Pamphili and her Letter from Sardinia 1662–1664

Costanza Pamphili (Pamphilj; 1627–1665) is special because at last we hear from a woman in her own words. She adds as a postscript to the letter she wrote to her niece from Sassari on 1 December 1662, 'Please excuse the bad handwriting, but I am writing to you while sitting on the floor.'

Born in Rome, the daughter of Pamphilio Pamphili and Olimpia Maidalchini, Costanza was also the niece of Pope Innocent X. In 1644, aged 17, she married, as his third wife, Niccolò Ludovisi, Prince of Piombino, Marquis of Populonia, Duke of Fiano and nephew of Pope Gregory XV. Pope Innocent conducted the marriage. In 1660, Niccolò was made Spanish viceroy in Aragon and then, in 1662, viceroy of Sardinia. Costanza accompanied him there from the beginning, three children in tow.

Ludovisi's entry by Giampiero Brunelli in the *Dizionario Biographico degli Italiani* (2006) notes that he 'arrived in Alghero in November 1662. After a few weeks of rest in Sassari, he took the oath on 21 February 1663 in Cagliari.' Brunelli does not mention that Costanza was with him, and he might have written differently if he had known of her letter. I learnt of it quite by chance from Caroline Castiglione's *Accounting for Affection: Mothers, Families and Politics in Early Modern Rome* (2015) in which she quoted just Constanza's postscript. She did, though, explain in a footnote that the complete letter was in the Vatican Library, and gave the reference details, so that I was able to apply for a copy. Costanza was right to apologise for her writing: even with help, I do not have a complete transcription in Italian or English, but enough to convey the essence.

The viceregal party almost did not make it to Sardinia: the vessel carrying them from either the Italian mainland or Spain was attacked by Turkish

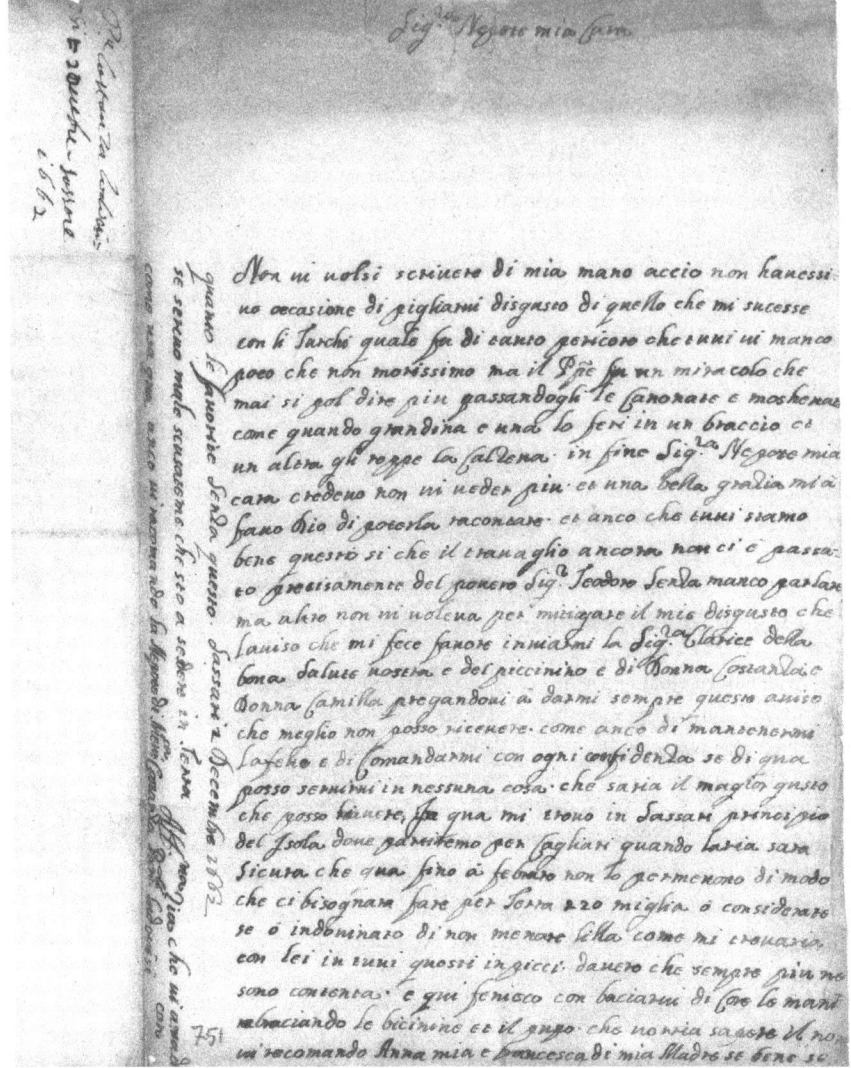

13. Page of letter from Costanza Pamphili, courtesy of the Vatican Apostolic Library

pirates. Costanza is not entirely explicit when she writes – in the translation kindly made for me:

> I did not write personally in order not to be ashamed to talk about what the Turks did to me. It was so grave that we were very close to die, but the Lord did a miracle and amidst the hail of cannonballs and musket bullets he injured one arm and broke the keel of the ship. ... In fact my dear niece I thought we would have not seen each other again. God gave me the Grace of being able to tell the tale. Even though we are well, the upset is still with us mentally, especially regarding poor Mr Teodoro [illegible].

What is extraordinary is that, in spite of diligent searching, I can find nothing about this obviously noteworthy incident, but it is not surprising that the party rested for some weeks at Sassari. After her brief description of the attack, Costanza goes on to other matters but, towards the end of the letter she writes of a more practical reason for the delay in departure:

> We will be leaving for Cagliari when the road will be safe, which is impossible here in February, in such a way that we will have to travel 220 miles or if I made the right decision not to bring Silla [?] as we would have been in all this trouble; that makes me feel happier.

Once in Cagliari, the family seems to have settled down though, as Brunelli explains, Ludovisi 'found the island's coffers exhausted and even had to use his own assets to cover the defence costs'. Details of his wealth make clear this was not an onerous burden for him, but it does show the state of Sardinia's economy, and the ramifications of it with which as viceroy he had to deal.

On Christmas Eve 1663, Costanza gave birth in Cagliari to **Ippolita Ludovisi** (1663–1733). All seemed well in the Ludovisi family itself, but it was not to last. Niccolò died on Christmas Day 1664 from an unspecified cause, and Costanza died in childbirth on 3 September 1665. She was 38. I have found no explanation of why, following the death of her husband, the viceroy, Costanza did not leave Sardinia; she was only just pregnant and probably did not know that she was, assuming that the months of their deaths are accurate. The son born then, named after his late father, died the following year. Ippolita, the only Sardinian-born child to survive, was left without a mother aged barely two. She was brought up in Italy by a much older sister-in-law, married well and had six children, including a daughter called Costanza. In 1701, Ippolita inherited the Piombino title and family fiefs from her sister **Olimpia Ludovisi** (1656–1700), six years old when the family arrived in Sardinia. She had become a nun and is clearly not the rather colourful Olimpia Maidalchini Pamphilij who earlier married into a branch of the family and whose lost portrait by Velasquez surfaced in 2019. But it is possible that 'I made the right decision not to bring Silla [or Lilla]' in Costanza's letter refers to a pet name for Olimpia.

The next viceregal wife to arrive in Sardinia left a different legacy.

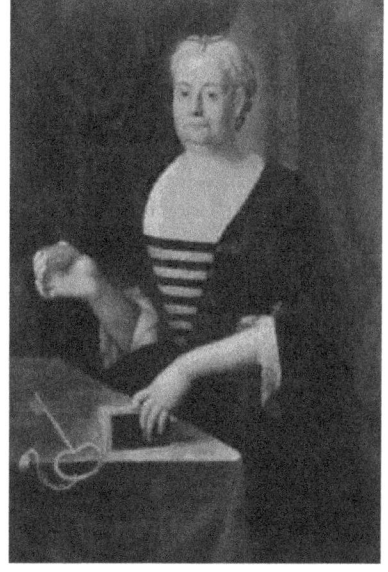

14. Ippolita Ludovisi, from the internet

Francesca Zatrillas: *Cherchez la Femme* 1651–1673

An interim viceroy followed Niccolò Ludovisi's death but, in 1665, Manuel de los Cobos, 4th Marquis of Camarassa was appointed; it was a punishment posting because he had mishandled his earlier one as viceroy of Valencia. He lasted only until his assassination on 21 June 1668 and, as not infrequently in murder stories, the best option is *cherchez la femme* or, in this case, two women.

Camarassa's time as viceroy was one of political upheaval and rival factions, so that the two assassinations and, later, several murders and executions, are sometimes portrayed as political, and this version is described in some detail by, for example, Giovanni Murgia. Put most simply, in Sardinia, at a time when Spanish imperial influence had declined, Madrid, in the person of its viceroy, was under increasing pressure from the *stamenti*, or parliament, particularly when Spain required it to finance a war against France; it was as if the viceroy was totally unaware of the poverty the recent disasters had exacerbated. In addition, Sardinian nobles were in a power struggle, not just with all that the viceroy stood for, but also with Spanish newcomers. And Sardinian noble extended families, too, vied with each other, and within themselves.

But other accounts of the Camarassa conspiracy (*Camarasa Conjura*) see it as driven by love or, at least, lust. And in yet another version, it is two rival women attempting to escape the straitjacket of the period placed on women, particularly those of the highest social class, by manipulating events from behind their husbands. And, as so often, there are different versions of all three, creating the need to steer as convincing as possible a course between them.

One of the first accounts was probably that of Pietro Giannone, early eighteenth-century Italian philosopher, historian and jurist in *Storia del Regno di Napoli* (1723), with its English translation, *The Civil History of the Kingdom of Naples* (1729–31). He implicates not only **Francesca Zatrillas** (1642–1671), most commonly regarded as the guilty party, but also the viceroy's second wife, **Isabel de Portocarrero y de Luna** (1627–1694). Isabel's role is developed by Carla Torres Llop in the paper '*Marquesa di Sietefuentes: Victima y Culpable de la Conjura Camarasa*' (2017) (Victim and Guilty of the Camarassa Conspiracy).

Francesca, Sardinian born, in Cuglieri, did not need to marry for position, status or wealth. Her father was Giambattista Zatrillas, Marchese di Sietefuentes, Conte di Cuglieri, of distant Spanish origins, but committed to Sardinia (Cuglieri had been in the Zatrillas family since 1421). Her mother was **Ana Maria de Castelvi y Lanza**, from an old Sardinian family. When her father died in 1651/2, Francesca, after a bit of an intra-family dispute, inherited his titles. She did not marry until 1665, when she was already 23, and then only on the death of her mother. The man she married, as his second wife, was her maternal uncle, Agostino de Castelvi y Lanza, Marquéz de Laconi, Visconte di Sanluri, and they had a son. It was, seemingly, an inter-family political marriage, not a love match.

Laconi was, according to genealogical sources, born in 1626 and, therefore, 16 years older than Francesca, which does not seem much of an age gap today. Although Carla Torres Llop describes him as 'a man of boisterous character, and restless', she adds that he was 'an aged man who had carved a reputation in the parliamentary political panorama of Sardinia'. And Dionigi Scano's 1946 biography, *Donna Francesca di Zatrillas*, has him as 'a crumbling and venerable old man'. An internet source sees him as 'gloomy, irritable and passionate'. If the genealogies are correct, he was only 42 on 20 June 1668; however Murgia says that he was 58, which is more in keeping with the descriptions, and makes him 32 years older than Francesca, while Federica Ginesu (2016) in *DonnaSarda* says that he was 25 years older. Whatever the truth about his age, that was the day on which he was murdered, on a street in the Castello, now the Via Lamarmora. As Francesca wrote to the queen regent of Spain, Mariana of Austria (1634–1696), he was killed treacherously by police officers who stabbed him many times.

It was initially seen as a political assassination: Laconi was a leading opponent of Camarassa. Pietro Gionnone, in his 1729–30 study, writes:

> It was rumoured that this murder was committed by order of D. Isabella di Portocarrero, Marchioness of Camarassa, with the knowledge and consent of the Viceroy her Husband, in Revenge of the Opposition made by D. Agostino in the Parliament. ...

Carla Torres Llop claims that the 'viceregal court was directed in practice by the Marquise de Camarasa, Isabel de Portocarrero, she also had conversations with her husband's parliamentary adversaries, threatening and coercing'. And she adds that 'The Conjura Camarasa is ultimately reduced to a confrontation between Donna Francesca de Zatrillas and Donna Isabel de Portocarrero'. Gionnone's account adds flesh to the suggestion that Isabel was behind the assassination of Francesca's husband, and Francesca's part in the retaliation:

> Upon this Rumour D. Giacomo Artal di Castelvi, Marquis of Cea, D. Silvestré Americh, D. Antonio Brondo, D. Francesco Cao, D. Francesco Portugues and D. Salviono Grizzoni met in the palace of D. Francesca Zatrillas, Marchioness of Laconi, the Deceased's Wife, where they agreed to put the Viceroy to death.

The name that springs out from that list of eminent Sardinians, relatives of Laconi, is that of Silvestré de Aymerich y Cervellon, Francesca's 21-year-old cousin. William Henry Smyth, a commander in the Royal Navy, writes of how things looked in the early nineteenth century when he was surveying the coast of Italy, one result being the publication of *Sketch of the present state of Sardinia* (1828); it was not Isabel who was behind the murder:

It appears that Francesca, Marchioness of Laconi, having an illicit commerce with Don S. Aymerich, induced him to assassinate her husband, and then propagated a report of the Marquis of Camerassa having committed the deed, which, as the deceased had recently been deputed to Madrid by the *stamenti*, to complain of the Viceroy's exactions, easily obtained belief.

Aymerich had apparently wooed Francesca when his mother lived opposite hers, or when her husband, who also had a mistress, was absent from Sardinia at Queen Mariana's Court in Madrid. There he was unsuccessfully pleading Sardinia's cause, including uproar over Camarassa's dissolution of the *stamenti*. Francesca was only too ready to respond.

A month and a half after Laconi's death, on 21 July, Camarassa, Isabel and their children were returning from mass at the church of our Lady of Mount Carmel in the Stampace district when, just as they passed the palace of Don Antonio Brondo y de Castelvi, assassins struck, firing into their carriage from the palace and killing Camarassa. As punishment, the palace at 32 Via Canelles was razed to the ground. When a new one was erected in its place, a plaque was affixed to it perpetuating the names of the assassins, including that of Francesca, and their infamy.

Francesca and Isabel came face to face, according to Carla Torres Llop, when the widowed vicereine summoned Francesca to a 'Royal Audience' before her and a lawyer of the 'Royal Hearing' to clarify the crimes that both women had claimed in letters to Queen Mariana. That is at odds with Gionnone's 1723 account which has Isabel fleeing immediately to Spain and safety, leaving Francesca 'at full liberty to enter into an Action against her in the Royal Tribunal of Cagliari and to charge her with the murder of the Marquis her Husband'. The queen, meanwhile, had moved quickly to appoint a successor to Camarassa; he arrived with a strong contingent of soldiers and instigated a hunt for those accused of his predecessor's murder.

Francesca fled to her castle in Cuglieri, north of Oristano, with her lover – the 'guilty paramours' as Smyth has it; and there she was reported by a visiting priest to flagrantly lead the high life with him – 'with marvellous boldness and licentious indecency' – making no attempt at discretion. It was not that the neighbours could look through the windows, as the Castello di Montiferru was perched high on a crag. It did not help her reputation that she married Aymerich only three months after her husband's murder.

A trial took place at the end of which, Murgia explains, by manipulating the evidence, the conspiracy against the viceroy was made to appear 'like a personal story of two young lovers who had ordered the murder of a husband who was in the way'. On 5 July 1669, death sentences were passed on Francesca, Aymerich, the Marquis of Cea and the others. Francesca and Aymerich, hearing that a commissioner leading a troop of knights was on his way from Oristano to Cuglieri, fled first to the church of San Lorenzo, then made their way to the coast and took a boat to Livorno; from there to Nice. The others charged with the assassination of Camarassa had at first taken sanctuary for a month in the Convent of San Francisco in Cagliari, then went into hiding first in northern Sardinia. They finally took refuge in Nice under the protection of the Duke of Savoy.

When the Duke refused to cooperate in extraditing them, an envoy was sent to convince them that Sardinia was ready to revolt. Murgia notes that there was, indeed, fear of an insurrection following Camarassa's murder, and a Spanish fleet left Naples to prepare to sail for the island, an order then rescinded when all stayed calm. When those beguiled by the envoy arrived in Sardinia some, including Aymerich, were murdered in their sleep; the others were dragged in chains to Cagliari where they were publicly executed in the main piazza of the Castello. The decapitated heads of Aymerich, Cao, Portugues and the Marquis of Cea were exhibited in the Torre del Elefante where they remained for 17 years.

Francesca, meanwhile, had given birth to Aymerich's son in March 1670, but on hearing of her husband's death, she retreated to the Santa Maria Convent in Nice where, after years dedicating herself to prayer, she died, in 1673, aged only 31, her reputation, at least there, saintly. Carla Torres Llop sees the explanation of the Camarassa conspiracy and the treatment of Francesca's reputation as a need to punish an adulterous woman, one who had stepped out of line, and as a warning to others. As Federica Ginesu on the *DonnaSarda* website interprets the attacks on her, she was described as the Lucrezia Borgia of Sardinia. And if the whole affair could be blamed on a woman, it was less likely to disturb delicate relations between Sardinia and Madrid.

Francesca's son with Laconi does not seem to have thrived, unlike that with Aymerich who was to inherit the properties, confiscated but later restituted, and the titles, of both Francesca and Laconi. He married well, twice, had several children, and died in 1716. Whatever the properties he inherited, the feud of Cuglieri was sold, but Francesca's Castello Montifferu there was abandoned in 1670 and fell into ruin. The best way to see and appreciate its powerful remains is via a short aerial video on the internet. According to *DonnaSarda*, Francesca's soul still roams there at nightfall!

In the grounds of the Palazzo Aymerich in the heart of the

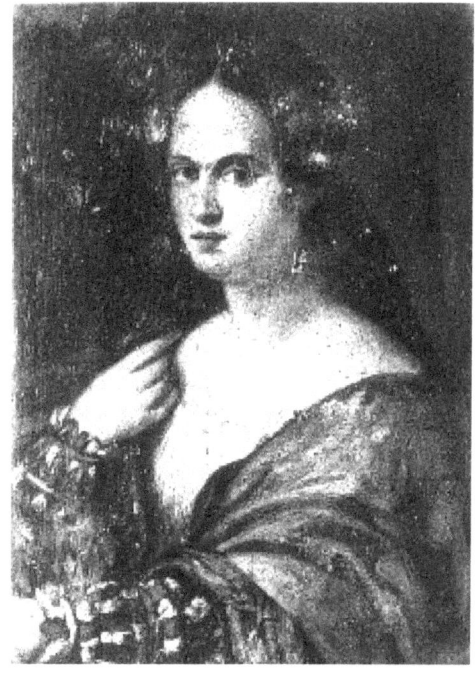

15. Donna Francesca Zatrillas, from the internet

village of Laconi not only is there a botanical paradise of rare plants but also the Civic Archaeological Museum of prehistoric sculpture dating back to the fourth and third millennia BC. So perhaps some good came from descendants of Francesca Zatrillas.

Rosaria Guiso's Lament

Unlike Francesca Zatrillas, little is known about Rosaria Guiso, except that she came from Orosei, was born into the noble house of Guiso, lived some time in the eighteenth century, and sparse details about what inspired her to write the poem that survives. It is published, and accessible online, in both *Ichnussa* and *Limbo* which specialise in poetry written in Sardo. Those sparse details introduce the poem, and they are a reversal of Francesca's reputed actions.

Beautiful Rosaria married a certain man known only as Toto, and had a son by him. On their way to church to baptise the baby, her husband was killed by a 'rival in love', or the murder was organised by this nameless rival. At the time it seems that Rosaria did not know the identity of the murderer, nor his motive, for she later married him. But he made the mistake of confessing to her what he had done to gain her, at which she 'drove him away furiously and would not see him'. Part of the poem, *Po dare pen'a mie* ('To give me pain again'), written in Logudorese, in six verses, reads:

> He lost his precious life
> My only loved one
> The one I'll always call
> The one I'll always mourn
> From deep of my own heart
> That handsome flower of mine

It is hardly surprising that it is not easy to fit Rosaria into the Guiso family history, for much of the history of Orosei itself, a town today in the province of Nuoro, on the banks of the Cedrino, 2.5 km (1.5 miles) from the east coast, is linked to that family. It is fair to assume that she is sandwiched between two extremes in time. Salvatore Guiso bought Orosei for a tidy sum in 1449, together with a barony. His eldest son died without heir, a pattern often repeated, and a number of determined women through the centuries passed the inheritance on. Worth mentioning is **Donna Francesca Guiso** whose father named her his heir, but the notarial deed could not be found. The incident provoked the intervention of the Assets Tax Office which ruled that Francesca and her sisters had no title to the succession. But in 1552, sister **Donna Violante** succeeded in obtaining recognition of the feud for her son who, having no heir, left it to his sister **Donna Angela**.

Fast forward to 2000, Don Giovanni (Nanni) Guiso founded the museum named after him. Housed in a seventeenth-century palazzo, it contains miniature theatres and puppet theatres from eighteenth- to twenty-first-century Europe, together with paintings, haute couture garments and a sixteenth-century marriage chest made for the Caponi family. The museum can be visited on request; details are on the internet.

The End of Spanish Sardinia

The War of Spanish Succession (1701–1714) which brought to an end four centuries of Hispano-Aragonese rule in Sardinia, was caused by the death of the heirless Carlos II in 1700. Spain lost all its possessions in Sardinia, Italy and the Low Countries. They were given to Austria, except Sicily which went to the Duke of Savoy. Sardinia became Austrian in 1708, confirmed by the Treaty of Utrecht in 1713. Even then, Spain tried to retake the island, hoping to use it as a strategic base from which to regain its Italian possessions. A successful expedition was sent there from Barcelona in 1717 and it is suggested that Sardinians cooperated, preferring Spanish rule to Austrian. But Spain's action caused the War of the Quadruple Alliance (1718–1720). The Austrians, French and British demanded Spain's withdrawal. Under the Treaty of London, signed in Aix in 1720, Sardinia was handed over to the House of Savoy; Victor Amadeus II of Savoy became King of Sardinia. Murgia ends the story of that era with the suggestion that Savoy 'inherited a land in which the language, culture, traditions, practices and customs, religious institutions and rituals recalled its secular bonds with the Spanish royalty'. The new Kingdom of Sardinia comprised Piedmont on the mainland, as well as the island, creating a considerable territory. It also elevated the status of what were then Savoyard kings.

6 – Sardinia Under the House of Savoy 1720–1861

Introduction: Dukes of Savoy, Kings of Sardinia

In 1720, the island that had been under the lordship of Aragon and Spain for 400 years came under that of the house of Savoy whose duke was, in addition, raised to king of Sardinia. The kingship was to last until the unification of Italy in 1861. The court of King Victor Amadeus II was based in Turin (Torino, Piedmont), and the kings and queens of Sardinia seem to have had no occasion to visit the island until 1799, when they had no choice, and were only too glad to find refuge there.

In 1720, little changed in the lives of most Sardinians. Until 1827, they were still subject to the laws of Eleonora d'Arborea's *Carta de Logu*; until 1836, they still laboured under feudalism; they were still governed by foreign viceroys; and there was still nepotism, mainland favouritism and corruption. These indulgences were to lead to rebellion.

Corruption, the Tonduts and Rebellion in Sassari 1733–1780

One of the most explicit examples of these indulgences and, indeed, the resulting rebellion, concerns the Tondut (Tonduti) family of Sassari. The family was originally from Lombardy, then established itself in Nice towards the end of the fourteenth century. By 1733, Carlo Francesco Tondut, a military man, was governor of Sassari, a posting that was to last until 1745. As Federico Francioni tells it in *'La Storia di una Sassari Ribelle'* (2017), both Tondut and his wife, **Angela Maria Germano**, appear to have been equally corrupt. Not only that but, as Francioni describes Angela in *Vespro Sardo* (2001), she was 'a woman of despotic temperament'. In 1739, a *Representation*, that is, a memorial of Sassari nobles and notables, was sent to Turin to the government of King Carlo Emanuele III, in which detailed accusations were levelled at the couple (Sardinia may have been between viceroys that year). As a result they were subjected to examination by the Savoy authorities for embezzlement, corruption and abuse of office; they were charged with corruption, favouritism and bad government, as well as arrogance towards the inhabitants of the island. Not surprisingly, they qualified as *scrocchi* – cowards and scoundrels.

An example of their misdemeanours is told in an internet teaching aid – *'Sardegna del Settecento Come Stato d'Antico Regime'*. The University of Sassari had been founded in 1617 and the couple – again the two of them – persecuted the university professor Antonio Murgi Liperi who was 'guilty' of sponsoring a divorce case. It is surprising that in a deeply religious Catholic island, where divorce then would not have been generally acceptable, nor easy, this should have been held against the couple. Their persecution must have been egregious.

Neither the investigation, nor the charges, seem to have unduly damaged Tondut's career: the *Dictionnaire de la Noblesse* (1786) lists him as lieutenant general in the Savoyard army 'in the war of 1747' (the War of Austrian Succession 1740–1748). That might have appeared to be the end of the Tonduts in Sassari but, as things turned out, it was not.

There may have been at least two Tondut daughters who married the same man or, as often, the sources are confused. What is not in dispute is that in 1772 Cavaliero Alli di Maccarani (also confusingly known as Marchese della Planargia – not the one later assassinated in Cagliari) became governor of Sassari. Francioni says that he was married to **Maria Genoveffa Tondut**, and a separate internet genealogy agrees (Maria-Genoveffa Tonduti de l'Escarène). But a footnote in *Il Dizionario Bibliografico degli Uomini Illustri di Sardegna* (1838) has him, patron of the Academy, firmly married to **Luigia Caterina Tonduti dell Scarena**. No amount of digging for the women of the Tondut(i) family clarifies either the mother's background or which of her daughters married Maccarani; another daughter, Anna Maria, married elsewhere. Maccarani's governorship was to last almost as long as that of his father-in-law (1772–1780), but his end was to be rather more ignominious; what came in between his arrival and departure in many ways followed the Tondut precedent he had been set.

The events of 1780 have been called 'The Bread Uprising' (*Rivolta del Pane*). It is worth noting that the immediate spark for both the French Revolution nine years later (the march of the women on Versailles), and the Russian Revolution of February 1917, was shortage of bread.

The cause and progress of the bread uprising in Sassari are usefully told by the scholarly Antonio Sisco, father of the Franciscan Order in Sardinia, in an eye-witness account introduced by Antonio Meloni in *La Nuova Sardegna* (26 March 2001). It is generally accepted that the social unrest culminating in days of violence was justly seen as the fraudulent management of the 'public' grain by Governor Maccarani.

The uprising started on 23 April by the poor, lacking anything to eat, particularly bread, normally provided from public stocks of grain. The palace of the Magistrate was the first to be sacked, not only the furnishings, but also the archives – papers thrown out into the street were then burnt. Only the images of the crucifix and the king were spared as the crowd chanted 'Long live the king, out with Maccarani and his bad government.' After evening prayers, shops were plundered.

After the mob had vandalised the house of the priest attached to the nearby Santa Chiara Convent, they set off towards Seminario Canapolense, for the house of **Giovanna D'Antona**, widow of lawyer Andrea Sadis Pilo. Father Sisco does not say what the lawyer is alleged to have done to merit this attack on his widow, but it cannot have been of little import because the mob turned its attention to the couple's daughter, paralysed for many years, throwing her off her bed, leaving her sprawling on the floor, and making off with her bedding.

After midnight on 25 April an attempt was made to break into the Santa Chiara Convent where it was believed that the rich had deposited money, silverware and other objects of value. When the door began to give way, the inmates rang the bell in desperation; someone ran through the crowd to call the troops and the thieves dispersed.

All through the uprising, though, the greatest venom was directed, in every district of the city, and by all classes, including women and children, at Maccarani, the 'nothing man'(?) (*Nardo del Nardo*). They chanted 'Out, Out' at his every appearance, mangling his name to an insult. When Maccarani appeared at a city gate, doffing his hat to those usually assembled there, they kept their caps on and turned their backs on him. 'And they did the same with the Marquise, his consort, and their children.' As far as they were concerned, he was totally corrupt – 'a leech on the blood of the poor'; he paid for neither what he bought, nor the wages of the workers; he had amassed a fortune through greed which was his god. His creditors who approached government house came away empty-handed.

Eventually news of the uprising reached Turin, and King Vittorio Amedeo III arranged for large quantities of wheat to be sent to Sassari from Nice; he also sent mediators to attempt to calm the situation. They arrived on 14 June and began looking into the cause of the uprising. On 12 July a new governor arrived to replace Maccarani who left at dawn on the 17th with his family for Livorno, hoping to avoid further trouble. He died in Livorno in November that same year, 1780. What became of his wife and children, not surprisingly, history does not relate. But several involved in the corruption under his governorship were exiled; and several of the rioters were executed. Many scurrilous poems against Maccarani were published, as well as a composition in Latin prose, probably 'written by an ecclesiastical man, highly versed in Holy Scripture' – '*Civitas Sassaritana, terra olim promissionis*' ('City of Sassari, once the promised land').

The Sassari uprising of 1780 is deemed to be the forerunner of that in Cagliari which was to explode on 28 April 1794, reinforced, perhaps, by the French Revolution.

Women and Feudal Rights Under Savoy 1723–1836

The sale of fiefs in Sardinia was always part of the financial policy of the House of Savoy. It was particularly marked while Conte Vittorio des Hayes was viceroy of Sardinia (1767–1771) with Gian Battista Bogino as the Savoyard Minister for Sardinian Affairs (1759–1773). Women often had to claim their rights to family fiefs through either formal or informal dispute resolution, often at some cost. At least two such cases are usefully described in Marzia Erriu's doctoral thesis '*Il Viceré Des Hayes e il Governo del Regnum Sardiniae*' (2012). This provides an opportunity to follow women connected with those who had their own earlier struggles of one sort or another.

Don Francesco Castelvi died in 1723 without any direct heir to the marquisate of Laconi. But he did have a niece, **Donna Maria Caterina Castelvi y Sanjust** (1694–1772), second wife of Gabriel de Aymerich y Zatrillas, son of the notorious couple Francesca Zatrillas and Silvestre de Aymerich whose exploits are described in chapter 5. By rights Caterina should have become 7th Marchessa de Laconi, Viscountess of Sanluri. Unfortunately for her, the tax authorities seized the opportunity to take over the fief and titles. Caterina went to law, in the end successfully, but the case lasted until 1733; not only that, she borrowed increasing sums of money to persevere. The debts accumulated and, in 1769, fell on the shoulders of her grandson and heir, Don Ignazio Aymerich when he became 8th Marchese di Laconi. He was not 'distinguished for parsimony or sobriety'; indeed, he preferred a life of luxury and 'appearance' which started with his 'magnificent' marriage to **Maddalena Zatrillas y Manca Giuso** (1735–1815) of the marquisate family di Villaclara. They were to have eight children, but you have to wonder about Maddalena's matrimonial well-being. Ignazio was of high rank in the military, and a delegate to the military *stamenti* (one of the three branches of the parliament); he led a dissipated life, accumulating yet further debts. Finally the government removed from him the management of his assets, putting them into the hands of an administrator.

A term that often arises in land disputes in feudal Savoyard Sardinia is *allodi*. Allodial lands are the opposite of feudal: they are held by the owner in their own right, not touchable by those distributing fiefs; therefore, the Crown had limited powers of intervention. To curb the increasingly burdensome Iberian presence in Sardinia – a leftover from its Spanish past – it would be necessary for the sovereign to purchase fiefs in order to re-distribute them to loyal Sardinians. Claiming that lands were *allodi* was, therefore, a useful negotiating ploy. The 1733 success of Donna Caterina Castelvi in claiming allodial rights led the way, and it was to be one followed by, for example, **Maria Faustina Tellez Giron, Duchess of Benavente and Gandia** (1724–1797), daughter of the 7th Duke of Osuna, and second wife and widow since 1763 of Francisco Alfonso Pimentel y Borgia, 11th Duke of Benavente.

In 1740 the family's claim to its Sardinian lands was questioned, but Faustina argued that she was the legitimate heir with allodial rights. She was anxious to preserve the interests of her young daughter, **Maria Giuseppa (Josefa) Alfonso Pimentel** (1750 or 1752–1834). Faustina reminded Bogino by letter of other 'examples of justice rendered by his Sovereign Majesty to similar Spanish houses of her class'. She assured the king of her gratitude, and it was 'my precise wish that my interests and advantages should not be separated from the service and contemplation of His Sovereign Majesty'.

The case lasted until 1767 when at last the sovereign, through his attorney, acceded to her claim via 'a friendly adjustment' of her dispute; that is, the case was mediated in favour of her daughter, Maria Giuseppa. In March that year, the minister presented a proposal which, 'due to its righteousness and magnanimity, was gladly accepted by the duchess and approved by the sovereign'.

The confirmation of the feudal concession was guaranteed. For 25 years the sum of 2,500 Sardinian *scudi* was to be donated by the Spanish title holder towards the protection of those suffering through wars and plague, and also to root out the evils of banditry. Another goal was the promotion of agriculture and commercial development, including through identifying a number of poor girls and boys willing to cultivate the land who would be given the means to marry. Another sum was put aside for foreigners to graft olive trees for the production of olive oil, and the formation of artificial meadows, for the treatment of hay, for plantations and factories. Workers should be equipped with a home and the necessary tools. The establishment of a hospital in the village of Ocier (?Ozieri, Osilo) ended the agreement.

At this point the agreement started to unravel; the hospital project met with the hostility of the Duke of Bejar and Mandas, a relative of the duchess. Although Des Hayes' announcement of the agreement with Countess Maria Giuseppa was published on 28 July 1767, the expected benefits were delayed; the royal intentions immediately disappointed, expectations frustrated. Blame was put on the indolence of the inhabitants of the duchy of Monteacuto, Anglona, and Manguini on the subject of the dowries and attributed to misunderstanding by the villagers. Bogino wanted to reprint the announcement with further explanation and with, above all, a version in the Sardinian language. The convoluted details of this mediation are recorded differently in other sources. But the result was that Giuseppa (Josefa) Pimentel assumed many titles, including, as one of those other sources lists, Princess of Anglona, Duchess of Monteacuto, Marquise of Marghine and Countess of Osilo and Coghinas. These were as well as the Spanish titles she had inherited from her father, Duchess of Benavente and Duchess of Gandia.

In 1771, she was to assume another Spanish title, Duchess of Osuna, when she married her first cousin Pedro de Alcántara Téllez-Girón and Pacheco, 9th Duke of Osuna; born in 1755, he was only 16, either three or five years younger than her. The couple moved in rarefied circles in Madrid, playing a prominent role there. Josefa, as she was called in Spain, was said to be sharply intelligent, enlightened, elegant and composed; she maintained one of the most important literary salons in Madrid and was admitted to two societies, in one of which she was one of only two women members. The couple supported the arts, particularly the work of Goya, who painted portraits of them both, and one with four of their children. (Josefa gave birth to nine children, but four died in childhood.)

This contribution to the life of the Spanish capital was all very well but what connection did Josefa have with Sardinia, apart from owning lands, reaping financial benefit, and holding titles from those lands? Did she ever even visit Sardinia? That is not clear, but it does lend weight to the early nineteenth-century opinion of William Henry Smyth RN, gleaned during his visits to the island:

The contempt in which the inhabitants of the plains are viewed by those of the mountains, and the large proportion of fiefs intrusted to indolent 'podatarii', by non-resident Spanish nobles (as the Marquis de Quirra, the Marquis de Villa-Sor, Count Montalvo, the Duke of Mandas, the Duchess of Gandia, and others) are also serious obstacles to improvement.

The Duchess of Gandia was still Josefa at the time Smyth was visiting Sardinia. A source in Italian and French on the Bortigali (Nuoro) website clarifies and elaborates Josefa's position and behaviour:

As it was with a number of other villages of Marguine, relations with their new feudal landlords were not easy for the fief was administered by unscrupulous Spanish functionaries. In fact, between 1774 and 1785, she openly refused to pay the taxes.

The traveller and writer Antoine-Claude Pasquin Valéry, travelling in Sardinia in 1834, the year of Josefa's death, wrote of her and her feudal income in *Voyages en Corse, a l'Île d'Elbe et en Sardaigne* (vol. 2, 1837): 'In 1834, eighteen hundred inhabitants paid just to the Spanish Duchess of Gandia, Princess of Anglona, the sum of sixteen thousand seven hundred and thirty eight francs, the justice that she rendered costing each of them three thousand five hundred and eighteen francs.'

It seems clear that Josefa was held up as a prime exemplar of non-resident Iberian feudalism, the abolition of which was not long in coming.

A third example of women possessing fiefs concerns the family of Jewish origin from Alghero, the Carcassonas, who, as described in chapter 5, converted to Christianity following the 1492 Spanish expulsion of Jews from their territories. This time the fief holder was, at least, Sardinian.

In 1749, the fief that encompassed the villages of Serdiana and Donori a few miles north of Cagliari came into the possession of **Francesca Brunenga Carcassona** (b. 1714), together with the title **Marchesa di San Saverio**. She was the daughter of Don Domenico Brunengo Pilo Boyl Cervellon, 1st Count

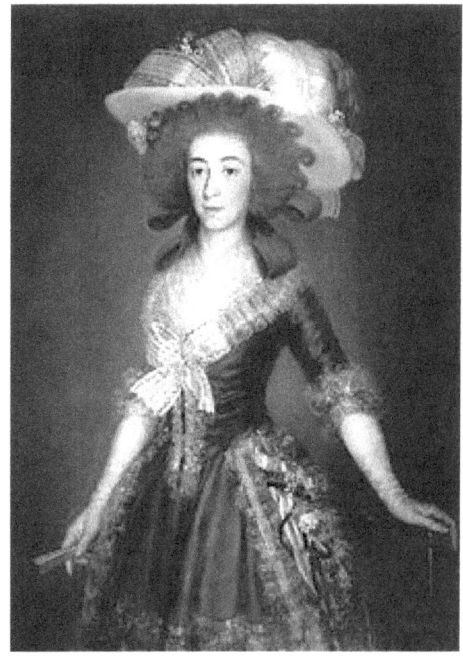

16. Duchess Benavente by Francisco Goya, 1785, from the internet

of Monteleone; which of his wives was Francesca's mother is unclear. In 1737, Francesca had married, as her second husband, the Spanish captain Don Francesco Carcassona Manca who left her widowed. With the fief and title, Francesca also acquired civil and criminal jurisdiction over her fief.

It appears that, in 1728, the fief had been forfeit and reverted to the Crown. The Royal Department of Internal Revenue auctioned it and Francesca, then aged 35, paid 27000 scudi for it and her title; a further 1000 scudi was due in subsequent years. An online history of Serdiana says that the inhabitants – anyone over 18 – continued to be burdened by tax, part in produce, part in money, as Francesca tried to recoup the large sum she had paid for the fief.

On Francesca's death, her son Efisio Luigi Carcassona took over and, the economic situation in Sardinia having improved, so did the lot of the inhabitants of the two villages. Efisio died in 1801 without a male heir, but he did have two daughters, the elder of whom, **Francesca Carcassona, Contessa di Monteleone** (d. 1823), was named after his mother; her title came from her great-grandfather via her great-uncle. In 1789, she had married Don Carlo Queseda and ten years later, when the Savoyard royal family took refuge in Sardinia, the couple both held royal appointments.

Francesca inherited the fief and Saverio title from her father. But that inheritance, according to a near contemporary, Sardinian politician and writer Giovanni Siotto-Pintor, was not unopposed. In his *Storia Letteraria di Sardegna* (1843–44), he wrote of:

> Judgment in favour of Francesca Carcassona, Contessa di Monteleone against Giovanna Carcassonna, Marchesa di San Tommaso for the succession of the Marquisate of San Saverio, Sassari, 1803.

Confirmation that Giovanna Carcassona was Francesca's younger sister comes from looking into how she came to be Marchesa di San Tommaso. And it starts with another enterprising woman. In 1747 the Marquisate of San Tommaso (Tomaso or St Thomas), encompassing the villages of Gesico and Goni north-east of Cagliari, was taken into the hands of the tax authorities following a long family dispute. **Giovanna (Juana) Maria Cervellon** snapped it up for 9000 scudi. The following year, she married Tomaso Nin. Their grandson, also Tomaso, then the Marchese of San Tommaso, married **Giovanna Carcassona y Pilo**, who thus became the Marchesa.

But why would the younger daughter lay claim to the fief and title of San Saverio over her older sibling? I have translated '*per la successione*' as 'for the succession', but I suspect it more accurately means 'concerning'. That there was a great tangle of a dispute, involving several intermarrying extended families following the death of Efisio, is clear from the compilation concerning the Manca family made by Paolo Amat from the Cagliari archives. It details the intricacies of a court case that rumbled on from at least 1810 to 1814 and includes references to the parents and two husbands, one an Amat, one a Manca, of the first Francesca. To attempt to disentangle it would not be appropriate for this account, though I would just add that one party of claimants was the heirs of **Giovanna Amat Brunengo** (1736–1806), wife of Antonio Manca-Amat, 1st Duke of Vallombrosa and Asinara. Anyone could get confused! More relevant is the extract from the February 1813 record,

> The Marchesa of San Tommaso Donna Giovannna Nin Carcassona claims, in the inheritance of her late Marchese of San Saverio parent, the figure of 20,000 scudi that constituted her dowry just after the marriage clauses stipulated in April 1795. Donna Giovanna had to give to her elder sister 2,750 scudi.

Those first years of the nineteenth century were not easy for the fief of San Saverio. There was smallpox in Serdiana and a lack of drinkable water. Then, 1812 was known as 'The Famine of the Twelve' (*su famini de s'annu doxi*). When Francesca died giving birth to her first child in 1823, she left everything to her sister Giovanna.

Giovanna's status as Marchesa of San Saverio and of San Tommaso obviously ensured her advancement in the world, one following her sister's earlier royal connection. Another entry from Siotto-Pintor's 1843–1844 history reads,

> Nin di S Tommaso, Marchesa Giovanna born Carcassona, a person already noted as matron of honour to SAR Princess Maria Anna Empress of Austria and Queen of Hungary.

Maria Anna, Princess of Sardinia (1803–1884) was the daughter of King Vittorio Emanuele of Sardinia, and married Ferdinand of Austria in 1831. He became Emperor in 1835 and Anna was crowned Queen of Bohemia. This gives some idea of the timing of Giovanna Carcassona's royal position which may even pre-date the princess's marriage. This portrait is of Giovanna in 1866. Her daughter, **Maria Luigia Nin** (1800–1866), was in turn to become Marchesa di San Saverio and di San Tommaso.

In 1839, three years after King Carlo Alberto abolished feudalism in Sardinia, the fief of Saverio was ransomed from Giovanna by its inhabitants. But Giovanna kept not only the title, but also the family castle in Serdiana. Indeed, Luigia's husband, Edmondo Roberti Castelvero, was to add to it. It is noticeable that this Sardinian aristocratic and feudal family did not just own the fief from the days

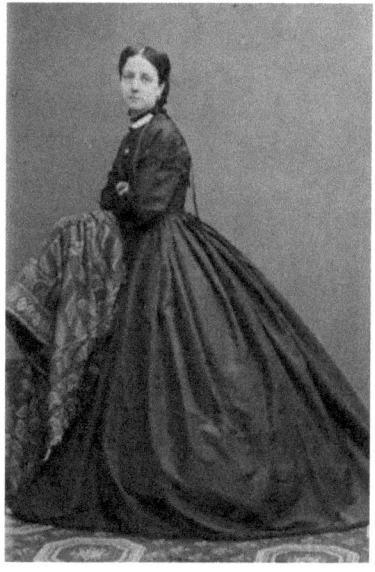

17. Giovanna Roberti Nin Carcassona, 1866, from the internet

of its purchaser, matriarch Francesca, but she and her Carcassona women descendants lived there. The castle, known as both Castello Roberti and Castello Carcassona, still stands, together with its chapel dedicated to Saint Anthony of Padua in which members of the family were buried. It is Serdiana's most imposing sight.

There are also two palaces in Cagliari connected with the family: Palazzo Roberti Nin di San Tommaso is at 122 Via Lamarmora, and Palazzo de Magistris at number 120. From their marriage in 1829 Luigia Nin and Edmondo Roberti Castelvero had one son and seven daughters. Edmondo was twice mayor of Cagliari between 1846 and 1875, and the couple's daughters all married within the nobility.

The saga of the Carcassona women shows how the converted Jewish family from fifteenth-century Alghero had merged seamlessly into the highest Sardinian Christian aristocracy by the eighteenth and nineteenth centuries, even mixing effortlessly with European royalty. What the material apparently available lacks, however, is detail of what must have been interesting, perhaps fulfilling, lives lived, apart from inheritance disputes and feudal dues. Where, for example, did the impetus come from to purchase a fief with all that must have entailed, and what talent or education must have been needed? How responsible were the women for at least supervising the administration, given that they lived locally? I suspect the widowed first Francesca, at least, was.

The Sardinian Vespers: *Sa Die de Sa Sardigna* – Rebellion 1793–1796

The Napoleonic Wars fought between France and a coalition of other European countries, including the Kingdom of Sardinia, followed the French Revolution of 1789, and lasted, with a short break in 1802, from 1792 to 1815.

In January 1793, a French fleet arrived in the Gulf of Cagliari, having earlier been welcomed in Carloforte on the Sardinian island of San Pietro. (The attack on Carloforte in 1798 by Berbers from North Africa and its dreadful aftermath are described in chapter 8). But Cagliari itself resisted the French bombardment and a landing of troops on the mainland coast; they were defeated by the Sardinian army on 14 February 1794. A similar attempt from Corsica led by the young Napoleon Bonaparte on the northern island of La Maddalena was also repulsed.

The bare facts record little of what the French attack and the continuing war with the French meant to the ordinary people of Sardinia, particularly its women. But **Maria Baule**, citizen of Poaghe, a commune a few miles southeast of Sassari, wrote a poem that gives a hint of what they went through. Little is known of the woman described as a celebrated improviser. Her 82-line poem, written in Logudorese, was included in *Canzoni Popolari di Sardegna*, collected by the foremost linguist of Sardinian dialects, Giovanni Spano, together with other patriotic and revolutionary songs and poems, and published for the first time in 1857. Maria's original has been republished in recent anthologies and is available online.

A short description of Maria's poem – *Ancora Semus in Guerra* (We are Still at War) – suggests that it is a hymn exalting the actions of the Ploaghesi, and their neighbours the Chiarmontesi, who helped prevent the French from landing in Sardinia. There seems to be no English translation, nor even one in Italian, but I needed to know what Maria wrote. I approached Barbara Costa, a Sardinian-born scholar working in Oxford, who had already helped me, and she, with the help of family and friends, translated it first into Italian, and then into English. I quote some lines from the beginning and the end:

> We are still at war./ We are still fighting/ against the Corsicans and the French;/ three years have passed/ along the sea/ because they want to destroy/ the holy and good law./ If they come back to Sardinia/ we will chop off their heads./ ...
>
> ...The pastor of Ploaghe offered himself/ as a good person./ I'll take care of you, come to my house./ Numerous landowners added to the poor,/ he divided all he had at his disposal into equal parts./ They left at two in the afternoon,/ on horseback,/ while the bell rang,/ and the priest blessed them/ and the Blessed Sacrament was shown./ 'Rather than you,' he said, 'I should die, my children./ If God wants you will come back alive from this expedition.'/ And the desperate mother of the parish priest:/ 'O my God, my son,/ if they meet the French/ they will never come back, unless God helps them.'/ Three years have passed/ and we are still at war.

Because there are no biographical details available for Maria, except that she is from Ploaghe, we don't know if any man connected to her took part in the campaign against the French, but it is possible to read between the lines to imagine that there would have been local women facing the prospect of losing loved ones, or already mourning them, or caring for the wounded. The poem is perhaps more an exercise in reportage or, as one source has suggested, a hymn to those prepared to sacrifice themselves.

More than once Maria writes of chopping off French heads. This may be a reference to the use of the guillotine in France, starting with the execution of Louis XVI on 21 January 1793, and ending in the summer of 1794, after 2639 had been guillotined. But it may also refer to the unverified suggestion that victorious Sardinians dismembered the dead French soldiers and carried their body parts round as trophies.

Among the other protest *Canzionari* Spano collected were some that were anti-feudal and anti-Piedmont. *'Su Pariottu Sardu a Feudatarios'* has even been called 'the Sardinian Marseillaise'. Although the Sardinians were against the French trying to invade their island, many were not averse to espousing their revolutionary ideas. And they definitely expected to be rewarded with reform for their defeat of the French, particularly with preferential treatment for Sardinians in place of the Piedmontese who held the highest positions.

They were outraged at what passed for their reward:

- 24 gifts of 60 crowns to be distributed annually to poor spinsters;
- The foundation of four free places in the College of Nobles of Cagliari;
- The granting of two places in the College of Nobles in Turin;
- The annual grant of 1000 crowns for the Civil Hospital of Cagliari;
- Amnesty for all crimes committed before the war.

The villages which had sent their men voluntarily to defend Sardinia had expected compensation; there was none. Not surprisingly, this resulted in discontent. Pressure was put on the *stamenti* to negotiate demands with the Piedmontese government. Eventually a series of demands to be presented was agreed upon:

- The convening of general courts to deal, above all, with aims beneficial to the public;
- The confirmation of all the laws, customs and privileges of the Kingdom of Sardinia;
- The right of employment for Sardinians (except for the highest institutional positions);
- The establishment of a Council of State which had to be consulted on all matters that once depended on the arbitrariness of a single secretary;
- A distinguished minister of Sardinian affairs in Turin.

The demands were intended to provide an administrative role for the Sardinian nobility and the burgeoning professional middle class, to provide some autonomy.

Sardinian delegates arrived in Turin to present their demands in early September 1793 but were left kicking their heels there for three months. They had been preceded by messages from the viceroy advising the king to reject the demands and to attempt to bribe the delegates. What is more the rejection was conveyed not to the delegates but to the viceroy.

Then two notable figures from the so-called 'Patriotic Party' were arrested. It was all that was needed to spark the revolt that had been simmering since that in Sassari in 1780. What came to be known as *Sa Die de Sa Sardigna* (The Sardinian Vespers) broke out on 28 April 1794. What then happened is only briefly sketched here because this account is concerned with participation in events by women, and the effect upon them.

The revolt spread to Sassari and Alghero, and then throughout the island. On 7 May 1794, the viceroy and other Piedmontese officials were forced to leave the island. The *stamenti* took control. Eventually, rioting turned to violence, including, on 6 July 1795, the murder of two top officials – the Intendent General and the Commander of Arms – who had tried to introduce repressive measures.

A new viceroy had arrived in September 1794 and he appointed the reformer Giovanni Maria Angioy – judge of the *Reale Udienza* (Royal

Hearing or Supreme Court) – to attempt to bring some order. Angioy's brief made him in many ways a substitute viceroy, but he was a republican and anti-feudalist and he led the uprising and the calls for reform, particularly against feudalism, for the next two years.

It is worth noting how earlier Angioy became increasingly radicalised, bolstering the influence on him of the 1789 French Revolution, because it concerns his marriage. In looking at that, a picture of a particular Cagliari bourgeois family, and the background of the marriage, also emerge. The story is best told in Pierluigi Serra's *Sardegna Misteriosa ed Esotica* (2018).

In 1781, aged 32, Angioy had married 17-year-old **Annica Belgrano** (1764–1791), daughter of Ramon Belgrano and **Donna Giuseppa Novaro**. The Belgranos were a rich bourgeois family of Genovese extraction who lived in an extended family house, sometimes called the Palazzo Belgrano, in Via Sant'Eulalia, the Marina district of Cagliari. They tended to establish relationships, alliances and marriages within the same Ligurian circle. Sardinian Angioy was different: he came from a middle class farming background around Bono in the Sassari district. By 1781 he was an ambitious lawyer who had taught at the University of Cagliari since he was 21. He was introduced into the Belgrano family by the merchant Onorato Cortese, husband of Annica's elder sister **Giuseppa Belgrano**. In entering this circle he came in contact with a group of politically aware men. To marry Annica was to cement himself firmly into this circle and gain access to the useful echelons of politics, religion and the military.

But the birth of the Angioy-Belgrano couple's daughter **Speranza** in 1782 brought about a crisis. Young Annica was used to living a comfortable, unemotional life, with little inclination to frequent the salons and debates that were integral to her husband's needs; not only that, but he fretted on the first floor of the family home in Via Sant'Eulalia under the watchful eye of his mother-in-law. When he could no longer contain his frustration, he sought lodgings in the Castello district and went to live in a property owned by **Ignazia Cordiglia**, wife of a judge of the *Reale Udienza*. This move may have allowed him to breathe more freely, and the contact with the judge may, in due course, have advanced his career, but it led to upset and gossip, not only within the extended Belgrano family and circle, but also in Cagliari itself.

Such a situation could not continue. Donna Giuseppa therefore asked the Bishop of Cagliari to mediate between her daughter and son-in-law, which he seems to have done. As a result, Annica joined Angioy in the Castello. In the next three years, two more daughters were born – **Giuseppa** and **Angela** – who were to 'live in an atmosphere of serenity, spending their days between school and social commitments'. But in 1791 Annica, aged 27, contracted tuberculosis or some other pulmonary illness, like many young women in the Marina district, and she died. Her funeral took place in the nearby church of Sant'Eulalia, the Belgranos' local church where the couple had married and where records show the three Cortese-Belgrano daughters were baptised between 1781 and 1794. This drawing of the church and its environs is

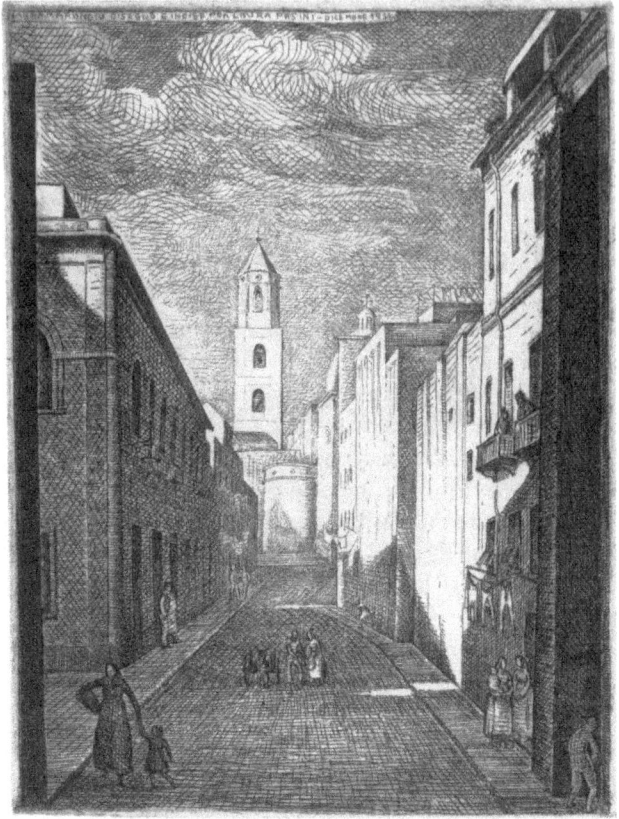

18. Campanile di S Eulalia, 1938, by Anna Marongiu, courtesy of Paolo Marongiu and heirs of Anna Marongiu Pernis

by the Sardinian artist Anna Marongiu, a member of the extended Pernis family; she and the church appear in detail in chapter 10.

The Angioy family's peace that had been restored was, not surprisingly, shaken by Annica's death; she had acted as the glue between her husband's 'passions' and her daughters' 'expectations'. Angioy was torn between parental duties and public political and social commitments. The girls were sent to the boarding school of the nearby Santa Lucia convent on the advice of the nuns. This was the convent founded in 1539 by viceroy's wife Maria Cardona (described in chapter 5). By the end of the eighteenth century it had 40 nuns and concentrated on the education and training of the daughters of the Cagliari nobility. But the convent, according to Pierluigi Serra, who subtitled his book *Il lato occulto, maladetto e oscuro dell'isola più magica del Mediterraneo* ('The occult, cursed and obscured side of the most magical island in the Mediterranean') indulged in supernatural and superstitious practices. Learning of this, Angioy removed his daughters and asked Onorato Cortese to take them back into the Belgrano ancestral home in Via Sant'Eulalia.

The girls' stay in the convent seems, however, to have changed their characters and attitudes, especially towards their father. Their maternal grandmother took them in hand, not only working on their faith but inculcating in them the indefinable qualities of the Belgrano and Novaro women. Pierluigi Serra suggests that the Genovese merchants had brought to Sardinia wives who themselves believed in the supernatural, resulting in strange happenings in the household. Angioy's daughters were to retain their distance from their increasingly politically active father, whose elevation to the *Reale Udienza* took place in 1794, the year that the viceroy appointed him to sort out the unrest on the island.

The scene now moves to Ittiri, a commune a few miles south of Sassari. There the feudal counts of Ledà were increasingly unpopular, even among landowning families of high rank. Among them was the extended Serra family, the most active of whom was Vincenzo Serra-Dologu, also known as the Jacobin. In 1758, when they were both 27, he married **Maria Caterina Salis-Dantona** (b.1731), a member of the enlightened Sassari bourgeoisie. They had eight children, only two of whom survived, **Marianna Serra** and Giovanni.

In 1785, at the age of 15, Giovanni married **Maria Teresa Pes** of Ittiri and moved there. When Vincenzo's wife, Caterina, died, he went to join his son in Ittiri, taking young Marianna. Vincenzo soon became a leader in Ittiri, acknowledged not just by fellow landowners, but also by those who worked on their properties, and anti-Ledà disputes continued over the years.

In 1794, Vincenzo, Marianna and Giovanni, together with Vincenzo's uncle, Professor Gavino Serra, became supporters of Angioy and closely involved in the anti-feudal revolt. Federico Francioni in his *Lingua Cultura* article 'La Presenza delle Donne' wrote of how the revolt saw the emergence of women and the parts the new atmosphere of the era enabled them to play. He tells of Marianna walking in public with Maria Giovanni Angioy and unafraid of speaking out in favour of a republican Sardinia. She took part in spreading propaganda during the struggle in the countryside. So effective was it that in December 1795 women were among the anti-feudal army of 3000 peasants, labourers, landowners and priests who first besieged and then took Sassari.

In February 1796, Angioy headed towards Sassari and made a triumphant entry. It may well have been then that Marianna walked boldly through the streets in his company. But his success was not to last: by June 1796 he was defeated and dismissed, and later that month he left Sardinia via Porto Torres for Paris where he died in exile and poverty in 1808. When he left Sardinia, he seems to have been in debt to a particular unnamed woman. When she went to Sassari, she tried to claim repayment from Angioy's daughters who, Pierluigi Serra suggests, sought to change their surname. Widowed Giuseppa Belgrano Novaro seems still to have been alive in 1807.

Whatever Angioy's reputation in Belgrano Novaro circles, he was regarded as a hero in his home town, and still is. The Sardinian artist **Liliana Canu** (b.1924) was commissioned to paint a mural in the Piazza Bialado in Bono to commemorate him and the anti-feudalism struggle so much associated with his name.

Wasting no time after the collapse of the revolt, the viceroy started a ruthless hunt for Angioy's supporters: some went into hiding or exile; hundreds of arrests were made and charges laid; they were tortured and some were executed. In Ittiri, Don Vincenzo and his followers prepared to repel forces sent against them, but the troops did not take the road to Ittiri. In due course, Giovanni Serra and Professor Gavino Serra were captured and imprisoned in Sassari. But Vincenzo, perhaps because he was 65 years old, and Marianna, perhaps because she was a woman, were put under house arrest in Sassari. Ittiri split into factions. Don Giovanni died in Ittiri in 1802, Don Vincenzo in 1803. What became of Marianna does not seem to have been important enough to record. Soon after the revolt, feudal forces and conservatives in Cagliari and the Sassari region regained political and social control.

War and Royal Exile in Sardinia

The Sardinians had withstood French invasion twice in 1793, in the south and the north; it was not so easy for the Piedmontese Court in Turin in 1798.

In 1750, **Maria Antonia Fernanda of Spain** (1729–1785) married Vittorio Amadeo of Savoy. In 1773, when he ascended the throne as Vittorio Amadeo III, she became Duchess of Savoy, Queen of Sardinia. Not only that but, of the couple's 12 children, three sons also became king of Sardinia. The first of these was Carlo Emanuele who, in 1775, aged 24, married 16-year-old **Princess Marie Clotilde of France** (1759–1802), sister of Louis XVI. Although the marriage was arranged, the couple quickly became devoted to each other, and the carefully and piously brought up young woman easily fitted in with the strict court rules of her mother-in-law. In spite of the strictures that this entailed, Clotilde was able to maintain her strong personality, and her rather passive husband, who was also in poor health, came to lean on her. Federica Contu, in the chapter 'Sovereign and his wife "Minister"', uses a quotation describing Carlo Emanuele as 'affected by epilepsy, sickly, psychologically fragile'. This may have contributed to Clotilde's failure, after eight years of trying, to provide the required heir.

Following the French Revolution of 1789, and the imprisonment and then execution of her brother and sister-in-law, Clotilde provided refuge in Turin to various other members of the French royal family. Her father-in-law promoted an anti-French coalition of the Italian states; the French alliance, which Clotilde's marriage had cemented, no longer existed. In 1792, the French occupied the Duchy of Savoy, and they easily took Nice.

Carlo ascended the throne of Piedmont Sardinia in 1796 as Carlo Emanuele IV with Clotilde at his side. Two years later, the French First Republic declared war on Piedmont; French troops marched into Turin, and the king was forced to abdicate from all his territories on the Italian mainland. In 'The Old World Prince' (1895) Bessie Rayner Belloc (1829–1925) drew on the diary of Carlo Emanuele's younger brother Carlo Felice (Charles Felix). She writes of what happened when the family had to flee in December 1798:

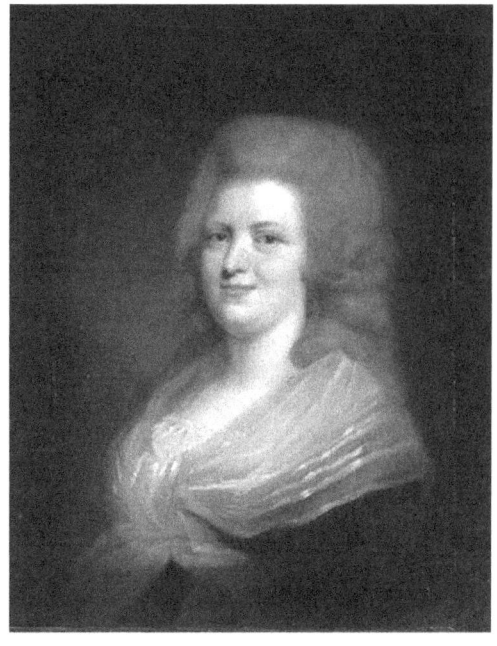

> On the 10th, a Monday morning, the royal family of Sardinia set out early by torchlight. In the darkness those who first got out of Turin waited anxiously for those who were belated. At last all the young men were got together, and the carriages started for the place of rendezvous by different roads. They intended to meet at Leghorn [Livorno], but the old king [Carlo Emanuele was 47], who had gone round by Florence, fell ill in that city, and there they all waited for two months; not till the twenty fourth of February did the English fleet take them in charge and land them in Cagliari, where the people received them with joy and greeting, and where Charles Felix was destined to dwell for sixteen years without ever revisiting his native Piedmont.

19. Queen Clotilde by Johan Julius Heinsius *c.*1790, from the internet

There is evidence that Carlo Felice started keeping a diary following the French Revolution. Bessie Rayner Belloc, poet, essayist, and feminist campaigner and educationalist spent some years on the Continent and mentions a volume she came across in Hautecombe; that is the only clue she provides of the diary and her interest in Carlo Felice's story. Her rather purple essay on him and his place in the House of Savoy is included in her anthology of biographical studies, *In a Walled Garden* (1895).

Henry Smyth RN does not seem to be aware of the time lag quoted above when he writes of the king, 'and hurrying to Leghorn, he gladly received the deputies from the *stamenti* of Sardinia, assuring him of the entire devotion of the Sards'. Conveyed by an English frigate, the royal family, with their suite, arrived at Cagliari on the 3rd of March 1799.

Before leaving Turin, the 'old' and sickly king wrote in his own hand, as Federica Contu quotes, confirming the part Clotilde played and was to continue to play:

I was forced to stay at home, so weak of mind and body that I was not able to provide for the least thing so that she (the queen) was responsible for all, and she had to govern the house and ensure that provisions were taken in our critical circumstances.

When they arrived in Cagliari in the spring of 1799, they moved into what had been the viceregal palace, now called the Royal Palace (Palazzo Regale) in the Castello and open to the public. It was the first time the Sardinians had seen their sovereign. There, perhaps being reassured by his kingship of Sardinia, Carlo Emanuele declared his earlier abdication of the crown of the Kingdom of Sardinia void. Although he and Clotilde, though not the rest of the family, were to leave Sardinia that September, it is worth quoting from a reply she wrote to a correspondent from their continuing exile in the south of Italy (first Rome, then Naples) of 17 March 1800, for it suggests the part she probably played in Sardinia during their six months there. It is not necessary to explain the intricacies of her subject matter, nor note either Clotilde's grammar or the translation:

> I have read your letter carefully, and I frankly declare that neither the King nor I have the slightest desire to use the protection of the King of Prussia, and much less of his mediation in France, with which, although there may be of precious in the world, he absolutely does not want to enter into negotiation ... the recommendation that the emperor of Russia to the King of Prussia have caused a great sorrow to us ...; but I hope that it was only a sort of courtesy of Paolo to sugar the pill that made us swallow. However we are in the hope of the returning of Russian troops and that the two imperial Courts are brought together.

Federica Contu also quotes one of Clotilde's correspondents, remarking on how she showed 'a diplomatic skill never suspected until now ... so that it would be difficult to recognise the hand of the "pious and devoted" Queen, who used to write [primarily] to nuns and [her] spiritual directors'. And she adds her own comment:

> Speaking on behalf of her husband, she maintained a semblance of subordination, but at the same time she showed an autonomy which, of necessity, changed her from a queen consort to a ruling queen. Carlo Emanuele delegated his own power, unofficially, making Marie Clotilde a key part of their reign.

The king's other brother, Vittorio Emanuele, Duke of Aosta, who with his family had fled first to Tuscany and then to Sardinia, tried to prevail upon him to abdicate again, but Clotilde strengthened his resolve to resist. The **Duchess of Aosta**, born **Archduchess Marie Teresa of Austria-Este** (1773–1832) wrote of her sister-in-law,

The Queen is the one that does all, the King believes that he does not have to take any advice except his own (this is what the Queen wrote to my husband from Caserta), while she writes everything so as not to strain his eyes. He does not speak to Aosta about anything ... the Queen is the Minister.

But then fate took a hand: Clotilde, aged 42, died in Naples on 7 March 1802, of what sources do not suggest, and was buried there. The bereft widower left for Rome in May and, on 4 June, he abdicated in favour of his brother; the Duke of Aosta became Vittorio Emanuele I, and Maria Teresa his queen consort. On 10 April 1808, the title of Venerable was conferred on Marie Clotilde, beginning the process of beatification.

The new king and queen were still in exile in Cagliari with their 10-year-old daughter **Princess Maria Beatrice** (1792–1840). In August 1799, their only son had died of smallpox, aged three; a daughter born in November 1800, probably in Cagliari, died at two months. This may be why, in 1803, they crossed over to Rome for the birth of twin daughters **Princess Maria Teresa of Savoy** (1803–1879) and **Princess Maria Anna of Savoy** (1803–1884). They were to spend most of their childhood in Sardinia. Another daughter, **Princess Maria Cristina of Savoy** (1812–1836) was to be born in Cagliari; she was the last of their seven children.

It is worth noting that it was the British who transported the royal family from the Italian mainland to safety in Cagliari at the beginning of 1799. Relations between Britain and the Royal Court in Sardinia were to fluctuate during the years that followed. In many ways, Sicily was more important strategically, but Sardinia not only had to be kept from the French but also provided a useful base, particularly its northern island of La Maddalena, from where Nelson and his fleet kept the French Toulon fleet hemmed in between 1803 and 1805 – a story to be told in chapter 9.

As well as Sardinia providing a useful naval base in the north, Cagliari proved an excellent listening post to the interchanges between the royal families of Europe. William Noel-Hill, 3rd Baron Berwick, was the British Minister to the exiled Court there and his despatches from June 1808 to May 1816 provide a useful barometer of relations between Britain and Sardinia, the ups and downs of Sardinian harvests and pecuniary importunities, and royal activities and gossip, including those connected to the brief outline of the family introduced above.

Regarding the latter, the births of princesses, Hill wrote on 4 April 1812, 'The Queen is supposedly pregnant and the King is anxious, as there is no male heir for the elder branch of this family'. The queen was by then 39. On 20 May, he added: 'The Queen is advancing happily in her pregnancy.' He concluded on 15 November:

The Queen of Sardinia has safely delivered a princess on 14th November, and the British Legation attended the baptism of **Marie Christina Gaettana Giuseppa Effina**. The disappointment of the Royal Family and the people of Sardinia is very great as they wished for a son and heir for the House of Savoy. The King is still in hopes of having a son in the future though W. Hill reports that until this birth the Queen had not been pregnant for nine years.

It looks as if these and subsequent dispatches were written on instruction through the good offices of an attaché, and the Italian spelling of names is not necessarily used.

Hill's despatches regarding the marriage of the eldest daughter, Princess Beatrice, 22 when the subject was first raised, record the weighing up of the advantages, diplomatic, political and financial, of various suitors; alliances being particularly important during the war. It is worth quoting Hill in some detail as rarely does such an opportunity arise to note the behind-the-scenes negotiations using royal daughters as pawns. He wrote on 12 May 1811,

> Archduke Francis has been staying in Salonika. From information Mr Canning sent from Constantinople the Archduke Francis is to ask [for] the hand of Princess Beatrice & the Queen of Naples wishes the Prince Leopold [of Sicily] to marry her Royal Highness, whilst Abbe Taillie who came with the Queen of France's corpse is in favour of an old candidate the Duke of Besny [sic] whose portrait he has brought with him. The Archduke appears to be the favourite.

The frontrunner, 32-year-old Archduke Francis of Austria-Este, was Beatrice's maternal uncle. On 19 May, Hill recorded, 'Archduke Francis has arrived at Malta and intends to proceed immediately to Cagliari'. His despatch of 20 June nicely illustrates the political ramifications of this marriage proposal:

> Archduke Francis arrived in Sardinia on 31 May, accompanied by three officers ... Count de la Tour visited W. Hill and asked to have as frequent opportunities of talking with him as possible. He also indicated that the Archduke was anxious to have the opportunity of seeing W. Hill alone. Previously most profound secrecy observed. Neither King nor Queen admitted into any of Archduke's plans, other than his good wishes to the British Cause. The idea of marriage with Madame Beatrice serves as a good cloak. The Queen favours the match & the marriage might usefully unite Archduke's interests with those of the King of Sardinia. As yet nobody knows of the secret. Queen of Naples extremely anxious to learn something and has set her spies to work. Her Majesty wants Olivieri, Bishop of Arethusa, one of her emissaries to acquaint her with whatever he can discover & he has sailed to Sicily on an English transport. He can only confirm the expectation of the marriage. Queen of Naples has also spoken to Mr Meyer at Constantinople with marks of great jealousy regarding General Nugent who has been arranging plans of which she has been kept in ignorance for nearly a year. Her majesty wondered how the

Archduke could be preferred to Prince Leopold whose father can bring 20,000 men into the field.

What Hill does not seem to have occasion to note was the already existing link between the royal families of Sardinia and Naples and Sicily. In 1807, Vittorio Emanuele's youngest brother, Carlo Felice, Duke of Genoa, and already viceroy of Sardinia, had married **Maria Cristina de Bourbon, Princess of Naples and Sicily** (1779–1849), daughter of **Maria Carolina Queen of Naples and Sicily** (1752–1814). As the queen often appears in despatches, it is worth pausing to put her in context.

Maria Carolina was born a princess of Austria, 13th (and sixth surviving) child of Francis I, Holy Roman Emperor and Maria Theresa of Austria, Queen of Hungary and Bohemia. She was the sister of Marie Antoinette. Aged 16, Maria Carolina was married to King Ferdinand of Naples as part of an Austro-Spanish alliance; it was not a love match, and they did not find each other attractive; they did, however, have 18 children, of whom seven survived to adulthood. In spite of constant pregnancies, Maria Carolina increasingly became de facto ruler, assisted by her French-born English favourite, John Acton, 6th baronet.

Following the French Revolution, and in an attempt to please Britain, Queen Maria Carolina struck up a friendship with Emma Hamilton, wife of its ambassador. When war broke out against the French, she arranged a treaty of alliance with Britain. But in 1799, the French took Naples and the royal family and, indeed, the Hamiltons were forced, with Admiral Nelson's help, to flee to Sicily. She was able to return to Naples in 1802, but had to flee again to Sicily in 1806. In due course, the British were to have enough of the Queen of Naples and Sicily, as Hill's despatches will suggest. But it was perhaps natural that she had a vested interest in the royal family into which her own daughter had married.

On 25 June, Hill again described conversations with Archduke Francis who always used his visits to the Court as a cloak because 'Cagliari is full of spies'. Hill records a conversation and the Archduke's plans in some detail, and continues,

> Mention made of his near connection to the King of Sardinia which would be strengthened by his marriage to Princess Beatrice, of his Austrian connection with Milan, of his connection with Tuscany of which his Uncle was sovereign, of the near Austrian connection with Venice, with his connection with the Queen of Naples. The Archduke had received a letter from the Queen of Naples in which it would appear she was piqued at not knowing [that] the motive of his touring was his probable marriage which frustrated the views of Prince Leopold. ...

A despatch of 10 July 1811 illustrates the Queen of Sicily's wiles: 'A letter sent by La Tour's brother to General Nugent was confiscated by the Queen of Sicily.' He goes on to detail various aspects of the plan and then continued,

'Necessary to keep Queen of Sicily calm and the Archduke hinted that the King of Sardinia had been inquisitive and knowing the archduke's claims on Modena the King of Sicily was likely to be suspicious, but the Archduke was not averse to any alliance with the King of Sardinia.' He ended, 'The Archduke also wanted to know what the British government's opinion of his marriage to Princess Beatrice [is]. He did not believe the King of Sardinia averse to it.'

It is noticeable that no one seems to have asked Beatrice herself what she thought of the various suitors for her hand, though her father did give some thought to what might be best for her. On 18 July 1811 Hill reported:

> The King of Sardinia wanted confidentially to let the King of England know that [of] all the candidates offered for Princess Beatrice's hand he preferred the Archduke. The King of Sardinia knew personally Prince Leopold, a good young man richer than the Archduke, but thought that neither the Duke de Berri [sic] nor Prince Leopold were calculated to make the Princess so happy as the archduke whose character he greatly admired. He thought the Archduke's situation precarious, having in a manner abandoned Austria. King of Sardinia added that had his daughter married Duke de Berry the British government would settle 3000 per annum on the Duke in addition to his present allowance and if England were in favour of this marriage the King of Sardinia would readily consent. Both the King of Sardinia & the Archduke required urgent reply. King of Sardinia uneasy as Prince Leopold of Sicily to visit Sardinia. Archduke stated as a political reason for England to favour his marriage that secrecy was still recommended to be preserved. The alliance would prevent all jealousy on the part of the King of Sardinia when the Archduke's plans should become known.

On 1 September Hill started his despatch, 'Archduke confirmed he wanted a guarantee of 5000 per annum and the settlement of 3000 per annum desired by Sardinian Majesties for Princess Beatrice until the Archduke could settle something.' Finally, and at last, Hill wrote on 26 May 1812, 'Their Majesties of Sardinia have given their consent to the marriage of Princess Beatrice and Archduke Francis. The marriage to take place towards the end of next month.' The marriage did, indeed, take place on 20 June 1812, with Francesca Queseda Carcassona, Countess of Monteleone, her 'Grand Madam' in attendance. (The position of Giovanna Carcassona, Marchesa of San Saverio and San Tommaso with Beatrice's younger sister, Princess Anna Maria, is detailed earlier).

The Archduke kept what is little more than an engagement diary, noting where he went and when as he travelled round Sardinia, visiting archaeological sites and towns of interest. Paolo Cau published it as an article with an introduction putting it in context, as *'Dal Diario di Francesco d'Austria-Este: I due Soggiorni in Sardegna'* (2014). It raises a wry smile to read that on 1 May 1812, not even a month before her parents gave their consent, the Archduke wrote 'One begins to talk of the wedding with Princess Beatrice'.

After a brief line about the wedding itself, on several subsequent days he mentions Beatrice having riding lessons.

The newly married couple left Sardinia on 15 July 1813. In 1814, the Archduke became Duke of Modena, and Beatrice the Duchess. They were to have four children. Francis was to become known for his tyrannical rule, behaviour which for Beatrice's sake one hopes was not practised on his family. Francesca Carcassona continued to be lady-in-waiting and confidante to Beatrice in Modena.

There is a tailpiece to the story of Beatrice which Hill does not mention: the Jacobites, who strove to gain the British crown, recognised her as 'Princess Mary of England, Scotland, France and Ireland' and, when her father died, as the rightful Queen Mary III. She never pursued any such claim, and I have seen no evidence that the British government was even cognizant of the matter.

When Giovanna Carcassona inherited the fief and Marquisate of San Saverio in 1812, she was, as earlier described, confronted with 'The Famine of the Twelve'. The royal family had more to worry about than Beatrice's marriage, or the queen's pregnancy. Hill, in his despatch of 9 March, wrote:

> There is an extreme state of famine in Sardinia, and the government has just begun to become alarmed. After an examination of the granaries, it has been deduced that only 6 weeks worth of consumption remain. However, the people in the villages have been reduced to eating acorns and roots. Insurrection is beginning to take root. The Sardinian government has not the money to solve the crisis nor to maintain the soldiers needed to control the populace as the main source of their income had been exporting grains.

On 16 March Hill reported: 'Six or seven small vessels have arrived in Sardinia laden with corn. The Sardinian government has detained these vessels, and it is hoped that this will allow them time until harvest.' But on 28 April he had to add, 'There were rumours of an insurrection in Cagliari due to the famine and the sentries have been put on alert.' Before reporting, on 23 May, 'The harvest in Sardinia appears to be favourable,' Hill sneered, 'The King's financial plans are based on what W. Hill believes to be imaginary silver mines.' Hill may have been less aware of Sardinia's history than he was of contemporary royal to-ings and fro-ings: silver had been mined in Sardinia for millennia; indeed, its extraction there was one of the earliest in Europe.

Hill had one more relevant piece of royal gossip to relate. On 15 November, when he had reported how the queen had given birth to a daughter, he added, 'PS, The Queen of Naples intends to take up her residence at this Court, and though preparations have been made in the Palace of her son-in-law the Duke of Genevois [Genoa], the King of Sardinia does not want the Queen of Naples to come.'

Although King Vittorio Emanuele and Queen Maria Teresa were to remain in exile, mostly resident in Sardinia, until the defeat of Napoleon, on ascending the throne in 1802, he appointed his youngest brother, Carlo Felice, Duke of Genoa, viceroy of Sardinia. As viceroy, Carlo Felice tended to judge disputes in feudal jurisdiction more in favour of vassals than feudal lords, and he exerted pressure on the *stamenti* to have the poorest classes exempted from tax; he also brought about some improvements to agriculture and the economy. Nevertheless, he earned the sobriquet '*Carlo Feroce*' not only for a government that was rather rigid and authoritarian, including police spying and censorship of letters, but also because of a special court set up to clamp down on oppositional activity and his harshness in attempting to suppress crime, particularly in the use of the death penalty.

Lord Byron and John Cam Hobhouse, travelling on the Continent, and on the last stretch to Sardinia joined by John Galt, arrived in Cagliari on 27 August 1809. The party soon caught up with William Hill, who filled them in on the island's criminal scene; Hobhouse recorded in his diary:

> At Mr Hill's I learnt that the property was feudal – that murders were every day committed and often by men of rank, that one *seigneur* would often steal three or four hundred sheep, and shoot the horses of another – as formerly in the highlands of Scotland – that no man therefore travelled, not even five miles from town, without a gun, which is a weapon of which they are very expert. That one ... had the other day been convicted of sixteen murders, but was only outlawed because the crime for which he had been immediately apprehended was not quite proven. This fellow had, with his own hand, cut the throat of the son of the *seigneur* at whose house he had been brought up from an infant, and the day after his outlawry was seen arm-in-arm with one of the Queen's equerries, and at his box in the opera. He said that men procured their pardon by the distribution of money, which they all kept for these occasions. At this time there are seven or eight hundred men, bands of robbers in arms, in the mountains – the King cannot collect his taxes – and is chiefly supported by £12,000 per annum which he receives from England.

There were women bandits, as well as men, and the next chapter concentrates on them.

On 27 August, Hobhouse's description of the royal family was rather more anodyne:

> Mr Gault [sic] and myself walked ... went to the church – saw the King of Sardinia, Emanuel III [sic] with the Queen and Madam Beatrice, rather pretty, and the King's brother, his heir [Carlo Felice] and his wife. King's brother very like the Duke of York – the Duke of Orleans, I was told, observed the same.

Although 42-year-old Carlo Felice had initially opposed his 1807 marriage to 28-year-old Princess Maria Cristina of Naples and Sicily, he was persuaded that the royal family had to have an heir. It is hard to be sure that Cristina's mother, the ever-conspiratorial Queen Carolina, was trying to be helpful when she wrote to her future son-in-law:

> My dearest son, your future bride is good, pious, honest and has a gentle nature, solid and virtuous, which makes up for her lack of beauty in face or figure. She is only too conscious of this lack, but many solid qualities protect her from what she lacks in brilliance.

This portrait of Maria Cristina painted in Naples in 1790 by the French refugee artist Elisabeth Louise Vigée LeBrun shows a pretty young girl, though the artist's many finely executed self-portraits are fit to adorn a chocolate box, and later portraits of Cristina are less flattering. This Vigée LeBrun portrait of Queen Maria Carolina was painted the following year.

As it turned out, the couple was to remain childless; in spite of that, theirs seems to have been a close partnership, and Ilaria Muggianu Scano's 2016 *DonnaSarda* biographical entry for Mimi, as she was familiarly called, suggests that she was '[her husband's] great councillor, especially in education and relations with the Sardinian subjects'. Her diary, like the Archduke's, little more than an engagement record, does not contain sufficient detail to confirm this. She also promoted the fine arts and her diary does record the concerts and operas they attended. As well as the contribution she sought to make to her husband's work, and Sardinia's well-being, Mimi made friends easily among Cagliari's female nobility, and was not averse to a little gossip.

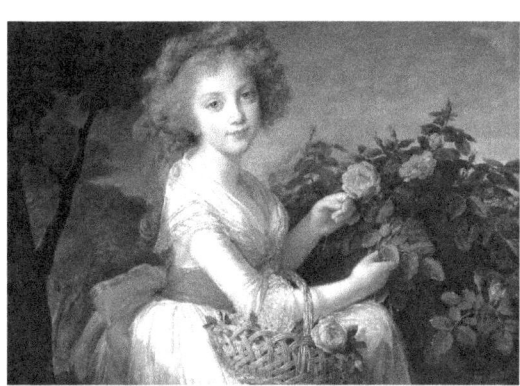
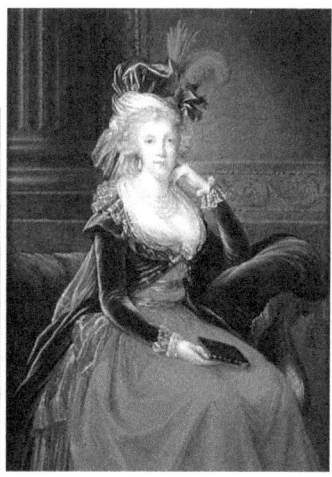

20a. Princess Maria Cristina, 1790, by Elisabeth Louise Vigée Lebrun, *su concessione del Ministero per i Beni e le Attività culturali – Museo e Real Bosco di Capodimonti*, Naples

20b. Queen Maria Carolina of Naples, 1791, from Billio, *Elisabeth Louise Vigée Lebrun 1755–1842*

The viceregal couple spent much of their time, from their marriage in 1807, at the Villa d'Orri, a finely furnished and elegant country house and agricultural estate at Sarroch a few miles from Cagliari on the west coast of the gulf, and with a wonderful park stretching down to the sea. It is an area now marred by oil refineries which, nevertheless, have improved the local economy. Their hosts were Stefano Manca, 2nd Marchese di Vallermosa e Santa Croce and his wife since 1804, **Anna Maria Manca Amat** dei Duchi dell'Asinara. (This dukedom, dating from 1774, will appear briefly in chapter 11.) Carlo Felice had written to his close friend recommending his future wife on 1 December 1806:

> She is not beautiful, but she is tall and well built; blonde and pale skinned and enjoying excellent health and, what is most essential, she is an angel, also called a saint in her family. She has all sorts of accomplishments – she sings very well and plays the harp reasonably. I have given you the full picture of her here, going into all these little details, being convinced that they will not bore you, knowing the interest you take in all that concerns me.

Whatever Carlo Felice's legacy as viceroy, his wife was well-enough regarded to have the imposing neo-classical Porta Cristina in the Castello named after her; it replaced an earlier gateway, and Carlo Felice approved its design. Decorated with a Latin inscription, it still links the Viale Buoncammino to the Piazza Arsenale. The Villa d'Orri contains vestiges of the royal couple's long stay of historical importance, and is protected by the Ministry for Cultural and Environmental Heritage. The villa itself is not open to the public, except on special 'open monuments' days, but one can visit the grounds on 1 May, when the procession of Sant'Efisio takes place through the Sarroch area and rests in the villa's chapel. It is possible to appreciate the villa and grounds through more than one YouTube tour; that with the scholarly Italian commentary is the best.

At the end of the royal family's exile in Sardinia in 1814, the Court, including Carlo Felice and Maria Cristina, returned to Turin. But after a brief stay the couple went back to Sardinia. Carlo Felice remained viceroy until 1821, though Turin was his base.

There is some ambiguity about either the movements or the activities of Queen Maria Teresa during the period 1814–15. It is raised in both Gian-Carlo Tuscero's 1998 online history of the Maddalena archipelago, and Antonio Frau's 2013 *Millelire*, a family history elaborated upon in chapter 9; I have not found the evidence elsewhere. It would appear that the queen did not leave Sardinia with her husband but that she was in effect regent there in a period that could have coincided with the viceroy's absence in Turin. Up until now, all that has been said of the queen in Sardinia has referred to the death of her only son, the birth of three daughters, and the marriage of Beatrice, her eldest.

Still in Cagliari, Maria Teresa, as regent, reprimanded Admiral Des Genys, stationed at La Maddalena, it appears on evidence brought to her by an enemy of his. It concerned ships from Genoa carrying grain supplies which, before reaching the capital, docked in the archipelago. She even went so far as to challenge the admiral with some illicit gains. Nothing came of it, but the queen never admitted that she had erred. In the *Millelire* version it is Agostino Millelire, commander of the islands, who was alleged to allow vessels coming from areas of risk concerning public health, and for allowing two convicts to apply for a 'penalty discount'. In her letter she warned him that in future he should be more cautious in

> appraising similar questions and not even taking responsibility for them, since for crimes of this nature no one should implore grace and much less who is in charge of the command and in charge of their safety.

This brief regency in Sardinia seems to have spilled over into Maria Teresa's attitude when she was back in Turin. The French occupation of Savoy-Piedmont had introduced reforms there. Although the queen was initially warmly welcomed back, she immediately took it upon herself to attempt to undermine, even abolish, them, and to treat those who had cooperated with the French with contempt. It is suggested that her behaviour was one of the reasons for the unrest, leading up to rioting in 1821. During the riots, she even declared herself willing to become regent. Instead, when her husband, King Vittorio Emanuele, abdicated that year, she followed him to Nice. But, when her childless brother-in-law Carlo Felice ascended the throne, she tried, unsuccessfully, to persuade him to name her brother, Archduke Francis of Modena, husband of her daughter Beatrice, as his heir. Because of the hostility towards her, she was not allowed to return to Turin following her husband's death, until 1831, the year before she herself died.

There was civil unrest in Turin in 1821 which led to Vittorio Emanuele's abdication; Carlo Felice ascended the throne, with Maria Cristina as his queen consort. His rule generally is beyond the scope of this account, but it was he who replaced Eleonora d'Arborea's *Carta de Logu* with The Civil and Criminal Laws of the Kingdom of Sardinia. Of real benefit to Sardinia, and in particular to slaves there or who might be traded in future, was the abolition of the slave trade.

Carlo Felice died in 1831 and Carlo Alberto (reigned 1831–1849), a distant Savoyard cousin, inherited the throne. Although he was conservative, he was also a reformist. Feudalism in Sardinia was abolished from 1836, and in 1847, apparently prompted by Sardinian middle-class liberals, he introduced *Fusione Perfetta* (Perfect Fusion). By this, the administrative differences between Sardinia and the mainland states of Savoy and Piedmont were abolished. The last viceroy left in 1848 when the new legal system came into effect, the island divided into three provinces, each governed by its own prefect, as had been introduced in Piedmont in 1815. This was supposed to spur economic development and increase Sardinia's importance; in reality, the island lost what little autonomy it had and, in the process, became an even more marginal part of the kingdom. In the long term, this was to fortify a distinct and separate Sardinian identity, not only politically but also culturally, exemplified by the Sardinian dialects, Logudorese and Sardo. A more immediate result was, as the next chapter suggests, an increase in criminality and banditry.

Queen Maria Cristina had died 10 years after her husband, in 1841, and was buried beside him in Hautecombe. With her death, the royal family's close personal ties with Sardinia came to an end.

The Cholera Epidemic of 1855 in Sassari

This chapter started with corruption in Sassari under the rule of the House of Savoy; it ends with a different sort of attack on the well-being of the city.

A family portrait, painted in about 1828, shows **Donna Luigia Ledà d'Ittiri** (b.1790), her husband Raimondo de Quesada Delitala, 1st Marquese di San Saturnino, and five of their children. Raimondo, Marquese since 1813, was a judge and criminal councillor to the governorship of Sassari. Among posts, he was secretary of state for war and, since 1813, gentleman of the bedchamber to Vittorio Emanuele I, King of Sardinia. The couple sit close to each other on the sofa in a salon furnished in the Empire style typical of the Sassari aristocracy of the day. Three of their daughters are engaged in embroidery or reading, an absent fourth is already a nun. Luigia, wearing a lace cap, is working on lace, while listening to her husband talking to their elder son, Cristoforo, who stands in the circle of his arm. Raimondo will die in 1849, and Cristoforo will inherit the title of Marquese of San Saturnino. Some time before 1850, Cristofero will marry **Felicita Guidobono Cavalchini** (b.1812) – they will have had five children before 1855.

The year before, a ship sailed from India to England with cholera on board. From London, the infection jumped to Paris and Marseille, and then to Genoa, spreading throughout Italy, especially Tuscany. From Leghorn it travelled by boat to Porto Torres in the north of Sardinia. It reached Sassari on 23 July 1855. The city, an administrative and judicial centre, with an ancient universi-

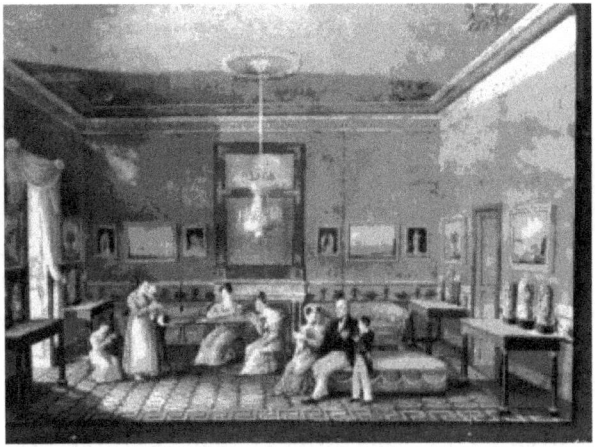

21. *Ritratto Famiglia de Raimondo de Quesada di San Saturnino, c.1828*, from the internet

ty, was so ill prepared that the usual procession of the Virgin of the Angels was allowed to take place on 2 August when the vast crowd prayed for salvation, inadvertently helping to spread the lethal bacterial infection. By 3 August, 266 were dead. Many tried to flee, as corpses piled up in the streets and pitiful cries for help filled the air. Among measures hurriedly taken was roping in prostitutes to help the dying in the *lazaretto* where those with cholera were taken into isolation.

Among the 5000 or so of the 23 000 inhabitants of Sassari who died during the epidemic were 67-year-old widow, Marquessa di Saturnino, Luigia Ledà, on 4 August, and her 33-year-old daughter-in-law, the Marquessa Felicita, who died a day later; 308 others died that same day.

Death from cholera made no distinction between the aristocracy and the very poor such as **Giovanna,** *La Povera*, surname and parentage unknown, who died on 8 August. At the end of Eugenia Tognotti's *L'Anno del Colera: Sassari 1855* (2000a) is a 37-page list, drawn up from the archives by Silvia de Franceschi, of the dead of four of the five Sassari districts. The original records in the local church registers were meticulous, as are their reconstruction, as often as possible giving the names of spouses and parents, age and date of death. To go through the list death by death is to have emphasised the extent of the tragedy that befell Sassari in five short weeks. I have counted 1242 women, girls and baby girls – women as old as 90, babies as young as a month.

Caterina and Antonio **Baldino** lost five daughters ranging in age from one to 12. The widow **Anna Maria Usai Torelli** (58 years) died on 20 August; one of her twin daughters, 27-year-old **Grazia**, had died on 3 August, the second twin, **Albertina**, died on the 22nd. **Angela Maria Polo** lost her husband and three children ranging from nine to 13 years old. The Uzano Pintus family lost mother and four children. There are too many similar examples.

In the *Regie Carceri*, the San Lorenzo prison opened that year – where lower-class prisoners were held under appalling conditions – women as well as men died. They, too, are on the list, with their then place of domicile. The higher class of prisoner was detained in the Castello. Out of the 297 prisoners in both prisons, 70 died, but not Michele Delitala, who might have wished that he had. Many doctors, priests and lawyers died (22 are named on the list), but not apparently Michele's top-class lawyer who had tried, but failed, to save him from the death penalty yet to come.

On 30 August 1854, 29-year-old army officer Don Michele Delitala called at the home of 19-year-old **Giovanna Maria Queseda** (1835–1854). He was passionately in love with Minnia, as she was known; she returned his affection. Although their families were friends, perhaps even related, Minnia's mother, **Donna Giuseppina Quesada** (1805–1865) had twice rejected his proposal of marriage. Reasons are not immediately obvious but, as was customary, the matriarch was the guardian of whom her children should marry, and that was according to social rules of hierarchy. The Quesada were of ancient nobility, the Delitala of minor island nobility. This time, Michele was not to be gainsaid: he came armed with a sword, two pistols and a dagger. Donna Giuseppina opened the door to him and he asked her again for Minnia's hand, and was again refused.

Michele lifted one of his pistols and fired. But Minnia had followed her mother to the door and, seeing in that instant what was happening, threw herself in front of her, taking the bullet in her chest. Michele, beside himself, slashed at Giuseppina with his sword and fired at Minnia's father, Antonio, who came to see what the commotion was, and her uncle. None of them was badly hurt, but Minnia died six days later, on 5 September. Michele was taken into custody and, following his trial, was sentenced to death.

While prisoners about him were dying of cholera and, outside, the death toll mounted daily, Michele's mother, **Donna Domenica Villa Delitala**, harped on one train of thought. Eugenia Tognotti paraphrases the will drawn up by Domenica at the time of the cholera epidemic, one full of the bitterness of a family struck by misfortune; only their sorrow was of any consequence, and she itemised the financial expenditure that had been showered upon Michele, for his education and the best lawyers hired for the appeal court in Sassari and the court of cassation in Turin: 1200 francs for studies when he undertook military service; 960 francs when he had conferred upon him the rank of second lieutenant; 1000 francs when he left for Lombardy; 1440 francs spent on taking counsel in the days before his arrest; 480 francs given to him on the day of his incarceration for daily provisions and other small expenses; 1000 francs paid to the lawyers Ferracciu and Mancini to defend him before the appeal tribunal sitting in Sassari and the court of cassation in Turin.

There was not a word of pity following that itemisation for the unhappy young man who awaited death in the awful tower of the Castello prison; her thoughts are all for the praiseworthy son Antonio, now seen as the family's heir, and beloved in retrospect as an obedient son.

In the various accounts of the family's tragedy, Francesco, father of Michele and Antonio, is mentioned only in passing. And there seems to be no mention of him in Domenica's will. Sardinian women managed their own property and the dowry that came with them from their family. Nor is there any evidence available, in spite of the will, that she died, though she may have expected to do so. Any connection between Minnia's family, or Michele's, with the Quesada Delitala, of the marquisate of San Saturnino, eludes me, as does any relationship with 43-year-old **Donna Giuseppa Quesada**, wife of Efisio Martino who died of cholera on 24 August, nor of 70-year-old **Nobile Donna Rosalia Delitala** of Corsica who died the day before.

Eugenia Tognotti draws conclusions from the wills she has studied concerning the social and economic effects of the cholera catastrophe. There was no doubt that the disappearance of so many rich members of the aristocracy and the merchant class made available new resources, modified social hierarchies, made a sudden remixing of fortunes and opened up new possibilities for individuals and groups.

As for Michele Delitala, on 19 May 1857, at dawn, a horse-drawn cart left through the great gate of the old Castello. In it sat a pale man with a black moustache and long hair curling around his shoulders. It made its way to the Campo di San Paolo and there Michele was hanged.

As already intimated, the next chapter shows a different sort of violence and retribution, mostly in a distinct area of Sardinia.

7 – Vendetta, Vengeance, *Banditesse* and Resistance 1733–1917

Introduction

Eleonora d'Arborea's 1392 *Carta de Logu*, the code of laws extended by the Spanish to the whole of Sardinia, and in place until 1827, took account of two realities: the agricultural and pastoral life of most of its inhabitants, and the position of its women. Clauses contained in the *Carta* saw how rural disputes might arise and not only sought to prevent them but also included processes to resolve them. Other clauses were tailored to prevent inheritance disputes. Integral to the *Carta* was equality before the law; this recognised that rural women in particular were naturally the head of the family and its decision making, particularly as the men were often absent tending sheep.

But over the centuries, and in particular in the Barbagia region of the mountainous east of the island, which even the Romans had been forced to leave to its own devices, the rule of the state's law was seen to work against the people, not for them. Increasingly they took the law into their own hands in the resolution of disputes. This led to feuds, or vendettas, between families, vengeance, including a vengeance code known in Barbagia as *codice barbaracino*, and banditry (*banditismo*), all of which involved women, including several known women bandits (*banditesse*). Added to this an enclosure act of 1820, which deprived rural people of their traditional rights regarding communal land, led to the 1868 resistance known as *Su Connottu*, in Nuoro led by a woman.

Feuds, Vengeance and Reconciliation as Seen by Foreigners

The essentially Sardinian nature of feuds, vengeance and banditry was of especial interest to visitors to the island; after all, it spiced up the books they wrote following their short visit, or even their extended stay there. Often they were not fully aware of background and context. A good example of this is contained in both William Henry Smyth's *Sketch of the present state of the Island of Sardinia* (1828), and *Sardinia* (1874) by Mary Davey. They both tell of the assassination in 1820 of the wealthy shepherd Andrea Scaccatos, of Limbara range, Gallura, and his two older sons by the brothers Puzzu (Putzu) of a rival family. One of the Scaccatos sons was just married to a Puzzu sister – **Caterina Puzzu**. Only **Dame Scaccatos** (**Maria Azara**), though wounded, survived the massacre, and the youngest son whom she hid, knowing what the banging on the door and the sound of a Putzu voice presaged. Her husband, too, had foreseen events: he had recently shown her where their considerable wealth in coins was buried. The day of the funeral arrived and Mary Davey recounts how her informant, the local priest, described it:

Then forth came Dame Scaccatos, holding in one hand the bloody shirt of her murdered husband, with the other leading the youngest and now only son, a slender, shrinking boy of nine years.

'Swear, Lorenzo, my son,' said she, pointing to the figure of the father more especially, and then pointing to the blood-stained garment as she looked steadfastly into the young child's troubled face; 'swear that thou wilt avenge this foul deed. See thy dead father, see thy young brother and the bride of yesterday; note them well. See this bloody shirt, descending now to thee, my Lorenzo. Behold the deed of the spoiler, and swear that thou wilt take no pleasure, that thy soul shall know no ease, until he be laid low in his turn. Swear! I, thy mother command thee; swear by all the saints in Paradise, and let the oath grow with thy growth and strengthen with thy strength – yea, until thine arm be strong and thine eye steady to do the deed of just and righteous vengeance.

The young boy did, indeed, swear, and was made to do so on each following anniversary. Dame Scaccatos was, however, too impatient to wait for her son to grow up and avenge the dead; the state did, after all, have something to offer:

No, she had within her power the means of punishment, and right vigorously and ably did she enforce them. She applied to Government at once, and appealed so successfully that the detestable villain Giovanni Puzzu was executed at Sassari, and his two wicked brothers, Leonardo and Pietro, were exiled to the little island of 'La Maddalena' … Five others of this vile family, fled to the mountains under sentence of death.

Smyth's version, written a few years earlier is much the same, though he does give more Putzu background – Pietro, for example, was British vice consul in Terranova (earlier, and later, Olbia) at the time of one of his visits. He wrote nearer the time of the massacre's occurrence than Mary Davey's version, though she is not drawing on his: she was told it by a priest who knew the family well, and had, indeed, warned Dame Scaccatos against her son's marriage into 'that terrible family; their hands are red with blood'. Smyth's book tends to be thematic – indeed, it jumps hither and thither as an idea takes him – rather than chronological, but surely he is writing of the same massacre, when he writes a hundred pages earlier, changing some facts and without mentioning names:

The widow of a murdered man carefully preserves her husband's bloody shirt, and displays it at stated periods to her children, who are bound to revenge their father's death as soon as they become capable. Just before my last visit to Maddalena, a little boy was brought thither from the opposite coast of Gallura, who had been desperately wounded in an attack which proved fatal to his father, two uncles, and a brother, and the rival family thought all their enemies were destroyed. But a shepherd conveyed the stripling safely over in the night – with the assistance of a surgeon he was speedily recovered, and his mother is now rearing him in daily execration of those 'that have *eaten* his father'.

Did Smyth just need a good editor, or did another family go through similar trauma? As for Dame Scaccatos, she retired to a convent at Tempio, much admired for having rid Gallura of the family that abused their power there from the end of the eighteenth century and into the nineteenth. The accusation explored in an undated Olbia internet piece – '*Il caso dei fratelli Puzzu: fu vero "banditismo"?*' by Federico Bardanzellu – is that the two foreign writers had added rather too much local colour, and been seemingly unaware of the more nuanced details of the long-established Puzzu family.

Mary Davies and her two years in Sardinia (1848–50) appear in more detail in chapter 11.

Feuds could last for years, and could be caused by, or trigger, strange events; these could even lead to reconciliation. John Warre Tyndale, lawyer, traveller and writer read up on Sardinia and then visited it in 1843. The result, published six years later, was the multi-volume *The Island of Sardinia, Including Pictures of the Manners and Customs of the Sardinians* (1849) which was later republished, and more accessible, as *The Island of Sardinia*.

While travelling in the mountainous Marghine, in the central western area of the island, Tyndale learnt of an incident that had taken place 'a few years since'. A party of six young women were performing a novena at their local church when bandits who knew some of them descended from their hideaway to pay them a visit. The women were sweet-talked into joining the bandits for supper, followed by singing and dancing. The women felt safe enough to spend the night there and were carefully and honourably guarded by their hosts. The next day was one of amusement, then they descended to complete their novena. But all was not well:

> In the interim, their absence had been discovered, and a report circulated in the villages that the banditi had not only carried them off, but had used every species of violence and insult towards them, made their enraged relatives arm themselves, and set off for the purpose of rescue and revenge.

By chance, the rescue posse was climbing up, as the armed party of bandits and young women was descending. The rescuers lay flat amid the shrubs, 'as was the custom', ready to ambush their prey; from there, guns cocked, they sprang up and demanded the release of their women.

> But there was no threat of firing, except on the part of one of the villagers; for, according to etiquette … the presence of women in the party prohibits the fulfilment of a vendetta; and so a truce was demanded, and a conference took place. It was, however, obtained with much difficulty; for the villager, who still held his gun in the same threatening position, was the bridegroom of one of the novenanti females, and the bandito against

whom it was levelled had formally been his rejected rival in her affections; from which cause disputes and vendetta had arisen, – they had attempted each other's lives, – the unsuccessful desperado had retired to the hills, and they had now met for the first time since their mutual attack on each other.

A standoff followed, each man with his gun in his hand:

And a minute more [they] would in all probability have terminated both their lives, had not the young bride at that instant discovered her husband, and rushed into his arms. She seized his gun, discharged its contents into the air, and then, placing herself in front to protect him, led him up to the bandito, from whom she demanded his gun.

He gave it up without demur, and she emptied that, too, and handed the gun back to him. The whole party then joined in the conference. The bandits explained the position, which the women corroborated. The whole thing was turned into a joke, and,

it subsequently ended in one united feast, during which some of them had an opportunity of mentioning and clearing up the causes of the disputes which had produced their existing vendetta and the scene eventually terminated in a mutual forgiveness.

This photograph by Charles Wright of a party of women and men on horseback on their way to visit a chapel, with food for a feast in their travel bags, gives a flavour of the more peaceful aspects of that event.

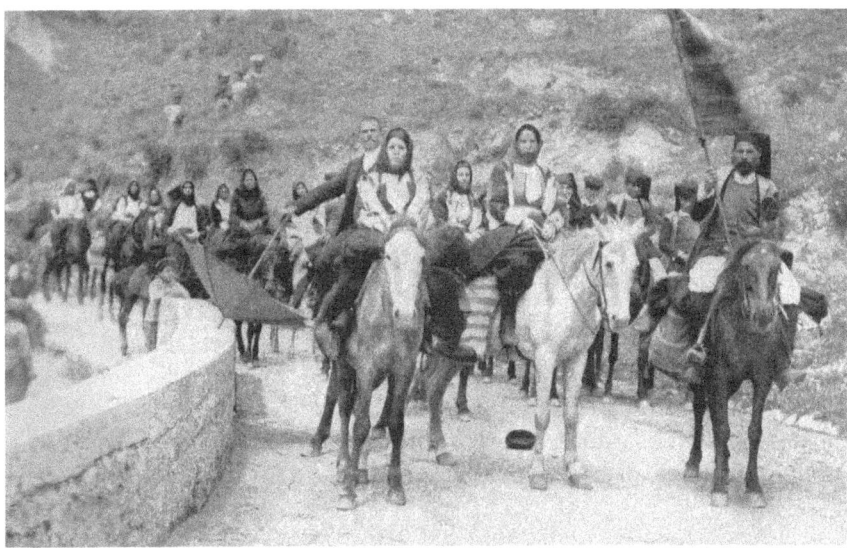

22. Cavalcade of horsemen and horsewomen, photograph by Charles Wright for Helen Dunstan Wright, 'Little-known Sardinia' from the *National Geographic* magazine, August 1916

The etiquette of vendetta – that you did not attack if a woman was present – was clearly not always observed, though it could be at the perpetrator's peril. Tyndale's descriptions of banditry were so well received in Britain that an anonymous contributor to *Blackwood's Edinburgh Magazine* of July 1849 quoted more than one example, including one of non-observance, and the consequences:

> A brigand was conducting his wife on horseback through the mountains when he suddenly met his adversary, who, regardless of the conventional and living flag of truce, attacked and slew him, together with his pregnant wife. The relations and friends of the deceased were not the only outraged parties: a general feeling of indignation and vengeance was kindled throughout the whole province. Every bandit felt it to be a breach of their laws of honour, and even the murderer's partisans not only denounced the act, but 'refused him the kiss of peace'. The mangled corpses were conveyed home, and the friends of the deceased having sworn, on the body of the unfortunate **Teodora**, a perpetual Vendetta against the family of the assassin, a system of revenge and bloodshed was framed and carried out to such an extent, that hundreds of victims, perfectly innocent of even indirect participation in this single act of dishonour, fell in all parts of Gallura.

As the example of the young woman who emptied the guns of two rivals has shown, it was possible for a vendetta to be brought to an end. Tyndale describes at some length two more formal types of reconciliation; for the first he draws on a 'Sarde author'. This reconciliation is performed by the local priest, and takes place amid much initial groaning and wailing, followed by tears on the part of the women, the emptying of guns and then feasting, dancing, singing and the exchange of gifts (*s'imbiatu*) – gifts being the women's responsibility. 'The *paci* [peace] thus established are generally perpetual,' and are sealed by the '*Danza di Sangue*', the dance of blood.

Tyndale suggests that the second method, 'private arbitration "by their peers" is preferred'. The arbitrators, known as both '*Ragionatori*' and '*Saggi*' (wise men), appoint a day and place for their adjudication before the two parties, their witnesses and kindred. Having explained the system, Tyndale describes an example: 'It was the case of a young shepherd who had been too ardent in his advances to a young maiden.' The shepherd did not care for the result of the arbitration, so the *ragionatori* turned to go. But an uncle detained them '"Stop, friends!" he exclaimed, "the thing must be finished at this moment."' And he reprimanded his nephew, who 'approached the offended party, and sued for pardon'.

> The uncle thus satisfied, advanced and demanded for him the hand of the maiden; the betrothal took place, and things having thus happily terminated, they betook themselves to prepare the feast. This is the whole expense incurred by the parties. Through the mediation of these good

old men, lawsuits have frequently been settled in one day which would, perhaps have been carried on at the price of half a patrimony, and have lasted many years; and, what is more important, bitter dissensions and bloody feuds have been thus extinguished by these solid reconciliations.

Although the anecdotes about vendettas, vengeance and reconciliation in Sardinia are readily accessible in the nineteenth-century written accounts of visiting foreigners, exploration of the subject, and that of banditry, is increasingly explored by today's Sardinian and mainland scholars of the island's history and culture.

The Sardo and Sardinian View

It is a pity that to reproduce a poem in Sardo in this study would prove inaccessible to many readers: one can only hope that a translation captures some of its essence: in *Malas Mutas*, which is translated as 'Bad Tidings', poet Antonella Anedda writes in *Archipelago*:

They shot the two brothers in the face.
The nape of their necks bend the bush down,
and make it darker than grapes in a barrel.

The moon rocks inside the island's heart.
Silence digs a ditch in Dead Throat Gulch.
As in Roman times, they dump carrion into pits
that smoulder with vendettas year after year.

Now lead is sewn into the hemlines
to make the widows' weeds
hang sheer and straight.

That last stanza, surely, cannot fail to strike home.

Feuding families is a ripe subject for the novelist imbued with the spirit of Sardinia, and no writer was more steeped in all its lights and shades than **Grazia Deledda** (1871–1936); indeed, she so captured a certain period of a certain part of Sardinia that in 1926 she won the Nobel Prize for Literature – only the second woman, and the second Italian, to do so. Born into a middle class family in Nuoro, and educated at home, she read avidly and started writing when she was very young. Her work, inspired by the peasants of her region and their struggles, appeared in magazines from 1890, and her first novel was published in 1892; her first real success was *Elias Portolu* (1900). Although after her marriage in 1900 she lived in Rome, she continued to write about Sardinia. Many of her novels, such as the best known *Canne al Vento* (1913; 'Reeds in the Wind'), have been translated into English but not *Colombi e Sparvieri* (1912) most easily translated as 'Doves and Hawks'.

Colombi e Sparvieri is set in a village Grazia Deledda calls Oronou, 'set on a granite peak', but which was actually Orune. The book was based on an episode of which she became aware in 1908. So that summer she spent a few days there to get the feel of the place, as she always did as part of her writing process. It tells the story of two young people, Columba and Jorgi (Giorgio) who come from two families traditionally separated by enmity and rancour, typical of the type of feud that was often passed down through the generations, though the authorities, bishop and prefect, have done their best to bring about a formal peace. The young couple are also separated by wealth and poverty; he is a poor but educated shepherd. Everything is done by her family to foil the relationship. On his side, Jorgi's relative is a fugitive who refused to accept the mediation; the patriarch of her family has been his rival. Eventually her relative accuses Jorgi of theft. Columba is influenced; he doesn't understand her change of heart, breaks off the engagement and leaves for Nuoro (25 km or 15.5 miles away). More detail would spoil the story!

Should you decide to visit Orune, on the trail of Columba and Jorgi, bear in mind that nearby is the Nuragic site of Su Tempiesu-Orune with its *pozzo* (sacred well). From this site, as chapter 1 relates, came the statuette of 'A Couple Making an Offering'. Could it have been to resolve a dispute?

Dolores Turchi (b.1935) was born in Oliena (Nuoro province) to Tuscan parents and became a primary school teacher, but she also researched local culture and tradition assiduously and published widely, including about Grazia Deledda. Her work, written in Italian, unfortunately remains untranslated. But an interview entitled 'The "Attitos" of Sardinia' (1988) by **Martha King** (1928–2011), Grazia Deledda's English translator and biographer, provides some useful hints. Martha was an American Italianist who settled in Italy in 1978; Dolores provided the introduction to her translation of Grazia's *Reeds in the Wind*. Where introducing Dolores is concerned, it is best to let Martha speak in her own words:

> The 'wild' Barbagia region in central Sardinia where the ethnologist Dolores Turchi was born and has lived and taught for many years is also the area of her research of orally transmitted legends, stories, and improvisatorial funeral poetry. In Oliena, Orune, Orgosolo, Nuoro, Bitti and other small, remote isolated villages, she listens to and records what has been passed down from generation to generation. ...
>
> ... Turchi has been able to record one aspect of Sardinian folklore that has all but vanished – except in the most isolated areas of Orgosolo and Orune where bandits and acts of vengeance still flourish and strong passions have not been diluted by technological change. In those villages the funeral lament or *attitos*, as improvised for the occasion by natural poets, still serves the important function of inciting revenge as well as providing an emotional release for the mourners.

Dolores Turchi was able to record a number of funeral chants recalled from *attitos* improvised in the 1930s, 50 years before the 1988 interview.

The most apposite quoted by Martha King is the cry of a young bride from Orgosolo whose husband had been murdered. As usual, the chant was in the local language; this is Martha's translation:

> On my twenty-first year
> I have dyed my dress!
> At my year twenty-one
> I have dyed my clothes black!
> It seems like a curse!
>
> You are dead to me, Carlo
> ruddy and handsome.
> Addio to the world!
> you are dead to me, Carlo
> handsome and ruddy.
>
> Get up and caress me;
> because I am still young!
> Get up and caress me;
> I'm young and not old!

Dolores Turchi explained that the Church was opposed to what it saw as a pagan practice:

> Not only did it perpetuate a pagan ritual, but it contrived to continue the *disamistades*, that is, the continual chain of murderous vendettas between families. 'Sangue chiama sangue.' 'Blood claims blood.' The religion of forgiveness never existed in the Barbagia. It entered only as a varnish applied by the church.

I might have translated that idiom 'Blood calls out to blood.' What I like best about the interview is one of the footnotes, not only because it brings full circle the relationship between Dolores Turchi, Martha King and Grazia Deledda, but also because it shows that Grazia, for all her entrée, sieved through her imagination, into the culture of her region, did not always gain access to an important tradition:

> When Grazia Deledda ... Tried to persuade some women to 'attitare' so she could transcribe verses for her *Tradizioni popolari di Nuoro* (1894) 'no one wanted to comply at any cost.' No one would cooperate because they thought it might bring bad luck – death in the house, explains Dolores Turchi. In Deledda's novel *Via del Male* (1896) she describes the custom of women improvising funeral poetry, but she gives no examples of it.

Carlo Levi briefly, but importantly, combines Grazia Deledda and her novel *Colombi e Sparvieri*, Orune and the *attitos* in his travel account of

Sardinia, *Tutto il miele è finito* (All the Honey is Finished or, There is no More Honey, 1964). It is a travel account, yet the writer, artist, anti-Fascist and physician intended rather more in his accounts of travels to the poorer reaches of Italy: they are at their core political. In both his visits to Sardinia, in 1952 and 1962 – during which he travelled widely – he visited the Barbagia region, and Orune was key, because the title of the book comes from there. Levi writes, of the commune generally, 'Orune, in the saying of the inhabitants of other countries, has a reputation (I don't know how justified) to be the first country of sheep thieves, but it also has a more glorious fame, and this certainly real, to be a country of poets.' More specifically he writes,

> Friends take me to see the fountain south of the square, linked to the memory of Grazia Deledda; and from there to the house where the student lived and died, the protagonist of the novel *Colombi e Sparvieri*. Here the young Deledda came to visit her friend. In the room an old woman recounts her memories of the writer, and sings me the *attitos* sung then for the funeral lament of the student, who was her grandson; in a corner her daughter breastfeeds the baby under the eyes of her husband.

The content of the *attitos* is significant: the young man who has died, probably murdered, is considered the honey in the family; with his death *Tutto il miele è finito*: there is no more honey in the house. Levi remembered so clearly

> those mountains, that April wind, and the old kitchen, black with ancient smoke and the *attitos*, and the poems, and the Sardinian dances, and the shepherds, and the sheep thieves, and the fugitives of an archaeological and present world.

The Introduction to Levi's book is rather long and discursive, but one relevant sentence stands out: 'there are few references in *Tutto il miele è finito* to the most famous Sardinian writer, Grazia Deledda; there is an indirect nod to an article of 1895 [1894?] on the magic words in use in Sardinia, remembered by the socialist shepherd who explains the words of the songs of an old woman from Orune.'

Grazia Deledda died of breast cancer in Rome aged 64. Her last novel published in her lifetime, *La chiesa della solitudine* (1936) is a semi-autobiographical description of a young Italian woman coming to terms with her breast cancer. *Cosima* (1937) – the manuscript of which was found after her death – is also an autobiographical novel. Her home town of Nuoro is filled with memories of her, including the family's house in the Santu Predu district (Via Grazia Deledda), which is now a museum devoted to her, including her archives. She was buried on the nearby Monte Ortobene; it is not clear if her remains are still there.

The illustrations of vengeance and vendetta described above have, not surprisingly, focussed on women, often central to the cause, as well as to what followed. But it is worth mentioning another cause relevant to a pastoral community. Much of the *Codice Barbaricino* dealt with forms of *abigeato*, the theft of livestock, and its just retribution. A local saying, in the local language, summed it up, *Nehe o no nehe, prange berbehe*. 'Guilty or not, it is always the sheep that cry.'

Banditesse: Sardinian Women Bandits

'The character of Sardinian women is dominant, firm and proud, and she has played a crucial role in Sardinian banditry, not only in supporting and developing the phenomenon since the early beginnings in the 1800s but also experiencing it as a bandit.' This is how Laura Baccaro, psychologist and criminologist specialising in violence against women, introduces Maria Silvia Todde's article '*Banditesse in Sardegna: il fenomeno del banditismo al femminile*' (2010). That article and Franco Fresi's *Le Banditesse: Storie di Donne Fuorilegge in Sardegna* (2015) help unravel the lives of the several known women bandits from 1733 to 1905. They are by no means the only works on the subject, or those that include it.

As chapter 6 intimated, from 1720, and the change of overlords in Sardinia, it was difficult for the authorities to deal with the crime and upheaval that prevailed. The first woman bandit (*banditessa*) made her mark in 1733. Her story is most succinctly told in Laura Candiani's internet article '*Lucia Delitala Tedde: Quando le Donne Sarde Cominciarono a "Banditare"*' (When Sardinian Women first turned to Banditry) (2019). The author, a former teacher, is now a consultant to the Women's History and Stories section of the Lucchese Historical Institute in Pescia, Tuscany. She has written not only about Lucia, but also about the *banditessa* who follows.

It was during the War of Spanish Succession which led to Spain losing Sardinia to Savoy that **Donna Lucia Delitala Tedde** (1705–post 1760) was born in Nulvi into a noble Sardinian family. Her father was Don Francesco Delitala, her mother **Donna Giovanna Maria Tedde**. The Delitala family had obtained cavalier status in 1636 and entered the nobility in 1641. They were rich by not always lawful means, including smuggling and banditry, and family members had participated in the anti-Savoy riots of 1720. Though Lucia had a sheltered childhood, in the background was a feud between the Tedde and the Delitala of different political persuasions. Not surprisingly, she grew up a rebellious tomboy, and is said to have taken embroidery scissors into church to attack the garments, ribbons and lace of women of different factions, particularly supporters of Savoy. The portrait of her overleaf, which shows her most elegantly dressed, is rather contradictory.

Encouraged by her father, in due course Lucia turned to banditry and writers are agreed that her activities as a *banditessa* were as much those of a patriot as of a lawbreaker. She did not act alone, but assembled an itinerant military body around her which attacked Savoyard troops. She was soon

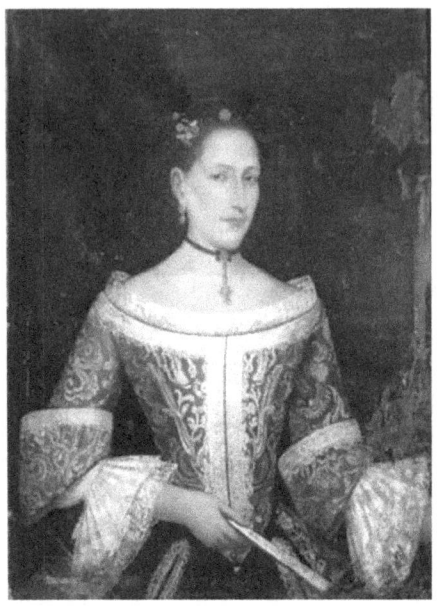

23. Lucia Delitala, from the internet

feared and respected, and seen as a warrior queen, an Amazon. When her lawlessness came to the attention of the authorities, the viceroy wrote to King Carlo Emanuele III that she would not marry because she refused to be dependent on a husband, and he described her, without having seen her, as having the moustaches of a grenadier and using weapons and her horse like a gendarme. Laura Candiani begins to explain the moustaches: she wore a mask to hide her identity. She also writes that 'She used the arched gun, with a flintlock primer, or the rapier, lighter than the sword, as she travelled Gallura with her beloved horse Tronu.'

Lucia's troop did not hesitate to use their weapons. It is said that there was a massacre of a company of dragoons in charge of prisoners and money that caused 'such a sensation that the Jesuit Father Vassallo gathered in Nulvi the leaders of the two factions, Giovanni Tedde and Antonio Delitala, to stipulate a lasting peace between them at least'.

Lucia did not hesitate, either, to form alliances with other bandit groups; typical was that with Giovanni Fais who was accompanied by his wife **Chiara Unali**, both from Chiaramonti. Her father was also a bandit leader. And she emulated Lucia in courage, determination and ability to use arms and to withstand the hardships of their violent itinerant life, in spite of travelling with a young son. Lucia considered her a sister. Fais went on to kill Giovanni Maria Tedde of Chiaramonti, perhaps to please Lucia. This sparked a vendetta, followed by a three-day fight with Tedde's relatives during which Fais was wounded and a brother of Chiara taken prisoner and tortured. Chiara and Fais fled with their son; but little Matteo started crying, threatening their discovery by their pursuers, at which his father, attempting to silence him, did so for ever. (Some sources say the child was a girl called Mattea; Chiara certainly had a sister of that name). The promptness and determination of Chiara made sure that the murder of their son was not added to her husband's other crimes. Fais was finally apprehended, betrayed by two friends, and hanged in Sassari in 1774. What happened to Chiara does not seem to have been recorded.

According to versions such as Federica Ginesu's entry for Lucia on the late *DonnaSarda* database, Lucia was, in 1733, taken to Cagliari to stand trial. She was accused of many crimes, and charged with the murder of a member of the Tedde family, probably he whom Fais had killed. Because of her noble status she was under house arrest there. She was ordered to pay the Royal Treasury 1000 crowns and to be confined to the *Castrum* for five years, but was free by 1735. Thereafter, her life becomes legendary: it is not known what became of her. It is not known when she died – perhaps some time between 1755 and 1767 – or how. Was she, as some say, killed in an ambush, or did a servant strangle her, or did someone set fire to where she was staying and did she die there in the arms of a nameless lover, as Franco Fresi says in *Le Banditesse*? There is no trace of her in the family tomb in Nulvi.

Lucia is said to have left ten thousand lire for the Jesuit college of Ozieri. When in 1848 the Jesuit order was suppressed, both monks and nuns being expelled, the parish priest of Chiaramonti made good use of the funds. In the goods listed in her will is a red silk dress to be made into vestments.

Women's involvement in banditry did not disappear with the departure of Lucia Delitala Tedde and Chiara Unali from the scene, but rose again, at least where there is recorded evidence, with the arrival of the next well-known *banditessa*. Not only did banditry continue to be widespread but there may be *banditesse* in their own right still to be discovered. And as has already been described, it was women who, typically, incited family members to revenge. This often meant those involved in vendettas and vengeance taking to the mountains. As Laura Baccaro makes clear, women would protect, feed and hide them as necessary, not only from the other side seeking them but also from the authorities trying to wipe out banditry and criminality.

By no means all bandits were fighting the authorities out of Sardinian patriotism: for some it was out of financial necessity; sometimes the motive was as base as greed. And wealth did not come only from ambushing: Giovanni Fais, for example, violent though he was, and a known criminal from the age of 15, sentenced to death in absentia, was so respected as a bandit in the countryside around Chiaramonti by local shepherds and farmers that they gave him annual gifts. This could, of course, be seen as protection money.

The 1890s were a time of particular lawlessness in Sardinia. The notorious *banditessa* who flourished then was not in the same 'patriotic' mould as her predecessor *banditessa* Lucia Delitala Tedde, but her story, too, is usefully told by Laura Candiani in '"*Sa Reina" Nuorese: Maria Antonia Serra Sanna*' (2019).

Maria Antonia Serra Sanna (Mariantonia, b.1866–?) was born in Nuoro, in the centre of the lawless Barbagia, in 1866. Her father was Giuseppe Serra Sanna, her mother's name is apparently unrecorded. Perhaps more important to her story, though, are the names of her brothers, Elias and Giacomo, who led one of the many bandit or brigand gangs who terrorised the region in that decade – anyone who failed to respond to their demands was brutally punished – but the brains behind them belonged to their sister. The family built on the wealth of their father who had started life as a shepherd but in due course became a landowner, with several houses and many animals.

Mariantonia was not only clever but a beauty who decked herself in jewels and fine clothes and paraded through the streets of Nuoro where she was admired, feared and respected – hence the sobriquet in all that is written about her, *Sa Reina*, the Queen. Without naming the Serra Sana family, but nevertheless apparently writing of Mariantonia, Grazia Deledda described her in *Cosima* as very beautiful, tall and trim with fine features in a pale face, two big black eyes and two thick, merciless and diabolical eyebrows.

Although Mariantonia had not gone into hiding like her brothers, it is said that she sometimes wore men's clothes to reach them on horseback in the inaccessible places of the Supramonte. The *DonnaSarda* website adds to that picture: 'Dressed in breeches and *mastruka*, fake beard and rifle on her shoulder, she galloped like a wild devil to bring to her brothers gunpowder, food and news about what was happening in the city.' The fake beard might hint at an explanation of Lucia Delitala Tedde's moustaches. My guess at the meaning of *mastruka*, as a jerkin, was not far off, but I sought clarification from my Orgosolo informant who wrote,

> Mastruca is a paleosardinian word (lat. mastruca) – sort of goat or sheepskin leather, without sleeves, almost to the knees, worn by Sardinian shepherds. My grandfather used to wear one in winter. In Sardo Orgolese it is called simply *sas peddes* (the leathers, being made of different pieces of leather).

In 1895 Mariantonia was arrested and held in prison for a few months, but then, as Laura Candiani explains, 'the accuser, terrified by the possible consequences, had retracted and she was released'.

Mariantonia did much more than parade her wealth: she also managed the family estate and had infallible methods to increase it. As Laura Candiani puts it: 'She visited friends and acquaintances and kindly asked for little favours and concrete gifts (weapons, ammunition, money, cattle and sheep) on behalf of her brothers that naturally could not be refused. Finally she issued a receipt.' Visits to creditors were not so kindly: Franco Fresi explains that if Mariantonia received the slightest complaint she would reply coldly, 'I will speak to Elias.' The complainant knew only too well what that meant.

Between 1897 and 1899 Mariantonia was often accompanied on visits by a friend, **Giuseppa (Peppa) Lunesu**, who is best described by Maria Silvia Todde: She was 'very clever, shrewd, ambitious, from a wealthy family. She had graduated from the Royal Normal School for

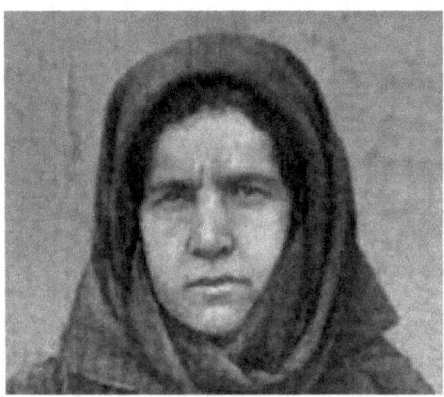

24. Mariantonia Serra, from the internet

Females.' And 'with two dark eyes that enchanted you but, at the same time, frightened you'.

There was no lack of wealthy landowners willing to court Peppa, because she was interesting and attractive and, presumably, because her family had money, 'but they were held back and alarmed by the close friendship that bound her to Maria Antonia Serra Sanna'. Make of that what you will, but Maria Silvia Todde goes on to say, 'And to make matters worse, she had fallen in love with a fugitive.' Who he was is not reported, but there were plenty to choose from.

Peppa was obviously a bit of a Mata Hari because:

Even an officer of the carabinieri had fallen in love with her; many spoke of true love, others spoke of a 'screen' used by the young man to learn from the beautiful woman useful information for the capture of the outlaws; actually the exact opposite had happened, since the officer was hurriedly transferred, because of the '*decoro* [possible misuse?] of his weapon', but also and especially because he had let slip some confidential information.

There was certainly information to let slip because, by 1899, it was no longer possible for such widespread lawlessness to continue, and it would take more than a posse of carabinieri to round up the gangs. On the night 14/15 May 1899, as Franco Fresi tells it, Nuoro was divided into seven districts; soldiers and carabinieri divided into seven groups with access to piles of handcuffs, chains and ropes, set about their task. Just after midnight, Mariantonia's 75-year-old father hearing the kicks and musket blows on the family's front door, knew what it meant and refused to open up until he was told that the door would be broken down if he didn't. He shouted, 'like a madman' as the authorities searched the house for his 'children'.

Mariantonia was found in her bedroom up a wooden ladder and forced to get down. A lieutenant, fearful of her reputation, and her ferocious look, waited outside as she dressed in a skirt and scarlet jacket. As she left the room she glanced at a chest in the corner. It was enough to alert her captors. Inside was jewellery of all kinds, together with a powerful telescope, 'a box of English brand gunpowder', and perhaps most important, documents that proved her guilt. Just from the Serra Sanna house 6000 lire worth of assets were recovered. And during the night 600 were arrested in the town.

Maria Silvia Todde adds an interesting side-story to these arrests which had been planned for months; suspects were to be arrested without a warrant, the omission of which would be regularised later. These were formalised enough to be known as 'preventative arrests'. As it happened, the following month King Umberto I of the recently united Italy, and his wife **Queen Margherita of Savoy** (1851–1926), were due to unveil a monument to his father, King Vittorio Emanuele II, in Sassari's Piazza d'Italia. The arrests, not only of brigands, but of anyone deemed lacking in enthusiasm for unification, were not unconnected with security for this visit, and every precaution was taken surrounding the couple's journey to Sardinia and then to Sassari.

During the round-up of suspects, several carabinieri had been injured and the king and queen visited them in hospital in Sassari and presented them with silver medals. To celebrate the unveiling, a spectacular cavalcade of thousands of horsemen in traditional costume from all over the region took place. Inspired by the cavalcade, every year a similar event still takes place, with participants from 70 or so surrounding villages, to celebrate both their common origin and their interesting differences. Ironically, the following year Umberto was assassinated on the mainland.

Mariantonia's brothers were not arrested; instead they were hunted by a force of 200, literally as wild boars would have been, with men acting as beaters, until on 10 July, their band was run down at Morgogliai, between Oliena and Orgosolo. The battle, and their reign of terror, ended with the deaths of 27-year-old Elias and 34-year-old Giacomo.

In 1900, Mariantonia, aged 33, was sentenced to 20 years incarceration, the harshest sentence meted out; she learnt in prison of her brothers' deaths. She served 18 years in Nuoro's 'La Rotonda' (which no longer exists). On her release, according to Laura Candiani, by then aged 50, she married a man from Orgosolo, brother of a cellmate, and they lived for a while in Nuoro. Then even family members lost track of *Sa Reina*, and all that remains of her is the legend of her life as a *banditessa*.

Although sources suggest that Mariantonia served 18 years of the 20 to which she was sentenced, there is a discrepancy: my Orgosolo informant, who will let no fact go unexplored, has found her marriage certificate. She did indeed marry, in Nuoro, a man from Orgosolo, Giovanni Andrea Marrosu, but the date of the marriage was 1908 – eight years after her incarceration, and her age was given, confirming the different timing, as 42. It is, perhaps, just conceivable that she was let out of prison to marry. But I am satisfied that she served at most eight years of her 20-year sentence – long enough for *Sa Reina*.

Maria Silvia Todde recounts what happened to Peppa Lunesu: 'A few days after the arrest, the charming Lunesu, able as always, managed to prove her innocence and came out of jail, as can be seen in the annex to the case file.' Of the 600 arrests made in May, called 'the night of San Bartolomeo', half were released immediately and most of the rest were acquitted for lack of evidence; only 150 were brought to trial.

Maria Silvia Todde adds a tailpiece about another bandit family to her account of Peppa's fate:

> **Eufrasia Lovicu**, mother of two bandits of Orgosolo, Pasquale Manca and Leonardo Mureddu, shared with them seventeen years in hiding in the Supramonte. When her two sons died in 1937 and in 1938, she went back down to Orgosolo, but always remained in isolation on the outskirts.

Never has it been brought home to me so sharply how versions of history can markedly differ, depending on one's sources, than with the story of **Paska Devaddis** (1888–1913). (Although Paska is the spelling of her name in most sources, in her home town of Orgosolo she is known as Pasca, pronounced Pasha, the 'h' with a glottal stop). She was the first *banditessa* to receive newspaper treatment of fancy and exaggeration. In an invented interview she was depicted as a 'tough virago', and a 'virgin Amazon' who was said to ride wearing the traditional Orgosolo headscarf in yellow. The reality was rather different, as Dr Anna Tilocca Segreti, one time director of Sassari's archives, found among documents there. Paska was small, delicate and sickly, though not lacking in courage.

Paska was caught up in the feud, called in accounts *disamistades* (enmity), that swept through the Barbagia town of Orgosolo between 1905 and 1917. Several families became involved in it, principally the Cossus and the Corraines. The Devaddis, a well-off family of the town, were drawn in, particularly on 3 April 1905 when Carmine Corraine was murdered. A further killing, this time of a member of the Cossu family, was said to have been committed by Paska's brother.

So far so good, but the versions I first came across go on to say that because she was a witness to the murder, when an arrest warrant was issued, Paska was forced to become a fugitive in the mountains and, thus, labelled a *banditessa*. It seems that the man to whom she was betrothed was also a member of the band of which she became a part.

Not surprisingly, those versions continue, the harsh life of the mountains played havoc with Paska's fragile health. She may have been a fugitive, and she may have had the courage to try and withstand the rough mountain life that was then her lot, but there was no evidence that she participated as a *banditessa* in the way that Lucia and *Sa Reina* did. Indeed, it was only a few months before her fragile health gave way and she died in a cave, probably of tuberculosis.

Paska was obviously much loved by her companions. They knew that Orgosolo was barricaded and filled with troops; they also knew that, by tradition, a person who dies in hiding far from home is dishonoured for ever. So, during a 'night without stars', they carried her body down to the town and to her family home, by then closed and empty, dressed her in her wedding dress, and laid her on her bed. What provoked amazement, given the reputation that had been fabricated for Paska, was that an autopsy revealed her to be a virgin.

The account up to Paska witnessing the murder is accurate enough, apart from the newspaper embellishment. But there is more than one version that differs substantially.

When there was a killing, all members of the family of the perpetrator became outlaws subject to arrest, often so that they could be forced to confess the whereabouts of the fugitive; and, indeed, Paska's younger sister, **Carola Devaddis**, was arrested. And Paska did have a fiancé, Michele Manca, who was a bandit. But Paska was known to have tuberculosis, and some said that during the time she was supposedly in the mountains, she was, instead, hidden in various friends' and relatives' houses in Orgosolo,

Lodine and Gavoi; this theory was first aired by anthropologist and ethnologist Franco Cagnetta in *Banditi a Orgosolo* (1975).

Another version given to me by an informant was that in reality Paska never moved from her late mother's house in Orgosolo. Even so, she was regarded as a fugitive and, thus, a *banditessa*; but the police, knowing of her ill health, and that she would probably soon die, never searched for her. It was there that she did die and her body, dressed by relatives, was found stretched out on a length of azure and gold brocade.

A similar if much more detailed and convoluted story, that Paska never took refuge in the mountains, but died in the family home, was told to Maria Silvia Todde and is included in her *'Banditesse in Sardegna'*, under the sub-title *'La vera storia: Intervista alla nipote di Paska Devaddis'* ('The true story: interview with Paska Devaddis' niece'). Maria Silvia is careful to warn that the story told to her in 2010 may have been subjective when told by Paska's sister to her daughter, as well as then being dragged back from long ago memory.

The 2019 version which I now choose to settle on comes to me via Pietrina Rubanu of Orgosolo, a former teacher, who is not only the author of *Murales politici della Sardegna* (1998), and an activist in the preservation of Orgosolo's murals, but also a fount of knowledge about her place and with useful connections. Pietrina has worked tirelessly to get the story right for me. As near reality as we are likely to get comes via Pietrina talking to **Francesca** (b.1950) and **Pasqua** (b.1953) Muggianu. They got it from the grandfather in whose house Paska finally took refuge.

This is their version. Soon after Paska was wanted by the police, she lived in the house of family friends in Fonni, a village about 30km (18.6 miles) from Orgosolo. She was forced to leave there when someone from the opposing faction found out where she was. She was already ill then, but not yet dying. She was then taken to the house of her cousin, **Pasqua Antonia** (b.1890), grandmother of Francesca and Pasqua. There she stayed, in a room without windows, looked after by her cousin, as her health deteriorated, and visited daily by the family doctor, who pretended that he was visiting another member of the family. And there she died, aged 25, and weighing less than 22kg (3 stone and 6.5 lb). It was that doctor who certified her death and declared that 'She is as her mother made her', that is, a virgin.

It was only after her death that Paska was taken back to her family home. Her parents were already dead, so it was her sister Carola, by then released from prison, who received her body and laid her out dressed in her wedding finery.

Whatever sympathy may remain in Orgosolo for Paska, caught up in the feud's tragedies, the betrothed of Carmine Corraine, **Juvanna Moro**, has not been forgotten. The Corraine house at Corso Repubblica 103 has been turned into an ethnographic museum by **Maria Corraine**. As well as being furnished as a typical Barbagia house of its time, it contains a costume of Zia (aunt) Juvanna, as Maria Corraine knew her.

Since the middle of the twentieth century, Orgosolo has become famous for the murals that decorate the facades of many buildings; some of them tell the story of historical events or characters, many of them revolutionary, some are pointedly political, including pacifism and anti-Fascism, some topical in other ways, and some reinforcing ethnic pride and resistance.

Don't be led astray by a website illustration suggesting that it shows a mural of Juvanna Moro, described as Carmine Corraine's 'wife', holding a baby, with a group of men to one side. This is a police public relations mural showing how they protect citizens. But there is one that illustrates the battle of Morgogliai of 11 July 1899, when *Sa Reina*'s brothers were killed by those hunting them; it is entitled 'Big Game' which is how it was described at the time, and is the title of a book written by a participant.

Most of the artists appear to be men, but there was a women's group of painters called *Le Api* (The bees), usefully described in Bill Rolston's article, 'Resistance and Pride: The Murals of Orgosolo, Sardinia' (2014). They tended to paint iconoclastic scenes that were not generally appreciated; indeed, they were whitewashed over, or partly so. The group no longer exists.

I like the mural of three women in traditional costume sitting outside a house, one of them sewing; it is called '*Saggezza Antica*' ('Ancient Wisdom'). Less peaceful is a mural of the 'Mothers of the Plaza de Mayo' who demonstrated year after year from 1973 on behalf of their daughters and sons who had 'disappeared', usually tortured and killed, during the military dictatorship of Argentina.

The 'headscarf' worn by the sewing women, and that worn by Paska Devaddis as she allegedly rode up to the mountains, needs to be explained.

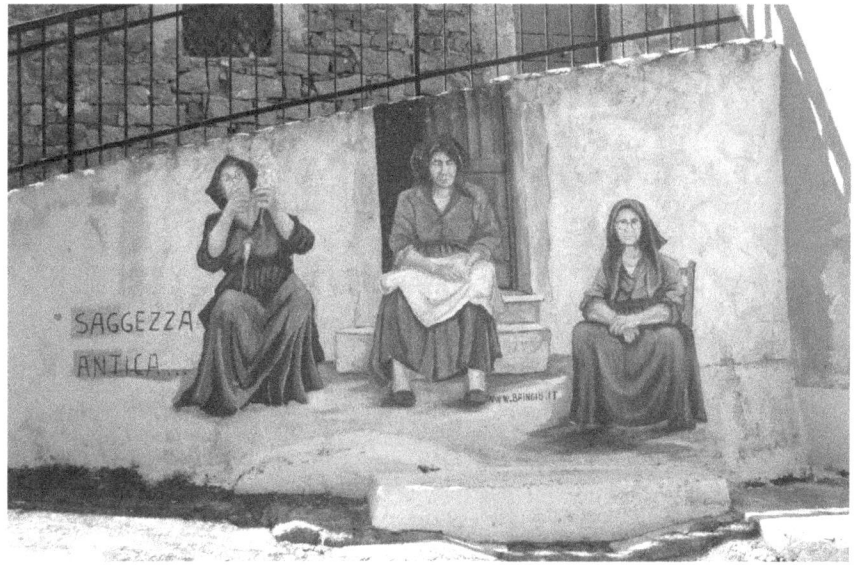

25. *Sagezza Antica*, Orgosolo, photograph by Bill Rolston

I am able to, thanks to Pietrina Rubanu. The 'headscarf' – traditional, and still worn headwear of Orgosolo women – resembles a cross between a hijab and a nun's wimple. The married woman's version is called *su lionzu*, that of the unmarried, *su panniheddu 'e pilos*, meaning headscarf with hair, because the only ornament consists of the long brown silk threads around it.

The 'headscarves' are made of silk, not any silk, but that made in Orgosolo from silkworms called Orgosolo. You can see a more formal picture of the 'headscarf' in the internet article by Angela Corrias, 'Preserving Ancient Silk Art in Orgosolo, Sardinia, with Master Maria Corda'. The 'Master', Maria Corda, is devoting her life to preserving this skill, form of art, that she inherited through her maternal line.

But even more exciting is a YouTube video (Google 'YouTube seta Orgosolo') – the link sent to me by Pietrina Rubanu. It starts with an ancient *cinquecento* driving out through Barbagia countryside to a stand of mulberry trees. Two elderly women in traditional dress of long black skirt, top and 'headscarf' then gather large baskets of mulberry leaves which you see them carrying home on their heads to feed their silkworms. You then see the whole process, step by step, in a way that brings to life something you may never have fully understood, until, with the help of several other women, long skeins of silk yarn are skilfully wound. You see the yellowish silk thread being traditionally woven on a loom into fine cloth.

Finally, you see a young bride being dressed up in an elaborate bridal costume, including a version of the 'headscarf' and a multi-coloured and magnificently embroidered 'apron', resembling that in which Paska Devaddis was laid out. It is nothing like the white wedding dress with which many of us are familiar today.

So particular to Orgosolo is this bridal costume, and so haunting is the story of Paska, that the Sardinian poet, Antioco Casula, better known as Montanaru (1878–1957), wrote in his own language a 38-stanza poem, 'A Pasca Devaddes' [sic]. It is available on the internet under that title, its original date, and the name of the poet's collection in which it appeared, not given. Pietrina Rubanu has perfectly performed the difficult task of translating the 36th stanza from Logudorese:

La ponzein pianu in d'una mesa
E sa este nodia de sa festa
Li ponzein indossu. Ite grandesa
De sarda gentilesa manifesta

They laid her gently on a table
and dressed her in the wedding dress.
What magnificence then was displayed
of the kind Sardinian soul!

Silk-making was relatively common even in Pietrina Rubanu's childhood: she tells me that

When I was a child, I went, together with my sisters and friends, to bring fresh leaves for the little worms. This happened every day, and we also moved the tiny larvae from old to fresh leaves using the eye of a needle. At the time lots of families bred them.

Silk was not the only craft particular to Orgosolo: Pietrina also writes, 'My mother [**Michela Rubanu** (1921–2009)] was one of the best apron embroiderers in Orgosolo, the piece is called "*s'antalena*".' This black and white illustration of the 'apron' does not begin to do justice to the colour, but does suggest the intricacy of the embroidery. The only photograph of Paska is a grainy black and white one of her on her deathbed which does not seem appropriate to include here.

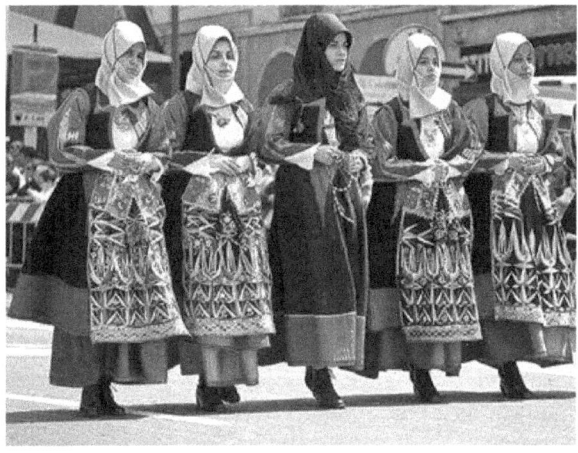

26. Orgosolo women with embroidered aprons, thanks to Pietrina Rubanu

There is more to learn about Orgosolo than feuding and all its ramifications and, if you are lucky enough to have access to a contemporary oral source for recreating history, you can count on being nearer to what really happened.

Dr Adelasia Cocco in Barbagia

Sometimes vendetta, vengeance and banditry have ramifications beyond what might be expected. And so it was with **Adelasia Solinas Cocco** (1885–1983), named after *Giudicessa* Adelasia of Torres, and daughter of Grazia Deledda's intellectual friend Salvatore Cocco Solinas. Adelasia became a doctor in the isolated Barbagia village of Lollove – where Grazia Deledda, possibly as a result of Adelasia's stay there, set her bleak novel *La Madre* (1919/20) (*The Mother*, translated 1989) – because her predecessor was mortally wounded by bandits in an ambush.

The road towards Adelasia's appointment was not an easy one. She had entered the Pisa Faculty of Medicine in 1907, and received a doctorate in medicine from the University of Sassari in 1913. She was the second woman to qualify in Sardinia (following Paola Satta – see chapter 12). In 1914, she had the effrontery to apply to go to Barbagia, an application which was deemed 'irreverent and shameless', and throughout her life she ignored a professor's words, 'no woman is able to reach an eminent place in the medical profession'.

Adelasia was first sent to the Seuna ward in Nuoro. In 1915, she applied to go to Lollove. There she took care of the 400 inhabitants in that small village lost in the mountains and beset by vendetta and banditry. Its ambience is so well conveyed in *La Madre*, but Lollove has history that predates the novel and Adelasia. Its inhabitants remember an ancient curse hurled on the village by some nuns of the seventeenth-century church of Santa Maria Maddalena. They left the village horrified at the behaviour of some of their sister nuns who had preferred the charms of the local shepherds to the rigours of monastic life. 'You will become as the waters of the sea – you will never grow old and you will never die,' they prophesied as they abandoned the village. (The church is integral to the climax of *La Madre*.)

All this Adelasia took in her stride. She travelled along dusty roads, and forded rivers, on horseback, with only one companion (in 1919, she was to be the first Sardinian woman to get a driving licence), bringing healing and succour to her wretched flock. She later wrote,

> It was a beautiful experience, in contact with the poor, the peasants, shepherds, almost as a missionary. I had to fight everyone in a sometimes hostile environment; they wanted the weaker sex relegated to the kitchen stove. But in the end I won the appreciation of the population.

In 1928, she became Sanitary Health Inspector for Nuoro, and in 1935 Director of the Institute of Hygiene and Prophylaxis. She and her husband Giovanni Floris had one son who died of scarlet fever. She lived to the age of 98. A sports park in Sassari is named *Parco Solinas-Cocco*. She appears again in chapter 13 on women and anti-Fascism.

In 2016, Lollove, without shops and schools or even a doctor, had only 26 inhabitants, most of them elderly. It attracts both scholars and photographers. It is well worth looking at the YouTube presentation of the village (Lollove YouTube).

Accabadora: Woman of Violence?

In Laura Baccaro's introduction to Maria Silvia Todde's work on *banditesse*, she describes a different sort of 'violence' when she writes, after itemising the several ways in which women are involved in a vendetta and the accompanying banditry:

Women with the same rights as men, perhaps even greater, so much so that the important task of helping the dying to die, with a precise blow of the hammer to the head, is entrusted to the female agabbadori. Women 'bandits' therefore are not considered deviants but respected women, of family, who perform their role as is expected of them.

In translating the passage, I failed to recognise the word *agabbadori*. Needing to appreciate what was obviously a key term, I emailed Laura Baccaro who explained her take on the woman described, including 'she is the Great Mother; she embodies the pities [*la pietà*] and she is the one who helps to bring about death out of pity and love.' But I then had cause to feel foolish for she mentioned Michela Murgia's debut novel *Accabadora* (2009, translated 2011), which I had, indeed, read a couple of years previously; I had failed to recognise a different spelling. Laura also sent me her article 'Sa Femina Accabadora: donne magiche o assassine?' (2016) in which she elaborates her theme.

Accabadora comes from the Spanish, meaning to finish or complete. One of the two main characters of the novel, Bonaria Urrai, is an aging, wealthy, but lonely, seamstress; she is also an *accabadora*, an angel of death, of mercy, who, visiting at night, helps her neighbours to die, when their situation is hopeless, by administering a quick blow to the head. Earlier in the day, she will have received their, and their family's, consent, sometimes explicit, sometimes tacit. Her position in the 1950s rural, gossip-filled village is common, and accepted, knowledge, as is her 'adoption' of Maria Listru, her soul child, whose birth mother cannot afford to keep her.

But Maria does not know about *Tzia* Bonaria's mission, to bring quick release at the end of life, and is devastated when she finds out. This remarkable story, of an archaic and culturally accepted euthanasia, is beautifully and heart breakingly told. Michela Murgia (b.1972) shows a recurrent interest in women's issues in her fiction; she has already appeared as author of *Viaggio in Sardegna*, a guide to her native island.

Paskedda Selis Zau and Uprising Against Enclosure: *de Su Connottu* 1868

As the introduction to this chapter suggests, banditry was not always caused by vendettas and vengeance; another cause, particularly in the Barbagia region, was the urge to rebel against a distant non-Sardinian bureaucratic, sometimes tyrannical government which understood nothing about the lives of its people, notably of its peasants and pastoralists. A law enacted in 1820, and built upon later in the nineteenth century, proved, eventually, to be the last straw.

1820 was the penultimate year of the reign of King Vittorio Emanuele I of Piedmont Sardinia; his brother, Carlo Felice, came to the throne in 1821 and, in 1827, replaced Eleonora d'Arborea's *Carta de Logu*, with its protections concerning land, with new legislation. By 1868, when the uprising known as *Su Connottu* (literally, 'the known') took place, Italy had been unified since 1861; government was then even further removed from the people of Sardinia than it had been under earlier Piedmontese rule, and the more recent 'perfect fusion'.

The first Enclosure Act (*l'Editto delle Chiudende*) came into effect in 1820, overturning generations, centuries even, of land usage. The mass of people depended on the land for their very existence. For landowners, however, such as those described earlier, land was a means of accumulating wealth and status. The Act meant the enclosure of land that had until then been under collective ownership by introducing de facto private property. Those it most affected began action against the law but, though sometimes violent, it was sporadic. The situation was worsened when the law was strengthened in 1858. State-owned land on which the villagers had previously had grazing and wood collecting rights by dint simply of long-term traditional use (*ademprivio/ademprivili*) was alienated. It was divided up and sold off, to be enclosed by wall, fence or hedge, creating what were known as *tanca*. Rumblings of rebellion gathered momentum in 1866, the climax of which was reached with riots in Nuoro in April 1868 when pastoralists were given three days to vacate the land on which they depended.

Su Connottu, the cry of the protesters of the Nuoro uprising, was led by **Paskedda Selis Zau** (Paschedda, Pasca, Pasqua; 1808–1882), a commoner, a widow with 10 children. You have to see her, on Sunday 26 April, marching at the head of what started as a demonstration, with her petticoat on a stick hoisted high instead of a flag, and accompanied by her daughter **Tonia**, together with **Tonia Porcu** and **Tonia Ormena** – 300 people in all. What they were determined to obtain, as they harangued the crowd, and called out to City Council members, was the restoration of the old and well-known system of land management. The demonstration turned into a riot, with an attack on the town hall (Palazzo Martoni), the tearing down of its doors, and the burning of archives, particularly the documents of sale of the former communal land. Not content with that, the crowd also burnt furniture, and generally looted the place, having snatched the rifles of the national guard attempting to exert control.

How far the above details have been exaggerated is unclear, as is how far Paskedda and the other women took part in the rioting and destruction. Certainly there were other women there, wives and daughters of the men involved. Sixty-nine were eventually arrested, and charged with causing a riot and looting. Ten were charged with instigating the riot, mostly men of standing, among them the priest Sebastiano Deledda, Grazia Deledda's uncle. They were sent for trial to the Court of Appeal in Cagliari. Paskedda's name was not one of them. What happened to her and her family after 26 April eludes me. In any case, as *Su Connottu* came to be seen as a struggle by the poor for their survival, the Minister for Justice decreed the granting of an amnesty to the defendants which was signed on 29 November by the king.

Also in November that year, a parliamentary commission of enquiry was set up which went to the island in 1869. There Ignazio Aymerich, Marquese

Laconi was one of those who vainly attempted to explain the economic problems of the island to the commissioners. The only positive result was a useful report on mining. With the unification of Italy came exploitation of Sardinia's natural resources: new mining laws were introduced, and deforestation was increasingly apparent. Mining is one of those industries in which Sardinian and foreign women played a part, as chapter 10 shows.

A poem, *Passio – A su Connottu*, by a witness of events, anti-clerical Salvatore Rubeddu, highlighting the part Paskedda and her women companions played in the events of 26 April 1868, does suggest that they took part in the sacking of the town hall. (The poem is written in *latino maccheronico*; to translate this as pig Latin is too simple a description of the melange of languages, but it is rather inaccessible to the uninitiated; it is available on the internet by typing in that title). A Pasca Selis Zau Association in Nuoro is behind theatrical events to keep her memory alive and, in 2019, a new piazza in the historic quarter of the town, Santu Predu, was named Paskedda Zau in her honour.

In his article 'Sea and Sardinia: Pax Britannica versus Vendetta in the New Italy' (2007), Owain Wright gives a useful general conclusion when he writes,

> In Sardinia, the prevalence of vendetta, livestock-rustling and banditry ensured that defiance of state authority lasted until well into the twentieth century, when ethnologists examining its endurance came to the conclusion that the Sardinians have been in a constant state of rebellion for two millennia.

Where women are concerned in this prevalence of vendetta, vengeance, *banditesse* and resistance, conflicting truths are apparent. Women are both strong and active in events, and victims. Judgements by mainland Italians, let alone complete foreigners, are best kept sparing. Even Sardinians from other parts of the island may find their fellow citizens sometimes difficult to fathom, as also even to understand each other's dialect. What the story does begin to show is the variety and richness of Sardinia's history, particularly that of place, a history which, inevitably, feeds the present.

8 – From Tabarca to Carloforte, San Pietro 1738–1918

Introduction

Just as chapter 7 concentrates on the region in the east of Sardinia, so this chapter tells how the small island of San Pietro, off the main island's coast, to the south-west of Cagliari, came not only to have its distinctive past and culture, but also to play a particular part in the history of Sardinia and its women.

Tabarca 1540–1737

In 1540, in the Bay of Tunisia, opposite the town of Tunis, lay the small, rocky island of Tabarca. That year Count Agostino Lomellini of Genoa obtained a concession to Tabarca from the Bey of Tunis and, in 1542, 300 families, about 1000 people, emigrated to Tabarca from Pegli near Genoa and other places in Liguria where the Lomellini had lands. They were primarily to exploit the coral banks that abounded around Tabarca, but they also developed trade in fish, cereals, legumes, oil, honey, wax, wool and leather between Tunisia and the Republic of Genoa. What part women played in this does not seem to be recorded, but it is easy to suppose that it was all hands to the pump. The Tabarchini were to live there for two centuries, ensuring profit for the Lomellini family who had a monopoly over the coral and so grew increasingly rich and powerful. In the early years, it made little difference that in 1574 the Ottoman Turks conquered Tunisia, for Tabarca can be described then commercially as a free port and, thus, religiously a link between Genoese, Arabs, Turks and Jews.

In 1731 Stefano Lomellini, Doge of the Republic of Genoa, ceded Tabarca, with its 2000 inhabitants, to his cousin Giacomo. Incursions by pirates, deteriorating relations between Genoa and Turks, depletion of coral stocks and over-population had made the island unprofitable and unsustainable. As a result, in 1737, Lomellini asked the new king of Savoy, Carlo Emanuele III, whose territories included Sardinia, to cede an uninhabited island 10 miles off the main island to the Tabarchini. The reason for the king's positive response was that a fortified and inhabited island should help to keep marauders away from Sardinia. Agostino Tagliafico, aged 47, a leading light of Tabarca, made a two-day survey of the island.

San Pietro 1738

In February 1738, led by Tagliafico, the first group of 86 settlers arrived in Cagliari from Tabarca. They were followed in April by another 302, in all 100 families. By then, the Tabarchini had moved to San Pietro. Twenty-six families, 79 people, then arrived from Liguria. The island had not always been uninhabited; pre-Nuragic and then Nuragic remains, such as a *Domus di Janas*, have been found. The Phoenicians arrived there in the eighth century BC. The Romans called the island Accipitrum Insula (Island of Sparrowhawks); in Italian it became Isola degli Sparvieri. And, indeed, it is noted for what are often called Eleanora's falcons, in honour of the *giudicessa* who sought to preserve them.

Tagliafico's wife was **Maria Nicoletta Luxoro**, born on Tabarca, mother of six daughters. What is more, Nicoletta was pregnant during the journey and gave birth to a son soon after arrival, because the list of arrivals says it was a family of nine. Their son died, though, either later that year or in 1740, depending on sources (of which these events have many on the internet available to mine and piece together with discretion). The first baptism, in July, was of **Maria Caterina** (b.1738), daughter of 35-year-old **Maria Felicia** and Nicola **Ferraro** who had married in Tabarca in 1735. They were to have eight children in all, and already had two other daughters when they left Tabarca. Little Caterina was on the passenger list from Tabarca but, as she was said to have been born in 1738, the list may have been made later than the party's first arrival in Sardinia.

By the time of the christening wooden houses were being built, and the development included cisterns for water, a church and fortifications against the fear of invasion from the Berbers of North Africa. The new settlement was named Carloforte, in honour of the king. Its inhabitants were to be called both Tabarchini and Carlofortini (or Carolini, after the Latin version of the king's name, Carolus), and their language to this day is particular, akin to Ligurian, their culture, including cuisine, is a mixture of Ligurian, Sardinian and North African.

It is worth pausing for a moment to imagine what it was like for the women arriving, most of them with several children who had to be kept warm, fed, and protected from harm and sickness. As well as six daughters to care for, Nicoletta Tagliafico would be grieving for her dead son. Perhaps the women remained in Cagliari until some building had been done, but that July baptism is said to have been in Carloforte, so they were by then already on the smaller island, and there is nothing to suggest that the Tabarchini women were anything but hardy.

The men were certainly on San Pietro by May. Three delegates were elected to travel then to the church in Portoscuso, which faced Carloforte across the water, to swear an oath of loyalty to King Carlo Emanuele. They were Agostino Tagliafico, who was made Count of San Pietro, Francesco **Vacca**, whose wife was **Maria Antonietta**, mother of four, and Simone **Rosso**, married to 33-year-old **Apollonia**, both born in Pegli. They had six children. Family names recur through the years and close relationships through marriage between families in both the small island communities of Tabarca and San Pietro are obvious.

In January 1739, a fire destroyed 22 of the wooden houses; they were rebuilt in brick, but not until 1744. I have found no evidence of casualties, but it must have been a frightening experience, as well as the loss of precious property such as furniture, clothing, utensils. In 1746 a malaria epidemic hit the island; among the deaths was that of Agostino Tagliafico, leaving Nicoletta with their six daughters to look after.

Meanwhile, in 1741, the Bey of Tunis with 300 men on eight galliots invaded Tabarca, dismantled the fortifications, destroyed the church, warehouses and houses and took 840 prisoners, its remaining inhabitants, reducing them to slavery. The last of them were eventually, in 1753, liberated through the efforts of the Pope, who freed some Mohammedan prisoners in exchange, Carlo III of Spain and Carlo Emanuele, as well as being occasioned by the death of the Bey's son. One of the negotiators was the Genoan Giovanni **Porcile**, who had married Tagliafico's eldest daughter **Elisabetta**, and whose granddaughter, **Anna Porcile**, is to feature largely in the later story. Many of the slaves who had survived were brought to Carloforte. Some went to the neighbouring island of Sant'Antioco and founded Calasetta.

During the war that followed the French Revolution of 1789 France had, as has been described earlier, declared war on the kingdom of Sardinia; its court in Turin, Piedmont, had joined the Coalition against France. In January 1793, a French fleet, which had been baulked by a gale from attacking Cagliari, occupied San Pietro as a naval base. The only obvious result for the Carolini was that they hid the 1786 statue of Carlo Emanuele with its two figures crouching at his feet – a Muslim Turkish slave, and a Christian Tabarchina woman slave with a child in her arms. Somewhat damaged, the retrieved statue is still there. In May, the French were expelled by Spain, another member of the Coalition, at the behest of the viceroy of Sardinia, and replaced with Spanish troops. However benign the occupations, mothers would doubtless have feared for the well-being of their daughters. The legacy of the French campaign was a revolt in Sardinia against the Savoyards, discussed in chapter 6.

September 1798

During the night of 2–3 September 1798, the worst fears of the Carolini Sardinians of Carloforte were realised: 600–700 Berbers from Tunis arrived. They stayed for several days, laying waste to Carloforte – setting houses on fire, and killing many inhabitants.

Richard Zacks, in *The Pirate Coast* (2005), suggests the reason for this attack: for the Bey of Tunis this was a legitimate war against Sardinia 'which had refused to pay tribute to him for the right to navigate the Mediterranean'. But 'to the rest of the world, these seven ships were Barbary pirates, part of a centuries-old extortion scheme'. There was a twist to it. Not only was the leader of the attack an Italian converted to Islam – Muhammed Rumelli – but, according to Zacks, the nameless pilot from Capri who led the vessels safely into the harbour at Carloforte had a personal reason for his betrayal. He had married a woman from San Pietro who had abandoned him; he was convinced that she was now 'cuckolding' him on the island. 'He had turned Turk to seek his revenge.'

The raid was heard about in the outside world on 4 September. A rescue was attempted by the French frigate *Bandine*, which happened to be in Cagliari, but adverse winds thwarted the attempt. A French naval officer who arrived after the raiders' departure, found five women dead in their beds from knife or scimitar wounds; one of them was the 'unfaithful wife'. A Sardinian historian later called her **'fishwife Helen'**.

Other murdered women are more fully named by 'AntonRiva' in the 2016 blog *'Invasione Barbaresca di Carloforte 3 Settembre 1798'*; details are added from my internet searches in 'MyHeritage Family Trees'. **Maddalena Ageno** (née Vian), 48-year-old mother of 10, desperately hanging on to the body of her 58-year-old husband Filippo, from whom she could not detach his killers, was pinned to him through her throat. **Maria Armeni**, wounded by a gunshot, saw her husband taken away to die, and was suffocated with her baby suckling at her breast. Pregnant **Rosa Parodi** was killed as she begged in vain for mercy for her unborn child. **Anna** (Antonietta) **Leone** (née Pittaluga?), 28-year-old mother of six, mortally wounded, was left carelessly to die. Her youngest child seems to have been born that year. These women were descended from, or had married into, families which had sought refuge on San Pietro from Tabarca.

More precious even than the loot the attackers piled into their vessels was their human cargo, which could be either sold as slaves or ransomed. On 6 September, they took 950 (or 825) Carolini, mainly women and children, into servitude, throwing most of them, dressed as they had been in bed, into the ships' holds for the four-day journey to Tunis.

The Dutch consul in Tunis, Antoine Nyssen, recorded details of their fate in his diary (as recorded in Marco Sioli's article, *'Una Schiavitu Impossibile: Anna Porcile e William Eaton'* (An Impossible Slavery). Among those kept above the holds were six *'jeunes filles'*:

> Young girls whom, alas, that they were still so, were selected by the Rais [captains] to serve their filthy desires, and the most disgusting forms of volupté were their pastimes during the voyage.

Among the captives were Agostino Tagliafico's nephew, Carlo, his wife **Maddalena Pittaluga** and her sister-in-law **Anna Tagliafico**, married to Sebastiano Repetto. Another family, one related by marriage to the Tagliaficos, was the Porciles – **Barbara Porcile** (née Onnis) and her husband Antonio. They had married in Carloforte in 1772 and the first of at least five daughters was born a year later. Three of the five were among those abducted with their parents; the only one whose presence is certain (because of her fate) was, as already noted, 12- or 13-year-old Anna. Antonio's father, husband of Elisabetta Tagliafico, Count of Antioco Giovanni Porcile, the negotiator of 1741, was by then nearly 80 years old, and a year later was sent by the King of Sardinia to Tunis to attempt to negotiate the freedom of the captives. But it came to nothing and a careful Porcile family tree on the internet site has his death in 1799 in Tunis.

For some reason, the English consul in Carloforte was not captured. Although one source says that his house was the only one left untouched, a more likely explanation is that he was among those who managed to escape to the mountains or by boat to Portoscuso. Although the French vice-consul, Louis Rombi, his wife and children were taken, they were almost immediately released in a boat without rudder or oars.

Another captive, details of whose fate is well known, was nine-year-old **Francesca Rosso** (c.1789–1848). Five nuclear Rosso families were among the captives, according to the detailed '*Tabarquins*' (2006) by Josyanne Massa and George Gander, drawing on five years of research by Guy-Joseph Fouché, a Rosso descendant. But Francesca's family does not appear to have been among them. Although another source speaks of her twin sister **Teresa** being taken, I can find no other mention of her, though the same source says that she remained in Tunis at the time of liberation. Their mother was **Anna Sofia Cappai**, wife of Bartolomeo **Rosso,** and they had three other children. The Massa documents talk of Francesca (no mention of Teresa) being torn from her mother's breast. But why was their mother not taken or killed? How most of the family escaped captivity, but not their young daughters, is puzzling. An answer concerning Sofia will emerge later.

It is fair to assume, in view of what happened to her afterwards, that Francesca Rosso was not among the '*jeunes filles*' sexually abused on the voyage to Tunis. A first-hand picture of the slaves as, on arrival in Tunis, they were forced to walk for two hours to the Bey's palace, was captured by Nyssen:

> I saw them harassed by blows, destroyed by fatigue, covered with dust and dying of thirst, dragged into the scorching streets without shoes and hats. There was a large crowd drunk with joy at seeing so many Christian victims of the courage of their soldiers.

The Story of Francesca Rosso (Jenet Lela Beia) 1798–1806

At the Bardo, the Bey's palace, he inspected the 950 captives, 702 of them women and children. To him, each one had a monetary value – women were double the value of men; virgins were at a premium. According to Zacks, the foreign consuls begged the Bey not to split up the families, nor sell them to Algerian slave traders. He seems to have listened because, for example, each Rosso family became the possession of leading citizens of Tunis, including foreign consuls. One family went to Maitre Don Ignazio Soler who, it is assumed, was the Spanish consul. All, that is, except Francesca. Speculation is that the girl was kept at the Bardo to be a companion to two other girls of the same age. Did the same happen to her twin sister?

That seems to have worked until the succession of a new bey whose younger brother, Sidi Mustafa, took a shine to Francesca. His mother disapproved of a relationship with a Christian girl and had her dispatched to the home of the English consul, Corsican Perkins Magra. History does not relate how she then could not have been released. But the prince found her and his mother gave in, recalling Francesca to the Bardo.

Dates may be confused in what followed, and it is certainly complicated to disentangle the Beys of Tunis to fit. But the couple are said to have married in 1810 when Francesca was 21. She forsook her Christian faith and took the name Jenet Lela Beia, and her husband agreed to a monogamous marriage. The most detailed source says that their son was born that year, yet his biographical details and lists of Beys of Tunis say that he was born in 1806. Another source says that Francesca was married at 17 (at the same time sticking to the 1810 date of the marriage, which would not fit if she had been nine in 1798). The younger age seems more likely. I therefore suggest that she was married in 1806, the year of her son's birth. There is no suggestion that he was born before the marriage. The story of Francesca, her son and, indeed, her mother, will be resumed a little later; it is necessary now to return to the other captives.

Return to Freedom 1803

Some criticism has been made by readers of this chapter in draft of the profusion of women's names. My objection to omitting some names to please them is that this is the one chance the women have for the unique story of their lives to linger here in context. I feel responsible, particularly after all they went through. You can always skip them, though their descendants may not want to.

It was to be five years before most of the Carolini slaves were released and returned home. Although almost immediately the Pope assigned funds from ecclesiastical benefits to meet the ransom demands, and a financial treaty was signed between the Bey and the Court of Sardinia, the Court failed to meet the large demand in the limited time. Eventually those still alive were released, partly through the intervention of Napoleon, partly ransomed, partly in exchange for Tunisian prisoners.

Of the names that are already familiar, the following are on a 1799 list, published as '*Les Tabarquins de Tunis 1741-1799*' published in *Revue Tunisienne* (1943); it is not clear if this refers to those captured, with the number of family members in brackets: Rosso (58), Leone (52), Ripetto (27), Ferraro (23), Vacca (12), Rombi (42), Parodi (41), Armeni (7), Pittaluga (2), Tagliafico (5) and Vian (5). There is something more to be said about three other names: Moretto (7), Gierra (12) and Porcile (7).

On 15 November 1800, a young Carolino slave, Nicola Moretto, took advantage of a moment of distraction by his master to wander off. Just beyond the beach, near the town of Nabeul, between a lemon tree and a date palm, he found a dark wooden effigy of the Madonna that probably came from the prow of a ship, and was somewhat damaged by the elements. Wiping it clean, he hid it under his jacket and took it away. For safety's sake, he gave it into the keeping of a Carolino priest. When news of the find leaked out, the community of slaves took heart, seeing it as a divine sign that gave them hope for the future.

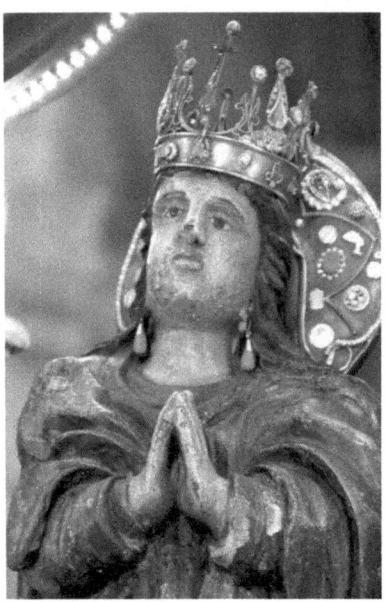

27. Simulacrum of Madonna of the Slave, from the internet

When the slaves were freed in 1803, the sacred relic accompanied them back to Carloforte and, in 1807, construction began on an oratory to house it on what is now Via XX Settembre. The Oratorio dello Schiavo (the Oratory of the Slave) was completed, after some delay, in 1815. For some time the date of enslavement was marked; more recently 15 November, the day of the effigy's discovery, is a public holiday when the Madonna, given a crown in 1964, is carried in procession through the streets in remembrance of both slavery and liberation. The Oratory, known as Gexetta d'u Previn, is open in the morning when the Madonna can be seen in the apse above a small altar. The Madonna of the Slave is the protector of the Carlofortini.

But 117 Carlofortini died during their years of enslavement. Among the 12 **Gierra** taken were Giovanni Battista, 34 in 1798, and his wife, 29-year-old **Nicoletta** (née Ferraro). It is not clear how many children they had at the time, but they appear to have been with their parents. Wife and husband may have gone to different masters, as suggested in the Italian internet source on Hiera.it – 'The return of the slaves (not all)'. But they must have been able to meet, because in 1800 another son was born, and died the same year. Giovanni was badly treated, beaten and insulted. He complained to the negotiator Count Porcile who begged a certain Giuseppe Perasso to redeem the family, and Perasso did so. But it was in vain where Giovanni was concerned because he died of pestilence before they could return home, leaving Nicoletta in debt to Perasso and unable to repay him because the family had lost everything in the looting of Carloforte. She petitioned the King of Sardinia for help, the outcome of which eludes me. It is hard to imagine what Nicoletta went through from the moment of the raid, and any end to her troubles leaves no trace.

The Story of Anna Porcile 1798–1826

Ten young women remained in Tunis at the time of liberation. The source that mentions Teresa Rosso includes her and her twin Francesca among them. The fate of seven of them has left no trace that I can find, but that of Anna Porcile is another exception.

According to consul Nyssen's diary, Anna was one of the *'jeunes filles'* sexually abused on the voyage from Carloforte. Certainly because she was nubile and apparently lovely, Rais Muhammed Rumelli was ready to make her his own once they reached Tunis. Marco Sioli draws, too, on Richard Zacks' account, and on a letter in Italian which Anna wrote from London in 1805 – a letter which he was good enough to send me the original of and then, at my request, to make a typescript of. (Maurizio Piga generously translated the not-always-easy handwriting for me.)

From these various sources, much of Anna's story can be told – the gaps have to be filled in by hypotheses. However much her life diverges from Sardinia, she was Sardinian. And, through all that is to follow, we have to remember that not only was she barely 13 at the beginning, but that she came from the top drawer in Sardinian society: her grandfather was a count,

28. Last page of Anna Porcile letter, 1805, thanks to Marco Sioli

her uncle Don Vittorio an admiral in the Sardinian navy. She would have been gently brought up and probably unfamiliar with hardship before that night in 1798.

Rumelli would give Anna up for 16000 piastres; he demanded an immediate answer. It is not clear how Anna's family appear to have been able to move around Tunis, but her father, Don Giovanni Porcile, turned to a Tuscan merchant in Tunis who lent him the entire sum. But she was not free, for she was the collateral for her father's loan. He was then allowed to travel within Europe to raise funds; but in the chaos of the Napoleonic War, he failed. So the Tuscan sold the debt to the Tunisian prime minister. 1799 came to an end; negotiations all round to free the slaves ground on; the prices of women dropped; some of the women had given birth. On 10 October 1800, the 87-year-old prime minister holding Anna's debt died, it passed to the Bey – who demanded that the family repay it immediately, or she would either enter his seraglio or be auctioned in the slave market at Istanbul.

Anna's father was still abroad trying to raise money; her mother and sisters went through the possibilities of doing so via one of the consuls, a Catholic Redemptionist charity or moneylenders. It was only a day later that they presented themselves at the house of the United States consul since the previous year, William Eaton. The 35-year-old former army captain, who had already been shocked by the slavery rampant in Tunis, could not withstand the tears of the three women. He later wrote, 'Imagination better than language can paint their distress.'

I have seen no evidence that the Porcile family spoke English, or that, at that stage, Eaton spoke any language other than English. What would he have done? For that immediate meeting, the participants might have muddled through with some help from Eaton's staff. But the relationship with Anna was to last some months. From her 1805 letter, it is clear that she taught Eaton Italian, but that would have taken time. He needed to be able to communicate precisely with the Porciles. This is where supposition must intrude.

By 1805, Anna was no longer Porcile, but Hargrave(s). By determined digging, the full name of her English husband – Lewis Chadwick Hargrave – emerges. He had lived and worked on the Barbary coast for 30 years, probably officially as a merchant, unofficially, I suggest, paid to provide information to the British government. Later evidence shows that he was an unofficial vice-consul, probably an unpaid position. In a Memorial he wrote to the Foreign Office in July 1804, he says that, in addition to English, he spoke Italian, French, Spanish and Arabic. His grandfather had been governor of Gibraltar; his father was chief engineer in Mahon, when it was a British naval port and capital of the Balearic Islands, and Hargrave was later to spend many years as consul there. And he not only knew but also worked with Eaton.

Among the papers in the Library of Congress of the then US Secretary of State James Madison is a letter of 14 December 1801 to him from Rufus

King, US Minister to London, which provides convincing evidence for such suppositions:

> By the annexed Copies of Letters respecting the articles prepared and preparing as a present for the Bey of Tunis you will perceive how far this business is completed. Mr Hargraves, by whom we have Sent the Box of Jewels, has been many years settled at Tunis; and although it would have been better to have Sent the whole of the articles had they been all ready, as Mr Eaton has repe[a]tedly informed the Bay that they would be sent by Hargraves, I was apprehensive that it might involve Mr Eaton in new Difficulties should Hargraves return empty handed.

There are remarks concerning insurance, ending, 'whether Hargraves proceeds from Gibraltar in an American Frigate to Tunis, or continues his voyage in the English Frigate to Algiers, and then by Land to Tunis'. From this, it is easy to suggest that Hargrave and Anna met through Eaton, initially when he was called upon to act as interpreter.

Following the meeting with the Porcile women, Eaton agreed to guarantee a six-month loan to Anna's father, as Zacks says, 'allowing himself to stand as surety for the repayment of $5,000'. As Eaton was later to write to Porcile, 'I ransomed your daughter because being in my house, both the honour of my flag and my own sensibility dictated it.' But he had no funds of his own and no authority from his government to back up his guarantee.

At the end of six months, Porcile had no money to repay the implied loan, but Eaton was required to do so, and was forced to borrow the money from a Tunisian merchant. It would require too much space to quote from the spate of letters over the years from Eaton to Porcile asking for repayment, and the internal letters within the US administration because the debt was eventually $22000 and caused real problems to the US navy and the consul who took over from Eaton when he left his posting on 10 March 1803. Porcile eventually thanked the US President for his help in the rescue of his daughter, while Eaton seethed at his cheek.

Meanwhile, Anna was living in Eaton's house. It is suggested that she was Eaton's secretary; it was presumed that she was his concubine. This is where one must turn to her 1805 letter and read between the lines. By the time she wrote that letter, and it was to Eaton, she had been in London with Hargrave since January 1804. She talks of three children. At first you assume that they were Hargrave's by a first wife; it is fair to assume that he was 50 or so by the time he met Anna. And to read his will of 1834, eight years after Anna's death, you would assume that was so. His son James Augustus, as the only male, is given precedence in what was a considerable estate, mostly in land and its rents, which had been inherited through Hargrave's extended Chadwick family; his daughter Louisa Maria is left £4000, and the children of his by-then-deceased daughter Carolina Catherine, are left the same.

But Anna's letter makes it quite clear that the children are hers; she talks of them as 'my disgraces'. Somehow, between 1798 when she was barely 13, and the end of 1805 when she was but twenty, she had had three children, she makes clear that none had been born in England – though all three reply to her Italian in fluent English. In an email to me, Marco Sioli suggests that James was the result of the sexual abuse Anna had undergone at the beginning of her captivity. But not only does Hargrave's will make it clear that James is his, but after his father's death, James takes on the long-running court case connected with the complicated Hargrave/Chadwick family inheritance. What is more, internet chat, between descendants and responses to them regarding Hargrave and his children, lists Carolina first, suggesting that she was the first born. And would Anna have named a child conceived by rape after her sisters Carolina and Caterina?

When you search for clues as to Carolina's father, Anna seems to provide them. When she writes to Eaton of 'our dear Carolina' she could be talking about the daughter of her and Hargrave, but she starts by referring to all three as 'my'. Then in a subsequent paragraph she writes 'and in particular your beloved Carolina begs me to cordially revere you'. It is interesting that Zacks should mention Eaton's 'deep-set large blue eyes' because Anna, in what to me is code between her and Eaton, writes: 'our dear Carolina is more and more lively, brave and pleasant with her beautiful blue eyes.' And there is a PS to the letter: 'Carolina sends you hugs in return.' (Marco Sioli suggests in an email that the reason Carolina is called that is because she is a Carolina from Carloforte, however her life unfolded. That could be an added factor.)

And yet! Also in that letter Anna writes,

> I heard the story of Miss Nissen [the Dutch consul's daughter] becoming Mrs Humbert. This would have given an example to the bad people of Tunis: before talking about others one needs to look at oneself.

Was she referring to rumours about relations between Eaton and herself? Or about her relations with Hargrave, and her pregnancies? When they married, if they did in fact do so, where and when was it? I can find no record, though it is perfectly possible that they did so in Tunis, perhaps even before Carolina was born. It is striking, though, that when Anna was buried in a Gibraltar cemetery in 1826 she is called Hargrave's 'unnamed wife'. Perhaps she simply referred to gossip about **Teresa Nyssen** and Jean-Emile Humbert before their marriage. But several sentences make it clear that there had been gossip about her and Eaton who, it should be noted, had a wife and family in the United States. And it is clear, too, that she is replying to a letter of his:

> The gratefulness that You favour me with reminds of those times of your so unpleasant and dangerous illness [and] make me say that the assistance I provided you had no other aim than that of my friendship and esteem that I felt towards You; and I repeat that I will always [be] willing to do the same if I had to face the same situation, regardless of the negative

gossips while I believe (and this is my belief) that an act of humanity and sincerity cannot possibly be disapproved unless by people without principles, without feelings and of an evil heart; therefore you are not in debt of any gratefulness other than friendship, since I am fully satisfied to have deserved your gratitude.

Is she saying that she and Eaton never had sexual relations, whatever the gossips said? The worst offender, excoriated in a second PS, is the British consul, Magra; though the 'us' may well be Anna and Hargrave: '[He] has missed no opportunity to do us down with his beastliness, but the truth will always prevail. Enough! You know his character. It is unnecessary to say more.'

In such a long letter, touching on so many subjects, it is strange that she never mentions the large sum of money that her father owed Eaton, and later the US government, particularly as ransoming her had caused him so much trouble. But then there are a lot of gaps.

Anna did not go to Carloforte, as Eaton apparently supposed, when she left Tunis, probably some time early in 1803. Possibly because of her 'disgraces', she did not feel able to, and now she was Hargrave's wife and she would expect to go to England if he went. They did not leave Tunis together, though; what is more, as she details her itinerary to England she says only 'I' – no mention of her children. She travelled first to Mahon, Minorca, and there she waited for nine months for Hargrave, or 'Mr H', to join her. Although she does not say so, Hargrave would have had long-standing contacts there as a result of the family connection. Is it possible that she was pregnant when she left Tunis and gave birth to Louise there? She gives no hint. After Hargrave's arrival, they travelled to Almeria in Spain and from there to Gibraltar, again no mention of children. They had the bad luck there of just missing a convoy to England – it was still wartime; 'Therefore we were obliged to stay there for three months up to the departure of another convoy which situation faced us with huge expenses and time wasted.' She did not mention the expense of nine months alone in Mahon. Finally they reached London on 22 January 1804.

It is worth pausing to take account of Anna's journey from Tunis – one that took over a year, much of it without Hargrave. Counting the months backwards, she must have left early in January 1803. She was 17 or 18 years old; she may have had children with her. Her years since 1798 would undoubtedly have hardened her, made her resourceful, but one needs only imagination to follow her until Hargrave's arrival with his contacts and know-how.

Further trouble awaited the Hargraves in England:

> Mr H left no stone unturned in order to apply for public employment. The tragedy has been that all the Ministers have been changing quite often, and therefore the friends of one Minister are not friends with a different Minister. Every care that had been taken was useless, so that nearly 20

months have gone by without Mr H getting not only any employment but no promise to get a position either.

Hence Hargrave's Memorial of July 1804, and its apparent unsuccess, and hence one of Anna's purposes in writing as she did to Eaton: she begged him to find Hargrave a job. The Memorial, the application for a consular post, says that Hargrave had been vice-consul in Tunis for six years, and then proconsul for three, following the death of the British consul, James Traill. But David Wilson's exhaustive list, 'Consular Officials in the Ottoman Empire', does not contain his name in Tunis, leaving the supposition that it was an unofficial posting, known about in the Foreign Office for its usefulness, and therefore able to be mentioned in the Memorial, but not formalised. The irony is that the only job that came up in 1805 was to take them back to the Barbary Coast:

> At present, thanks to some friends of Mr H, he found two merchants' Houses willing to start trade in Algiers; ... Mr H accepted the offer, and therefore we will all leave together on the first ship to the Mediterranean, which is thought will leave in February.

She was not looking forward to it. And it is unclear whether or not they went. All that we know, for the moment, is that Lewis Hargrave was consul and consul general to the Balearic islands, based in Mahon, from 1811, continuing after Anna's death in 1826, and probably until almost his own death in 1837, though he drew up his 1834 will in London. There is something ineffably sad that Anna Porcile Hargrave, with a young life of such moment, should thus disappear from history. But her children had children. Carolina was to marry Joseph-Louis Kuhn, paymaster of the Marine Corps of the United States, which may, or may not, be significant. Her children were living in America in 1834.

The Nightmare Returns 1815: Sant'Antioco

Unfortunately for the descendants of the Tabarchini on the two islands of San Pietro and Sant'Antioco, 1798 was not the last raid resulting in killing and enslavement, in spite of strengthened fortifications. This time it was Sant'Antioco that was to suffer. On 16 October 1815, a hard-fought resistance failed to save 150 of the inhabitants from capture. The commander of the fort, Efisio **Melis-Alagna** was killed. His wife, **Angelica** (Angelina) was there too, and worked alongside him carrying munitions for the soldiers. She was taken into slavery, alongside **Scolastica Mainas** and **Agata Deidda**, wife of a corporal, and her two daughters and two girls she was looking after. Some differences stand out. The rest of the 150, listed in full in the internet archive posting *'Assalto a Sant'Antioco'* were men; many wives and children were left; many of the wives were pregnant; and the names of those on the list were not the family names of either the original Tabarchini, or those Carolini from neighbouring San Pietro who had been enslaved in 1798. In that earlier raid, several Carolini had escaped from Carloforte to Sant'Antioco.

Bey Mother Jenet Lea Beia Reunited with Family 1837–1848

Some 10 years or so after Anna Porcile Hargrave, aged only 40, was buried in the 'old' graveyard, Santa Gracia, Gibraltar, Jenet Lela Beia, formerly Francesca Rosso of Carloforte, was reunited with her mother and sisters. Her husband had succeeded his brother as Bey in 1835. Their son was educated in Paris, but when his father died in 1837, she recalled him and he became Ahmed Bey, known as 'the Sardinian'. Under his rule, many reforms took place, including the abolition of slavery in 1846. He died in 1855 under mysterious circumstances, it is assumed because of his Christian blood and education.

As time went by, and memories of 1798 and 1815 faded, Carolini ventured, with permission, into Tunis waters to fish for tuna. Guy-Joseph Fouché describes what followed in *'Francesca Rosso et les Carlofortins'*. Francesca, by then Bey Mother, hearing of the presence of the Carlofortini, made herself known to them and asked if her own mother was still alive. When they answered yes, she burst into tears. Thereafter, they were made welcome at the Bardo. There came the day when she asked if they would bring her mother, and other Carlofortini familes to Tunis. After consideration, Sofia Cappai Rosso, in her eighties, set out.

On her arrival, she was led into a salon at the Bardo in which there were several women; she went to pick out the daughter she had not seen since she was dragged from her 30 years previously. I had thought that in the 1798 raid Francesca's mother was absent or in some way had escaped with the rest of her children. But that detail of their parting, if true, suggests that Sofia was left in Carloforte because she was pregnant.

All those years later, shaking with emotion, Sofia had no trouble recognising the splendid woman, now in her forties, from a large mole above her breast. She stayed with Francesca for several weeks. Relatives stayed longer, her older brother finally settling in Tunis. He brought Francesca's younger sister, **Antonietta** (b.*c*.1794), to her, and her son, Bartolomeo Giuliano, by her Italian husband stayed on in the Bardo, eventually becoming a colonel in the Turkish army. When Francesca's son, the Bey, died, she and his wife remained alone in a society full of pitfalls and perils. While her daughter-in-law hastened back to her own country, Francesca remained in Tunis until her death in 1848. There is a street named after her in Carloforte.

29 April 1918

There was one more danger and death to be faced by women of Carloforte. Towards the end of the First World War, following the torpedoing of two ships in a British convoy by a German submarine, the damaged ships took refuge in Carloforte's harbour; the submarine followed them in. The fort and the submarine exchanged cannonades and eight British sailors were killed. A plaque on a wall in Via XX Settembre is a memorial to two Carlofortini deaths; translated into English it reads:

At dawn on 29 April 1918, on the balcony above,
from a cannonade during combat
between the German submarine Ub-48
and English ships at anchor,
Mariangela Novella, 59 of Carloforte was killed
And **Giuseppina Nanni,** 29, of Iglesias.
May the weapons be silent and the peoples live in peace.

That is a later version of the plaque; an earlier one, probably dating from 1919, was taken down during the Fascist period:

At dawn on 29 April 1918 a German Submarine
Commanded by Lieutenant Steinhauer
fired five shots against the town.
Angela Novella and Giuseppina Nanni were killed here.
Remember it to eternal infamy.

Chapter 13 will tell the story of Sardinian women as anti-Fascist activists. Chapter 9 is about the women of two other Sardinian islands.

9 – The Other Islands: La Maddalena and Tavolara

Introduction

La Maddalena Archipelago, which lies a short distance off the northern coast of Sardinia, comprises seven main islands, including the eponymous one from which it takes its name. Santo Stefano, to the south of it, is known chiefly for the presence there until 2008 of an American naval base. The poet Antonella Anedda was born in Rome, but her family, of Sardinian Corsican descent, originated from La Maddalena and that is where her writing often takes her. In 'September 2001, Maddalena Archipelago. Island of S. Stefano' she writes lines about that familial descent that convey the more typical life of the island's earlier people:

> This small island riven underwater by US submarines,
> where my great-grandfather planted citrus fruits and vines,
> built cowsheds and brought ten cows from the mainland.
> Their trembling hoofs on the boat, the wind on their backs
> Only struck till then by rain from the north.
> They're still there, horns mingled with the sand,
> Deep-rooted skeletons, close up to the rocks, no longer afraid,
> No longer distinguishing pasture from sea.

Two other poems in Logudorese by Antonella Anedda from the collection *Archipelago* (2014), translated into English on the opposite page by fellow poet Jamie McKendrick, appear in earlier chapters.

In *Isolatria: Viaggio nell'Arcipelago della Maddalena* (2013), Antonella Anedda goes back earlier in time, writing of how the archipelago came to be called 'La Maddalena':

> [It] is said to be named after Mary Magdalene, not only because of her pre-eminence in the Christian story but also because legend has it that after the death of Christ, the saint was driven away from Palestine and, in her flight towards Marseille she came ashore on the island. They also say that her cult, not very widespread in Italy, but much taken in the south of France, explains the presence of the first Corsicans who came to the island on the track of the saint. At sunset every 22 July, her statue, with its long chestnut hair, is carried from the church dedicated to her in the middle of the town to the port, and from there to the Sardinian coast.

It is worth noting that the name Santa Maria Magdalena was not given until the sixteenth century, becoming in due course La Maddalena. And the church that bears that name only began to be constructed in 1780 and has undergone many changes since then, including a larger church built on the site in the years 1814–1819. Malta, too, lays claim to have been the island resting place of Mary Magdalene on her journey into exile, though in that case she is said to have been shipwrecked. What does remain in reality is the procession on La Maddalena of the statue, which Antonella Anedda vividly recollects, at the same time confirming the historical and continuing link with Corsica:

> The statue has a beautiful round face painted white, a green robe and a red shawl. In one hand is a book, in the other a skull. The procession used to pass twice under our window going one way to the Via Garibaldi, coming back the other by Via Amendola. Everyone was silent, standing outside the shops. Men and women, some in Gallurese costume, processed behind the statue of the Maddalena, praying at the tops of their voices. The mayor took part, and the bishop of Ajaccio [Corsica] and, when the American base was here, their commandant also processed. Every year we leant out and watched the procession while they disembarked the statue and then carried it back, at first on a lit up boat, then carried it again in their arms to the church. Meanwhile, the relics stayed in a shrine held by the bishop of Ajaccio and returned there at the end of the ceremony. The fiesta is simple, almost modest, apart from the fireworks.

It would be a pity to leave out a later sentence: 'On La Maddalena ... the statue is carried through the town like a family member, as if she were a sister a little under the weather in need of a breath of sea air.'

Nelson and his use of La Maddalena as his naval base between 1803 and 1805 was presaged in chapter 6. Like much in Sardinia's history, a good story tends to gain credence. Although it is known for a fact that during the 15 stays of Nelson and his fleet in La Maddalena he never went ashore, a romantic liaison with a local beauty was put about. She was said to be Signorina Leone which may be a confusion with his mistress Emma Hamilton whose maiden name was Lyon. Nelson was, however, concerned about two island women, the wife and daughter of Agostino Millelire, the commander of the island's port. He had overall responsibility for the victualling on each visit of Nelson's fleet with its 6000 men – an exercise that required him to reassure the island's men, of the population of 1200, that their women would be safe from predatory Jack Tars. It was not always easy as John R Gwyther relates in 'Nelson and Agostino Millelire' (2005): following the attempted rape of a shepherd's wife, a group of islanders fired on and seriously injured an officer who had gone ashore searching for some sailors.

At the same time, Millelire also strove to maintain the strict neutrality that was the policy of the government. But so civil were the relations between him and Nelson that he was invited to dine on board the admiral's flagship in May 1804. A letter of 12 May survives from Nelson to Millelire written in the hand of Alexander Scott, Nelson's chaplain and foreign language secretary. Its PS reads, translated here from the Italian, 'You do not inform me about the Signora's health, nor about the Signorina's. Is there a reason?'

It is not clear if Nelson had met the two on board and had since heard of ill health; if he had invited them and they, for cultural reasons, had given ill health as an excuse; or if Nelson, out of courtesy had simply asked after Millelire's family and been told that his wife and daughter were unwell.

In 1784, Millelire had married **Santa Zicavo**. They were to have 10 children but by the time of Nelson's visits, the two oldest boys were already dead. In May 1804, Santa probably already knew that she was pregnant with a son born that September, and that may have been the cause of her ill health. The signorina in question was probably 15-year-old **Maria Maddalena** (b.1789) who was to marry that September and whose reputation would need protecting.

The Millelire household had been involved earlier, when the viceroy and other Piedmontese officials were forced to flee Sardinia following the rebellion *Sa Die de Sa Sardigna* which started on 28 April 1794, as chapter 6 relates. Before they finally left Sardinia, and in the hopes of being able to return to Cagliari, they took refuge on La Maddalena in the new Millelire house on the waterfront. It is not clear if the family moved out, at some inconvenience, or if Santa Millelire, whose second son was born that year, had to cater for her 'guests'. The house still stands, on Cala Gavetta; this watercolour, by the later English Maddalena inhabitant William Craig, shows it straddling the Via Vittorio Emanuele. The image comes from *Millelire: Una Famiglia e le Sue Mille Storie* (Antonio Frau et al, 2013), a useful account of the extended Millelire family, including family trees. Millelire died at the end of 1816, and his widow was granted an annual pension of 200 new lire.

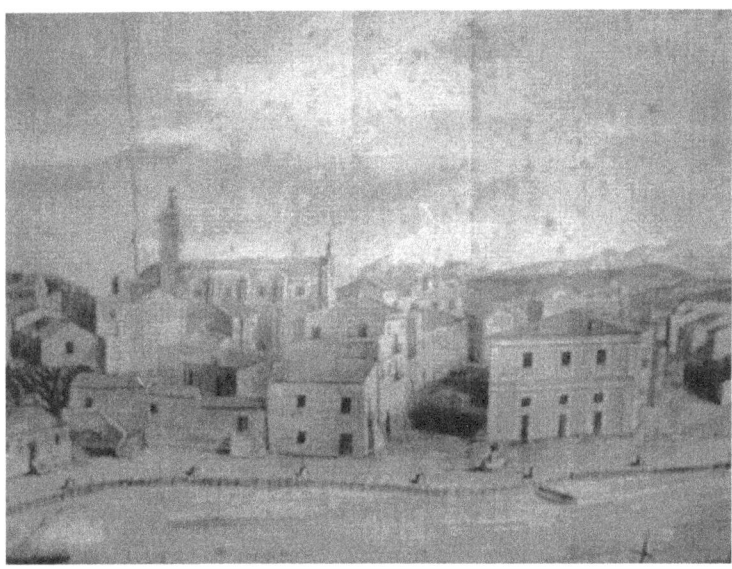

29. Millelire House, by William Craig, post-1848, from Frau, *Millelire*

Nelson was not the only important person to be connected to this northern archipelago in more modern times: of more interest to Sardinians and, indeed, Italians, was how their hero Garibaldi came to make his home on the nearby island of Caprera in 1855. There he lived with more than one wife, and children, and there he received women admirers. He was not the only resident: even before his arrival, several foreigners, starting in 1821, also found it an attractive place to settle or to exploit its natural resources.

William Craig, Women Lichen Collectors and the La Maddalena Family

William Sanderson Craig (1796–1867) is perhaps best known as British vice-consul, and then consul and busy merchant and entrepreneur in Cagliari between 1843 and 1867. There he was liked and respected. Mary Davey, arriving in Cagliari probably in 1848, writes of him in *Icnusa* (1860) where she calls him Mr Cg.:

> He is from the North Countrie, and one can see it in every curve and line of his honest, kindly, worthy face, which though not handsome, is lighted up with an expression at once so courteous and urbane, and with now and then a brightening flash of drollery, and a smile so pleasant that it gives one the idea of a sunbeam on a picture.

She continues by describing Mrs Craig:

> Mrs Cg. is sitting by his side. She is real Scotch, and a very kindly Scot too; and it is very piquant to hear her genuine hieland accent, for she 'minds the dear old countrie weel'.

That is all well and good, but much lies behind that account, for Craig's time in Sardinia starts in about 1821, when he was in his mid-twenties (at least one source suggests 1818 and his early twenties). He arrived then in La Maddalena, having been sent there by George Macintosh, his boss at a Glasgow tweed-making firm. His brief was to have collected and sent back to the firm in large quantities the lichen, *Roccella Tinctoria*, which grew abundantly on the islands' inaccessible rocks, and which was used to produce a much sought after purplish-red dye. I was interested to know who had the onerous task of collecting the lichen and was prompted to write to Dr Tiziana Cossu at Kew Gardens London who, with the link she sent me, confirmed what I had suspected:

> Women, girls and a few old people were mainly employed in this activity, both because they were paid much less, according to how things were then, and because men were engaged in forestry, hired to sail private boats, or were gardeners, shepherds or fishermen.

Craig was to tell Mary Davey about his time in La Maddalena, from 1824 until at least 1834, leaving out rather a lot of detail, though, as he said, 'I will pledge my word that it is true'; (what he told was the prelude to a ghost story which is not relevant here):

> The little town of Maddalena is a straggling place, containing upwards of 1600 inhabitants; they are very poor, and their island is very barren, save that their shores abound in valuable lichens and mosses used in dyeing, and their bays in nacres, nautili, and shellfish. I had settled in the island, for the purpose of collecting these lichens, and had taken apartments in an old house at the outskirts of the little town.

He did not mention who actually collected the lichen; it is not hard to imagine that it was back-breaking work and how it would be easy to cut oneself on jagged rocks, and even to fall and have more serious injuries. I'm told that they would not have worked in the heat of the day, but I wonder. Might there not sometimes have been time pressure caused by the imminent departure of a ship?

Craig continued in that account by describing his domestic arrangements, making a link with the feuding that was so much a feature of chapter 7:

> My housekeeper, **Paulina**, was a Corsican woman; she was descended from a race of bandits; she was tall, handsome, commanding, and seemed utterly insensible to fear. It was well she was so, for many a victim of lawless revenge would take refuge on our shores, and many a startling tale of horror greeted our ears.
>
> At the time I am speaking of, I had some very valuable merchandise concealed in the magazine, or ground-floor of the house; and for additional security, had been provided with a sentinel from the picket on guard at the fort.

In that account, Craig is leaving out much about his Maddalena life, the details of which are best told in the chapter 'William Sanderson Craig: Commerciante e Console Inglese' in *Inglesi nell'Arcipelago* (2005) by historians of La Maddalena Giovanna Sotgiu and Alberto Sega. In their account they write of Mary Davey's Craig story, 'If he really had a housekeeper who fits that description for any length of time, we certainly don't know about it.' And they continue:

> We know for sure that from 1823 until he left, perhaps in 1837, he lived with a young Maddalena woman (whose parents were from Caprera) called **Caterina Zagaglia**. This was an uninhibited family among which were many illegitimate births. ... Thus we know that from 1824, Caterina, living in sin (*'peccaminoso' rapporto*) with the Englishman William Craig, had six children, three of whom died very young.

A footnote gives the names and birthdates of these children, dates that are useful in piecing together contemporaneous aspects of his life:

Guglielmo – 1824
Maria Anna – 1826, died at 3 months
Anna Maria – 1827
Maria Francesca – 1831, died at 1 month
Maria Francesca – 1832, died at 5 months
Maria Francesca – 1834

But on 7 October 1828, confirmed in a marriage record that I have before me, William Sanderson Craig married in Glasgow **Jessie Fleming,** the Scottish Mrs **Craig** described by Mary Davey. That same Giovanna Sotgiu footnote lists Mrs Craig's children with her husband, though I do wonder about the date given for the first:

Jessica, born Glasgow 1825
William, born Palermo 1838
Cristina born Cagliari 1843

It seems unlikely, even with Craig's record with women, that Jessie Fleming, living in Scotland, would have had a child by him three years before their marriage, though they did have a daughter called Jessica. I suggest that the date in the record was unclear, and **Flora** and **Guglielma** are left out. But certainly Craig continued to have children by Caterina in La Maddalena after his marriage to Jessie. The birth of William in Palermo suggests that after Craig left La Maddalena, he spent some time, or years, in Sicily, accompanied by Jessie.

You would have thought that with his irregular lifestyle in La Maddalena he would be shunned by the local community. On the contrary, quickly fluent in Sardo, he became deeply embedded and accepted there, particularly by members of the long-established *gente per bene* who acted as godparents to his children by Caterina; Giovanna Sotgiu even lists them: 'Doctor Agostino Nicolari and his wife **Maria Domenica Susini**, Cavalier Benaglia, Francesco Susini and his wife **Anna Maria Millelire** ... the English vice-consul Domenico Peretti and his wife **Santa Susini**.'

Not everyone accepted the situation: a priest appointed as tutor in the local school blew the Craig/Caterina relationship into a scandal. He pointed out to his pupils that the Englishman had not been chastised under article 6 in an 1824 regulation which called for imprisonment for concubinage. He criticised the connivance of those, such as the godparents, in that state of affairs, drawing attention not only to Caterina having already had four children by Craig, but that she was pregnant again. He even suggested that Caterina's sister, **Maddalena Zagaglia**, was also Craig's concubine.

There is no evidence that anything changed as a result of that exposure. And the circumstances of their birth did not appear to affect the marriage prospects of the Craig Zagaglia children: Anna Maria was to marry English lawyer Edward West who also settled in the archipelago. As for the Craig children born to Jessie, Jessica and Cristina married the prosperous merchants, brothers Alfonso and Benvenuto Dol.

Settled in Cagliari, at least by 1843 when their daughter Cristina was born there, Craig and Jessie lived in the Marina area. He died in 1867, and was buried in the Bonaria cemetery. His widow and children – their son and two of their daughters – remained in Cagliari. The marriage records show that William, named as Guglielmo, married a Sardinian there the year before his father died. And there is evidence from a notice of a court case involving Jessica Craig Dol, by then a widow, in 1886. Caterina Zagaglia may have ended up in Genoa, if the records of her children in the archives there are anything to go by.

Craig's reputation remained intact, the Italian soldier and naturalist Alberto Della Marmora, for example, describing him after his death as 'A studious and intelligent man, loved by all for his virtue both in private and as a citizen'. It would have been interesting to have the opinion of the women in that private life. While the part played by foreign entrepreneurs such as Craig helped, as he claimed himself in an 1852 report, to drive Sardinia's economic progress in the nineteenth century, it can also be seen as self-serving, sometimes exploitative. Other members of that foreign fraternity, and the women who accompanied them, appear in chapter 10.

Emma Collins and Garibaldi

If it were not for Italian revolutionary hero Giuseppe Garibaldi (1807–1882) **Emma Claire Collins** (1811–1869) would not even be a footnote in history. As it is, she merits a place here in the history of women in La Maddalena, as well as in Garibaldi's time there. The only detailed source for Emma is the novel by Barbara Minniti, *Casa Collins: La Memorie della 'Segretaria Inglese' di Garibaldi* (2008). It has an introduction by Annita Garibaldi Jallet, a great-niece of Garibaldi, and an 'editor's preface' by Professor Gavino Puddu of Sassari University, giving it some apparent authenticity; he suggests that some manuscript papers written by Emma were found in the Sassari archives. In addition, some facts were confirmed by Emma's niece, Fanny, about whom little more is revealed.

Annita Garibaldi, obviously named after Garibaldi's beloved first wife and comrade-in-arms, begins her introduction:

> Emma ... one of the names of women most present in the life of Giuseppe Garibaldi. But no memory erases another [ie Anita?]; one is love, the other is friendship, the third is a boat. Love is Emma Roberts. The friend is an English lady, Emma Clare Collins, who shares with Garibaldi a secret, a perfume, that of Caprera, when spring comes with its infinity of flowers.

Some time between 1852 and 1854, Garibaldi, visiting Paris, met the talented musician, widowed **Emma Roberts**, and became enamoured. During his stay in London in 1856 they became engaged. With her friend, **Jessie White** (1832–1906), Emma visited Garibaldi in Nice and Sardinia. Jessie was to become dedicated to Garibaldi's cause, to speak and write about it and human rights abuses, particularly in Sicily, to practise as a nurse to his soldiers, and to write a biography of him. But the relationship between Emma Roberts and Garibaldi was not to be. Nevertheless, Emma was to look after the youngest of Garibaldi's children by his wife Anita, and the much-prized cutter she presented him with was named after her. That is two of the Emmas accounted for.

Garibaldi set foot on La Maddalena for the first time in 1849. He was arrested while trying to flee Rome, a flight during which Anita, pregnant with what would have been their fifth child, died of malaria. He was supposed to be sent to Tunis, but the Bey demurred, so the Millelire who commanded the vessel taking him there was ordered to put into La Maddalena instead. Garibaldi was to spend just one month there, but it was long enough to forge deep friendships among the Susini and Millelire families, develop a liking for the place, and to collect admirers, including Emma Collins.

Yorkshire-born Emma and her husband Richard had arrived in the archipelago in 1832 (or 1834) having fled England – perhaps they had eloped – with just a few guineas. Eventually they managed to buy land and build a house. Emma, in the novel at least, explains her first contact with Garibaldi:

> I myself, when I saw him for the first time in September 1949 at the Susini vineyard, was moved. Of course I had heard of him and not just for Italian events. My brother Jack, an officer of the British navy, had come into contact with him in South America where England favoured the independence movements and the rich traffic of goods. In several of his letters he had, among other things, told me of the battles of a group of privateers led by the Italian. ...
>
> ... Sitting in a circle in the Susini mansion after the tiring day of harvesting, in the still warm evening air of the beginning of autumn, we listened to the story of his most recent earth and sea vicissitudes.

After returning from another of his adventures, in the early 1850s, Garibaldi decided to set up home in La Maddalena, and he preferred the island of Caprera across a narrow strait from the east of the main island (now connected by a bridge) where he bought some land from local owners. He still hoped initially to share his life there with Emma Roberts. The details of his extended family, as it became, follow this concentration on Emma Collins.

While Garibaldi's friendship with his neighbour Emma was never to fail, Richard Collins, who already had problems with the Susini family, took an increasing dislike to him, probably not helped by Emma's admiration. Relations deteriorated still further when Richard Collins' pigs trespassed on to the half of Caprera sold to the revolutionary soldier turned farmer and caused damage. The dispute was mediated by Royal Navy Captain Daniel Roberts, another Englishman settled in the archipelago, though without a wife.

The best view of Emma Collins is obtained from the account by Elpis Melena (pen name of Baroness Espérance von Schwartz), *Recollections of General Garibaldi; or, Travels from Rome to Lucerne* (1861); the author will be explained in the next section because, in 1857, she was on La Maddalena in order to visit Garibaldi. Espérance was obviously rather taken with Emma, but she did tend to take to people, causes, scenery and flowery language; she wrote of Emma at some length, slightly curtailed here:

> In about an hour we reached the Punta della Moneta, at the extremity of which stood the white mansion of Mr C, built in the Moorish style, and we arrived there, after a short walk along a picturesque terrace, where bloomed the cactus and the Indian fig. ... Mrs C is one of those extraordinary women whom England alone can create ... she advanced towards us as far as the door of her romantic habitation, begged us to enter a pretty room even with the terrace, expressed her regret that her husband was not there to receive us.
>
> Mrs C might be about five-and-forty, still very agreeable in person, and her manners evidenced the distinction of her birth. She had resided here for twenty-five years, and I believe that some catastrophe had condemned her to this voluntary exile. I longed to know the mystery of this destiny, but all I could learn was that she ordinarily accompanied her husband on his long excursions on horseback and in the chase, and even in his fishing voyages – a passion for which they both possessed, to the extent of being several days absent on the open sea.
>
> Mrs C seemed to penetrate my wishes, but she only gratified them so far as to tell me that by birth she was a lady, by choice a gipsy, and by necessity a farmer's wife. I can only say that her behaviour evinced perfect contentment; and, notwithstanding the complete isolation in which she was placed, without children and without domestics, her life, perhaps affords more real interest than the existence of some of our queens of fashion ... Exclusively devoted to the care of her household and farm, she had formed for herself a circle of activity, that ennui could never reach her. I was told that for seventeen years she had never set foot in the town of La Maddalena. A pleasant fireplace, a choice library, a writing-table covered with books and papers, showed that many calm evenings might be enjoyed in this room.

The discussion of the two women turned to horses, particularly the small Sardinian variety, and Espérance was invited to see Emma's special pride:

> She went out into the garden, and one call of her well-known voice served to bring from his stall the prettiest little horse of dappled grey. He put up

his bright eye, and shook his head with a proud but docile air, and followed his mistress, who, having a sieve in her hand, attracted the attention of all the other quadrupeds and all the fowls of the farmyard. Two dogs came out to greet her, wagging their tails. Some pigs, of a kind peculiar to Sardinia, a flight of pigeons, and many fowls with bright red crests, came running to pick up the grains that fell. A bank of laurels, roses, and exotic plants formed the frame of this living picture, the serene beauty of which reminded one of the pastoral manners of the golden age.

In spite of this apparently idyllic life, Richard Collins had some problem for which he turned increasingly to drink. This made him more morose than ever, and began to affect his health, so that he died in 1864. At this stage Emma sold the rest of Caprera to Garibaldi. She was to remain friendly with him and, indeed, to help him to leave the archipelago for yet another Italian adventure.

The long letter Emma wrote to her dead husband from their home on La Maddalena, La Moneta, on 19 September 1868, is claimed as genuine; it was presumably written in English, though Emma was fluent in Italian, was translated into Italian, and now roughly into English, that is, not exactly what Emma originally wrote. Some paragraphs from it bear quotation:

The General has long bought everything, even our beasts. I did not resist and indeed, I am happy that our island be all his. I am old and tired and everything, without you, seems tiring and useless. ...

... I must also confess that in part I myself was a voluntary instrument for an event that will surely have its place in history. I do not know if the same would have happened if you had been present, since your subtle hostility to the General, which I wanted to interpret as expressed jealousy, would have pushed me to keep myself away from heroic ambitions.

However, being dragged into the events of Italy, at least allowed me to leave my tormenting melancholy next to that wall inside which your mortal ashes were enclosed, to dedicate myself to the destiny not of another man, but of an entire nation. I am English by birth, but Italian by choice and full of gratitude for the many days of happiness I enjoyed here. ...

Now I will have intrigued you, although you did not have too much interest in his affairs (how many times have I reproached you for your stubborn and unexpected indifference to a noble cause) even when he especially loved talking about crops, cows and horses to tame. ...

Before returning to our country from which we fled with a few guineas many years ago, rich only in our exclusive and overwhelming love, the only food we needed to live, I will leave these few sheets hidden in a tin box. The one you used to store hooks and small tools for fishing. I'll hide it under that wall that once marked the boundary between the two properties, necessary to prevent our pigs and goats from invading the possessions of the General with whom we have often fought about this.

And how many times, my beloved Richard, did we use our blunt weapons, so useless and ridiculous, against that titan with a persuasive voice and hypnotic smile with which he was able simply to regain a friendly look from us. It was enough to see him from afar sitting on a rock with the sun on his face at sunset, busy sewing the buttons on one of his worn red shirts, to think affectionately about him. ...

... Goodbye, my beloved Richard, have peace. I leave you in our little paradise.

Yours forever

Emma

It does not appear that Emma did return to England: it is said that, instead, she died on La Maddalena and was buried in the local cemetery, as if she were, indeed, a *maddalenina*. When the Collins headland, Punta Moneta, was expropriated by the government, her husband's bones (ashes?) were recovered from where Emma had buried him (them?) in the garden and taken to be re-buried beside her.

As for the help she gave Garibaldi hinted at in her letter, that happened in 1867 when he was attempting to leave Caprera for Italy without being intercepted. Having managed to cross by night from Caprera to La Maddalena with the help of friends, he was held up by the sound of shots being fired. It was, therefore, decided, as they were near La Moneta to take refuge with Mrs Collins. Cautiously Garibaldi approached the house and, with his walking stick, tapped on a windowpane. Emma, already alerted, had expected him, and was ready to open the front door and welcome him. There he spent the night and was able, the following morning, to leave for the mainland where he arrived safely, the government assuming that he was still a hostage on Caprera.

The gossip that Emma and Garibaldi were lovers following Richard Collins' death may or may not be true. Stefano Giani's internet piece 'L'Ultima amante di Garibaldi e la fuga da Caprera' (2008) claims that there are letters from Garibaldi to Emma that suggest intimacy. The chronology of his amours certainly allows it in 1864–65, but she was not the last, as the next section shows.

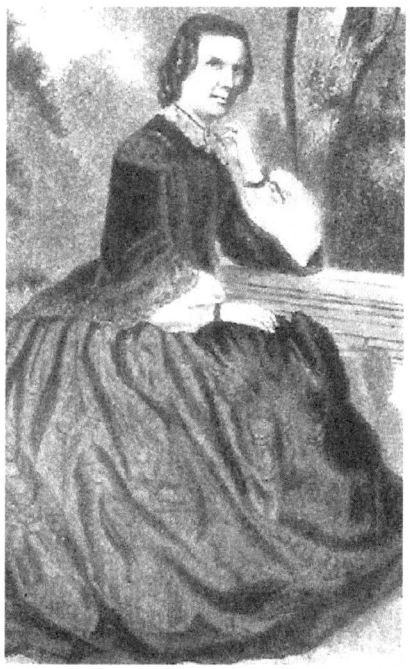

30. Baroness Espérance von Schwartz (Elpis Melena), from Hoe, *Crete: Women, History, Books and Places*

Garibaldi on Caprera: Wives, Mistresses and Daughters 1855–1959

In spite of Garibaldi's occasional absences on military or political adventures, the 'White House' on Caprera, with its surrounding farm, although part of his heroic identity, was essentially a family home, however sometimes irregular that family was. He had had four children with Anita: Domenico Menotti (1840–1903), **Rosita** (1843–1845), **Teresita** (Teresa, 1845–1903) and Ricciotti (1847–1924). Rosita had died in Latin America, hardly more than a baby, but the other three were with him from the beginning on Caprera.

Not surprisingly, the heroic and handsome man continued to be attractive to women and, from the record of his entanglements, to have been attracted to them. Espérance von Schwartz was one of them following her visit to him mentioned above. **Mary Espérance Kalm Bandt** (1818–1899) was born in London, the daughter of a Hamburg banker resident there. (Her mother was Susanne Stephanie Sylvestre.) Although Espérance spent little time in England in the years that followed – living in Italy, Germany, Greece, Crete and Switzerland – she retained British nationality. Her first husband was a banker cousin who made her unhappy and committed suicide, her second (1842) was the banker Baron Ferdinand von Schwartz. They travelled widely and adventurously, using her eight languages, and she became a writer, adopting the pen name *Elpis Melena* – the Greek for Hope (Espérance) Black (Schwartz).

Espérance's marriage was dissolved in 1854, and her friendship with Garibaldi was to date from the 1857 visit to him; at some stage they became lovers, and Garibaldi hoped to marry her, but Espérance prevaricated and by 1866 their intimate relationship was over and she went to live in Crete where she involved herself in revolutionary causes. (I describe her time there, and take the above details from *Crete: Women, History, Books and Places*.)

To detail Espérance's description of Garibaldi's Caprera home would be too much; it is similar in style to her description of Emma Collins' lifestyle, but it starts:

> The beautiful appearance of this mode of construction is extremely agreeable to the eye; and, on entering the house, I found that the interior corresponded in character with the façade ... Every room was ample and well ventilated. The harmony of their proportions proved that the architect thought more of producing becoming apartments than of submitting to the mere rules of his art.

But her description of Garibaldi's 12-year-old daughter, however overblown, is entirely relevant, as it may be all there is; he went to look for Teresita while his guest describes the books in the room in which he left her. Then, she notes:

The entrance of the youthful Teresa ended my literary review. I saluted with much interest this beautiful girl, in whose regular features I recognised the traces of her father's countenance, while the flexible firmness of their movements reminded me of the Brazilian origin of her mother. Never did a complexion of golden brown so harmonize with light-coloured hair. Was it the softness of her dark chestnut coloured eye, or the expression of a physiognomy which at one time betrayed the petulance of a young maiden, which gave so great a charm to her entire person? In honour of our visit, she had assumed 'a toilette extraordinaire', but I would rather have seen her in her usual costume, with the sling which she uses so adroitly thrown over her shoulder. Curious, that this oldest instrument of war and the chase should still retain its position in this kingdom, and that the form of the Sardinian 'Fionda' should be so identical with that which David used in his combat with Goliath!

A woman of the household that Espérance does not describe was **Battistina Revello** (Teresa Battista Raveu; 1830–1906) whom Garibaldi, then living in Nice, had hired to look after his children; she went with the family to Caprera. In May 1859 she gave birth to Garibaldi's daughter **Anna Maria Imeni** (**Anita**; 1859–1875). Apparently, out of a sense of duty, he nearly married Battistina, but he was still hoping that Espérance would say yes. In due course Anita went to Crete to live with Espérance with whom Garibaldi was still friendly, indeed, his letters to her started *'Speranza Amatissima'*. Anita was educated by Espérance in Chania, and perhaps also at boarding school in Switzerland starting in 1868, but she was 'a difficult young woman who tended not to appreciate her benefactor's ministrations'.

In 1875, for reasons which no one, least of all Espérance, explains, her long friendship with Garibaldi came to an end. Anita left her house and, within a year, was dead, aged about 17. An online source, Evelyne Castelli's *'Garibaldi et les Niçois'*, suggests that, when visiting her father on Caprera, she may have contracted 'fulmanant [sic] hepatic encephalopathy after eating seafood'. She was buried in what became the family plot on the island. Continuing my own account:

> Espérance, feeling betrayed, continued to live in [Crete] until 1896. She had published her version of Garibaldi's autobiography – the manuscript of which he had entrusted to her – in 1861; in 1884, two years after his death, she published his letters to her. Their authenticity has been questioned, but they ring true to the uninitiated, and are fascinating, given Garibaldi's place in history. They are available in English.

Some of Espérance's account of her visit to La Maddalena is disputed, particularly concerning earlier history of the archipelago which she learnt from an old man while out walking during a sleepless night. That does not apply, though, to what she wrote of her visits to Garibaldi and Emma Collins. Perhaps her informant's mind was wandering or perhaps, as often happens under such circumstances, indigenous people spin yarns to please eager and credulous visitors.

It did not take long for Garibaldi to become once again romantically entangled. This time it was with **Giuseppina Raimondi** (1841–1918), the natural daughter, recognised but not legitimised, of the Marquese Giorgio Raimondi Mantica Odescalchi. Like many women who moved within Garibaldi's orbit, she was involved in revolutionary activities. Garibaldi fell in love at their first meeting, but she did not respond, not even to his passionate letters. The reason, it appears, was that she was in love with one of his officers, a love which was, indeed, consummated. Perhaps she was pregnant when she at last responded warmly to a letter from Garibaldi; at some stage she had a child that did not survive. Whatever the chronology, and her reasons for giving in to his blandishments, she and Garibaldi were married on 24 January 1860. Somehow, later that day, Garibaldi discovered that she was still attached and sexually active elsewhere, perhaps to and with more than one lover, even just before the wedding – which, when pressed, she confirmed – and he immediately repudiated her and the marriage. When Garibaldi was later wounded in battle, she wrote him a letter in solidarity; he did not reply and refused to see her even when she arrived on Caprera to talk to him. The annulment of their marriage did not come through until 1880.

Meanwhile, Battistina, at an unspecified date, returned to Nice. Her mother had died earlier, but her father was still alive until 1867, and she had several siblings. She remained unmarried and worked as a laundress, a common occupation in Nice. Gianluigi Alzona tells the story of Battistina and her life with Garibaldi in *Battistina e la Piccola Anita* (2013).

The year after Garibaldi's short-lived marriage to Giuseppina Raimondi, his daughter Teresita, aged barely 16, married Stefano Canzio, a Garibaldian officer eight years her senior. The wedding took place on Caprera. Teresita, born in Uruguay during her parents' time as freedom fighters in the jungles of South America, accompanied them to Europe in 1848. Following her mother's death, she was looked after first by her paternal grandmother in Nice and then family friends, before, aged 12, she joined her father on Caprera. Espérance von Schwartz's meeting with her, and the description, must, therefore, have been soon after her arrival.

Teresita and Stefano were to have either 14 or 16 children, the first born in 1862; four died early and, **Annita Canzio** (1866–1878) seems to have been one of only two daughters. She was born on Caprera, but died in Genoa aged 11. The second daughter, called Annita after her dead sibling, was born in 1879. When Garibaldi left his exile on Caprera in 1867 with the help of Emma Collins, described above, Teresita, the apple of her father's eye, joined her husband and Garibaldi on his next adventure. She spent the last years of her life in the archipelago, dying in 1903 aged only 58; she, too was buried in the family cemetery on Caprera.

Francesca Armosino (1848–1923) was hired in 1865, aged 17, to be nanny to Teresita's children. She was the descendant of a noble Armenian family which had emigrated to Italy to escape the persecution of Christians by the Turks. In spite of their age difference, Garibaldi was by then 58, they fell quickly in love. Teresita, perhaps through jealousy, disapproved of the relationship and, indeed, did all she could to thwart it, going so far as to accuse Francesca of theft. Her efforts were in vain; they served only to strengthen the relationship and Francesca had three children with Garibaldi: **Clelia Garibaldi** (1867–1959), **Rosa** (b.1869) who died aged 18 months, and Manlio (1873–1900). When the annulment by the Court of Appeals in Rome of Garibaldi's marriage to Giuseppina Raimondi came through in 1880, they were able to marry, and legitimise their two surviving children. On Garibaldi's death two years later, in 1882, Francesca divided her time between their home on Caprera and the house she had bought in Livorno in order to be near their son Manlio, cadet at the naval academy. When she died in 1923 on Caprera she, too, was buried in the family cemetery where her two children, Rosa and Manlio, also lay.

Clelia was briefly married in Turin to a professor but by 1889 the couple had separated. Thereafter she devoted her life to the memory of her father, taking care of the house/museum on Caprera, welcoming guests and visitors, writing a memoir of her father (*Mio Padre*, 1948) and involved in good works in the archipelago, especially those concerning children. She was comfortably off following an annuity granted to Garibaldi by the government in 1876. In 1948, she not only had published her father's novel *Manlius*, but also was nominated to hold a seat for the Republican Party in the Italian Senate. (See chapter 14 for women in post-war politics.) She died aged 92 and was buried beside her mother, brother and sister in the family cemetery on Caprera.

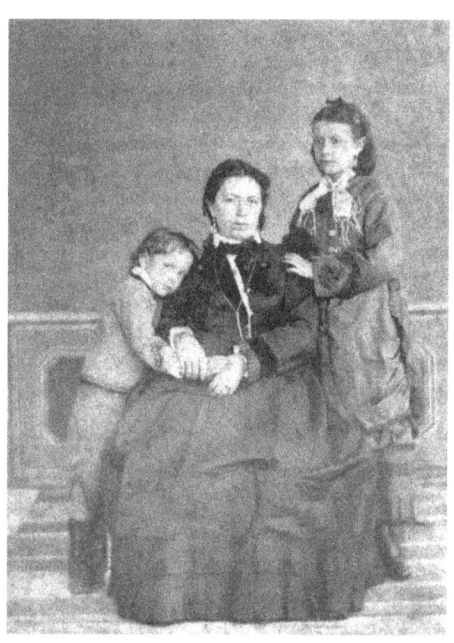

31. Francesca Armosino, Clelia and Malio, from Garibaldi, *Mio Padre*

The Garibaldi house/museum is open to visitors. Although it is a shrine to the great man, it is worth visiting, too, for the women – daughters and granddaughters – who were an important part of his life there. If you don't have time, or the means to make the short journey over the bridge to Caprera, you can spot the white house in the distance while taking a bus tour of La Maddalena.

Maria Webber Tamponi

Another house that is easily spotted during a bus tour of La Maddalena, this time not very far from the road, is the Villa Webber in the Padule district on the outskirts of today's town. Be sure to ask the tour guide to point the house out, as **Maria (Marietta) Webber Tamponi** (1845–1928) and her time there are not part of the patter, or were not until I asked.

Espérance von Schwartz allows us to see, in 1857, the sort of set-up that was to welcome Maria, and the man at the centre of it:

> Mr Webber's house ... is situated about a mile from the shore, and forms, with the surrounding grounds, an object sufficiently imposing to produce a desire to view it more nearly. We approached it by a newly-formed carriage drive. The power of riches displayed itself on all sides; and if La Maddalena had but a few more such wealthy colonists, to whom money makes everything easy, the dreamy solitude of the island would quickly be replaced by noise and bustle.
>
> The greatest activity prevailed without and within. Troops of labourers worked in the plantations and in the buildings. Several grooms were dressing the shining coats of spirited horses, while other servants were opening cases of elegant furniture. The rooms were full of Genoese artificers [skilled workmen], laying variegated parquets and pavements. The noise of their hammers kept time with their songs. Some were whistling and some talking, and yet all so entirely devoted to their employments, that it was difficult to find anyone to announce our arrival. We were introduced into a room *encumbered* with works of art, pictures in magnificent frames, and books in resplendent bindings; and in the midst of all this we could not but perceive that our visit, though politely received, was singularly inopportune. Mr Webber was quite preoccupied with all his treasures, and with the appointment of Vice-Consul, of which he had just received the official announcement.
>
> I afterwards heard that the new Vice-Consul had made a large fortune in Australia, where he had passed ten years in making and selling hats, a circumstance which decreased my wonder at his having, in the pride of his riches, displayed all the magnificence of cities in the rural plains of a remote island like this. The building was a kind of Moresque Italian style, and well placed in an amphitheatre of hills.

Espérance's account may sometimes rely too much on local gossip. Brian Walsh, in *James Phillips Webber: the Man and the Mystery* (2008) suggests that contrary to her claim about the origins of Webber's fortune being the making and selling of hats, that occupation probably occurred after he left Australia. While he was there he was a landowner, magistrate and convict master, and that was the source of his fortune.

The *Sydney Gazette* of 1834 suggests that Webber was leaving Australia for family reasons; the Walsh account adds that local conflicts could also have been a factor, as could ill health. His life between 1836 and 1850 when he decided to settle on La Maddalena is even less known about, except for the hat clue. Equally mysterious is why he travelled there on a diplomatic passport. Mussolini, who was confined in the Villa Webber for three weeks in 1943 wrote in his diary:

> The villa which I have been taken to belonged to a British citizen, Mr Webber, who, very strangely, among all the places in the world where he could have settled down, has chosen the most lonely and arid island of Sardinia ... Intelligence Service? Perhaps!

And Walsh comments that some residents of the island believe that even today – La Maddalena being chosen because of its naval significance, already illustrated by Nelson. Whatever the reason, Webber purchased land there in 1851, and began construction of the villa in 1855, completing it at the time of Espérance's 1857 visit.

To add to the Webber mystique is the adoption as his son and heir, some time between 1852 and 1854, of a young Neapolitan, Luigi Russo (b.1829), who added the name Webber. He had accompanied Webber to La Maddalena in 1849–50, perhaps as a servant, though it is also possible that his father was a picture dealer in Naples from whom Webber bought paintings.

Maria, the daughter of Martino Tamponi of Tempio and **Elisa Spano**, married Luigi Russo Webber in 1859. It seems that she was then barely 15; the 1871 census gives her age as 26; Luigi was 43. Some of the detail that follows regarding Maria's immediate family and, indeed, her extended family, was gained from a 2002 interview between La Maddalena historian Alberto Sega and a member of the family. Her father was a man of some substance, involved in shipping; so presumably he moved from Tempio, inland Gallura, to Olbia (then known as Terranova).

That same interview compounds the ambivalence over who built the Villa Tamponi in Olbia, the extensive grounds of which can still be seen as you drive round the city. The interviewee, who wished to remain anonymous, suggests that it was Martino, in 1867; another source has it that it was Maria's brother (she had four of them), Giovanni Battista Tamponi, also involved in shipping, who built it in 1870. A handwritten note on the typed interview script says that it was Maria herself, with means which will become clear.

There is an intruder into this account, stemming from Owain Wright's 2007 article, 'Sea and Sardinia: Pax Brittanica versus Vendetta in the New Italy (1870)'. In it he tells the story of a Martino Zamponi who, in 1870, was serving as British vice-consul in Olbia (a post created in 1859). As he was also vice-consul for France and Spain, this created a power struggle and a feud between two local families. So much heat was generated that, as Owain Wright records,

The feud later resulted in the murder of the vice-consul's son and the death threat against Zamponi himself, having escalated 'on account of some property' and also 'on account of some lady'.

The story is told in much more detail than is appropriate here, including the relevant background to Britain's relations and similar activities in the Mediterranean at that time. But it is worth noting that, when the Italian authorities failed to intervene, at the instigation of the British consul in Cagliari, a Royal Navy gunboat was sent to the island in the hopes that its mere arrival would help the beleaguered Zamponi. Italy felt humiliated and the incident caused a diplomatic upset in relations.

When I originally read that article, I tried to track down more about Zamponi's 'lady', without success. But Owain Wright, on reading my text, tells me that he has seen Zamponi written as Tamponi. While this information does not clarify, it certain adds to the story. Of course, what I want to know is, who was the 'lady', and how was she involved? Was she the mother of the child who was murdered? I now take it as read that Martino Tamponi and Zamponi are the same. So we know that Tamponi was married and, with his wife, had Maria and four sons. Was Elisa Spano Tamponi still alive and, if so, how does she fit in? One thing is clear, Martino Tamponi/Zamponi was a man more than once involved in disputes.

Adding to Maria's background is an entry in Casalis's *Dizionario Geografico, Storico, Statistico* (1833–1856), stating that a Martino Tamponi was involved in a physical set-to in Tempio in front of the cathedral in 1848; severely wounded, he departed for Turin. If that was her father, Maria would then have been about three. The altercation was probably political: the Sega informant suggested that Martino and his brother were republicans and were at some stage arrested. In due course, Martino must have found himself back in Sardinia, and in Olbia doing well for himself.

There may have been a political link between Martino and James Webber, accounting for Maria's marriage to Luigi. Giovanna Sotgiu and Alberto Sega concentrate entirely on Webber in their chapter about him in *Inglesi nell'Arcipelago* (2005), without even mentioning Maria by name. They suggest that her father and Webber had maritime business links. In her chapter 'Marietta Tamponi' in *L'Isola e le Donne* (2016), Giovanna Sotgiu adds that Luigi, on a hunting trip near Olbia, saw Maria and fell in love with her beauty.

Maria had joined her husband and his adopted father at the Villa Webber by 1860: four of their five children were born on La Maddalena, the first in 1862, and a daughter, **Elisabetta Russo Webber** in 1864. It is clear that Maria settled well into the household and became close to her adoptive 'father-in-law', though Giovanna Sotgiu suggests that it was a rather enclosed life; Maria was certainly not seen round and about in town. It is fair to assume, though, that she met Garibaldi. On that occasion in 1867 when he spent the night at Emma Collins' house on his way from Caprera to the mainland, he went the following morning, accompanied by two comrades, to meet his friend Pietro Susini at the Villa Webber, and it was from there that they left. In 1866 Emma Collins, noted by Walsh, had written to Garibaldi asking for help for a local man:

> I am so sorry to disturb you in your solitude with these requests, and I had made up my mind that I would not intervene on behalf of those who asked me to, except for Mr Webber or for dear Captain Roberts, or maybe for Fanny [her husband's niece].

What caused the breakdown of Maria and Luigi's marriage and, apparently, an estrangement from his adoptive father, seems to have no record, though there is some suggestion that he was a violent man. Whatever the cause, he left the villa and La Maddalena for Livorno in 1872 to live in a house that Webber had purchased. Maria stayed on with James Webber and was there when he died in Pisa in November 1877. What is more, in his English and Italian wills, as Walsh writes, he left everything to her:

> all his property in New South Wales and the United Kingdom ... for her sole use, free of control and debts of her husband Luigi. He also gave Maria life tenancy of Villa Webber, while ownership of the Villa passed to her son Lorimer. James' brother, Edward Affleck Webber, also left 1,000 pounds to Maria Russo Webber in his Will.

This inheritance gives credence to the suggestion that it was Maria who built the Villa Tamponi (Via Principe Umberto) in Olbia. Confirmation was suggested by a handwritten note: 'As the villa's outer gates are strikingly similar to those of Villa Webber'.

Maria lived on in the Villa Webber, more a crenellated castle or walled fortress surrounded by pine forest, until her death aged 73 in 1928, and that of her eldest son Lorimer. What sort of a life did she live there? In her chapter on Maria, Giovanna Sotgiu sees it through the eyes of **Marianna Mura**, who came to be her personal maid in her later years. Marianna had not left Dorgali in the Barbagia region of mainland Sardinia before and her first impressions were 'engraved on her memory'. So she remembered:

> The caretaker of the villa, zi' Stefanu who was waiting for her with the coachman Ciccittu to take her to her destination and the three gates that closed behind her as the carriage entered the vast property. The young woman reported an unpleasant impression, almost of imprisonment, although veined with curiosity about that strange place.
>
> In fact, the villa, completely detached from the city, seemed to fall in on itself in an isolation exacerbated by the high walls, the gates, the shady and dense park that constituted an impenetrable barrier to the north, from the entrance of the house itself which, turning its back on the sea, on the sun, on the road and its passers-by, opened onto a walled courtyard with a little gate turned towards the shade of the trees.

Though Maria continued to live isolated in the villa, its contents, such as 31 paintings, which should have included a possibly valuable one of 'Susanna and the Elders', had, apparently, been auctioned in 1920. There may have been something underhand about the sale: that painting was not on an 1882 inventory used for it.

Giovanna Sotgiu does not mention any missing paintings, but she does recount a visit to Maria made by Luigi in 1882, an unpleasant occasion which she tried to avoid by appointing a lawyer. Luigi, while disinherited by Webber, had lived on a pension provided by Maria. But she had reduced it when her investments yielded less. Luigi reacted by asking a judge for a general inventory of her assets, and by accusing his former wife of bad management. His demands were petty, asking that the inventory include even the children's toys, and he increased the value of the house contents – books, paintings and carpets were counted and any reduction in their value seen as another example of Maria's bad management. Although neither Giovanni Sotgiu nor Alberto Sega's interviewee makes a link between this occasion and any paintings that went missing, it is difficult not to do so.

The villa itself remained the family's property until it was requisitioned during the Second World War. It was then that Mussolini was briefly held there. After the war, ownership of the villa was restored to the family, but by then it was in a poor state of repair. Thereafter, the family sold the villa and, as Walsh writes in 2008, 'it remains in a sad state, its future uncertain'. The same state of affairs was noted in a cultural and architectural report of 2013, but the two architects who made the study and compiled the report were in fact responding to a rumour that the owners of what was private property were planning to build houses in the park. As one of them, Monica Morbidelli, an officer in the Italian Ministry of Culture, responsible for the north of Sardinia, made clear in answer to my email, they felt the need to ensure protection of both the villa and the surrounding park as a monument of historical importance; a restraining order was, therefore, put on the property.

A more up-to-date (2019) report on the position of the villa comes by email from Alberto Sega. It continues to be private property, now owned by a company; it seems that recently they have been given permission to use part of the park to build tourist accommodation, despite the earlier restraining order. The villa itself is inaccessible, its windows and doors boarded up as much for health and safety reasons as against intrusion: its condition continues to deteriorate. What the future holds seems unclear. There are, however, plenty of photographs of its exterior on the internet, and you can glimpse it in the distance from the road. For its interior, one needs to go back to the 1857 description by Espérance von Schwartz, and to imagine the house full of fine furniture, an extensive library and many works of art.

To visit La Maddalena Archipelago, you leave from Palau on the mainland by ferry. We went on a touristy tour which stopped at several of the islands and didn't leave enough time for exploring the main island, with its over-busy though picturesque and historic town, let alone Caprera.

A coach tour round the island was the best we could manage. This way of going is not an unalloyed pleasure.

The fate of the Villa Webber was by no means the end of Maria's branch of the Tamponi family. In 1882, aged 18, her daughter, English-educated Elisabetta, married her uncle, Maria's brother Girolamo Tamponi, British consul in Olbia. Marriage within the extended Tamponi family was commonplace, presumably to safeguard assets. There is no way of knowing the feelings about this of the parties concerned, nor is the age difference in this instance known.

The couple built the Villa Tamponi in Golfo Aranci not far from Olbia where the family also had shipping interests. Mario Spanu Babay includes a photograph in *Figari* of the 'agenzia di navigazione' there, as well as of the villa. There is also a photograph of a woman with Edwardian hairstyle and dress on the terrace of the villa with a child clinging to her skirt which I like to think is Elisabetta. The family was involved in good works, including, in 1913, the donation of land for the building of the new San Giuseppe church. When visiting Golfo Aranci, don't forget the island – Figarolo – just offshore where Roman Atte may, or may not, have had a villa.

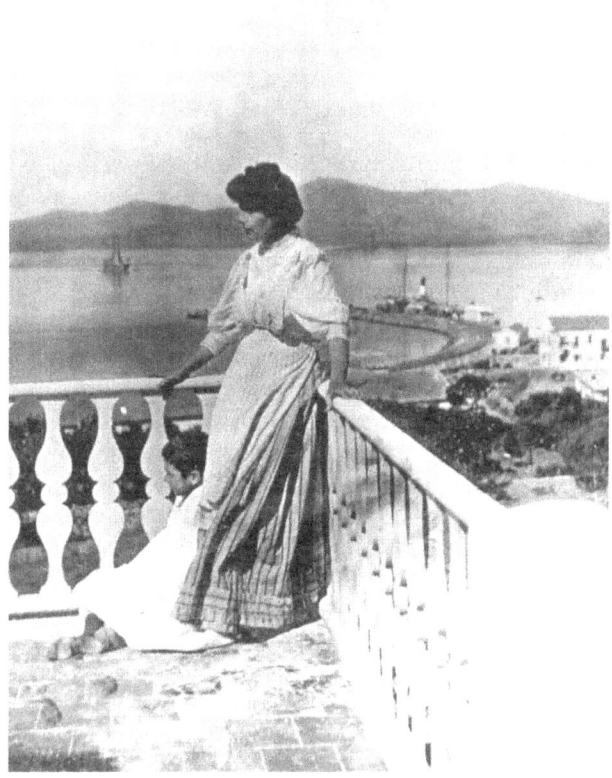

32. Edwardian woman on terrace of Villa Tamponi, Golfo Aranci, from Spano, *Figari*

Many members of the extended Tamponi family lived at least part of the year in Golfo Aranci, including Maria's granddaughter, daughter of Lorimer, **Dolores Russo Webber** (1910–2012). When she died, aged 102, she merited an effusive obituary in the Olbia edition of *La Nuova Sardegna* – 'The Tamponi have always been part of the city's nobility'. An anonymous 2006 article in the same newspaper, '*Vincolo su Villa Tamponi*', suggested that it was her husband, a cousin, who built the Olbia Villa Tamponi in Viale Principe Umberto early in the 1900s. That seems unlikely, as he had died in 1882. The sale of the Olbia villa could not go ahead because of a restraining order placed upon it when it was discovered that Punic and Roman archaeological remains lay under its parkland full of rare and exotic botanical specimens. The house is still in private Tamponi hands; it may be possible to visit the grounds if you have strings to pull, though part of it has been sold to private entrepreneurs and construction of a building begun. The situation may change, as it could with the Villa Webber on La Maddalena. When visiting Olbia, don't forget that the nuragic well, Sa Testa, is just outside.

Unhappily, Dolores' three daughters living in Golfo Aranci, Olbia and Cagliari, have been particularly noted for the court cases in which they have been involved concerning the family inheritance, as well as access to their mother, sometimes resulting in fisticuffs. That is fortunately outside the scope of this narrative; internet material is endless.

From La Maddalena to Tavolara: The Royal Bertoleoni Dynasty

Tavolara is a small island 6 km (3.7 miles) off the north-east coast of the main island of Sardinia, just beneath the Gulf of Olbia. Its prehistory is of current archaeological interest, particularly to scholars such as Paola Mancini, author of *Gallura Orientale* which I found so useful for chapter 1. In 2016, she headed the dig at Spalmatore, south-west of Tavolara, which discovered pottery dating to 2800–1900 BC, from the Monte Claro period. Archaeologists have also found the remains of an Iron Age Etruscan settlement dating from the ninth century BC. In Roman times, the island was known as Hermea and, in the ninth century AD, it was used as a base by Arab ships for attacks on Sardinia. In the 1730s it was abandoned because of North African piracy in the area and thereafter it was uninhabited. Of particular interest to this chapter, though, is its nineteenth- and twentieth-century link with La Maddalena.

Giuseppe Bertoleoni (1778–1849) was a shepherd on La Maddalena who appears to have been an educated man. His antecedents remained a mystery, though not without romantic speculation – perhaps he was even the lost dauphin of France. Another source suggests that his family arrived in Corsica from Genoa and then across the strait to La Maddalena.

In 1798, he married **Maria Laura Ornano** (b.1780), eldest child of Salvatore Ornano and **Mariangela Altieri**. Married in 1781, Mariangela was widowed in 1794, following an engagement involving the Sardinian navy, in which her husband was an officer, with North African pirates. He died of an infected wound leaving her with six children, the youngest of whom was two years old.

The Ornano Altieri couple's third daughter, **Maria Caterina Ornano** (1784–1856) married aged 14, but she too, was widowed. She moved in with Laura, her husband and their son Paolo, and soon became Giuseppe's mistress. In order to avoid scandal, he moved both women and their children into the old church of Santa Maria. This arrangement worked well enough, at least for Giuseppe, for some time, but then his mother-in-law, Mariangela, who had remarried after two years of widowhood, intervened: she reported him to the local Maddalena commander. Giuseppe was to be arrested and the children baptised.

Giovanna Sotgiu discusses the moral environment emanating then both from the State and the community in the chapter '*Gli Scandalosi, Ovvero Concubinari, Adulteri, Pottane*' ('The Scandalous: Concubines, Adulterers, Prostitutes') in *L'Isola e Le Donne*. A few lines sum up the situation in 1817: ' the parish priest … asked his bishop … to intervene at government level, punctiliously noting the presence of couples living together outside marriage, the cases of adultery and sinful women.'

(The book is a treasure trove of the women of La Maddalena – not only the sinful – too many, unfortunately, to include in this chapter.)

Ever alert to dangers and possibilities, Giuseppe arranged for Caterina and children to be looked after by friends on mainland Sardinia. By some means, he already had a stake in Tavolara and it was there that Caterina and family – she had a son by her earlier marriage and two children by Giuseppe, Giovanni and **Pasqua** – were moved next. Eventually, both women, their children and Giuseppe lived on Tavolara. They were the only inhabitants. If the date of that final move is uncertain, Giuseppe was certainly there in 1836 because that was when King Carlo Alberto visited the island to hunt.

During the royal visit, Giuseppe presented the king with some island sheep and goats. The king asked what Giuseppe would like in return. The reply of a pound of gunpowder not seeming of sufficient value, the king, interested in such an educated man in such an out-of-the-way place, gave him instead, verbally at the time, the title King of Tavolara. His eldest son, Paolo, was to be a prince, the younger ones each to be Lord of the Islands and each of his daughters, *Signora del Mare*. I have not seen either Laura or Caterina called queen, though later wives of the king used that title.

It may sound like a fairy story, but it isn't. In 1839, Paolo went to Turin and obtained a royal charter from the king. In 1845, Giuseppe, who could not be prosecuted for bigamy because of his title, passed the kingdom to Paolo, before dying in 1849. After the creation of the Kingdom of Italy in 1861, King Paolo I of Tavolara pressed for and obtained recognition for the island from King Vittorio Emanuele. When Paolo became ill in 1882, his wife, **Pasqua Favale**, acted as regent until his death four years later. They had two children. Carlo I ruled from 1886 to 1887, but his elder sister **Mariangela Bertoleoni** (1841–1934) acted as regent from 1927 to 1929 on behalf of Carlo's son and successor Paolo II while he was absent from the island

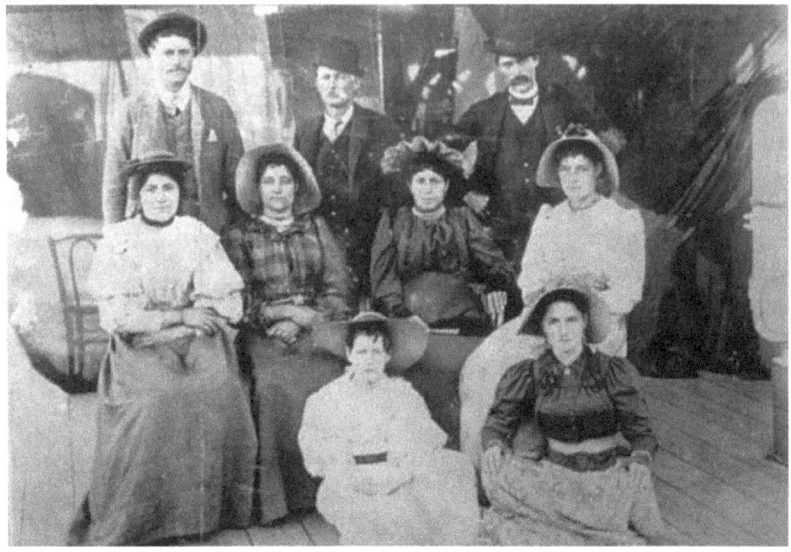

33. King Carlo I and Bertoleoni family, from the internet

looking for a job. She and other family members are buried in a family cemetery on the island.

Paolo II married **Italia Murru** (1908–2003) in 1930. When he died in 1962, the widowed queen retired to Porto San Paolo, a fishing village on the main island across from Tavolara, wintering in Capo Testa, the furthest point north-west of Gallura, still apparently a wonderful place to visit and to winter. She died aged 95 and you can somehow picture her queenly until the end. But her husband was the last Bertoleoni king to actively rule Tavolara with its approximately 50 inhabitants. At the end of his reign half the island was occupied (1962) by a NATO military installation. This means that the eastern half is restricted to military personnel. The distinctive island goats were moved off the island. More positively, the island is now, since 1997, surrounded by a national marine reserve.

In spite of the hiatus at the end of his father's reign, Carlo II came to the throne; he married but had no children and died in Capo Testa in 1993. His aunts, **Maria Molinas Bertoleoni** (1869–1974), and **Laura Molinas Bertoleoni** (d.1979), daughters of Mariangela and her husband Bachisio Molinas, both laid claim to the vacant throne in the 1960s and 1970s. The image of the competing duo is intriguing.

Carlo's brother Antonio (Tonino), well into his eighties, owns Da Tonino, the only restaurant on the island, open in the summer, and now run by his children **Princess Loredana** and Prince Giuseppe. At one time his sister, **Princess Maddalena**, married to an American naval officer, owned the nearby La Corona restaurant and assumed governmental duties of the island. But the restaurant, then run by another family, was closed down by sanitary inspectors in 1995.

When Tonino's wife, **Queen Pompea Romana**, died in 2010, aged 78, *La Nuova Sardegna* called her the wife of the last reigning monarch of Tavolora, the smallest monarchy in the world. Her widowed husband, in a 2016 article, said of himself, as he buried his feet in the sand, 'I am probably the world's most ordinary king.' He added, 'My family have had a beautiful past.'

10 – Women and Sardinia's Economic Development 1735–1919

Introduction

'Silk is as yet produced only for amusement', wrote William Henry Smyth RN in *Sketch of the Present State of Sardinia* (1828). And he continued,

> except at Dorgali, where a coarse kind is wove for sale. The towns of Galtelli, Sassari, Cuglieri, and Nuoro, have yielded a few pounds of inferior silk; but the process throughout is ill understood, and a proprietor at Alghero is actually obliged to send his cocoons to Cagliari to be reeled off.

His information was limited, as suggested by Cristina Grassi's internet piece, 'Claudia Casu's "*Filindeu*"' (2018) (mostly about pasta) where she wrote:

> I surprisingly found myself immersed in a wonderful journey in the past, searching for thin threads that could link my homeland, Sardinia, to the Orient; I also discovered the amazing history of Sardinian silk that, for centuries, has been worked with great skills in our Island. Introduced from China by the Jesuits in the seventeenth century, the silk is still worked in Orgosolo (Nuoro) and used to make the beautiful headscarf of the traditional dress, *su lionzu*.

Chapter 7 has described the continuing production of silk for *su lionzu* in Orgosolo, but it is useful to know how it came to be introduced to Sardinia. And, of course, the silk made with silkworms feeding on mulberry leaves is distinct from the sea-silk produced on the Sardinian island of Sant'Antioco with the help of the bivalve *pinna nobilis*, as described in chapter 2. Sea-silk, rather irritatingly, comes up endlessly when searching for more details on the internet about the less esoteric variety of Sardinian silk. But that very predominance also shows that the story of sea-silk's continuing production is not without controversy, as a Wikipedia entry about silk production worldwide attests:

> 'Project Sea-silk' from the Natural History Museum of Basel is collecting extensive data and studies on the subject, and informs the public that a couple of other women still produce and work today with byssus in Sant'Antioco in Sardinia, such as the sisters **Assuntina** and **Giuseppina Pes** which contradicts the claims of Chiara Vigo who is credited as having invested with an extraordinary imagination her own story of sea-silk and [spinning] it tirelessly and to the delight of all media on and on. In 2013,

Efisia Murroni, a 100 year old sea-silk master weaver nicknamed 'la signora del bisso' (born in 1913) died and her work is now shown in the Museo Etnografico di Sant'Antioco, with other artefacts being already on display in various museums throughout Europe.

Donna Francesca Sanna Sulis, The Lady of the Mulberry Trees

Francesca Sanna Sulis (1716–1810), entrepreneur and philanthropist, was to take Sardinian silk-making to a new level and, with it, seemingly to be the first woman involved in expanding Sardinia's economy in modern times – Claudia Atte could perhaps lay claim to that in the Roman era, as chapter 2 describes.

Francesca was born in Muravera, 45 km (30 miles) north-east of Cagliari, to Francesco Antioco Sulis, a landowner wealthy from farming and cattle ranching, and **Caterina Porcella**. Caterina was his first wife, with whom he had three children, including another daughter, **Barbara Sulis** (b.1714). Three other wives followed. The second wife, married 1719, also had three children; and the fourth wife, **Maddalena Sanna**, married 1736, had two children. Although Francesca's mother died when she was very young, she gradually came to be surrounded by a large and cultured extended family. Her father had imbibed the ideas of the Enlightenment and it was he who early spotted and encouraged her potential.

In the reconstruction of Francesca's life, Cagliari community activist Ada Lai draws on the earlier biographical work of Lucio Spiga for her novel *La Straordinaria Storia di Francesca Sanna Sulis Donna di Sardegna* (2016). She notes that after Francesca's childhood in Muravera, she moved to Cagliari, to a house in the Via Dritta in the Castello, which is described as 'teeming with life, commerce and intellectual stimuli. It was in Cagliari that Francesca's life blossomed: in a world that was rapidly evolving, the role of women also needed to be revised, and with it clothing.'

In 1735, aged 19, Francesca married Pietro Sanna Lecca, lawyer of the Court of Cagliari and 'regent of Toga' to the Supreme Council of Sardinia at Turin which gave him access to the king; in due course he produced for Carlo Emanuele III a compendium of the laws enacted during the first half-century of Savoyard domination of Sardinia. The couple were to divide their time between his family property at Quartucciu, then a commune 8 km (5 miles) north-east of Cagliari, now part of the metropolitan city, and 61 Via Lamarmora in the Castello. They were to have two sons and a daughter, **Maria Michela Sulis Sanna**, who entered the convent of the Cappucines in Ozieri (Sassari), and eventually became its abbess. But the marriage was to be much more fruitful than that.

Ada Lai writes, 'We often hear that behind every great man there is a great woman, but in this case the opposite is true: Donna Francesca's dream would not have materialised without the support of an open and equally visionary husband.' With that support and the backing of his family wealth, and in the warehouses that existed on their property in Quartucciu, Francesca set up her enterprise. Thanks to her husband's position, she was able to take advantage of an agrarian law that facilitated the cultivation of mulberry trees. Hundreds of them were planted on the surrounding acres and, in the warehouses which became workshops, every step of the process of silk production took place using the latest technological innovations.

There was rather more to this enterprise than family wealth creation. A large part of Francesca's dream was not only to provide employment for girls and women, particularly those experiencing poverty in precarious times, but to set up professional courses for them in spinning and weaving; and the course included other basic educational subjects. At the end of the course or, when, as was traditional, a woman was expected to stop work on marriage, and perhaps to move away from the Quartucciu area, they would be given a loom as a marriage present. That meant that they could continue work even after marriage and be economically independent. They were also encouraged to pass on their skills. Hundreds of young women from all over Sardinia attended these courses, as did those from further afield, from Italy and Savoy. Over time at least 750 women were trained and worked in Francesca's silk-producing establishment. Adding to her advanced views on women's needs, and how she could help to meet them, Francesca also set up nursery schools for the children of those workers.

The soft climate of the area allowed an early hatching of the silkworm cocoons, enabling Francesca to get her silk to market 20 days earlier than that made elsewhere, and soon it was considered to be of the highest quality, not only in Sardinia but throughout Europe. Not content with producing highly esteemed silk, Francesca then started designing clothes. By the end of the eighteenth century these were being worn by the smartest women, not only including royal women of the House of Savoy but also Maria Teresa of Austria and Catherine the Great of Russia. Ornelia Demuru, in her 2012 internet article 'Francesca Sanna Sulis: "La Signora dei Gelsi"' (mulberries), suggests that there is a *c*.1780 portrait of Catherine by Fyodor Rokotov in St Petersburg's Hermitage dressed in a costume designed by Francesca. Count Giulini, Lucio Spiga discovered, opened the first boutique in Milan and had to hire six ships to transport all the silk that was ordered.

Francesca's sons died early and her husband did so in 1780, but she did not stop working. It may be that, with the death of Pietro, who had strong ties with the House of Savoy, Francesca then felt politically unconstrained. From her residence in the Via Lamarmora she could see the 1783 French attack on Cagliari, and there is some evidence that she was so friendly with Giovanni Maria Angioy, with his opposition to the Piedmontese regime, that she opened her house up to the conspirators planning the Sardinian Vespers of 1794 described in chapter 6.

Francesca herself lived until she was 94 and her will, written two years earlier, in 1808, shows that, with her death in mind, she continued along the path which she had travelled for so many years. First she instructed that she should have the simplest possible funeral, one 'without pomp'. She made bequests to the poor of her birth family's properties in Muravera. Bequests went to women without husbands so that they would neither have to depend financially on their families, nor have to marry. She left money to a hospital in Cagliari to pay for the medicines and social care of poor patients. A further bequest was to clothe poor primary school children. Another bequest went towards the release of enslaved Christians. However Cristina Muntoni, in her 2014 biographical entry for the *DonnaSarda* website, continues with a less happy outcome: two years after Francesca's death, money which should have been distributed to the church went missing and the land that had been covered in mulberry trees became orchards.

Francesca is, however, remembered in several ways, one of which continues to promote women's skills. In 2004, the authorities of the Sarrabus sub-region set up an art centre in the old carabinieri barracks at 74 Via Guglielmo Marconi in Muravera. In part of it is the Donna Francesca Sanna Sulis Museum, often subtitled Museum of the Entrepreneurship of Women. It is inspired by the work of Francesca and displays some of her work, but it is more than that, it is also a showcase for the continuing traditional handicraft activities of women, often passed from generation to generation – for example, weaving, sericulture, embroidery, fabric dyeing, macramé and the making of candles. It is a living museum, continuously evolving through workshops, demonstrations and dialogue with the community.

In Quartucciu, the Francesca Sanna Sulis Municipal Library is at 19 Via Nazionale and, in the same street, there is a plaque on the house in which Francesca lived until her death. In Cagliari, in the Castello, marking the bicentenary of her death, a plaque on 61 Via Lamarmora reads, 'Here lived Donna Francesca Sanna Sulis – entrepreneur – stylist – educator'.

The Pernis Family 1832–1941

'I went with Mamma and Auntie for a walk to Mr Pernis', wrote Florence Piercy in her diary on 9 January 1873. And she continued, 'We ordered many English things. Mrs Pernis was in the shop.' Without this hint, I might never have happened upon the extended Pernis family. As for the Piercys, they will feature in chapter 11.

It is not possible to be sure that Florence was writing about **Catterina Pernis** (1804–1879): she would have been 69 by then; and was the Mr Pernis, shopkeeper, Josias, who was then 76, but still very active? She could have been referring to the next Pernis generation. Nevertheless, it would not be a surprise if the founders of the dynasty were still in harness then. The extended family across generations will allow me to divert a couple of times from the theme of this chapter.

Catterina – her will makes it clear that she spelt it with two t's – born in Cagliari, was the daughter of the Genovese couple Giuseppe Sesselego and **Maria Pasterino**. In 1819, aged barely 15, she married Emanuele Costa with whom she had a son who died young. Her husband died in 1825. Pasterino family members were pharmacists from Genoa; this probably included Catterina's maternal grandfather, and there is some evidence that at some stage, probably when she was a widow, she worked in the family business in Cagliari. Three of the four witnesses to Catterina's will many years later were pharmacy apprentices from the Pastorino pharmacies scattered around Sardinia. Another source, a 2013 internet article about Mediterranean consulates (*Bollettino Storico*), suggests that she had work involving the supply of naval contracts. In 1829, aged 25, Catterina married 32-year-old Josias Pernis (1797–1895). They were to have seven children, two of whom died young. Some of their children, and their descendants, will feature in what follows.

Josias Pernis was born in the Swiss Canton of Grisons where his name, later Italianised, was Pernisch. He came from a family of merchants and winemakers who lost their assets during Napoleonic invasions. Josias fled to Trieste where he was given refuge by an uncle who taught him trading and navigation. In 1816, on a ship taking him from Genoa to London, he was shipwrecked on the coast near Cuglieri (Oristano). From there he made his way to Cagliari where, aged 19, he gained employment in Andrea Odone's shipping agency. His trading knowledge and languages enabled him to advance between 1820 and 1826 so that when he married Catterina in 1829 they both brought useful business experience to the marriage. Indeed, there is a suggestion, in the 2013 article, that Catterina met Josias through her work. Useful information about him comes from the website of the Bonaria cemetery where he was buried.

The Pernis Commercial House became the owner of large vineyards, and traded mainly in salt and wine, both locally and in the firm's own ships to France and the Veneto region and from there to Switzerland, as well as to England, Sweden and Norway. On the return trip, lumber and ice were imported from the north to Sardinia.

It was not all plain sailing for Catterina, as attested by the convoluted details of a family inheritance dispute that is to be found in an internet exploration of what houses were in which streets of a particular Cagliari quarter ('*Cagliari: le case della Marina*'). It seems that several of the families concerned, the Pernis – Catterina and Josias, the family of Andrea Odone (head of the shipping company for which Josias had first worked) and Catterina's siblings – lived in the Marina area of Cagliari. The area included Via Sant'Eulalia, near the church of that name, where Catterina and Josias had married, and Via Barcelona which runs past the church of Santa Lucia. The church is the earliest in Cagliari; it was built before 1119 and was demolished in 1947 but its remains are still to be seen. These mostly narrow streets still exist. Nineteenth-century Cagliari was not a particularly clean or tidy place, but the houses were probably not as decrepit as they are now, and some have been pulled down for more modern constructions. To wander through the area is, however, still useful in imagining the inhabitants' lives.

The dispute, which arose from the death of Catterina's father, Giuseppe Sesselego, in 1825, reached a climax in 1832, and concerned the Sesselego family home. Catterina's sister **Michela Mura Sesselogo**, married to the hairdresser Giuseppe Mura, and her brother Giacomo, who was a chemist, sued

Catterina and Josias, accusing them not only of taking possession of the family property as their family home, but of administering the assets badly – the house in Via Santa Lucia, a fishing boat and its cargo, and an equipment shop in Via Barcelona. For some reason, the asset whose possession seems to have most rankled was a press for making pasta. And there was some involvement of Andrea Odone, and the debts of Josias Pernis. The account seems more concerned with the story of the houses than of the outcome of the dispute. I surmise that the modern café opposite the remains of Santa Lucia, now a wire-fenced archaeological site, stands where the house in question was.

Whatever the outcome of the dispute and the truth of Josias being 'overwhelmed by debts', it obviously did not affect his rise to be one of the most important citizens of Cagliari, not only an entrepreneur, banker and founder member of the local chamber of commerce, but also a benefactor of the city. Catterina and Josias' son Eugenio, born in 1834, married **Mirra Serpieri** (1840–1890), daughter of the mining entrepreneur Enrico who arrived in Sardinia with his family when Mirra was 10. Together he and Josias established a bank in 1869 to provide lending and deposit services to local merchants, industrialists and artisans. Josias became its chairman. For many decades he was British consul and vice-consul of Norway and Sweden. It is not fanciful to assume that Catterina, having started their marriage as a working woman, offered practical support throughout her husband's upward progression; they certainly worked together at the beginning of their marriage when her Sardinian connections were useful to the young Swiss.

It is this eminence of Josias that sows doubt about the identity of the Mr Pernis, 'shopkeeper', in 1873 when young Florence Piercy accompanied her mother to his shop, and that of the Mrs Pernis who was present, though not necessarily working there. I suggest that the Mr Pernis was Eugenio, who I know took over that side of the business, undoubtedly rather grander than a little corner shop. The Mrs Pernis would, therefore, have been Mirra. It is thanks to the couple's descendants, who so kindly and invaluably helped with my Pernis research, that I know of that transfer to the next generation. They were even able to tell me the exact location of the building, which eventually combined both business and family home, enabling me to walk to the far end of the very smart arcaded shopping street of Via Roma, facing the waterfront, to the side street Via Porcile. Across that street there is an old building, also looking out over the water, that fits the bill. Josias had the necessary pull to ensure that it was not demolished, as most buildings were, for the construction of the Via Roma.

Was it Josias in later life, or Eugenio, about whom Florence Piercy wrote in her diary on October 1872, when one of her sisters had a high

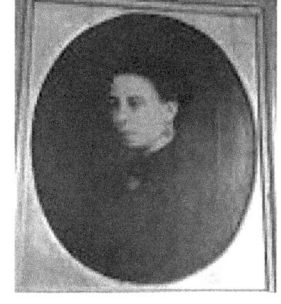

34. Mirra Pernis, photograph by Anna Maria Spinas

fever, 'Mr Pernis thought it was diphtheria; he gave me a pomegranate.' The Pernis and Piercy families had every reason to move in the same circles: from 1871, Benjamin Piercy was responsible for the construction of Sardinia's railway system which benefitted Josias' business interests.

Mirra and Eugenio had three children. The eldest, **Nelly Pernis**, married ophthalmologist Efisio Marongiu. Their daughter, **Anna Marongiu Pernis** (1907–1941) was the artist whose painting of the church of Sant'Eulalia appears in chapter 6. It was also the family church of the Belgranos who, a generation or two earlier, lived in the same area as the Pernis family.

Initially self-taught, and early revealing a talent for illustration and caricature, as Maura Picciau writes in the Italian biographical dictionary, Anna, after studying as a lawyer, became a well-known artist who lived between Cagliari and Rome where she had studied at the British Academy of Arts. She is particularly noted for her 15 views of Cagliari – *Vedute di Cagliari* – which she painted, engraved and printed between 1936 and 1941. This was at a time when it was rare for a woman to be an engraver, it being considered a masculine art form. '*Via Roma a Cagliari*' shown here is also one of those scenes.

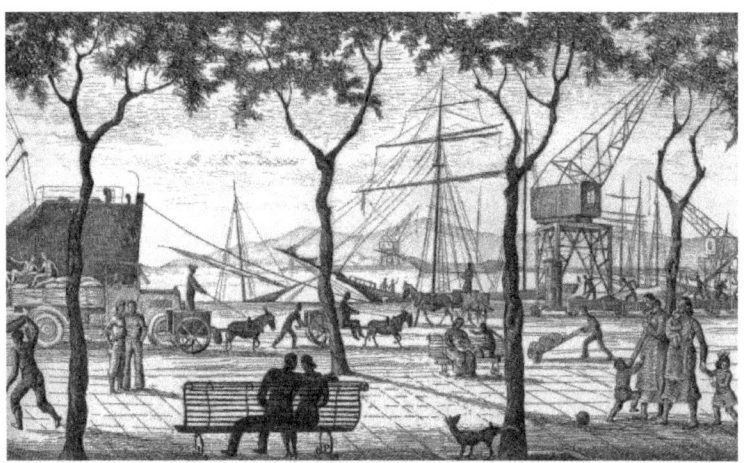

35a. '*Via Roma a Cagliari*' by Anna Marongiu

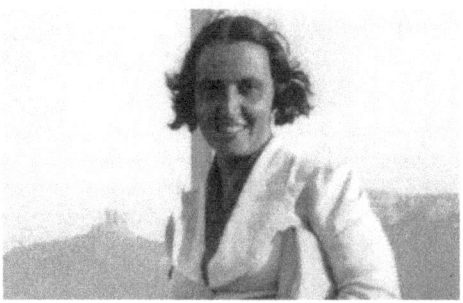

35b. Anna Marongiu, by permission of the
Ministry of Culture/University Library of Cagliari

War came and, on 30 July 1941, the seaplane in which 34-year-old Anna was travelling from Ostia near Rome to Cagliari crashed, and she was killed. Her parents gave much of her work to the Cagliari University Library. In London, her 1929 illustrations for 'The Pickwick Circuit' – 29 watercolours and 226 drawings depicting the characters in the novel – are housed in the Dickens House Museum at 48 Doughty Street. These, too, were donated by the family. Illustrating works of literature made up a large part of Anna's work throughout her artistic life. Happily, if you cannot manage to see the originals, you can see images of many of them on a YouTube video, also accessed through the Museum website. If you want to see the originals, you need to contact the Museum and discuss such a visit with them. They have recently been seen in Sardinia: in 2020 they formed part of a retrospective exhibition of Anna's work in Nuoro.

To detail the many branches of the Pernis family, even of its women, would be straying too far from the subject, but of the invaluable informants for this section, two of them, sister and brother, Anna Maria Spinas Pernis and Edoardo Spinas Pernis, are second cousins of Anna Marongiu. On the apartment walls of one of them is the portrait of their great-grandmother Mirra Pernis Serpieri which they kindly photographed while I was there. And it was they who thought that perhaps their grandmother, Caterina (Lina) Tronci Pernis who married her cousin Romolo Pernis, had been a women's suffrage activist. In an attempt to substantiate that, they got up on the internet, on the *DonnaSarda* website, information about suffrage activism in Sardinia. It was headed '*La Storia delle Suffragette Sarde*'. Unfortunately, by the time I was home and tried to retrieve that page, the *DonnaSarda* website had ceased to function and, despite concerted effort, I have got no further in accessing it, even from the author of the entry Federica Ginesu. It is no bad thing to have to start from scratch with one's own digging so, what I have found out about the women's suffrage movement in Sardinia, with some help from Cristina Muntoni, appears in chapter 12. Lina Pernis appears in detail there.

My third Pernis informant, Angelo Meridda of Milis, became interested in the Pernis family because of Benvenuto Pernis, son of Catterina and Josias's son Guglielmo, and his connection with Milis. Benvenuto made a fortune, no doubt benefitting from his connection with Josias Pernis, which had enabled him to build the Villa Pernis in Milis, acquire and breed from it a stable of the famous Anglo-Arab-Sardinian horses destined for the army, and become known too for the property's citrus and olive production. In addition, by marrying **Donna Enrichetta Cao di San Marco** (1870–1924), he acquired a noble title. She was one of the four daughters of Conte Battista Cao di San Marco and **Giovanna Palomba Miglior**. Like similar well-to-do families in Milis, the couple used their position to contribute usefully to the community.

I am going to suggest, without evidence, that, while Benvenuto occupied himself with his horses, Enrichetta was responsible for its gardens which today are the venue for an annual floral event – 'Spring in the Garden'– which involves the town and beyond. As Elena Macellari describes in '*La

Primavera nel Giardino delle Esperidi: I tesori di Milis e dell'entrottera Sardo' (2015), nurseries from far afield exhibit, and other participants include organisations concerned with Sardinia and Italy's environment, conservation and bio-diversity. In 2015 there was an exhibition of the flower and plant paintings of Sardinian artist Marina Virdis which was intended to stress the continuing importance of Sardinian women's defence of the traditional botanical knowledge passed down through the generations.

I've allowed myself to linger in Milis because of the 'Places' component of my title; Milis is, in this respect, a place of some consequence. It starts with its early association with Queen Tocoele whose story is told in chapter 4. Angelo Meridda was anxious that I include in the history of Sardinia's women the Milis-born **Donna Maddalena Vacca Salazar** (1783–1816), daughter of Giovachino Vacca and **Maria Grazia Salazar**. In 1800, she married Marquis Vittorio Pilo Boyl di Putifigari at Iglesias. Members of the royal families of Europe have apparently descended from the Vacca-Boyl union.

What is known as the Palazzo Boyl in Piazza Martiri, Milis, came to Maddalena's husband as part of her dowry, while she acquired his title. The palazzo was built in 1600 on the site of a fourteenth-century manor house. Vittorio enlarged the palazzo which was owned by the Boyl family until 1978 when it was sold to Milis town. It now houses a traditional costume and jewellery museum, and an amphitheatre in the courtyard seats 700 spectators. The palazzo is open all year round. It is noted for the famous people who visited the family there; in the early twentieth century it was a literary meeting place; visitors included Sardinia's Nobel prize-winning writer Grazia Deledda.

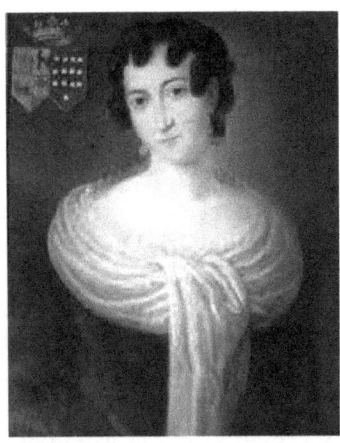

36. Donna Maddalena Vacca Salazar, Milis, thanks to Angelo Meridda

Milis, set in a valley, and in Roman times a military outpost (*miles* = soldier), is more than the Pernis manor house, and the Palazzo Boyl with the fine gardens and parks of both and, indeed, the women who have lived in them: it is famous for its orange trees, the fruit of which is sweet and succulent. They not only proliferate in the large properties but also line the streets. The introduction of orange trees dates back to the thirteenth century and the arrival in the area of the Camaldolese monks of the monastery of Bonarcado, and their flourishing is thanks to what is called *La Vega*, the Spanish term for fertile soil rich in water. French traveller Claude Pasquin, known as Valery, in his *Voyage en Sardaigne* compared the orange groves of Milis to the mythical North African Garden of Hesperides. The orange groves, the sight of them in full blossom, and the perfume that fills the air, not only are a delight to visitors but their existence has driven the economy of Milis.

Be careful if you are prone to hay fever.

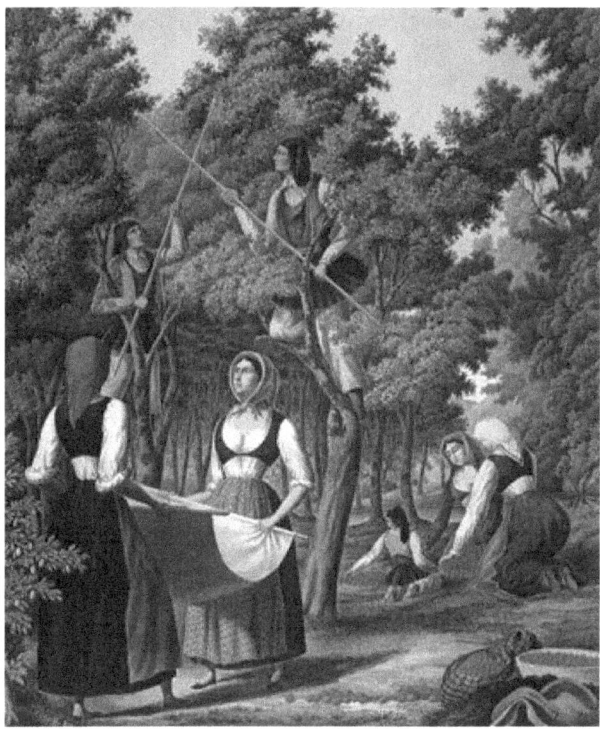

37. Women collecting oranges, Milis, by Simone Manca di Mores, from the internet

Sardinia's Mining Sisterhood 1851–1918 (Introduction; Elena Poinsel and the Rosas Mine, Zely Sanna-Castoldi, Montevecchio and its Women Workers; Helen Dunstan Wright, Idina Brassey and the Ingurtosu Mine)

Introduction

In 1832, the year that the inheritance dispute between Catterina Pernis and her family came to a head, the presence of lead, zinc and copper was discovered in the lee of Monte Rosas, named for the rose-coloured quartz (rosasite) also prevalent, in the Sulcis Iglesiente region of south-west Sardinia. This find by a businessman from Iglesias – the capital of Sardinia's mining area – was, by the second half of the nineteenth century, to introduce women as major participants, at least one of them an owner, in Sardinia's mining enterprises.

Mining of various stones and minerals was hardly new in Sardinia. Chapter 1 describes the mining of obsidian in Neolithic times. Silver extraction was among the earliest in Europe. Under the Romans, Sardinia was to rank third in the empire for the quantity of metals worked. And mining continued thereafter, often known about because of the tools left on site;

by the beginning of the nineteenth century 59 mines produced mainly lead, iron, copper and silver.

Elena Poinsel and the Rosas Mine

With the discovery of what came to be known as the Rosas mine, the nearby village of Narcao, 40 km (25 miles) west of Cagliari and about 15 km (9 miles) east of Carbonia, mushroomed: as Rita Cannas of Cagliari University notes in her internet article 'The Sustainable Tourism Management of Cultural Heritage' (2016), it grew from 561 inhabitants in 1824 to 2316 in 1858. Whole families moved in, including young boys who worked underground, and women and children who dressed the ore at the surface.

There is little more frustrating than to come across a woman of obvious consequence about whom so little is known, and about whom the sources differ. Some say that **Elena Felicia Poinsel** was from Marseille; at least one source, the website for Minerals of Sardinia, says that she was Belgian. I can find no dates for her, and no parentage. But she did have a brother called Emilio who was apparently in business with her. In 1851 the Unione Sulcis e Sarrabus mining company, of which Elena and Emilio were major shareholders, seems to have acquired several mining concessions in Sardinia (Gibbas, Perdarta and Peddiattu). As that same source suggests that it was a Genoese company and, given her brother's Italian name, it may be that the family of French or Belgian origin had at some stage moved to Italy.

In 1863, according to the internet article '*Narcao: La Miniera Rosas*', Elena purchased the concession of La Rosas for £9765. That concession was then merged with the other three her company mined. Elena's ownership of those concessions lasted only until 1869 when, because of poor revenue, they were sold to the Cagliari Mining Company. Not only do I lack confidence in the facts that I have presented, but it is impossible to tell of, or even guess at, Elena's involvement. Did she ever go to Sardinia? If she did, did she have anything to do with the management of the mines? If so, what was her attitude to the workers, women, children and men? Where did the £9765 come from? Was it family money, or a bank or other loan? There must be evidence of answers somewhere, but it continues to elude me.

The Rosas mine passed through several hands after Elena Poinsel's, and suffered the same vicissitudes as many mines during the First World War: male labourers were replaced by women, children and prisoners; it closed temporarily in 1918. There were problems, too, before and after the Second World War. It closed permanently in 1980 because of the depletion of lodes and the soaring cost of mineral extraction. But it was deemed of sufficient cultural significance, as Rita Cannas describes with photographic illustrations, to gain recognition as a UNESCO heritage site in 1998, and, under those auspices, it was opened to visitors in 2009.

Rita Cannas goes on to describe the current complex ownership, management and funding of the mine and the village of Narcao:

The municipal authority of Narcao is the only one in Sardinia to have full ownership of their own site, while mining heritage overall is under the management of the Geomineral Park and other individual authorities and is owned by the Sardinian regional government. This aspect is crucial because, as the legal owner of the mining complex, the Local Council of Narcao was able to apply directly for funding made available by the European Union for projects such as the restoration of the ex-mining site, and to closely follow its path of development.

This ownership was explained to the blogger 'Kernowclimber' in 2012/13, prompting the internet description of what it means for the visitor:

This has engendered a sense of democratic ownership of the eco-museum. Indeed the home cooked lunch we are consuming with gusto has been prepared by the wives and daughters of the former mineworkers as the restaurant, a building that was once the mine post office, is run by the Association of former Rosas Miners.

The lunch consisted of 'many courses including blue fin tuna, a local pasta dish and roasted suckling pig washed down with a fine Sardinian red wine'.

It may be a bit fanciful to suggest that what is now an apparently flourishing eco-museum owes something to Elena Poinsel: can it be seen as a monument to her? Perhaps not, but she does seem to have been unusual, and is the beginning of a trend of middle-class women's involvement in mining establishments. That of working-class women is most noticeably apparent in the Montevecchio mine described next.

If La Rosas appears attractive enough to warrant a visit, it would be a pity to miss the remains at the nearby hamlet Tarraseo of a Phoenician temple dedicated to the goddess Demeter. The original sections and the Roman reconstruction are clearly visible and have not completely altered the original floorplan.

Zely Sanna-Castoldi, Montevecchio and its Women Workers

The story of **Zely Sanna-Castoldi** (1852–1932) and the mine of Montevecchio is quite different from that of Elena Poinsel and La Rosas: so much more is known about her, for a start, her dates and parentage. She was the daughter, the youngest of four, of Giovanni Antonio Sanna of Sassari and **Maria Sanna Lambi y Casas** (b.1820). Maria, whom Sanna had met and married in Marseille where he went as a young man to make his fortune, was the daughter of a Spanish businessman, no doubt a useful connection. In 1875 Zely married Alberto Castoldi, who had been born in the same house in Via Sant'Eulalia in the Marina district of Cagliari, four years before her. This is an area with which we are becoming increasingly familiar. They were to have two children, **Enedina Castoldi** (named after one of Zely's sisters) and Giovanni Antonio (Nini).

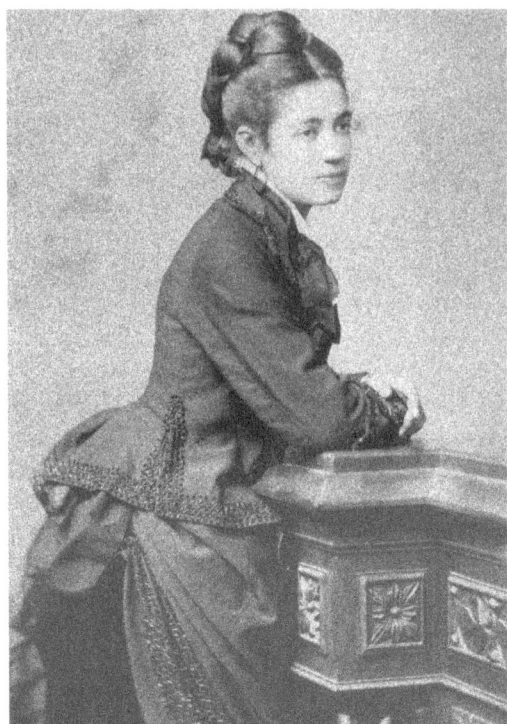

38. Zely Sanna Castoldi, from Fadda, *La Montevecchio di Alberto Castoldi*

Alberto's father died in 1855 of cholera during a well-documented epidemic in Sassari (see chapter 6). Zely's father, who had already left Sassari in 1842, and thereafter begun to make his fortune, sought a mineral concession west of Guspini and Arbus, an area where both the Phoenicians and Romans had mined. To do so, he set up the Society for the Mining of Lead and Silver at Montevecchio. By 1848 this had developed into Montevecchio I, II and III, for which King Carlo Alberto signed an act of perpetual concession. By 1865, Montevecchio employed 1000 workers mining for silver, zinc and lead, making it the largest mine complex in the Kingdom of Italy. It is said that the lead for the roof of Notre Dame Cathedral in Paris came from Montevecchio in that same year.

In 1870 Sanna built at Montevecchio what became known as 'Palazzina della Direzione' where Zely must have lived as a young woman. In 1871, he founded and became president of the Sardinian Agricultural Bank. Its Sardinian manager was lawyer Lorenzo Castoldi, the uncle of his future son-in-law, and the Rome branch was managed by Alberto Castoldi's brother. The two families already knew each other, having moved in the same circles in Sassari.

Alberto Castoldi was bright, particularly at mathematics and, having obtained a scholarship to the University of Padua, graduated with a degree in pure mathematics. It was not surprising, therefore, that Sanna, with an eye to the future of his mine, should have supported him in his studies at the Institute for Mining and Engineering at Freiberg, from where he graduated in 1874. By then he was clearly a suitable husband for Zely, and the couple married in Rome a few months after Sanna's death there in 1875. From there they moved to Montevecchio.

In Montevecchio, the couple acquired a large property near the mine which was developed into a modern farm. They also bought the house in Sant'Eulalia. In 1877, Alberto was made director of the Montevecchio mine.

They were thus obliged to live there for eight months of the year, and they did so initially in the house they called Genna Serapis, named after the nearby Monte Genna Serapis. (The name of the mountain apparently refers to the Greco-Egyptian goddess Serapide, guardian and protector of the underworld, invoked by slaves who at the time of Roman domination worked in the mines of the area.) In due course, they moved into the Palazzina della Direzione, attached to which, in 1880, Alberto built the chapel dedicated to Santa Barbara, the patron saint of miners. Much of the information for Alberto, Zely and Montevecchio comes from Paolo Fadda's *La Montevecchio di Alberto Castoldi* (2014) which I bought there. Carefully mined, enough can be gleaned about Zely.

Although the contrast is made in some sources between the 'humble dwellings' of the mine-workers and the 'luxurious' Palazzino della Direzione where the Sanna-Castoldi family lived, and where the management of the mining complex had its offices, Zely was by no means unaware of the workers' conditions and needs. As early as 1885, she convinced Alberto to build a 36-bed hospital – four rooms with nine beds in each – with the sort of advanced medical equipment that would ensure that the workers and their families had top-quality health provision run by an expert medical staff. The hospital, overlooking the main Montevecchio square, was renovated and expanded in 1905. For a time it was said to be one of the most modern hospitals in Sardinia. In addition, a mutual aid fund and organisation was set up to look after the miners and their families in case of accident; £1200 was paid into it annually.

Running in tandem with the comfortable, if benevolent, life of Zely Sanna-Castoldi was the rather harder and more precarious life of the women who worked at the Montevecchio mines. Their story is invaluably told and illustrated in *Donne e Bambine nella Miniera di Montevecchio* (2005) by Iride Peis Concas which was brought to my attention and generously bought for me in the carefully stocked bookshop run by two women interested in my project in the nearby town of Guspini where Iride Peis was born.

The jobs of the women and girls, usually wearing traditional headscarves, were to deal with and sort out what came up from the mines and ran past them on a conveyer belt, or to hold two ends of a large industrial sieve full of stones to be shaken over a suspended box, or to wash them in a container inside another, by pulling on a chain suspended over the arm of a post. There is also a photograph of a line of women walking along the ridge of an open mine – men digging in the background – with large, full baskets on their heads. 'The abandoned mining area of Montevecchio-Ingurtosu' (2001), a technical article by Stefania da Pelo et al of the Department of Earth Sciences at the University of Cagliari, adds an explanatory note in connection with the building of a new washing plant in 1877: 'Here Women and children handpicked the ore, to separate gangue material from the ore, that was then carried to the washing and grinding plants.' Gangue, I discover, is commercially worthless material that surrounds, or is closely mixed with, a wanted mineral in an ore deposit. So women and children's work is as essential a part of the process as that of the men.

The photographs in Iride Peis Concas's book are well worth their inclusion, but would not be effective in reproduction here. The only one I have chosen shows the exact location of Montevecchio, and the two women inset gives an idea of one of their tasks.

It does not take much imagination to conclude that the women's work shown in the photographs was back-breaking and sometimes head-numbing and hot, but other photographs suggest that there was camaraderie among them which helped them to survive it. There was, though, rather more to what they went through. This is what happened in 1871, before even the young Sanna-Castoldis's marriage, let alone their arrival at Montevecchio.

Iride Peis Concas writes up the incident:

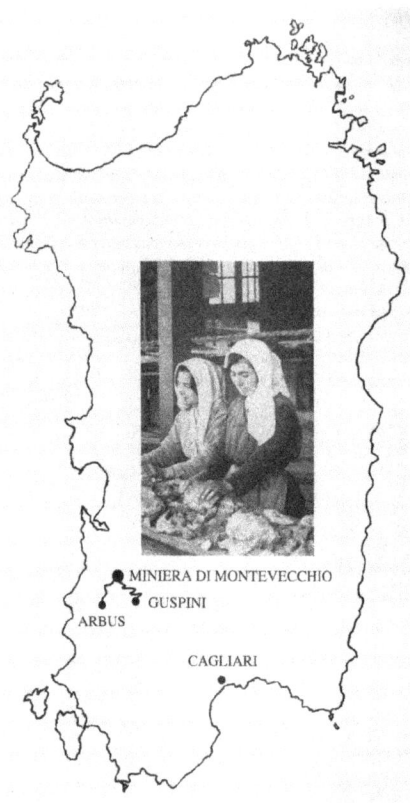

39. Women workers inside Map of Sardinia, from Concas, *Donne e bambine nella miniera di Montevecchio*

Around 6.30 in the evening of 4 May 1871, at the Atzuni yard of the Montevecchio mine, Guspini, about 30 women and girls left their daily work to return to their dormitory. Above this an 80 cubic metre water tank had recently been installed for the laveria [for washing the minerals]. Just as they were going in, the side of the tank was smashed by the volume of water which was hurled against the dormitory wall. This caused the roof to collapse onto the women below. 11 of them died instantly. Four others were got out injured, though not critically. Nine of the victims came from the neighbouring village of Arbus, the other two were from Guspini. Of the wounded, three came from Guspini, one from Gonnosfanadiga, the other from Nurri.

The 11 dead are listed below that account, together with their ages and home villages. Two of them, **Anna Peddis** and **Anna Pusceddu**, were only 14; **Rosa Gentila** was 15; the oldest, **Rosa Vacca**, was 50.

As a result of the work of Iride Peis Concas, the tragedy has, not surprisingly, struck a chord with today's Sardinian women writers, and their comments don't make happy reading concerning the treatment of the island's women workers in the past. Several writers have chosen either an anniversary, or 8 March, International Women's Day, to remember women who might have slipped away from Sardinia's memory. The blogger Doriana Goracci, in '*Una Miniera di Donne Dimenticate*' (2017) quotes from a 2015 *DonnaSarda* article by Cristina Muntoni who describes the women walking towards the dormitory as 'annihilated by fatigue. They had broken and bagged stones all day long with rough and calloused hands. They had done it, as always, since dawn, in strict silence.'

Doriana Goracci goes on to explain that 'the powers-that-be could not tolerate people talking and the punishment would cost the whole day's pay. The blackmail of bread. A cost too expensive for those who work to survive.' The walk back to their village, after such a day, required effort the women – 'widows of miners, wives with too many children to feed left behind to take care of each other' – no longer possessed. If that was the case you could stay at the construction site and 'rest on the cots, in dormitories without toilets or any kind of comfort'.

In '*4 Maggio 1871: La tragedia di Montevecchio – Muoiono in Miniera 11 Operaie*' (2016), Veronica Secci pronounces judgment:

> With regard to the tragedy – one of the darkest pages in the history of women's work on the island – an investigation was opened, which ended with the full acquittal of all the leaders. Nobody – it was said – could be considered responsible for the accident, if not fate. What is certain is that in Sardinia, at the end of the nineteenth century, occupational safety and the protection of workers' rights – and, above all, those of female workers – enjoyed very little attention. Poor pay, exhausting shifts and almost total subordination to the work of their male colleagues: this was the condition of the workers employed in the numerous mines of the island. A despised, difficult and dangerous job, which was accepted as a necessary evil, given the precarious social and economic conditions of these young and very young women, often orphans or widows.

There is a YouTube presentation that shows most of the photographs in Iride Peis Concas's book and tells the story of the 1871 tragedy. I'm not sure about the swelling background music by Nino Rota.

With the fuller picture of the lives of women workers, the initiatives of Zely Sanna-Castoldi at Montevecchio are given a new context. She would have known what happened in 1871; was she trying to make sure that such a tragedy could never happen again, and if there were to be an accident of any sort, there was now a safety net? It is a fair assumption.

In 1880, aged 32, Alberto Castoldi entered parliament as deputy for Iglesias, which assumed responsibility for Montevecchio, a seat he kept until 1913. He remained director of the mines until 1915, when Sollmann

Bertolio, husband of his daughter Enedina, took over. Alberto was said to be rather conscious of his position, seeing himself as 'sovereign of his empire'. Three cannon shots would announce his arrival perhaps as his carriage passed through the triumphal arch 2 km (1.2 miles) out of Montevecchio (still there today). Zely, on the other hand, remained unconscious of hers: she continued gentle, generous and displaying 'love of her neighbour'.

An informant, knowing of my interest in his family place of Guspini, told me of an innovation that took place in 'around 1913', perhaps in Zely's time, and she may, I suggest, have been responsible for it. The story comes from Aunt N, born in 1940, who got it from an aunt:

> Her mother, **grannie Delfa**, raised her family in the mining district of Montevecchio, where she worked as a mineral polisher. With the younger siblings of Auntie F, she did not have time to leave the work place and Auntie F used to bring the little ones to her mother to breast feed them in the middle of the hall where they worked, without any privacy. Upon seeing Auntie F bringing her brother to grannie Delfa to be breast fed, the mining director was shocked and decided to introduce a breast-feeding break for all the mothers with little children.
>
> Back then, poverty for the mine-workers was astonishing, Auntie F remembers that one of the remedies for disinfecting the wounds used by her mother was human urine.

A rather different story is told by Rosalba Mariani in her novel *Miniera* (The Mine, 2011) based on 1000 family letters bequeathed to her by her older sister, **Silvia Mariani**, already 20 when Rosalba, the last of seven children, was born. The book is partly a history of her family, particularly its strong women – her lace-making grandmother, ready to cross the island for love, her beloved sister and surrogate mother, Silvia, who felt no need to marry, and the family cook Elfisia who would wring a chicken's neck without turning a hair. It is also the story of Montevecchio with added touches of twentieth-century Sardinia.

Attilio Mariani, Rosalba's father, arrived at Montevecchio as a doctor in 1907. Awaiting him was the state-of-the art hospital built at Zely's instigation. He brought his wife, **Maria Mariani Cucca**, there in 1911. This portrait of them dates from then. Attilio had been considered a suitable *partie* by Maria's father, who was also a doctor. As a professional, he and his family moved in the highest Montevecchio circles, hobnobbing with the Sanna-Castoldi and other profes-

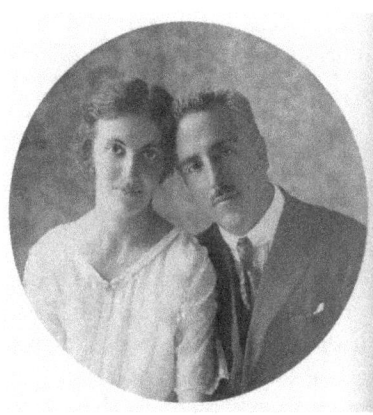

40. Maria and Attilio Mariani, *c*.1911, from Mariani, *Miniera*

sionals, managers and technicians, chemical engineers and geologists. It is a bourgeois family life that Rosalba describes; her father practised there for 50 years. But, as will be revealed, she ends the book elegiacally and inclusively.

Following Alberto's death in 1922, Zely turned her attention, between 1926 and 1932, to funding the establishment of the Archaeological Museum in Sassari's Via Roma so that it could house her father's large collection, which she had donated to the city as early as 1878. As a result of her bequest, all Sardinian museums are free to women on 8 March. Zely was 79 when she died in 1932, after a life in which, whatever had gone before her at Montevecchio, she had made, and left, her mark.

Montevecchio did not close until 1991. Today it is one of eight sites in the Geo-mining park of Sardinia, as well as being a UNESCO World Heritage Site, and you can take the full tour. Even if you don't do that, not only can you drive past the mines, visible where they are open-cast, but the headquarters complex, built around a square, is eminently visitable. It is so apparently unchanged, though slightly as if preserved in aspic, that it is not hard to imagine all that went on there. The Palazzina della Direzione has opening hours which allow the visitor to see the 'sumptuous Blue Room', in its heyday used for receptions; both it and the hall are decorated with frescoes. There is apparently a museum there now. Unfortunately, we did not choose the right time to visit and find the building open. Walk round the back and you can see the chapel; from the front of it, the valley stretches out before you to the south.

Rosalba Mariani ends *Miniera* poetically, not neglecting the women who had worked at Montevecchio before its closure, and the ghosts that were left behind:

> The person who chooses to live at Montevecchio needs to relate to the past, does not fear solitude and lives as if nothing had happened, as if the mine still worked. By day they go looking for mushrooms or asparagus and at night they wait for the herds of deer that live there now, alongside the humans, which come to look for food almost in front of their houses.
>
> In short, Montevecchio is not a ghost town today, but it is inhabited by ghosts, and perhaps Attilio and Maria pass by them and look at their house, so poorly reduced, with regret, while Giovanni Antonio Sanna observes his palace, just as he left it, with pleasure.
>
> Even the eight little ones who graded stones, dead from the collapse of a tank, and all the women who exhausted their bones in the mine, and those who sold vegetables on payday, are there at the foot of the Leone Rock and wait for someone to speak about them again.

Helen Dunstan Wright, Idina Brassey and the Ingurtosu Mine

La Rosas mine briefly re-enters the picture because in 1909, a man mistakenly called Karl William Wright, said to be an English engineer, took over, or came to direct, the mine, bringing with him his young wife. A strange story built up around her, an interim source for which may be a chapter in Antonio Maccioni's *101 Tesori Nascosti della Sardegna* (2012). She was said to be an albino whom the locals called 'The White Woman' who walked around the garden of their residence at night alone reading a mysterious book by the light of the candle she held. It is hard to find a grain of truth in this story.

Charles Will Wright was, indeed, a mining engineer, but he was American. When his father died, his mother took her three children to Germany; there Charles studied at the Freiberg School of Mines, as his father had done before him and as, indeed, Alberto Castoldi of Montevecchio did. During the family's time, his mother, **Caroline Cox Wright**, went to Sardinia to visit friends of her husband, and that presumably began a Sardinian connection.

In 1909, the year he started at La Rosas, perhaps as the owner, Charles married **Helen Bree Dunstan** (1882–1975), daughter of a lieutenant governor of Michigan, and a graduate of Vassar College, and she did, indeed, accompany him to La Rosas. There is, however, no evidence to link her to a man of a similar but different name, nor any nocturnal wanderings. But it may be that his time in Germany allowed the name Karl to creep into sources. How long the couple remained at La Rosas is unclear, but probably a short time, nor whether or not his time there was part of his 10-year contract with a British mining company.

The more substantial part of Charles's mining life in Sardinia, once again accompanied by Helen, was at the Ingurtosu mine, where silver, lead and zinc had been extracted since 1853, not far from Montevecchio; indeed it was part of the same mineral seam. There he was deputy director in the British mining company – Pertusola Limited – of which Thomas Allnutt Brassey was owner and managing director. The Wrights were to live in Villa Wright, in the nearby village of Pitzinurri, and to stay at Ingurtosu until the outbreak of the First World War. There was probably not yet a midwife at the mine, as there was to be later, because their daughter Janet was born in Genoa in 1911.

Thomas Allnutt Brassey (known as TAB), Eton,

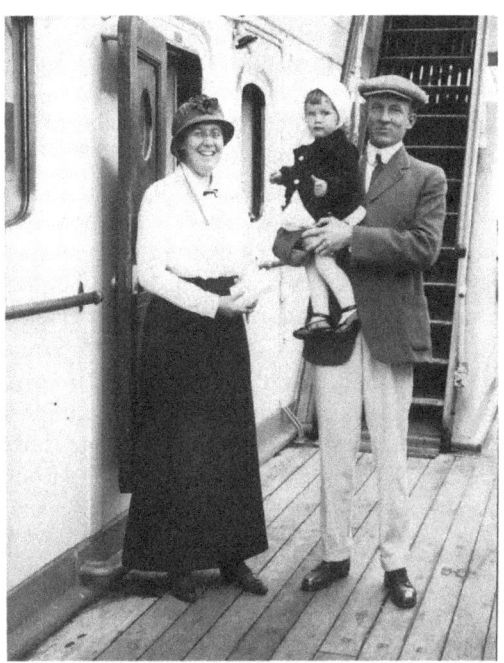

41. Helen and Charles Wright, thanks to Maurizio Piga

Balliol College, Oxford, and Captain in the Imperial Yeomanry, is often called Lord Brassey in sources, but he did not inherit that title from his father, the 1st Earl Brassey, until 1918, the year before his own death; his formal title until then was Viscount Hythe. In 1889, Thomas married Lady Idina Mary Nevill, daughter of William Nevill, 1st Marquess of Abergavenny and Caroline Vanden-Bempde-Johnson. It was a big society wedding and an account of it from the *Boston Evening Transcript* – 'Lady Athletes in England' – gives a flavour of the **Lady Idina Brassey** (1865–1951) who was to feature at Ingurtosu:

> Only this season, at the marriage between the Hon. Thomas Brassey and Lady Idina Nevill, the bridesmaids were arrayed in serge gowns with loose shirts, and the colours of the cricket club which the bride had so often captained with success; and the marriage does not seem to have interfered with Lady Idina's devotion to the national game, for in spite of the counter attraction of the London Season, she appears to be in very good form this year: at any rate she has been scoring well.

By 1903, and after 14 years of marriage, little had changed: an article in the *New York Times* supplement 'Women Here and There' reported:

> Lady Idina Brassey, who with her husband Mr Tom Brassey, arrived in New York last Saturday for a short stay here and a trip to Canada, is a very handsome woman. ... She is intensely fond of all outdoor sports, and is one of the best cricket players in England, where women have taken up the game quite seriously. She is an excellent shot, and she has made several long tours of the Continent and in Scotland on her wheel.

These descriptions of Idina, as determined, talented, slightly eccentric, were to last, perhaps to increase, until her death at the age of 85. Much more about English women's cricket and the part played in its development by Idina and her sisters is to be found in Timothy Dudgeon's *Bats, Baronets and Battle: A Social History of Cricket and Cricketers from an East Sussex Town* (2013). As a member of the White Heather Club, Idina was said to have bowled 'undeniable chisellers'. The club did much for the involvement of working-class women in sport.

The Pertusola Mining Company, as detailed by Frank Partridge in *TAB: A Memoir of Thomas Allnutt Brassey,*

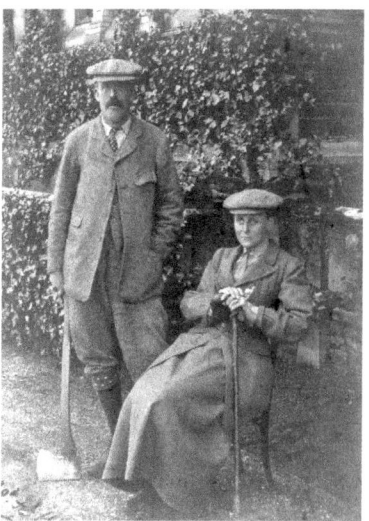

42. Idina and Thomas Brassey, courtesy of the Bexhill Museum, East Sussex

Second Earl Brassey (1921), had been set up by Thomas Brassey's grandfather and had mines, a smelting works and a shipyard in Italy. Eventually these came into his grandson's hands. By 1896, in spite of his political and military commitments in Britain, Thomas Brassey entered the Sardinian Mining Association and was its president in 1914. He bought the Gennamari-Ingurtosu mines in 1899 and expanded them with an investment of about 4000000 lire (about 1.5 million Euros).

Brassey, a paternalistic liberal, was to make many improvements to the mines, not only in infrastructure, such as the palatial *laveria* (mineral washing – 'dressing') building, built at Naracauli in 1900, but also in the conditions of the workers. And while he is credited with them, care needs to be taken over who inspired them; that is, what part Idina played. My reason for this caveat is that he is credited in, for example, the internet piece 'An English Man in Arbus: Lord Brassey', with having had built the church dedicated to the miners' patron saint Santa Barbara which stands on a hill above the main road. It is known that it was built at the instigation and fundraising not only of Idina, but also of Helen Dunstan Wright who was obviously a friend and collaborator in improvements. The two of them lobbied Thomas to contribute and in addition to approach the Bishop of Cagliari for funds; the bishop must have persuaded the Pope to help. Thomas was certainly at the church's inauguration in 1916; Idina might well have been but it wouldn't have been thought worth mentioning; the same applies to Helen.

The Brasseys travelled to Ingurtosu together at least once a year; Thomas was usually there every six months. An evocative account of their time there, dating from 1910/11, comes from *Social and Diplomatic Memories* (1922) by Sir James Rennell Rodd, British ambassador to Rome. It illustrates generally prevailing foreign attitudes towards Sardinians then, in this case the Sardinian workers and their families; at one time the population of Ingurtosu reached 6000, 2500 of them mine-workers. Sir James starts, 'I had long promised a visit to the Brasseys, who spent a month every spring on their mining estates in Sardinia.' He then explains a family bereavement, and continues, also describing the delights of spring the Brasseys enjoyed there:

> Sardinia, where I could only remain three or four days, was in early May a paradise of wild flowers. The dark macchia jungle looked as though snow-sprinkled with the white stars of the cystus. There were wild peonies, stocks and lavender. The curious Pancration lily with its fretted white blooms grew in the folds of the hill near Ingertosu. There were slopes steel blue with rosemary and rocks carpeted with the mesymbrianthemum in full flower. That good fellow with the unfinished manner and the warmest of hearts whom we loved as Tab Brassey had been, here and everywhere, active in endeavouring to improve the lot of his fellowman. The cottages built for the workmen at the Brassey Mines were solid and comfortable, and every year he and Lady Idina offered a number of prizes for the cleanest and smartest houses and for the best-kept gardens. There was eager competition to win them. Sardinia, with customs and traditions

and almost a language of its own, is remote from contact with the march of progress. I felt proud of my countryman who was thus endeavouring to humanize its primitive sons.

Another example of attitudes towards the Sardinians at Ingurtosu comes not necessarily from the Brasseys themselves. Thomas is said to have been well liked by the workers; in turn he 'loved' to have lunch with them all. His car was among the first in Sardinia and the people who saw it for the first time called it '*Sa carrossa chenza des Cuaddusu*' ('a carriage without horses') as they looked 'from all sides to see where the horses were hidden'. The introduction of the car must have made travelling to Ingurtosu from San Gavino railway station easier for the Brasseys and, indeed, to Villa Ginestra, also known as Villa Idina, their quite isolated residence in the hills above the mining complex.

As at Montevecchio a generation earlier, and perhaps inspired by Zely Sanna-Castoldi's prompting of her husband, a hospital was built at Ingurtosu in Brassey's day; the midwife introduced there must surely have been the initiative of Idina or Helen, or perhaps both. Partridge, quoting from a report made originally in Italian by Thomas, gives an overall picture. Having mentioned the building of the much-needed hospital, Thomas continues:

> Having provided for work, bread for the workmen and the care of the sick during the first three years of our management, we were able in 1902 to tackle the problem of improving their conditions of life, which were very similar to those of the population of the poor Irish provinces, which I have repeatedly visited in order to inspect … improvements made … Our workpeople lived in very small houses, often without windows, to be ruled out from the sanitary point of view. Many lived in huts made of branches. Down in the valleys, many were suffering from malaria.

It is not surprising, therefore, that much was done to improve housing, taking care to build on higher ground for fresher air, important, especially for the children, and quinine was purchased from the government, and mesh put over the windows, to combat malaria. Access to good water was another innovation. The purpose of the prize-giving is also explained, not so much paternal as practical:

> It would have been useless to provide good dwellings if means of encouraging cleanliness had not been provided as well. For this purpose we give prizes each year for the best-kept houses in each section and in the whole of the Mine. … The prizes are given by my wife, and one of our lady friends. … when visiting the houses, the workpeople and their families become acquainted with their employers, and we with our workpeople. We hear their grievances and we see their difficulties.

He felt that education of the children generally was the responsibility of the commune, but 'When education is given to adults or juvenile working people, this must, of course, be at the expense of the Company. We have already tried evening schools for workmen.'

In 1905, his men asked Thomas to become president of the *Circolo Operaio* (Workingmen's club) the object of which was threefold: to advance education amongst the workmen; to prevent useless strikes, and to establish a Mutual Provident Association.

Without detailing Idina's involvement in the Brassey improvements, the biographer does, though, add:

> Lady Idina, whose achievements in raising the standard and general tone of the district were second only to his own, was often there. To the untutored mind of the Sardinian workman and his wife both of them appeared as something more than human. If they were not gods, they were at least divine. Perhaps this is not to be wondered at.

In spite of the remarks in what is rather a hagiography, it seems obvious that, the Ingurtosu and Montevecchio mines being so close together, Idina Brassey, Helen Dunstan Wright and Zely Sanna-Castoldi must have known each other. It is also quite likely that the older, and longer-established woman at Montevecchio inspired her neighbours with her improvements at her husband's mines. I can find no mention of the women mine-workers at Ingurtosu. Presumably they performed the same functions from 1899 onwards that are described so vividly at Montevecchio, though, all being well, under improved conditions. Did the women members of the families in their improved housing also work at the mine?

In 1918, a large mineralised mass was discovered in the mine of San Giovanni which took the name Idina, as did the mine's *laveria*. But at the end of the following year, Thomas was knocked down by a taxi in London and killed.

That the people of Ingurtosu appreciated Idina as much as they did Thomas, is suggested by the message they took the trouble to send to her, and in English:

> Deeply sorry for the unexpected and tragical death of our Master well loved Lord Brassey, we beg your Highness to agree our hearty condolences. He was the best Man in our world and we shall always remember him with deep sadness.

Thomas's death inevitably ended Idina's Sardinian days, but not her community involvement in England that hints at her mostly unrecorded involvement at Ingurtosu. During the First World War, in connection with her work with the Red Cross, she had turned the family home, Normanhurst, near Battle, into a military hospital and become its commandant. Tim

Dudgeon softens that superior, rather militaristic, image: he records that 'Lady Idina worked tirelessly as part of the nursing staff'.

During the First World War, after they had left Sardinia, Helen and Charles Wright were giving their support to Italy, each in their own way. Charles was a captain of engineers in the Italian Army. Helen worked for the American Red Cross and raised $50000 from family and friends to build a hospital in Cagliari for Sardinian soldiers. In a letter to the *New York Times* of 20 May 1917, she sought funds for a tuberculosis treatment plan in Sardinia for returning soldiers. She received the title of *Gran Dama della Regina* from the King of Italy for her service.

Sardinia in peaceful times remained on Helen's mind, and her article published in the *National Geographic* magazine's August 1916 issue seems to have been looking forward to tourism and Sardinia's post-war economy. The first paragraph includes the passage:

> The tourist seldom includes a trip to Sardinia in his travels, as neither of his advisers, Thomas Cook nor Baedeker, recommends it to him. It, however, is one of the few foreign fields that has not been overrun and overfed by the tourist, and in many of the villages a traveller is still regarded as a guest and not as prey to be pounced upon.

Anyone hoping, though, for some insights into her life at Ingurtosu will be disappointed: it is really for potential tourists. This is a good example:

> Unfortunately, the general impression outside of Sardinia, even in Italy, is that the island is more or less overrun by bandits; this is not true, and a traveller on the island today is even safer than he would be in southern Italy or Sicily.

The many photographs that illustrate the article, mostly taken by Charles, are both lively and informative, as those used in chapters 7 and 14 show. If only Helen had written for publication about those scenes set in their context.

By early 1919, the Wrights had already returned to Italy – a son was born in Rome in January. In 1920 they settled in Merano, in the southern Tyrol, where Charles operated mines he had bought, though Helen had a second daughter in Rome in September 1921. In Merano, she formed an association of American women to help destitute Englishwomen and Russian refugees. They left Italy when Mussolini began confiscating the property of foreigners, and returned to the United States where Charles became chief of the Mining Division of the Bureau of Mines, and Helen continued her good works. She died seven years after Charles, at the age of 93.

Following Thomas Brassey's death, Idina, in her long widowhood, was a Justice of the Peace and Parish Councillor, as well as active patron of many charities and institutions. Her presidency of the board of trustees of the St Catherine's Convalescent Home for Gentlewomen after the Second World

War is ineffably captured in Victoria Seymour's *Letters from Lavender Cottage: Hastings in World War One and Austerity* (2002). In a 1949 letter the correspondent writes of Idina and St Catherine's,

> The Patron is a countess but if you saw her you would conclude that the charlady had volunteered to act in that capacity. The poor old dear is over 80 and one can't hear a word she says but still, a countess is a countess, even in Socialist England.

Idina, who is also described elsewhere as wearing man's clothes, not very 'charlady', but certainly eccentric, died in 1951, crippled with arthritis. The White Heather Cricket Club, perhaps because shorn of her support, ceased playing cricket in 1957.

I really wanted to see Villa Idina and the Santa Barbara church at Ingurtosu, with their Idina Brassey and Helen Dunstan Wright connections, and to go to Montevecchio where Zely Sanna-Castoldi lived. It seemed impossible as our situation made car hire out of the question, but a very kind friend, whose original home place was nearby Guspini, offered to take me to both. It was also an opportunity to see the landscape from Cagliari to the mining district. Our first stop was to be Villa Idina, and you really needed to know where to go, though it looks as if there may be instructions online. It also helps to be in a four-wheel drive vehicle, the road up to the deserted, desolate ruins of the house being as neglected as the house itself. But it was a magical moment to arrive.

The position of the Villa Idina was obviously carefully chosen for its spectacular view over the valley stretching to the sea. In spite of the condition of the three-storey house today, it is easy to imagine Idina sitting on the veranda that ran along the length of the front. In spring, the garden, before the land slopes away, would have been full of those flowers described by Sir James Rennell Rodd. She and Thomas would have driven back from a demanding day at Ingurtosu and just sat and gazed and breathed in the pure air. After Thomas's

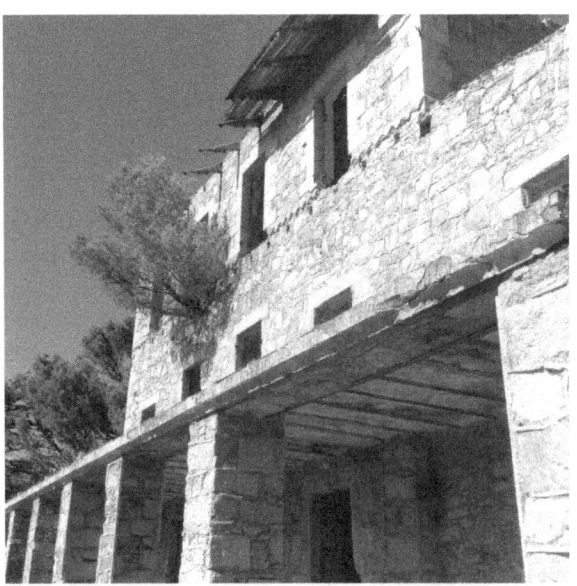

43. Villa Idina, Ingurtosu, 2017, photograph by the author

death, it was used as a guesthouse for executives and guests of the mining company – it is not their ghosts that inhabit it.

Back on the main road, you come to the Santa Barbara church on the hill above, a tall obelisk to Thomas in front. It was not possible to see inside. We did not have time to turn into what remains of Ingurtosu itself, which I regret. In 1965, after years of running at a loss, the Pertusola company was taken over, but the mine closed for good in 1968. It, too, is now part of the UNESCO recognised Geomineral Historic and Environment Park of Sardinia.

Today Ingurtosu is abandoned and dilapidated, though what was the Palace of Management – Il Castello – remains, as does the hospital building, with plans to make tourist use of it, perhaps as a hotel. In the hospital's heyday a study was made there for the prevention of silicosis, which was prevalent, often causing death to the miners comparatively young; tuberculosis was another scourge. The hospital's doors were open to the sick from the surrounding villages. In the village of Pitzinurri, the Villa Wright still stands, as do the imposing ruins of the Brassey dressing plant on the river Naracauli.

It is still possible to gain an impression of Ingurtosu as a flourishing small town from a YouTube video. A couple of post-1968 retired miners, one of them a bit of a joker, take you round showing you what each boarded up, often crumbling, building represented in the mine's heyday: post office, butcher, baker, cobbler, post office, tobacconist; there was even a cinema. They talk, too, about the football team and a strike they remember, and there is a photograph of a lively procession to the Santa Barbara church. The background piano music to this video is appropriate. But there is no mention of women, either as workers or widows when their husbands died young.

The SS126 main road is the more comfortable but much longer way to travel between Ingurtosu and Montevecchio, though it is not direct: you need to turn on to a strada provinciale to complete the journey. There is, however, a very-much-unmade, but shorter, road, which is the one we took, willing the car forward as we gingerly progressed. You might find it closed. Did Idina and Thomas Brassey drive over to Montevecchio to visit Zely and Alberto Sanna-Castoldi in the 'carriage without horses'? One can only imagine.

11 – More Foreign Women in Sardinia 1848–1966

Introduction

Some foreign women in Sardinia in the nineteenth century have already appeared, namely those relevant to earlier chapters such as Jeannie Craig, Elena Poinsel, Helen Dunstan Wright and Idina Brassey. Mary Davey appeared but only in connection with what she wrote about Jeannie, her description of Paulina, William Sanderson Craig's housekeeper in his pre-marital home on La Maddalena and, for a different chapter, a bandit saga in which women were involved.

Mary Davey 1848–1850

Mary Davey is a bit of an enigma. She published two books about Sardinia, *Icnusa, or Pleasant Reminiscences of a Two Years' Residence in the Island of Sardinia* (1860) and *Sardinia* (1874). The two years were probably *c.*1848–1850. The books are similar in many respects but, apparently, tell the story of those two years from the point of view of two different people, one herself, the other ostensibly someone called Charley, who may have been a brother. He is obvious as a character by name, but only in *Icnusa*; nevertheless, *Sardinia* seems filled with his account. Neither book makes clear the author's purpose in Sardinia. In spite of the mystery, Mary Davey tells some interesting stories about the island and her stay, and her name is not a *nomme de plume*, as two letters from Alfred Lord Tennyson attest. On 15 March 1854 he wrote to John William Parker, editor of *Fraser's Magazine*:

> My dear Parker,
> A Mrs Davey (a friend of mine many years ago) has been living at Cagliari in Sardinia and has written a tale illustrative of Sardinian customs. Her friends want her to publish. She thinks that would be a troublesome and expensive proceeding and prefers insertion in a Magazine and applies to me thinking a word of mine will be sufficient to procure the admission of her story into any Magazine whatsoever; but I am not so sanguine. You are the only Magazine Editor I am personally acquainted with. I have told her to forward her papers to you and assured her you will give them due consideration …
> Yours very truly
> A Tennyson

Tennyson wrote to Parker again on 23 November; it would appear that Mary had heard nothing:

I enclose you a letter from Mrs Davey author of the Sard tale. I have promised to let her hear from me. It may be a difficult matter for you to answer if you have made up your mind to reject the contribution. However write me a note which I may send on to her if you prefer communicating through me.
Ever yours,
A Tennyson

That the poet laureate, who had that year published his celebrated poem 'The Charge of the Light Brigade', should continue to take an interest in Mary's work confirms his suggestion that she was a friend, and one with whom he sympathised. But that information takes us little further in accessing Mary's background and the puzzle of the two different versions of her Sardinian stay. In the end, *Icnusa* was accepted by a Bath publisher and, 14 years later, *Sardinia* was published by Oxford: Clarendon for the Christian Knowledge Society.

Having read reprints of the books side by side, trying to disentangle the discrepancies between them, I have deduced that Mary wrote *Icnusa* as her story, but when it came to *Sardinia*, published 14 years later, she decided to include Charley's material that she had previously left out, that is assuming that there was such a person as Charley. I can think of only one explanation: that she had a male informant who relayed to her interesting details of his travels around the island with a group of men. Why wasn't she with them? Probably because, as a woman, such journeying on horseback, spending the night in various, sometimes odd, places, would either not be fitting or be too gruelling. Not only that but Sardinia was well known as a dangerous place, as chapter 7 illustrates. She refers to a Charley in that group without specifying who he is, but it is possible to infer that he is her informant: Charley did this, Charley did that in her account. That is why I feel that he is deputed by Mary to seem to be the author of *Sardinia*.

In *Icnusa* Mary never identifies the 'we' who arrive in Cagliari, probably in 1848; in *Sardinia* the author writes 'We were four in family – my father, mother, my sister and myself'. If Mary was, indeed, in a family of four, was she sister or mother? Given that she had been a friend of Tennyson's 'from many years ago', it is perhaps more likely that she was mother, and he calls her Mrs Davey. They were more than mere visitors; they were there for some purpose, but what was it? The only hint is given at the end of *Sardinia*:

> Soon after the departure of MacLean, my father decided on returning to his own country; not, as he then imagined, to remain, but to induce a party of friends to join him in making a purchase of certain lands in the 'Capo di Sopra' in a very fine situation, where the air was free from taint, finely wooded, and well watered. Society, he thought was all that would be required to make life pleasant in such a locality. Thus, he, too, left us by the steamer.

'Capo di Sopra' may refer to a wide area encompassing Sassari and Nuoro provinces – central-northern Sardinia. The fact that *Sardinia* was published by the Christian Knowledge Society, may hint that 'Charley' is talking about the establishment of a religious community, but neither text suggests that. Mary is obviously Anglican, and not slow to make clear her views on Roman Catholicism, but there is no suggestion of proselytising in Cagliari or through her books. Whatever the purpose, it was to come to nothing because, a few paragraphs later, 'Charley' writes: 'Our letters from England brought us startling news. My father had purchased a house, and had finally made up his mind to abandon all hope of returning to the ancient "Ichnusa".' In the last pages of *Icnusa* (even the spelling in the two accounts is different) Mary writes of 'Charley and his mother'; presumably not herself.

In *Icnusa*, William Sanderson Craig is C ... g; in *Sardinia* he is 'Cairne'. There is nothing in Charley's account about Craig's domestic arrangements in La Maddelana described by Mary. It is impossible to begin to detail the many descriptions in either that touch upon women, often regarding dress or their participation in saints' celebrations, or gossip with or about fellow British Cagliari friends, or Sardinian acquaintances. There is, however, a description in Mary's account, not in Charley's, that I had an interesting time getting to the bottom of regarding place. I shall tell the story of Donna Margherita, partly in Mary's words, mostly paraphrasing several pages, then I'll jump to the twenty-first century and the part I played.

It starts at a tea party in Cagliari attended by both Mary and Charley, in the palazzo of the Regent of Sardinia at which the 'Regentessa' is hostess. It is not at all clear who Mary is talking about, as no year is given for the story and several changes took place around 1848. The last Viceroy, who left that year on 2 March, and then became prime minister of the Kingdom of Sardinia, was Claudio Gabriele de Launay who, in 1806, married a French noblewoman, **Camille Angelique Caze de Méry** (*c*.1793–1875); they had four children. What is noticeable throughout the story is Mary's mocking tone. The 'pretty salon' is 'furnished somewhat *a l'Anglaise*' because the Regentessa

> much affects what is English: accordingly, she indulges her guests with their national beverage, if that pale, straw-coloured liquid can be called tea, which the little lady is cautiously distributing from a huge coffee-pot, not at all *a l'Anglaise*. She is somewhat profuse, too, in the matter of sugar, and totally oblivious of milk.

The compensation is 'delicious water-ices'. What emerges at the end of the tea party is that there is

> a cloud, however, on many a brow; for that lovely girl, sitting so calmly and majestically apart, is taking her leave of the world; she is about to become a nun. Yes, Margherita G, the daughter of the Regent, a young and lovely creature, of scarcely seventeen years, with the world all bright

before her, has chosen her part. There are many comments, some of high commendation, others the reverse.

Mary records several of the comments. In due course, the scene switches to young Margherita's big day. There is 'quite a throng on the bastion Santa Caterina, before the doors of the chapel of the convent dedicated to that saint'. One of the male guests from the tea party, a Sardinian, who was particularly critical of both Margherita's future and the girl's mother, addresses the Regentessa:

> 'Vossignora looks charming to-day; your maternal heart is no doubt bounding with exultation, at the idea of the high vocation the Damigella Margherita has chosen.'
> Regentessa, though by no means sharp at repartee, or, indeed, at anything else, feels the sarcasm: it seems to dance amid the artificial floral decorations of her very artificial little head, and so to percolate unto her very hard and artificial little heart. She can but make an artificial smile and bow; but a colour by no means artificial tinges her cheek and spreads over every feature.

Finally the ceremony of admission of Donna Margherita begins:

> The grille, or grating, communicating with the interior of the convent, is unclosed – one feels almost a cold tremor, even at this hot season, as one peers into the cavernous depths of that large, dreary, vaulted chamber; every sound echoes and re-echoes along those mysterious corridors; and, as the soft wind eddies through them, it seems to bring back the sighs of broken-hearted and departed sisters.
> But hush! Softly, very softly, and in the far distance, one hears a sweet melody of many voices, most seraphic; nearer it comes, and more distinct and nearer still, and now, two and two, with slow and measured step, each with a large lighted taper in her outstretched hand, appear the veiled forms of the sisters; onward they come, into the centre; the stately abbess takes her canopied chair opposite the grating; then slowly the line divides, and singing still, they form a circle on each side. Alone, on a cushion, close by the grille, kneels the lovely Margherita, bright and brilliant, with a crown of flowers on her fair young brow.

There are reams more, as the ceremony progresses; then:

The nuns surround their young companion, the beautiful glossy brown hair is cut off tress by tress, a pall is drawn over her, and the funeral service read, in all its thrilling solemnity.
Margherita G is dead; dead to the world – to all who love her; her very name is erased from the annals of the living. She is Margherita no longer!

The pall is withdrawn, and a veiled nun is kneeling in her place. She is henceforward the sister Agata.

As if to emphasise the enormity of what has happened, Mary ends her account of the ceremony and the family gathering afterwards where all are wet-eyed or weeping: 'The young brother comes in, and drawing from his vest the knot of glossy hair, weeps over it, as the last remaining relic of his lost sister.'

Not surprisingly, I was keen to discover the Santa Caterina convent, so made my way to the fine Remy Bastion on the edge of the Castello, and up to that of Santa Caterina. There was no obvious convent, just one large dusty-rose-coloured building standing in the hot sunlight overlooking Cagliari far below. I went round the side and into a courtyard where two women were talking. Apologising for disturbing them, I explained what I was looking for. They responded enthusiastically: their primary school (*Scuola Elementare Santa Caterina*) had been the convent in an earlier incarnation. They were so interested in hearing about Mary Davey's account of Donna Margherita that they took me inside to meet the headteacher, who was equally interested to learn a little more of the school's earlier history.

The convent, belonging to the Dominican Order, with its attached church, was built in 1641. Tragedy struck a century later, as Giovanni Spano related in *La Guida della Citta e Dintorno di Cagliari* (1861). At about 9pm on 27 December 1747, the part of it with a portico that towered over Via Fossario collapsed, falling into the embankment below. Twelve nuns and 10 boarders were killed, and the chronicle names the nuns, two pairs of whom have the same surname, so could have been closely related. This damage to the structure was to lead to a deterioration of the whole over the years. That was not helped by nearby building works in 1882 and, in 1893, the Cagliari Municipal Council made improvements in the Via Canelles running alongside it which exacerbated its condition.

In 1896, the Council determined that a school was needed in the Castello, and that it should be on the Caterina Bastion, indeed, that it should occupy the site of the convent where two elderly nuns still resided. Could one of them possibly be Sister Agata? She was only 17 some time between 1848 and 1850. In 1906, the convent was demolished, the school was built and ready to open in 1910. Some internet sources, for example, blulassu, suggest that the convent was destroyed by fire in 1800, which does not fit with Mary Davey's account, but I do like their suggestion that within its walls the 1668 conspiracy to assassinate Viceroy Camarassa, described in chapter 5, was hatched. Certainly the shots were fired from a palazzo in the Via Canelles.

I offered to send headteacher Anna Puscedu and my original teacher guide, Carmen Storia, the details of Mary Davey's book, although, being in English, it would not be readily accessible, and the reprint is rather poor. But I was able to do more than that. Following my return home, and after an internet trawl of anything about Mary Davey's book, I discovered that Maria Antonella Capula, of the Memoriale Giuseppe Garibaldi, Caprera, had, using a microfilm from the British Library, translated *Icnusa* into Italian for her 1998 thesis in the faculty of Foreign Languages and Literature, University of Sassari. I emailed her and asked if the Santa Caterina school could have a copy. With the generosity that I soon came to expect from Sardinian scholars, she was more than willing to provide it, and they were, not surprisingly, grateful to receive it. Donna Margherita/Suor Agata has found a niche that ensures she is not forgotten, and Mary Davey's book has a practical purpose that would surely have pleased her.

The Piercy Family 1872–1966

If this were a general history of Sardinia, I would be concentrating wholly on Benjamin Piercy, responsible for the construction of the main railway system in the island, to the great advantage of its economy and people's lives. But as it is, instead, a history of women, then his daughter Florence's diary is fascinating for the insight it provides into the life of British expatriates in Cagliari in the late nineteenth century.

Florence Ada Piercy (1859–1958), born in Wales, was 13 years old when the family arrived in Sardinia in December 1872. *Florence's Diary* (2006), published with a foreword by her great-niece Giorgina Giustiniani Mameli, has the original English version facing an Italian translation. The little volume of the manuscript diary was rescued from oblivion by Florence's niece, **Vera Norina Piercy** (1896–1979), Giorgina's mother. Giorgina (under the name Giorgina Mameli-Piercy Giustiniani) published her version of the family story – *Tra il Galles* [Wales] *e la Sardegna; Storia della Famiglia Piercy* (2019). In it she makes use of her mother's diary. That has allowed me to flesh out some family members, including Florence in her later life. Some time after I had finished this chapter, Giorgina arranged an Italian translation and publication (2020) of what her mother wrote – *Nel mezzo della vita* by Donna Vera Mameli Piercy.

The diary of Florence's brother, Vera's father, Benjamin Herbert Piercy (Bertie), has also been published only in Italian – *La Sardegna dei miei ricordi* (2008). Bertie was the last of eight children (five daughters, three sons) born before the family's

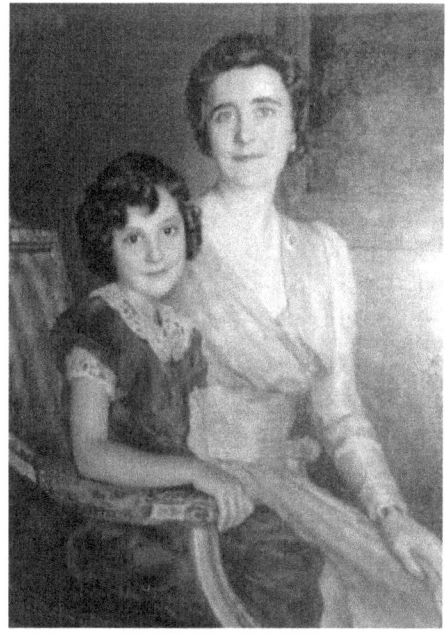

44. Vera Mameli Piercy and Giorgina as a child, from Giustiniani, *Tra il Galles e la Sardegna*

arrival in Cagliari. Because he was born in 1871, and was little more than a toddler in the early days, his book does not keep pace with Florence's diary of those first years, and is not in the same mould.

Florence first describes the journey to Sardinia, starting on 24 November 1872, followed by that to Cagliari where they arrived on 31 December. Her diary then covers the period 1873 to April 1874, though the family lived in Sardinia until some years later, it is not clear when, though Benjamin Piercy himself was there until 1883.

In 1855, Benjamin Piercy, engineer, had married **Sarah Davies** (c.1833–1912). She was the daughter of the owner of the hotel where he was resident while his railway designing work took him to Wales. With blue eyes and strawberry blond hair, she 'had all the grace and sweetness of her 17 years'.

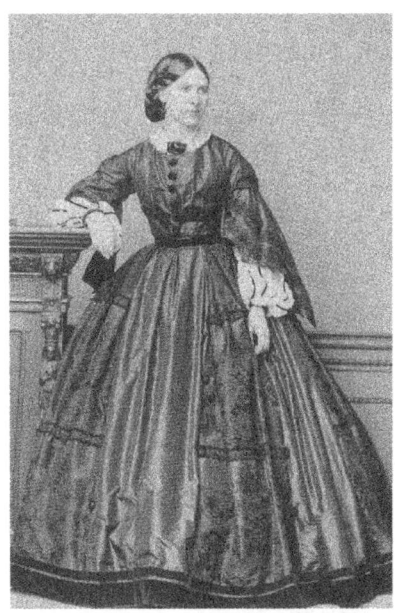

45. Sarah Piercy (née Davies) from Giustiniani, *Tra il Galles e la Sardegna*

At 34, Sarah must have been just pregnant with their eighth child during the journey to Sardinia from Paris, where they had been living while Benjamin supervised a development of the French railway system. Florence writes on 11 July 1873, 'A little baby arrived at five, consequently we did not bathe'. That sixth daughter was christened **Helen Louise Piercy** (1873–1943), known as Nellie. So, pregnant, and with eight children, one child still hardly more than a baby, Sarah had made what was then an onerous journey via mainland Italy, of over a month. She did have help: **Miss Maslin** (Mazzie), the children's English governess, **Mlle Piat**, their French governess, **Carry**, the child minder, and Benjamin's sister **Jane Piercy** (Jinny; 1834–?1891). The party also consisted of the cook, **Marguerite**, who was probably also French, Robert, Benjamin's brother, Charles and William Davies, Sarah's brothers, Emanuele, manservant, and Peter, the handyman. The logistics of the journey are awe-inspiring.

It was as early as 1862 that the Anglo-Italian Royal Sardinian Railway Company sought the advice of Benjamin Piercy, Chairman of the Institution of Engineers, and his brother-in-law concerning the Company's concession to build 250 miles of railways on the island. He was able to simplify the plans already in place, and is responsible for the lines that link Cagliari to Porto Torres (on the north coast), and Cagliari to Olbia and thence to Golfo Aranci (on the east coast). He was also to build a harbour at Golfo Aranci.

Benjamin seems to have visited the island first in 1862, again in 1865, and to have been there working on the project from 1870. He will, therefore, have organised the family's accommodation, and he met them in Livorno (Leghorn) from where they sailed to Porto Torres. From there they made their way in stages down to Cagliari, first by carriage, then, from Oristano, by train.

The party settled into what was more a palazzo than a house, probably facing both Via Genovesi and Via Lamarmora in the Castello. It belonged to Baron Rossi and his wife. A footnote in Florence's diary, without a first name, gives details that seem to refer to very rich entrepreneur Salvatore Rossi who was made a baron in 1848. But, if more than one source is correct, he was born in 1775 and is unlikely, therefore, to have been alive a century later; he had three daughters, at least, with **Grazia Vodret**, and a son, Francisco; Salvatore certainly owned several palaces.

More likely, the baron was Salvatore and Grazia's son Francesco Rossi, born 1807, and the baroness his wife **Delfina Meloni**. In 1877 Francesco owned a palazzo in the right location in the Castello; in 1891, Delfina, presumably then a widow, owned it. They appear to have had 10 children. The period 1873/4 was one of both happiness and grief for the couple. In August 1873, their 24-year-old daughter **Giulia Rossi** married 34-year-old Francesco Serra; but just over a year later, in November 1874, their son Massimo, aged only 22, died. There are several 1873/4 entries about Baroness Rossi in Florence's diary, though the diary ends before Massimo's death: 'The Baroness and her daughters came to pay us a visit and stayed two hours.' On another occasion she came to see how Nellie, when rather sick, was progressing and, in September 1873, 'The Baroness, her daughter and Mme Rogers called but all they wanted to know was whether we were leaving the house for always (for we intend going into the country in November).'

One of the first things that Florence writes in the Cagliari part of her diary is a description of their accommodation:

> Our house is the highest and best in Cagliari. It is situated at the top and is very prominent. It belongs to Baron Rossi and the two top floors belong to us. The stairs are in marble. The lower floor has rooms with passages, namely kitchen, room between kitchen and dining room, diningroom, drawing room, Mamma's bedroom, bathroom, Auntie's bedroom, Bob's bedroom, office, passage, Uncle Will's bedroom, Peter's bedroom, Papa's private office, another office and the coaling water place with passage. The floors are made of polished and coloured bricks, which are the best floors in Cagliari. The walls are papered and, as for the ceilings, they are all colours. Upstairs there is the hall, the breakfast room, the woman's bedroom, the passage, Lily and Eva's room, Bella's room, the room between Bella and Miss Maslin, or box room, Miss Maslin's room, my room, the study, the passage, the nursery, Harry's room, Marguerite's passage and kitchen.

At the age of 13 Florence has already picked up foreign attitudes towards Sardinians as revealed in the writing of other nineteenth-century visitors. In a general description of Sardinia, she writes, 'The civilisation in *Sardegna* is a hundred years behind England, the place being crowded with brigands and convicts.' After unpacking all morning on 6 January, members of the family went for a walk down to the port and she saw her first women of that area without us learning anything more about them than a judgement on their appearance:

I nearly burst out laughing at the awful chignons they wear here, dear me! They are a mile high and the Sards dress so peculiarly too! Just fancy they will wear a blue and red striped petticoat, a pair of gilt stays with a chemise with low neck and long sleeves. Over their heads they wear half a dozen shawls.

We might wonder, after that mockery, what sort of girl Florence was otherwise. The most revealing passage, a self-analysis, was confided on 16 August 1873 when she had been in Sardinia for seven and a half months;

I was just wondering this morning what I should be when I grow up, whether I should be a governess, a poetess, an authoress, a painter or whether I should marry. I must be clever. I must do something someday. I shall have to earn my living and I don't want to be tied to a man. What shall my future life be? This is a very serious question and no doubt some of my little readers may think it a silly one; but it is not so, let that be impressed on you: learn while you have time or you will come to ruin. I have heard of a lady who, when a little girl, would not learn, was idle and naughty. Consequently, after her father died, she, having no money became a char-woman. Let this be a lesson to you my young friends – be industrious, be obedient, be good and in fact do all you are told.

Her writing, a page of which illustrates the published diary, and is shown

46. A page from Florence Piercy's diary, from Manca, *Florence's Diary*

here, is surprisingly adult; one entry notes a lesson in calligraphy. The education of all the older children is scrupulously supervised, both in and out of the home, presumably by their mother, as their father is often absent. The entry two days earlier than the passage above gives some idea of how Florence is preparing herself for her future, and of the family ties:

> It is Thursday today, a half-holiday at our school so consequently I did not work after twelve. We are getting on in Italian famously. Papa is soon leaving now. I am very sorry. It is so nice to have him with us. Nellie is getting such a nice little girl. Mamma is so fond of her.

It becomes clear that Florence is a 'Daddy's Girl' – there are several entries about how much she wishes he were there – and in such a large family and entourage, relationships did not always run smoothly. On 7/8 January 1873, she wrote, 'Bella got in a temper and was rude to Mademoiselle, who screamed at the top of her voice, much to our disgust.' And on the 15th, 'Lily and I had such fun. We ran away with Mademoiselle's things and teased her into a rage.' **Lily** (Lilian, 1862–1920) was 11. And Mademoiselle was obviously an endless target as yet another spat, on 9 February, attests: 'Mademoiselle got in such a rage 'cause Lily, seeing her garter was a very ragged green silk one, said to her "Give me that pretty piece of ribbon to tie my hair up with."' One can only hope that the obvious brat said it in French. And it was not only with the children that the French governess had a problem. On 3 May, 'Another noise with Mademoiselle. She is so rude and impertinent with Mamma.' Things were coming to a head: on the 5th, 'We are not to have any more lessons with Mademoiselle.' And, after retiring to her bed – 'Mademoiselle pretended to be ill'. On the 14th, 'Mademoiselle went off today while we were at lunch. Mamma telegraphed to tell Papa.' Poor Mamma, plagued with staff: on 4 February, 'Mama and Miss Maslin had a quarrel.'

More dramatic was what happened on 13 April 1873:

> Uncle Charlie and Will had a quarrel with Mamma. At last Uncle Charlie rose from the table, took up his napkin and said 'Sarah, you have turned me out of the house. I'll write and tell your husband'. And, so saying, left the room. Uncle Will stopped eating his dinner and made his cigar, then in a vacant manner looked up and said, 'Sarah, you have turned me out too', and he also left.

Three days later, 'Uncle Charlie and Mamma made friends'. But on the 17th, 'Uncle Charlie takes his meals with us, but Uncle Will is not out of his sulk.' You have to wonder about childhood relations between Sarah and her brothers. Uncle Charlie, incidentally, had earlier taken Mademoiselle's side, and 'was very rude to Mamma'. By May, he had left Cagliari, but he came back. All this time, Sarah Piercy was in her last months of pregnancy with Nellie. A month after she gave birth, a new governess arrived.

The reader gets the impression that Sarah Piercy was, not surprisingly, rather harassed, not just by domestic wrangles, and the need to keep the household running smoothly, but also by baby Nellie's serious illnesses, and her husband's constant and long absences. The introduction to *Florence's Diary*, written by one of the editors, Christine Tilley, as well as the Preface written by Giovanna Cerina, lean, rather like Florence herself, in favour of his virtues and talents, giving him the credit for the careful education of his children in all respects. They imply, because of Florence's obvious preference for her father, that Sarah was a rather background figure which I don't think can have been so, with a family and household that size in a strange country. It was easier for the *pater familias* to seem perfect, arriving home as he did from his absences 'always smiling', untainted by constant presence. And it seems true that Sarah, with her responsibilities in the home, was less proficient in Italian than her children who sometimes needed to interpret for her in the outside world.

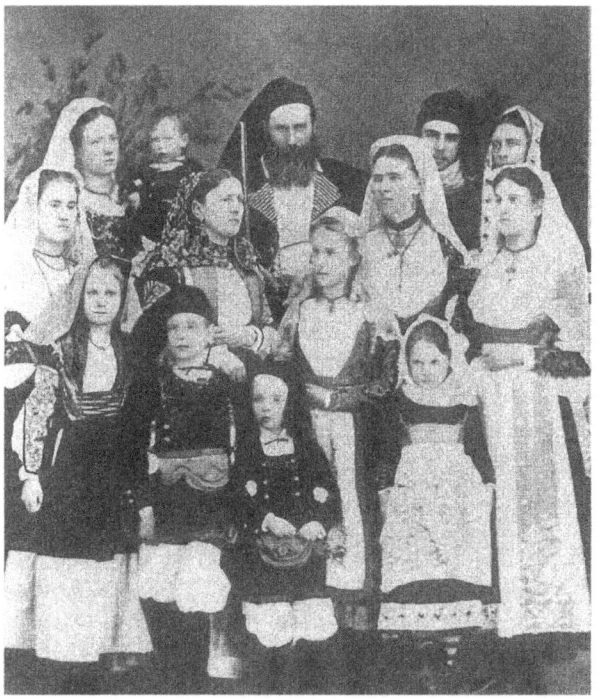

47. Piercy family in Sard costume, from Babay, *Figari*

It is worth noting that Florence quickly made friends among her Sardinian school-mates and, indeed, her school mistress: several names appear in her diary and she writes on 9 October, 'Miss Borghi and six of her pupils came to dinner. We went for a walk notwithstanding the rain.' The family soon had a wide circle of friends and acquaintances, expatriate and Sardinian; they flit through the diary entries.

Cagliari was very much a cultural city: going to the opera is mentioned frequently, though *Macbeth* was a failure – the men too 'puny'; and there is a sad opera entry for 21 January 1874: 'It was the benefit night of Amelia Bettini and, there being few people, she got in a rage and would not sing.' I work it out that **Amalia Bettini** (b.*c*.1813), in her heyday in 1837, would have been 70 then. There were saints' processions and carnivals, though they didn't always work out for the family: on 15 February 1874, Florence noted, 'It is the last Sunday of the Carnival, so we all went out but missed the procession, which put Miss Bella in a rage.' Her eldest sister, not yet 16, was probably at a difficult age.

The last entry in Florence's diary is for Sunday 19 April 1874, when the family was no longer living in Cagliari which they left for the Sassari area, though not all together at the same time. Florence gives no reason for stopping then and from the last few entries it is not clear where they were living; it would appear in new quarters that were not quite ready for them.

The Oxford Dictionary of National Biography supplies the useful bare bones of Benjamin Piercy's life in Sardinia. As early as his first visit, he had been given a tract of farmland near Macomer; this was apparently added to in 1865 as a reward for his various activities, and he also purchased additional land. There, at Baddesalighes, he gradually developed an agricultural experiment. He built 50 miles of roads on his estate and it came to include a village of forty houses accommodating 97 settlers and 210 inhabitants. He introduced new breeds of Sardo-Welsh livestock, particularly cows and horses, and modernised their management; he built a dairy and cheese factory using the latest technology. By extensive draining he had swamplands turned into a perfect garden filled with rare species of exotic plants garnered from his foreign travels, and he had planted thousands of eucalyptus and other trees, Sardinian and Welsh, which improved the residents' health. Garibaldi loved to hunt at Baddesalighes, and was impressed by Piercy's achievements; they became so friendly that Piercy was godfather to his son Riciotto, who also became his pupil. King Umberto made him a commander of the Italian Crown.

With all this activity, it appears, though, that construction on the four-towered Anglo-Italian style Villa Piercy on the 37000 hectare estate of Baddesalighes was not started until 1879, and completed in 1883. And where Piercy's family fitted into his schemes is not clear. An online journal (Brozu 2016) only tantalises when it suggests that Sarah 'would have helped her husband, looking after the ill workers suffering from tubercolosis'. By 1881, his railway work in Sardinia appears to have been completed, though he continued to take an interest in his Baddesalighes property. He also bought a large property in Wales which allowed him to concern himself with Welsh railways, for which he is also well known.

In 1888 Benjamin Piercy died unexpectedly following pneumonia contracted from attending a City of London dinner and then a cardiac arrest. By then he had amassed considerable wealth – £324574. You can find speculation about the contents of his will online, but his great-granddaughter Giorgina Giustiniani Mameli has now published an obviously more accurate, detailed and exhaustive account, including of what followed. The charitable institutions that benefitted were hospitals, railway benevolent institutions and Wesleyan and Methodist chapels. Then there was his wife Sarah, siblings, Jane and Robert Piercy, and nine children to consider. A fifth of his wealth was to go to Sarah, the rest was to be divided equally between his children and his siblings. Sarah was to live for a further 24 years; his youngest child, Nellie, was only 14 when he died.

Then there were Benjamin's Sardinian assets to consider; that was more complicated because he was aware of how little interest his children had shown in the agricultural and breeding activities he had undertaken 'with much ardour and passion'. It would be difficult, anyway to 'assign equally to the various heirs the parts of land and buildings due to each one, which were rather substantial and extensive'. What happened, in fact, was years of legal wrangling initiated by his eldest son, Robert, concerning the validity of the will. This involved a case which went first to the court in Cagliari, then the Supreme Court in Rome, then to the Appeal Court there. From there it went to the High Court in London. That is, necessarily, a very truncated sketch. There are no remarks about Robert attributed to his niece Vera.

Meanwhile, Bertie, the youngest of the three sons, who was only 18 when his father died, had grown rather fond of Baddesalighes. He had, therefore purchased, with the help of his other brother Henry, all the livestock, and signed a lease effectively taking ownership of the production company, including Villa Piercy.

Where was Florence in all this? She was to live until she was 99, and it is thanks to Vera that we know a little of her later life. She spent some time in Rome; there she was welcomed into the grandest houses, including at receptions given by Queen Margherita, apparently 'for the sheer joy of looking at her'. She was courted by, among others, Prince Agostino Chigi, but she returned home unmarried. He was later killed during the Abyssinian war. Florence did marry, though not until 1903, when she was 44. Her husband was Major Graham Egerton Rickman of the Welsh Fusiliers. Vera, whose life at Villa Percy was spent among the best-bred horses in Europe, adds a rather delightful note to her mention of the prince her aunt did not marry: when dining at the Hunting Association in Rome, she would look up and see on the wall his portrait as master of the Rome hunt and 'although Uncle Graham was so nice, I regretted that lost love a little.'

Of Florence, her great-niece, Giorgina Giustiniani Mameli, writes in the foreword to Florence's diary that

> She was both beautiful and kind, beloved by all who came in contact with her, especially her nephews and nieces whom she spoiled no end, perhaps seeing in them the children she never had.

There is no evidence that Florence fulfilled her girlhood dream of becoming a writer or artist.

As for the 'brat' (my judgement) Lily, her niece Vera nicely captured the girl who appeared in Florence's diary:

> The least lovable but the most cheerful who always sang and laughed. She sang all the way to Hong Kong with George Coxon, an employee of the firm Jardine Matheson [whom she married in 1888], thus forging the first links in the chain that would link the family with that firm.

Lily did have children, two of them. Two years after her marriage, her sister **Eva Piercy** (1864–1960) continued the Jardine Matheson connection by marrying its director, James Jardine Bell-Irvine whom she met when visiting Lily. He was also a member of the Legislative and Executive Councils of Hong Kong. Giorgina also gives biographical details, and, usually, her mother's opinion of them, of the rest of Florence's siblings.

Baddesalighes (Valley of Willows) lies between Bolotana and Bonorva in the Marguine region of central western Sardinia. Following Bertie's acquisition of Villa Piercy, he and his family were to make it their home. His three children with his first wife, **Mildred Sawrey-Cookson** (1875–1908), two boys and a daughter, Vera Norina, grew up there. Mildred was the daughter of a famous horsebreeder; such an upbringing fitted in well at Baddesalighes, but she died in Rome, aged only 33, when Vera was 12. A year later her father married **Daphne Beatrice Hardwick** (1880–1971), and had another son. Daphne was said to be very beautiful but with little brain.

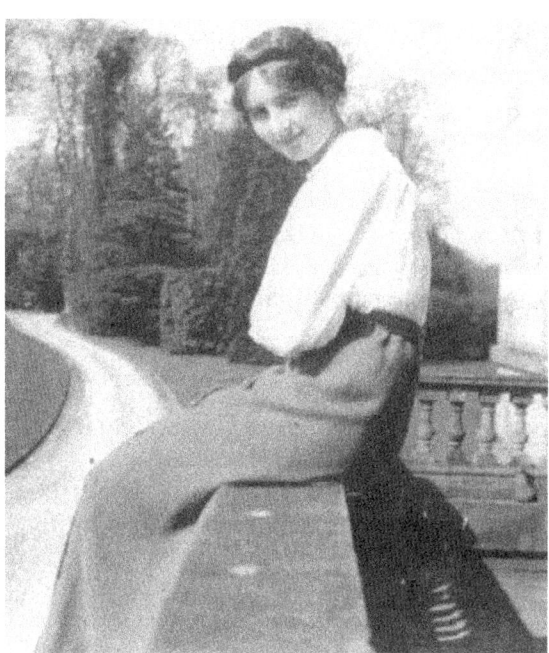

48. Young Vera sitting on a wall, from Giustiniani, *Tra il Galles e la Sardegna*

Bertie died in 1941. Following a land reform act of the 1950s, all agricultural land in Sardinia exceeding a certain size was to be acquired compulsorily by a Land Reform Board for the purpose of being resold to small farmers who did not hold sufficient land of their own; that included Baddesalighes. The villa itself remained in family hands. When Vera married Count Giorgio Francesco Mameli, Italian ambassador to the Holy See, she became known as the Countess of Baddesalighes, and her life included rubbing shoulders with the nobility and, even, royalty, of Europe, often at the Villa Piercy. It was not to last and financial difficulties meant that in 1966 she had to sell the property.

Until 1965, the villa was the home of her daughter Giorgina Mameli (b.1934; later Giustiniani). Giorgina now lives in the Veneto region of Italy but, when re-visiting the villa in 2010, she was able to point out which had been her bedroom, and she still keeps alive the Piercy family flame, as her most recent book attests. The villa, with much of its surrounding beauty intact, is now owned by L'Unione dei Comuni del Marghine. It is a symbol of a bygone age, a little bit of the history of Sardinia and the women for whom it was home. As at present advised, the house can be visited at weekends with a tour guide.

Isabelle Eberhardt 1900–1904

'Cagliari, 1 January 1900: I am alone, sitting facing the grey expanse of the shifting sea', wrote 22-year-old **Isabelle Eberhardt** (1877–1904), in a way reminiscent of Florence Piercy's 1873 Cagliari introspection aged 13. And yet Isabelle's is on a completely different level, for her life until then had been rather removed from that of the sheltered Welsh girl with her stable background. Isabelle continued,

> I am alone … alone as I've always been everywhere, as I'll always be throughout this seductive and deceptive universe … alone, with a whole world of dashed hopes, disappointments and disillusion behind me, and of memories that grow daily more distant, almost losing all reality.

Annette Kobak usefully distilled her biography, *Isabelle: The Life of Isabelle Eberhardt* (1988) for the Introduction to *The Nomad: The Diaries of Isabelle Eberhardt* (edited by Elizabeth Kershaw, 2012) and it is this latter book that I have drawn on.

At the age of 19, Isabelle's Russian mother, **Natalia Eberhardt** (1838–1897), born out of wedlock, married 63-year-old widower General Pavel de Moerder, a member of the Russian Tsar's entourage. With that marriage, Natalia inherited two stepdaughters and a stepson and, with the general, she had two sons and a daughter before leaving Russia to convalesce in Switzerland. Accompanying her were her children, her stepson and the children's tutor, Armenian-born, married, former priest, anarchist, Alexander Trophimowsky. In Geneva, Natalia gave birth to another son, Augustin, whom her husband acknowledged as his; four months later she received news of the general's death.

Four years later, still in Geneva, Natalia gave birth to Isabelle; it is assumed that Trophimowsky was the father, but Isabelle's birth certificate did not name one, and she was given her mother's maiden name. Her 'father' whom she called 'Vava', continued to live with the family, although the other children left as soon as they could. Natalia's eldest son, joining the Tsar's Ministry of Foreign Affairs, began to harass the man he cited as his mother's lover and murderer of his father. Isabelle was aware of all this from the age of 11, though her mother never admitted that Vava was her father.

It is against that background that Isabelle grew up, home-educated by Vava who believed in equality between the sexes. She wrote her diaries mostly in French, but they are sprinkled with words in the other languages in which she was fluent, Latin, Greek, Italian, German, Russian and Arabic. That last was to be the most important for her future and, when she spent the month of January in Cagliari in 1900, she would soon be on her way to North Africa, the area that was to dominate the rest of her life. It would not be her first visit: she had been there with her mother in 1897 – indeed, Natalia had died there from a heart attack – and on her own in the summer of 1899, following Trophimowsky's death. Not only the loss of her mother and Vava, but the suicide of her elder brother, Wladimir, in 1898, as well as the precariousness of her finances, combined to explain the tone of that 1 January 1900 diary entry, and her lonely stay in Sardinia.

There is a suggestion in *Great Women Travel Writers* (ed. Alba Amoia, 2006) that the reason for Isabelle's stay in Cagliari was that she would meet her brother Augustin and his wife Hélène Long there. In 1895, Augustin had joined the Foreign Legion and was stationed in Algeria. That may be why mother and daughter had gone to North Africa in 1897. But there is no mention of him or Hélène in her Cagliari diary entries; indeed, there is no mention of meeting, or talking to, anyone at all.

Isabelle made several Cagliari diary entries, a few extracts, of necessity substantially cut, give a flavour of her poetic sensibility and the political leanings that were to emerge, too, in the considerable body of writing, published and unpublished, that she left. On 7 January she wrote an original and deeply personal description of the city and its environs,

Impressions in a park, around 5 p.m.
A savage landscape, the jagged outlines of deeply gutted hills of either a red or grey colour; cavalcades of maritime pines and Barbary fig trees. Greenery so lush it is almost out of place in the heart of winter. Salt lagoons with surfaces the colour of lead, dead and immobile like desert shotts [shallow, seasonal, lakes in North Africa]. And up there at the very top, the town's silhouette straddles the steep furrowed hillside. Ancient ramparts and a square, odd, crenellated tower, levels of geometrically shaped roofs, all of it cast in pink, standing out against an indigo sky. ...

... Dark, old churches full of marble statues and mosaics, objects of sheer luxury in a country where poverty is the rule. ...

... Doors lead to vast cellars below street level where whole poverty-stricken families live in age-old dankness. Other entrances afford glimpses of vaulted hallways and tiled stairwells. ...

... There is an Arab beauty about the women. The expression in their language [languid?] and melancholy, large, jet-black eyes is resigned and sad like that of wary animals. ...

The contrast between that description of the women, and Florence Piercy's first view of them, is marked. At 5.30 pm on 18 January Isabelle reverts to introspection:

I realise that the fairly restful winter I am spending here is but a breathing spell from the kind of life that will be mine until the very end. In a few days' time, my true way of life and its aimless wanderings will take over again. Where? How? Only God can tell. I must not even dare speculate any longer: just as I was about to stay on in Paris for months on end, I ended up in out-of-the-way Cagliari of all places.

Her last Cagliari entry was written on 29 January:

The brief interlude in this ancient Sardinian town has now come to an end. Tomorrow at this time I shall be far from these Cagliari cliffs, on the leaden, grumbling, turbulent sea.

Last night, Cagliari was booming with the echo of the sea's rolling thunder ... Today it was its most ominous; it had a dull and glaucous shimmer. This beloved hovel looks a desolate wreck in tonight's grey sunset, the very image of departure and upheaval, and I am full of the sorrow that goes with changes in surroundings, those successive states of annihilation that slowly lead to the great and final void.

And what will be the next stage?

She was to spend the next few months unhappily between Paris and Geneva. But on 22 July 1900 she was in Algiers. She was to remain in North Africa thereafter, often dressed as, and passing for, a young Muslim scholar called Si Mahmoud Essadi. This was to make living there easier (though she had also cross-dressed as a child in Augustin's clothes). She became deeply imbedded in the region's everyday life, culture and Islamic religion, and writing about it, including in her diary; she was to leave behind two thousand pages of notes, articles and fiction. She had met a young Algerian soldier, Slimene Ehnni, whom she married in October 1901, a marriage which she did not intend to let curtail her independence. She became friendly with French Marshal Lyautey, who was preparing the eventual take-over of Morocco, and liaised between him and local leaders, her sympathies remaining with their people. There was an attempt on her life with a sabre, in which she was wounded, and her letters to the local papers pardoning her would-be assassin, and calling for a lesser sentence, brought her to a public attention that was to begin to create what was to become her legendary reputation.

In the autumn of 1904, she was in Lyautey's barracks town of Aïn Sefra in the Atlas mountains being treated for a fever. Elizabeth Kershaw describes what happened next:

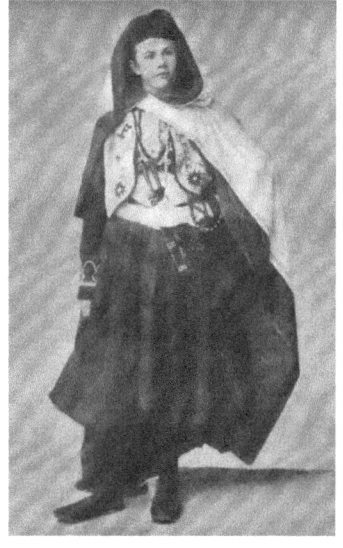

49. Isabelle Eberhardt, from Blanch, *The Wilder Shores of Love*

On 21 October, the day after Slimene's arrival, the town of Aïn Sefra was struck by a freak flood; torrential mountain waters rushed down the *oued*, engulfing houses and claiming the inhabitants. Slimene escaped. Isabelle Eberhardt was killed, aged just twenty seven. Her body was discovered crushed by rubble. She was dressed as Si Mahmoud, her arms clasped above her head in a final gesture of defence [defiance?].

So 'romantic' was her life to appear following her death that much was written about her in several genres; for example, she is included in Lesley Blanch's *The Wilder Shores of Love* (1954) alongside other women of her era beguiled by the desert. The portrait of her comes from there. Lesley Blanch sums her up:

In her brief lifetime she aroused violent interest. She was loathed or loved, respected or despised. No one was indifferent to her. Her echoes have never died. No one who knew her ever forgot her. Those who had never known her felt the strange, compelling force of her character. She was a legend during her lifetime. After her death the legend grew monstrous and distorted. *La Bonne Nomade, L'Amazone du Sable, L'Androgyne du Desert*, or *le Cosaque du Desert* ... these were romantic, but reasonable epithets. But she was also vulgarized as *l'Esclave Errante* in a cheap farrago of nonsense played at the Theatre de Paris in 1924. In 1939 she was *Isabelle d'Afrique*, in another lamentable piece which would have revolted her fastidious nature. For fastidious she was, and naïve and dignified, and pious. All these, in spite of excesses and brutalities of living which would have made a Légionnaire recoil.

Apart from serious biographies, there have also been a modern play about her (*New Anatomies* by Timberlake Wertenbaker, 1981), a film and an opera. A trailer for the opera *Song from the Uproar: The Lives and Deaths of Isabelle Eberhardt* by Missy Mazzoli, first performed in New York in 2012, can be seen on YouTube. I broke off from writing to listen to it, and then ordered the CD, which I have since listened to. The one word that comes to mind is 'thrilling'. It seems to capture at least one of the spirits of Isabelle, as does the quotation from Isabelle used on the disc cover:

> What urges me to restlessness and keeps thrusting me onto life's roads is not the wisest voice in my soul. It is a side of me that finds the earth too limited, and is unable to find in myself a sufficient universe.

I have written about Isabelle Eberhardt in some detail because the one month that she spent in Cagliari seems to provide a link between her former life and what followed. She thought her time there, before the real adventures of her life began, important enough to commit to her diary, as she tried to sort out the roads for her future. It seems to have been a crucial time and place for reflection.

The Strange Case of Ellen Giles 1906–1914

The American **Ellen Rose Giles** (1874–1914) had a similar aptitude for learning languages as a result of a European education as the Russian Isabelle Eberhardt: by the time Ellen had finished her studies – in Germany (the University of Berlin), France (the Sorbonne), Tuscany, Africa, Australia and the Middle East – she spoke Italian, French, German, Spanish, Arabic and Chinese, and had a working knowledge of Greek and Latin. Both women chose a distinctive way of life and work: Ellen was artist, photographer, philosopher, journalist, archaeologist, anthropologist and ethnographer. And both women died by surprising means. But, while Isabelle spent only a month in Sardinia, Ellen lived there between 1906 and 1914. Her life and death were considered interesting enough to merit an exploration, followed by a biography by Alberto Mario Pintus and Maria Giovanna Cugia of the Sassari Historical Society – *Il Caso Giles: Un misterioso fatto di cronaca nella Sassari del primo novecento* (2011).

Ellen's father, George Giles, was an American financier who died when she was young; her mother **Anna Rose Giles** (1848–1937) was involved in nurturing the family's considerable finances which led to travels in Europe without any financial worries. That is how Ellen, following time at Bryn Mawr women's college, Philadelphia, began travelling with her mother, grandmother and sisters. Ellen, at least, studying as she went, ended up in Florence in 1898, and spent eight years there. She was already known for her competence in the decryption of cuneiform tablets of Babylon and Nineveh, but she was by now drawn towards ethnography and something about the island across the water from Tuscany caught her fancy.

Ellen, aged 32, arrived with her painter and travelling companion mother in Cagliari in 1906; it did not take her long to realise that Sassari, to which she travelled on horseback, was the place she should make her base. In a

2011 article in *La Nuova Sardegna* – 'Miss Giles' – Daniela Scano suggests that she used her education in the service of 'militant ethnography' – an intriguing description. At the centre of this was her interest in the centuries-old use of sheepfolds (*tanca*) and the life of pastoral people. So she soon made sure that she was conversant with the local Sardo language.

The Sardinian-born art historian Enrico Pusceddu, at the University of Barcelona, was interested in the work Ellen's mother, Anna, did on the Catalan-influenced art of Sardinia in collaboration with Georgiana King – whose story will follow Ellen's. But in his chapter '*I Retabli Sardi nella Storiagrafia Americana del Primo Novecento*' (2013), he includes an invaluable description of Ellen's ethnographic explorations, this time apparently setting out from Nuoro:

> An American miss … left [Nuoro] at the most unusual hours of the day and night – on foot, on horseback or in the rustic carts of the local peasants. She visited the most remote *tancas*, approaching everyone, men, women and children. One winter evening, when an inch of snow lay on the ground, they saw her mysteriously start from Nuoro towards the mountain. Where did the strange young lady go. They had told her that … the dead were buried at dawn, and she had immediately climbed on horseback and all alone, along uncomfortable and dangerous ways, she went to attend the macabre ceremony.
>
> The eccentricities of the daring signorina certainly did not go unnoticed and the popular imagination leapt to a thousand romantic assumptions. But the imperturbable miss, armed with camera, palette and revolver, minutely visited every corner of Sardinia, staring at the impressions recorded on the [camera] plate and on canvas and especially in her brain. She could certainly say that she knew Sardinia.

That account suggests that much of Ellen's research was carried out in the Barbagia region. What her biographers also suggest was her interest in bandits. They note that she interviewed members of the Corraine family of Orgosolo whose vendetta with the Cossu family was at its height between 1905 and 1917. This feud and its ramifications are detailed in chapter 7, concentrating particularly on Paska Devaddis, so-called *banditessa*.

Ellen made copious notes as well as taking photographs and painting images; not surprisingly, she intended to write a book based on her material; indeed, her proposal had already

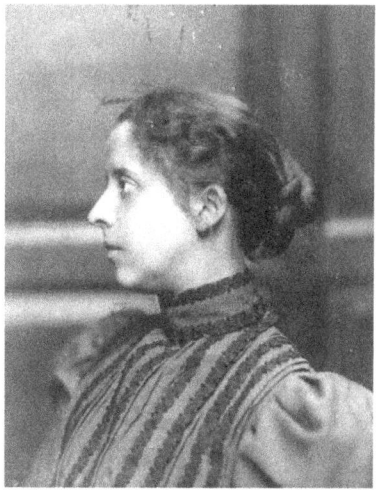

50. Ellen Giles, courtesy of Bryn Mawr College Special Collections

received interest from foreign language publishers. But it was her revolver and 'romantic assumptions' that were to lead to the lasting interest in her still unresolved story.

At the beginning of 1914, Ellen, aged 39, was living at 87 Via Roma in Sassari; she was in the process of transcribing her notes. But at 3pm on 15 January, she was found dead by her maid, **Maria Filippa Rovetti**, with a gunshot wound in the chest; the bullet had passed through her heart. A revolver was found on the floor, the one that Ellen had bought a few days earlier. It suited the police, and then the local magistrate, to see it as an open-and-shut case of suicide committed by a non-conformist, nosey foreign woman. But the bullet had apparently passed through her dress leaving the cloth intact.

The local press accepted the verdict of suicide, while the *Washington Post* and *New York Times* headlines read 'Girl from Bryn Mawr killed in Sardinia'. Nearly a century later Maria Giovanna Cugia, who was working on a volume on the Sassari Monumental Cemetery, came across Ellen's simple marble slab covering a niche in a wall with just a name, no dates, no nationality, no designation. Her interest, and that of her colleague Alberto Pintus, was piqued and exploration into her life and death became irresistible. They noted that Ellen was said to have had a lover, and that, at the time, a young Sassari nobleman, whose name still eludes them, hurriedly left town. They speculated that Ellen had been naked at the time of her death, and that someone had hurriedly dressed her. They were not helped by the fact that there was no trace of her in the archives.

Ellen is described as the 'last guest' in the Sassari Monumental Cemetery. Her niche is in the peripheral wall facing the new part, a few metres on the right beyond the side gate entrance off Via Caniga.

Anna Rose Giles and Georgiana Goddard King 1906–1939

Before she died in 1937, Ellen's mother Anna Rose Giles is said to have donated her daughter's notes to the University of Sassari Library. But in reply to an email, Enrico Pusceddu says that there is no sign of those notes there. And I can find no mention of them having been unearthed elsewhere and made use of.

For reasons which Ellen's biographers and those who have followed the story of her life and death cannot understand, Anna continued to live in Sardinia for the next 23 years. I suggest the reason was simply that she was already established there and her subsequent activities confirm that she was already interested in, and becoming something of an expert on, the church paintings of Sardinia, an expertise that was to be drawn upon by art historian Georgiana Goddard King.

But Anna's artistic interests were much wider than churches and Sardinia, and she was prepared to draw on her Bryn Mawr contacts, as is revealed in the letter she wrote in November 1914, the year of her daughter's death, and soon after the beginning of the First World War; it was published in *The*

College News in January 1915, and is quoted in Enrico Pusceddu's 2016 article about the American Hispanic Society:

> Will not our American Art, Architectural, Archaeological and Historical Societies, our Universities and Colleges, raise a strong and united protest if not elsewhere, at least in the American newspapers against the destruction being carried on in Europe of art treasures that are the property not only of the countries where they are, but also of the civilized world? And will not Bryn Mawr lead in such a protest? Germany dreads the unfavourable public opinion of the United States, and England and France would certainly gladly join in any measures Germany could be got to agree to for the protection of art monuments. If such a protest were too late to save the art treasures of Belgium still remaining at this moment, it would not be too late to protect Venice whose peril will be great as soon as Italy moves and as she certainly will move before long.
> Anna Rose Giles, Sassari, Sardinia.

It is likely that Anna's continuing artistic interest and experience encouraged her friendship with the Sardinian artist Carmelo Floris which, in turn, led to her move, as a result of that friendship, to settle in the parsonage of the parish priest, Carlo Nonnis, of Ollolai, in the heart of the Barbagia region. On the death of his father when Floris was two years old, Nonnis, his maternal uncle, had looked after him. Anna's move, perhaps away from Sassari where her daughter had died, provided a secure life, while at the same time allowing her to work, including on behalf of Georgiana King.

After some time in Spain, **Georgiana Goddard King** (1871–1939) arrived in Sardinia for the first time in March 1920. She was drawn there by three complementary factors: her work on medieval Spanish paintings and architecture, about which she had already published; Catalan influence on Sardinian art, as a result of the island's time under Spain; and the fact that her old friend Anna Giles was living there. Not only did Anna know her way around, she was conversant in the local languages, and they had already worked together – Anna illustrated Georgiana's *Comedies and Legends for Marionettes: A Theatre for Boys and Girls* (1904).

Georgiana was, as the *Dictionary of Art Historians* details, the daughter of a railway employee, Morris Ketchum King, and an educated mother with strong literary interests who died when her daughter was 10. So she and her siblings were brought up by a maternal aunt. She was a student at the women's Bryn Mawr College, the first to offer graduate degrees. It is fair to assume that that is how she knew the Giles family. After graduation, first in English (1896), then a master's degree in political science (1897), Georgiana travelled in France, and then taught at a boarding grammar school until 1906, during which time she published two books. She then returned to Bryn Mawr to teach English. In 1910 or 1911, she was asked to teach courses in Gothic and Renaissance art, alternating with her literature course. She began to focus on art history and was promoted to lecturer in 1911; in 1913 she founded a separate department of history of art in which the first graduate courses on Spanish art in the United States were offered. By 1916 she was a full professor. She had varied artistic interests and friends among famous modern artists and writers such as Gertrude Stein. But it was her work and publication on Spanish architectural history for which she was, and is, best known, and which was most relevant to her interest in Sardinia.

There can be nothing more frustrating to the re-creator of history than to know that some work crucial to your narrative has been done, then not to be able to access it. Because the invaluable *DonnaSarda* website is no longer available, I have not been able to read 'Georgiana Goddard King: Una Suffragetta Americana in Sardegna', nor to track down another version of it. A hunt for anything else that elaborates that thesis comes up only with Janice Mann's remark in *Romanesque Architecture and its Sculptural Decoration in Christian Spain, 1000–1120* (2009),

> A former student reported that King frequently told her all-female classes, 'I have done everything known to man.' She clearly believed that she was entitled to occupy the public sphere of erudition so often associated with the masculine and to extend her research into any uncharted area of the discipline.

It was not only her overwhelming self-confidence as a woman scholar that disconcerted some of her students, in spite of the progressive and feminist ambience created by the college's president: Georgiana also lectured without notes, in her black gown, in the dark, so that her students could not take notes. In spite of my frustration, Enrico Pusceddu reassures me that, having read the *DonnaSarda* entry himself many years ago, he can confirm that it did not add anything new. It would appear, therefore, that Georgiana may have confined her suffragette activities to the United States and the article's title may simply have been an indication of her identity on arrival in Sardinia.

When Georgiana published *Sardinian Painting: The Painting of the Gold Backgrounds* in 1923 (translated into Italian in 2000), she thanked Anna Giles warmly for her contribution. That it was well deserved is attested to by a letter Anna wrote on 22 March 1922 to Professor Pietro Meloni Satta, a famous citizen of Olzai, concerning the terrible floods in the town the previous year, and how they had affected her. She had gone there to study, among other works of art, the altar

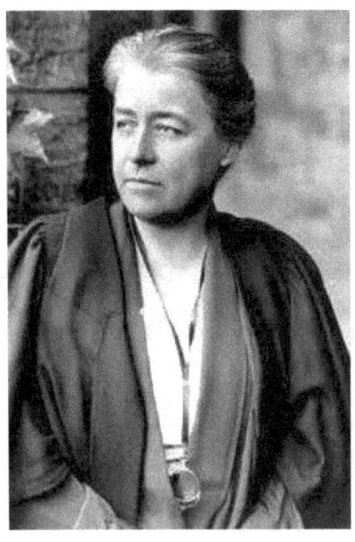

51. Georgiana King, courtesy of Bryn Mawr College Special Collections

painting on wood (*retablo*) of the 'Maestro di Olzai', dating from some time between 1300 and 1600, in the Santa Barbara church. The letter reads, translated from the Italian,

> I arrived in Olzai the day before the terrible storm and I was in the church library when it broke. Having to spend the night in the kindergarten, I drank water believing it to be from the source; instead it was from a well polluted by the flood. I was sick for a long time, and weakened for many weeks. I stayed in Olzai for about a month, studying and copying in the library, when I had the strength, and found a lot of value. Afterwards I was in Oliena and Ozieri, returning home on 22 October very sick. I was sick and weak for a long time. I am fairly healthy now.

Anna's research visits to churches in the towns and villages of Barbagia and elsewhere in Sardinia, and the photographs she took, were greatly to enhance Georgiana's eventual work. Anna also helped by introducing her friend to Sardinian scholars on whose expertise she could draw, not only for the paintings themselves, but also for the historical text in which she set them.

The 1923 publication was intended as a first volume; the second was to have concentrated on Renaissance and Baroque painters, and another letter from Anna to Professor Melonia Satta, of 1925, mentioned by Pusceddu, preceded a visit by Georgiana in 1926; it seems, too, that Georgiana visited Sardinia and Anna several times in subsequent years, but nothing came of her second volume.

Meanwhile, as a report of Georgiana's sabbatical year in Europe 1930–31 suggests, Anna had a project of her own:

> Mrs Giles is collecting every piece of Sardinian Religious Drama and is making a line-for-line translation. This work will be complete and the only one its field. Miss King is writing the introduction and Bryn Mawr is to have the honour of publishing it.

There is no evidence that anything came of that either.

Anna Giles died in Sardinia in 1937, aged 89; and she was buried in Sassari. Georgiana died two years later, aged 68. Anna's will contained the following clause,

> I give and bequeath to Miss Georgiana Goddard King, Professor in Bryn Mawr College … , all my jewelry and laces, free and clear of all taxes whatsoever. I know that Miss King will carry out my wishes in regard to the distribution of a part of the articles in question.

Anna may have made her will before 1935, as Georgiana retired from teaching at Bryn Mawr that year. As far as the College itself was concerned, a report of 1939 reads,

From the estate of Mrs Anna Rose Giles we received a unique collection of over one hundred books on Sardinia and the Sard language. Mrs Giles had lived in Sardinia for many years and had made a study of the folklore and religious drama of that country. The books form the nucleus of a collection for any one who wishes to continue the study.

Although it is said that many boxes of Anna's papers passed to Georgiana and reside in the college archives, that is not borne out by the facts; just the books were received. Somewhere, surely, the papers of both mother and daughter must have been deposited; but they have not been unearthed by determined scholars such as Enrico Pusceddu who continues to work on the three women.

Anna and Ellen both gave to and received much from Sardinia; indeed, it was central to the latter part of their lives. In spite of the detective work already done, there is still more to be discovered, and they really do need to be remembered. As for the missing article about Georgiana and women's suffrage, as far as Sardinia is concerned the result of my own digging on the subject more generally is in the chapter that follows.

Amelie Posse-Brázdová, Alghero 1915–1916

The year after the death of Ellen Rose Giles, and the start of the First World War, **Amelie Posse-Brázdová** (1884–1957) arrived in Alghero. But, whereas Ellen and her mother chose to live in Sardinia, Amelie's sojourn was as a form of detention. Nevertheless, the book she wrote as a result – in English translation from the Swedish, *Sardinian Sideshow* (1933) – is a joy to read, capturing, as it does, several strata of Sardinian society in the Alghero area in a style that manages to be not only historically informative but also amusing and moving.

Amelie was the daughter of Count Fredrik Arvidsson Posse, a builder of railways, and Auda Gunhild Wennerberg, intellectual, artist and singer. Although Amelie was a sickly child, she was educated in languages, including Italian, singing and art. Aged 20, she married a criminal psychologist, but they were divorced in 1912. After studying art in Copenhagen, she moved to Rome; there she met and married, in 1915, the Czech bohemian artist Oskar (Oki) Brazda.

The first few chapters of Amelie's book deal with her Roman period and the early days of her relationship with Oki, lived in a bohemian, artistic, penniless and international community set in a beautiful park; friendships thrived, a lot of fun was had, creativity flourished. As war started to make an impact, and sides were taken, she and Oki actively espoused the cause of Czech independence from Austria. After May 1915, the position of foreigners in Rome became precarious. In spite of their anti-Austrian sentiments, in marrying Oki Amelie took on his nationality and, as Italy and the Austro-Hungarian Empire were on different sides in the war, they became enemy aliens. On 8 July an order came for internment in Sardinia. It was possible to choose where on the island they wished to be sent, so Amelie took advice from a Sardinian acquaintance. She writes,

> As I had met Grazia Deledda several times, I went to her, to find out something about her native land. She gave me letters of introduction, and much good advice as to the best way of handling her stiff-necked, primitive, but in reality good-natured countrymen. Afterwards, I was to realize how sane and true her psychological analysis had been. Many a time I met types and even individuals, especially among the peasantry, whom I seemed to recognize from her books. This was before she achieved fame and won the Nobel prize.

Amelie's description of her time in Sardinia, including its people, particularly its women, starts immediately on her landing in Olbia, still called Terranova, and catching the train. It is worth comparing her first sight of local women with the accounts of Florence Piercy and Isabelle Eberhardt:

> I did not bother any longer with a first class ticket; the third class looked far more interesting. I climbed into a carriage where the costumes of the peasant women especially delighted me, and immediately fell in love with the wonderful shapes of their head-kerchiefs, and a little, too, with their stern, rather pathetic faces. ...
>
> ... The girls, too, had their little tricks of secretly expressing their heart's desire, strictly though they were looked after on the island. There was another complicated language in the folding and knotting of the wool or silk ribbons, which discreetly advertised what the modestly lowered eyes concealed.
>
> It was only by slow degrees, of course, that I learnt all this; on the journey their dialect alone was puzzling enough for me to understand. They themselves thought that they were talking Italian, and I thought they were talking Sardinian. Actually, it was a mixture of both. Sardinian proper is a language by itself, and quite impossible to understand at the first hearing.
>
> As usual, I made plenty of friends on the journey, and I soon found out that it was a matter of indifference to them whether I was an Austrian or not. ... on the other hand, when they found out that I was not a '*continentale*' (Italian from the mainland) they grew obviously more friendly.

Amelie continued that passage with the one I have included in the Introduction concerning relations between Sardinia and the 'mainland'.

There is far too much of Amelie and Oki's life in Catalan-imbued Alghero and its environs in her book to do more than touch on it; I really do recommend it, particularly if you live in Alghero or are planning to visit it. Worth quoting is her first description of the town:

The houses round the harbour were painted in bright, cheerful colours. Several had loggias and arcades, and some had terraces with geraniums and oleanders growing on them. But the town itself with its narrow, dark medieval streets and lanes, dirty and overcrowded, was very different. Here and there one came across old palaces fallen into sad disrepair, or an occasional better-kept convent; and there was a very lovely old cathedral, with a baroque interior, and a spire that looked like a carrot. It was chiefly the colours of the flat, tiled roofs which gave the town its character. They glowed in every imaginable shade from yellow and blood-red to darkest purple, against the background of blue sea.

Amelie describes many of the characters with whom they interacted during their year in Alghero, not only Sardinians but also other internees of several nationalities. Most important to their lives was Maddalena who flits in and out of the story; she arrived after a bit of a setback:

Signora Marietta had found me a servant who she declared was a perfect treasure. She was an elderly widow, dressed from head to toe in funereal black. When she had been with us for a day or two, I remarked to our landlady that I could not think how the woman could bear to wear woollen stockings in that tropical heat. She said I must be mistaken as she was always bare-footed. And, sure enough, when I looked more closely I saw to my horror that what I had taken for black wool was the accumulated layers of sixty years' dirt, so ingrained that not even her toes were distinguishable. When I discovered that she always put both fish and fowl into the oven without cleaning or washing them, so that 'the aroma should not be spoilt in the water', and that she never washed her hands either, she left at a moment's notice.

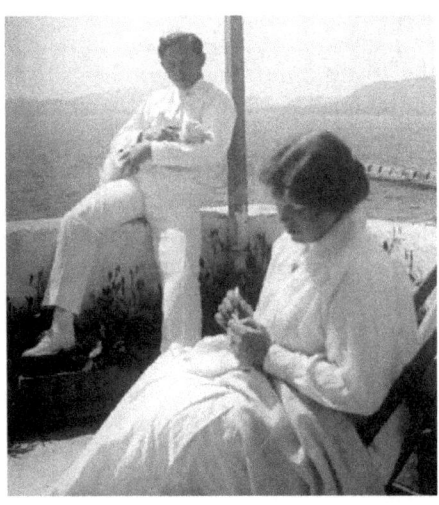

52. Amelie Posse-Brázdová and Oki on balcony, thanks to Gianni Usai

After a few days' search I found another servant. Her name was Maddalena. She was only thirty-two, pretty, quick, and according to Sardinian standards, wonderfully clean, although I had to teach her certain elementary rules, and do most of the cooking myself. She stopped with us the whole time we were interned, and shared all our ups and downs.

So many other characters appear, often more fleetingly; I rather like this one met at a dinner party:

The guest of honour had been **Baroness Fanni di Villanova**. It was she who wanted to meet the two interned, and the dinner had been arranged for her benefit. She was a full-bosomed lively lady who liked a little variety, and she already knew everything there was to know about officers in the town. She arrived in a very décolleté red satin dress, a huge plumed hat of the kind that had been fashionable on the 'Continent' five years before, black glacé kid gloves, which she kept on all through dinner, and an enormous feather fan behind which she flirted boldly in the most devastating manner.

Although, as chapter 7 has indicated, banditry, often as a result of feuds and vendettas, was most prevalent in the Barbagia region, Amelie makes clear that there were still vestiges of it in the west of the island. And her first hint of it is reminiscent of the Charles Wright photograph that illustrates chapter 7:

When those black-bearded, fine-featured Sardinian herdsmen came riding into town on market-days, their guns slung across their shoulders, and their wives '*a groppa*' (i.e. perched behind the saddle with their feet to one side) and their cloaks drawn up over their heads, you could not help a little shudder. You remembered all the old folk's tales about their young days when vendetta was at its height, and banditry reigned supreme and unchecked throughout the island.

That description is merely a snapshot, but Amelie and Oki made friends with a man who vividly brought the past of banditry much closer to home.

As often as possible they got away from Alghero and into the countryside, and Amelie explains why:

Life in small provincial towns, where scandal and intrigue are the only means of diversion, is often very unpleasant, but here it was a hundred times worse. It seemed as if the constant inbreeding, the extraordinary high percentage of cripples and degenerates, and the Spanish pride and indolence, hung like a miasma in the air. One had to go out into the country or on the sea, in order to breathe freely and get away from the fusty atmosphere in the narrow streets, from all the din and quarrelling and petty bickering.

A whole chapter – 'Our Friend Sor Giovanni' – is devoted to this escape from town and the learning of their friend's bandit heritage. Amelie sets the scene:

Sor Giovanni's wife owned a house in the town, in one of the darkest lanes, where she reigned supreme over their twelve children. They lived by selling the produce of the market-garden. The wife kept a shop, and the various children went round the town with either a donkey-cart, pushcarts, or baskets which they carried on their heads. But Sor Giovanni lived outside the town and no longer concerned himself with buying and selling.

The interned couple would go out into the countryside and spend time with Sor Giovanni, helping him in his vegetable plot, mostly channelling water on to the beds, which 'was great fun'. Work done for the day, they would throw themselves down, hot and tired, beside the fire, while Sor Giovanni cooked extraordinary vegetable stews in a tin, which Amelie describes in detail. But just as enlightening was listening to him yarning. In this way they came to learn about his father, a younger son of a family of tough lads 'when the romance of banditry was at its height'.

As it happens, the youngster was outlawed for a murder that he did not commit: it was his brothers who had fired the shots. He himself had lowered his gun at the crucial moment with the thought 'Have I really any right to send another to his death before his time?' But he would not desert his brothers, so fled with them, hunted by the carabinieri, 'feared and respected as if he were a real bandit'. Because of this status, a pretty girl became his wife, joining him in the cave among the rocks,

> She was beaming with pride at belonging to the most famous bandit for miles around. It was in this cave that our Giuannu first saw the light of day. Three swarthy bandits were midwives. A goatskin slung by a couple of rocks was his cradle, a tame fox his earliest companion.

The false bandit could not keep up the pretence however: the truth came out and his wife began to be sullen. But all went well between peace-loving father and growing boy; Giovanni regaled his listeners with stories of his happy childhood learning country lore. But his mother became more irritable and unbearable.

> What annoyed her most was the shameless way in which she had been deceived by her husband. Instead of a bold awe-inspiring bandit whom a woman could honour and look up to, he was nothing but a milksop, a weak-kneed coward. Not a whit more wonderful or *glorioso* than any ordinary herdsman in the neighbourhood. ... She grew even more bitter and bad-tempered, and did nothing but mutter and grumble about how foolishly she had wasted and thrown away her life.

Then one day her husband saw her laughing and joking with his youngest brother who had just escaped from prison. The boy's father became more and more gloomy: husband and wife changed places:

> His mother sang from morning till night and hurled scoffing gibes at him whenever she saw his gloomy face. She went about with a red flower in her hair. One day she came in with a brand-new coral necklace and

another day with a pair of long glittering ear-rings. Then one night she was gone for good.

Her husband searched for her, and then one day his son was taken on a journey to an aunt in Alghero. That evening his father kissed him and said 'God bless you, *figlio mio*! Remember what I have always told you. Live in peace – never kill.' Then week after week went by as the boy fretted at the absence of his father, finding solace in the friendship of a market-gardener. Finally the climax of the story unravelled:

> One morning, when he came home, he found his aunt crying and wailing, and neighbours standing round her helping with the dirge. He paused on the threshold, astonished and frightened. When they caught sight of him, they all rushed towards him and the howling rose higher than ever. It was some time before he could make out what they were saying, or understand why he was the centre of all this lamentation, but at last he realized.
>
> News had come from the south of a dreadful deed. His father had succeeded in finding his youngest and best-beloved brother. And with him he had found his wife. For a long moment he stood staring at them, while they lay paralysed, incapable of saying a word or making a movement to defend themselves. Silent and terrible, that man who had always been so gentle and peaceful had raised his gun and shot first his brother and then his wife. Afterwards he had said a prayer, made the sign of the cross over them, and turned the gun upon himself.
>
> They were all buried together, and the crowds who had come from far and near wept and praised his action. That was a death worthy of a great and honourable bandit.

At the beginning of 1916, Amelie found that she was pregnant and would give birth in September. She started looking into the facilities for giving birth in either Alghero or Sassari. She found them seriously wanting, as she describes in detail. She requested permission to return to the mainland but was refused. Plans began to be hatched. Suffice it to say that Amelie and Oki's child was not born in Sardinia. It would be a pity to spoil the end of the story by telling it here, but you probably could not make it up.

The rest of Amelie's life, and particularly her political activities, are not part of *Sardinian Sideshow*: they included a few more years in Rome, and years in Czechoslovakia, where she became known as a democrat and pacifist. I have not been able to clarify her relations with Oki following her next move. In 1938, she returned to Sweden after the Gestapo had ordered her arrest. In 1940 she was one of the founders of a discussion club in Stockholm, formally about culture, but its true purpose was to work against the expansion of Nazism in Sweden. The club was inaugurated the same day, 9 April 1940, that Nazi Germany occupied Norway. It was to be used as the centre of the Swedish resistance movement should that country ever be occupied. Amelie was, like other members of the club, listed in German records as 'Untrustworthy Swedes'.

Amelie, and the others exiled to Alghero because of their Austrian connection, had it relatively easy. Between December 1915 and March 1916, 23339 Austro-Hungarian soldiers arrived on Asinara, a straggling and rugged island off the north-west tip of Sardinia, second only in size to Sant'Antioco; they were prisoners of war, and their conditions were inhospitable.

Evidence suggests that habitation on the island dates back to Neolithic times. In the sixteenth century it was used as a base by Saracens for incursions into the main island. For protection, several towers were built which were occupied by French pirates in the seventeenth century as a base from which to attack Alghero. When in 1720 Sardinia was ceded to Savoy, Asinara started to be populated by shepherds and their families from Corsica. In 1767, two French brothers, the Velixandres, expropriated the land of the shepherds and settled there, instead, 150 French colonists. Because of the brothers' fraudulence, that did not last long. In 1774, Don Antonio Manca Amat, Marquis of Mores, having acquired the title of Duke of Asinara, brought a number of Ligurians on to the island who developed agriculture and fishing. These various groups of inhabitants would have included women and children, but I can find no details about them. Life would have been demanding.

In 1885, prompted by a serious cholera outbreak on the main island, those last islanders were forced to leave when the Sardinian authorities established an infectious diseases hospital in Cala Reale on the north-eastern coast of Asinara, its harbour known since ancient times as one of the most natural in Europe. And, in due course, a penal colony for Italian prisoners was established at Cala d'Olivia further round on the east coast. The prisoners of war were housed in detention camps there and, during their stay, 7000–8000 of them died of infectious diseases, mainly cholera. In July 1916, about 18000 left for France. There is no evidence that there were any women among them; that was to change in the late 1930s when the island was to have yet more new inhabitants.

The year before Amelie Posse-Brázdová returned to Sweden, in 1937, a number of Ethiopian women arrived on Asinara and were interned under rather less happy circumstances, and with much less freedom, than the exile she had enjoyed in Alghero.

Ethiopians Exiled to Asinara 1937–1940

Italy had had its eye on Ethiopia since the nineteenth century. Fuelled by Mussolini's dream of colonial expansion, the Second Italo-Ethiopian War (also known as the Second Italo-Abyssinian war) was fought between October 1935 and October 1937. It was a brutal war in which many war crimes were committed by both sides, and success swung back and forth until, finally, Italy prevailed. One of the Italian Fascist commanders, Rodolfo Graziani, was particularly harsh; in March 1936, for example, he authorised the bombing of the city of Harar. An assassination attempt on him in February the following year led to what is known as the Yekatit massacre, during the three days of which the Ethiopians claimed that 30000 civilians were killed. According to the Italians it was only a few hundred, while a 2017 source puts the number at 19200.

As a result of the assassination attempt, many Ethiopian nobles – the educated elite – were rounded up and executed; 284 others were sent to be detained on Asinara, including 43 women and 27 children; among them was a daughter of Emperor Haile Selassie and his first wife Woizero Altayech. They joined a few anti-Fascist activists already imprisoned there, as well as Libyan notables exiled from 1930 onwards.

Princess Romanework Haile Selassie, or the Princess of the Golden Pomegranate as she was also known in Ethiopia (1909–1940), was married to Major-General (Dejazmach) Beyene Merid, governor of Bale. They had four sons. While she and her sons were captured and sent, first to mainland Italy, and then to Asinara in 1937, her husband remained at liberty and was a leader of the resistance until he was executed later that year.

One of the two most useful accounts of the women's detention is that of Carlo Hendel who was stationed on Asinara between 1982 and 1987 as Agrozootechnical Director of Asinara prison house. In November 2019 his article *'Asinara, un posto nella storia Etiope'* was posted on the *Isola Asinara* website. A bonus of the article is the photographs, particularly that of the princess with two of her very small sons (which, unfortunately, I have been unable to reproduce). The other account is that of an interview given to a researcher in Addis Ababa in 2010 by **Yeweinshet Beshah-Woured** (b.1931) who was six years old when she was deported to Asinara with her 27-year-old pregnant mother **Sara Gebruyesus Beshah-Woured Habtewold** (b.1920), and brother; her father, a government official close to the emperor, had been shot by the Italians. Unfortunately, her aged mother was too ill to be interviewed, but Yeweinshet has a quite vivid and useful memory of the family's detention and, indeed, that of Romanework, and two other women, one called **Woizero Sanabedjus** who was distantly related to her father; she died on Asinara. The other was **Woizero Seledo** who died not long before the interview. (Woizero appears to be a female title).

Of the princess she wrote,

> Then there was the Emperor's daughter. Yes, Woizero Romanework and her children. I think she had been caught. Her husband was one of the big fighters and died in the war. And maybe she was somewhere near her husband and she was arrested by the Italians and they took her. And I think she had more problems than we did. With her more children. With hindsight I believe they took her off the island, because of that. And they took her away from us.

In some ways the 28-year-old princess was more protected than others because she had a retinue with her, and she was comfortably enough housed. The detainees lived in what were called 'pagodas'; the food available was serviceable if unexciting. In spite of being educated, even the little Yeweinshet whose father had insisted she should be, the Ethiopians did not speak Italian. This no doubt increased their feeling of isolation. One of Hendel's informants, the photographer Gianfranco Massida, told him 'I remember Princess Woizero Romanework walking away along the paths of Cala Reale, always accompanied by a lady-in-waiting and under the watchful but discreet eye of the carabinieri.'

Whatever her privileges, Romanework's suffering must have been acute when one of her sons fell ill and died. She, herself, seems to have caught tuberculosis and so was taken off the island and settled in Turin, where she died in 1940, aged only 31. Hendel includes a photograph of her tombstone. A second son also died in Turin. Yeweinshet's mother was in the same party leaving the island, because she was pregnant, and her second son was born in a maternity hospital in Rome, leaving her ill for some time. Another pregnant woman, **Woizero Touawitch**, did not survive childbirth there. In June 1938, the repatriation of the detained Ethiopians on Asinara began, following case-by-case examination, starting with the women and children. Yeweinshet's extensive interview includes an account of the family's life on their return to Ethiopia and for some time thereafter.

To get a real insight into the sort of Ethiopian women sent to Asinara, you cannot do better than to read the short-listed Booker Prize novel of 2020, translated into English as *The Shadow King* (2019). Its author, Maaza Mengiste, has put herself into the skins of her women protagonists of 1935 who, as she relates, played a major part in what was, on the Ethiopian side, mainly a guerrilla war against Italian tanks, bombs and gas. She has been helped in doing this not only because she is Ethiopian, but also because, as she discovered, her great-grandmother and her grandfather were involved in that war. She learnt Italian to access relevant archives and better to understand the protagonists – Italian Fascists – on the other side.

The two leading women in the novel are aristocratic Aster, and Hirut, dogsbody in the house because Aster's husband undertook to be guardian to the young orphaned woman when her parents died. The three of them lead an intertwined life full of tensions and, often, cruelty, described poetically, sometimes opaquely, almost mystically. You soon know which side you are on as war hits the women and their compatriots and, until you finally put the book down, you are enabled to become Ethiopian.

In 1997, Asinara was established as a National Park, and is now a nature reserve. Visitors interested in exploring can do so with Sealand Asinara, a social co-operative of women graduates which aims to educate people on environmental and sustainability issues on island tours.

The next chapter includes a return to the First World War; chapter 13 is about Sardinian women who actively opposed Fascism.

12 – The Twentieth Century: Literature, Politics, War, Science and Art 1875–1950

Introduction

In *Sardinian Sideshow*, as chapter 11 suggests, Amelie Posse-Brázdová paints a lively picture of what it was like to be a foreigner interned in Alghero during the First World War. Although she also displays an ethnographic sensibility, she could not write about the effect of the war on the families of the many Sardinian men who fought on the mainland; she was only interned for a year, between 1915 and 1916, and she was not free to roam too far from Alghero.

In '*La Sardegna durante il ventennio fascista*' (2010), M Garroni gives some statistical idea of the war's results, alongside which it is not hard to use one's imagination. Sardinia's population at the beginning of the war was 870000; mobilisation between 1915 and 1918 was almost 99000 – 11.8 per cent of the total population, and the fallen and missing were more than 17000, almost 17 per cent of those called to arms and 2 per cent of the inhabitants of the island. 'So if you take into account the population scarcity, it can reasonably be argued that few other Italian regions have paid a price as high and bloody as that of Sardinia.' The experience of war touched all the villages on the island. Those fallen and missing would have had mothers, wives, sisters, daughters, sweethearts who would be left not only grieving but perhaps the sole breadwinners for the family.

Almost all those Sardinians who fought did so in the 'Sassari Brigade'; among them was Emilio Lussu, who is to feature later in the story of the Sardinian women fighting against the Fascism that grew into prominence in the 1920s. Garroni draws on Lussu's writing to suggest the background of the fighting men: they were farmers and shepherds, workers, miners and craftsmen. With the men dead, who would look after the sheep, for example; who would replace the miners; and who feed their families?

This chapter describes how women, particularly of the middle class, rallied around the war effort, but Luisa Maria Plaisant, director of the *Istituto Sardo della Resistenza e della Automomia* suggests in *Le Donne Cagliaritane e la Prima Guerra Mondiale* (2018) that there were also those who protested. In October 1917 a decree was issued that provided for large fines or imprisonment for anyone who exhibited or promoted manifestations of defeatism or even of pessimism or mistrust. **Maria Immacolata Pellegrino**, teacher of history and geography in a Cagliari normal school, was tried on just such a charge. Although the charges were not proved and she was, therefore, acquitted, she was suspended from her job and remained unpaid for 10 months – not easy for a mother of two. The accusation against her could well have been because her husband was an Austrian detainee.

Drought caused price rises which led to inflation and, therefore, to a decrease in real wages. This, together with the requisition system and limitations on the export of island products, led, again in the autumn of 1917, to demonstrations, mainly by women. Not only were they the main purchasers for the family but, also, many men were away at war. The demonstrations took place particularly in the cities; in Sassari groups of women threw stones at vehicle headlights and shop windows, and tampered with loads of wheat. In Cagliari that August, stones caused injury and the administration resigned, so that there, and in Sassari, the municipalities were run by prefectural commissioners until 1920.

Little seeped through to Sardinia of what was happening in the war, but there was more to it than fighting, as Garroni, again drawing on Lussu, attests. The experience of both men and officers was broadened and they had more to do with each other. The officers, almost all voluntary, were employed professionals, young graduates and students – the small and medium bourgeoisie; he notes:

> The experience of the trenches strengthened the link between the representatives of the urban and village middle classes and the rural proletariat and it became not only a school of war, but also a 'political' school. Above all there developed in Sardinians the awareness of their own strength and the need to resolve the serious economic situation which the island was facing, caused by the inadequacy of the old Sardinian political class.

Post-war Sardinia was, therefore, to be an increasingly different, more politically conscious, activist place. Women's political consciousness was also raised, as was their consciousness as women, though the seeds of this were sown even earlier.

Late Nineteenth and Early Twentieth Century Developments

The contribution made by **Caterina Faccion Berlinguer** (1839–1909) to the advancement of Sardinian women is a useful place to start piecing together its progress. She was born in Sassari to a military father, Giuseppe (or Antonio) Berlinguer, a member of the town's progressive bourgeoisie, and **Maria Marogna Satta** from a well-off family from Sorso not far from Sassari. Educated by nuns, Caterina became a teacher in a private school, presided over a women's club, translated from English and French, and loved reading and writing. Among her reading were biographies of renowned Italian women, the writing of Cristina Pisani (Christine de Pisan) who, based in Paris in the fifteenth century, was to have such an impact on women's development, and John Stuart Mill's *Subjection of Women* (1869), which she must have read in English. It is fair to suggest that several strands fed into Caterina's political and social awakening: her reading, background and parental influence, and marrying Antonio Faccion Valentini, a Venetian lawyer, in political exile in Sardegna having fled the Hapsburg police.

In July 1875 in Sassari, Caterina founded and headed *La Donna e la Civiltà* (Women and Civilisation), the first Sardinian periodical aimed at women. It had numerous features in common with many of the Italian women's magazines of the second half of the nineteenth century: it supported the struggle for the protection of women's rights, looked in depth at educational issues, and disseminated rules of hygiene. Caterina edited in particular a series of articles entitled *'Pensieri* [Thoughts] *sull'educazzione'* in which she promoted the importance of education and upbringing in order to enhance the role of women and mothers. As she wrote, quoted in Federica Ginesu's 2017 internet piece about her, 'Wide and deep education must not be feared by women.'

In her first editorial, Caterina had written, 'Many difficulties arose before me, because it was not easy after the experience of many periodicals born and died, to give rise to a new one especially of women and without material means.' It was not surprising, therefore, that her publication was short-lived: at the end of 1876, for lack of subscribers to keep it financially afloat, it had to close down. Undefeated, Caterina continued to write, including a verse, a rough translation of which reads:

The women came in excellence,
Having taken care of each Art.
And whatever histories give warning,
She still feels a dark hunger for it.
If the world has long been without it,
The bad influence does not last for ever.
And perhaps their honourable dues have been hidden
By the envy and unknowing of writers.

Two of Caterina's younger siblings were, in their own way, to be as politically active as she was. Both her sister **Edoarda Berlinguer** (later Cardia, 1841–1931) and her brother Enrico (b.1850) were committed followers of Giuseppe Mazzini, spearhead of the Italian nationalist movement, known as the *Risorgimento*. Edoarda, an elementary school teacher, wrote under the pen name Ava in *Giovine Sardegna*, an adjunct of *Giovane Italia*, the secret revolutionary society which Mazzini had founded in 1831. As part of her work as a Mazziniana, she was also, according to a 2019 article about Garibaldi by Gianfranco Murtas, president of a female workers' group which met in the Via Arborea near the University. Chiara Valentini, in her Italian-language biography *Enrico Berlinguer* (2014) of the twentieth-century Communist leader, Enrico's grandson and namesake, briefly mentions Edoarda. She describes her as one of 'the singular female characters, independent up to the point of extravagance, of which this family history is rich'.

An anonymous 2017 article from the *Unione Sarda* website about Edoarda's niece Ines Berlinguer suggests that Edoarda founded a periodical called la *Donna Mazziniana*, but I can find nothing further about that. Ines, who was, it seems, inspired by her aunt to be politically active herself, finds her place in chapter 13.

Enrico, the youngest of Caterina's six siblings, having graduated in law from the University of Turin, returned to Sardinia, a lawyer and jurist, and became active in politics: as a municipal councillor he led the Republicans to a majority in the Sassari municipal council; in 1891, he was one of the founders of *La Nuova Sardegna*, the main newspaper in Sardinia even today.

It may not be possible to know how far journalist and newspaper editor **Maria Manca Colombo** (1851– ?) was influenced by Caterina Berlinguer's earlier publication. Born in Turin, Maria became Sardinian by adoption. After moving to Cagliari, she met and married Cesare Manca, an employee in the construction of the railway between Mandas and Nurri, an employment which ties in with the work of Benjamin Piercy described in chapter 11. The couple set up home in Sarcidano in central Sardinia, and there Maria's first cultural interests were born, ready to be channelled into her future project.

Moving back to Cagliari, Maria was conscious of the conservatism of the capital, even of hostility towards women, whose only function was seen as wife and mother. They did not have the right to vote and they were excluded from administrative and political office and education. She saw the need for their more general education and to do that, in 1898 she set up the publication *La Donna Sarda*. It is not too much of a leap to suggest that the late twentieth century internet platform, now defunct, *DonnaSarda*, was the granddaughter of Maria Manca's publication.

Grazia Deledda, already a well-known writer (see chapter 7), was among those whom Maria Manca persuaded to write for her, as was feminist and activist Anna Maria Mozzoni. As early as 1877, the Milanese **Anna Maria Mozzoni** (1837–1920) presented a petition to the Italian Parliament calling for women's suffrage. In 1878 she represented Italy at the International Congress on Women's Rights in Paris. In 1879 she published her translation from English into Italian of John Stuart Mill's 1869 essay *The Subjection of Women* – the English edition of which had influenced Caterina Berlinguer. How far Anna Maria's contribution to *La Donna Sarda* was overtly feminist, whether or not it talked of women's suffrage, I have been unable to determine. It may be that the *DonnaSarda* internet contribution by Federica Ginesu 'La Storia delle Suffragette Sarde', which has proved frustratingly inaccessible now that the website has closed down, would suggest the answer. My lack of access has, however, spurred me into my own concerted exploration of twentieth-century Sardinian women activists.

Maria Xanta of Sassari, who wrote with masculine assurance, turned out to be, indeed, a man, as Michela Deriu reveals in the internet piece about Maria Manca's work, '*Nessuno è perfetto!*' (2014). Michela Deriu also suggests that 'In England in those years a movement of women was born, fighting for the right to vote. In Sardinia, the women of the enlightened bourgeoisie decided to formulate their opinion in writing. In the baggage of our history this is not an unimportant detail.'

La Donna Sarda was of a price, no doubt caused by the economy of scale, only affordable by the 'enlightened bourgeoisie', and its life, though in some ways productive, was brief: by 1901 it had ceased publication. Maria Lidia Contu's internet piece, '*Maria Manca Colombo: La Prima Giornalista che Diede Voce alle Donne Sarde*', starts with an illustration of the front cover of the *Periodico Mensile Feminile* [Monthly Female Periodical]; *dalla Signora Maria Manca.*

If Maria Manca appears something of an admirable woman in advance of her time, and if one imagines that those who agreed to write for her admired her, one's hopes are dashed by the supposed opinion of her held by Grazia Deledda. Grazia might even have been grateful, given that Maria had her to stay when she visited Cagliari from Nuoro in 1899. Instead, her 2005 English-language biographer, Martha King, quotes from her 1936 posthumous autobiographical novel *Cosima* of being met by the 'overzealous editor' at Cagliari station, a quotation that continues in that vein:

> A woman dressed in an almost comic way, all flutter and fringe, with her hat awry on her sparse yellow hair, jumped toward the girl, took her almost in flight from the train steps, hugged her to her thin bosom, covered her face in kisses. Her porcelain blue eyes were shining with tears that ran down her aquiline nose and mixed with saliva squirting from her mouth. With a convulsive sob she called the girl by her first and last name in such a loud voice that she embarrassed Cosima; people were looking at her.

Maria lived in Via San Lucifero, the same street that the male protagonist in Grazia's novel *Cenere* lived in. On that same 1899 visit, Grazia was to meet the man who became her husband and with whom she moved to Rome, but to begin with they were apparently to live at Maria Manca's place, or an apartment she owned, and Grazia gave all sorts of rather unpleasant instructions, quoted by Martha King, for dealing with Maria. I have been unable to discover when Maria died, but hope it was before 1936, so that she never read what Grazia thought of her.

Grazia Deledda's novels, many of them translated into English, are an education regarding an aspect of the old Sardinia, particularly Barbagia, and she well deserved the Nobel Prize for Literature she received in 1926, but I'm not sure that I like her as a person! So celebrated was she by 1909, and living in Rome, that she was deemed the ideal woman to put forward as a parliamentary candidate; she was to be a kite flyer for women's suffrage. Martha King tells the story in some detail, mostly using direct Grazia quotations:

> In early 1909 something unexpected occurred without her consent or knowledge. Deledda was put up as a candidate for the national Chamber of Deputies. A group of citizens of Nuoro, headed by Sebastiano Satta [poet and Nuoro lawyer] wanted her as an opposition candidate to a certain outspoken, anti-feminist lawyer… . Deledda learned of it from a Sardinian newspaper on the Monday after the election – in which she

received only three valid votes. Of the thirty-four votes cast in her favour, thirty-one were invalid because they carried messages of protest against the other candidate. *La Tribuna* of Rome made light of her candidacy, saying that as mother of fine children and writer of good novels, she would have made a poor deputy because she wouldn't have known how to read the budget. Deledda defended herself by saying that though she and her children got a good laugh from the whole episode, she would have gone to the Chamber if she had won, but to do what she didn't know. She was asked the question: why would you go then? 'Out of curiosity, to study the environment, to reproduce it, to see politics with my own eyes. They say it is a very ugly sight up close.' She went on to say that she was not interested in politics herself, but felt that women who were educated for it should have the opportunity [to] go into public life. To the interviewer's insistence that women already played a large part in the public sector, Deledda agreed: yes, but almost as machines – as telegraph operators and workers under men's direction. Only when women can become members of the parliament and heads of business organizations would the situation change. Men are eligible for parliament at thirty, but because women have children, most of them can't take part until they are in their fifties. How unattractive that would be, responds the male interviewer, to have a room full of 'venerable matrons.' Malicious observations such as that always convince her of the futility of pursuing such topics. 'On the other hand, if a woman wants to take part in public life, why renounce her energy at the age when her mental faculties are most developed; the age when the so-called weaker sex has an undeniable superiority over men? ... Yes, I know that is dangerous ... The best thing is to let the world go the way it will, without forcing its inclinations too much; without opposing it too much either. As for myself, I am completely disinterested in the question; I have my books, my work and my children; I don't have time to bother with politics'.

Deledda never allied herself with feminism as such, though she attended the First National Congress of Italian Women held in Rome in 1908, and was friends with some of the avowed feminist writers in attendance ... 'I have never wanted to be associated with certain manifestations of modern "Feminism" ... but that doesn't mean that I think a woman who participates in some measure and with much circumspection in public demonstration is foolish or imprudent.'

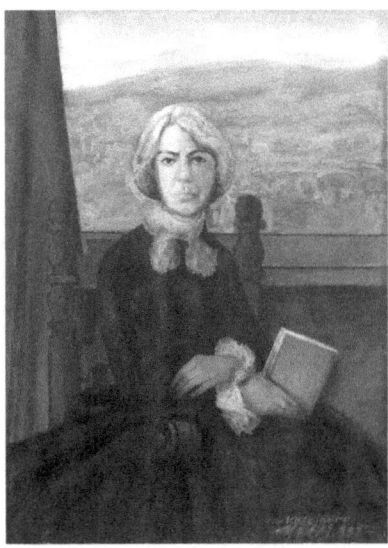

53. Grazia Deledda, by Melkiorre Melis, from the internet

The First World War and the National Women's Union (*l'Unione Femminile Nazionale*) 1915–1924

Although Italian women gained the right to vote in local elections in 1925, they were not able to vote nationally until 1945/46; but that by no means prohibited them from making their talents and voices heard before either of those dates. One of the ways in which they did that was, in 1915, during the First World War, to set up the Sardinian chapter of the *Unione Femminile Nazionale* (UFN). This union of women had been founded in Milan in 1899 by a group of likely mainland women, with the Milanese **Ersilia Bronzini Majno** (1859–1933) as its first president. She was the daughter of a small entrepreneur whose family business went bankrupt, interrupting the education of his daughters. But with the help of a graduate brother, Ersilia educated herself, and her marriage to Luigi Majno, a socialist lawyer committed to the struggle for women's emancipation, enabled her to fulfil her own feminist ambitions. The death of her daughter Mariuccia in 1902 prompted her to set up the Mariuccia Kindergarten which she ran until her death. This was but one of her projects.

The UFN's main, but by no means only, objective was the emancipation of Italian women through the acquisition of political, social and civil rights, including suffrage and political representation. A petition of 1905 was signed by 10000, asking for 'recognition of the administrative and political right to vote and eligibility for women'. The campaign continued throughout the years that followed.

In May 1915 Italy entered the First World War, and that year chapters of the UFN were set up in Sardinia, in Macomer and Cagliari. Macomer, though away from the centre of political life, was an important railway junction between north and south; less seems to be known about its UFN activities than about those of Cagliari, but they certainly took place. The Cagliari headquarters seem to have been in the premises of the workers' society. Many women were to be involved, and many activities took place, particularly in support of the war effort in which, as the introduction to this chapter details, Sardinian soldiers who formed the Sassari Brigade played a major part.

Among the founders of the Cagliari chapter was **Dr Paola Satta** (1877–1974) who is famous for being Sardinia's first woman to qualify as a doctor; more recently she is noted as the first president of the Cagliari UFN. Born in Thiesi, in the north-western Logudoro region of the island, to Leonardo Satta and a mother whose name eludes me, she attended Cagliari University, starting in the academic year 1896–7, and graduated in 1902. By 1903, in the Institute of Hygiene, she was already publishing a learned article, and she continued to do so after she had moved to the Obstetrician-Gynaecology Institute. In *'Medicina: una carriera anche per le donne'*, Enrico Fanni elaborates on her medical contributions, as well as noting that soon she was distinguishing herself not only as a practitioner but also for her social commitment.

Dr Paola was interested in the fate of prisoners of war, and Fanni's Facebook article, '*Paola Satta, la Prima Donna Medica Sarda*', suggests that she was a volunteer in the Red Cross. Although his enquiry to that organisation's archives did not confirm that, Luisa Maria Plaisant's later writing clarifies that she was: she writes that Dr Paola was 'prominent' in the Red Cross headquarters set up in the civil hospital in Piazza del Carmine.

Perhaps because she was the first Sardinian woman doctor, she continues to be of interest to researchers, particularly Elena Branca, member of the Italian Society of the History of Medicine, and a scholar of the history of the Red Cross. In '*Dottoresse al fronte*' (2016) she mentions Paola in a list of women doctors active in 1911 at the time of the Balkan War and the Italo-Libyan or Turkish war – Libya was then part of the Ottoman Empire. In a separate internet piece – *Paola Satta* (nd) – edited from archives, she has Paola living in Turin in 1911, presenting herself to the Military Corps of Turin on 21 March 1911 (on the occasion of the Libyan War) with 'an application for enlistment, accepted on 10 April'. By 1915, she was back in Cagliari.

The Red Cross played, as usual, a major role in treating the war wounded and the ties between it and the UFN were strong, doubtless assisted by Dr Paola. Gianfranco Murtas's May 2015 piece written for the 60th anniversary of the Cagliari chapter of the Italian Federation of Women's Arts, Professions and Business (FIDAPA) contains many useful details for this period. He suggests that Paola also concerned herself with the soldiers at the front, particularly their health, as well as members of their family, some of whom became widows and orphans. (FIDAPA may or may not be a descendant of the UFN.) Later details about Dr Paola seem to be obscure, perhaps because in September 1917 she married the soldier Edoardo Somma. Paola Satta Somma is the name used when she applied to re-enter the medical register in 1929. It is known that she died aged 96. Elena Branca has established that it was in Rome, where she is buried in the Verano cemetery.

Caterina (Lina) **Tronci Pernis** (1865–1967) was a member of the extensive Pernis family whose business activities are detailed in chapter 10. She was the daughter of Luigi Tronci and **Antonietta Pernis**, daughter of the original couple, Joseph Pernis and Catterina Sesselego. As she herself was to say, she was born at a time when the needs of the working middle class needed to be taken account of. As was not uncommon then, she married her cousin (Romolo) Enrico Pernis, a leading Cagliari Freemason and president of the Civil Hospital. It is worth noting in passing that Freemasonry was prevalent in many philanthropical activities in Sardinia, including those undertaken by the Pernis family, particularly Enrico's father Eugenio; connections between Freemasonry and the UFN were, therefore, not to be unusual. It is also necessary to note that Lina and Enrico's son was also, a little confusingly, called Enrico.

In the family home beside the Salesian Institute on Via Merello, which became Via Baccaredda, Lina and Enrico and other activists prepared a large number – well over thirty thousand – 'warmers'. They were paraffin-soaked

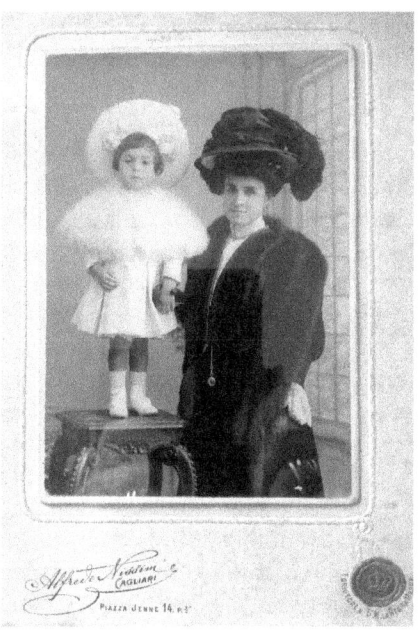 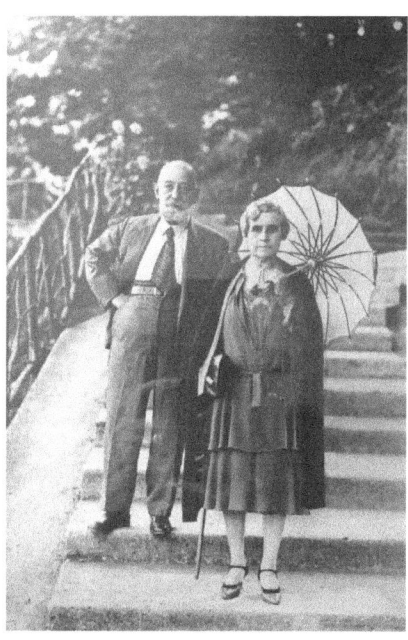

54a. Lina Pernis and little Enrico, courtesy of Anna Maria Spinas Pernis and Edoardo Spinas Pernis

54b. Lina Pernis and her husband Enrico, courtesy of Anna Maria Spinas Pernis and Edoardo Spinas Pernis

newspaper pages compressed into rolls which soldiers at the front could use to heat their meals. Also packaged in Lina's garden, according to Luisa Maria Plaisant, were wool and cotton garments for the troops made by volunteers through a competition with prizes.

As the war came to an end Lina was president of the Casa delle Madri (House of Mothers), part of the UFN's continuing work for the care of children. Under Lina's authoritative presidency, as Francesca Vardeu, an authority on Sardinian women's First World War activities, informs me by email, important initiatives were taken and structures put in place for the help of soldiers, as well as the children, mothers and relatives of the military. With the help of the obstetric clinic of the University, and with an endowment of some 12000 lire, about 80 children, from one to three years old, were taken in on weekdays and looked after by lay and religious staff and paediatric doctors. Paola Satta is not mentioned but, given her experience, it seems likely that she, too, was involved. Lina lived until she was 102, after being widowed in 1933. She and Enrico had the unhappy experience in the 1920s of their 18-year-old son Enrico bringing Mussolini supporters into the house.

Sassari-born **Bastianina Martini Musu** (1892–1945) was in her early twenties, and maybe already married to Domenico Musu, when the war started and she immediately recognised a need: knowing that 60 per cent of the island's population were non-literate, she set up a correspondence office in Sassari. This allowed families to communicate with the men at the front. She and her colleagues took down dictation about news from home of domestic and island goings on, and asking for news about the health of the recipient who was continually at risk, often in the trenches or taking part in assaults. Bastianina's office provided not only envelopes but also the postage which families could ill afford. Similar correspondence centres were set up elsewhere, for example in Cagliari. Another office, chaired by **Luisa (Gigina) Serra Rossi**, provided news to soldiers' families who approached the office with trepidation to ask after their loved ones; that news increasingly made the recipients aware of the harsh reality of war. In due course, Bastianina was to become fully involved in the struggle for women's emancipation and suffrage; her story continues in chapter 14.

The aftermath of the war, including the international influenza epidemic of 1918/19, called for continuing activity by women. Prominent among organisations was the Cordeliane set up in 1920 in the Via Lamarmora in Cagliari's Castello by the writer from the mining area Iglesias **Amelia Melis Devilla (1882–1956)** who became its president. Amelia had moved to Cagliari in 1911 following the death of her father, emeritus professor of engineering and pure mathematics. She soon became known as a writer, her well-received first novel, *Faula de Orbaci*, being published in 1913 and printed by the newly founded Sardinian Printing Company.

The Cordeliane association took its name from the publication for girls *Cordelia* (1881–1942) founded in Florence. The Sardinian association went in for a mix of welfare and cultural activities. Prompted by Amelia, it contributed to the paediatric ward for poliomyelitis of the Binaghi Hospital in Cagliari. It raised money by concerts and fetes on behalf of the Casa delle Madri. Relief work was offered via appropriate institutions to the blind and those mutilated during the war. It managed to obtain funding to develop girls' and women's arts and crafts; it held lectures and exhibitions and took parties to visit museums, monuments and factories. It encouraged the production of such natural comestibles as confectionery.

Ten years after its founding, the marine colony for scrofulous children, with their tuberculosis of the lymph nodes, entered the Cordelian charitable agenda chaired by **Dina Pisano Azzolina**. Because she was married to the renowned professor Liborio Azzolina, she could call on all sorts of useful contacts.

With the coming of Fascism in the 1920s, Amelia bowed out: she would have nothing to do with it. She moved to Rome in 1921 with her sister, to be near their brothers, one an economic journalist, later head of the press office of the capital's municipal authority, the other an architect and engineer, professor at the Polytechnic of Turin, and founder of several connected periodicals. The siblings formed an intellectual trio. Amelia continued to write, journalism and literature. She produced several books, usually about Sardinia, until the outbreak of the Second World War, the best known of which, not only in Sardinia and Italy, was the novel *Alba sul Monte* ('Sunrise on the Mountain') (1931). It investigated the realities of the mining world of the Iglesias region, an industry described in its earlier years in chapter 10.

Not only was Grazia Deledda an admirer of Amelia's work but their writing is compared by Ilaria Muggianu Scano and Mario Fadda in *Grazia Deledda e Amelia Melis de Villa: Due Protegoniste del Romanzo Cattolico Italiano* (2014). There is a Via Amelia Melis de Villa in Iglesias.

The Cagliari chapter of the UNF ceased to be active in 1924 because its welfare activities and ideology were inimical to the Fascist regime then becoming entrenched in Italy and Sardinia. As Francesca Vardeu put it to me, 'My impression is that women, rather than join in the structures and activities of the fascist regime, withdrew into the private sphere, waiting for better times and a more favourable political situation which happened in another form probably after the Second World War.' The Macomer chapter, though, continued until 1938. Some women may have withdrawn from social and political activity, but a brave band of sisters was openly active in the anti-Fascist movement, as described in chapter 13.

Science and Art between the Wars

Fascism and anti-Fascism were to be a preoccupation of many in the inter-war years, and, indeed, during the Second World War, but it was also possible to pursue intellectual and artistic pursuits. What is noticeable where artistic and intellectual endeavour is concerned is how often it ran among female siblings.

Eva Mameli Calvino is not noted for being a sibling but because her son was the famous writer Italo Calvino. That, though, was only one of her successes in life, and not the most noteworthy.

Giuliana Luigia Evelina Mameli Cubeddu (Eva, 1886–1978) was born in Sassari, the fourth daughter of upper middle class parents, colonel of the Carabinieri Corps Giovanni Battista Mameli and **Maddalena Cubeddu** from Ploaghe (Sassari). The secular couple transmitted to their children, without sex discrimination, the same values of education, of knowledge, and the importance of a full commitment to one's life and work. Early on Eva shared an interest in nature with her favourite and older brother Efisio. She was the first and only girl to attend the then Technical and Nautical High School Pietro Martini, graduating in 1903. Then, having shown an interest in science, she enrolled to study mathematics at the University of Cagliari. In 1905/6 she was the first woman in Sardinia to achieve the licence in mathematics.

Following her father's death, Eva and her widowed mother moved to the mainland, to Pavia, where Efisio was a lecturer in organic chemistry at the University of Pavia. In 1907 she completed the degree in natural sciences that she had started in Cagliari, at the same time attending a laboratory which boasted a high scientific reputation for being one of its kind in Italy. She studied particularly 'lower' plants such as algae and mosses that had proved of importance for the physiology, pathology and ecology of plants. She was ready to proceed up the scientific ladder. Her first publication was in 1906 – a paper entitled in English translation 'Of some species and varies of the genus Fumaria new to the Sardinia Flora' – and, in 1915, she was the first Italian woman to obtain a teaching certification in botany. From 1907 to 1920 she was a research assistant in botany at the University of Pavia.

During the First World War, Eva worked as a Red Cross nurse and was decorated. Immediately afterwards, aged 34, she was faced with a difficult choice: her main teacher was dead and Efisio had transferred to the University of Cagliari where, in 1921, he was to be a founder member of the Partito Sardo d'Azione (the Sardinian Action Party). Eva was alone and rudderless in Pavia. Then in 1920 she met again agronomist Mario Calvino with whom she had been acquainted some years before. He had multiple scientific, social and educational commitments which took him to Latin America and Cuba. As director of the Experimental Agricultural Station in Santiago de las Vegas, he was looking for someone ready to be employed in plant genetics. Eva accepted his marriage proposal and they settled in Cuba where they were able to lead a peaceful life of work and study in tropical surroundings. In 1923 their son Italo was born and, by 1924, she was head of the botany department and teaching botany.

In 2013 Professor Elena Accati of parks and gardens attached to Turin University, herself a distinguished floriculturalist, gave a paper in the Sassari University Library at a Garden Club study day – *'Un Esempio di Donna Dotata di Straordinario Talento per la Ricerca'* ('An example of a woman gifted with an extraordinary talent for research'). In it she gave a flavour of Eva in Cuba:

> There she worked intensely on sugar cane, a crop of primary importance to the inhabitants of the island, achieving absolutely innovative results of great usefulness to the local population. In addition she devoted herself to work on behalf of Cuban women, to try and elevate them culturally.

In 1925, the couple returned to Italy, taking with them novel palm trees, grapefruit and kiwi fruit. Mario was to be director of the flower-growing Experimental Station 'Orazio Raimondo' of San Remo, the plans for which he had earlier drawn up with his friend after whom it was named. They settled there, acquiring a family home, with Eva as assistant and deputy director. Meanwhile, though, she pursued her independent professional career: she won the competition for the chair of botany in Catania (Sicily) and, shortly after that, in Cagliari.

From 1925 to 1929, as well as having a second son in 1927 (Floriano who became a geologist), she not only taught botany but, from 1926, she was also the director of the Botanic Garden of the University – the first woman. Among her projects, she resurrected the vegetable garden abandoned during the war, and reintroduced rare plants in memory of the natural vegetation of the island before the changes made by the Carthaginians. It is that period, as well as her early educational achievements, that are of particular importance to the history of women in Sardinia.

From 1929, and her return full time to her husband in San Remo, instead of commuting from Sardinia, she continued to work with him at the floriculture experimental station. In 1930 they founded the *Società Italiana Amici dei Fiori* (Society of Friends of Flowers) and the publication '*Il Giardino Fiorita*'. During the Second World War, the couple offered asylum to partisans and Jews, for which Mario spent 40 days in gaol and Eva was forced to attend two mock executions of her husband by the Fascists. In 1950 she took over from Mario as director of the Orazio Raimondo; he died a year later. Eva held the post for eight years, continuing her research, publishing widely, including about Sardinia, well into her retirement. She was also one of the first supporters of the movement for the protection of nature in Italy. In her 2013 paper, Elena Accati added her impression of Eva in later life (1976): 'I had the privilege of knowing Eva Mameli Calvio when she was 80 and working on a large etymological dictionary on flower species. I was amazed at her liveliness, her intellectual curiosity.'

Much has been written about Eva, as a woman pioneer and about her botanical importance to Sardinia and to the wider world. There is even a book for children in the series 'Women in Science' – *Fiori in Famiglia: Storia e Storie di Eva Mameli Calvino* (2015) by Elena Accati. It purports to tell Eva's story in her own voice. In 2018, Elena Accati published a biography, *Eva Mameli Calvino*. A raft of other distinguished botanical scientists contributed to a symposium in honour of Eva at Cagliari University in 2014.

In the hopes of finding a trace of Eva in the Cagliari Botanic Garden, I visited it in the autumn of 2017, having first sent an email enquiring about her, but received no response. I was disappointed to find, on my arrival, that the staff did not know who I was talking about. And yet, in November 2016, during the celebrations of the 150th anniversary of the Botanic Garden held by the Botanic Gardens and Historical Gardens Group of the Italian Botanical Society, the lecture hall was renamed in honour of Eva Mameli Calvino. The keynote address, 'A Portrait of Eva', was given by Maria Cristina Secci of Cagliari University who a year later published *Eva Mameli Calvino: Gli Anni Cubani (1920–1925)* (2017). Eva may be well known among the scientific and botanic community, and perhaps those researching the history of Sardinian women, but she is worthy of being more widely known to visitors to the Botanic Garden. Elena Accati ended her 2013 paper with the suggestion of how Eva contributed towards Italo Calvino's literary development:

> In addition to being a scientist and scholar, Eva Mameli was a sensitive and loving woman able to create a home laboratory of the so-called two cultures, as she dealt not only with science, but also with art and literature, factors that favoured and helped her son in his growth and in becoming a great writer.

Italo Calvino apparently wrote his first short stories in his parents' laboratory. He noted, 'My mother … never left the garden, where every plant was labelled, the house swathed in bougainvillea, the study, with its herbariums

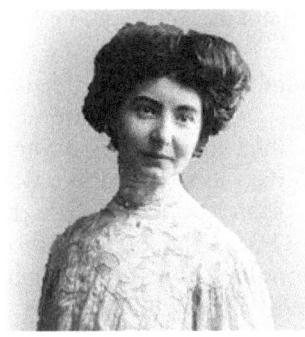

55. Eva Mameli, from the internet

and the microscope under its glass dome.' His writing shows her influence; indeed, a paper by Paola Govino of Bologna University is entitled 'The Making of Italo Calvino: Eva Mameli-Calvino and her Laboratory Garden' (2009). He was to call Eva 'the good sorceress who cultivates irises'. And he sums up her life appropriately when he describes her as 'a pacifist, educated in the "religion" of civic duty and science'. She died in San Remo aged 92.

The two most famous women in Sardinian history are probably Eleonora d'Arborea and Nobel Prize winner Grazia Deledda. But how many people have heard of her sister **Nicolina Deledda** (Allina, 1879–1972), eight years her junior, seventh and last daughter of Giovanni Antonio Deledda and **Francesca Cambosu** (c.1832–1916)? Just as Grazia was a self-taught writer, so Nicolina was a self-taught artist. Like many of the Sardinian women artists of her time, such as Anna Marongiu whose life and work are described in chapter 10, Nicolina was primarily an illustrator; indeed, she illustrated several of Grazia's short stories published in national magazines, one of them as early as 1894 when Nicolina was only 15. They also worked together on many of Grazia's folkloric articles. A portrait of Grazia by her sister dates from 1908. The writer is roughly outlined in pencil with her eyes half-closed. I have tried, without success, to find an image of it, or, indeed, of any of Nicolina's work. Apparently, what survives is in private collections.

Nicolina is said to have been 'particularly graceful and sensitive to fashion's charms'. But something happened in 1906, when she was 27, which was to have a bearing both on her life as an individual, changing her perception of herself, and perhaps on why she is not better remembered as an artist. That year she had an ear infection which made her very ill and needing to have several operations. Grazia's biographer Martha King quotes a letter in which the older sister wrote, 'It's terrible to see a dear, young, and intelligent person suffer day after day, one who loves life and feels like she's been rejected.' Whether or not the operations were a success as far as hearing is concerned is not clear but, as a result, increasingly in later life, Nicolina tended to stay close to home because of what she considered a 'facial disfigurement'. In spite of that, in Nuoro, the family's home town, Nicolina was friendly with leading figures in the Sardinian intelligentsia.

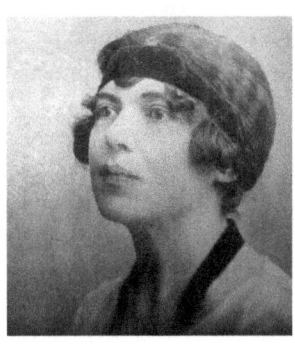

56. Nicolina Deledda, from the internet

Following her marriage in 1900, Grazia moved to Rome. Nicolina left Nuoro to join her in 1913. They lived next door to each other at 15 Via di Porto Maurizio, their houses divided only by a courtyard at the back, a border of flowers at the front. They saw each other daily and became increasingly close. In due course they were joined by their sister Peppina (**Giuseppa Morelli Deledda,** 1877–c.1938) and, in the 1930s, Nicolina looked after Peppina's children.

In spite of her self-consciousness, as Grazia also wrote, in 1920, 'Nicolina continues to make her ever more beautiful drawings ... They have also asked her to make a cover for Donna ...'. Martha King does not elaborate on what 'Donna' was, but there was a periodical for women called *La Donna* at the time. As she had in Nuoro, Nicolina was involved in Rome in the current art scene, in particular the Arts and Crafts movement into which Grazia had entrée, and the sisters continued to work together.

As Margherita Heyer-Caput has it in *Grazia Deledda's Dance of Modernity* (2008), the art historian Maria Elvira Ciusa 'has analysed the deep relationship between the sisters. She traces the intriguing complementary evolution of Grazia's writing and Nicolina's painting from naturalism to impressionism, symbolism, and expressionism on the wavelength of European avant-garde movements to modernity'.

As Martha King points out, 'A consistent feature of [Grazia] Deledda's fiction is the frequent comparison of moods and landscapes to paintings'.

In spite of her increasing preference for staying at home, in 1920 (or 1923), Nicolina's work was part of an exhibition in Rome, together with that of Melkiorre Melis who drew a 'tender caricature' of her in one of the lovely little hats she favoured. An image of that, too, unfortunately eludes me. His artist sister follows this story of Nicolina.

Grazia won the Nobel Prize for literature in 1926, attending the ceremony in December 1927. From Stockholm she wrote to Nicolina, illustrating the preference both of them had to be 'home bodies', 'The world is beautiful and varied as Bertoldo said, still one of the most beautiful places in between via di Porto Maurizio and Via Trapani.' As is described in chapter 7, Grazia died of breast cancer aged 64 in 1936, but Nicolina lived until she was 93.

Melkiorre Melis belonged to what is known as the *Fratelli* [brothers] *Melis*, and it is certainly true that he had two other brothers who were 'artists' in the broad sense: one was a ceramicist, the other an illustrator and designer. But the name should more accurately be *La Famiglia Melis* because an integral member, the first born of the four siblings, and perhaps the most successful financially, was **Olimpia Melis Peralta** (1887–1975). She introduces an important craft element into the term 'artist'.

The four artistic Melis siblings were born in Bosa, in the west of Sardinia, to Salvatore Melis and **Giuseppina Masia Melis,** and the couple also had four other children. In about 1911, Olimpia married Lorenzo Peralta and they had three children. At some time between 1910 and 1920, Olimpia set up her business in Bosa; it is likely that, in the years leading up to the decision to do so, she had herself been practising her craft, enabling her to see a market and the expansion needed to meet it. Whether or not her husband or her parents provided the initial financial outlay to set up the enterprise I have been unable to ascertain; she may well have saved any profit from her own sales to do so.

The craft was traditional to Bosa and is commonly called *filet* (*rete* in Italian, 'net' in English). At first glance this looks like lace, and it is sometimes called filet lace, but it is in fact a form of embroidery on linen or cotton. The technique uses a wide square mesh warp (the 'net'), and the square in the empty field on which the geometric motifs are embroidered, using a long blunt needle, in the contours represent themes, the oldest examples of which are religious, among them the peacock, a symbol of fertility and eternal life. Soon Olimpia had many women *filet*-working in her establishment, fulfilling orders from Rome, Paris and New York for a variety of newly designed furnishing pieces, among them curtains, tablecloths, bed surrounds and covers, and trims.

What I find frustrating is the apparent lack of detail about the working of Olimpia's enterprise. Did she still practise *filet* herself? Was she responsible for training the other women? Was she responsible for the designs they worked on, and the nature of the pieces they made? Who promoted the work produced, so that there were sales abroad? Who dealt with the sales, and the finances?

On the Corso Vittorio Emanuele, the main street in Bosa, is the Museu Casa Deriu comprising several floors. It most clearly houses work by Melkiorre Melis, the most sought-after of the '*Fratelli*', but if you look carefully at photographs of the museum's contents, you can see examples of *filet* work covering, for example, a bed in a furnished room. Whether or not they are Olimpia's own work would be good to know.

Just as Olimpia and her brothers were known as the *Fratelli Melis*, Albina and Giuseppina Coroneo were, and are, known as the *Sorelle Coroneo*. That was because **Giuseppina Coroneo** (1896–1978) and **Albina Coroneo** (1898–1994), initially creators of small illustrations and cloth collages, were inseparable in life and in their work. What is more, they preferred to work away from the public eye, so that it is only quite recently that their work has become appreciated for its delicacy and lyricism, and its contribution in a modern way to Sardinian folkloric tradition. Art historian and member of women's associations, Lidia Piras, whose thesis was on women's work, describes in her *Enciclopedia delle Donne* entry, '*Albina e Giuseppina Coroneo*' the sisters' work as divided into two periods. In the first, which ended with the Second World War, they dealt with illustration or made small cloth paintings, with stylised figures, very close to Art Nouveau taste; in the second they gave shape to almost expressionistic characters obtained with poor and recycled materials.

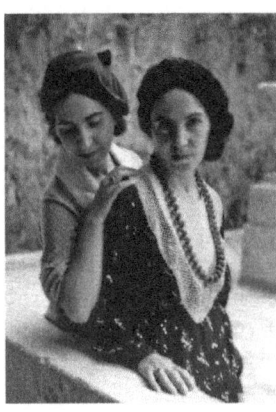

57. Coroneo sisters, from the internet

Although Giuseppina obtained a diploma from the Technical Institute and Albina at the Magistral Schools, the sisters did not have real artistic training. They learnt their craft in the back room of their father's haberdashers and antiques shop in the Castello district of Cagliari where he also repaired dolls. That is how they first practised their manual skills. Visually, they learnt from the illustrations in women and children's magazines, often ones drawn by readers. They began to make themselves known through contributing their own decorative cut-outs.

Their work was first shown at a craft exhibition in Cagliari in 1929 called 'Sardinian Spring'. When it began to be better known, and they to be called artists, in the 1940s, particularly when they exhibited their artefacts at the Milan Triennale, they replied simply that they were needleworkers and their work coloured papers. Lidia Piras elaborates on their work, dismissing someone's definition of it as dolls and puppets:

The early period includes the Deco-style fashion sketches designed by Albina, but, above all, the collages in cloth and trimmings, which represent short landscapes or profiles of girls and boys in clothes inspired by traditional Sardinian costume. The sisters cut and sewed essential figures, then they profiled them with borders and coloured ribbons, completing them with elegant touches of brush and ink. A small lyrical and stylized picture emerged, but always connected with the concreteness of everyday life.

Following the bombing of Cagliari which reached a crescendo in May 1943 (see chapter 13), the sisters abandoned the refined subjects of the earlier period, favouring rougher works, mainly by Giuseppina. These are figures around 20 cm (8 in) high, made of wood and wire, straw and rags. With them, they reconstructed often grotesque street scenes, populated by drunks, bloated ladies, boys, prostitutes, sick or abandoned old people. These works were not generally for sale, the potential customer had to convince those who had crafted them of their respect and humanity. Sometimes they would only be given away.

From the Castello, the sisters' workplace moved to Via Baylle in the Marina district. There Giuseppina died aged 82, and Albina aged 96. The first major retrospective of their work was shown at the Civic Palace in Cagliari in 1996, and it could be seen again, representing Sardinia, in the exhibition 'The Treasure of Italy' at *Expo Milano* 2015. But it can best be appreciated now on YouTube which shows it chronologically, from the 1920s to the 1950s, with a text indicating the change of decade. There are also photographs of the two. There are several versions; I found the one without commentary, but just piano music, the most pleasing. See the later grotesque figures and street scenes, you wonder where these apparently sheltered women saw such sights: it must have been during the war when much of Cagliari was razed to the ground.

Perhaps the best known of the artists were the Altara sisters – **Lavinia Altara** (1896–1975), **Edina Altara** (1898–1983) and **Iride Altara** (1899–

1981). The most prolific of them, and the best known, is the middle sister, Edina. Her renown and talent are confirmed and augmented by the beautifully and lavishly illustrated *Edina Altara* (2005) by Giuliana Altea. Most of the text and illustrations are, not surprisingly, about and by Edina, but the other two and their work are included.

The sisters were born and brought up in Sassari by the bourgeois couple ophthalmologist Eugenio Altara and **Gavina Campus**. Only one sister, Aurora, was not artistic. Like most of the other women of the period, the three artists were self taught. Edina started producing work in the form of collages as early as 1914, aged 16. The following year, there were plans for a Sardinian exhibition in Rome, in which she was to feature, but it was scuppered by the First World War. Her collages were, however, exhibited in 1916 in Sassari, and she also won a silver medal in Rome; there followed exhibitions of Sardinian work in Milan and Turin. Other exhibitions followed in the 1920s. In 1922, she married the illustrator Vittorio Accornero de Testa whose name as an artist was Max Ninon and, in due course, the couple moved to Milan where they sometimes collaborated artistically.

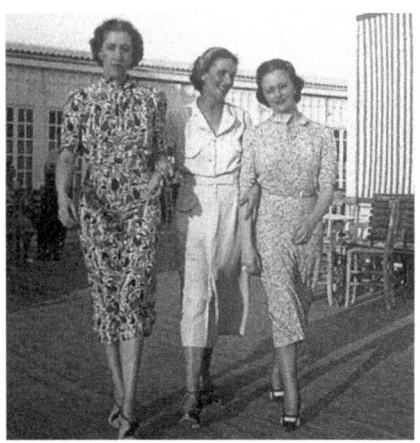

58. Altara sisters: Iride, Lavinia, Edina, 1937, courtesy of ILISSO Edizione

During the long period of her artistic life, Edina was painter, ceramicist, decorator and fashion designer. Her ceramics, for example, were mainly plates and tiles; on them she painted Sardinian women in the traditional costumes of their place. These were sold in a Sassari shop. The mock-ups for the ceramics are paintings in their own right.

Following an amicable separation from her husband in 1934, Edina opened her own studio in Milan, hiring three or four seamstresses and attracting a sophisticated clientele. But during the war it had to close. Her sketches for the clothes she designed are both meticulous and fun. Between 1941 and 1943, she worked with the magazine *Grazia* and illustrated over 30 children's books and magazines. Those bare bones don't begin to do justice to her work, for that you need either an exhibition or, as I have done, to acquire *Edina Altara*. From that I notice that she painted the cover of the magazine *La Donna* in 1931, as well as several that were appropriately stylish for *La Bellezza* in the 1940s.

In 1918, Lavinia married the dermatologist Saverio Granata and moved to Cagliari; they were to have four children. Any dreams of being an artist were in the future. In the 1940s, Lavinia and Iride collaborated with Edina. Their joint work was sold in Sassari through their friend there, **Maria Serra**.

It was only in the 1950s, when they went to stay with Edina in Milan, that they blossomed artistically in their own right.

Lavinia's work is mostly strange little terracotta figurines, human, animal and plant, but she did paint as well. It is impressive that by 1971, when she produced the painting I have chosen as the cover for this book, she had only started painting in oil two years earlier. I chose *Ricordo d'Infanzia: Il Bagnetto di Portotorres* not only because of the liveliness and colour, which seem to embrace Sardinia, but also because of the rather incongruous sheep on the hillock overlooking the pier and bathing huts full of people – sheep being so much a feature of Sardinian country life. Although Lavinia painted the scene in 1971, four years before her death, the memories of childhood which she captures would have been Edwardian; the bathing costumes and some of the hats the women are wearing support that. It is noticeable that, whereas Edina tended to paint in sombre colours, Lavinia had a lighter touch when she started painting in oil in 1969. She exhibited several times thereafter.

Iride married the Sassari lawyer Francsco Nonis in 1924. But her artistic endeavours also only started in the 1950s in Milan. Her work consisted of paintings on artefacts such as boxes and mirror surrounds, and even stranger figurines, such as Christ on the cross and Neptune, than those made by Lavinia. They almost look as if they were made out of pipe cleaners but the material is, in fact, plaited copper wire. Giuliana Altea describes Iride as 'the one of the three sisters who reveals the strongest taste for whim and the bizarre'. Lavinia and Iride had their work shown for the first time at a craft exhibition in Sassari in 1956.

With the death of Iride in 1881, Edina lived with Iride's daughter until, showing signs of dementia, she went to a care home in Sassari. But she refused to stay there, moving first to Cagliari, then to Lanusei, a mountain village near Ogliastra (Barbagia region), where she died in 1983, aged 85. At least two exhibitions of the Altara sisters' work have been held in the twenty-first century: one in 2005, and another in Cagliari called '*Femminilità, Follia, Evasione*' (Femininity, Madness, Escape) in 2015. To add to Giuliana Altea's *Edina Altara* are two wonderful YouTube versions of Edina's work; in part 2, I particularly like a young girl sitting on a stool watching a hedgehog drink from a saucer at her feet.

I started my account of women artists with two sisters, the famous one a writer, her less well-known sister an artist; I end the other way round: the famous one an artist, her sister a writer.

Maria Lai (1919–2013) and (**Rosa**) **Giuliana Lai** (1921–2012) were born in Ulassai, near Ogliastra (Barbagia) to veterinarian Giuseppe Lai and **Sofia Mereu Lai**, two of five children: another sister who died aged seven, and two brothers. Maria was the artist but that word is far too restrictive: she lived and worked into the twenty-first century, so that many influences were available to her, though she was entirely original. In her work she made use of paper (written words, drawn lines, straight or tangled, and figures drawn with crayon, pencil or charcoal), fibre, ribbon, wool, woven cloth, embroidery, pages of fabric or canvas sewn together, stone (sculpted or arranged), ceramic and terracotta, or anything else that took her fancy and imagination. She believed that you should not grow out of the playfulness of childhood, that people generally benefit from holding the sun in their hand. She was to say of herself, 'I played with great seriousness, at a certain point my games were called art.'

Sometimes her work is an art installation. Typical was *'Legarsi alla Montagna'* ('Bind to the Mountain') in 1981 when the villagers – women and men, old people and children – wound almost 27 km (nearly 7 miles) of blue ribbon round the balconies and doors of the houses and the Gedili mountain, in order to unite human beings and nature, and the people with each other. An attractive 2013 account of it, posted online by journalist and writer Sandra Petrignani, elaborates on that last theme, as well as providing details about other aspects of Maria's life and work:

> Maria had been asked by the municipal administration for a monument to the fallen, but with the anarchy that characterised her every choice – not only artistic – counter-proposed something that 'served for the living, not for the dead'. The living ones were quarrelsome people. They agreed to knot, yes, but only with the villagers with whom they got along. It took a year and a half to convince them to be together in such a bond. And we came up with a compromise suggested by the artist's serene mind: the ribbon would go straight where there was a grudge, it would create a knot (intertwined with *pintau* bread) where the person recognised friendship, and even a bow where there had been love.

Maria's work is also infused with the spirit of place, the area round Ulassai, even though some of her artistically formative years were spent away from it. It is necessary, therefore, to know a little about Ulassai, and useful to look at a couple of the many YouTube videos of her work, particularly those that show Maria and her mountainous place. (It's best to put 'work of artist Maria Lai, Ulassai' into your browser. Having watched that first one, continue with *'Inventata da un Dio Distratto'* ('Invention of a Distracted God').) It is not only the mountains, but also the prehistory and its remains that draw her in. Ulassai made her, and she put Ulassai on the Sardinian and international map.

Ulassai lies in the most inland part of the province of Ogliastra, at an altitude of almost 800 metres, surrounded by mountains, valleys and gorges. Before the advent of the railway in 1893, the village was connected to nowhere outside the region; that led to the preservation of old, even ancient traditions: particularly festivals and theatre, sometimes connected with the nearby prehistoric archaeological sites; the use of the horizontal loom; the artisan production of cheeses and hams; and bread-making in wood-burning ovens still in use. The valley of the Pardu river to the east is cultivated with olive groves and vineyards producing olive oil and Cannonau wine. Strawberry tree honey and local dishes such as *culurgiones a ispighitta* and *coccoi prena* are also well known. (These are somewhat similar in that they are pasta parcels filled with potato, pecorino cheese and mint; the boat-shaped *culurgiones* are then served on a bed of tomato sauce, as a main dish, while the *coccoi prena* are dry, differently shaped, and eaten with your fingers.)

If you are taken with the idea of *culurgiones*, perhaps as an entrée into Sardinian cuisine, you cannot do better than to get hold of Letitia Clark's *Bitter Honey: Recipes and Stories from the Island of Sardinia* (2020) – the title taken from the honey produced from the nectar of the strawberry tree's blossom. This former chef from Devon may not be Sardinian, but she has lived there for some years, initially with a Sardinian, Luca, who, with generations of his family, introduced her to Sardinian food, about which she writes:

> Sardinian food is a distilled version of Italian food, simpler, more rustic, more wild. The emphasis on tradition and of the importance of eating well is even more pronounced here on this forgotten island. Even more of its ancient delicacies are preserved, even more of its produce grown or made at home.

She tells how Luca 'described an island of deliciously simple food, abundant produce and unspoilt countryside where people lived forever, forgetting to die'. And it is certainly true, as is illustrated by the women who fill my pages, that many Sardinians lived, and live, to a great age. As has also been suggested, outsiders' view of Sardinia and its people was, and is, not always complimentary: '"An island of goats and gangsters" my father blustered when I announced my intention of going there.'

The joy of this copiously and beautifully illustrated, and rather large, heavy book – not one to put in your knapsack – is that it is also full of the recipes and background of the dishes Letitia has collected and learnt to cook, including *culurgiones*. She also gives a titbit of the history of Cannonau wine, originally thought to have been introduced by the Aragonese in the sixteenth century but, as she writes,

> Recent archaeological studies, however, have discovered remains of vines dating back to 3,200 years ago, which suggests that the grape is in fact indigenous and that Cannonau is the oldest wine in the Mediterranean basin.

It is against this background that Maria and Giuliana Lai grew up, and grew old. To gain a more particular insight into both sisters, three generations of their ancestors, the family's large house on a hill overlooking a *nuraghe*, the landscape in which they flourished, and their communal relationships and customs, you cannot do better than to get hold of Giuliana's memoir *L'Erede* [Heir] *del Corbulaio*. Written in secret over the years, its publication in 2001 was enabled by Maria as an 80th birthday present to her younger sister. Although it first appeared relatively recently, the book only seems to be available in or from Italy.

Corbulaio is not, as it might appear to a non-Sardinian, the name of a family but that of a seller of corbulas (baskets), probably an itinerant pedlar who sang out his wares to encourage women to come out from their houses to purchase them. They were woven of reed or willow and asphodel (a type of long-leafed lily), and they were carried on a woman's head, as this photograph illustrates, full of flour which she had picked up from the mill to take home for baking bread. A 2010 internet review of the book by the writer from nearby Orani, Bastiana Madau, suggests that the use of *Corbulaio* is poetic, perhaps a pedlar of poems, dreams, imagination, appropriate to the sisters. (As an aside, nonetheless important for being a diversion, I had to ask my Orgosolo informant, now surely a friend, Pietrina, about the meaning of *Corbulaio*. Following my use of her explanation above, she sent me two more images, one to show that today in Sardinia silver and gold are woven as a pendant to resemble a slightly curved *corbula*, usually quite small and delicate, the other of a very small *corbula* that she had woven herself with thin reed and raffia to contain a square silver *corbula*, a present from a friend. I found it easy to buy online a small round silver *corbula* pendant sent from Sardinia.)

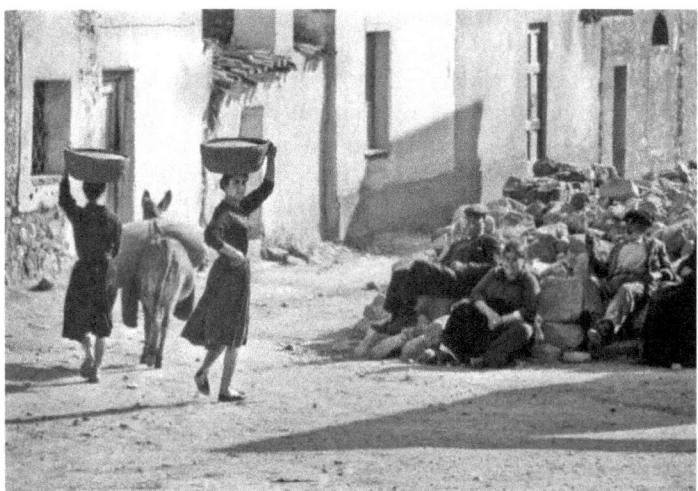

59. Women with corbulas on their heads, thanks to Pietrina Rubanu

How did Maria become the artist she did? Her upbringing differed from that of her siblings: in poor health, she was given in a form of adoption to a childless uncle and aunt to rear as a *fill'e anima*, daughter of the soul, so vividly described in Michela Murgia's novel *Accabadora*, the details of which appear in chapter 7. Not only did Maria have four parents, but those years were spent not in Ulassai, but in the nearby but isolated village of Giaro where her second parents were agricultural traders. In the winter months she couldn't get to school, and it was in that isolation that she discovered a talent to draw. Giuliana was to write of this period of her sister's life, 'This uncle and aunt kept Maria and made her a perfect, disciplined, sensitive child. Maria lived in a world different from ours.' Paraphrasing Giuliana's memoir, Sandra Petrignani continues,

> a richer, citizen world, of which she was the beloved queen and to whom was granted an unusual freedom. In the country house, she was allowed to paint the walls of her room as she liked, which were repainted in white only so that she could start writing and drawing on it with charcoal as on a blackboard. Some itinerant circus performers came to the house as guests for more than a year, teaching their children – and Maria with them – juggling exercises and acrobatics. When the caravan moved on, little Lai hid in the caravan to escape with them. And no one scolded her when she was discovered and brought home. She also ran away and hid because she loved 'listening to silence'.

When her uncle and aunt died, Maria joined her birth family, and Giuliana writes,

> When she was with us, we communicated above all through the drawings she did with charcoal on the terrace paving. We lay around her for hours, full of amazement. She drew and told: small scenes were born and animated by moving figures and far-fetched stories. We always started from objects at hand, such as stones, shells, cane fronds, pieces of cork; we lived those stories firsthand because we were assigned a role and a character.

Maria was sent to school in Cagliari aged 15. There she had an exceptional Italian teacher, the writer Salvatore Cambosu who was the first to recognise her artistic and little fairy (*jana*) qualities. He brought Latin and poetry to her attention, and taught her 'the value of the rhythm of the words that lead to silence' which were to become two key components of her work. From Cagliari, she was sent to an artistic high school in Rome where she studied sculpture and made important connections. Then, in 1940 Italy entered the War and she was unable to return to Sardinia; instead, cut off and short of money, she went to Venice and enrolled in the Academy of Fine Art under Arturo Martini who was a misogynist and humiliated her. As Maria was to say later, 'There wasn't much space there for women.' And she added, 'He thought that art was a very serious and difficult path to tread, unsuitable for women. It was not something to possess, but to conquer. Only those who resist have the right to call themselves artists.' But in the three years under his direction, Maria learnt a great deal.

In 1945, Maria returned to Sardinia perilously, in a lifeboat from Naples to Cagliari, and she was to remain on the island until 1954. She met up again with Salvatore Cambosu and taught drawing and art history in elementary schools in Cagliari, where she had a studio, and in other regions. After 1954, she returned to work on the mainland. They were years of artistic progress but also of drama and distress: on one of her return visits there was a kidnap attempt in Ulassai on her and her brother Lorenzo, thwarted only by the intervention of a passing truck of American servicemen, but then Lorenzo was murdered in 1963 in a shootout between bandits, and her other brother Gianni died in a plane crash in 1971.

Eventually, in older age, by now not only an established artist, but famous, with exhibitions internationally, Maria returned to Ulassai and moved to a house in nearby Cardedu. In July 2006 in Ulassai, she inaugurated and donated 140 or so of her works of art to, the Museum of Contemporary Art, better known as *Stazione dell'Arte*, set up in three buildings belonging to an old railway station. That is what now draws visitors to Ulassai.

Giuliana had married and had children with schoolteacher Luigi Pisu, and then grandchildren. She was not only a writer but an artist in her own right. Her art, or craft, was weaving silk and damask fabrics. The difference between her and Maria's art was that Giuliana's was practical – rugs, fabric bags and cases, and dolls. She waited patiently for her sister's return, whitewashing the walls in anticipation. When Maria did so, Giuliana by then widowed, both in their eighties, they became inseparable. Maria used the whitewashed walls and, indeed, white tablecloths. In the house among olive and lemon trees, vines and a vegetable garden, they would also sit in the courtyard sewing and embroidering.

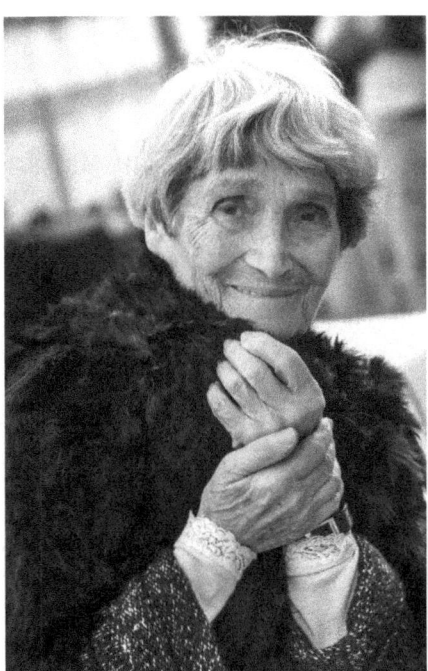

60. Maria Lai, photograph by E Loi, courtesy *Fondazione Stazione dell'Arte Ulassai*

Giuliana died in 2012, 12 days before her ninety-first birthday. Just before, she had received the first copies of her book *Ritagli* (Remnants) in which she said that not only did she like listening to music and watching football, but she was also trying to learn how to use the computer. Crying silently in her bedroom when she learnt of her sister's death, Maria, nearly 93, pronounced, 'I've lost my little sister, and art has lost its great and humble interpreter'. Maria died barely a year later. Giuliana had summed up their relationship, 'We who have the loom, which does not cut but binds, say: sister women they weave the threads of destinies with each other; they mix lives in a single carpet. We have been good, good artists.'

All these artists lived through the Fascist period in Italy, and were apparently unaffected by it. But Maria Lai's misogynistic teacher in Venice, Arturo Martini, has been dubbed the semi-official sculptor of the Fascist regime. Edina Altara's work was much admired by **Margherita Sarfatti** (1880–1961), journalist, art critic, patron, collector, but also prominent propaganda adviser of the National Fascist Party; she was also Mussolini's biographer, as well as his mistress. And one artist about whom I have not written, **Francesca Devoto** (1912–1989) of Nuoro, because her work was introduced to the public by the Fascist Union of Fine Arts of Sardinia. It seemed somehow inappropriate, given how the next chapter begins. But perhaps she felt that she had no choice in 1935 if she wanted her work recognised, and her career to progress, than to show in the 'Sardinian Spring' exhibition held in Nuoro. Her five paintings certainly received attention and admiration. But, as chapter 13 shows, several women knew exactly what they felt about the Fascism that had been well entrenched for some years in Italy and Sardinia by then, and how it was to be fought against.

13 – Anti-Fascism 1920–1943

Introduction: Fascism and its Appearance in Italy and Sardinia

In March 1919, Mussolini founded the first Italian Combat Leagues (*Fasci Italiani di Combattimento*). He failed to win a parliamentary seat in the elections of that year, but was elected in 1921. Even without a seat, his 'Blackshirts' militia squads (*squadristi*) had begun to throw their weight about – in 1920, for example, breaking up a general strike at the Alfa Romeo factory in Milan. The first women's Fascist group was founded in May that year. But Fascism really made its mark most firmly with the March on Rome (*Marcia su Roma*) – an organised mass demonstration – in October 1922, a precursor to a planned armed insurrection. That was not necessary because, following the march, the king appointed Mussolini prime minister.

A most useful account of Fascism in Italy in general, and in Sardinia in particular, is by Sardinian Emilio Lussu (1890–1975) who appeared briefly in the introduction to chapter 12. Born in Armungia (Cagliari Province), and graduating with a law degree in 1914, he had fought as an officer in the Sassari Brigade during the First World War and was to fight with just as much commitment and carelessness of his own well-being against Fascism from its inception in Italy. He was also to prove an inspiration to the women anti-Fascist activists in Sardinia. In *Enter Mussolini: Observations and Adventures of an Anti Fascist* (1936; 2013), Lussu describes how during 1921 Fascists began to organise themselves in Sardinia. He wrote:

> They had little success at first. The commune in which, during the election I had lost both votes and wallet, was among the first to have a regular 'Fascio' but its members were not numerous. I went there only once more, this time without money in my pockets, and I observed no trace of political activity. Fascism was resting on its oars after its electoral successes.

He goes on to describe in some detail the success it did have in the mining area of Iglesias. Only one woman is included in this description, and it is by no means clear that she was a supporter of Fascism. She was married to a local Fascist leader named Mocci, whom Lussu describes as a 'queer character'. He had fought during the war and thereafter practised 'precariously as a lawyer'; he had also spent several years in a 'lunatic asylum'. Usually mild, he could become violent.

At these times, if his wife were at home, he would beat her; if she was absent he would organise punitive expeditions against 'Bolshevik' workers. Usually, on these occasions, he was brought back on a stretcher with injuries of some

> description, and his wife, who was a good hearted woman, would not know whether to be glad or sorry that she had been out of the house. …

Later on, at the time of really violent conflict between Fascists and anti-Fascists he used to declare that he would have my head. One evening he came to my house. It was very late and I naturally imagined that he was accompanied by a force of Fascists. His wife must be away from home, I said to myself, as I let him in. He entered timidly, and I, ready to defend myself, asked what it was he wanted. Much embarrassed, he politely begged me to excuse his presumption, and asked for my opinion on a translation he had made of one of Horace's odes.

A useful description of the position of women under Mussolini's Fascist regime is given by Nicole Robinson of the University of California:

While Fascism's rhetoric of the ideal woman and its practices day-to-day were not necessarily one and the same from 1922 to 1945 ... being a woman in Italy involved delicate balance and manoeuvring between the advancement of modernity and the celebration of femininity equated with motherhood. By coupling the future and tradition, women were expected to fulfil a paradoxical role that ultimately denied their freedom.

Several noted women have left their mark on the anti-Fascist history of Sardinia, and their stories follow. But it would be remiss not to include more general instances of women's defiance against the regime; glimpses are to be found in official records.

Silvia Seu in '*Frammenti di dissenso*' (2020) explains that the prefects and quaestors of the provinces were obliged to report any manifestation of dissent registered among the population. Their reports were sent first half-yearly, then quarterly, to the Ministry of the Interior. These reports on the situation and state of mind of Sardinians show a profound dissatisfaction concerning economic difficulties, unemployment, increase in taxes and prices and the interference of the regime in the sphere of private life. There are also notes on protests against *Il Duce*, the identification of the underground press, and the emergence of anti-Fascist groups.

Women were in the forefront of dissent in, for example, Jerzu, Ollolai (both of Nuoro province) Seui and Portoscuso. In Nuoro in 1930, the population were reported as suffering from the economic crisis, particularly because of the decrease in the price of milk, cheese, wine and oil which constituted the main resources of the area. In Jerzu on 9 and 10 December 200 women demonstrated on the first day against the application of the council tax. Between 8 and 10 June 1932, the women of Seui and Ollolai demonstrated.

Under a heading, 'Reports of non-aligned citizens are becoming the more numerous', it was reported on 21 June 1932 that 'A woman from Sindia [Nuoro Province], **Francesca Palia**, is arrested for singing *Chi se ne frega della galera, camicia nera brucerà* (who cares about prison, black shirts will burn)'. If I understand correctly, Francesca was turning a recognised Fascist (black shirts) song into an anti-Fascist one.

On 9 April 1934, the report of the Prefect of Cagliari read:

> Some small demonstrations have occurred in some municipalities due to the state of unease. In Portoscuso, for the light touch used by the Tax Collector in making the foreclosures and withdrawing the foreclosed effects, there was a demonstration of women who managed to take possession of the foreclosed objects deposited in a room of the Town Hall by bringing them back to their respective homes.

The censors also had their say: on 8 May 1937, a report noted that a letter sent by a nun in Bosa told her correspondent in France that 'In Bosa they burned the photographs of the King, Queen and Mussolini and that there was a real revolution in Cagliari where they hoisted a red cloth on the city's flagpoles and on poles at the head of a procession.'

Dated 9 April 1937, a long report presented by the Quaestor of Cagliari noted the words 'Viva Lussu – Viva Libertà – Viva Lenin' on a wall in Serramanna, 30.5 km (19 miles) north-west of Cagliari.

The Sardinian Connection (Joyce Lussu, Ines Berlinguer, Lina Merlin, Sister Giuseppina Demuro and Fulvia Riccardino)

Some further account of Emilio Lussu is necessary as background to the anti-Fascist women who follow. In 1921, he founded the *Partidu Sardu-Partito Sardo Azione* (The Sardinian Action Party, in Sardo and Italian), very quickly banned under Fascism. That same year, aged 31, he was elected to the Italian parliament. In 1926, having been physically attacked several times, he shot one of the *squadristi* in self-defence. He was charged, tried, acquitted, but then retried and sentenced to five years' imprisonment on the island of Lipari, near Sicily, from where he escaped in 1929. He reached Paris where, with others, he formed the anti-Fascist movement *Giustizia e Libertà* (Justice and Freedom). He then took part in Spain's civil war. Numerous reports indicate that Lussu, after being confined and escaping, continued to be a leading figure in Sardinia's anti-Fascism.

Biographical sources state that in 1938 in Geneva the exiled Lussu met the poet and translator Joyce Salvadori (Gioconda Beatrice Salvadori Paleotti). But it seems more likely that they had met briefly as early as 1932 when, as a member of *Giustizia e Libertà*, Gioconda, better known then as Joyce Salvadori and later as **Joyce Lussu** (1912–1998), had been asked to deliver a message to him. There was apparently an immediate rapport between them. Silvia Ballestra, born in Porto San Giorgia, Joyce's ancestral home place, describes her then as 'twenty years old, beautiful, tall, blond, cultured and elegant'; Lussu was 22 years older, with the irresistible aura of the courage and energy of his achievements.

Joyce was one of three children born in Florence to Guglielmo Salvadori Paleotti and Giacinta Galletti. Giacinta was better known as Cynthia and that name, and Joyce's, arose from the fact that both maternal and paternal grandmothers were English. Upon marriage they settled with their Italian husbands in Porto San Giorgio, in the Marche region of eastern Italy. Joyce's parents were aristocratic, intellectual, secular, progressive and anti-Fascist. Because of that, and following the torture of her father in 1924, the family had sought exile in Switzerland. Joyce was educated there, moving in 1931 to study philosophy in Heidelberg, which she left the following year on the advent of Nazism. Not surprisingly, she spoke Italian, French, English, German and, later, Portuguese. Guided by her parents, she developed her feminism early, and she printed her first collection of poetry in her teens.

Joyce and Lussu met again in 1938 and their life-long relationship dates from then. Joyce's previous few years are often skated over. Although she was to write two autobiographical volumes, she leaves her early marriage out of both. This is described instead, in both the text and a footnote in Noemi Crain Merz's *L'Illusione della parità* ('The Illusion of Equality'; 2013) and in Nicole Robinson's article 'Return from Exile: Joyce Lussu's Many Autobiographical Voices' (2015).

In 1934, Joyce had married Aldo Belluigi, a young landowner from Tolentino (Marche region) and they had gone to live in Kenya where he and Joyce's brother set up an agricultural enterprise. When it failed, he returned home, but Joyce stayed for a while in East Africa, apparently working in a factory that polished rice. At some stage Belluigi was, or became, a Fascist. Given her family background and future anti-Fascist activities, Joyce must then have left him.

Following their meeting in exile in Europe, Lussu and Joyce lived together in the Latin Quarter of Paris. They had a 'political wedding' and were an acknowledged couple in their anti-Fascist exile and, later, in resistance and partisan circles, and she took his name. Their relationship was, however, always one of equals, in spite of the title of Noemi Crain Merz's book. At some stage Joyce divorced Belluigi and she and Lussu were able to marry officially on 6 June 1944, two days after the liberation of Rome, and a few days before the birth of their son. Maria Paola Fiorensoli uses a perfect quotation from Joyce at the beginning of a review of Noemi's book.

> Being a woman I have always considered it a positive fact, an advantage, a joyful and aggressive challenge. Someone says that women are inferior to men, that they cannot do this or that. Ah, yes, I'll show you! What? Is there anything to be envied about men? All they can do, I can do it too. And, in addition, I can also have a son.

More appropriate to the history of women in Sardinia is a quotation from Agnese Onnis's *'Giorgino: Una Targa* [Plaque] *col Nome di Joyce Lussu'* (2014) concerning her meeting with Lussu:

> So it was that I fell in love with a Sardinian and also with Sardinia, and to me who didn't know it, it seemed fabulous and remote. When I met him, it became my homeland. Of homelands, it is good to have more than one,

indeed, the more the better. In addition to the roots, there are also the grafts, which multiply leaves and fruits.

Joyce was later to use the metaphor of grafting, and was to write much more about Sardinia, but it is noteworthy how much has been written, and is still being written, about her.

Still in exile during the early years of the Second World War, the couple worked in the Resistance; as well as being involved in risky operations, Joyce's particular forté was the forging of identity documents. They apparently collaborated with the British Special Operations Executive (SOE), even trying to get clearance for an anti-Fascist uprising in Sardinia. In 1940, when the Germans entered Paris, they moved to Portugal.

Following the armistice of 1943, they returned to Italy and became involved with the partisans, work for which Joyce was later awarded the silver medal for military valour. In 1939 she had started to write *Fronti e Frontiere* (1945), describing those years of struggle and activism. She substantially rewrote the book for its 1967 edition, and it was this version that was translated into English in 1969 as *Freedom has no Frontier*.

In 1944, before the end of the war, Lussu took Joyce and their newborn son to Sardinia, and his home place, Armungia, for the first time. As a result, Joyce was to write the semi-fictional *L'Olivastro e l'Innesto: L'incontro con un uomo, la sua isola antica e la sua gente* ('The Olive and the Graft: meeting with a man, his ancient island and his people'), though it was not published until 1982. It is a book of both reportage and fantasy. In it, she wrote two particularly moving and pertinent passages:

> I saw Sardinia for the first time in September 1944, humiliated and impoverished by fascism and the war. The island then entered my whole life, with its villages and its stone paths, its mastic tree and its asphodels, its homes and its lament.

And:

> I have no roots in Sardinia. My ancestors are buried in different and distant lands. Love for a Sardinian brought me to Sardinia, and this love was also the acquisition of a world, with its history and its present, its ancestral crystals and its future buds. I grafted on Sardinia, and since then we have grown up together.

She explored the island, starting with the area round Armungia, then going up to the Barbagia region and down to Campidano, in the south-west. While Lussu had his post-war Senate commitments in Rome, and those as Minister of Aid, Joyce was to spend time in Sardinia, listening to farmers and shepherds, and paying particular attention to the condition of women. Initially, she travelled round the island by truck, together with Ines Berlinguer, when they became provincial inspectors for war assistance to the island. She was able to see daily lives of misery, children dying of malnutrition, malaria and tuberculosis. What is more, she noted that not much had changed in the mining district since the hard times described in chapter 10. She observed the inhuman condition of the women and their hands 'that never stopped' as they selected and broke the stones brought up from the mine. She wrote, quoted by Agnese Onnis:

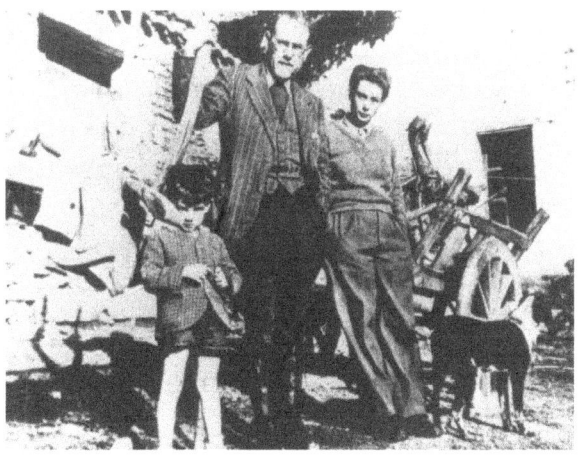

61. Joyce and Emilio Lussu, from Lussu, *l'Olivastro e l'Innesto*

> Giovanna has seven children, the last two twins. During her pregnancy, three teeth fell out. ... Now that she is not pregnant, her body is hollowed out like an arch, her spine is curved and her breasts hang long and empty under the cotton dress, but certainly her husband will impregnate her even more times. Giovanna is twenty-seven years old.

She was particularly interested in the education of children. She wrote, 'Sardinian childhood is the image of these sufferings and these injustices: and looks at us with wide eyes.'

When the *Partito d'Azione* was disbanded in 1947, she and Lussu focussed on the *Partito Socialista Italiano*, and Joyce was a leader in *Unione donne italiane*, publishing feminist essays. At the Stockholm Peace Conference in 1958 she met the Turkish poet Nazim Hikmet; he would recite and explain his poetry to her in French, and she would translate it into Italian. She continued her translation work, turning to that of African poets, and publishing 13 works of translated poetry.

Joyce also continued with her own writing: in all she was the author of 24 original works, both poetry and prose. Of Sardinia she wrote, for example (in rough translation):

> Sardinia, splinter of an older continent
> rusty eroded ridge
> like a forgotten sword
> that nobody collects.
> They are not your remains
> beautiful that I seek, for the joy of my eyes ...
> ... I look for the image of life in your effort
> difficult, in your granite cliffs
> in your expanses of greens and resin ...

To celebrate the anniversary of her marriage to Emilio in 1944, Joyce wrote a wonderful poem dedicated to him which was eventually contained in *L'Olivastro e l'Innesto*; it starts:

> For thirty years, partner mine, for thirty years
> our lives have been intertwined
> like the wicker of a basket,
> like the olive and the graft,
> like two stories told
> through the same voice.

Joyce was widowed a year later, in 1975, but lived on for another 23 years in her original family home in Porto San Giorgio, Marche, on the east coast of the mainland. There she started writing, 40 years after her autobiographical memoir *Fronti e Frontiere*, her official autobiography, *Portrait* (1988), published when she was 76 (this has not been translated into English). If you are interested in an analysis of Joyce's life and work, Nicole Robinson's article concentrating on these two books is for you. You might, however, prefer to let Joyce speak for herself. This necessarily long quotation from *Portrait* manages to encapsulate, and sum up, her long activist life, and her various identities, looked back upon in her older age. It is particularly revealing about her relationship with Lussu, and how others saw it. It is clear that, following their meeting, Sardinia was very much part of her life. She wrote,

> During the preparation of the conference, I had been able to meet many women of the Sardinian agro-pastoral world, very different from those of the other southern regions, and much less repressed and depressed. They never expressed themselves in clichés and ready-made sentences, but in a language full of images and ironic wisdom; and men used discretion and respect towards their wives. On the one hand, it was nice to be welcomed by the elderly as '*sa mulleri de su capitanu*' [the wife of the captain], or '*sa bobidda d'emilieddu*' [wife of Emilio], and by young people as 'Emilio's partner', because this opened many doors for me and allowed me to forge intense and friendly relationships with many people. But when the comrades of Carbonia [set up under Fascism in the mining district] offered me the candidacy and preferential votes for the Chamber of Deputies (Emilio stood for the Senate), I understood that there was suspicion. Although I knew I was well-qualified, it was clear that such a career would be based on exploiting Emilio's position.
>
> I left Sardinia with regret, because I was much attached to it, and I became increasingly active in the Peace Movement around Europe to oppose the Cold War. But also in Vienna, in Moscow, in Stockholm, the first thing I heard was 'Ah, Lussu! Are you related to Emilio Lussu?' It is not easy to be a well-known politician. However you put it, in today's societies there is always something wrong. During the struggle against

fascism and the partisan war, the question did not arise at all. We were two activists who were worth what they were doing at the time, without implications of prestige or social 'role'. The fact that Emilio was more mature and better than me, did not at all relegate me to a subordinate position. I liked to learn from him (I always liked being with people who knew more than I did), but nobody considered me his appendage or his reflection, except perhaps the Ovra [Fascist security] and the Gestapo.

The difference in age did not matter, because we did the same things and lived our lives together, even if now and then we had to separate. Now, in the republican and anti-fascist legality, but still always traditional, this element also weighed more, because it took us to separate spheres. Emilio was going to places where I could no longer enter – the Ministry, the Senate, the Party leadership – and I was running around where Emilio no longer had time to come. If I was in politics, everyone wore written on their face that I used the name of Emilio; if I wrote, they said I copied his style. I was looked down on by male chauvinist companions and their wives who resigned themselves to their role.

Emilio was completely different: he was free and decent; he encouraged my autonomy and I was not forced to compromise. It wasn't his fault that he was like a big oak tree, in whose shadow I always found myself unable to be directly in the sunlight. I was very envied for the husband I had; it was as if I had won him in the football pools. 'How lucky you are!' my companions said. 'Such a charming husband.' 'Not luck,' I replied, 'I had to chase him for ten years.' 'But weren't you afraid of losing him, one from here, one from there, in the midst of so many adventures?' 'I would have lost him if I had stayed at home waiting for him while he did interesting things. What would I tell him when he came back? I would have bored him.' And when I wanted to be malicious, I would add: 'As you bore your husbands.' They ganged up on me then and made my life hard in political organisations.

Of course, outside the big and small powers, there were also very good ones. But I must say that in general I found myself better with the girls of '68 or the young feminists of today than with the communists and socialists of that time. The politicised feminists who concern themselves with everything, as opposed to those confined to one sector who instead reproduce the ancient division of roles: sex and the psyche for women, politics and power for men.

Joyce died in Rome aged 86, ten years after the publication of *Portrait*.

The Museo Storico Emilio e Joyce Lussu is based in the Casa del Segretario in Armungia. It concentrates mainly on Emilio, who was born there and is a figure of great importance in Sardinian history but, in 2012, the centenary of Joyce's birth, an exhibition, 'Joyce Lussu, the journey of a woman in the history of the 1900s', was inaugurated. She is also honoured in Porto San Giorgio: not only is there a Joyce Lussu Study Centre but, in

November 2012, it held 'Spaces and Collective Rights: Study day in memory of Joyce Lussu'.

Ines Berlinguer (1899–1994) who, with Joyce Lussu, was a provincial inspector for the war assistance of Sardinia, was the niece of Caterina and Edouarda Berlinguer who appeared in chapter 12. Born one of seven children into the Sassari Berlinguer family, one of the most prominent in the city, Ines eagerly imbibed the progressive ideas of that family, particularly its women. By the age of 16, she was already a republican. During the First World War, as a student at Sassari University, she was president of Young Italy, a student organisation allied to the Red Cross, created to help families whose loved ones were missing. By this time she had met her future husband, Stefano Siglienti, known at Fanuccio, who was at the front.

With the arrival of Fascism after the war, because none of the Berlinguer family joined the Party, they were stalked and persecuted, but that failed to instil fear; indeed, as Ines wrote, 'We keep a supply of pebbles and stones on the windowsill: bad boys often try to break the glass, but we fight back.'

Ines and Fanuccio married in 1923, with her nephew, little Enrico Berlinguer, the future leader of the Italian Communist Party, as special page boy, and Emilio Lussu a witness. In 1926, they left Sardinia to live in Rome where Fanuccio worked for the *Credito Fondiario Sardo*, eventually becoming deputy director general; by this time Ines was pregnant with the first of four children. He joined Lussu's *Partito Sardo Azione* (Action Party) and *Giustizia e Libertà*, and the couple became involved in anti-Fascist activities which was quickly noted by the authorities. Following the arrest of a group of members of *Giustizia e Libertà* in 1931, the Siglienti home in Via Poma became a bulwark against the regime and a political school for young Enrico Berlinguer. With the signing of the armistice in 1943, the situation worsened, though they were still able to accommodate those who needed a safe house, two of whom were Joyce and Emilio Lussu on their return from exile. In *Portrait*, Joyce tells an intriguing anecdote of their arrival:

> Arriving in Rome we went to the house of Ines Berlinguer who lived then near Piazza Mazzini, deposited the bundle and went to rest, having cycled the equivalent of a stage of the Giro d'Italia. Ines dragged the bundle into their bedroom and, in the presence of the leaders of the Action Party who had immediately rushed over, opened it and spread the contents over the double bed. The objects on which the eyes of those present were pinned were very strange: black pieces of carbon coke, green cones similar to those of the pine, oblong boxes like glasses cases, fountain pens of an unusual shape, grey but strangely-light river stones, and more.
>
> Since there were also wires, Ugo la Malfa suggested that they were camouflaged radio sets to be assembled, while Visentin suspected a joke in poor taste, and Oronzo Reale proposed throwing everything into the Tiber. They were practically fiddling with it when I arrived from the kitchen and, in a low voice, begged them to lay everything on the bed with the utmost caution. It was, in fact a collection of the most deadly

sabotage ordnance invented up until then, which, when put on the track or in a hold, could blow up a train or a battleship. If only one of them had fallen to the ground, it would have been the end of Ines's house and of the Roman leadership of the Action Party.

In November 1943 Fanuccio was arrested in his office as a leading member of the Action Party, denounced by a former employee whom he had dismissed. Emilio Lussu wrote, 'We have lost the most important pillar of our organisation; it is the hardest blow we could suffer.' Ines refused to give up hope and helped Fanuccio to flee in the aftermath of the 24 March 1944 massacre of the *Fosse Ardeatine* when 54 Action Party activists and nearly 300 other political prisoners were killed by German occupation troops in reprisal against Partisan activity.

As Sandro Gerbri tells the story, published in the *Corriere della Sera*, 19 November 1993, as '*Una Bella Storia Antifascista*', Ines had been able to visit her husband in prison, and studied the situation and layout. Those who escaped did so dressed as women after she and another wife managed to bribe two Austrian prison guards. As they waited for their husbands to arrive, on 25 March Ines wrote in the diary intended for her grandchildren:

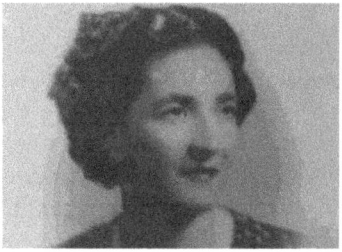
62. Ines Berlinguer, from the internet

> Again at Cecchignola, this time in a carriage! Loads of food, spare clothes, razors and other comfort. We rely on a family of caretakers who provide us with a bedroom with two camp beds; we explain that the husbands will be arriving, having finished their shift at the Anzio front. Meanwhile, we pay for the rooms and give the children meat and pasta. We are very anxious, it is getting dark and our husbands are nowhere to be seen. We both go out on patrol; at some point we hear suspicious steps, they are Germans who follow us. We are afraid and run away, and they are behind us. Finally we see a Red Cross sign, and we knock on the door. Fortunately, a woman who had seen us the night before, says they are our friend and accompanies us without trouble to the caretakers' house. Maybe, we think, our husbands can't find the house. Let's go back out, I to one side, Muscetta to the other. Nothing! We are truly afraid. We go home and they, thank God, are there waiting for us. They are free, we are mad with joy.

And on the 25th she wrote,

> We spent a sleepless but happy night, laughing and joking about the strange situation of the two escapees with their wives, almost in the same bed! Our hosts, oblivious of the truth, had confided to us that the Command of the SS of Cecchignola was upstairs! We couldn't have been

better protected. Early in the morning, after a careful cleaning up of our husbands, shaved, with polished shoes, ironed trousers, we leave the house and make for Rome. Muscetta realises that her husband has no documents, she is desperate. Fanuccio has a bilingual card, issued before the arrest by *Credito Fondiario Sarda*; let's try our luck. We are asked to show documents at a barrier: the bilingual card, German and Italian, gives the green light to Fanuccio and me. Muscetta does not lose heart and, as a good Neapolitan, says, 'I am with them!' And she passes through with her husband. A terrible wind blows, we keep the husbands moving forward, and we lean on them. We made it! You can see the church of St Paul from afar; it never appeared to us and it will never do again, so beautiful and resplendent.

After the war, Fanuccio, like Emilio Lussu, became a minister in the Italian government. Following her 1951 stint with Joyce Lussu as inspector for war assistance in Sardinia, Ines left the island to return to her family. In Rome she worked trying to help the families of those who had been shot in the massacre at Fosse Ardeatine, and the Siglienti home was always open for Ines's favourite nephew, Enrico Berlinguer.

At the age of 94, the year before her death in 1994, Ines received a medal for military valour for her activities during the harrowing war months. She not only lived to see Enrico Berlinguer become leader of the Italian Communist Party in 1972, a position he held until his death, but she also outlived him.

Sardinia has traditionally been a dumping ground for those inimical to the mainland. Claudia Atte was exiled there in Roman times, admittedly comfortably, when her presence in Rome had become an embarrassment to Nero; Tiberius had to do the same with his de facto wife, Berenice, Princess of Judea; the loving couple Atilia Pomptila and her husband were sent there for political reasons, and died there, in the first century AD; Amelie Posse-Brázdová was exiled there as an enemy alien during the First World War; and Mussolini was to be imprisoned for a short time on La Maddalena in 1943. The fate of Lina Merlin resembled that of Mussolini, in that she was a prisoner sent from the mainland, rather than an exile, but her views were hardly his.

Angelina (Lina) Merlin (1887–1979) was born in Chioggia, a seaside town south of Venice, to Fruttuoso Merlin, a municipal secretary, and Giustina Poli, a teacher. After completing her master's degree at the Institute of the Canossian Sisters, Lina moved to France to deepen her knowledge of French and French literature, and became a teacher. Because of her interest in women's issues, friends tried to persuade her to join the Fascist movement in 1919, but she preferred to join the Italian Socialist Party, starting to collaborate in the periodical *La Difesa delle Lavoratrici* (The Defence of Women Workers), of which she became the director. After a political assassination in 1924, Mussolini consolidated his power, and Lina's fate was sealed: in less than 24 hours she was arrested, the first of five times; in 1926 she was dismissed as a teacher for refusing to take the oath of loyalty to the regime, mandatory for public employees.

She moved around to make it more difficult to be traced, but she was on a list of subversives, found, arrested, sentenced to five years' confinement, and sent to Sardinia, first to Nuoro; but that was considered 'A lair of Sardisti opposition to the regime' so, after three days, she was moved to Dorgali; after three months she was moved again, this time to Orune. There she gained respect and trust, particularly of women whom she taught to read and write. She seems then to have been moved back to Nuoro because she wrote to her mother from there:

> Since I have been in confinement, this is the fourth accusation or, rather, slander, made against me. The first was in Dorgali, but nothing was registered to me, and cost me the transfer to Orune. I was only the scapegoat of local quarrels. The second in Orune, when I was searched to find out if I had clandestine correspondence with a Communist. And nothing was found, because I had never had relations of any kind with Communists. The third time was here in Nuoro, when he claimed to have seen me enter Mastino's study, and I proved without trouble that I had no relationship with that gentleman: I was only giving lessons to the daughter of one of his sisters with the permission of the prefect Dinale. Then I turned to the Quaestor, asking to make sure that in future I was not moved too easily by unfounded accusations. Now too much facility is added to the form, which I could not define, because if any official has the right respect in the exercise of his duties, it seems to me that he must also respect, and, if anything, give a more considered tone to the warning, which should be accompanied by the detail necessary to clarify the source from which they come.

In post-war years Lina was to become involved in Italian politics at the highest level, in both Parliament and Senate – in 1948, she was the first woman to speak in the Senate – and to introduce reforming legislation, such as that concerning prostitution.

Sister Giuseppina Demuro (de Muro, Demuru; born Rosina, 1903–1965), though Sardinian, is best known and esteemed for her work in a Turin prison under Fascism, particularly during the war. Then, with German control of Piedmont, many of the prisoners were political, and the Catholic Church's attitude towards the regime was ambivalent.

Rosina was born in Lanusei (Nuoro), the second of nine children to Francesco and **Matilde Floris** – an affluent family with a wine, almond and pecorino cheese business. By the age of 20, she had gone to Cagliari and entered the convent of the Daughters of Charity (*Le Figlie della Carità*) of St Vincent de Paul, an Order that insisted on the dignity of women prisoners.

In 1925, Giuseppina was transferred to Turin where, in the Order's convent in the San Salvario district, she took her vows. On the last day of that year, she entered the women's section of the Le Nuove prison as part of a small community of nuns living with the prisoners, eating and sleeping alongside them. But it is in 1942, when she was put in charge of that section, that her story in detail begins. And it is best told by English human rights journalist and biographer Caroline Moorehead in *A House in the Mountains: The Women Who Liberated Italy from Fascism* (2019). Be alert, though, Sister Giuseppina is not in the index under any of her names, but can be found under Turin/prison. The Daughters of Charity website is also informative.

Women in the prison often had their children with them so, at an unspecified date, Sister Giuseppina set up a nursery school for infants up to the age of three. She also set up classes teaching mothers reading, writing and arithmetic, as well as those for sewing, knitting, embroidery and ironing. She taught herself to play the harmonium, so as to provide the solace of music to the women, as well as consciously increasing her own learning. She was concerned for the inner growth of both herself and the prisoners.

In 1942, Sister Giuseppina, born organiser, determined and friendly, not above using her charm, was made mother superior and director of the prison's women's section in one of the six wings. But her subterfuges to ameliorate conditions and treatment extended, whenever and wherever possible, to the five wings of the men's section as well. During the 1920s and 1930s, the prison held, among criminals, hundreds of anti-Fascist activists on their way to penal colonies; Sister Giuseppina arrived there just as 'Mussolini's Special Tribunals were sending the first Piedmontese women to jail for defying his regime'. By 1942, Le Nuove was a 'holding pen' for partisans and Jews from all over Piedmont. At one time, there were 150 women political prisoners.

Among Sister Giuseppina's first tasks, during the bombing of Turin, when two prisoners were killed, was to move the others to the safety of the cellars. When the Germans commandeered part of the prison, declaring that Jewish partisan women detainees were to reside there, she knew what to do. Caroline Moorehead details too many of her successes to include them all here, but some examples of her 'guile', determination, ingenuity, courage and charm are instructive:

> She convinced the commandant, an SS officer called Siegel, to let the women live in her own wing, returning there after interrogations, on the understanding that they would be kept separate from the criminal prisoners. She offered to do his laundry, then to have her nuns to keep his office clean. Siegel was seduced. When his men demanded the keys to the cells of the prettier women, a furious Suor Giuseppina clipped the keys to her belt and defied them to come and get them. ...
>
> ... Common criminals had food brought in by their families, but since the right was denied to the political detainees, many were slowly starving to death. Suor Giuseppina made contact with the partisan networks and the Catholic charities in Turin and arranged for secret deliveries of fruit. She told Siegel that it was for the pigs being reared in an inner courtyard, asking him whether a little of it could go to his prisoners. Siegel, who was not heartless, agreed. ... [She] used her deliveries to learn the names

of those detained, so that she could tell the partisans in the city. When a leading partisan was brought in, badly wounded, she arranged for his X-rays to be swapped with those of a man who had just died of tuberculosis; the partisan was moved to a hospital, from which he was soon rescued.

Against the fate of some prisoners, Sister Giuseppina was powerless, even if she could provide some small mitigation: 'She was forced to see her Jewish female prisoners depart on convoys bound for Auschwitz, providing them with as much food as she could muster for their journeys.' And when men faced execution in an internal prison courtyard, she arranged for them to have a nun at their side for their final hours. Some Jewish prisoners she did, however, manage to save, including a husband and wife; and she got the death sentence of at least one man revoked.

Sister Giuseppina remained at the prison after the war and was still able to continue achieving improvements. For example, she set up the Casa del Cuore (The House of the Heart) for homeless former prisoners, particularly those with financial difficulties and under-age children. She only gave up following a number of strokes, dying aged 62, and was buried in the crypt housing the relics of other mother superiors in the convent.

Sister Giuseppina may not be much known about in Sardinia, or even in her home town, but she is certainly remembered in Turin. The Order's website – headed under her name, 'A strong and bold woman with a boundless love and an unshakable will' – contains the city's commemoration of her:

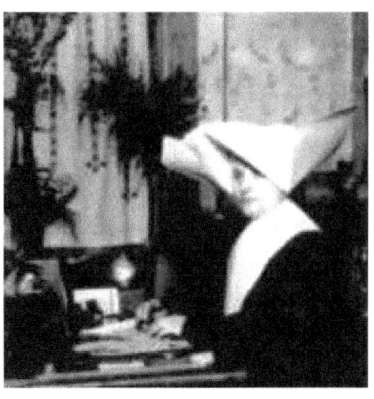

63. Sister Giuseppina, from the internet

> Sister Giuseppina ... knew how to put into practice the precepts of the Gospel with a spirit of charity, she knew how to give herself without counting the cost, and without seeking credit for the work she accomplished. She was a woman of boundless love, without prejudices, she was authentic, gentle, with a great Charity. She is a shining example for all those who believe in justice, in mutual respect, in reconciliation and the power of love as the way to peace.

And, on 8 March 1976, the municipal nursery school in Via Michele Lessona was named after her – 'so that her name remains among those to which Turin owes admiration and gratitude'.

Fulvia Riccardino (1928–1983) is best known as the first Sardinian woman engineer, but, still in her teens, she was also a partisan on the mainland during the war.

Although her father, Spartaco Riccardino, was a writer from Turin, by the time of her birth, he was director of the boarding school Vittorio Emanuele in Via Manno, Cagliari. When he died of diabetes in the early years of the war, he left his pregnant wife, **Anna Pau**, to bring up two daughters, **Fernanda Riccardino**, who was later to become a doctor, Fulvia and, in due course, a son, in their home in Via Sardegna in the Marina district.

With Italy's entry into the war came the bombing of Cagliari, which is described in more detail below, at the end of Fulvia's story. It was particularly heavy in 1943 and that was when Anna decided that they must escape the city and take refuge on the mainland, in her late husband's home village of Chiaverano near Turin. The family found that, although they had escaped the bombs, they had landed in an area of the Resistance against the Germans. Aged only 15, Fulvia became employed as a partisan support; she grew up quickly. During one of her many missions, she was captured by the Germans and put against a wall waiting to be shot. This death sentence is said, without detail, to have been foiled by the intervention of her companions.

At the end of the war, when Fulvia was 17, the family returned to Sardinia. With everything to live for now, and encouraged by the independent spirit of her mother, Fulvia decided to follow her interest in technical science, and entered the Mining Engineering Faculty of Cagliari University. There she met her future husband, Franco Meloni, from the Barbagia region, sharing with him a passion for physics and mathematics. Aged 24, with a thesis entitled 'Iron and Steroid Graphite', she graduated as an engineer in 1952, and she and Franco married in 1955. They were to have five children, which did not deter Fulvia from pursuing her career; at the same time, the couple ensured that their children received a humanist education. As well as being engineers, Fulvia and Franco themselves enjoyed, always together, going to concerts, visiting art galleries, watching sport. Their second son, Bruno, who was to become an artist, wrote of his mother at a time of student unrest:

> Our house was always open to all our friends and peers which, as can be imagined were many since we children were born so close chronologically. I remember that for all of them our mother was a point of reference, an institution and a confidant, because of her great openness. I remember that to us, perhaps not to impress us too much, she did not talk in detail about her partisan days. Minimizing made us understand that doing what was necessary and love for those people had made her brave.

Teaching, perhaps to fit in with her family, perhaps because of her empathy with students, determined the course of the rest of Fulvia's working life. She taught at the Scano Industrial Institute, founded in 1826 with the transformation of the Hospice for the Poor of San Lucifero. It went through various stages of development until, in 1946, it became a technical industrial institute, named after the engineer Dionigi Scano. Among subjects Fulvia taught over the 30 years when she saw entire generations of students pass through her hands, were electrotechnics and electrical measurements. Her students were waiting for her to arrive at the beginning of the academic year in 1983 when she failed to turn up: she had been caught by a freak wave swimming off Chia beach near Cagliari and drowned, aged only 55. This was hardly a fitting end for a woman who had been bombed in Cagliari, and put against a wall to be shot.

It may be useful here to put the bombings, particularly those of 1943 from which Fulvia's family escaped, into context. They were a series of military operations conducted by the Allies – British and American – in order to destroy the aeronautical installations of the Axis forces which used their airfields for attacks across the Mediterranean, as well as diversionary raids to distract Axis attention from the forthcoming attack on Sicily. Although most attention was focused on Cagliari, Alghero, too, was bombed.

The official entry of Italy into the conflict on 10 June 1940 had caused only minor disturbance to the citizens of Sardinia's capital, though there was rationing of foodstuffs which produced hardship in some quarters – hardship which would have mainly affected women trying to feed their families; this was exacerbated during the course of the war. The first bombing raids started as early as 2 June 1942, but February 1943 saw a considerable increase. Indeed, on the fateful day of 13 May, between the hours 13.35 and 14.45 and then between 22.50 and 23.07, squadrons of 200 bombers poured almost 500 tons of explosives on the city, reducing what was left of it to rubble – it is said that, by the end, four-fifths of it had been destroyed; 40000 had lost their homes; and 70 per cent of the city's cultural heritage had been damaged. Casualties could have been worse, but many inhabitants had left the city – after the May bombings, only 10000 remained, and they were left without functioning utilities. The final estimate of fatalities was somewhere between 1000 and 2000. Incursions ended with the 8 September armistice and Italy's surrender. Allied troops arrived on the island and, within a few days, the German troops were expelled and left for French Corsica.

One of the difficulties of writing about Sardinia is that being conversant with the Italian language is not always enough: some of the best writing, particularly poetry, is often in a local language. I have mentioned Sardo and Logudorese more than once, and have imposed more than once on someone to translate from them for me. Now, when I need the translation of a poem about the bombing of Cagliari, written in the dialect of Cagliari, or the Campidano region (Cagliaritano), I feel I have imposed often enough. I will quote the first verse of *Bombas in Casteddu* (1943) to illustrate, for English and, perhaps even Italian, readers, the problem:

Chini ascurtara mi crétara in fueddu
cussu chi contu no esti esagerau;
is fattu veru chi esti incapitau:
é s'orrori deis bombas de Casteddu.

The poet was **Teresa Mundula Crespellani** (1894–1980), the fourth of five daughters of lawyer Carlo Mundula and **Nepomucena Zuddas**. The family was prominent in the civil, political and cultural life of Cagliari, and the daughters were well educated. Two of Teresa's sisters, **Mercedes (Mercede) Mundula Romanelli** (1890–1947) and **Francesca Mundula** (1892–1961), hardly less well known, also played their part in the intellectual and cultural life of Italy, particularly in Rome – Mercedes specialising in the biography of famous women, Francesca as professor of Fine Arts and Pedagogy.

Teresa studied chemistry and biology at the University of Cagliari and then taught experimental physics at the university's Physics Institute. In 1922, she married the lawyer Luigi Crespellani who, post-war and post-Fascism, and as a Christian Democrat, was to become the first elected mayor of Cagliari (1946–1949), then the first President of the region of Sardinia (1949–1954), and was elected to the Senate of the Republic (1958–1967). Her husband's career and the birth of four daughters made it easier for Teresa, in due course, to devote her life not only to her poetry but also to the language in which she wrote. She carried out, for example, a study to safeguard Cagliari's linguistic variant. As a port city, it drew in external influences which inevitably changed its character in both positive and negative ways. The period 1940 to 1950 saw a flourishing of the greatest creativity in Cagliaritano. Teresa only occasionally wrote in Italian.

From the 1943 wartime period, Teresa wrote not only the poem specifically about the bombing of Cagliari that February, seen from the family home at 26 Via Macomer, but also about the black market (*Sa Martinica*), and the fleeing of homes (*Sa Fuirura*). Of her husband's political life she wrote *Mariru Miu Presidents* (1949–1953). In 1967, following his death, Teresa collected and had published three volumes of her poetry, which are not very accessible. More accessible is *Bello, Bello Anche il Mondo di Quaggiù: Letteratura e Poesia nella Cagliari del Novecento* (Lovely, Lovely Even the World Down Here, 2007). Although it is said to be by the three sisters, Mercedes, Francesca and Teresa, it is more a collection of their work compiled and edited by Teresa's daughter, **Maria Crespellani** (b.1925), artist friend of Maria Lai and art historian, with a foreword by another daughter, **Giovanna Crespellani** (b.1924) who followed in her father's footsteps, becoming the first Sardinian woman lawyer; the other two daughters, Margherita and Teresa, became engineers.

La Triade Femminista Sardista Antifascista (Mariangela Maccioni, Graziella Sechi Giacobbe, Marianna Bussalai)

Three women make this section easy by being known as the 'Sardinian Feminist Anti-Fascist Triad'. These comrades-in-arms were, in date order of birth, **Mariangela Maccioni** (1891–1958) from Nuoro, **Graziella Sechi Giacobbe** (1901–1973) from Nuoro and **Marianna Bussalai** (1904–1973) from Orani. It is noteworthy that all three were from the Barbagia region which, as early as Roman times, tended towards intransigence. It is no wonder that, when Lina Merlin was imprisoned in Nuoro, it was described as 'A lair of Sardisti opposition to the regime'. Among Nuoro's approximately 13000 inhabitants, there were 700 members of the National Fascist Party and about 100 anti-Fascist 'subversives'.

Mariangela's father, Sebastiano Maccioni, was the only graduate in a family of small landowners. He was a teacher who would teach for 40 years, a committed socialist and founder of the first workers' association in Nuoro. It was, therefore, he who, it is fair to assume, instilled in Mariangela the teaching and political commitment she was to espouse.

After primary school in Nuoro, she attended the *Scuola Normale Femminile Margherita di Castelvi* in Sassari. In 1909 she graduated with a teaching qualification and that autumn, aged 17, she started teaching in Mamoiada, a small town 11 km (7 miles) south-west of Nuoro. She was assigned to a first year class of 90 children aged between six and 10, with desks and chairs for barely half of them. That sorted itself out because there was a 50 per cent drop-out rate during certain times of the year – presumably because children were expected to work on their family's agricultural smallholding. This set the pattern for her future teaching commitment. In Orani in 1911, she was in charge of an all girls class, and the following year she passed the competitive exam and become a probationary teacher at the *Scuola Normale* in Nuoro, thus becoming a colleague of teachers who had taught her as a child.

During the First World War and in the lead-up to 1920, her father died, her two brothers went into exile abroad and then died under tragic circumstances. Mariangela found herself alone with her widowed mother **Giuseppina Maccioni**, who was becoming increasingly disabled through blindness. In spite of any dreams she might have had of moving to Florence or Rome, she was now committed to staying in Nuoro. During the early stultifying years of the Fascist regime, she found solace in turning her home in Via Barisone into a literary and anti-Fascist coterie with her friends Marianna Bussalai and Graziella Sechi (whose daughter Maria Giacobbe would later become one of her students). And she expanded that into little public acts of anti-Fascist defiance.

In 1923, she refused to attend the official ceremony commemorating the March on Rome. In 1924 she signed a petition in support of Giacomo Matteotti, the Italian socialist politician who in May that year alleged in the Italian Parliament that the Fascists had committed fraud in the recently held elections, and denounced the violence they had used to gain votes. Eleven days later he was kidnapped and killed. In 1926 she refused to give a lecture extolling the greatness of *il Duce*; instead she encouraged her students to sing the Communist anthem, *La Bandiera Rossa* (The Red Flag). She did everything she could to mitigate the oppressive Fascist school system and curriculum that had been imposed, the Fascist circulars and

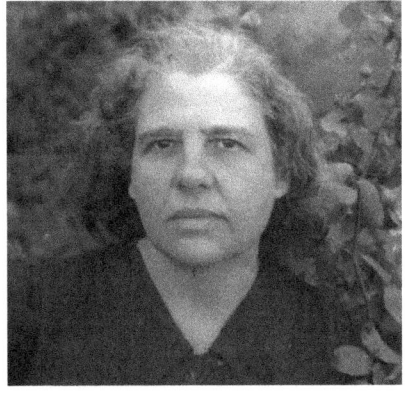

64. Mariangela Maccioni, from the internet

ministerial injunctions which sought to inculcate the iron ideology. She was a sympathiser of the Sardinian Action Party. For these activities she underwent petty persecution by the authorities who controlled her correspondence and teaching allocation. She earned the sobriquet '*la maestra resistente*' (the teacher who resisted).

Mariangela had good women friends other than the other two members of the Triad. A letter to her from Grazia Deledda of 22 December starts, 'Mariangela Carissima'. She had other friends she could count on in Nuoro. One of those was Dr Adelasia Cocco who appeared in detail in chapter 7. In 1914, after the previous doctor had been killed in a bandit incident, she had struggled, as a woman, to be sent to practise in Barbagia, a struggle in which she was successful. By 1928 she was a sanitary officer of Nuoro and it may be during that tenure that she drew up a medical certificate for Mariangela stating that 'she cannot attend ceremonies that are emotional'.

In 1935, Mariangela married Nuorese anthropologist and sociologist Raffaello Marchi, an anti-Fascist who became her soulmate. They might have preferred to live together more unconventionally, but that would have created unnecessary difficulties under the law and its hold on Nuoro at the time; it was bad enough that, not even betrothed, they had a scandalous friendship, going for long walks together unaccompanied. Their home was to become a cultural and political meeting place, as Mariangela's home had been previously.

On 17 April 1937, her 46th birthday, a squad of the Fascist police, OVRA, arrived and found Mariangela with a bouquet of roses in her arms. They searched the house, finding not only anti-Fascist books, but also a letter to her from Graziella Giacobbe expressing sympathy for a young man from Orgosolo who was killed fighting against Franco in Spain. For these she was arrested, charged and spent a gruelling 39 days in prison, unable to be visited by her husband, and only released on health grounds. The charge led to her being suspended from teaching and the consequent withdrawal of her salary. She did, accordingly to Maria Giacobbe, teach older girls without charge.

Mariangela's case was taken up by the anti-Fascist lawyer Filippo Satta Galfre but it was not until 1 March 1944, following the downfall of Mussolini, that she was readmitted to her post; she was also appointed director of the Sebastiano Satta Municipal Library. After the war, she collaborated in editing the social and cultural periodical *Aristocrazia* which she and Raffaello had founded. For her, their work together was always equal to reading Latin lyrics, French philosophers, and treatises on the history of Eastern religions. Emilio and Joyce Lussu were friends of the couple.

Cristina Chirra, in a 1995 internet article, '*Nuoro e il Fascismo*', suggests that 'Maccioni was a real suffragette who, clearly, fought for the rights and vote of women'. In 1946, she was nominated as a candidate for the municipal council, but was unsuccessful. She had been a member of the Action Party but later she joined the Christian Peace Movement and in 1948 stood for the Popular Front. In 1953, exhausted, Mariangela retired and devoted herself to writing her autobiography, *Il Mio Romanzo. La Mia Famiglia*, set against the background of Sardinia's tumultuous first half of the twentieth century. She died, aged 67, before she could finish it. Raffaello, who lived until 1981, edited it and it was published in 1979 under the title *Le Memorie Politiche*.

Because of her love of flowers and plants, a friend wrote that inside Mariangela were 'the strength and kindness of an ancient olive tree'. Nuoro's Middle School 4 is named after her, to honour her commitment as a teacher. There is a quirkily modern mural dedicated to her and, indeed, depicting her, in the Piazza Italia, Nuoro. The best way to view it is to put the artist Francesco del Casino into YouTube, then you can watch four images, of which that of Mariangela is the third, shown to the stirring partisan anthem '*Bella Ciao*', which is still sung on 25 April to honour the Resistance. The *Istituto Superiore Regionale Etnografico* (ISRE), set up in 1972 to celebrate the centenary of Grazia Deledda's birth, has taken over the archive of the Raffaello Marchi Mariangela Maccioni Foundation. It includes the letter from Grazia to Mariangela.

Fellow Nuorese Graziella Sechi Giacobbe was imprisoned with Mariangela in 1937; it was her letter that had incriminated her friend. Graziella was accused of militancy against the regime. Ten years younger than Mariangela, Graziella Sechi was the daughter of Giovanni Sechi and **Maria Francesca Guiso Pirari**. Graziella became a primary and secondary school teacher in Nuoro. On his return from the First World War, she married architect, engineer, anti-Fascist Dino Felice Giacobbe whose father was from Genoa, and his mother from a rich Bosa family, but he had been born in Dorgali near Nuoro. Dino was something of a hero, having been decorated for his part in the war, and was a founder, with Emilio Lussu, of the Sardinian Action Party. The couple were to have four children, including the well-known writer Maria Giacobbe who, she records in an interview, was born into the Sardinian Action Party.

The letter that incriminated both Graziella and Mariangela concerning the death of a young Sardinia killed while fighting against the Fascists in Spain was regarded as particularly heinous. The Spanish civil war had wide resonance in Sardinia, and prefects and Quaestors were required to signal any support in the population for the anti-Fascists fighting there. Graziella spent 26 days in prison, Maria Giacobbe describing the prisons of Nuoro as 'hell – dirt and insects of all kinds, tortured cries'. While Mariangela Maccioni was dismissed from her teaching post – probably as a deterrent to others, I suspect that by then, with four children of her

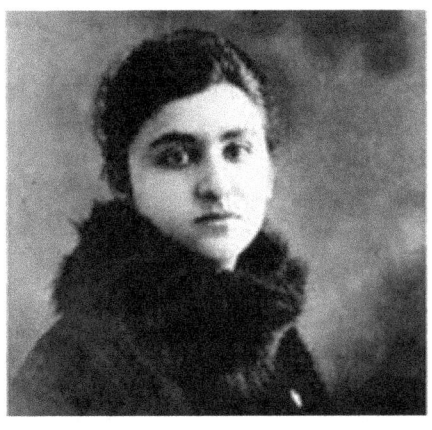

65. Graziella Sechi Giacobbe, from the internet

own, Graziella had given up teaching. But there were other ways she could be further punished.

The Nuoro Fascist newspaper, *Nuoro Littoria*, published an article describing Graziella and Mariangela as 'two passionate lesbians'. Dino Giacobbe challenged the author to a duel. Because duelling was against the law, he was arrested. The newspapers increased attacks on him; he was stripped of the public employment he had won in competition, and it became difficult for him to practise as an engineer. Fascist surveillance was stepped up.

Dino realised that fighting Fascism would be more effective in Spain than in Sardinia. Another daughter, **Simonetta Giacobbe**, writes,

> On 2 September, Dino left Sardinia clandestinely. He reached France, at that time ruled by the Popular Front, with the intention of going to Spain where civil war had turned into a frightening international confrontation between fascism and democracy.
>
> Graziella, who espoused the same belief which she had openly expressed during her interrogation in prison, would have gladly followed her husband if she had not had four children to protect.

Remembering that time in the internet piece 'The memories of a schoolgirl' (2005), Maria Giacobbe described her feelings:

> When my father, persecuted by the regime, left, I was eight years old. I was very sensitive and felt the pain of my mother, too. ... I thought that, in order to never displease her, I had to adapt myself one hundred percent to what surrounded me. I misunderstood, why, after all, she had not adapted at all.

From Spain, Dino went into exile in the United States. During all those years, he and Graziella exchanged letters which often came from him by circuitous routes: they might pass through Argentina and Switzerland, changing envelopes and stamps so as to mislead the Italian-German espionage system. In 1944, Graziella and Maria, then aged 15, travelled to Cagliari in the hope of making contact with a member of the United States military to try and restore the correspondence with Dino. Later Simonetta was to publish some of the letters her parents exchanged as *Lettere d'Amore e di Guerra. Sardegna-Spagna (1937–1939)* (1992). The title shows that the love between the couple remained strong, however hard it was for Graziella to bring up four children, the oldest, her only son, aged 12 in 1937.

Maria Giacobbe was to become a well-known author. At the age of 17 she had an article about the children of Orgosolo published in Mariangela Maccioni and Raffaello Marchi's periodical *Aristocrazia*. From 1949 to 1951, she gave evening classes teaching literacy to adults. From 1952 to 1956 she studied philosophy and theoretical pedagogy at the University of Rome. Then, like her mother and Mariangela Maccioni, she became a primary school teacher. Her first published book, the novel *Diario di una*

Maestrina (1957), was based on her own experience, 1956–57. While her period of teaching in the area around Nuoro post-dated that of her predecessors, and probably her role models, by a couple of decades, little had changed in the Barbagia region in spite of the war.

Maria wrote not as an observer, but as a participant: she immersed herself in the reality of her pupils, dealing with local customs, ancient traditions, banditry, Fascism, emigration, hunger and war with, as reviewer Rosella Canudu put it, 'disarming simplicity'. Poverty stalked the families of farm workers and shepherds. The need for survival trumped reading, writing and arithmetic: children, especially girls, were expected to help in the house, sometimes to work in that of a rich neighbour in return for a few hot meals (*s'adju*'). Working in the fields, or in the mountain pastures increasing the size of your father's flock, beat school lessons. Maria was at first regarded with much suspicion but in the end managed to prevail. Unfortunately, 'Diary of a School Teacher' is not yet published in English, though it has been widely translated, particularly into Danish; Maria settled in Denmark with a Danish husband, and still lives there, aged 92, as I write.

Her autobiography was published in Danish and, later, in Italian as *Le Radici* (Roots, 1975); unfortunately that, and others of her books published in Danish incorporating aspects of her childhood, and therefore of her mother, have not been translated into English either.

Le Radici is more than an autobiography; like the accounts of other women, such as Joyce Lussu, it is a history of family, of family place and of country; in the case of Maria Giacobbe, of Nuoro, and its region, and Sardinia. She writes,

> The house where I was born, where my mother was born, where grandmother got married, and that grandfather had enlarged and embellished for her ... that house still exists, although now almost unrecognizable ... Only by closing my eyes can I find it.

She had an ancestor who was a famous marauder, but in the end altruistic; her great-grandfather established the family in Nuoro; her grandmother was 'an old woman who barely knew how to read her black prayer books, with characters as big as ants'; Maria's mother passed on to her the 'vice of reading'. And some of those books would had have been those seized when Graziella was arrested. Through the family house during her childhood, 'a river of people entered and left without stopping': servants of different eras, shepherds and peasants, with their ancient traditions and customs, poor wives from neighbouring provinces, street vendors, wandering singers, anti-Fascists and other friends of her parents.

Maria's history of Barbagia includes those two nights known as *San Bartolomeo* in May 1899, described in chapter 7, when, in an effort to get rid of the scourge of banditry, a thousand people were rounded up, families torn apart – with Nuoro as the centre described as the 'delinquent zone' and crime 'a historical blood disease'. Her historical round-up also covers the

Island as a Spanish fiefdom, and then a Habsburg colony, the 'ownership transfers' about which Sardinians were not consulted.

By the late 1950s, when Maria was publishing *Diario di una maestrina*, and then emigrating to Denmark, her mother and siblings, too, were moving to elsewhere in Italy and the rest of Europe.

The third member of the feminist triad of anti-Fascists was the poet Marianna Bussalai. She described Mariangela Maccioni and Graziella Sechi Giacobbe as 'sweet and heroic friends', and her poem *'A GS Ardente Figlia di Nuoro'* (to GS Ardent Daughter of Nuoro), published in *Lumen*, was a disguised hymn to Graziella Sechi Giacobbe, following her signing of the petition in support of Giacomo Matteotti in 1924. Unfortunately, I have been unable to find the poem. Many letters between the three women show the warmth of their friendship and the feminist nourishment that the correspondence provided.

Lumen was 'a women's magazine for the youth of Italy', published between 1920 and the 1950s, originally edited by Rose Borghini in Abruzzo, on the eastern coast of Italy. It was used, for example, as a teaching aid for girls of school age. Marianna's first poem *'Rivelazione'* was published there in number 5 of 1923. Number 4 of 1924 was a competition in which Marianna came third for the novel in verse, *l'Anello della Felicità* ('the Ring of Happiness').

Marianna was well known as a poet, but there was much more to her activities and achievements, memories of which have long outlasted her, as are detailed in historian of Sardinia Francesco Casula's *Marianna Bussalai* (2013, in Sardo) and a chapter by him devoted to her in *Uomini e Donne di Sardegna: Le Contraversie* (2010). Mariangela Maccioni's husband, Rafaello Marchi, also wrote about her. Dr Marta Brundu, also from Orani, chose Marianna as the subject for her thesis, and is responsible for the website, www.mariannabussalai.org. There is a section listing, and allowing access to, Marianna's writing, including some poems published in *Lumen*, unfortunately not that devoted to Graziella Sechi Giacobbe. A comment on the site reads, 'I thank Marianna for conveying to me the pride of being a woman and being Sardinian.'

Marianna was born, the first of two daughters, in 1904 in Orani, a small town at the foot of Mount Gonare in the heart of Barbagia. Her father was Salvatore Bussalai, her mother his second wife, **Antonietta Angioy** (d.1909), descendant of the late eighteenth-century revolutionary Giovanni Maria Angioy (see chapter 6). The family was comfortably off, but Marianna's mother died when her elder daughter was only five, and **Ignazia Bussalai** (d.1995) even younger. Their father's work took him to Nuoro and then to Porto Torres, and he remarried, leaving his daughters in the care of **Graziette Angioy**, a maternal aunt. They lived in the eighteenth-century Angioy family house near Piazza Santa Gruche – a house full of legends.

On top of losing her mother so young, Marianna had an infection of the spine which deformed it. This was to disable her for the rest of her life and to confine her to her home and, mostly, to Orani. She was only able to attend primary school, rather than to progress to school in Nuoro, but this did not deter her from becoming self-taught, philosophically, culturally and politically, through reading classics such as Dante, Marx, Angioy, the Russians. She was later to write, in the letter from which I quote at the start of the preface to this book:

> My Sardism dates back to before the Sardinian Action Party arose [1921], that is, since, on the benches of elementary school, my humiliated self noticed that in the history of Italy there was never any talk of Sardinia. I decided that Sardinia was not Italy and had to have its own separate history.

At the age of 17, therefore, she decided to dedicate her life to Sardism, to women's rights, and the empowerment of Oranese people. Inspired by Emilio Lussu, she joined the anti-Fascist Sardinian Action Party at its inception, the first woman to do so, and regularly contributed to its information and cultural periodical *il Solco*. She was not only an admirer of Lussu but they became friends as well; at one time, when he was on the run from the Fascist police, she hid him in the cellar of her house, reached through a trapdoor. During constant police raids, Ignazia relates how Marianna, who risked imprisonment if Lussu were found, would sit quietly, embroidery frame in hand, patiently waiting for the search to end.

Though special, Lussu was one of a wide circle of Marianna's friends, correspondents, and those she influenced. The Angioy house with its large library which Marianna continued to share with Ignazia, her greatest supporter, was also a political, cultural and educational (for adults and children) meeting place; meetings of the Action Party were held there, attended by local miners, shepherds and agriculturalists. Marianna was to write of the literary gatherings, quoted in the 2010 blog '*l'antifascismo da madre à madre*' by Bastiana Madau whose grandfather attended:

> Our small group lived in an atmosphere of poetry and friendship that prevented us from lamenting the distractions of life. Our favourite authors, the intimate confidences, the fervent exchanges of ideas, replaced the external beauty that was missing from our life. Precious books, beloved authors kept in our youth, [took] the place of palaces and theatres, of dances and parties, of travels and loves, and offered us the universe in a compendium that barely left us to suspect its cruel disappointments and its infinite miseries. Delicious hours, generous friendships, first doors open on the ideal ...

Sardism, the demand for Sardinian autonomy, was Marianna's guiding light. To that end, also at 17, she made and embroidered a banner depicting the *Rossomori* (Four Moors) and the Action Party adopted the *Rossomori* as its flag. Marianna became known as *Signorina Mariannedda 'e sos battor moros* (Miss Marianna of the Four Moors). The origins and significance and, indeed the appearance, of the Four Moors (four black heads wearing bandanas, separated by a cross), the symbol of Sardinia dating back several centuries, is disputed, but it was to become the flag of the Autonomous Region of Sardinia in 1947. In the title of her *DonnaSarda* entry for Marianna, Virginia Saba calls her '*La Prima Sardista*'. Sardism can be seen as a continuation of Sardinia's historical struggle against the powers that dominated it, and the reinforcing of its distinctive and traditional social and cultural identity; this applied particularly to the Barbagia region, and included separateness from mainland Italy. From 1921 to 1943, anti-Fascism gave this full expression.

There were some in the Action Party who felt that to be trapped in the Sardinian chapter of it would be provincial and restrictive, but Marianna wrote to Graziella,

> Tell me why it takes a heart capable of being more militant in the Italian Action Party, and a lesser militant heart in the Sardinian Action Party. Undoubtedly Italy has a larger land surface than Sardinia; but breadth and narrowness of spirit cannot be measured in metres or square kilometres.

Among Marianna's best known writing are the *Mutos e Mutetus* (poetic structures particular to regions of Sardinia), satires written in the local language. The *Mutos* were to be translated and became the rebellious voice of Nuoro. Marianna also expressed her views in word plays such as '*mussi mussi*' (Latin, mus – mouse) warning of an approaching cat, satirising Mussolini who bitterly dubbed Sardinia '*l'isola refrattaria*' (the disobedient island).

Bastiana Madau explains that it was not so long ago that Sardinia's main language, Sardo, was not recognised as a language but 'identified exclusively as a rough and *natural* means of expression for daily needs'. And she quotes from a letter Marianna wrote to the poet Montanaru (pseudonym of Antioco Casula from Desulo in Barbagia), who had first drawn her to the expressiveness of poetry and whose poetry she early translated into Italian from Logudorese:

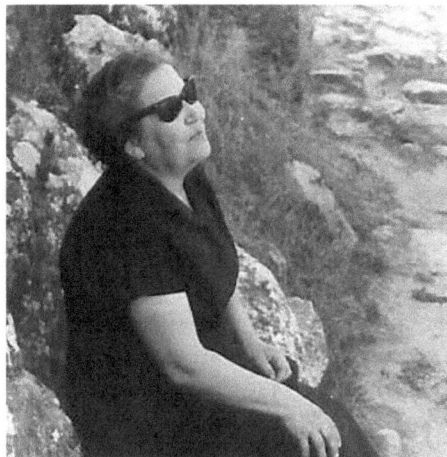
66. Marianna Bussalai, from the internet

> The rhapsodist does not deny it yet, and knows how to draw noble accents and admirable harmonies from it! And Sardinian women, quiet and ignored poet women of the shadow, when they free the naïve and passionate heart in

the *muttos* or *meste cantilene* [dirges?], they know how to sweeten it and soften it to perfection.

Marianna was only 43 when she died in 1947. Her coffin, which weighed little, was carried aloft by friends from the Angioy house to the church and through the alleys of Orani to the cemetery. People arrived from all the towns and villages of Barbagia, and from Sassari and Cagliari to say a last farewell to an exceptional woman. They said farewell, but she was not to be forgotten. Ignazia was one of those who made sure of that well into her old age and in poor health: at political rallies, for example, she would wave on high the *Quattro Mori* banner that her sister had embroidered.

Marianna lived to see Italian women being given full suffrage in 1945, though they could not vote or stand for election until the following year; they had been allowed to vote in local elections since 1925. She also lived to see Italy becoming a Republic in 1946, following a referendum. Dying as she did March 1947, what she was not to know was that in June that year the Constituent Assembly approved article 116 of the Constitution of the Italian Republic which included Sardinia among the Special Status regions, and with it granted the island domestic autonomy. It was only in 2016 that the European Parliament recognised Sardinia as having the special status of an island, giving it preferential and direct access to EU cohesion programmes – a status which the Italian Constitution does not yet recognise as I write.

Marianna may not have been able to take part in what was to follow the securing of Italian women's suffrage, but her name, and what she had stood for, survived well into the twenty-first century. Among other marks of her importance was the agreement, sent to the Orani regional council in 2014, for the setting up of the Marianna Bussalai Foundation which would not only promote the advancement of women in Sardinia but also house her archives.

Those anti-Fascist women activists whose names have lived on tended to come from the Barbagia region; but women's lives went on outside politics, and elsewhere, during the war and afterwards. A novel that illustrates that, without pushing it, but also captures the distinctiveness of Sardinians and how they were regarded by mainland Italians, is *Mal di Pietre* (2006) (translated into English as 'The House on Via Manno' (2009) or, in the version I read, 'From the Land of the Moon' (2010)) by Milena Agus (b.1959), one of Sardinia's best-known writers associated with the Sardinian Literary Spring.

The main protagonist is Grandmother (*Nonna*), a fey woman from a village in the agricultural Campidano region, north-west of Cagliari. Her family, small landowners, regard her, and treat her, as mad, and her behaviour is certainly rather eccentric, embarrassing even, particularly where potential admirers are concerned. And in 1943 she was rescued after throwing herself down a well. One of the English titles of the novel comes from how Grandmother would sit, 'as if she knew nothing, as if she had arrived from the land of the moon'. But she was artistic and painted murals on the walls of the house.

Grandmother's story is told through the eyes of her grandchild, and soon includes Grandfather (*Nonno*), a Communist atheist whose whole family was killed during his wartime absence when American bombs destroyed his house in Cagliari's Via Giuseppe Manno on 13 May 1943. He is prepared to take on Grandmother and eventually rebuilds the Via Manno house and takes her there. A flashback from this life of prosperity describes her wartime childhood of poverty not only because of the war but also because of the 1932 agrarian reform. Only the slices of bread needed were cut; jackets and coats were turned; jerseys unravelled to knit new ones; shoes re-soled 'a thousand times'; and water available on alternate days.

Grandmother has kidney stones – hence the Italian title – and goes to a spa on the mainland where she has an enigmatic attachment to a fellow patient which is the core of the story, and allows a nice twist to the ending. Meanwhile, one of her sisters has married a Sardinian and they have gone to find streets paved with gold in the north of Italy. When Grandmother and Grandfather go to visit them, the truth is revealed. This nicely illustrates the point of Marianna Bussalai's Sardism concerning the island's relationship with the mainland, and how Sardinians have been viewed from at least Roman times.

Don't be misled by the 2016 French film *Mal de Pierres* (with English subtitles called 'From the Land of the Moon') starring Marion Cotillard. It is loosely based on the novel, and worth watching if you are interested in anything connected with the original, but it is set in France, with the changes that suggests. Wasn't Sardinia interesting enough?

14 – Post-War Women and Politics 1945–1946

Introduction

'After the liberation of Italy from Nazi-fascism,' legal historian Michele Strazza started his article '*La Nascità dei Movimenti Politici Femminili nel Dopoguerra*' (The birth of women's political movements after the war) 'women, who had been an important presence in the partisan struggle, claimed a more incisive role in the political life of the country'. The women of Sardinia were as involved as any and, indeed, had been campaigning since before the War. They were to enter formal politics from a broad ideological spectrum, ranging from Catholic to Communist.

Bastianina Martini Musu; Nadia Gallico Spano; Maria Giulia Cocco; Ninetta Bartoli; Margherita Sanna

Bastianina Martini Musu's welfare work during the First World War – helping unlettered families in Sassari communicate with their fighting men – is described in chapter 12. But what she really strived for was women's emancipation, and the securing of Italian women's suffrage. The campaign for the right of women to vote was given its first impetus as early as 1877 when, as also described in chapter 12, Anna Maria Mozzoni presented a petition to the Italian Parliament. With the War over, Bastianina was free to concentrate once more on women's rights. Soon after the war, date uncertain, she and her husband Domenico moved from Sardinia to Rome; it was before 1925 because her daughter **Marisa Musu** (1925–2002) was born there that year.

In Rome, the centre of political power, Bastianina was able more easily to campaign. She contributed to the Republican newspaper *L'Iniziale*, and took the floor at conferences and the platform at rallies. During the Fascist era, the family home provided a clandestine meeting place for Democrats and during the partisan struggle she was active in the Action Party with Emilio and Joyce Lussu. She was also a member of the Women's Defence Committee, and among the signatories of the memorandum calling for women's suffrage delivered to the *Comitato di Liberazione Nazionale* (CLN). This was a political umbrella organisation and the main representative of the Italian resistance movement fighting against the German occupation of Italy in the aftermath of the 1943 Armistice. In 1945, she was appointed to the National Council (the body that preceded the Constituent Assembly) that was, among other initiatives, to call for the introduction of universal and, indeed, women's suffrage. But at that time she was diagnosed with a tumour, and so was unable to participate.

Italian women's suffrage was achieved in two stages, a decree on 1 February 1945, and a further decree on 10 March 1946. The second enabled women to stand and to vote in the elections of March/April 1946. On 2 June 1946, Italians voted in a referendum by which their country became a republic. Bastianina died on 21 October 1945, aged 53.

Marisa, who was to follow in her mother's political, partisan and anti-Fascist footsteps, also collected her mother's unpublished speeches after her death and a couple of her dictums usefully give a flavour of her beliefs:

> The political monopoly exercised by men is unfair and harmful to women ... the woman leaves the house not to destroy, but to create a family that conforms to the right of justice and freedom.

And:

> Today half of the human family, half from which we seek inspiration and comfort, half who take care of the early education of our children, is, by singular contradiction, declared civilly, politically, socially unequal, excluded from that unity.

Bastianina's ill-health and subsequent death precluded her from taking part in the Constituent Assembly for which her past experience amply qualified her. There is a Piazza Bastianina Musu Martini in Sassari.

Nadia Gallico Spano (1916–2006) is widely known as the Mother of the Constituent Assembly, a parliamentary chamber which sat between 25 June 1946 and January 1948. Its task was to write a constitution for the new Italian Republic. Nadia is also called Mother of the Constitution.

She was born at the height of the First World War in Tunis to well-to-do Italian immigrants residing there since the second half of the nineteenth century. Her father, Renato Gallico, was a lawyer who, from the early 1920s, worked in Italian with the local anti-Fascist press. She spent her youth in Tunis, taking an early interest in politics, and joining the clandestine Tunisian Communist Party in which, like three brothers, she was active. According to one source, she also enrolled in the Faculty of Chemistry in Rome, but I have found no evidence that she then went to Rome to pursue her studies.

On the eve of the Second World War, Nadia, aged 20, met in a ballroom and soon married, the Sardinian Communist and veteran of the Spanish Civil War, 31-year-old Velio Spano, sought throughout Europe for his anti-Fascist activities. He had been sent to Tunis by the PCI (*Partito Comunista*

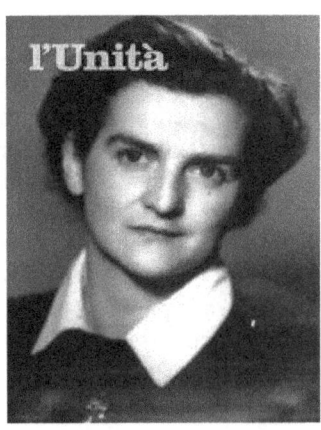
67. Nadia Gallico Spano, from the internet

Italiano) to promote action against Mussolini and make contact and work with members of the Party there. Tunisia was then a French protectorate and Tunis was a multi-ethnic city where Italians, and French, Maltese, Jews, Muslims, veterans of the Spanish Civil War, Communists and Gaullists, Catholics and free thinkers rubbed shoulders. Nadia was to write of her meeting with Velio in her autobiography, *Mabrúk: Ricordi di un' Inguaribile Ottimista* (2016):

> The Sardinian character peeped out from behind the convictions of the man open to the equality and freedom of women ... And anyway, I haven't danced since then.

Mabrúk in Tunisian means blessing, hope, and it is telling that Nadia chose 'Memories of an Incurable Optimist' as her sub-title.

Velio's political education had been received in the important mining centre of Guspini where the family had moved when he was 10. His first studies were received there and he got to know the struggles of the working class, particularly the miners. When he moved to Cagliari, he participated in the anti-Fascist campaigning that followed the March on Rome. In Rome, where he read law, he met Antonio Gramsci, also Sardinian-born, with whom he had long political discussions on 'the Sardinian question'. Velio was to write, 'I doubtless owe, at least in part, to those conversations that I became a Communist'. Following arrest, imprisonment and release in 1932, he had gone into exile in France, then, in 1937, to fight in Spain, finally on his mission to Tunis in 1938.

In 1940 Velio was arrested and imprisoned, together with other Communists. With the fall of France and the establishment of the Pétain government there in June 1940, the same month that Italy entered the war, he was released. By this time, Nadia's commitment to the Resistance against Nazi-Fascism was total, and she was, in due course, to be condemned for her political activities. In 1941, Velio reorganised the Party and became its de facto leader, establishing valuable contacts with other groups struggling against the Vichy government in France. That November, the betrayal of an informer led to the arrest of many members of the Tunisian Party. In the trial that followed, Velio, who had escaped capture, was tried and sentenced to death in absentia. He continued to work underground during 1942, when he was once more sentenced to death. At least one source suggests that Nadia was sentenced to three years' imprisonment for her own activities – a penalty that she evaded. With the fall of Mussolini's Fascist regime in June 1943, and the freeing of Tunisia, first Velio and then Nadia managed to escape Tunis and take refuge in the liberated south of Italy. They settled in Naples and took up PCI work there, Nadia assuming responsibility for women. By this time, the couple had two daughters, **Chiara Spano** and **Paula Spano**, who for a while they left behind in Tunis with Nadia's mother.

That same year, Nadia visited Sardinia for the first time when she was sent by the PCI to see how fertile the ground was among women. In Guspini, her father-in-law, Attilio Spano, had been municipal secretary of the Party for some years, and there were 300 members of the women's section. Nadia was struck by how 'proud and combative' they were. She spent two months touring the island.

She arrived in Rome in 1945 and started working for the Roman Communist Federation which dealt in particular with the problems of women living on the margins of society in peripheral neighbourhoods and towns; at the same time she was in correspondence with Sardinia concerning the creation of women's structures. She was involved with the 'trains of happiness' (*Salvare Infanzia*) which, in collaboration with the Rome Municipality and the Italian Red Cross, set up convoys for the transfer towards northern Italy of 70000 southern children from the areas most affected by the war. There they found temporary shelter with generous families who treated them as their own. Nadia also participated in the founding of the *Unione Donne Italiane* and, in 1944, of the weekly *Noi Donne*. She was quite clear that the first cover of the periodical should represent the future for women, not the present nor the past; to that end, it featured a smiling young woman, a student, rather than bowed-down women workers or tired post-war housewives, of which there were 13 million. That was not to say that she did not daily concern herself with the struggles of those women. Her autobiography has three small children on the cover. At some time during the post-Tunis years, a third daughter, **Francesca Spano**, was born.

From January to June 1946, Nadia devoted herself wholeheartedly to the election campaign for the Constituent Assembly, dividing herself between activism – meetings, rallies and lists – and her husband and their daughters. The excitement of election day – 2 June, her 30th birthday – arrived and she was to write, 'Velio voted from Sardinia and sent me two telegrams of good wishes'. The Republic won and she was elected to draft the Constitutional Charter – one of 21 women (of 530 members). She was to say in an interview with Antonella Restelli who directed a documentary about her:

> The women were not many, but they spoke for themselves and were decisive: our country has not only founding fathers, but owes its shape to this cohort of founders who have been able to hold firm to the point of equality for all. ... We weighed every word, every comma because what we were writing had to serve also for the future ... and we knew that for us women it was an opportunity not to be missed.

And the director added,

> I like to call her Mother Constituent, because it is also thanks to her that we today, girls and women, have taken a step forward in society and can enjoy those rights that during Fascism and in the first post-war period, women were, in all respects, subordinate to men, they couldn't even dream.

(Nadia's daughters, Chiara and Paola, were speakers at a showing of the film in Balsamo (Milan) on 19 April 2015.)

Nadia was subsequently to spend 10 years – 1948 to 1958 – at the Palazzo Montecitorio, the palace in Rome that was the seat of the Italian Chamber of Deputies, as a Communist parliamentarian representing Sardinia. She and Velio, who was also elected, lived between Rome and Sardinia where Nadia became President of the Union of Sardinian Women. They were also involved, through the PCI, with countries and movements in the Third World, such as Vietnam, South Africa, Sub-Saharan Africa, and the Middle East.

Velio died of a tumour in 1964 leaving Nadia to work alone for the next 42 years on securing the future: during the last years of her life she concentrated on spreading the values of the Constitution in Italian schools and the struggle for securing the rights of women. An encomium delivered on her death in 2006, by the mayor of Carbonia, makes clear her close links with the Sulcis mining basin in the south-west of Sardinia, sharing as he said, its difficult times. With her death, he explained, 'A great Italian woman disappears, the protagonist of the crucial period in the history of the last century that marked the defeat of Nazism and the foundation of the Italian Republic.' He noted that she had made one of her last appearances in Carbonia, giving a speech at the celebration of 25 April, the feast of the Resistance. As a sign of mourning, the city council decided to lower the flag to half mast on the day of her funeral. The Mayor ended,

> Today is a sad day for all women and men who believe in the values of democracy, freedom and justice. Nadia Gallico Spano, protagonist in the anti-Fascist and liberation struggle, joined the Constituent Assembly with the PCI group and then remained, throughout the history of the Republic, among the most intelligent and passionate women who, actively, have contributed to the most important political and civil battles for the improvement and growth of Italian democracy and the living conditions of workers and the weakest. Her strong bond with Sardinia and the Sulcis Iglesiente made Nadia and her husband Velio a constant point of reference for the workers in the struggles of the Sardinian autonomous workers movement. A delegation from the Sulcis-Iglesiente Federation will participate in the funeral on Monday in Rome, bringing the affection and esteem of our territory.

Nadia's autobiography was published just three weeks before her death. In March 2009, an article in *Noi Donne*, still going strong, but by then a monthly, featured Nadia as Woman of the Month; Maria Luisa Boccia ended it with reference to Mabrúk:

> It is a precious gift not only to know, through the memory of a protagonist, the history of the twentieth century, but to understand what political life is. In the twofold sense: of how a life is inextricably intertwined with politics and of how politics is, if we consider it in its making life, marking

the experience, relationships, ideas and choices, in short, the way of being and acting in the world of men and women. And it is no coincidence that it is a woman who offers us a book of memories in which politics is interwoven with life as life is with politics.

Just as Nadia Spano finished her two stints as a parliamentarian in 1958, **Maria Giulia Cocco** (1916–2013), ten years her junior, started hers, aged 42. Her politics, coming from Catholicism and the Christian Democratic Party (DC, founded 1943) could be said to be the opposite of Nadia's Communism. But each was committed both to Sardinia and to the emancipation and progress of women.

Maria was born during the First World War in Domusnovas (Domus Noas), in the mining Carbonia-Iglesias region where Nadia and Velio Spano had been particularly active. She was the eldest of five children born to a mother who was an elementary school teacher and a father who was a gunner then and who was to become an administrator and then a local judge – the names of neither appear to be available. During her secondary schooling at a time of Fascism she was a member of Catholic Action, and organised courses and regional groups. At the age of 19, she enrolled in the Faculty of Letters at Cagliari University, gaining a bachelor's degree in literature and, in 1941, during the Second World War, she moved to Rome to work on her thesis. After graduation in 1944, she went back to Rome where she met Catholic **Maria Federici**, a future member of the Constituent Assembly and Christian Democrat deputy; she was also founder president, in 1944, of the Italian Women's Centre (CIF) – a federation of Christian associations concerned with the social and cultural emancipation of women. As a result, Maria's interest in politics was strengthened and, on her return to Sardinia, she became the regional representative of the CIF, and responsible for its centre in Cagliari. In this role she organised courses in rural home economics, pedagogy and civic education. At the core of these were women and education – the two strands that guided her life's work. Her profession in a parliamentary biography is given as 'teacher'.

When Maria was elected to Parliament in 1958, she was the first Sardinian-born woman of only 27 others. She was to be a deputy for four consecutive terms, until 1976, representing Cagliari and Oristano, and in due course she became Under-Secretary for Education and of Health. Her legislative goal from the beginning was to improve the conditions of Sardinian women and children, those most affected by poverty and isolation on an island geographically and metaphorically separate.

An amendment Maria introduced in 1961 opened the way to the courts and the judiciary to women. Her slogan, 'No to women under guardianship', presaged perhaps the most important reform she initiated. This was the repeal of the rule of 1894 which provided for the right of a husband's opposition to all acts of the disposition of his wife's estate. She also called for, and obtained, the repeal of law 1179 of 1919, thus allowing women access to public executive positions. In this way she made it possible to comply with articles of the Constitution which provided for equality between the sexes and equal access to all offices and professions. Like so many of her Sardinian countrywomen, Maria was very long-lived: she died aged 96.

Ninetta Bartoli (1896–1978), mayor of the village of Borutta (Sassari) in Sardinia, is said to have been the first woman mayor in Italy, though more than one woman mayor was elected in Italy and, indeed, Sardinia, in April 1946. She was born, one of two daughters, into a local noble family, the status of which enabled her to make the right friends – such as **Laura Carta Caprino** (b.1896), daughter of a rich landowner, and destined to marry Antonio Segni, the first Sardinian to serve as Prime Minister, and later as President of the Italian Republic – and to go to the right school. Figlie di Maria, a boarding convent and the most exclusive school in Sassari, that aimed to turn her into the perfect young lady, with all the accomplishments necessary for her class, and to enable her to make a good marriage. She, however, eschewed marriage: she had more important things to do with her life: she was wedded to action and social commitment, and that in her home place, Borutta, with its 600 inhabitants. She acted as a link between there and the Sassari Christian Democrats, helped by the ties with Laura Carta Segni and her husband.

In 1945, straight after the end of the war, she took advantage of her opportunities by becoming secretary of the local branch of the Christian Democrats. This led her, at the age of 50, to stand for election to the council, winning 89 per cent of the vote, then to stand for mayor, voted for by 13 out of 14 councillors – she did not vote herself.

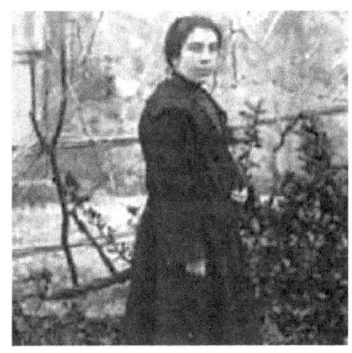

In a decade she had built, in poor and infrastructure-deprived Borutta, the aqueduct which supplied water to all the houses, the sewers and the power plant.

68. Ninetta Bartoli, from the internet

She was responsible for the rebuilding of the ancient and ruined Romanesque abbey of S Pietro di Sorres and many other infrastructural and social works, including a primary school, an orphanage, a cemetery, a communal hall, a milk and cheese-making co-operative, a care home and a branch of an agricultural credit cooperative.

As mayor, Ninetta was totally committed to the service of her community, managing to impose her political programmatic choices on the subordinate bodies, the province and the region, by sheer determination and the exercise of her authority. Although she was elected as a Christian Democrat, and although she managed to break the earlier patriarchal structure of her society, in some ways her power came from pre-ideological times, to when the local nobility held sway. Aged 62 in 1958, she was defeated by a young doctor. She died twenty years later and her funeral was held in Borutta's municipal hall officiated at by the prior of S Pietro di Sorres.

Margherita Sanna (1904–1974), also standing as a Christian Democrat, was, aged 42, elected mayor of Orune in the Barbagia region on 7 April 1946; she, too, was said to be the first woman to hold such a position in Sardinia though, in her case, the claim did not extend to Italy, at least in the account by Pasquito Farina in *'Il Ricordo di Margherita Sanna'* (2016). She was to be mayor for three legislatures, until 1956, and provincial councillor from 1964 to 1966, only retiring for health reasons. Farina writes of her:

> The memory of her presents us with a role of the woman in Barbagia who, despite living within rigid logics and social dynamics, has never been subordinate to that of man; different[,] yes, but never dominated. Her election as mayor, the first in Sardinia, demonstrates, if needed, that in our 'deep Barbagia' the foundations of equal opportunities were already well-established 70 years ago.

Margherita's parents, Pietro Sanna and **Cecilia Ruiu**, were part of a large family of Orune shepherds and academically she did well, graduating with a bachelor's degree in accountancy from Sassari University. But her early attempt to enter the job market was not so promising: although she won a competition to work for a city bank in Sassari, a man was appointed instead. Returning to Orune, she worked for a while in the secretariat of the municipality. It was not, however, what she wanted to do; in her unpublished diary, drawn on by Natalino Piras in the blog *'L'eroismo quotidiano di Margherita Sanna, sindaco di Orune'* (2011), she wrote of the boredom of 'the game of balancing the accounts, the precise succession of the work phases and the bureaucratic efficiency of forms, calculations and figures'. She may, though, have remembered that experience when she became mayor; at the time she decided instead to be a teacher and, in 1935, gained a diploma to teach in primary schools. Teaching became her vocation.

In order to be able to continue teaching, in 1939 she must have felt that she had no option but to join the National Fascist Party, but was opposed to Mussolini from the start, believing, as Piras noted, that his policy was leading Italy to war and catastrophe. Instead, as a woman of faith, she became active in the *Azione Cattolica*, a home which allowed her to campaign for the emancipation of women.

Her activities led her, in 1943, to be arrested by the Fascist regime and detained for two months in Cagliari's Buoncammino prison on charges of espionage on behalf of the British. She was accused of being part of the Nuorese group that was supposed to favour the Allied landing on the coast of eastern

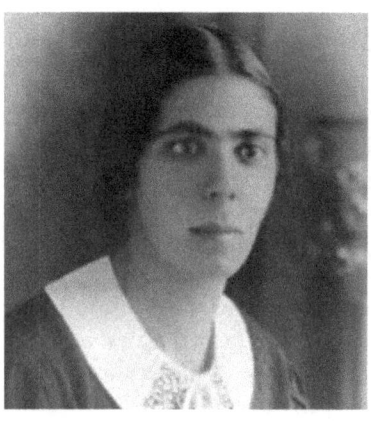
69. Margherita Sanna, from the internet

Sardinia. This was probably connected to Emilio and Joyce Lussu's enterprise from their bases in Paris and Portugal, noted earlier; Lussu's name, and that of Dino Giacobbe, were on a proscribed list, as were others with whom Margherita had connections through her own work. She had the added disadvantage of speaking English.

She continued to keep her diary in prison, noting, for example, as the British and Americans bombéd Cagliari, 'February 13, 1943, I am 39 years old. The music played for my party is not skimped. The last explosion was very close. ... great hustle and bustle in the corridors ... the prison must have been hit.' Despite that nerve-wracking hour, 'The rations arrived on time, but not a word about the bombing. I try to eat, although I'm not sure that I'll be here in a minute.' She was interrogated, asked 'crazy questions'. Back in her cell between 'this hell of whistles and bombs', she wrote, 'I have never argued against institutions ... I have always firmly wanted everyone to be aware of their own autonomy of thought and I am convinced that democracy arises from confrontation and debate.' Fascism was the denial of democracy. She continued, 'They accuse me of having immorally imposed my will on minors, referring to my activities in Catholic Action. The constant wear and tear of the arguments in my defence reduces my resistance.' She worried about her 'abandoned [school] children' and her mother's desperation. Even praying 'does not arouse new strength in the exhausted spirit'.

As early as 1933, she had wondered why the grandmother, the mother, the sister, had to 'spend so much time on household chores that numb the brain even if they keep the limbs elastic. I cannot understand the resigned strength of generations of women who sacrifice ten hours of their day at home on such things.' And, of women, she later wrote,

> If I had more time for them perhaps I could communicate this need for action and knowledge, this need to open the mind beyond the domestic walls, this passion for sacrifice that transforms resignation into constructive and operating strength of women capable of moving apathy, of minimising aggravations.

Of the children she taught, she noted in her diary some of the difficulties she faced: it was useless, for example, to insist on them writing of Mazzini and Garibaldi; they were more interested in the details of farms with which they were familiar. One thing was very clear – the stricture formulated when a pupil talked of being beaten:

> What is the sense of pain on the hand of a child? What is the sense of violence against the weak? Any punishment but not that blow. No more blows to my children. It is the maximum defeat of the teacher.

Her election as mayor 13 years later allowed her more scope to work for the emancipation of women, to do something about her earlier questioning about the trap of household chores. She ordered the construction of a municipal laundry so that the women of Orune would not have to go away via the dark mountain roads to do the laundry, illustrated by the photograph in Helen Wright's 1916 article. She supported the creation of a paediatric outpatients clinic and a kindergarten. But she did not neglect the wider community, creating new job opportunities, such as the first cooperative society of shepherds in Sardinia; a school canteen, and the start of reforestation work, in particular the establishment of a pine forest on Cucumache, the mountain above the commune.

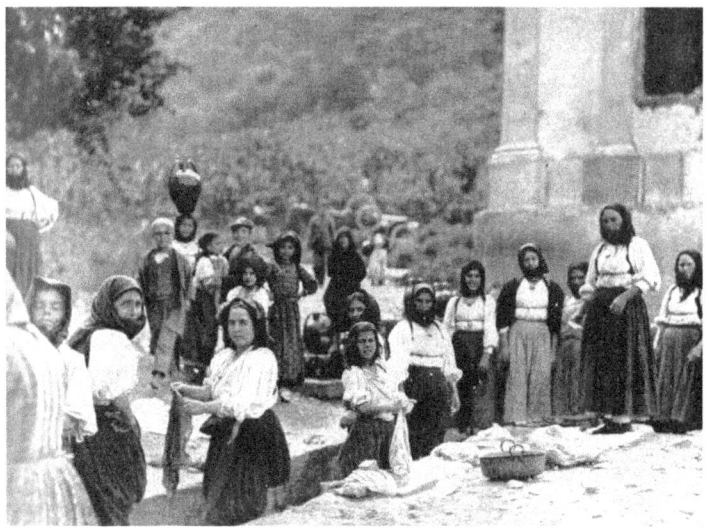

70. 'The Community Laundry Tub', photograph by Charles Wright for Helen Dunstan Wright, 'Little-known Sardinia' from the *National Geographic* magazine, August 1916

Margherita believed that, with education, legality and politics, everything, particularly the emancipation of women, and the general progress of the community, could be done if they were united with a culture of change. She kept in mind precepts, such as 'autonomy of thought' and the importance of debate, that she had noted in her prison diary. In spite of her powerful position, she did not give herself airs. Carlo Levi, anti-Fascist activist, as well as writer and painter, wrote of her in *Tutto il Miele è Finito* (1964; All the Honey is Finished), 'From the town hall – we are in 1952 – a grey-haired woman emerged wrapped in a peasant's shawl: she was the mayor of Orune.'

And, following her death aged 70, she was not forgotten: *La Nuova Sardegna* noted on 18 December 2016, the seventieth anniversary of Italian women gaining the right to vote, that the council chamber of Orune was named in her honour, as a plaque was affixed to the wall there. Many spoke of her, one suggesting that she represented the 'figure of mother, educator, Woman with a capital W'; another that she was 'the one who, after preparing the earth, sows the seed of progress with full hands'. The Orune poet Mario

Cherchi wrote his poem '*A Margherita Sanna*' for the same occasion. I have only been able to find the original Logudorese version, but some phrases stand out, nevertheless: 'humble person', 'Sardinian heroine', 'honour and honesty', 'Orune fell in love with you', 'Margherita Sanna bright mind'.

It is not my place, nor my inclination, to try and engage with, let alone unravel, Italian post-war politics. But a couple of loose ends need tying up concerning the women whose lives and politics feature in this and the previous chapter, and, indeed, their interaction with each other, with only scraps of information to go on.

However much Marianna Bussalai saw Emilio Lussu as the symbol of freedom and resistance, when between 1945 and 1947 he proposed uniting, or allying, the Sardinian Action Party with the Italian Action Party, she continued to fight for the island's independence from the mainland. Lussu left the Party in 1948 to found the short-lived Sardinian Socialist Action Party, which joined the Italians a year later.

As implied earlier, the Lussus tended to work together politically, but any change of political party was irrelevant to the women's congress Joyce Lussu mentions in the long passage quoted in chapter 13. It must have been the one that took place in the Teatro Massimo, Cagliari, starting on 9 March 1952, and described in an article on 7 March 2018. The First Congress of Sardinian women had 2200 delegates, 928 guests, and was decorated with a mass of mimosa and red carnations. The poster shows two peasant women, one holding a toddler, perhaps the Barbagia women Joyce described so admiringly.

Discussion focused, for example, on the problems of land: 10 per cent of Sardinians were absolutely destitute, wages were 10–30 per cent lower than those elsewhere and, for labourers, 50 per cent lower. In some municipalities there was no sewage system, while inhabited centres were without aqueducts. Infant mortality reached 40.4 per cent in the first year of life. Trachoma, like tuberculosis, affected adults and children. There were not enough schools and kindergartens. The school equipment provided barely covered 35 per cent of the needs. Misery, unemployment, degradation, housing, childhood were themes concerning many women. Parliamentarian Nadia Spano presented a motion on childhood; and Joyce Lussu one on municipal problems; other motions included female school conditions. These resulted in decisions to be presented to municipalities, regional 'councillors', and Parliament, calling for 'progress in Sardinia and the security of tomorrow'. The two women mayors, Ninetta Bartoli and Margherita Sanna, would have been involved, as would Maria Cocco, the other parliamentarian.

Mention of regional councillors requires something of an explanation here. The Regional Government of Sardinia, with its 60 Regional Councils, was introduced in 1949. Its details fall outside the scope of my necessarily sketchy and time-limited narrative, but Silvia Benussi's 2014 'A Historical Study of Gender and Representation in the Regional Council of Sardinia (1949–2013)' is helpful for those interested in pursuing the subject. It seems unlikely that the regional councillors who were to be approached in 1952 would have been women. Also discussing women's position too modern for my 'history' is Eugenia Tognotti's *'Considerazione generali sulla condizione femminile in Sardegna'* (2000), in particular the section *'Se le donne fossero protagoniste nella politica'*.

As well as women's position in Sardinia, Eugenia Tognotti, professor at the University of Sassari, specialises, as was suggested in chapter 6, in health and disease, both historical and current. The health of Sardinians was undermined from the earliest times by the prevalence of malaria. It was not until the early 1950s that international funding and concerted and scientifically led measures throughout the island brought about its eradication. This led to increasing prosperity, partly driven by the rise of tourism.

However recent, some political developments bear inclusion. As late as 2009, a regional, separatist political party was founded, the *Rossomori* (Red Moors) described as a left wing split from the Sardinian Action Party (Psd'Az). It was obviously connected not just with the Sardinian Flag itself, but also with Marianna Bussalai's embroidered banner of 1921 for the founding of the Psd'Az. Then, as is the way with Italian politics as far as an outsider can observe, two years later an article is to be found in *La Nuova Sardegna* entitled, *'Dimissioni in Massa del Circolo Bussalai'* ('Mass Resignation from the Bussalai Club'). Its first sentence reads, 'Cagliari. Resignation of the members of the "Marianna Busslai-Joyce Lussu" club in Cagliari from the Rossomori party.'

Marianna and Joyce were long dead. You have to wonder what they would have made of this outcome to all they had dreamed of, struggled for, cooperated over as sisters on behalf of the women of Sardinia. That episode may, or may not, be a fitting ending to an outsider's historical account of the centuries of women's multi-faceted lives on the island.

Bibliography

Books by and about Women, General Reader (in English and Italian)

Accati, Elena, *Fiori in Famiglia: Storia e Storie di Eva Mameli Calvino* (Florence, Editoriale Scienza, 2015)
Accati, Elena, *Eva Mameli Calvino: Una Straordinaria Figura di Scienziata, Moglie e Madre* (Turin, Libreria Cortina, 2018)
Agus, Milena, *Mal di Pietre* (Rome, Nottetempo, 2006)
Agus, Milena *From the Land of the Moon* (London, Europa Editions, 2010)
Altea, Guliana, *Edina Altara* (Nuoro, Ilisso Edizioni, 2005)
Alzona, Gianluigi, *Battistina e la Piccola Anita: due done sfortunate sullo sfondo dell'epopea garibaldina* (La Maddalena, Paolo Sorba, 2013)
Amoia, Alba ed., *Great Women Travel Writers* (London, Continuum, 2006)
Anedda, Antonella, *Isolatria: Viaggio nell'Arcipelago della Maddalena* (Rome-Bari, Editori Laterza, 2013)
Balducci, Carolyn, *A Self-Made Woman: Biography of Nobel-Prize-Winner Grazia Deledda* (Boston, Houghton Mifflin, 1975)
Blanch, Lesley, *The Wilder Shores of Love* (London, John Murray, 1954)
Clark, Letitia, *Bitter Honey: Recipes and Stories from the Island of Sardinia* (London, Hardie Grant, 2020)
Concas, Iride Peis, *Donne e Bambine nella Miniera di Montevecchio* (Viareggio, Pezzini Editore, 2005)
Costa, Enrico, *Rosa Gambella: raccontostorico Sassarese del secolo XV* (1897; Nuoro, Ilisso, c.2004)
Costa, Maria-Merce, *Violante Carros: Contessa di Quirra* (Oliena, Edizioni Iris, 2004)
Daniels, Elizabeth Adams, *Jessie White Mario: Risorgimento Revolutionary* (Athens, Ohio University Press, 1972)
Davey, Mary, *Icnusa, or Pleasant Reminiscences of a Two Years' Residence in the Island of Sardinia* (London, Binns & Goodwin, 1860) (also available in scanned reprint)
Davey, Mary, *Sardinia* (London, Christian Knowledge Society, 1874) (also available in scanned reprint)
Deledda, Grazia, *Elias Portolu* (Milan, Fratelli Treves, 1900) [There are multiple editions of all Grazia Deledda's novels, and it is not always easy to deduce the first]
Deledda, Grazia, *Cenere* (Milan, Treves, 1904)
Deledda Grazia, *Colombi e Sparvieri* (Milan, Fratelli Treves Editore, 1912)
Deledda Grazia, *Canne al Vento* (Milan, Fratelli Treves, 1913), translated into English by Martha King as *Reeds in the Wind* with an introduction by Dolores Turchi (New York, Italica Press, 1999)
Deledda, Grazia, *La Madre* (Milan, Fratelli Treves, 1920), translated by MG Steegman as *The Mother* (London, Dedalus, 1923)
Deledda, Grazia, *Cosima* (Milan, Fratelli Treves, 1937); translation and introduction by Martha King (London, Quartet Books, 1988)
Devilla, Amelia Melis, *Faula de Orbaci* (Cagliari, *Societa Tipografica Sarda*, 1913)
Devilla, Amelia Melis, *Alba sul Monte* (Rome, *Sapientia editrice*, 1931)
Dumas, Alexander, *Acté* (1838; Paris, M Lévy-freres, 1854)
'Fresi, Franco, *Le Banditesse: Storie di Donne Fuorilegge in Sardegna* (Nuoro, Edizioni il Maestrale, 2015)
Garibaldi, Clelia, *Mio Padre: Recordi di Clelia Garibaldi* (Florence, Vallecchi, 1948)
Giacobbe, Maria, *Diario di una Maestrina* (Bari, Lateresa, 1957)
Giacobbe, Maria, *Le Radici* (Cagliari, Edizioni, 1975)

Giacobbe, Simonetta, *Lettere d'Amore e di Guerra. Sardegna-Spagna (1937-1939)* (Cagliari, Datteria, *c.*1992)
Kershaw, Elizabeth ed., Introduction by Annette Kobak, *The Nomad: The Diaries of Isabelle Eberhardt* (Northampton, Interlink Books, 2012)
King, Martha, *Grazia Deledda: A legendary life* (Leicester, Troubador Publishing, 2005)
Kobak, Annette, *Isabelle: The Life of Isabelle Eberhardt* (London, Chatto & Windus, 1988)
Lai, Ada, *La Straordinaria Storia di Francesca Sanna Sulis Donna di Sardegna* (Cagliari, Palabanda Cultura, 2016)
Lai, Giuliana, *L'Erede del Corbulaio* (Cagliari, Arte Duchamp, 2001)
Lai, Giuliana, *Ritagli* (publishing details inaccesible; 2012)
Lewis, David, *Jessie White Mario: an English heroine in the liberation of Italy* (Oxford, Eureka Press, 2006)
Lussu, Joyce, *Fronti e Frontiere* (1945), translated into English as *Freedom has no Frontier* (London, Michael Joseph, 1969)
Lussu, Joyce, *L'Olivastro e l'Innesto: l'incontro con un uomo, la sua isola antica e la sua gente* (Cagliari, Edizioni Della Torre, 1982)
Lussu, Joyce, *Portrait* (Ancona, Transeuropa, 1988)
Manca, Maria and Tilley, Christine eds, *Florence's Diary: il diario di Florence Piercy, terzogenita di Benjamin*, with a foreword by Giorgina Mameli Giustiniani (Olbia, Editrice Taphros, 2006)
Mariani, Rosalba, *Miniera* (Sassari, Carlo Delfino Editore, 2011)
Melena, Elpis (Espérance von Schwartz), *Recollections of General Garibaldi, or, Travels from Rome to Lucerne* (1862; scanned reprint nd)
Mengiste, Maaza, *The Shadow King*, trans Robert Fagles (Edinburgh, Canongate, 2019)
Minniti, Barbara, *Casa Collins: le memorie della 'segretaria inglese' di Garibaldi* (Florence, Edizioni Polistampa, 2008)
Moorehead, Caroline, *A House in the Mountains: The Women Who Liberated Italy from Fascism* (London, Chatto & Windus, 2019)
Murgia, Michela, *Accabadora* (Turin, Einaudi, *c.*2009)
Murgia, Michela, *Accabadora*, translated Silvester Mazzarella (London, MacLehose Press, 2011)
Murgia, Michela, *Viaggio in Sardegna: Undici Percorsi nell'Isola che non si Vede* (Turin, Giulio Einaudi Editore, 2014)
Piercy, Donna Vera Mameli, *Nel mezzo della vita* (2020)
Pintus, Alberto Mario and Cugia, Maria Giovanna, *Il Caso Giles: Un misterioso fatto di cronaca nella Sassari del primo novecento* (Sassari, J Webber Editore, 2011)
Posse-Brázdová, Amelie *Sardinian Sideshow* (New York, EP Dutton, 1933)
Ronalds, Mary Teresa, *Myself My Sepulchre* (London, Macdonald, 1961)
Scano, Dionigi, *Donna Francesca di Zatrillas* (1946; Sassari, Nuova Sardegna, 2003)
Schwartz, Marie Espérance von, *Recollections of General Garibaldi: or, Travels from Rome to Lucerne* (London, 1861) (see also Melena, Elpis)
Secci, Maria Cristina, *Eva Mameli Calvino: Gli Anni Cubani (1920–1925)* (Milan, Franco Angeli, 2017)
Sotgiu, Giovanna, *L'Isola e le Donne* (La Maddalena, Paolo Sorba Editore, 2016)
Spano, Nadia, *Mabrúk: Ricordi di un 'Iguaribile Ottimista* (Cagliari, AM & D Edizioni, 2005)

Specialist Works by or about Women (may be available on the internet; *see also* Internet Material *below*)

Alba, Elisabetta, *La Donna Nuragica: Studio della Bronzistica Figurata* (Rome, Caracci Editore, 2005)
Artizzu, Francesco, 'Un Approccio al Condaghe di San Pietro di Silki' (2013) *Archivio Storico Sardo* 48 23–40

Baccaro, Laura, *'Sa Femina Accabadora: donne magiche o assassine?'* in S Borile, *Antropologia e Violenza*, pp185-191, Amon editore, 2016
Baillio, Joseph, *Elisabeth Louise Vigée LeBrun* (Fort Worth, Texas, Kimball Art Museum, 1982)
Balmuth, Miriam S, 'Ancient Copper and Bronze in Sardinia: Excavation and Analysis' (1976) 3(2) *Journal of Field Archaeology* 195–201
Barbagli, Marzio, *Marriage and the Family in Italy* (Cambridge, Cambridge University Press, 1991)
Belloc, Bessie Rayner, 'The Old World Prince' in *In a Walled Garden* (London, Ward and Downey, 1895)
Benussi, Silvia, 'A Historical Study of Gender and Representation in the Regional Council of Sardinia (1949-2013)' (2014) 34(1) *Parliaments, Estates and Representation* 95–113
Brozu, G, http:// giornale.liceobrozu, 2016
Budin, Stephanie Lynn, *The Myth of Sacred Prostitution* (New York, Cambridge University Press, 2008)
Cagnetta, Franco, *Banditi a Orgosolo* (Florence, Guaraldi Editore, 1975; 2nd edn, Nuoro, Ilisso, 2002)
Campi, Evangelina, *La Seta del Mare – Il Bisso* (Taranto, Scorpione, 2004)
Candiani, Laura, *'"Sa Reina" Nuorese: Maria Antonia Serra Sanna' Stories* No 17, 2019
Castiglione, Caroline, *Accounting for Affection: Mothers, Families and Politics in Early Modern Rome* (New York, Palgrave Macmillan, 2015)
Casula, Francesco Cesare, *La Carta de Logu del Regno di Arborea* (Sassari, Carlo Delfino Editore, 2008)
Casula, Francesco, 'Eleonora d'Arborea' and 'Marianna Bussalai' in *Uomini e Donne di Sardegna: Le Contraversie* (Cagliari, Alfa Editrice, 2010)
Casula, Francesco, *Marianna Bussalai* (in Sardo) (Cagliari, Alfa, Editrice, 2013)
Cocco, Maria Bastiana, 'La Schivitù nella Sardegn: Sintesi dei dati alla luce della documentazione letteraria ed epigrafica' in Monique Dondin-Payre and Nicolas Tran eds, *Esclaves et Maîtres dans le Monde Romain* (Rome, Publications de l école Française, 2017)
Contu, Federica, 'The Sovereign and his Wife "Minister": Charles Emmanuel IV and Marie Clotilde Adélaide Xavière of France. Interpersonal and Political Relations between the Sovereigns of Sardinia' in Elena Woodacre, *Queenship in the Mediterranean: The Role of Queen in the Medieval and Early Modern Eras* (London, Palgrave Macmillan, 2013)
De Michele, Stefania, *L'Arcano Minore Eleonora d'Arborea: tra mito e realità* (Oliena, Ethos Edizioni, 2010)
Demontis, Luca, *'Costanza di Saluzzo regina-giudicessa d'Arborea e fondatrice del Monastero di Santa Chiara di Oristano (1343)'* (2018) XCIII *Antonianum* 31–64
Deplano, Valeria, *'La Sardegna vista dai consoli inglesi (1830–61)'* in F Alzeni and A Mattone, *La Sardegna nel Risorgimento* (Rome, Carocci, 2014)
Ebrahim, Marina and Torrebruno, Aldo, 'Eleanora of Arborea' in *Queens of Italy: Women in power in medieval Italy* (Milan, Hoc-lab Politenico, 2015)
Ehrenberg, Margaret, *Women in Prehistory* (London, British Museum Press, 1995)
Enna, Francesco, *'Paristoria di Maria Giusta'* in *Sos Contos de Foghile* (Sassari, Gallizzi, 1984)
Ferrante, Carla and Mattone, Antonello, *'La Communità Rurali nella Sardegna Medievale (Secoli XI–XV)'* Diritto e Storia, 2004
Ferrante, Joan, biographical introduction and translation, *Epistolae: Medieval Women's Latin Letters* (available online)
Giacobbe, Maria, 'Memories of a schoolgirl' (2005)
Giustiniani, Giorgina Mameli-Piercy, *Tra il Galles e la Sardegna; Storia della Famiglia Piercy* (Sassari, Carlo Delfino Editore, 2019)
Govino, Paola, 'The Making of Italo Calvino: Women and Men in "Two Cultures" Home Laboratory' in P Govino and ZA Francheschi eds, *Writing about Lives in Science (Auto) Biography, Gender, and Genre* (Goettingen, Vandenhoweck & Ruprecht, 2014)
Hayden, Christopher, 'Public and Domestic: The Social Background to the Development of Gender in Prehistoric Sardinia' in Ruth Whitehouse ed., *Gender and Italian Archaeology: Challenging the Stereotypes* (London, University of London Institute of Archaeology, 1998)

Heyer-Caput, Margherita, *Grazia Deledda's Dance of Modernity* (Toronto, Univesity of Toronto Press, 2008)
Hoe, Susanna, *Crete: Women, History, Books and Places* (Oxford, HOLO Books: The Women's History Press, 2003)
Hoe, Susanna, 'Pope Gregory the Great and the Disputes of Sardinian Women 591–604', (2018) 34(4) *Arbitration International*, December
Hoe, Susanna and Roebuck, Derek, *Women in Disputes: A History of European Women in Mediation and Arbitration* (Oxford, HOLO Books, 2018)
King, Georgiana, *Sardinian Painting: The Painting of the Gold Backgrounds* (London, Longmans, Green, 1923)
King, Georgiana, *Pittura Sarda del Quatrro-cinquecento* ed. Roberto Coroneo, trans. Stefania Lucaente (Nuoro, Ilisso, 2000)
Lalli, Virginia, 'Eleanora of Arborea' in *Women in Law* (Bloomington IN, AuthorHouse, 2014)
Llop, Carla Torres, 'Marquesa di Sietefuentes: Victima y Culpable de la Conjura Camarasa' (part of *Asparkia: investigació feminista*, núm 30, 2017)
Lo Schiavo, Flavia, 'The Bronze Age in Sardinia' in Anthony Harding and Harry Fokens, *The Oxford Handbook of the European Bronze Age* (Oxford, Oxford University Press, 2013)
Lo Schiavo, Flavia and Milletti, Matteo, 'The Nuragic Women: Facts and Hypotheses' in Stephanie Lynn Budin and Jean MacIntosh Turfa eds *Women in Antiquity: Real Women across the Ancient World* (London, Routledge Taylor, 2016)
Maccioni, Mariangela, *Memorie Politiche*, ed Raffaello Marchi (Cagliari, Edizioni della Torre, 1988)
Mancini, Paola, *Gallura Orientale: Preistoria e Protostoria* (Olbia, Editrice Taphros, 2010)
Mann, Janice, *Romanesque Architecture and its Sculptural Decoration in Christian Spain, 1000–1120* (Toronto, University of Toronto Press, 2009)
Marongiu, Ann, *Vedute di Cagliari: Un'artista Cagliaritana nell prima metà del novecento* (Rome, Instituto Nazionale per la Grafica, 1938)
Martyn, John JC, *Pope Gregory and the Brides of Christ* (Newcastle-upon-Tyne, Cambridge Scholars, 2009)
Martyn, John JC, *Queens to Slaves: Pope Gregory's Special Concerns for Women* (Newcastle-upon-Tyne, Cambridge Scholars, 2011)
Meir, Amira, 'La Ketubbah di Selomoh Carcassona ebreo Sardodel XV secolo' in *Materia Giudaica: Rivista dell'associazione Italiana per lo studio del giudaismo* (XIV 1–2, 2009)
Merz, Noemi Crain, *L'Illusione della Parita: Donne e Questione Femminile in Giustizia e Liberta* (Nuoro, Franco Angeli, 2013)
Mussi, Margherita, 'The Venus of Macomer: A little-known prehistoric figurine from Sardinia', in P. Bahn, ed. *An Enquiring Mind, Essays in Honour of Alexander Marshack*, pp 193–210 (Harvard University, American School of Prehistoric Research, 2009)
Oppo, Anna, '"Where There's no Woman There's no Home": Profile of the Agro-Pastoral Family in Nineteenth-Century Sardinia' (1990) 15(4) *Journal of Family History*, October 483–502
Pinna, Tomasino, *Storia di una Strega: l'inquisizione in Sardegna: il processo di Julia Carta* (Sassari, EDES, 2000)
Pisano, Raimondo, *Il Gabinetto delle stampe 'Anna Marongiu Pernis' della Biblioteca Universitaria di Cagliari* (Cagliari, Sezione sarda dell'associazione italiana per le biblioteche, 1948)
Poli, Fernanda, *Ardara: La Chiesa Palatina di Santa Maria del Regno* (Sassari, Carlo Delfino, 2014)
Puglia, Andrea, 'Interactions between lay and ecclesiastical offices in Sardinia' in Frances Andrews ed and with Maria Agata Pincelli, *Churchmen and Urban Government in Late Medieval Italy c1200–c1450* (Cambridge, Cambridge University Press, 2013)
Pusceddu, Enrico, 'L'incarico dell'Hispanic Society of America a Georgiana Goddard King per lo Studio dei "Primitivi" Sardi' in Rosa Alcoy i Pedrós, *l'Art Medieval en Joc* (Barcelona, Universitat de Barcelona Edicions, 2016)
Robinson, Nicole, 'Return from Exile: Joyce Lussu's Many Autobiographical Voices' (2015) 10 *Carte Italiane*

Rubanu, Pietrina, *Murales Politici della Sardegna* (Balsano and Cagliari, Massari e Dathena, 1998)
Ruggeri, Paola, '*Olbia e la Casa Imperiale*' in Attilio Mastino and Paola Ruggeri eds, *Da Olbia ad Olbia: 2500 anni di storia di una città mediterranea* (Sassari, Editrice Democratica Sarda, 2004)
Ruggeri, Paola, '*La Vestale Massima Flavia Publicia*' in Javier Cabrero Piquero and Luca Montecchio eds, *Sacrum Nexum: Alianzas entre el poder politico y la religión en el mundo romano* (Madrid-Salamanca, Signifer Libros, 2015)
Ruggeri, Paola, '*Un Nuovo Bollo Laterizio dalla Necropoli Romana di Monte Carru Alghero (SS)*' in J Bonetto et al., *Alle Origini del Laterizio Romano* (Rome, Edizioni Quasar, 2019)
Sanna, Claudia, '*Cosi mangiavano i nuragici? Le scoperte dal primo Festival della Civiltà Nuragica di Orroli*' (2017) *Archeologia*, 28 March
Scano, Ilaria Muggianu and Fadda, Mario, *Grazia Deledda e Amelia Melis de Villa: Due Protegoniste del Romanzo Cattolico Italiano* (Cagliari, Akadema Editore, 2014)
Sioli, Marco, '*Una Schiavitu Impossibile: Anna Porcile e William Eaton*' in 2 *Quaderni Tabarchini*, Carloforte, Saphryina, Associazione Culturale (nd)
Sorlini, Giulia Battiti, 'The Megalithic Temples of Malta' in Anthony Bonanno, *Archaeology and Fertility Cult* (Amsterdam, Gruner, 1986)
Sotgiu, Giovanna, and Sega, Alberto, 'William Sanderson Craig: *Commerciante e Console Inglese*' in *Inglesi nell'Arcipelago: da Nelson alla fine dell'ottocento* (La Maddalena, Paolo Sorba Editore, 2005)
Strazza, Michele, '*La Nascita del Movimenti Politici Femminili nel Dopoguerra*' (nd)
Tasca, Cecilia, '*La Comunita Ebraica di Alghero Fra '300' e'400'*' in *Revista del'Aguer* pp 140–66 (Centre de Recercas i Documento 'Eduard Tola' 84, 1900)
Todde, Maria Silvia, '*Banditesse in Sardegna: il fenomeno del banditismo al femminile*' with an introduction by Laura Baccaro (2010) III (3) *Rivista di Psicodinamica Criminale*
Tognotti, Eugenia, *L'Anno del Colera: Sassari 1855: uomini, fatti e storie* (Sassari, EDES Editrice, 2000)
Tognotti, Eugenia, '*Considerazioni generali sulla condizione femminile in Sardegna*' in *Le donne e l'università: prima indagine conoscitiva* (Sassari, Edizioni Gallizzi, 2000)
Virdis, Maurizio, ed., *Condaghe di Santa Maria di Bonarcado* (Sassari, Centro Studi Filologici Sardi, 2002; Cagliari, CUEC, 2002)
White, Evelyn, 'Land Reform in Sardinia: The Work of EFTAS', (1961) 42(494) *Blackfriars*, July/August 320–322

Poetry by and about Women (*see also* on the internet)

Anedda, Antonella, trans Jamie McKendrick, *Archipelago* (Hexham, Northumberland, Bloodaxe Books, 2014)
Baule, Maria, '*Ancora Semus in Guerra*' in Giovanni Spano, *Canzoni Popolari di Sardegna* (1857; Nuoro, Ilisso, 1999)
Bussalai, Marianna, '*A GS Ardente Figlia di Nuoro*' in *Lumen: Rivista per la Gioventu Femminile d'Italia*
Bussalai, Marianna '*Mutos e Mutetus*' (in Sardo; further details not available)
Casula, Antioco, '*A Pasca Devaddes*' (no details available; original on the internet)
Colombo, Salvatore, *Poesie in Limba dal 1700 al 1900* (Nuoro, Editrice Archivio Fotografico Sardo, 2008)
Crespellani, Maria, *Bello, Bello Anche il Mondo di Quaggiù: Letteratura e Poesia nella Cagliari del Novecento* (2007) (see internet sources for Teresa's mentioned poems and add to browser: *Bombas in Casteddu*; *Sa Martinica*; *Sa Fuirura*; *Mariru Miu Presidents*)
Ichnussa: la biblioteca digitale della poesia sarda (eg Teresa Mundula Crespellani)
Lumen: Rivista per la Gioventu Femminile d'Italia
Mundula, Mercede et al, *Bello, Bello Anche il Mondo di Quaggiù! Letteratura e poesia nella Cagliari del novecento* (Cagliari, AM & D, 2007)

Rubeddu, Salvatore *'Passio – a su Connottu'* (no further details available; original on the internet)

Films, Plays and Operas about or featuring Women with Sardinian connections

Agus, Milena, *Mal de Pierres*, film of *Mal di Pietre/From the Land of the Moon* (starring Marion Cotillard)
Dessi, Giuseppe, *Eleonora d'Arborea* (play) (Nuoro, Ilisso, 2011)
Mazzoli, Missy, *Song from the Uproar: The Lives and Deaths of Isabelle Eberhardt* (first performed, 2012; CD available; *see also under* YouTube)
Mozart, WA, *La Clemenza di Tito* (1734) (Berenice)
Pasca Selis Zau Association, Nuoro, theatrical events
Wertenbaker, Timberlake, *New Anatomies* (1981)

Books, General

Alexander, Michael C, *The Case for the Prosecution in the Ciceronian Era* (Michigan, University of Michigan Press, 2002)
Andrews, Frances and Pincelli, Maria Agata, eds, *Churchmen and Urban Government in Late Medieval Italy, c1200–1450* (New York, Cambridge University Press, 2013)
Anedda, Antonella, *Geografie* (Milan, Garzanti, 2021)
Atzeni, Sergio, *Passavamo sulla Terra Leggeri* (Nuoro, Ilisso, 2009)
Babay, Mario Spanu, *Figari: Storie del Golfo e di Golfo Aranci* (Olbia, Editrice Taphros, 2004)
Beattie, Blake R, *Angelus Pacis: The Legation of Cardinal Giovanni Gaetano Orsini, 1326–1334* (Leiden, Biggleswade, 2007)
Bonazzi, Giuliano, *Il Condaghe di San Pietro di Silki: testo Logudorese inedito dei secoli 11–13* (Sassari-Cagliari 1900; reprint, Sassari, Dessi, 1997)
Davis, John A and Ginsborg, Paul eds, *Society and Politics in the Age of the Risorgimento: Essays in Honour of Denis Mack Smith* (Cambridge, Cambridge University Press, 1991)
Della Marmora, Alberto, *Viaggio in Sardegna* (Turin, Fréres Bocco, 1860)
Dudgeon, Timothy, *Bats, Baronets and Battle: A Social History of Cricket and Cricketers from an East Sussex Town* (Bloomington IN, AuthorHouse, 2013)
Dyson, Stephen, and Rowland, Robert J jr, *Shepherds, Sailors and Conquerors: Archaeology and History in Sardinia from the Stone Age to the Middle Ages* (Philadelphia PA, University of Pennsylvania Museum of Archaeology and Anthropology, 2007)
Fadda, Paolo, *La Montevecchio di Alberto Castoldi* (Sassari, Carlo Delfino Editore, 2014)
Francioni, Federico, *Vespro Sarde: Dagli esordi della dominazione Piemontesse all'Insurrezione del 28 Aprile 1794* (Cagliari, Condaghes, 2001)
Frau, Antonio et al, *Millelire: Una Famiglia e le sue Mille Storie* (La Maddalena, Paolo Sorba Editore, 2013)
Giannone, Pietro, *The Civil History of the Kingdom of Naples* vol. 2 (London, W Innys, 1729–31)
Hobart Michelle, ed., *A Companion to Sardinian History, 500–1500* (Leiden, Brill Academic, 2017). *See also under* Chapters in Hobart, Michelle, ed., *A Companion to Sardinian History 500–1500*
King, Georgiana, illustrations by Giles, Anna Rose, *Comedies and Legends for Marionettes: A Theatre for Boys and Girls* (London, Macmillan and Co, 1904)
Lang, Cecil Y and Shannon, Edward Finley, *The Letters of Alfred Lord Tennyson 1851–1870* (Cambridge, MA, Harvard University Press, 1987)
Lecis, Vindice, *Buiakesos: Le Guardie del Giudice* (Cagliari, Condaghes, 2014)
Levi, Carlo, *Tutto il Miele è Finito* (Turin, Einaudi, 1964)
Lilliu, Giovanni, *Sculture della Sardegna Nuragica* (Cagliari, Edizioni della Zattera, 1956; Nuoro, Ilisso, 2008)

Lussu, Emilio, *Enter Mussolini: Observations and Adventures of an Anti Fascist* (London, Methuen, 1936; London, Taylor & Francis, 2010)
Maccioni, Antonio, *101 Tesori Nascosti della Sardegna: da vedere una volta nella vita* (Rome, Newton Compton Editori, 2012)
Martini, P, *Storia delle Invasioni degli Arabi e delle Pirateri dei Barbareschi in Sardegna* (Cagliari, A Timon, 1861)
Mastino, Attilio, *Storia della Sardegna Antica* (Nuoro, il Maestrale, c.2009)
Melis, Paolo, *Civiltà Nuragica* (Sassari, Carlo Delfino Editore, 2003)
Melis, Paolo, *The Nuragic Civilization* (Sassari, Carlo Delfino Editore, 2003)
Mill, John Stuart, *The Subjection of Women* (London, Longman, Green, Reader & Dyer, 1869)
Monier, MH, *Lettres sur la Sardaigne* (Lyon, Léon UOITHL, 1849; facsimile reprint available)
Partridge, Frank, *TAB: A Memoire of Thomas Allnutt Brassey, Second Earl Brassey* (Portsmouth, Partridge, Frank, Bishop, 1921)
Piercy, Benjamin Herbert, translated Raffaele Cherchi, *La Sardegna dei Miei Ricordi* (Cagliari, Zonza Editori, 2008)
Pintor, Giovanni Siotto, *see* Siotto-Pintor
Rodd, Sir James Rennell, *Social and Diplomatic Memories* (London, E Arnold, 1922)
Ross, Alan, *South to Sardinia* (London, Hamish Hamilton, 1960)
Rowland, Robert J jr, *The Periphery in the Center: Sardinia in the Ancient and Medieval Worlds* (Oxford, Archaeopress, 2001)
Serra, Pierluigi, *Sardegna Misteriosa ed Esotica: Il Lato occulto, maladetto e oscuro dell'Isola piu magica del Mediterraneo* (Rome, Newton Compton Editori, 2018)
Seymour, Victoria, *Letters from Lavender Cottage: Hastings in World War One and Austerity* (Hastings?, printed 2001)
Sienkiewicz, Henryk (Marie Doran), *Quo Vadis* (London, Dent, 1897)
Siotto-Pintor, Giovanni, *Storia Letteraria di Sardegna* (1843–4; reprinted Bologna, Forni, 1966)
Smyth, William Henry, *Sketch of the Present State of the Island of Sardinia* (London, John Murray, 1828)
Storrs, Christopher, *War, Diplomacy and the Rise of Savoy 1690–1720* (New York, Cambridge University Press, 1999)
Todde, Giovanni, *Storia di Nuoro e delle Barbagie* (Cagliari, Editrice Sarda Fossataro, 1971)
Tolomeo, Claudio, *Geografia* (*c*.AD 15; Venice, Vincenzo Valgrisi, 1561)
Tyndale, John Warre, *The Island of Sardinia, Including Pictures of the Manners and Customs of Sardinians* (London, R Bentley, 1849; available scanned in separate volumes – BiblioBazaar)
Valentini, Chiara, *Enrico Berlinguer* (Cagliari, Feltrinelli Universale Economica, 2014)
Valery, Antoine-Claude Pasquin, *Voyages en Corse, a l'Île d'Elbe et en Sardaigne*, vol. 2 (Paris, L Bourteois-Maze, 1837)
Varro, Marcus Terentius, *De Re Rustica* (1st published 39–36 BC; London, Loeb Classical Library, 1934)
Walsh, Brian, *James Phillips Webber: the Man and the Mystery* (Paterson NSW, CB Alexander Foundation, 2008)
Webster, Gary, *A Prehistory of Sardinia 2300–500 BC* (Sheffield, Sheffield Academic Press, c.1996)
Zacks, Richard, *The Pirate Coast: Thomas Jefferson, the First Marines, and the Secret Mission of 1805* (New York, Hyperion, 2005)

Articles and Chapters, General

Babbi, Andrea, 'Clay Human Figurines from "Nuragi" Sardinia' XLIV 2009 *Riunione Scientifica – la preistoria e la protoistoria della Sardegna*
Bruce, Travis, 'The Politics of Violence and Trade: Denia and Pisa in the eleventh Century', (2006) 32 (2) *Journal of Medieval History*, 127–142
D'Oriano, Rubens, '*Kouroi* in Sardinia' (2004) 21 *Quaderni*

Gwyther, John R, 'Nelson and Aostino Millelire' (2005) 15 *The Trafalgar Chronicle: Year book of the 1905 Club*
Lebeuf, Arnold, 'The Nuragic Well of Santa Cristina, Paulilatino, Oristano, Sardinia. A Verification of the Astronomical Hypothesis: Work in Process, Preliminary Results' (2008) 10 *Archaeologica Baltica* 20 September
Reidy, Denis V, 'Lord Nelson, HMS *Victory* and Sardinia – A Forgotten Episode?' (2007) 2 *eBLJ*
Rolston, Bill, 'Resistance and Pride: The Murals of Orgosolo, Sardinia' (2014) 3(1) *State Crime* 73-101
Soddu, Alessandro, '*I pàperos ("poveri") nella Sardegna giudicale (XI–XII secolo)*' (2008) 29 *Acta Historica Archaeologica Mediaevalia* 29 205–255
Strinna, Giovanni, '*La Carta di Nicita e la Clausula Defensionis*' (2009) II *Boletino di Studi Sardi*
Strinna, Giovanni, '*Monache Viaggiatrici tra Sardegna e Toscana: Le badesse di S Maria di Asca e S Pietro di Silki*' in Gemma Colesanti et al eds, *I Monachesimo femminile nel mezzogionro peninsulae e insulare (XI–XVI secolo): fondazioni, ordini, reti, committenza* (Cagliari, Istituto di Storia dell'Europa Mediterranea, 2018)
Tangheroni, Marco, 'Sardinia and Corsica from the Mid-Twelfth to the Early Fourteenth Century' in Rosamond McKitterick et al, *The New Cambridge Medieval History*, vol 5 (Cambridge, Cambridge University Press, 1995)
Wright, OJ, 'Sea and Sardinia: Pax Britannica versus Vendetta in the New Italy (1870)' (2012) 37(3) *European History Quarterly* 398–416
Wright, OJ, 'Between Italy and Africa: British Perspectives on Nineteenth-Century Sardinia' in Stefano Villani et al eds, *Travels and Translations: Anglo-Italian Cultural Transactions* (Amsterdam and New York, Rodopi, 2013) 11–134
Zedda, Corrado, '"*Amani Judicis*" o "*la manu judicis*"? *Il ricordo di una regola procedurale non rispettata in una lettera dell'arcivescovo Guglielmo di Cagliari (1118)*' (2012) 9 *Revista dell'Istituto di Storia dell'Europa Mediterranea* December

Chapters in Hobart, Michelle, ed., A Companion to Sardinian History 500–1500 (Leiden, Brill Academic Publishers, 2017) (also available as an e-book)

Galoppini, Laura, 'Overview of Sardinian History (500–1500)'
Hobart, Michelle, 'Sardinia as a Crossroads in the Mediterranean: An Introduction'
Martorelli, Rossana, 'Cagliari: Historiography and History of the Archaeology of Cagliari'
Milanese, Marco, 'Catalan Alghero'
Murgia, Giovanni, 'Spanish Sardinia: Conflicts and Alliances'
Ortu, Gian Giacomo, 'Establishing Power and Law in Medieval and Modern Sardinia'
Tasca, Cecilia, 'Jews in Sardinia'
Turtas, Raimondo, 'The Sardinian Church'
Zedda, Corrado, 'A Revision of Sardinian History Between the Eleventh and Twelfth Centuries'

Dissertations

Anon (B042857), 'During the period of Carthaginian colonial presence on Sardinia, to what extent should the Carthaginian relations with the Sardinian population from the sixth to the second centuries BC be regarded in terms of either dualism or hybridization?' (Ancient History and Classical Archaeology (MA) (Hons) (nd)
Bruce, Travis, 'The Taifa of Denia and the Medieval Mediterranean' (509, Western Michigan University, 2010)
Cocco, Maria Bastiana, '*Servi e Liberti nella Sardegna Romana alla Luce della Documentazione Epigrafica*' (Dipartimento di Storia, University of Sassari, 2009–10)

Erriu, Marzia, *'Il Viceré Des Hayes e il Governo del Regnum Sardiniae'* (Universita degli Studi di Cagliari, 2012)
Pilkington, Nathan, 'An Archaeological History of Carthaginian Imperialism' (Graduate School of Arts and Sciences, Columbia University, 2013)

Newspapers, Magazines and Articles in them (also available on the internet)

Anon, *'Qyel Tessuto Ce Viene de Mare'*, *La Nuova Sardegna* (2004)
Anon, *'Vincolo su Villa Tamponi'*, *La Nuova Sardegna* (2006)
Blackwood's Edinburgh Magazine (1849)
Bassu, Antonio, *'Lina Merlin, Esiliata in Barbagia'*, *La Nuova Sardegna*, 8 March 2008
Boccia, Maria Luisa, *'Nadia Spana: La Donna del Mese'*, *Noi Donne* (2009)
'Dimissioni in Massa del Circolo Bussalai', *La Nuova Sardegna* (2011)
Farina, Pasquito, *'Il ricordo di Margherita Sanna'*, *La Nuova Sardegna* (16 December 2016)
Floris, Carlo, *'Il Mistero dei "beronicenses": antichi cortigani della regina?'*, *La Nuova Sardegna* (2007)
Gerbri, Sandro, *'Una Bella Storia Anti-fascista'*, *Corriere della Serra* (19 November 1993)
Giles, Anna Rose, letter, (Bryn Mawr) *College News* (January 2015)
'Girl from Bryn Mawr killed in Sardinia', *Washington Post* and *New York Times*
La Donna e la Civilità, Sassari (1975)
Hoe, Susanna, 'Pope Gregory and the Disputes of Abbess Pomponiana of Sardinia', *History Today* (June 2018)
'Il Buddenrook sassarese che fece di Montevecchio una capitale mineraria europea', *La Nuova Sardegna* (18 October 2010)
'Lady Athletes in England', *Boston Evening Transcript* (5 September 1889)
Mameli, Giacomo, *'Addio a Giuliana Lai, Compagna di Sogni della Sorella Maria'*, *La Nuova Sardegna* (8 July 2012)
Meloni, Antonio, *'Il Racconto della Sommossa del 1780 di Frate Sisco'*, *La Nuova Sardegna* (26 March 2001)
New York Times (20 May 1917) (letter from Helen Dunstan Wright)
Nuoro Littoria [Fascist newspaper re lesbians]
Paradiso, Max, 'Chiara Vigo: The Last Woman Who Makes Sea Silk', *BBC History Magazine* (September 2015)
'Paska Devadis, amore e disamistade' based on work of Anna Tilocca Segreti, *La Nuova Sardegna* (27 March 2009)
Sana, Roberto, *'Il Condaghe Svela il Medioevo Silki, I Benedettini Raccontano'*, *La Nuova Sardegna* (2 March 2014)
Scano, Daniela, 'Miss Giles', *La Nuova Sardegna* (2011)
'Women Here and There', *New York Times Supplement*
Wright, Helen Dunstan, 'Little-Known Sardinia (1916)' XXX(2) *National Geographic* magazine Washington, August (published in Italian as *Sardegna quasi sconosciuta*, Zonzi editore, 2005)

Manuscripts and Unpublished Documents

Borbone, Maria Cristina di, *il Diario 1813–1814* (Biblioteca Studi Sardi del Commune di Cagliari)
Desogus, Francesca and Oppo, Anna Maria, notes on 'Il Diario di Maria Cristina di Borbone', paper given in 2012, *Biblioteca Studi Sardi del commune di Cagliari*
Hargrave, Lewis, 'The Humble Memorial of Lewis Hargrave...' 16 July 1804, ref U840/095, Kent History Library
Hargrave, Lewis, 'Will of Lewis Chadwick Hargrave, His Majesty's Consul General for the Balearic ...' 12 July 1838, ref PROB 11/1898/45, National Archives, Kew

Hargraves, Anna Porcile, letter of 31 December 1805, written from London to William Eaton, Eaton Papers, Huntington Library, Los Angeles
Ludovisi, Costanza Pamphili, letter written from Sassari to Olimpia Giustiniani Barberini (1 December 1662) Rome, Vatican Library, BAV Barberini Carteggi 41, 751r
Scott, Alexander John, 'Autograph letter, 4th May 1804, signed to Agostino Millelire (Alexander John Scott, 1768–1840, Nelson's Chaplain and Foreign Language on Board "Victory")'

YouTube Videos

Anna Marongiu
Bella Ciao
Castello Montiferru (Francesca Zafrillas)
Edina Altara
Ingurtosu
Iride Peis Concas
Lollove (Barbagia)
Lugherras
Maccioni, Mariangela, mural by Francesco del Casino (3rd image)
Mazzoli, Missy, trailer for *Song from the Uproar: The Lives and Deaths of Isabelle Eberhardt*
Museo Storico Emilio e Joyce Lussu, Armungia
Pozzo La Testa
Seta Orgosolo
Sorelle Corneo
Villa d'Orri, Sarroch
Work of Artist Maria Lai, Ulassai, Sardegna

Reference (may also be online)

Abulafia, David, ed., *The New Cambridge Medieval History*, vol V, *c.*1198–1300 (Cambrdige, Cambridge University Press, 1991)
Artizzu, Francesco, '*Benedetta di Massa*' in *Dizionario Biografico degli Italiani* (Istituto dell'Enciclopedia Italiana, 1966)
Aubert de la Chesnaye des Bois, Francois Alexandre, *Dictionaire de la Noblesse: Contenant les généalogies, l'histoire et la chronologie de familles nobles de France* (1876)
Barnett, RD, *Tharros: A Catalogue of Material in the British Museum* (London, British Museum Publications, 1987)
Bernardini, Paolo et al, *Il Museo Archaeologico Nazionale di Cagliari* (Sassari, Carlo Delfino Editore, 2016)
Brunelli, Giampiero, 'Niccolò Ludovisi' in *Dizionario Biographico degli Italiani* (Istituto dell'Enciclopedia Italiana, 1960–)
Casalis, Gofreddo, *Dizionario Geografico, Storico, Statistico, Commerciale degli Stati di SM il Re di Sardegna* (Turin, Presso G Maspero, 1833–1856)
Catholic Encyclopedia: Sardinia (online edition)
Christiani, Kerry and Garwood, Duncan, *Sardinia* (Lonely Planet Publications, 2015)
Dictionary of Art Historians: A Biographical Dictionary of Historic Scholars, Museum Professionals and Academic Historians of Art, Lee Sorenson ed. http:/www.arthistorians.info
Dictionnaire de la Noblesse (Paris, La Veuve Duchesne, 1770–1786)
Dizionario Biografico degli Italiani (Italy, Istituto dell'Enciclopedia Italiana, 1960–present)
Dizionario Bibliografico degli Uomini Illustri di Sardegna (Turin, Tipografia Chirio e Mina, 1838)
Guide to Archaeological Sites in Sardinia: The 100 most important monuments from the Neolithic to the Roman Age (Nuoro, Imago Multimedia, 2010)
Ilan, Tal, 'Berenice' in *Jewish Women: A Comprehensive Historical Encyclopedia* (Jewish Women's Archive, March 2009)

Nora Tourist Guide (Olbia, R Balzano Edizione, 2016)
Oxford Dictionary of National Biography, The (Benjamin Piercy) (Oxford, Oxford University Press, 2004–)
Picciau, Maura, 'Anna Marongiu Pernis' in *Dizionario Biografico degli Italiani* (Istituto dell'Enciclopedia Italiana, 1960–)
Pupurello, Alfredina, *Tavolara: Paesi, Citta, Regioni della Sardegna* (Sassari, Carlo Delfino Editore, 2012)
Sardinia, Insight Guides (nd)
Singer, Isidore ed., *The Jewish Encyclopedia: A Descriptive Record of the History, Religion, Literature, and Customs of the Jewish People from the Earliest Times to the Present Day* (New York, Funk & Wagnalls, 1901–1906; reprinted 1960s; now in public domain)
Spano, Giovanni, *La Guida della Citta e Dintorno di Cagliari* (Cagliari, Timon, 1861; 2nd edn 2012)

DonnaSarda Website (in abeyance since Autumn 2017)

Atzei, Annachiara, '*Donna Violante Carròs, la contessa dissortada*' (2015)
Atzei, Annachiara, '*Giuanna Zonca, Quando l'anima vuole tornare a casa*' (2015)
Atzei, Annachiara, '*La Leggenda di Luzia Arrabiosa*' (2016)
Atzei, Annachiara, '*Rosa Gambella la nobile tradita dall'onore*' (2016)
Atzei, Annachaira, '*Sofia Bonorcili, vita violate dai pirati rinnegati*' (2016)
'*Georgiana Goddard King: Una Suffragetta Americana in Sardegna*'
Gianfico, Matilde '*Sa Reina nel regno del crimine: regina di giorno e brigante al notte*' (2016)
Ginesu, Federica, '*Mariangela Maccioni la maestra resistente che sfidò il fascismo*' (2014)
Ginesu, Federica, '*Adelasia Torres, l'altra giudicessa*' (2015)
Ginesu, Federica, '*Lucia Delitala Tedde: la nobile bandita fuorilegge*' (2016)
Ginesu, Federica, '*La Storia delle Suffragette Sarde*' (2016)
Ginesu, Federica, '*L'Indomita Marchesa, Donna Francesca di Zatrillas*' (2016)
La Leggendaria Fulvia Riccardino, Cagliaritana Classe 1928: La Prima Ingenera della Sardegna
Muntoni, Cristina, '*Francesca Sanna Sulis: l'imprenditrice del gelso*' (2014)
Muntoni, Cristina, '*Benedetta, la Giudicessa di Cagliari che cedette Castello ai Pisani*' (2015)
Saba, Virginia, '*La Prima Sardista: Marianna Bussalai tra poesia, ironia e femminismo*' (2014)
Scano, Ilaria Muggianu, '*Atte, amante di Nerone. La Sardegna come via di scampo*' (2016)
Scano, Ilaria Muggianu, '*Mimi di Borbone: Una regina alla moda alla corte di Carlo Felice*' (2016)

Internet Material (website not always given here; best to put name, author or title into browser; dates often missing online)

Accati, Elena, '*Un Esempio di Donna Dotata di Straordinario Talento per la Ricerca*' (2013)
Amat, Paolo, '*Notizie sui Manca desunte dale Regie provisioni dell'Archivo di Cagliari*' (1810–1814)
'An English Man in Arbus: Lord Brassey' (Blue Mines, nd)
AntonRiva (blog), '*Invasione Barbaresca di Carloforte 3 Settembre 1798*', 2016, www.carloforte-isoladisanpietro.over-blog.com
http://araldicasardegna.org/genealogie/albe
Archeologia mineraria in Sardegna, htpp://minieredisardegna.it (eg Elena Poinsel)
Ardu, Anna, '*Tharros in Età Romana*' (nd)
'*Assalto a Sant'Antioco*' in Sant'Antioco Gestione Archivi, www.studio87.it (2010)
Atzei, Giampaolo, '*Politica e Società nella Sardegna Mineraria del Novecento*' *Ammentu*, n.3, gennaio-dicembre 2013
Bardanzella, Federico, '*Il Caso dei fratelli Puzzu: fu vero "banditism"?*' (nd)
Beshah-Woured, Yeweinshet, 2010 Testimony, conducted by Roman Herzog, 18 April 2010
Blog, Eretz, '*31 Marzo 1492: Edicto de expulsion de los judios*', 2007

Bollettino Storico, Archivistico e Consolare del Mediterraneo (2013)
Bonaria Cemetery *see* chs 10, 13
Branca, Elena, '*Satta, Paula*' (nd)
Branca, Elena, '*Dottoresse al fronte: l'esordio vitaminevaganti*' (2019)
Byron-Hobhouse Correspondence, 1808–1812 (Spain and Sardinia, July 24th–August 30th 1809) http://petercochran. files.wordpress.com
'*Cagliari: le case della Marina*' http://storiadicase.jimdo.com
Candiani, Laura, '*Lucia Delitala Tedde: Quando le Donne Sarde Cominciarono a "Banditare"*' (2019) *le Storie, Numero 16, Storie e Filosofia*
Cannas, Rita, 'The Sustainable Tourism Management of Cultural Heritage: The Case of the Rosas Mine in Sardinia' (2016) 14 *Journal of Tourism, Culture and Territorial Development*
Canudu, Rosella, '*Il Diario di una Maestrina del 1957: Maria Giacobbe, l'insegnante che (per fortuna) non va in vacanze*' (2012)
Castelli, Evelyne, '*Garibaldi et les Niçois*' (2012)
Cau, Paolo, '*Dal Diario di Francesco d'Austria-Este: I due Soggiorni in Sardegna*' http://quaderniestensi.beniculturali.it (2014)
Chirra, Cristina, '*Nuoro e il Fascismo*' (1995) http://*comune.serdiana.ca.it*
Congiu, Francesca, 'Contested Places: Carlo Levi's post colonial discourse in *Tutto il Miele è Finito*' (2012)
Contu, Maria Lidia, '*Maria Manca Colombo: La Prima Giornalista che Diede Voce alle Donne Sarde*' (2018)
Corrias, Angela, 'Preserving Ancient Silk Art in Orgosolo, Sardinia, with Master Maria Corda'
Cossu, Carla and Angiolillo, Simonetta, '*Lo Sapevate? Un tempio dedicato ad Adone e Venere dove oggi sorgono le poste di piazza de carmine*' (2017)
Da Pelo, Stefania, 'The abandoned mining area of Montevecchio-Ingurtosu' (2001)
Demuru, Ornelia, '*Francesca Sanna Sulis: "La Signora dei Gelsi", una Donna Sada Dimenticata per Troppo Tempo*' (2012*)*
Deriu, Michela, 'Nessuno è Perfetto!' (2014)
Di San Raimondo, Luigi Orrù, '*Albergo Genealogico della Famiglia Porcile*', http://famiglienobilidisardegna.org
Fanni, Enrico, '*Paola Satta, la Prima Donna Medica Sarda*', facebook (nd)
Fanni, Enrico, '*Medicina: una carriera anche per le donne*' (nd)
Farina, Pasquito, '*Il Ricordo di Margherita Sanna*' (2016)
Fiorensoli, Maria Paola '*Parità è illusione: il percorso delle donne in Giustizia e Libertà nel Partito d'Azione*' (2016)
Fonnesu, Federico, '*La città scomparsa: Santa Igia, l'antica capitale del giudicato di Cagliari sommersa dal cemento tra costruzioni e strade nel moderna Sant'Avendrace*' (March 2017)
Fouché, Guy-Joseph, '*Francesca Rosso et les Carlofortins*' in Josyanne Massa '*Tabarquins*'
Francioni, Federico, '*La Presenza delle Donne*', Lingua Cultura (nd)
Francioni, Federico, '*La Storia di Una Sassari Ribelle*' (2017)
'*I fatti – 29 Aprile 1918: Il Sommergibile entro in porto …*' www.isoladisanpietro.org
'*Il Nome Tocoele*', Associazione Archaeologica Culturale Tocoele
'*Il Rientro degli Schiavi (non di tuti)*', www.hieracon.it
Garroni, M, '*La Sardegna Durante Ventennio Fascista*' (2010)
Gasperetti, Gabriella, et al, '*Viaggi, Navi e Porti della Sardinia e della Corsica Attraverso La Documentazione Epigrafica*' (2014)
Giani, Stefano, '*l'Ultima amante di Garibaldi e la fuga da Caprera*' (2008)
Ginesu, Federica, '*Caterina Berlinguer, la prima donna a dirigere un giornale in Sardegna*' (2017)
Grassi, Cristina, '*Claudia Casu's Filindeu*' (2018)
Goracci, Doriana, '*Una Miniera di Donne Dimenticate: le cernitrici di Montevecchio e le altre*' (2017)
Govino, Paola, 'The Making of Italo-Calvino: Eva-Mameli-Calvino, and her Laboratory Garden' (conference paper 2014)

Gregory, Tessa, 'Ancient Phoenician DNA Tells a Story of Settlement and Female Mobility' (Plos Research News, 2018)
Gwyther, John R, 'Nelson and Aostino Millelirc' (2005)
Hendel, Carlo, '*Asinara, un posto nella storia etiope*', in (2019) 1 *Academia, Ambiente, Cultura ed Arte*, November
Hill, William Noel-, Dispatches from Cagliari to Foreign Office, from 13 June 1808–21 May 1816. http:/search.shropshirehistory.org.uk
'*I Congresso Donne Sarde' di Assarchivi*', 7 March 2018
'*Ines Berlinguer: protagonista della Resistenza*', *L'UnioneSarda.it*
'Kernowclimber at Purple Peak Adventures: A blog devoted to outdoor pursuits and adventure travel' (2012/13)
King, Martha, 'The "Attitos" of Sardinia: An interview with Dolores Turchi' (1988)
King, Rufus, Letter to James Madison of 14 December 1801, James Madison Papers, Library of Congress
Lemaire, JB, '*Apel a Temoins Recherchons "Tabarchins"*', www.bone.piednoir.net
'*Les Tabarquins de Tunis 1741–1799*' in (1943) 53 and 54 *Revue Tunisienne* 1er et 2éme trimester, www.procida-family.com
Longu, Pierpaolo and Ruggeri, Paola, '*Un Nuovo Bollo Laterizio dalla Necropoli Romana di Monte Carru-Alghero (SS)*' (nd)
Macellari, Elena, '*La Primavera nel Giardino delle Esperidi: I tesori di Milis e dell'entrottera Sardo*' (2015)
Madau, Bastiana, blog, '*l'antifascismo da madre à madre*' carteblancheblogspot.com (2010)
Madau, Bastiana, blog, '*Le eredi del corbulaio*' (8 March 2010) cartebianche.blogspot.com
Malgosa i Morea, Assumpció (see Piga)
'*Marchesa del Marghine, La Duchessa di Benavente e Gandia e il concordato con il Regio Fisco*' (Associazione cavalieri Macomer)
'*Maria Cocco, paladina della magistratura al femminile*' (Unione Sarda, 2017)
Massa, Josyanne and Gander, George, '*Tabarquins: Les Rosso de Carloforte Pris en Esclave en 1798*' (2006)
Mastino, Attilio, '*Persistenze preistoriche e sopravvivenze romane nel Condaghe di San Pietro di Silki*' *Diritto e Storia*, UnissResearch, 2002
Matisoo-Smith, E, 'Ancient Mitogenomes of Phoenicians from Sardinia and Lebanon: A Story of Settlement, Integration and Female Mobility' (Plos, 2018)
Meridda, Angelo (re: Pernis and Milis) http://angelomeridda.it
Message boards, www.boards.rootsweb.com
Murgia, Giangavino, '*La Tesimonianza della giornalista Americana Anna Rose Giles*', '*La Cronaca dell'alluvione del 10 settembre 1921*', '*OLZAI, Appunti per una Storia: l'arginamento nel rio Bisine*', 20 September 2014
Murtas, Gianfranco, '*La questione femminile al convegno del 60 della FIDAPA Cagliaritana*' (2015)
Murtas, Gianfranco, '*Nel Camposanto di Bonaria, Celebrando le Memorie dei Massoni Cagliaritani di Fine Ottocento/Primo Novecento*, 2018, http://fondazionesardinia.eu
Murtas, Gianfranco, '*Fra Garibaldi il sardo universale e Goffredo Memeli martire della Republic Romana*' in *Massonicamente: Laboratorio di Storia Grande Oriente d'Italia*, n 16 set-dec 2019 (Edoarda Berlinguer)
'*Nadia Gallico Spano, madre della costituente*' (*L'Unione Sarda*, nd)
'*Narcao: La Miniera Rosas in attività 1851 al 1980*' http://www.myheritage.com
Onnis, Agnese, '*Giorgino: Una Targa col Nome di Joyce Lussu*' (2014)
Patatu, Carlo, '*Il celebre bandito Giovanni Fais*' (Chiara Unali) 2007
Petrignani, Sandra, (blog) '*Ricordo di Maria Lai*' (il Foglio, 18/5/2013)
Pi, Effe, '*Cagliari: L'Archeodisastro di Santa Igia*' (nd)
Piga, G et al, 'A Case of Semi-combusted Pregnant Female in the Phoenician-Punic Necropolis of Monte Sirai (Carbonia, Sardinia, Italy)' *Journal of Comparative Human Biology* (Teeside University's Research Repository, 2015)
Piras, Lidia, '*Albina e Giuseppina Coroneo*', *Enciclopedia delle Donne* (nd)

Piras, Natalino (blog) 'L'eroismo quotidiano di Margherita Sanna, sindaco di Orune' (2011)
Plaisant, Luisa Maria, 'Le Donne Cagliaritane e la Prima Guerra Mondiale' (Consiglio comunale di Cagliari 20 novembre 2018)
'Poemas del rio Wang: Treasure of the Jews' (including marriage of Bella bat Merwanha ha-Sheniri), blogspot, 2015
Portas, Sergio, 'Una Fiaba d'Altri Tempi Pensando Alla Lontana Montevecchio: Incontro a Milano con Rosalba Marianni per il Libro "Miniera"', 2012
'Processo per il Possesso di Servi' Materiali Barisone, Condaghe di San Pietro di Silki n.205, 2013
Pusceddu, Enrico, 'I Retabli Sardi nella Storiagrafica Americana del Primo Novecento' in Pusceddu, Enrico, *Joan Barceló II (gia Maestro di Castelsardo): Questioni di pittura in Sardegna intorno al 1500* (Universitat de Barcelona, Department d'Història de l'Art, 2013)
'Ritratto di Don Raimondo de Quesada Famiglie Nobili, genealogia ed araldica in Sardegna' (nd)
Rivano, Antonello (blog), 'Francesca Rosso: da Schiava e Sposa e Madre di Bey', 2016, www.Caroloforte-isoladisanpietro.over-blog.com
Ruggeri, Paola, 'La Liberta Amata da Nerone, Claudia Atte' (2015)
Ruggeri, Paola, 'Esiliati in Sardegna: Claudia Atte, la Liberta Amata da Nerone ad Olbia' (2017)
Ruggeri, Paola and Cocco, Maria Bastiana, 'Nel Segno di Sardo: Donne di Potere, Donne di Popolo: Il lavoro delle donne in Sardegna in epoca romana', 8 March 2012
Sanna, Claudia, 'Il Culto di Santa Giusta, Santa Giustina e Santa Enedina in Sardegna' (Mare Calmo, 2017)
'Santa Chiara: Oristano, Viaggio Attraverso l'Architetettura' (nd)
'Sardegna del Settecento Come Stato d'Antico Regime' (nd)
'The return of the slaves (not all)' Hiera.it
Scano, Ilaria Muggianu, 'La Scrittrice delle Miniere: l'Opera Letteraria della Semisconosciuta Amelia Melis De Villa' (2012)
Scano, Ilaria Muggianu, 'La Cosa Legava la Figura di Ellen Rose Giles alla Sardegna? Un caso ancora insoluto' (2015)
Secci, Maria Cristina, 'Ritratto di Eva Mameli Calvino' (talk given, l'Hortus Botanicus Karalitanus, Dipartimento di Filologia, Letteratura e Linguistica, University of Cagliari 2016)
Secci, Veronica, '4 Maggio 1871: La tragedia di Montevecchio – Muoiono in Miniera 11 Operaie' (2016)
Serra, Efisio Lippi, *Storia, leggende, arte e culto dell'acqua in Sardegna e nel mondo* (2003)
Seu, Silvia, 'Frammenti di Dissenso' (2020)
Strazza, Michele, 'La Nascita dei Movimenti Politici Femminile nel Dopoguerra' (nd) www.win.storiain.net num 191, art 4
Strinna, Giovanni, 'Monache Viaggiatrici tra Sardegna e Toscana. Le badesse di S Maria di Asca e di S Pietro di Silki' (2018)
'Suor Giuseppina De Muro FdC, Figlie della Carità di San Vincenzo de Paoli'
'Timbòra' in 'Personaggi, Re, Giudici (e mogli, figlie di giudici) della Sardegna Antica' (nd)
Tusceri, Gian-Carlo, 'La Maddalena, Base Inglese nel Mediterraneo Tra il 1794 e il 1805', (1998) 57(1) *Cahiers de la Méditerranée*, 125–130
Tuveri, Matteo, 'Sardigna de Lacon: La "Signora" del Romanico in Sardegna' (nd)
Usai, Alessandro, 'Cabras (OR). L'insediamento nuragico di Sa Osa' (2012)
Vulpes, Gianni, 'Don Vincenzo Serra-Delogu e la rivolta antifeudal ittirese'
Wilson, David, 'Consular Officials in the Ottoman Empire' (2011)
Zanda, Giuliano, 'I Pernis: una famiglia di imprenditori cagliaritani di origine svizzera e l'attività consolare svolta nel capoluogo sardo tra Ottocento e Novecento' Ammentu, n 3, gennaio-dicembre 2013

Index

For reasons of length, and possible confusion, it would be impractical to include here all the many women mentioned by name in the text. Included, therefore, are those who play a substantial or significant part there. Husbands are usually omitted, though if significant to the narrative they may be in brackets after their wife. In order to draw strands together, individual women may be combined into different categories; an example is that which begins the index – Activists during the First World War. There is also a separate entry 'Women' which lists other matters that concern them, such as equality, land owning, and pregnancy. Typical of other combined categories are Churches and Museums.

Activists and organisations (women) during the First World War
   Cordeliane Association 270; Amelia Melis Devilla 270–1; Bastianina Martini Musu 269–70; National Women's Union (*Unione Femminile Nazionale* – UFN) 267–9; Lina Tronci Pernis 268–9; Dr Paola Satta 267–8
Adelasia, *Giudicessa* of Logudoro-Torres 61, 68, 70–2
Alghero xiii, 28, 87–90, 97, 99, 113, 116, 118, 202, 252–8, 261, 301
Anedda, Antonella (poems and La Maddalena) 36, 143, 177–8
Angioy-Belgrano family (Marina, Cagliari) 118–22
Anti-fascist women activists (see also Lussu, Emilio, and Mussolini, Benito)
   Ines Berlinguer 263–4, 294–6; Marianna Bussalai xii, 1, 302–3, 308–12, 323–4; Sister Giuseppina Demuro 297–9; Graziella Sechi Giacobbe 305–8; Joyce Lussu 288–94, 296, 304, 307, 313, 321, 323–4; Mariangela Maccioni 302–6, 308; Lisa Merlin 296–7; Fulvia Riccardino 299–301
Archaeological phases and sites (see also Nuragic)
   Hunter gatherers (Stone Age) 4; Homo Sapiens 4–5; Neolithic (Filiestru Cave) 5–6; Bonu Ighinu (Cuccuru S'Arriu – Tharros) 6–7; Ozieri (San Gemiliano-Sestu – Gulf of Cagliari; Genna Arrele; Montessu – Villaperuccio, Serra Is Araus-Cabras (Oristano) 7; Monte Claro (Biriai – Oliena) 9–10; Bell Beaker 10; Bonnanaro – Sassari (Cave Lanaittu Valley – Dorgali; Sisaia) 10–11
Artists (women)
   Altara sisters (Edina, Iride and Lavinia) 277–9; Liliana Canu 121; *Sorelle* Coroneo (Giusepina and Albina) 276–7;

Nicolina Deledda 274–5; Maria Lai 279–86; *Le Api* 155; Elisabeth Vigée Lebrun 131; Anna Pernis Marongiu 120, 208–9; Olimpia Melis 275; Marina Virdis 210
Asinara island 115, 132, 258, 262 (see also Ethiopians and exile)
Attitudes towards and of Sardinians
   Foreign visitors 2, 36, 222–3, 230, 236, 244, 253, 281; Italians ('Continentals', relations between and Sardism) xii, 1, 253, 309–10, 312, 323; Romans 35–6

Baccaro, Laura 147, 149, 158–9
Banditesse (women bandits) 138, 147
   Paska Devaddis 152–6, 247; Giuseppa Lunesu 150–1; Marianna Serra Sana (Sa Reina) 149–52; Lucia Delitala Tedde 147–9; Chiara Unali 148–9
Barbagia region 33, 44, 138, 144–6, 149, 153, 155–9, 195, 247, 251, 255, 265, 279, 290, 300, 302, 304, 307–8, 310–11, 320, 323
Baule, Maria of Poaghe (poet) 116–17
Benedetta, *Giudicessa* of Cagliari 61, 71, 73–7
Berlinguer, Edoarda 95–6 (see also Magazines – Caterina, and anti-fascists – Ines)
Bertoleoni royal family (Tavolara) 198–201
Bonorcili, Sofia 94 (murdered in a raid)
Bosa 72, 89, 275–6, 288, 305
Britain (the British; relationship with) 107, 125–9, 139, 142, 170, 173–6, 180, 184, 188, 193–4, 197, 207–8, 220, 222, 230, 233–42, 290, 301, 320–1
Budin, Stephanie and sacred prostitution 45

Cagliari (see also Churches, Convents, and Museums)
   Caralis (early name) 27, 30, 34, 38, 41, 46, 49–50, 53, 77–8; Castello (district)

72, 75–6, 82, 89, 95, 103, 105, 119, 124, 203, 205, 232, 235, 270, 277; Marina (district) 119–20, 183, 206, 213, 277, 300
Calvino, Eva Mameli (botanist; University of Cagliari Botanic Garden) 271–4
Carcassona, family 89–90, 113–16, 128–9 (see also Feudalism and Royalty)
Cardona, Maria, *Viceregina* 95–6 (accused of witchcraft)
Carolini enslaved (1798) 162–75 (see also San Pietro island, and Tabarca)
Anna Porcile (Hargrave(s)) and family 168–74; Francesca Rosso (Jenet Lela Beia) and family 166–8, 175; Tagliafico family 162–5
Carroz, Violante, Contessa di Quirra (*La Sanguinaria*) 90–2, 94
Carta, Julia (accused of witchcraft) 96–7
Carthaginians (including Punic) 23–5, 29–35, 38, 44–5, 48–50, 198, 272
Ceramics and pottery 5–7, 9–10, 15–16, 32, 44, 198, 275, 278, 280 (see also Women)
Christianity and the Church (including establishment of; see also Churches and cathedrals, and Convents and nuns) 2, 40, 47–8, 54, 59, 66–7, 74, 89–90, 113, 145, 297
Churches, cathedrals, basilicas, abbeys (Santa, San, Sant')
Anastasia (Bonorcili) 94; Anna (Cagliari) 50; Antioco di Bisarcio (Ozieri/Ardara) 69; Antioco Martir (Sant'Antioco) 48; Barbara (Ingurtosu) 222, 226–7; Barbara (Olzai) 251; Bernardino (Mogoro) 94; Caterina (Castello, Cagliari) 232; Chiara (Alghero) 90; Chiara (Oristano) 78, 80; Cristina 24; Eulalia (Marina, Cagliari) 119–20, 206, 208; Francisco (Cagliari) 91–2; Gavino (Porto Torres) 64; Giovanni (Assemini, Cagliari) 59; Giusta (Oristano) 48; Lorenzo (Cuglieri) 104; Lucia (Marina, Cagliari) 206–7; Madonna di Bonacattu (Milis) 61; Madonna delle Grazie (Sassari) 73; Maria di Bonarcado (Montiferru) 62; Maria di Codrongianos (Sassari) 63; Maria Maddalena (La Maddalena) 177–8, 199; Maria Maddalena (Lollove) 158; Maria Navarese (Baunei/Tortoli) 2; Maria del Regno (Ardara) 72; Michele di Salvennor (Sassari) 65, 69; Michele di Therricellu 69; Our Lady of Mount Carmel (Cagliari) 104; Pietro di Zuri (Ghilarza, Oristano) 79; Salvatore (Sassari) 65; Trinità di Saccargi 68

Clothes (see also silk) 6, 14, 16, 20–2, 26, 55–6, 79, 97, 134, 145, 147, 149–51, 153–4, 156, 165, 197, 202, 204, 215, 226, 230, 236, 244–5, 248, 254–5, 265, 277–9, 291, 295, 310
Cocco, Dr Adelasia (Barbagia) 157–8, 304
Cocco, Maria Bastiana, 35, 37–9, 41, 44, 50–1
Confusions, contradictions, disagreements and hypotheses (see also Questions) xvii, 6, 15–16, 34, 45, 50, 66, 72, 81, 90–1, 94, 109, 115, 147, 167, 169, 175, 202, 268, 314
Convents and nuns (see also Pomponia, and Massimilla) 50, 53–6, 61, 63–8, 72–4, 78, 95, 124, 149, 158, 203
Santa Caterina (Castello, Cagliari) 231–2; Santa Chiara (Alghero) 90; Santa Chiara (Oristano) 78, 80, 98; Santa Chiara (Sassari) 90, 109–10; Daughters of Charity of St Vincent de Paul (Cagliari) 297; San Francisco (Cagliari) 92, 105; Figlie di Maria (Sasseri) 319; Santa Lucia (Castello, Cagliari) 95, 120; San Pietro di Silki (Sassari) 63–8, 72–3; San Pietro di Zuri (Ghilarza, Oristano) 79
Coral, 34, 88, 162, 256
Corbula (plant woven basket) 281–2
Corruption 35, 42, 54, 56, 96, 108–10, 134
Corsica and Corsicans 4, 71, 77, 86, 116–17, 136, 167, 177–8, 181, 198, 258, 301
Craig, William Sanderson and families (see also La Maddalena) 179–83, 228, 230
Crespellani, Teresa Mundula and family (poet) 31–2
Crete xii, 1, 22–3, 32, 188–9
Cuglieri 102, 104–5, 202, 206

Deledda, Grazia (novelist and Nobel Prize winner) 143–6, 150, 160, 210, 253, 264–6, 271, 275, 304–5
Di Roccaberti, Timbora 79–80, 84, 87, 90
Diet and food (including animals and livestock) 4–8, 11–13, 16, 19, 26–7, 33, 36, 141, 147, 149–50, 186, 189, 239–40, 259–60, 281, 295, 298–9, 301
Dispute Resolution (see Law)
DonnaSarda website 71, 77, 92, 103, 105, 131, 148–50, 205, 209, 217, 250, 264, 310

Education, female, teachers and teaching 80, 95, 116, 120, 123, 131, 136, 144–5, 147, 154, 204, 232, 237–8, 246–7, 249, 251, 261–5, 267, 271–2, 283, 291, 296–8, 300, 303–9, 314, 318, 320–2

Eleonora, *Giudicessa d'Arborea* (and *Carta de Logu*) 61, 72, 80–2, 84–5, 87, 108, 133, 138, 159, 163, 274

Environment, ecology and landscape (including drought and famine) 8, 12–13, 16, 19, 31, 36–7, 62–3, 98, 109, 115, 129, 132, 202, 210, 226–7, 243, 260, 273, 275, 280–1, 322

Ethiopians in Sardinian exile (see also Asinara Island) 258–60

Feudal and feudalism 87, 92–3, 108, 111–19, 121–2, 130, 133
  Francesca Brunenga Carcassona (see also Carcassona family) 113–14; Francesca Carcassona, Countess of de Monteleone 114–15; Maria Caterina Castelvi 111; Maria Faustina, Duchess of Benavente and Gandia 111–13; Maria Giuseppa Pimentel, Duchess of Benavente and Gandia 111–13

Foreign Women in Sardinia
  Mary Davey 1, 138–9, 180–2, 228–9, 232–3; Isabelle Eberhardt 242–6, 253; Anna Rose Giles 246–8, 250–2; Ellen Giles 246, 248–9, 252; Georgiana King 248–9, 251–2; Piercy family (particularly Florence) 205, 207–8, 233–42, 244, 253, 264; Amelie Posse-Brázdová 1 252–8, 261, 296

France (and the French, French adj.) 1–2, 8, 32, 73–4, 87–8, 97–8, 102, 107, 109–10, 113, 116–17, 119, 122–7, 129, 131, 133, 164–6, 170, 177, 193, 198, 204, 206, 210, 212, 230, 234, 237, 243–4, 246, 249, 258, 262, 288–9, 291, 296, 301, 304, 306, 315

Funerary Customs 10, 15, 30, 32, 38, 40–1, 59, 61, 95–6, 119, 138–9, 144–6, 204, 231, 254, 317, 319

Giacobbe, Maria (writer; see also Anti-fascist activists) 305, 308

Gambella, Rosa, 48, 93–4

Gardens and gardening (including botanic) 37, 67, 106, 180, 198, 209–10, 222, 226, 239, 272–3, 284

Giusta, Maria 19

Goddesses 7–10, 14, 22, 27–34, 37, 40, 45–6, 213, 215, 255, 257

Golfo Aranci xii–xiii, 22, 40, 197–8, 234

Greece (Ancient, including Greek influence) 23, 29, 31–3, 37–9, 42–3, 51, 58, 188, 243, 246

Guiso, Rosaria, 106

Guspini (see also mining) 214–16, 218, 226, 315–16

Health, general, disease (including cholera, epidemics, malaria and plague) xii, 1, 11, 30–1, 38, 80, 84, 86–7, 97–8, 112, 115, 133–7, 158, 164, 184, 196, 214–15, 223, 239, 258, 268, 270, 291, 304, 324

Honey 36, 146, 162, 280–1

Iglesias (see also mining) 9, 77, 86, 89, 176, 210–11, 217, 270–1, 286, 318

Islam (Islamic, Muslims, Arabs, Turks) 2, 39, 57–60, 94, 99–100, 162, 164–5, 170, 175, 191, 198, 209, 243–4, 246, 268, 291

Jewellery 9, 29, 32–3, 150–1, 210

Jewish women (including Judaism and expulsions) 42–4, 48, 88–90, 113, 116, 162, 273, 298–9, 315

La Maddalena Archipelago (see also William Craig, Barbagia, and Tamponi family)
  Emma Collins 183–7, 189; Giuseppe Garibaldi and families 180, 183–4, 186–9; women harvesting lichen 180–1; Millelire family 132–3, 178–9, 182, 184; Admiral Horatio Nelson 125, 127, 178–80, 193; Maria Webber Tamponi (see Tamponi family); Espérance von Schwartz (Elpis Melena) 165–9

Lai, Giuliana (writer, sister of Maria, artist) 279–81, 283–4

Land and landowning (see also under Women) 3, 63–5, 138, 159–60, 258, 323

Languages and dialects (of Sardinia) 249
  Cagliaritano 301–2; Logudorese 34, 63, 66, 71, 106, 116, 134, 156, 177, 301, 310; Nuragic 38; Punic 38; Sardo 36, 91, 106, 134, 143, 150, 182, 247, 288, 301, 308, 310

Law (including position of women, dispute resolution and lawlessness) 1, 19, 25–6, 40, 51–7, 61, 63, 67, 74, 82–4, 89, 104, 108, 110–12, 117–18, 130, 133, 135–6, 138, 141–4, 147, 149, 151, 159–61, 181, 185, 196, 203–4, 242, 256, 304, 306, 318

Lo Schiavo, Flavia (archaeologist) 11–12, 14–15, 21, 25
Lussu, Emilio (see also anti-fascist women activists) 261–2, 286, 288–93

Magazines (women's) and women founders 143, 263, 274, 277–8, 308
  Caterina Faccion Berlinguer (*La Donna e la Civiltà*) 262–4; Maria Manca Colombo (*La Donna Sarda*), 264–5
Maiore, Dario 23
Malta 1, 6, 126, 178
Mancini, Paola (including wooden statuette) 23–4, 33–4, 198
Martyrs, women (early Christian)
  Santa Giusta 48–9; Santa Restituta 49–50; Santa Rosa 48
Massimilla, abbess (and abbesses and nuns of San Pietro di Silki; see also convents) 63–66, 68–9
Mediterranean Sea 2, 4, 6–7, 9, 27, 29, 31, 33, 45, 57, 120, 164, 174, 194, 206, 281, 301
Minerals and metals (copper, obsidian, silver; see also mines) 4–5, 7–9, 15, 27, 211
Milis 6, 209–11
Mines, Mining and women involved (see also minerals)
  Idina Brassey (Ingurtosu) 220–27; Maria Mariani (Montevecchio) 218–19; Elena Poinsel (La Rosas) 212–13; Zely Sanna-Castoldi (Montevecchio) 213–19, 224, 227; Helen Wright (Ingurtosu) 19–20, 226–6; Workers (Montevecchio) 215–18
Monuments (including stelae, protomes and inscriptions)
  Domus de Janas 9–10, 95; Favonia Vera (Nora) 27, 46; Flavia Cyriace (Porto Tores) 51; Luxia Arrabiosa (Villaperruccio) 9; Maryam (Assemini, Cagliari) 59; Menhirs 8–9; Septimia Musa (Porta Tores) 51; Preziosa and Susanna, protomes (Sant'Antioco di Bisarcio)
Mountains (*monti*) 16, 33, 113, 130, 138–40, 142, 146, 149–50, 152–5, 158, 166, 215, 247, 270, 279–80, 307, 322
  Arci (Gulf of Oristano) 4, 7; Cucumache (Orune) 322; Cudias (Sarrabus) 91; Gedeli (Ulassai) 280; Genna Serapis (Montevecchio) 215; Gonare (Barbagia) 308; Ortobene (Nuoro) 146; Sirai (Carbonia) 28, 30–1
Mozzoni, Anna Maria (early suffrage petition) 264, 267
Muntoni, Cristina 205, 209, 217

Murgia, Michela (writer) 18–21, 159, 282
Museums
  Antica Palazzo di Città (Castello, Cagliari) 66; Aymerich Palace (Laconi) 105–6; Borely (Marseille) 32; British (London) 32–3; Corraine Ethnographic (Orgosolo) 154; Dickens House (London) 209; Diocesan of Sacred Art, San Michele Church (Sassari) 69; Don Giovanni Guiso (Orosei) 106–7; Donna Francesca Sanna Sulis (Muravera) 205; Eco of Rosas Mine 213; Ethnografico di Sant'Antioco 203; Garibaldi House (Caprera, La Maddalena) 191; Grazia Deledda House (Santu Predu, Nuoro) 146; National Archaeological (Castello, Cagliari) 27–9, 32–3, 40; National of Copenhagen 20; National Archaeological (Sassari) 34, 219; Natural History (Basel, Switzerland) 202; New York Metropolitan of Art 47; Oristano Archaeological 10; Palazzo Boyl (Milis) 210; Porto Torres 47, 51; Speleo Archaeological (Nuoro) 16; Witch House (Bidoni) 97
Mussi, Margherita (Venus of Macomer) 4
Mussolini, Benito 193, 196, 225, 258, 269, 285–8, 296, 298, 304, 315, 320 (see also anti-fascist women activists)
Myths and legends (see also controversies etc) 2, 9, 6, 18–19, 26, 39, 42–3, 45, 48, 50, 72, 87, 91–4, 97, 144, 149, 152, 177, 210, 243, 308

Navarra, Princess of 2
Nora 27, 29–31, 35, 44–6
North Africa (including Tunis and Tunisia), 25, 28–9, 31, 48–9, 57, 59, 116, 162, 164–75, 184, 198, 210, 243–4, 314–16
Nuragic people, sites, and figurines (see also Archaeological sites, and Wells, Sacred) Bronze Age
  Abini – Teti, Nuoro (*Donna Offerente*) 22; Cabu Abbas – Olbia (*Donna Offerente, Portatrice d'Acqua*) 21; Nuraghe Arrubiu-Orrol 15; Sa Domu 'e S'Orcu – Ogliastra (Mother of the Slain; *Madre dell'Ucciso*) 16–18; Santa Cristina – Paulilatina, Oristanto 21; Santa Vittoria – Giara Plain (*Donna con Adolescente, Donna con Bambino, Donna in Preghiera*) 19; S'Arrideli-Teralba, Oristano (*Donna in Preghiera*) 20; Su Nuraxi-Barumini 14, 19, 25–6; Su Tempiesu-Orone (*Coppia di Offerente*) 16

Orgosolo 144–5, 150, 152–7, 202, 247, 282, 304, 306
Oristano 4, 7–10, 20, 26, 31, 38, 44, 48, 61, 78–84, 89, 91, 94, 97–8, 104, 206, 235, 318

Palaces (*palazzi*)
Antica di Città (Castello, Cagliari) 66, 277; Ardara 69, 71–2; Aymerich (Laconi) 8–9, 105–6; Belgrano (Marina, Cagliari) 119; Boyl (Milis) 210; Castello Roberti Carcassona (Serdiana) 116; Don Antonio Brondi (Castello, Cagliari) 104; Don Giovanni Guiso (Orosei) 106–7; Goceano 69; Holy Office of the Inquisition (Sassari) 95; Magistrate's (Sassari) 109; di Magistris (Castello, Cagliari) 116; of Management (Ingurtosu) 227; Martoni (Nuoro) 160; Montecitorio (Chamber of Deputies, Rome) 317; Nin de Carcassona (Alghero) 90; Regale (Castello, Cagliari) 124; Roberti Nin di San Tommaso (Castello, Cagliari) 116; Rossi (Castello, Cagliari) 235; Vecchio di Rosa Gambella (Sassari) 93–4
Pamphili (Pamphilj), Costanza (*Viceregina*) and her letter 99–101
Pernis family (Cagliari and Milis; see also Activists, and Artists) 120, 205–11
Phoenicians (and Lebanon) 23–5, 27–31, 33, 49, 163, 213–14
Politicians (elected women)
Ninetta Bartoli 319, 323; Maria Giulia Cocco 318–19, 323; Bastianina Martini Mussu (see also Suffrage campaigners) 313; Margherita Sanna 320–3; Nadia Gallico Spano 314–18
Pomponia (and nuns in dispute) 52–4, 56–8
Porto Torres 47, 49–51, 64, 68–9, 121, 134, 235, 308
Portugal 2, 10, 290, 321

Queseda family (including death of Giovanna Maria – Minnia; see also Health) 135–6
Questions (still to be answered) 2, 4, 9–10, 12, 16, 20–1, 29, 31, 38, 43–4, 64, 70–1, 74, 92, 101, 110, 112, 114, 116, 144, 151, 166, 172–3, 181, 194, 205, 212, 224, 229, 276

Rebellion, revolt, uprising and demonstration 42–3, 64–5, 81–2, 93, 105, 108–10, 116–19, 121–2, 159, 160–1, 164, 179, 262, 286–8, 290

Roebuck, Derek xii, xiii, xvi, 23, 63, 82
Roman Women in Sardinia (see also Romans)
Aelia Cara Marcellina (Nora) 44; Atilia Pomptilla (Cagliari) 38–9; Atte (Claudia Augusti Liberata; Acte; Olbia) 39–42; Berenice (Beronice; Sant'Antioco) 42–4, 296; Claudia Calliste (Olbia) 40–1; Favonia Vera (Nora) 44–6; Galla Fundania (Tharros) 36–8; Maxima Flavia Publicia (Porto Torres) 47
Romans (ancient; see also Roman Women in Sardinia) 2, 23–7, 30–1, 33–50, 52, 57, 61, 67, 88, 94, 138, 143, 163, 197–8, 203, 210–11, 213–15, 296, 302, 312
Rossi family (Piercys' palazzo) 235
Royalty (families and refuge in Sardinia)
Clotilde, Queen of Sardinia (princess of France; and King Carlo Emanuele) 122–5; Maria Beatrice, Princess of Savoy (and Archduke Francis of Austria-Este) 125–30, 132–3; Maria Carolina, Queen of Naples and Sicily (princess of Austria; and King Ferdinand of Naples) 127–31; Maria Cristina, Queen of Sardinia (princess of Naples and Sicily; and King Carlo Felice) 127, 130–4; Maria Teresa, Queen of Sardinia (archduchess of Austria-Este, Duchess of Aosta; and King Vittorio Emanuele I) 124–30, 132–3
Rubanu, Pietrina 156–7, 282
Ruggeri, Paola 35, 37–40, 44, 47

Saluzza, Costanza di 98
San Pietro and Carloforte (see also Carolini enslavement 1798) 84, 116, 162–6, 168–9, 172–6
Sant'Antioco (earlier Sulcis) and 1815 enslavement 9, 27–8, 31, 42–3, 48, 57, 69, 88, 95, 164, 174–5, 202–3, 211, 258, 317
Sassari 6, 10, 34, 37, 39, 44, 60, 63, 68–9, 72–3, 89–90, 93–6, 99, 101, 108–10, 114, 116, 118–19, 121–2, 134–7, 139, 148, 151–3, 158, 183, 202–3, 213–14, 219, 230, 233, 239, 246, 248–9, 251, 257, 262–4, 269, 271–2, 278–9, 294, 303, 311, 313–14, 319–20, 324
Sicily 10, 69, 77, 86, 107, 125–8, 131, 182, 225, 272, 288, 301
Silk (*seta*) 42–4, 149, 156–7, 202–4, 237, 253, 284
Sisaia (S'Isaia; the Witch) 11–12

Slavery and slaves (see also Carolini enslaved, Sant'Antioco, and San Pietro) 3–4, 47–9, 51, 57–9, 61, 68, 93, 133, 164–8, 170, 174–5, 205, 215

Spain (including Catalans, Catalonia, Aragon and rulers and viceroys; see also War, Spanish Civil) 2, 58, 61, 70, 77–82, 84, 86–91, 93–5, 98–9, 102–4, 107–8, 112, 122, 147, 164, 173, 193, 247, 249, 253, 281

Suffrage, women campaigning for 81, 209, 250, 252, 264–7, 304, 311, 313–14, 319, 322

Sulis, Donna Francesca (Lady of the Mulberry trees) (see also silk) 203–5

Tabarca Island and Tabarchini 162–5 (see also Carolini)

Tamponi, Maria Webber and Tamponi family (La Maddalena and Olbia) 192–8

Tharros 6–7, 27, 29, 31–3, 36–8, 78

Tocoele, Donna (*Giudicessa* d'Arborea; Milis) 61–2, 78, 210

Tognotti, Eugenia 135–6, 324

Tondut family (corruption and uprising in Sassari; see also Corruption, and Rebellions) 109–10

Turchi, Dolores 144–5

Turin (*Torino*; court of Savoyard Kings of Sardinia; Piedmont and Piedmontese) 32, 107–8, 110, 117–18, 122–3, 132–3, 136, 159–60, 164, 179, 191, 194, 199, 203–4, 260, 264, 268, 270, 272, 278, 297–300

Ulassai 279–84

United States and American (including the Administration and Bryn Mawr College) 13, 81, 144, 170–4, 177–8, 200, 220, 225, 246–50, 284, 301, 306, 312, 321

Vardeu, Fancesca 269, 271

Wars and warfare (including warriors and society) 7, 11, 14–15, 17–18, 20, 45, 76, 81–2, 102, 112, 148, 164, 189
Abyssinian 240; Austrian Succession 109; Balkan 268; Cold 292; First World 175–6, 212, 220, 224–6, 248–9, 252–8, 261–2, 267–70, 272, 278, 286, 294, 296, 303, 305, 313–14; Italo-Libyan 268; Napoleonic 116–18, 122, 126–7, 164, 170, 173; Punic 33, 35; Quadruple Alliance 107; Second Italo-Abyssinian 258–60; Second World 50, 196, 209, 212, 225–6, 257–8, 271, 273, 276–7, 283, 290, 293–4, 296–7, 299–302, 304, 307, 311–16; Spanish Civil 288, 304–6, 315; Spanish Succession 107, 147; Thirty Years 97

Wells, sacred 16, 19, 21
Cabu Abbas (Olbia) 21; of Coni (nuragus, Cagliari) 20; Santa Cristina (Paulilatino, Oristano) 21, 24; Sa Testa (Olbia) 23; Su Nuraxi-Barumini 19; Su Tempiesu-Orune 16, 144

Women, Sardinian
Concubinage 25, 68, 171, 182, 199; difference from Italians 1, 83–4, 133, 253; discriminated against 158, 283, 304, 316, 320; equality of 25, 56, 83, 138, 203, 243, 289, 315–16, 319–20; feudal rights 110–16; independence of 3, 44, 62, 244, 263, 272, 300; life of, imagined (including victims of fighting, war, famine) 4–5, 18, 89, 92, 117, 163, 168, 181, 196, 219, 226, 265; land, ownership of 3, 41, 44 49, 55, 61–4, 66, 71, 75, 78, 88–9, 91, 94, 111–13, 197, 203, 205; makers of ceramics, pottery and clay figurines 5–7, 9–10, 14–16, 278, 280; marriage (Sardinian versus Pisan custom 83–4, 136; in politics (see Politicians (elected women), Activists during the First World War, Anti-fascist women activists, and Suffrage, women campaigning); pregnancy and childbirth 30, 33, 81, 86, 95, 101, 125, 126–7, 129, 142, 163, 165, 172–5, 179, 182, 184, 190, 234, 237, 257, 259–60, 291, 294, 300; Serfs and servants (including exploitation; see also Convents, Slaves, and Questions) 62, 64–6, 67–8, 82, 64–8, 82, 84, 88–9, 92–3, 192, 254, 307; spinning and weaving (see also Clothes) 8–9, 14, 26, 96, 202, 204–5, 284; status within family and society 3, 11, 25, 30, 43, 47, 52, 57, 59, 65, 74, 83, 88, 96, 102, 105, 149, 160, 319; victim of raids 5–6, 94–5, 98, 161 (see also Carolini); witches and witchcraft (including the Inquisition) 9, 11–12, 96–7

Zatrillas, Francesca (Camarassa Conspiracy) 102–6

Zau, Paskedda Zelis and *de Su Connottu* (see also Rebellion) 159–61